NATIVE TREES
FOR
NORTH AMERICAN
LANDSCAPES

NATIVE TREES

FOR
NORTH
AMERICAN
LANDSCAPES

From the Atlantic
to the Rockies

GUY STERNBERG
with **JIM WILSON**

TIMBER PRESS
Portland · Cambridge

Frontispiece: Osage-orange (*Maclura pomifera*) and other trees
at Starhill Forest Arboretum.
Dedication page: *Carya tomentosa*.

Published in 2004 by

Timber Press, Inc.
The Haseltine Building
133 S.W. Second Avenue, Suite 450
Portland, Oregon 97204, U.S.A.

Timber Press
2 Station Road
Swavesey
Cambridge CB4 5QJ, U.K.

Library of Congress Cataloging-in-Publication Data

Sternberg, Guy.
    Native trees for North American landscapes: from the Atlantic
to the Rockies / Guy Sternberg with Jim Wilson.
        p. cm.
    Includes bibliographical references (p.).
    ISBN 0-88192-607-8
    1. Ornamental trees—United States. 2. Ornamental trees—
Canada. 3. Landscape gardening—United States. 4. Landscape
gardening—Canada. I. Wilson, James W. (James Wesley), 1925-
II. Title.

SB435.5.S74 2004
635.9′77′097—dc22   2003053705

A catalog record for this book is also available from the British
Library.

Designed by Susan Applegate in Legacy Serif, Legacy Sans,
and Academy Engraved. Printed through Colorcraft Ltd., Hong Kong.

To
BILL & VIRGINIA STERNBERG
for their love of nature.

Contents

Acknowledgments

J
IM WILSON, my friend and coauthor, has been an inspiration and a motivating force. Several of the photos in this book were taken by Jim, and many observations about the nuances of these trees originated with him.

Artist Adelaide Murphy Tyrol of Oliphant Studios in Plainfield, Vermont, provided the silhouette drawings for the featured species. She has illustrated more than a dozen other natural history books, and her work has been displayed in numerous shows, galleries, and museums. She is foremost an artist but also a naturalist who brings life and realism to her portrayals of North American trees.

With the encouragement of my doting parents, I began studying trees seriously at the Morton Arboretum in Illinois in 1961 by picking the brain of my first mentor, Floyd Swink. I have visited many other great arboreta since then. Much of the information in these pages originated from working with people like Floyd. My friend and former professor at Purdue University, Harrison Flint, has been a fountain of knowledge and observations, not only about woody plants themselves but also about the right way to learn about them. During my decades of tree watching in Illinois I have been extremely fortunate to have had so many opportunities to learn from and so many people to learn with, including friends John Schwegman, Al Koelling, Henry "Weeds" Eilers, Earl Cully, and Larry Mahan. Time spent with each of them has always been well invested.

Respected tree experts like Ron Lance of Chimney Rock Park, North Carolina, Gil Nelson of Florida State University, Bob McCartney of Aiken, South Carolina, Steve Bieberich of Clinton, Oklahoma, and Michael Melendrez of Los Lunas, New Mexico, have taken me to some of the most obscure parts of North America and helped me become more familiar with the trees of their respective regions. Ron and Gil, who have written their own tree books, also offered to provide photographs for this book. Mike, Steve, and Bob manage native tree nurseries and are known nationally for their expertise and passion for trees and native plants.

The incomparable Benny Simpson of Texas A&M University taught me much about the trees of the Southwest. I wish he had survived long enough to teach me more. Countless friends from the International Dendrology Society and the International Oak Society have shared their knowledge more times than I can remember. My friends at American Forests generously provided access to champion tree records in advance of publication in the biennial National Register so that these records might be as up to date as possible for this book. State big-tree coordinators, district foresters, and natural heritage botanists from many states have also been extremely helpful. Their enthusiasm for their work shows in their willingness to devote so much of their personal time to helping people like me understand their respective corners of the natural world.

Native trees can be studied best only in the context of nonnatives. Many other tree friends from around the globe have assisted graciously and enthusiastically with fieldwork and logistics during trips to their countries, and with acquisition of the seeds needed to grow and study so many trees during the past forty years. Each of them is a resident expert for a region or a genus, and every day I've spent with them has been memorable. I have enjoyed learning from these people, more than they might imagine. I hope you will too, because this book represents some of their collective input as well as my own experience.

I have saved the best two for last. My wife, Edie, realized long ago that any trip we might take would have to be at least partly a tree trip, and any activities that we planned together would have to be designed around propagation season, seed-collecting season, transplanting season, blooming season, fall color season, and several other horticultural and photographic seasons. She adapted with grace and enthusiastically became my second pair of eyes when looking for seeds or setting up photographs. She often refers to herself as unpaid staff, but as her reward she has seen many wonderful, remote places with me worldwide that we never would have found at typical tourist destinations.

Finally, Timber Press has provided a rare combination of botanical knowledge, friendship, and editing skills coupled with the management ability to keep authors like me engaged at times when projects seem too daunting to complete. No reference book is simple to write, but I was encouraged to take as much time as I felt necessary to triple-check everything in order to produce the best possible book we could create together.

As for me, I'm still learning. I always welcome any useful information readers are willing to provide. Based upon past experience, such feedback often comes in too great a quantity to be acknowledged individually, but please be assured that it is appreciated.

GUY STERNBERG
Starhill Forest Arboretum
Petersburg, Illinois

Preface

Native Trees for North American Landscapes had its beginnings with the popular *Landscaping with Native Trees: The Northeast, Midwest, Midsouth, and Southeast Edition*, also by Jim Wilson and myself, but it differs in many ways. It provides expanded tree descriptions, additional species, and up-to-date information about cultivars and champions, covers more regions, and includes a useful Internet directory and selection lists. This new book also reflects the many lessons learned from the valuable feedback provided by my many tree friends who read the first book. It still deals exclusively with trees, unlike more general books that divide their attention among wildflowers, shrubs, vines, prairie plants, and wetland plants. The main portion of the book is the Menu of Native Trees. Ninety-six trees are profiled as featured species, while the remainder are mentioned more briefly as similar and related species. I have tried to be straightforward about the advantages and limitations of each native tree described and to provide valuable background information on native species issues, ecology, and tree care.

There are already many wonderful books available that emphasize exotic tree species from foreign lands or that limit their coverage to popular species. Others are beautiful coffee-table folios with inspirational photographs but no substantive information, and still others are scholarly manuals that convey useful information only to the scientists who are able to understand them. Somewhere within the perimeter defined by these extremes are the books most useful to the majority of us. They are accurate and complete without being arcane and are attractive without sacrificing utility. They are made for anyone who enjoys trees as a serious hobby, as well as for landscape architects, nursery professionals, arborists, and horticulturists who need a general reference source. Hopefully they are fun to read as well. This attempts to be such a book.

INTRODUCTION

THIS BOOK IS intended for anyone interested in, and fascinated by, our native trees and our natural environment. In it I focus exclusively upon the cultivation and preservation of native trees and cover a broad but surprisingly homogenous region in which hardiness zones, elevations, soils, and other parameters to plant growth merge gradually into one another without the abrupt influences of tropical climate, Mediterranean precipitation patterns, or high alpine conditions. This natural region is bounded by the Atlantic Ocean to the east, the high mountains of the Continental Divide to the west, the treeless tundra of northern Canada, and subtropical areas of Florida and southernmost Texas. When I refer to "our" forests or "our" trees I am referring to the forests and trees of the region covered by this book. Many of the trees and most of the concepts presented are suited to much of this botanically rich and diverse region, where Jim Wilson and I have both spent our lifetimes studying and admiring native trees and their environments. The rest of our native trees are more specialized, and some are uniquely adapted to thrive in some of the harshest habitats. There truly is a tree for every purpose.

So what exactly is a native tree? This depends on the context in which the term is used. Trees, like everything else in nature except our own species, do not recognize political boundaries, and therefore being native to a state or a county means very little. On the other hand, being native to a continent or region bounded by geophysical or climatological barriers, or to a habitat type that restricts the reproduction or survival of potential competitor species, means a lot. And being native to a natural community that has stabilized over millennia and established successful interactions among its component species means even more.

Most plants are native somewhere, excepting those developed through human tinkering and hybridization. Over time the definition of "native" must be flexible, since species adjust their ranges due to evolutionary adaptations and environmental changes. Some plants now considered native to the southern United States, for example, might have evolved in Canada during a warm-climate period millions of years ago. In this sense the only purely native tree is one that is growing in the same region in which it originated, and scientists call such species "autochthonous." Some plants are considered "endemic" to a particular area because they are not found elsewhere; others might be "pandemic" and distributed across a vast natural range, often with geographic races adapted to local habitats, or provenance.

In a more general sense, just as a weed is a plant out of place, a native plant is a plant that is very much in place. For the purposes of our discussion, a native tree can be considered a species that existed in what is now eastern North America prior to the arrival of European settlers

LEFT: Hardwoods (*Quercus virginiana*, *Q. geminata*, *Q. hemisphaerica*, and *Ilex vomitoria*) and palms (*Sabal palmetto*) line the banks of a salt marsh in the Deep South.

(as opposed to a naturalized tree, which has escaped into a new habitat due to human influence). More precisely, a native tree is a tree that has proven its adaptability to local climate and soil conditions over the past several thousand years. Each of us can make a contribution to our environment by helping to preserve such native trees and by using them in our landscapes.

Many of our common native trees would be the cream of any ornamental crop, although their outstanding characteristics are not always appreciated. These trees seem to belong here. They help to reinforce our sense of place, offering the familiar context for childhood memories that reassure us that this is indeed home. When treated with respect for their basic needs, these trees provide low-maintenance landscapes and all the aesthetic benefits and seasonal nuances that only the most well adapted plants—the natives—can provide.

For much of our history we in North America have sought the unusual and exotic: Old World crystal, tropical birds, imported sports cars, and the rarest or most flamboyant foreign plants. There is a movement afoot, however, to reassess our preferences—at least our horticultural preferences. We are beginning to appreciate native trees and other plants and to recognize imperfections among some exotics. There is a decided trend to use more native North American plants in residential and commercial landscapes.

What is so wrong with nonnative plants? Sometimes, nothing at all. Anyone with a genuine interest in horticulture must admit a certain fascination with a favorite Asian flower or European shrub. Many landscape trees imported from other regions are well behaved, attractive, and innocuous, and our meals would be quite dull indeed without some of the exotic food crops grown in our gardens or farms.

On the other hand, some of the plants we think of as native become nonnative when we cultivate them beyond their natural range or habitat type, or when we modify them by plant breeding. Many native plants have been "improved" for horticultural purposes by inbreeding or via the artificial infusion of a stray gene here and there from a foreign relative. This genetic manipulation is usually done to increase ornamental value, but the widespread cloning of such genetically engineered individuals can narrow the gene pool, with potentially disastrous results. Occasionally this must be done to impart resistance to a crippling disease. In many cases, such diseases have been spread by sudden, human-induced

exposure of a native plant to the same alien species from which the resistance gene was extracted, the alien species itself having carried the disease. We thus must accept responsibility for the adverse effects of our own interference.

In addition, many exotic plants have been moved into new environments without the limiting factors that controlled their reproductive or competitive abilities in their native habitats. As a result, some of these species have become the house sparrows of the plant kingdom: multiplying out of control, displacing beneficial native species, overwhelming nature preserves, and causing general ecological havoc. Most biologists, and quite a few gardeners, are aware of environmental problems caused by punk tree, Australian-pine, kudzu, Japanese honeysuckle, multiflora rose, autumn olive, purple loosestrife, and on and on through a litany of the ecological nightmares brought about by our previous meddling. Sadly, we humans have been slow to learn, and some weedy species are still propagated and sold in parts of the United States and Canada.

The majority of the exotic horticultural items we cultivate in our personal landscapes might never become such ecological pests, but they could still have some surprises in store. The "super" exotic plants, those that seem to do so well in North America in the absence of their natural predators and parasites from overseas, can eventually begin to experience difficulties as those debilitating organisms gradually find their own way here. Even in the absence of these controls, many aggressively marketed aliens simply don't live up to their glowing reputations as wonder trees, except under ideal situations.

In the meantime, other exotic plants require a lot of tender loving care when they encounter local conditions or abnormal weather patterns, and many may not be worth the effort. Some have very beautiful flowers—which might last for a few days each year if the buds aren't killed by a late frost in a continental climate zone for which they are not adapted. Many exotic plants lack significant fall color or have little resistance to leaf mildews and other problems because they evolved in a different environment. Some die back every few years as evolving climate extremes take their toll. Others are conspicuously out of place in most landscape situations because of silvery foliage or other evolutionary adaptations to their own native habitats—characteristics that might not fit well with the local garden environment or the native plants best suited to it. Many foreign plants also do not share the stable ecological relationships with native wildlife that native species have developed over thousands of years.

Then there is the investment factor. Herbaceous annual flowers from China or Africa are small, inexpensive, temporary condiments in the landscape. They are easily replaced, so their loss to winter cold or summer drought is of no great consequence. Trees, though, are the primary living structural elements of the outdoor environment—the meat and bones of the landscape. Tree planting is a lifetime investment, and such investments should be made with prudence. Native species have evolved with our climates, soils, pathogens, pollinators, and associated species over thousands of years: what you see is what you get. Not so with exotic imports, many of which have been grown under these conditions for only a few decades or less and have not been tested by the gauntlet the native plants have run for millennia. The next weather extreme—whether it occurs tomorrow, next month, or next decade—could trigger their collapse.

Scientists know from tree-ring analyses, fossil records, glacier ice cores, and other data that prehistory was punctuated by frequent environmental catastrophes only survived by the strong. We must presume that such eventful ecological times will return periodically, wiping the slate clean of some short-term pretenders to the throne. Hopefully none of those pretenders will be your own expensive exotic trees, which you may have nurtured for a decade or more.

Considering the human-induced threats to the environment—ozone holes, global warming, air pollution, soil disruption, habitat destruction, and the problems provided by our own introductions of exotic pests into new habitats—nothing is certain. We live in an evolving, dynamic system, and we are accelerating its spiral of change by our own actions, compounded by unchecked human population growth. It makes sense, for all these reasons, to dance with the beau who brought us—with the survivor that adapted to all the changes in our regional environment since time began, and that continues to grace our local wildlands unaided by (or in spite of) human intervention.

In this book you will find a comprehensive cross section of native trees presented for your consideration. Some are readily available at your neighborhood nurseries; others can be found through diligent searching through mail-order catalogs or can be propagated easily from seeds or cuttings. Some may be difficult to obtain through any of the above means, but they are suggested for selective preservation if they are already present on your building site or if they sprout as volunteers in a convenient location in your garden. Some are recommended simply for you to protect and admire in a nearby park or forest. Like wild animals, these trees are best untamed. Their value to wildlife, and to the entire web of life within which they have evolved and persevered, commends them to you as much as their aesthetic quality.

Join the vanguard of modern, responsible landscape design and management. Learn from nature, plant and preserve native trees, and take pride in a job well done. It will be good for garden design, good for the environment, and good for your spirit.

READING YOUR LANDSCAPE

WHEN CONSIDERING the options for the trees you would like in your landscape, you might be tempted to cheat a little and include a favorite native (or exotic) species that you know is not ideally suited to your site. Such decisions are to be expected; in fact, they can be what turns a landscape into a garden. When you do this, however, remember that the further you reach for special trees to achieve the desired effect, the more attention you will need to devote to site preparation and future maintenance. The basic premise of native-plant landscaping is to minimize the problems associated with exotic plants, whether they come from halfway across the county or halfway around the world.

Nature is a system of overlapping parts that fit together in a multidimensional jigsaw puzzle. Each species follows certain strategies for success in a competitive world where the right to every space capable of sustaining life is contested by myriad other organisms. Over time the contestants sort themselves into a predictable assemblage for each combination of the variables of soil, moisture, temperature, light, air quality, and various types of disturbance.

The superior trees and other organisms suited to a particular set of such conditions thus form a natural community type that can be found wherever that exact same set of conditions prevails. The balance of species can be so finely tuned that subtle changes in growing conditions from place to place result in different species dominating in different areas, or in some species being replaced by others in a particular natural community. Stochastic events might alter their proportionate dominance slightly, but the communities are amazingly predictable.

The level, timing, and duration of the minimum winter temperature in your area will dictate which trees are hardy there. Some southern species drop out of the picture at the first hard frost. Others are eliminated progressively as you travel northward, in a pattern reflected by the zones shown on the U.S. Department of Agriculture (USDA) Plant Hardiness Zone Map. Many species use a supercooling mechanism to prevent winter injury; this process, and the trees that use it, will fail precisely at –40°F (–40°C), which is the northern limit of USDA zone 3. Other trees tolerate even colder winter extremes, but many wither in the heat of a southern summer or are unprepared for a late killing frost in spring. Some survive winter cold without damage on well-drained soils but sustain cold injury on poorly drained soils; others need more ample moisture or protection from winter sun to avoid the freeze-drying effect of winter desiccation.

Your microclimate can explain a tree's ability to survive in certain portions of your site but not in others. This selective survival is increased by factors such as protection from drying winds, soil temperature moderation on north-facing slopes (or under mulch), and summer shade from the hot afternoon sun. It can be adversely affected by the heat-island effect of an urban setting and by the countless impacts of vehicles, pets, and daily

LEFT: Beech (*Fagus grandifolia*).

human activities. The genetic pattern of an individual tree also plays a part, with trees of local provenance frequently having an edge over trees of the same species from more distant areas.

Some species that succeed locally will overlap into adjacent areas where some, but not all, conditions are the same, as long as the primary factors that limit those species remain unchanged. Such species are often ecological generalists, capable of surviving reasonably well under a broad set of circumstances. Other species will specialize, becoming perfectly adapted to a narrow habitat niche at the expense of their potential adaptability to other niches. These specialists are indicator species; their occurrence on your site is strong evidence that certain growing conditions are present. Such specialists are often found on marginal sites where their competitors cannot thrive, but some will do fine under cultivation on more productive sites if competition is controlled.

Many trees prefer acidic soil, while others grow in limestone areas. Some require ample moisture, while others can compete under drier conditions; either type might be tolerant, or intolerant, of flooding, or of the poor drainage that accompanies tight, compact soils. Some trees are better able to resist damage from fires, wind, ice, insects, or salt spray. Some will take charge on ideal growing sites that offer everything in moderation but will fail under less perfect conditions. And some, called climax species, will succeed in displacing others

BELOW: Colorful trees such as paper birch (*Betula papyrifera*), sugar maple (*Acer saccharum*), and striped maple (*A. pensylvanicum*) enliven autumns in the Northeast.
RIGHT: The mesic forest of eastern North America, with red oak (*Quercus rubra*), white oak (*Q. alba*), beech (*Fagus grandifolia*), and various hickories (*Carya*) forming the main forest canopy.

over the long term as local conditions are changed by the growth of the first pioneer trees.

Such changes can be caused by the shade or leaf litter cast by the pioneer trees, resulting in suppression of weedy herbaceous plants or reduced evaporation of moisture from the soil. Other changes result from the establishment of forest-inhabiting mycorrhizal fungi, important to the survival of the trees that follow the pioneers. There might also be changes in wildlife composition, caused by habitat development, which affect herbivory or seed dispersal to favor some plants over others. Many plants are allelopathic, releasing chemicals that selectively retard certain competitors, thus assisting others. Usually the changes that affect seed germination and seedling establishment are the most important, since the seedling stage of a tree is its most vulnerable time.

You can read your landscape by studying the guilds of trees and other organisms that grow there naturally or that grow in adjacent uncleared areas. The presence or absence of certain species will be a sign of the various conditions that control tree growth on your property. Under your management some of those conditions, like competition from weeds and availability of water during droughts, can be manipulated. Such manipulation, even for only a short period of time, might allow a desired species to become established and, having done so, to survive without further intervention. Other conditions, such as summer heat or soil alkalinity, can be difficult or impossible to influence and must be considered permanent site limitations.

As you read about the cultural requirements and potential problems associated with each tree in this book,

BELOW: *Quercus oblongifolia*, *Q. grisea*, and *Q. arizonica* in a Madrean oak woodland in the Southwest. RIGHT: A mixed hardwood-conifer forest of eastern Canada, including *Acer saccharum*, *Acer rubrum*, *Quercus rubra*, *Betula alleghaniensis*, *Abies balsamea*, *Picea glauca*, and *Pinus strobus*.

you will notice that certain patterns begin to emerge. Groups of floodplain species, calcareous-soil species, xerophytic species, mesic-forest species, and other associations are typically found together in regions where their preferred conditions are present. Looking at the existing healthy trees on your property or in your neighborhood, you can presume that young trees of those same species will do well if you plant them. But as you become more familiar with forest guilds, you will begin to reason that certain other trees, often found under similar conditions in the wild, should also succeed for you.

Try to determine why such trees are absent. It might be due simply to the caprices of nature, wherein every tree can't be in every suitable place all at once. Perhaps they were removed by a timber harvest or during the clearing of your lot. Maybe the conditions required for germination of their seeds have been lacking, due to fire suppression, for example. A former land use, such as grazing or cropping, might have eliminated them. There might be other factors involved, such as a previous insect or disease outbreak. If such factors are no longer present or can be overcome, use your increasing awareness of forest guilds to guide your planting choices and enhance the diversity of your landscape.

Always consider the effects of human activities, such as winter salt spray, engine exhaust from highways, or soil compaction from traffic or construction, and use species that can adapt to those effects where they occur. Many swamp trees, for instance, tolerate poorly aerated soil, whether from natural flooding or from urban soil compaction. Trees from floodplain habitats are also more resistant to the soggy conditions caused by excessive turf irrigation. Prairie or savanna species are more tolerant than forest species to the competition and allelopathic effects from turf roots, and so on.

Many early-successional species from sunny open fields adapt to the increased heat of a planting site in the urban canyons of downtown or near a south-facing brick wall. Those accustomed to poor hardpan soils or caliche can be counted upon to adapt best to building sites where the natural soil profile has been destroyed by a careless contractor. If you are lucky enough to have great soil and careful enough to limit the encroachment of turf or pavement into the root zone of your planting area, be sure to take advantage of the magnificent classic tree species that settle for nothing less. Then complete the concept by incorporating appropriate native understory plants into the design of your ground-level space.

GETTING STARTED

THE TREES ON YOUR property will exist due to one or more of five options you face in the beginning. If you own a forested tract or wooded lot, your first option will be preservation. If you start with the blank slate of a cleared piece of land or wish to supplement or expand your existing forest with additional trees, you may choose from among the remaining options. These are, in no particular order, propagation, purchase, natural regeneration, and wild-collection. Each has its advantages and drawbacks.

It is never too soon to begin thinking about bringing in the new trees you will need. As a hands-on alternative, do not be afraid to jump into propagation mode. Many trees are easy to propagate, and some can be grown into handsome specimens in a surprisingly short time. Some people find great satisfaction in propagating their own trees from seed, or by cuttings or grafting. Some of us remember the first acorn we planted as a child and feel a special relationship with the tree that grew from it. Growing trees this way, from known sources, is also a good way to guarantee that your trees are from quality stock adapted to your local area.

As I discuss each species in the Menu of Native Trees, I will provide information on propagating and transplanting it, for those inclined to follow this approach. Always place yourself in the tree's shoes and try to learn how the tree has adapted to propagate itself and recruit new generations into the landscape. When is the seed

LEFT: Douglasfir (*Pseudotsuga menziesii*).

ripe, how is it dispersed, what weather conditions does it typically experience prior to germination, and on what sites can it successfully establish and compete? Does it cast its seed to the wind as spring floods recede, leaving freshly eroded seedbeds? Does it mature its seeds in fall and wait for completion of a winter season prior to germinating? Does the seed ripen in late summer and lie dormant in the moist soil through the warm fall months and the following winter before germinating? Do the seeds land on the surface of disturbed soil and germinate there under full light, or are they buried by siltation, animals, or falling leaves? Do the fruits appeal to vector animals that will distribute the seed and possibly scarify the seed coats in their digestive tracts along the way? How can you give the seeds what they want? Try to think like the tree.

If you have neither the green thumb nor the patience required for do-it-yourself tree propagation, you can be assured of obtaining a well-grown native tree by purchasing it from a reliable commercial nursery. Nursery professionals grow trees for a living, and most become very good at what they do. You may be able to see the growth form, fall color, flowers, and other characteristics of the tree before you buy it. Many nurseries will allow you to pick a tree with a particular branching pattern or fall color from the rows of trees in their fields, and will dig that particular tree for you. You can select a cultivar too, if you wish, and thereby obtain a tree with a proven track record of form, color, or vigor.

Good nursery-grown plants have been cultivated and

23

managed to assure successful transplanting and are worth a fair price in the long run. Assuming the plants are well rooted, vigorous, and healthy, the biggest problems you will face will be finding rare or difficult-to-grow species and provenance information. However, purchasing native species from a nursery can have a pebble-in-the-pond ripple effect, encouraging the production of additional native plants. You could be the first home gardener, landscape architect, or conservationist in your area to reach beyond the palette of exotic plants that most nurseries seem to stock in such great numbers.

You might have to insist that your local nursery special-order or custom-propagate native trees for you, grown from locally adapted seed. Most nurseries enjoy tinkering with new items as long as they have a guaranteed sale, and so will probably be willing to go the extra mile in this regard. All nurseries are businesses, and businesses produce what sells; but the best nurseries are also labors of love, and their plant-loving proprietors will jump at the chance to work with you.

Buying a nursery-grown tree allows you to choose from a variety of sizes, depending upon how much money you wish to spend. In general, field-grown trees up to 2 inches (5 cm) in diameter are reasonably priced and give good value for the money. Larger trees become

increasingly hard to handle and are proportionately more expensive due to the labor and equipment involved. Of course, the bigger the tree, the more time it will take to become established in its new location, but you might be surprised at the sizes of trees some nurseries are equipped to handle. If you have an open, accessible planting site and sufficient funds, there is almost no limit to the size of tree you can obtain.

Another option is to buy young trees at plant sales hosted by native plant societies or arboreta. These organizations frequently have the most unusual varieties not available in the commercial trade, and unlike most commercial nurseries they often keep track of the provenance data that can be so important in selecting special trees for your landscape. You are likely to acquire valuable information about your trees at such sales, and you may even meet some interesting kindred spirits. In addition, your purchase will help to support the benevolent activities of the organization. If you have such an organization in your area, become a member and watch the newsletters for announcements about the next plant sale. Then be sure to show up early, while the rarest selections are still available.

A favorite proverb among nursery professionals is "Don't plant a dollar tree in a dime hole." This is obvi-

ously an ancient proverb, written when a dollar was worth something, but the wisdom remains valid. Site preparation and maintenance will govern the success of your planting efforts. The entire planting area, not just the planting hole, should be loosened over a distance several times the diameter of the root ball you are transplanting, at least to spade depth. If your soil is heavy, the edges of the planting hole should be broken or scarified to encourage root penetration. Root regeneration complications, especially circling and girdling, can be a major problem for your tree years down the road if you plant it improperly.

If your soil is so poor that you need to add organic amendments, do so over a broad area and in moderation so that the roots are encouraged to disperse into the surrounding soil instead of hiding and circling in the benign environment of the planting hole. It is usually best to simply crumble the soil that came out of the hole and put it back in, using the surplus to build a small levee around the perimeter of the hole to facilitate watering. Organic mulch applied to the soil surface will break down gradually and be incorporated by earthworms, providing a sustained nutritional boost that is much more effective than any amended backfill.

Do not plant your tree any deeper than it grew in the nursery or in its container. If you plant a container-grown tree, eliminate any circling roots and loosen the outside and bottom of the ball to integrate its edges with the backfill soil. Water containerized trees carefully for the first year or two: they are equally sensitive to too much or too little watering, depending on variations in the texture of the container medium and the soil-medium interface. Factors such as drainage should also be addressed prior to planting—over the entire future root zone of the tree, if possible. Fertilize lightly at most, at least until the tree becomes established and demonstrates symptoms of nutrient deficiency rather than simple transplant shock. Minimize the effects of soil compaction and competition from turf roots by giving the tree a large mulched area free from turf and foot traffic.

Watering is the most critical factor in successful reestablishment of a transplanted tree. This watering should be done heavily, and frequently enough to keep the tree from wilting, but with "breathing" intervals to permit aeration of the root zone. The frequency will vary con-

LEFT: Mulch as large an area as possible around your trees. RIGHT: Plastic tree shelters can provide protection from animals, herbicides, and lawn trimmers.

siderably with your climate and soil, but a weekly watering during the growing season (in the absence of heavy rain) is a reasonable rule of thumb. Continue this watering for a period of one year per 1 inch (2.5 cm) of trunk diameter or until the tree shows obvious recovery of vigor, applying at least 1 inch of water over the entire root area each time. Another good rule of thumb is to apply as much water as you can carry in two 5-gallon (19-l) buckets each time you water a tree your own size. If the tree is twice as tall as you are, make two trips, and so forth.

After proper watering, the next most critical factor for your new tree is pest control. This includes elimination of all weeds and other competing plants within the root zone, including turf. Pull or scalp the vegetation and apply a good mulch layer in a wide circle around the tree to shade the soil and inhibit weed regrowth. New trees also require careful monitoring for insect pests, as trees under stress can emit biochemical odors that some insects find irresistible. What might be a tolerable insect infestation a few years down the road, when the tree is again growing vigorously, can be fatal to a new tree struggling to survive. Defoliators are the most conspicuous, sometimes able to strip a tree of foliage in a few days by feeding in groups. Luckily, they are also easy to control if found in time. Borers are more insidious,

doing their damage out of sight under the bark. The best deterrent is to maintain tree vigor, but sometimes a targeted spray program is also helpful. Aphids and their relatives can be controlled by natural predators or by directed water blasts or insecticidal soap. The other major pest category will be your local mammal population, including rabbits, deer, porcupines—even the neighbors' children!

Another tree option, especially if you are fortunate enough to have a large rural property, involves preparing a seedbed and allowing natural regeneration to take its course. If the mature, seed-bearing trees in your vicinity consist of a native species mix suitable for your needs and you are trying to encourage a wild, natural landscape, there is no better way to achieve a random pattern of species and spacing than to let nature do it for you. This method will provide many surprises; some will be delightful, and the others may be uprooted and given to your tree-loving friends before they become permanent fixtures in your landscape.

Plan to thin volunteer seedlings as they develop, with a careful eye toward their potential future size. Remember that a forest is a dense community of tall trees and understory shrubs racing for a piece of the sky, whereas a savanna is a scattering of full-crowned shade trees with a mostly herbaceous understory, so decide at the beginning what type of grove you desire. Also keep in mind that a grove is a living, growing, changing entity, so plan to do your thinning over a period of time as your trees develop.

This really applies to your entire landscape. A big difference between a building architect and a landscape architect is that the builder's project is done and begins to depreciate the day the contractor leaves the job site. It will never look any better or be any bigger than it is on the day the politicians cut the ribbon for the television cameras. Good landscape architects plan for a never-ending sequence of changes and developments, day to day, season to season—and for trees, decade to decade. They are working with the miracle of life, while the building architects are working with bricks and sticks.

The next option is one I must discuss with some reservation. This is the act of collecting wild trees and transplanting them to your site. A word of advice must be offered if you are considering digging native trees, or any other native plants, from wild, natural populations: in general, don't do it. Such collecting involves ethical, legal, and horticultural baggage. Minor collecting of common species from disturbed sites may be harmless,

but your first choice should always be to purchase well-grown, nursery-propagated native plants or to propagate your own. At its worst, wild collecting brings to mind terms such as trespass, larceny, liability, habitat disruption, and potential violations of endangered species protection laws. Most trees are easy to propagate or buy, and so wild collection should generally be disdained as a form of piracy. Yet there are circumstances in which it becomes a viable option, even a noble one.

Some trees reproduce on disturbed sites in numbers so dense that most seedlings die in a year or two. Pastures and field borders subject to periodic cultivation can be excellent places to find young seedling trees that would be doomed without relocation. Some species also send up suckers from their roots, often in places where those new stems are surplus or even detrimental to the parent plant. Under such conditions, with full permission from the landowner and with any applicable regulatory permits in hand, it may be appropriate to relocate surplus material if the species and circumstances are adaptable to your transplanting work. If nothing else, this does assure you that the trees are of local provenance and adapted to your local climate and soil.

There are many concerns involved with wild-collection of native plants, including young trees. An open hole left behind may create a legal liability for public injury litigation, as well as a resentful attitude on the part of the landowner who was generous enough to allow you to dig. Digging a wild plant in full view without explaining to onlookers the nature of your action can set a very bad example. Harvests of supposedly surplus material should be conducted in a way that will avoid any adverse impacts to the site.

If your situation justifies transplanting wild trees, don't try to move them from shady woods directly into sunny, exposed areas. Such trees will not be accustomed to the increased insolation and may sunburn. In fact, you may want to do what some wise old nursery professionals do: mark the south side of the tree before digging it, and replant it with the same side exposed to the sun. Dig an oversized root ball, since wild trees have not been root-pruned like nursery trees. Don't try to take a tree that is too big to handle, no matter how much you like it. Carefully backfill the hole you leave behind, taking care to avoid disturbing adjacent wildflowers as you dig. Conduct your collecting in the dormant season, when the transplanted tree is most likely to survive, not during the growing season when it is conspicuously in bloom. Unless you know enough about ecology, horticulture, and law to address these types of concerns, digging wild trees will be a mistake and should be avoided.

If you decide to collect wild trees, always ask permission, and never take a colorful specimen from a prominent location where it could grow to become the aesthetic focus of a landscape visible to the public. Do not take plants of any kind from legally designated natural areas. Become aware of which species in your area are protected by the U.S. Endangered Species Act of 1973 or by similar state or provincial legislation; a species might be common in your locality but nowhere else, and your activities might destabilize one of its last strongholds. And never allow exuberance to overcome restraint, with one major exception.

That exception is what landscape restoration ecologists call a rescue operation. Authorized plant rescues conducted one step ahead of bulldozers are generally commendable, though not always successful. When all attempts to prevent the impending destruction of a tree (or a whole forest) have failed, the time has come to break out the spades, wheelbarrows, volunteer helpers, and horticultural know-how. Even then, be sure to have permission, and advise the neighbors or the public of the benevolent objectives of your project. If endangered or protected species are present on the site, consult with your state or provincial natural resource management agency before proceeding.

If beautiful native trees already exist on your property, count your blessings and learn how to take care of them properly. Their replacement value can be immense, and the time you will save in preserving what you already have versus starting from scratch is precious. Preservation of native trees also carries a philosophical value. Any large, dominant living organism such as a tree is disproportionately important for ecological, biological, and aesthetic reasons. Large trees moderate their local environment, provide habitat for wildlife, and become the instant focus of any landscape by sheer virtue of size. The loss of a great tree, like the loss of a whale in the ocean or a grizzly bear in the mountains, affects the local environment much more than the loss of any single "lesser" organism.

Conversely, the presence of such a tree can inspire a human awareness and appreciation of nature in a way that nothing else can. While other organisms might pass from the scene without notice or concern, when a great

RIGHT: Young trees can sometimes be salvaged from areas scheduled for clearing.

tree is threatened by acts of human greed or ignorance it can inspire altruistic people to rally to its support in the same way they might respond to threats against spectacular wildlife species, such as elephants or tigers. The tree may be saved, and with it, everything ecologically associated with it, down to the smallest unnoticed microbes, which otherwise might have vanished under new pavement.

Those who already have existing trees or natural forest areas on their property thus have the opportunity to deal with this best of all options: preservation. This involves more, *much* more, than politely asking contractors not to run into the trunks of your trees with their heavy equipment. Any construction or other land-use activity will affect your forest to some extent. It is important that you evaluate your tree resource, determining your preservation priorities in the context of the

site's potential, and plan your activities in a way that will minimize and contain adverse impacts.

First, inventory your trees and identify the "keepers," those you intend to protect. Trees are preserved for various reasons. Some merely form part of the background matrix of your forest, and a few of these might be expendable if necessary. Some are locally rare and add to the biological diversity of the site. Some are particularly valuable for aesthetic reasons or for wildlife. Some are healthy and vigorous and might be favored over their stunted or less thrifty neighbors, given the choice of triage. The keepers might also be of a resilient species, better able to cope with the impact of construction activities than others and thus more likely to survive long term. Then there are the special trees that command extraordinary attention. Endangered species, historic trees, commemorative trees, giant monarchs (including champion trees), and picturesque specimens in highly visible settings are all unique and cannot be managed simply as the "renewable resources" of forestry parlance.

Each tree also grows through different stages that are of benefit to native wildlife. When young, trees provide browse for mammals and nesting sites for songbirds. As they begin to mature, many produce edible fruit, or nectar for butterflies. When they become older and craggier trees develop little nooks and crannies that are necessary for hibernation and breeding of bug-eaters like bats. Then, as they die and slowly decay, they pass through stages from hard deadwood to soft mushy wood, with each stage needed for different species of woodpecker and other cavity-nesting birds. When trees finally fall, they shelter salamanders and form the substrate for the next generation of forest. How much of this natural cycle can you preserve on your own property, or in your neighborhood?

For the sake of both the tree and the house, don't build too close to a large old tree (or a dead, woodpecker-inhabited tree), and consult with a certified arborist about things such as pruning, bracing, and lightning protection. If you have a special tree within the borders of your property, you have inherited a stewardship responsibility that should be taken very seriously. When

the time comes for you to pass this responsibility along to the next owner, do so with the knowledge that, at least on your watch, a priceless source of inspiration and a living connection to the past was preserved.

Historic trees have exceptional intrinsic value due to their associations with human history. As living, growing organisms, their mere mass can help to emphasize the passage of time, giving a perspective of age to their site. Knowing that a particular tree was planted or tended by Thomas Jefferson, for instance, provides a living link to the history of Monticello. Knowing that your own tree was associated with an important local event, or with an ancestor, can be equally valuable to you or your descendants.

The size and condition of a historic tree at the time of the historic period involved might be discernable from old photographs or drawings, making such trees among the best documented of all living organisms that predate the collective memory of the present human generation. Historic trees also lock within their layers of wood a chronological record of climate variations, fires, stray musket balls, old fence staples, original surveyors' benchmark spikes, and other signs of previous land use in the area, so they can be useful for research even after their death. The care of such trees in life, and their eventual potential for interpretation or science at death, should be given careful thought.

Just as our different life spans cause us to think of our pets' lives in terms of dog years (seven dog years for each human year), trees would probably look at us in terms of people years (perhaps five human years for each tree year, depending upon the tree species). Each of us can perform a service for posterity by helping to protect and preserve ancient trees that transcend human generations, even if we aren't the actual owners of the parcel of land where they grow. Surprisingly, this involvement is just as important for trees on public land as it is for those under private ownership. Many public agencies have no legal mandate, no budget, and little inclination to conserve the trees that happen to fall within their jurisdiction by the fate of a land survey. Some fail to even understand the significance of a truly historic tree.

Land managers with custodial responsibility for public lands must be specialists in their own fields—wildlife managers are trained in biology and game management;

historic-site managers are educated about old bricks, bones, and other artifacts; public administrators must become adept in negotiating the pathways of politics and bureaucracy—but few of them have any understanding of arboriculture. Each successive generation of such managers must be helped to understand and appreciate the venerable living resources placed temporarily under their care. Otherwise these timeless living treasures can, and much too often do, fall victim to inattention, misguided maintenance, or the senseless impact of poorly planned construction.

Many European countries have learned to appreciate these things and have established general laws to protect their trees, such as the English Countryside and Rights-of-Way Act, but we in North America have no such laws. Unless your municipality has a tree protection ordinance, you are free to make your own choices, good or bad, enlightened or otherwise. Our duty to nature and history is a voluntary one, and it falls anew upon each successive human generation.

A historic building can be renovated so many times that little of the original structure remains, and still be considered authentic; but it begins to deteriorate the day it is built. A historic tree, by contrast, will maintain itself, with a little human understanding of its needs, and will become more impressive with each passing decade. The building is merely a decaying artifact of human creation, while the tree is a living, growing link to the past. Such trees are the only living organisms with a life span sufficient to connect us with our ancestors. They're the spiritual food of the Druid in each of us. Eventually the tree rots or blows down, but with proper care it can survive for several centuries.

These, then, are the options you face when you want to enhance the tree resource on your own land or assist with tree management on public land. Preservation is unique among them in dealing with existing trees that might be centuries old or historically significant. There are no compromises in preservation; if a tree, or an entire forest community, is to be preserved, it must be dealt with in its present location and its present condition. The other options—propagation, purchase, natural regeneration, and wild-collection—allow you to begin the cycle so that future generations will have something to preserve.

LEFT: Indian trail marker trees such as this white oak (*Quercus alba*) are a living link to the history of our continent.

CONSTRUCTION AND LANDSCAPE MANAGEMENT AMONG TREES

TREES ARE LIVING organisms. Surprising as it might seem, this obvious fact and its implications can become lost amid the commotion of house construction or the routine activities of our daily lives. Because trees grow to be so big, live so long, change so slowly, and seem to function as part of the inert architectural framework—the bones—of our landscapes, we sometimes forget they can be injured or killed by our actions.

Just like turf, herbaceous ornamentals, and garden vegetables, trees require certain conditions for their survival. Two primary distinctions, however, separate trees from most other garden plants: first, trees are often slower to show the effects of their problems, due to the enormous food reserves they accumulate while they are healthy; and second, once a mature tree is beyond help it cannot be replaced as good as new in a single growing season, or sometimes even in a human lifetime. A mature specimen tree is, in terms of human time, irreplaceable.

This is why it is so important to devote more attention to the condition of your trees than to that of other garden plants. While this is not a book about tree protection and maintenance, it is necessary to touch briefly upon some of the factors you should consider. First I will present a battle plan to help you guide your trees safely through the potentially horrific impacts of house construction or renovation; then I will review some general procedures for long-term management of your trees.

LEFT: Red maple (*Acer rubrum*).

Construction protection does not begin when you notice that your contractor happens to be scraping the bark of your tree. It begins at the beginning—when you first decide to design your new house (or room addition, garage, patio, or pond)—with an inventory and evaluation of the trees and other plants present on the property, preferably with the assistance of a certified arborist or qualified urban forestry consultant. It continues with a site analysis in which priorities are assigned to individual trees, groups of trees, and patches of understory vegetation for preservation.

Next you work with your landscape architect to design the site in a manner that will allow the improvements you build to lie lightly upon the landscape, in accordance with the preservation objectives identified in your site analysis. The landscape architect and arborist should work together to resolve problems such as grade changes and construction-access protection for soils, and they should be given veto authority over the building architect and contractor in the event of any significant disagreement.

Heavy-impact activities such as concrete delivery might be timed so that they occur when soil conditions are at their least sensitive, either frozen or dry. Some trees might be pruned in advance, or even transplanted, if they will be serious obstacles to construction access. Utility trenching within the primary root area of a significant tree, especially within about 15 feet (4.5 m) of the trunk, should be routed in a pattern that is radial to the tree, rather than across the spokelike root pattern.

Boring under the trunk or root flare as necessary to avoid damage to major roots will minimize injury, because the pipes or wires can be slid under the roots without cutting them. Boring equipment can be rented inexpensively at many construction rental businesses, and there should be no excuse for not using it wherever needed.

Unavoidable earth-fills within critical root areas can be designed to incorporate a base layer of porous materials like washed gravel and inexpensive tile aeration systems. Vertical mulching (radial trenching or coring and soil amendment) can be specified to mitigate unavoidable soil compaction. If excavation for a footing would cut major roots, piles or pier bearings can be used to bridge the critical area. Your design team (architect, landscape architect, and arborist) may come up with other unique and creative techniques as well, specific to

the site conditions at hand, and many options can cost surprisingly little to implement.

Only when these measures have been resolved to your satisfaction does it become time to interview potential contractors. Such interviews should include references from other owners of wooded home sites where the contractor worked previously. It often takes several years for tree damage to become apparent, so don't be content to look only at last month's job. If the previous work looks good, former clients offer enthusiastic endorsements, and the contractor seems to have some tree savvy, you may have found the one who will give you the results you seek.

If possible, work out a stick-and-carrot contract. Include a generous bonus for your contractor taking the extra precautions necessary to preserve your trees, because these precautions may cost considerable money or time to implement. Couple that incentive with a penalty clause that deducts for any unapproved tree damage in accordance with standard tree-appraisal procedures adopted by the International Society of Arboriculture and administered by your arborist. Before construction begins, invite the arborist back to document preconstruction conditions, with the contractor present, so there will be no misunderstanding later regarding construction-caused damage.

While the arborist and contractor are together, ask the arborist to review the protection measures that should be used during construction. This will include the careful removal of any trees that are to be cleared and the installation of protective temporary fencing to limit construction traffic and material stockpiling to designated areas away from the roots of your most important or sensitive trees. It should also include a final walk-through of the field-staked design with the landscape architect to fine-tune the plans, especially if substantial grade changes are involved.

Once the project is underway, expect the contractor to perform exactly as you have agreed. Understand, however, that the contractor probably won't be on the job site every minute, constantly supervising his or her employees and subcontractors. Many of those workers will believe that a tree is a post with leaves and will think nothing of disturbances within the root zone as long as

LEFT: Trees should be respected as living organisms, not treated as architectural structures.
RIGHT: Bulldozer blight is the most common tree disease in North America.

they stay away from the trunk. They might not realize that spilled fuel, concrete slurry, mortar, and paint are toxic to the roots. They also might not realize that temporary stockpiles of soil or building materials can suffocate the roots, or that soil compaction from parking vehicles in the shade can do just as much harm.

Such workers also might not be aware that pruning of minor branches that are in the way should be done with a saw, not with a backhoe or the tailgate of a dump truck. They might not know that any necessary backhoe excavation within the root zone should be preceded by shallow root pruning with a trencher. The hoe work should be done from a radial position (facing the tree) with a vertical slicing motion, so that any unpruned roots are not wrenched in a lateral direction; and any broken or torn roots should be trimmed cleanly with a saw and kept from drying or freezing while the excavation is open.

Workers might not know such things, or they might not care, so keep after them. These are your trees, after all, and they are worth the trouble. Remember that you will only have to do this once, and that the effects of skimping on tree protection cannot be undone. If you weren't the type of person who feels your trees are worth the effort, you wouldn't be reading this book.

There is another side to construction protection. Until now we have been talking about protecting the trees from the construction or remodeling of the house, but it is critical that consideration also be given to protecting the house from the trees. A picturesque old tree on a hillside across the ravine from a house, silhouetted against a full moon with a resident owl perched on a craggy limb, can become a hazard the moment buildings, automobiles, or routine human activities are positioned beneath its weathered canopy. Hollow trees can live a long time, but they are more likely to break under the force of wind or ice than are solid, vigorous trees.

Dead or broken limbs high in the crown of a tree, resulting from wind, lightning, or root damage, are called widow-makers for a very good reason. Knowingly allowing them to remain in high-use areas can result in a negligence claim if someone is injured by one that falls. Live

branches that arch above a roof with reasonable clearance on a calm winter day can sag several feet under the load of foliage, fruit, or ice, sweeping away the surface of your shingles. Any branches in a position to sag or blow into overhead utility lines will also cause difficulties. Have the lines moved if possible, or have the branches pruned.

The part of a tree you don't see, the half beneath the ground, can invade porous tile lines, heave sidewalks, and crack footings if the tree is too close. Since tree roots do not need to support themselves against gravity, like limbs do, they taper rapidly to a long, slender ropelike configuration as they spread from the base of the tree. These ropelike roots don't expand much in diameter as they grow, so heaving sidewalks and bulging foundations can usually be avoided if the tree is no closer than about 10 feet (3 m) away. If closer construction is unavoidable, or the architectural element involved is particularly fragile, commercial root barriers should be considered.

The long, ropelike lateral roots travel like vines underground and can easily reach a tile line beyond the dripline of the tree's canopy. Once a root penetrates a crack or flaw in the line and finds the interior to its liking, it will begin to branch repeatedly, eventually clogging the tile. Inexpensive copper compounds are available to curtail such root penetration without harming the tree; they should be used annually if there is any potential for a problem.

Once the perils of construction have been negotiated, do whatever you can for the next several years to minimize stress on your trees. Insect outbreaks, droughts, and other routine problems that healthy trees take in stride will be more serious during the recovery period following construction. Sudden competition from turf roots, unknown in the forest primeval, may become a major problem for any tree in a newly created backyard. Poor soil aeration from compaction, drainage changes, frequent irrigation of a new lawn, or excessive moisture from a malfunctioning leaching field can cause root decay and even death.

A tree has likely survived construction if after a pe-

riod of several years there is no dieback or chlorosis occurring in the upper part of the canopy, no fungi are visible on or around the base, and the annual growth increment at the ends of the twigs has returned to the normal amount seen prior to construction activity. Once you are satisfied that your trees have recovered, you can relax your vigilance somewhat and slip into a more casual, long-term management mode.

This involves the obvious, such as deep watering during severe droughts, and organic mulching. Mulching, in fact, was recognized as a beneficial technique as early as 1627 by Sir Francis Bacon, who stated in his epic tree book *Sylva Sylvarum* that mulching "retaineth the moisture which falleth at any time upon the tree, and suffereth it not to be exhaled by the Sunne." Establishing a broad, shallowly mulched area around a tree remains one of the most effective ways to moderate weather extremes, control competing weeds, and simulate natural, woodsy soil conditions.

Such mulched areas need not be circular nor conform to any other specific shape. The bigger they are the more protected the root zone will be. Mulch should not be piled against the bark, which can cause fungus problems, and it need not be more than toe deep to be effective. Ferns, woodland wildflowers, spring bulbs, and other compatible understory plants can be inserted carefully to liven up the mulched area if desired, as long as you do not rototill the tree's root zone area to prepare it for planting. Spring ephemerals are particularly desirable because they become dormant in summer and do not compete with the trees for moisture during hot, dry conditions.

You might consider lightning protection if you have a valuable specimen or a tall tree on an exposed hill. Cabling and bracing can be a sensible investment if your tree has a structural weakness. These measures should not be considered do-it-yourself items, however: contract a qualified arborist. You might also ask the arborist to handle any pruning that is beyond your capability or comfort level, such as thinning the crown or removing high branches or very large limbs.

Don't ever ask arborists to "top" a tree, however, unless you are testing their knowledge. If they are willing to do such a thing, they are underqualified or unethical and

LEFT: Lack of attention to structural weaknesses in your trees can lead to massive storm damage.
RIGHT: Do not permit anyone to butcher your trees.

should not be hired. Topping destroys the tree's appearance and structural integrity, leading to premature death. It is only legitimate to top a tree if it is already damaged and temporary preservation of the trunk and lower crown is deemed preferable to immediate removal. Good arborists will often prune so subtly that when they leave it is difficult to determine they were ever there.

Prune young trees as needed when they are still small, removing double leaders, suckers, and parallel or clustered limbs to encourage a strong, aesthetic limb structure. Remove lower limbs gradually over several years, if at all, to raise the crown. Pruning recommendations have changed over the past few years based upon research into how trees grow, so read one of the many current books on pruning or seek advice from a knowledgeable person. Avoid leaving long branch stubs exposed to decay, but also avoid cutting through the thickened basal collar of the branch. This collar is formed from the wood fibers that bypass the limb to reach the rest of the tree, and these fibers will promote rapid overgrowth of the pruning scar if left undisturbed.

Trees often have a pleasant way of attracting wildlife. One member of that wildlife cadre, however, has become the scourge of trees and natural areas throughout much of North America: deer. These beautiful native animals are managed for hunters by some state wildlife agencies at population levels far in excess of historical densities, and we all pay a needless price for this mismanagement. If you live in deer country, your part of this price (from

your trees' point of view) could be crown deformation caused by excessive browsing of foliage, or girdling caused by antler-rubbing of stems each fall. Deer seem to know how to select the most prized specimens to attack, so be prepared with whatever solutions are effective in your situation. These measures may include using repellants (if you are willing to be vigilant about their frequent application), putting up fencing, keeping a dog nearby, and constructing barriers around individual trees.

The risk of antler damage is highest for young trees up to about 4 inches (10 cm) in diameter, especially those that are installed in the open or that have been exposed by brush removal around their bases during landscape development. Frequently all it takes to discourage deer is to set a few tall metal stakes around the tree. Try to use something that will blend in aesthetically, and encourage the tree to grow quickly to a size that will make it immune from further deer attacks. Those who plant trees in moose or elk country should also plan to establish a close relationship with an anger management counselor!

If you live in a rural area, livestock can present similar

problems. Horses and goats can be especially destructive and must be fenced away from trees. Horses have been known to girdle magnificent oak trees several hundred years old, killing them in the process, although this tendency varies with the individual animal and perhaps with its nutrition. Cattle and sheep are grazers rather than browsers and are therefore much less likely to cause problems unless they are present in such numbers that they cause soil compaction or ammonia toxicity under the shade of the tree canopy.

If some of your young trees were transplanted, or suddenly exposed to the wind by the removal of their neighbors, you might need to stake them for the first growing season. This should be avoided unless necessary, and any staking should permit the natural flexing that builds caliper and wood strength. The traditional practice of staking new trees is currently yielding to the ancient wisdom of Francis Bacon, who wrote, in 1627, that "binding doth hinder the natural swelling of the tree." Trees need to flex in order to build the taper that supports them as they grow, and they need to have room for diameter growth unimpeded by ropes and wires.

One problem that arises when densely wooded areas are thinned for construction is that some of the tall, slender young trees that had been forced to reach for the light are suddenly exposed to wind and sun. Some thin-barked species may be subject to sunscald damage, and the really slender ones that were previously able to lean on their neighbors for support might be bowed by a sudden wind or ice load, never again to stand erect. If your arborist is able to guy such trees very loosely for a couple of years, allowing them room to sway naturally but not to buckle completely, they will begin to build the caliper and stiffness necessary to survive in their newly exposed situation. The result will be tall, vigorous, stout young trees, as opposed to slender, arching stems with tips that reach down to sweep the ground and that must be removed.

Techniques for the management of insect and disease problems have evolved in stages over the years. In the first half of the twentieth century, North America was wallowing in the age of "modern" chemicals, and the accepted practice was to saturate the environment with the

LEFT: Wildlife can destroy unprotected young trees. RIGHT: If trees need temporary staking, tie them loosely so they can sway in the wind and develop strong stems. FAR RIGHT: Conks and burls are often harmless and add character to old trees.

most deadly toxic sprays available. Then we entered the age of *Silent Spring* and chemical backlash, and organic procedures came into vogue. This grew into the compromise age of integrated pest management (IPM), in which pest levels were monitored and actions were taken (with the least toxic alternative available) only if an economic or biological threshold of damage had been reached.

Finally we emerged into the age of plant health care (PHC), analogous to preventative health care for humans. Rather than wait idly for a problem to develop, we became proactive in maintaining health and vigor so that diseases and harmful insects were less likely to gain a footing. IPM, organic methods, and selected chemicals remain important parts of the process, but fertilizing, watering, mulching, correct pruning, and special treatments such as lightning protection and bracing also play important roles in maintaining tree health.

Regular inspection of your trees is a good way to identify potential problems before they become serious. Learn the primary problems to be expected with each species, or with each type of structural weakness, and concentrate your inspections in those areas and during the times when such problems are most likely to develop. Look for insect outbreaks when the critters are likely to be present but have not yet had enough time to do much damage. Look for splits and broken limbs after ice storms and windy periods. Check for disease problems at the stage when treatment, if needed, can be effective.

Examine your trees for abnormalities that might indicate something is wrong. Reduced growth rates, thin or pale foliage, fungi, heavy infestations of mistletoe, sprouts along the trunk, cracks and splits, holes from borers, large masses of gregarious caterpillars, wilting branches, and loose or cankered bark patches are examples of symptoms that can mean trouble. If you notice such signs, deal with them immediately or hire a professional who can.

If your inspection reveals that your trees are strong, healthy, and vigorous, the inspection time will not have been wasted. You will have become a little better acquainted with your environment and probably a little more appreciative of the trees that do so much to improve it.

MENU OF NATIVE TREES

SOME HOMEOWNERS PRESERVE what they can of their wooded sites, while others attempt to restore woodlands from the ruins of a former forest or create them from a farm field. Others never claim a piece of earth as their own, opting instead to live in a high-rise and connect with nature by hiking public parks, forests, or the wooded properties of friends and family. Whatever your situation, you will enjoy your environment much more if you learn about the trees that live there.

First let's agree on a definition for "tree." In the simplest sense a tree is a woody plant that, when mature, you can stand beneath, while a shrub is a woody plant you can stand beside. In definitions used to separate trees from other plant forms, size limits are frequently used, but they seem artificial and arbitrary. In addition, size is a contextual term: someone living in the pygmy pinyon woodlands of the Southwest might identify trees differently than someone living in an Appalachian cove forest. I like to give all candidates the benefit of the doubt and confer the honor of tree status wherever reasonably defensible.

I think growth habit is the most meaningful characteristic. Shrubs form clumps of canes or stems, none of which become dominant over the life of the plant, and maintain low crowns of foliage throughout their life spans. Some trees might also develop multiple stems, but the oldest stems remain dominant unless killed or

LEFT: White oak (*Quercus alba*).

injured, and the crowns generally elevate above eye level. This book includes some native species that others might consider large shrubs; in these instances the form of the mature plant guided my decision. Others are included if they become trees in part of their natural range, even if they remain smaller in other areas due to different habitat conditions.

Tree profiles are arranged alphabetically by scientific name, followed by the common name. Common names, which are not as uniform from region to region, are also listed in the index. In each profile, species not mentioned elsewhere in the book are emphasized with boldface for quick reference.

The information within each tree profile is given in the same sequence, beginning with a general description of the tree, including its potential size and special characteristics. The U.S. national champion trees, of record at the time the text was written, are mentioned to give a sense of the ultimate potential of each species. Synonyms are also included in cases where the scientific name recently changed or where such a revision is not universally accepted. For the sake of readability, I have avoided including technical references formally citing the taxonomic authority and original publication for naming each species, and I list only those synonyms that are most likely to lead to confusion.

Descriptions of leaves follow, since this is the feature most often noticed first about a tree. All leaves are assumed to be simple, deciduous, and alternately arranged along the twig unless otherwise indicated. Special attributes for each tree, such as interesting texture and fall color, are presented.

Flowers and fruit are described next, including ornamental and wildlife values, if they are significant, and very basic identification information. Some trees, such as dioecious species, have special flowering characteristics, and these are also noted. In the case of conifers, which have no true flowers, information is given about cones and seeds.

The tree profiles become a little subjective at this point as I offer my opinion regarding the best seasons for landscape value, listing each in order of preference. Your own viewpoint may differ with mine if, for example, you consider edible fruit more important than beautiful spring flowers; but I will give you my opinion just the same, and the reasons for it. Consider it a starting point in your appreciation of the best that each species might have to offer your landscape, and a clue as to how to combine different tree species for continuous landscape effect.

The overall native range of every tree species is described, along with the additional adaptive range where it might grow successfully under cultivation. Once again, keep in mind that provenance and habitat conditions influence the presence or performance of individual trees at specific locations. I use the USDA plant hardiness zones as a beginning because they are a widely accepted, uniform system. While these zones are actually divided into "A" and "B" components, this can be misleading and confusing, and since few authorities agree to that level of detail, subzones are not mentioned. Extent and timing of cold weather is more important than the subzone. Consider the zone ratings a general guide, nothing more. My personal experience with growing trees has been in USDA zone 5, so ratings given to that zone may be taken with a little added assurance.

There is much more to plant adaptability than tolerance of winter cold, so I offer cultural suggestions regarding soils, moisture, exposure, proper pruning, and other factors that can make or break a tree. I also offer information based upon my own lifetime of experience with transplantation and propagation.

Every tree has problems, and in each tree profile I discuss the main ones. Scientific names are given for insect pests and diseases so that you are able to look up more detailed information elsewhere, but the pest lists are not intended to be comprehensive. Physiological weaknesses inherent within each tree species, and any serious problems caused by the tree itself, are mentioned, as are sensitivities to environmental stresses.

Next is a discussion of cultivars available from nurseries, and the news concerning cultivars is both good and bad. The good news is that they consist of plants chosen for special virtues such as unique form or spectacular flowers or fall color, and that every plant of the same cultivar is genetically identical and predictable. The bad news is that reliance upon a few cultivars leads to genetic impoverishment in the landscape, and that some cultivars are selected for particular attributes, such as disease resistance or hardiness, at the expense of others. Some cultivars will not grow well except in their region of origin, and overuse of cultivars leads to a narrowing of the genetic diversity that can protect trees from quick-spreading plagues.

Strict reliance upon cultivars also eliminates the individuality of plants. With "natural" trees, grown from seed, there is the suspense of not knowing precisely what each tree will look like until it grows past adolescence. Depending upon your needs, this can be either exciting or frustrating. If you need uniformity or predictability, select an appropriate cultivar, if one is available. If you want a more natural variation or want to avoid having your trees be part of a narrow, potentially overplanted neighborhood monoculture, choose seed-propagated trees grown by reliable nurseries from a locally adapted seed source. As an alternative, propagate your own seedlings or cuttings from selected local parent trees with special characteristics you admire.

If you choose a cultivar, remember that true cultivar names (those that can be registered legally for plant patents) and trade names (those that can be registered as trademarks and copyrighted) are not the same. Clones may have both types of names, or neither one. Some so-called cultivars are actually seed germplasm selections propagated by seed from selected individuals or breeding groups, and these maintain some genetic variability. Patents, trademarks, and copyrights can apply to a tree, to one or more of its names, or to the business interests that own rights to it. Most popular horticultural reference books don't differentiate completely among these categories, and various nomenclature systems for trees are used interchangeably even at many botanic gardens.

This is not a book about cultivars or nomenclature. So, with sincere apologies to name nitpickers everywhere, I have decided to use the simplest names most likely to be recognizable in the trade in order to make it easier for you to find the specific plants you need. Nomenclatural lingo is worse than lawyer-speak, so you will not find long strings of alphabet-soup cultivar names with attributions in this book, followed by trade names, punctuated by various typographic symbols designating the present status of registration or patenting of a plant or its name, despite the fact that such lengthy name sequences are technically most correct.

If you wish to delve more deeply into the morass of horticultural nomenclature, you will find the best information in *The International Code of Nomenclature for Cultivated Plants* (Trehane et al. 1995), which is updated periodically. You'll find I like to tease taxonomists, but that's because some of them are my good friends (and they're so easy!). I must give a lot of credit to one such friend, Piers Trehane, and to his commission for trying to sort out this mess. I recommend their work to anyone who truly wants to know more about it, and it is mandatory reading if you are thinking about naming a plant.

Now that the nomenclature issue is behind us forever, let's return to the tree profiles. After cultivars I mention similar and related species, describing the main characteristics that make them different from the featured species. Some of these species are common in North America but similar to those already described, and some are shrubby relatives of the larger trees. Some are suggested for planting, others just to preserve and admire in situ for their beauty or for wildlife. I try to provide a little information on each tree's familial relationships and occasionally mention commonly encountered exotic trees related to the native species.

The final comments on each species are intended to spark your interest. Special wildlife values or historical associations are discussed, and I include some of my personal experiences. All trees have many stories. As you become more familiar with trees and live among them, you can begin to take increasing delight in adding your own tree lore.

Abies balsamea

BALSAM FIR

DESCRIPTION: Balsam fir is one of the most cold-hardy and aromatic of all conifers. It thrives in cold, moist climates throughout most of Canada, yet can be grown successfully down through the midlatitude United States in Iowa, Illinois, and eastward as far south as Virginia, from sea level up to the highest elevations that can support tree growth. Balsam fir, with its dense, pointed silhouette, is a common component of our boreal forests and has been named the arboreal emblem of New Brunswick.

The largest balsam on record in the United States is in a residential yard in Fairfield, Pennsylvania. It stands 100 feet (30 m) tall and almost 4 feet (1.2 m) in diameter and has a unique question-mark top, developed as the terminal shoot aborted high in the tree a few years ago. Even larger specimens may exist in Canada, but most balsams are medium-sized trees. Balsam fir often retains its attractive, dense habit and full, symmetrical, spire-shaped crown throughout its life.

LEAVES: Balsam needles are flattened and soft to the touch, less than 1 inch (2.5 cm) long, dark green on top with contrasting lighter abaxial surfaces, and arranged in horizontal ranks on the lateral branches. They are pleasantly aromatic when broken or scraped, making this tree a good selection for use in fragrance gardens. The persistent, user-friendly foliage and fragrance also make balsam fir a favorite Christmas tree.

CONES AND SEEDS: Staminate strobili sometimes show to advantage as they release their greenish yellow pollen. The female strobili, or cones, stand erect on the upper branches, about 3 inches (7.5 cm) long and sticky with resin. As is the case with other true firs, the cones disintegrate on the tree when ripe and don't pose a significant litter problem. Many are opened by chickadees, crossbills, purple finches, and grosbeaks for the nutritious seeds they contain; others are gathered intact by squirrels, who take them away to secret places when they think you aren't watching.

BEST SEASONS: WINTER (this is a classic evergreen that holds its rich green color well all winter). FALL (as an attractive foil for colorful maples and birches) and SPRING (the light green new growth contrasts well with mature foliage from the previous year). SUMMER (balsam is always good as a background plant or as an isolated specimen where an accent form is desired).

NATIVE AND ADAPTIVE RANGE: Balsam fir extends north in Canada to the Peace River in northern Alberta, around James Bay, and across to the coast of Labrador. It grows throughout much of northern North America, from northern Canada south into the Lake States and New England. It can be planted successfully from USDA zone 2 south, wherever summers are cool and moist. It does not perform well south of USDA zone 5 unless given a cool north-facing slope or a lakeshore site. Its natural range is a good indication of the area where it will thrive under cultivation without special attention.

CULTURE: Balsam can do well in shade or on seasonally wet soil, which are conditions fatal to many other conifers. It prefers acidic, organic, friable soil that is kept cool and moist during the growing season. If possible, southern plantings should be located next to cool springs, caves, or other features that provide a cool microclimate, and kept away from hot masonry walls or air conditioner compressors that generate heat.

Balsam is very easy to transplant and establish. I once transplanted a 15-foot (4.5-m) tree by hand, with no reduction in growth rate beyond the first season. Where its requirements for a cool, moist environment can be met, balsam is also one of our most smog-tolerant conifers. It is very resistant to attack by Gypsy moths (*Lymantria dispar*), which frequently defoliate much of the surrounding forest in the East.

PROBLEMS: This tree can develop a ragged appearance with age, especially if planted too far south of its natural range, in areas with hot summers. It is among the most susceptible North American conifers to browsing and antler rubbing by deer and moose. Balsam fir is sensitive to air pollution in hot urban areas and to windthrow on exposed sites. It can be damaged or killed by heavy infestations of the spruce budworm (*Choristoneura fumifer-*

RIGHT: Balsams (*Abies balsamea*) shedding snow in winter.

ana) or the balsam woolly adelgid (*Adelges piceae*), which was introduced into Maine from Europe in 1908. It can also be damaged by late spring freezes. In naturalized or wild stands, its low branches, abundant resin blisters, and thin bark make it very sensitive to wildfires.

CULTIVARS: No tree-sized cultivars are commonly available. Named globe and prostrate forms can be found in botanic gardens and dwarf conifer collections. Balsam is easy to graft, and attractive individuals can be propagated readily.

SIMILAR AND RELATED SPECIES: The Fraser fir (*Abies fraseri*) is confined in the wild to high altitudes in the Appalachian Mountains. Like balsam fir it is commonly planted at lower elevations for ornamental and Christmas tree purposes. It is very similar to balsam but more southerly and alpine in distribution, with shorter, more contrasting, less aromatic foliage. It requires better drainage but is less susceptible to spring freeze damage. Fraser fir is becoming an endangered species in the mountains of its natural habitat due to mortality from acid rain and the woolly adelgid. A reported hybrid between the two species, called Canaan fir, is grown by Christmas tree growers. Some botanists classify Canaan fir as *A. balsamea* var. *phanerolepsis*.

Many beautiful firs can be found in the western states and provinces. Some selections of the white fir (*Abies concolor*) of the Rocky Mountains also grow well in the East. This tree is one of the most adaptable and forgiving of all firs regarding climate conditions, and it is one of the most striking, with its long blue-green foliage highlighted by bright blue-white new growth in spring. It tolerates hot summers better than any other hardy fir and even grows reasonably well in urban smog conditions and somewhat alkaline soil. The U.S. national champion, found in northern Utah, is 94 feet (28.2 m) tall. 'Candicans' has especially long, colorful needles and forms a narrowly upright tree.

Subalpine fir (*Abies lasiocarpa*) and corkbark fir (*A. lasiocarpa* var. *arizonica*) are beautiful, spire-shaped western mountain trees but are best enjoyed in the wild because they are not fond of lower elevations. They are very tall and narrow in habit, the largest known example being 125 feet (37.5 m) tall with a wingspan of only 26 feet (7.8 m). Several exotic fir species are also common in cultivation.

TOP LEFT: Balsam fir (*Abies balsamea*). LEFT: Foliage of balsam fir. RIGHT: White fir (*A. concolor*). FAR RIGHT: Douglasfir (*Pseudotsuga menziesii*).

One dominant tree encountered in the foothills of the Rocky Mountains, and on up the slopes to fairly high elevations, is Douglasfir (**Pseudotsuga menziesii**), specifically variety *glauca*. Douglasfir is not a true fir, and it has an interesting taxonomic history, having been bounced around from one genus to another before finally being given one of its own. It has unique cones with forked, snake-tongue-like bracts extending from each scale. Like white fir (*Abies concolor*), this tree adapts readily to planting far beyond the limits of its natural range and habitat as long as it has sun and good drainage, and it is widely cultivated. Only the Rocky Mountain variety should be used in our region because the larger, more vigorous coastal *P. menziesii* var. *menziesii*, the state tree of Oregon, and the rare, large-coned **P. macrocarpa** of southern California are not reliably hardy east of their native ranges. *Pseudotsuga menziesii* 'Fastigiata' is a narrow, up-right cultivar, and 'Glauca Pendula' and 'Graceful Grace' are weepers.

COMMENTS: Many of us can remember attaching cover slips to microscope slides in science class with a sticky, fragrant substance called Canada balsam. It was a natural product: the resin of the balsam fir tree. Trimmings of balsam fir also make comfortable, fragrant beds, attractive holiday decorations, and great winter mulch for tender perennials.

Firs are important wildlife trees. My wife, Edie, and I once stood silently in a fir forest until the local red squirrels, emboldened by the quiet, began to bombard us with the cones they were harvesting for winter. The fragrant, flat boughs of balsam and Fraser firs also host a variety of rare mosses and liverworts and are preferred nesting sites for many birds.

Acer negundo

MANITOBA MAPLE

DESCRIPTION: The Manitoba maple—known as boxelder in much of the United States (though neither a boxwood nor an elder) and as *erable a Giguere* in Quebec—is a compound-leaved native maple, and the only maple we have that is consistently dioecious. It is able to survive under more adverse conditions than any of our other maple species and is widely planted throughout the world wherever a resilient, fast-growing tree is needed. However, it is also notorious as a weedy, short-lived, insect- and decay-prone seed machine with weak wood and relatively few other redeeming qualities.

Its fast growth and subsequent tendency toward structural damage and decay help Manitoba maple provide many cavity homes for wildlife in riparian agricultural areas previously cleared of forest habitat. Although it usually attains only a modest size, Manitoba maple can grow into a large tree. One tree in Lenawee County, Michigan, is 110 feet (33 m) tall and more than 5 feet (1.5 m) thick.

LEAVES: Manitoba maple leaves are always pinnately compound and opposite, with three to seven coarsely toothed leaflets of variable size on long petiolules. They occasionally turn a decent yellow in fall but often persist in their green summer color until scorched off by the first hard freeze. They resemble ash (*Fraxinus*) leaves in general form and phyllotaxy, which is why the tree is sometimes called ash-leaved maple. Some cultivars have been selected for foliage color.

FLOWERS AND FRUIT: Nature sometimes sorts these dioecious trees by gender on harsh sites. Manitoba maples growing along streams in such areas often tend to be female, while those surviving on adjacent uplands are usually male. This is due to complex and fascinating gender-biased, competitive evolutionary processes as yet only partially understood, relating to the metabolic costs associated with seed production for females and the effects of location upon optimum pollen distribution for males. The fruits are borne in pendent racemes that often persist into winter. While many of them are sterile, enough good ones are produced to enable this opportunistic tree to occupy every available nook and cranny in the landscape.

BEST SEASONS: SUMMER (especially for those cultivars with attractive foliage or where the shade from this tough tree provides a welcome refuge from the hot sun of the High Plains). WINTER (for vigorous young plants with brightly colored twigs).

NATIVE AND ADAPTIVE RANGE: Manitoba maple can be found in the wild from Vermont west across the continent into southern Saskatchewan, southwest to the California coast (as subspecies *californicum*), and south in suitable habitats to the Gulf Coast and into Mexico and Central America. It will adapt under cultivation anywhere in our region south of USDA zone 2, assuming local ecotypes are used, and can be found naturalized throughout Europe and many parts of Asia.

CULTURE: Some gardeners might advise you to plant it and then hurry out of its way. Many others would suggest you avoid planting it at all. Where its contributions are welcome, give this tree any reasonable soil and adequate moisture in full sun or part shade for best performance. Prune it while young to train it to a strong structural shape. Alternatively, it will survive nearly anywhere with no care whatsoever, albeit perhaps not as a handsome specimen.

Manitoba maple grows so easily from seed that it is frequently used as understock by nurseries for grafting other maples. The maple research program run by the Morton Arboretum in Illinois experiments with it in hybridization, attempting to blend its toughness with the ornamental qualities of other, less hardy maples.

PROBLEMS: The flowers of female trees are the primary food of the detested but harmless red-and-black boxelder bugs (*Leptocoris trivittatus*) that invade houses each fall. This problem, as well as unwanted seed litter, can be minimized by planting or saving only male trees. More often the concern with Manitoba maple is that it is invasive, weak wooded, decay prone, and generally the prototype of the weedy species. Still, beauty is in the eye of the beholder.

RIGHT: Manitoba maple (*Acer negundo*) shades a yard.

CULTIVARS: Several variegated Manitoba maple selections are useful even in the most refined, formal landscapes. 'Auratum' and 'Kelley's Gold' have yellow leaves, 'Elegans' has variegated yellow and green leaves, and 'Flamingo' is a dwarf female selection with variegated pink and white leaves. Its sterile fruit seems to make 'Flamingo' less attractive to boxelder bugs than most female specimens. The male 'Sensation' is unusual for its bright red fall color. 'Baron', from Manitoba, is an upright form with normal foliage. The western subspecies *californicum* has yielded two popular cultivars: 'Variegatum' with white variegation and 'Violaceum' with purple young leaves that later turn green. Maple experts often ponder the infraspecific taxonomy of Manitoba maple, and it is such a broadly adapted and variable species that classification of varieties should probably not be considered an exact science.

SIMILAR AND RELATED SPECIES: Three other native maples, shrubby species that sometimes become small trees, are among our most beautiful ornamental native plants where they are adapted to local conditions. Rocky Mountain maple (*Acer glabrum*) is a small, hardy species nearly as variable as Manitoba maple. Its leaves may or may not be compound (trifoliate), and occasionally both leaf types are found on the same tree. Leaves turn yellow in fall, contrasting nicely with the conifers that share this maple's natural habitat in the Black Hills and Rocky Mountains. It grows in the wild from Alaska south through the mountains of New Mexico. Striped maple (*Acer pensylvanicum*) and mountain maple (*A. spicatum*) are eastern and boreal understory species that cannot be established easily in hot, sunny locations or very far outside their natural ranges. In this regard, all three of these small maples occupy the opposite end of the adaptability scale from Manitoba maple. However, as native trees by the strictest of definitions, where they exist as natural components of the local forest, they are spectacular ornamentals and are especially cold hardy. Striped maple will survive north into USDA zone 3, and mountain maple grows north to USDA zone 2. Rocky Mountain maple is not seen frequently in cultivation and is happiest on well-drained sites at high elevations in western mountain ranges, north (actually, up) to at least USDA zone 4.

Striped maple is slightly larger than mountain maple and more often grows as a graceful, arching small tree with beautifully patterned bark. *Acer pensylvanicum* 'Erythrocladum' rivals the most colorful Asian coral-bark maples. Mountain maple and Rocky Mountain maple usually exist as large, erect shrubs or small, multiple-stemmed trees. The largest striped maple on record grows in Nassau County, New York, at the Bailey Arboretum and is more than 75 feet (22.5 m) tall and 15 inches (37.5 cm) in diameter, while the biggest mountain maple is in Houghton County, Michigan, and is about 60 feet (18 m) in height and 10 inches (25 cm) in diameter. These champion trees are exceptional, however, as most members of their species are much smaller. Rocky Mountain maple actually grows larger west of our area (as *A. glabrum* var. *douglasii*) than it does in the Rocky Mountains. The U.S. national champion tree, in Washington State, is about as tall as the champion striped maple and twice as thick.

LEFT: Spreading roots of Manitoba maple (*Acer negundo*).
RIGHT: A variegated form of Manitoba maple.

Striped maple leaves turn a bright, clear yellow in fall, while those of mountain maple turn a brilliant mottled orange. Both species have textured, rugose, opposite leaves that are ornamental in spring and summer, and both have attractive flower clusters—those of striped maple are pendulous, while those of mountain maple develop as erect spikes. These two small trees are among the most resistant of all maples to attack by the voracious Gypsy moth (*Lymantria dispar*) and should be used in areas subject to attack by that pest.

I have admired beautiful masses of mountain maple along shorelines in Quetico Provincial Park and along some of the northeastern tributary streams of Lake Superior in western Ontario. Equally impressive striped maples can be seen in the Adirondacks of upstate New York and across to Mount Desert Island, Maine. Where they can be grown, and especially where they occur in the wild, both maples rival the best Asian maples for fall color, bark, graceful form, and bloom.

Striped maple flowers are fascinating in that they may be influenced into being all female in any given year, on any given tree, by local environmental conditions; their gender is not determined until they begin to expand in spring. Dormant branches cut for forcing in early spring will be female and may be displayed indoors in a vase with confidence that they will not litter the room with pollen, while the branches left on the same tree might produce copious amounts of the stuff.

These three small maples are best adapted to cool, shady, moist areas and rocky soils. Striped maple and mountain maple do best in Canada, the northern Lake States, and the Appalachians, while Rocky Mountain maple grows best in sunnier, streamside habitats above 5000 feet (1500 m) in the western mountains.

COMMENTS: A well-grown Manitoba maple can be an attractive shade tree, and its early flowers add a pleasant froth of yellow-green above the banks of prairie creeks. In general, though, this species is most appreciated in those harsh areas of the High Plains where it is one of the few trees able to survive. Manitoba maple was cited in a conference on xeriscaping at the University of Saskatchewan as one of the best trees for drought toler-

ance. Still, it is happier along streams, where it has unlimited access to moisture, and is quite tolerant of seasonal flooding along rivers. The heartwood is subject to a rather innocuous fungus condition, *Fusarium roseum*, which imparts a striking rosy color.

This maple usually lives a hard life and consequently doesn't last too long, but there are a few old specimens. One stands at Cannonball House in St. Michaels, Maryland. Lanterns were hung from it to confuse enemy gunners during the War of 1812.

BELOW LEFT: Striped maple (*Acer pensylvanicum*) foliage.
BELOW: A striped maple in the forest understory.

Acer rubrum

RED MAPLE

DESCRIPTION: Red maple is among the most colorful and popular trees in the eastern United States. The state tree of Rhode Island (a translation from the original Dutch gives us "Red" Island), it is a tree for all seasons that develops into an attractive yard specimen under a great range of soil and climate conditions.

Similar to its close relative silver maple (*Acer saccharinum*), red maple grows fairly quickly in favorable situations and occurs naturally in habitats ranging from boreal forests to southern swamps, in full sun or shade. It can be found on shallow, rocky upland forest soils in deep shade, in wet interdunal areas along lakeshores, on old strip mine spoil banks, and on floating logs in the swamps and bayous of the South. Red maple generally develops a uniform crown of ascending limbs and can attain a very large size. The U.S. national champion tree is 179 feet (53.7 m) tall and nearly 6 feet (1.8 m) in diameter. Its canopy shades a considerable piece of real estate in St. Clair County, Michigan.

Typically, however, this is a medium-large tree. Although it is a soft maple (section *Rubra*), red maple is not as prone to storm damage as silver maple. Red maples selected from northern areas are extremely winter hardy, and those from southern areas are very heat resistant; the reverse, though, is not always true. Likewise, upland and swamp types might not always be at home in each others' habitats.

LEAVES: The opposite leaves of this species are variable from tree to tree, ranging from 2 to 6 inches (5 to 15 cm) long, from three-lobed to five-lobed, and from light green to woolly white underneath. The emerging spring color, and especially fall color, can be exceptional, but these characteristics also vary considerably.

FLOWERS AND FRUIT: True harbingers of spring, the flowers of red maple can provide a scarlet mist of color in the forest very early in the year, especially in trees that are predominately female. Individual red maple trees can be mostly male, mostly female, or anything in between, and some might change their dominant gender from year to year in response to stress. Red maple is actually one of the more uniformly dioecious maples, but both staminate and pistillate trees are attractive in bloom. The paired fruits, or samaras (also known as schizocarps by those who like to throw around big words), are bright red, and they mature in spring, unlike those of most other native maples.

BEST SEASONS: FALL (for the majority of individual trees, which display the magnificent scarlet fall color for which the entire species has become known). EARLY SPRING (for those with the best flower color). WINTER (for vigorous young trees, which have smooth, silvery gray bark). SUMMER (for those varieties with contrasting leaf surfaces that shimmer in the wind).

NATIVE AND ADAPTIVE RANGE: Red maple grows from Lake of the Woods in southeastern Manitoba across southern Canada to Lake St. John and the Gaspe Peninsula in Quebec, and southward throughout the eastern United States. Its western limit is closely linked to the boundary of the Prairie Peninsula, the eastern extension of tallgrass prairie into Illinois and Indiana. Red maple selections from comparable climate and soil areas can be grown in almost any location in our area of Canada and the United States that will support tree growth. However, none of them seem to enjoy dry heat, and they are not the best choices for exposed midwestern prairie sites or for soils with a pH above about 7.0.

CULTURE: This tree can be transplanted very easily at any size, preferably in early spring. Give it enough water and protect its thin bark from salt and sun exposure. Watch out for manganese deficiency chlorosis on high pH soils. Wild red maples in forest areas are very sensitive to fire, again because of their smooth, thin bark, but will resprout vigorously. If you prefer a seedling tree over a cultivar yet demand good fall color, select your tree at the nursery in fall when it shows its "true colors." Standard precautions about geographic provenance are particularly applicable to this species: always try to use locally adapted trees when planting a red maple.

PROBLEMS: Red maple can be damaged by sunscald, ice glazing, insufficient soil acidity, *Verticillium* wilt (caused by the ubiquitous vascular fungi *V. dahliae* and *V. albo-atrum*), and drought. Tar spot fungus (*Rhytisma acerinum*) causes unsightly but harmless blotches on the

leaves of this and some other maples in late summer. Leafhopper insects (*Alebra albostriella* and *Empoasca fabae*) sometimes cause considerably more serious injury, and many other insects will nibble here and there. The most serious new threat is the Asian longhorned borer beetle (*Anoplophora glabripennis*), which delights in carving finger-sized holes in the trunks of many maple species.

Most red maples are not very resistant to decay and begin to decline following any substantial structural damage or bark injury. This damage is often initiated by salt burn or sunscald in roadside plantings, especially if the trees are planted in hot, dry sites. Red maple is a preferred browse species for deer and moose, both of which cause heavy damage in some regions. Failure due to graft incompatibility (similar to organ-transplant rejection in humans) can be a serious concern with some cultivars, unless they are grown from cuttings or tissue culture.

Red maple (and probably other maples) can cause acute hemolytic anemia in horses if grown in pastures where its leaves are accessible for browsing. In some cases this affliction is fatal, so caution should be used when permitting horses to forage among these trees. A horse, of course, can also be considered a fatal disease of trees. Horses are best kept away from trees of any species, as individual animals can be very destructive if they develop a taste for foliage or bark.

Although red maple casts a relatively open shade that permits turf growth under the crown, its shallow roots can cause problems in neatly groomed lawns. Like the notorious Norway maple (*Acer platanoides*) and our native sugar maple (*A. saccharum*), red maple can become a weedy species in the understory of some mature forests that are not subjected to periodic ground fire, gradually succeeding other trees in the canopy and converting the woods to maple dominance. Fire will provide control of red maple where this control is wanted—and careless use of string trimmers will provide such control where it is not wanted.

CULTIVARS: The naturally occurring Drummond red maple (*Acer rubrum* var. *drummondii*) has large leaves with whitened woolly undersides and grows in southern swamps. *Acer rubrum* cultivars are too numerous to give a thorough account of here. Some are upright or fastigiate, like 'Bowhall', 'Columnare', 'Autumn Spire', and 'Karpick', while many others were selected for their exceptional fall color, like 'Autumn Flame', 'Embers', and

the red maples trademarked as October Glory, Firedance, and Red Sunset. October Glory and Red Sunset are among the most brilliantly flowered selections, as are 'Autumn Spire', 'Embers', 'Festival', 'September Song', and 'Shade King', all functionally female except for 'September Song'. The immature fruits of the females, which are the same color as the flowers, prolong the spring show.

A few, like 'Northwood' from Minnesota, 'Olson', and 'Phipps Farm', were introduced as colorful trees with tough foliage or extreme hardiness. 'Magnificent Magenta', propagated from a female tree found in northeastern Kansas, is one of these, with dramatic fall color and superior stress resistance. 'Autumn Spire', a product of the hardy plant research program managed by my friend Harold Pellett in Minnesota, is a cold-tolerant columnar selection. 'Autumn Flame', which tolerates higher pH soils and hotter conditions than most, 'Karpick', 'September Song', and some others are seedless males. 'Red Rocket' and 'New World' are newer selections that appear resistant to leafhoppers and cold climates while displaying outstanding fall color. 'Fairview Flame' is a colorful selection adapted to the Deep South.

SIMILAR AND RELATED SPECIES: Many people know silver maple (***Acer saccharinum***), somewhat unfairly, as a large, fast-growing shade tree with invasive roots, messy seeds, brittle branches, and a weak crown structure. It is also viewed with disdain as a "poor folks' tree" frequently planted in lieu of a more expensive, "quality" tree.

Silver maples can attain great size very rapidly, often

LEFT: Red maple (*Acer rubrum*) can be brilliant in fall.
RIGHT: Foliage and fruits of silver maple (*A. saccharinum*).

exceeding 100 feet (30 m) in height and 3 feet (0.9 m) in diameter. The former U.S. record tree, located in Columbia County, Wisconsin, is 115 feet (34.5 m) tall and almost 8 feet (2.4 m) thick. It grows as a clump, like most of its neighbors. A shorter specimen in Iowa has a trunk more than 10 feet (3 m) in diameter.

The branches of this species develop a characteristic sweeping pattern, with upturned ends, which can give such large old trees a graceful outline. Young silver maple seedlings frequently form dense "dog-hair" stands in abandoned bottomland fields, where the red color of their twigs en masse over the silver-gray bark of the lower

stems can make an otherwise stark floodplain landscape glow warmly on sunny winter days. The leaves can turn a good, clear yellow in fall, with some specimens being brighter than others.

One of silver maple's most valuable ornamental assets comes from the timing of the red flower clusters, which appear even before those of red maple and are among the first signs that winter is losing its grip on the cold northland, offering us hope for spring. Beauty is a comparative perception, and during the time when silver maples bloom, frequently glowing through coatings of ice, they are the belles of the ball. Like red maple, silver maple can be dioecious but is not predominantly so. The whirling airborne seeds add a dynamic life to the landscape but can be a real nuisance if they fall on patios or germinate (as they love to do) in flower gardens. Where this is objectionable, seedless male selections may be used. The fruit of silver maple, like that of red maple, matures in late spring just as the receding spring floods expose receptive new seedbeds in their riparian habitat.

Silver maple is a very hardy species, growing from Trois-Rivières, Quebec, south throughout the eastern and central United States to the coastal plains. Under cultivation it performs well north into USDA zone 3. It does better in cold climates than mild ones because cold areas experience more snow than freezing rain, which causes glazing damage, and because cold winters satisfy the dormancy requirements of the terminal buds. When these buds are unable to achieve total dormancy, they may not grow in spring and may instead be overtopped by growth from pairs of lateral buds, resulting in the V-shaped limb junctions that make this tree more susceptible to damage from wind and ice in the South.

Many books recommend silver maple for difficult or low-maintenance sites, but although it does tolerate such conditions, it performs best with reasonable care, as with any other tree. It can survive as a less-than-perfect specimen almost anywhere, but it prefers floodplains and seasonally wet areas with rich, porous soil, and it can become a majestic tree under such conditions. It will develop a good limb structure if careful attention is given to developmental pruning when it is young, to remove multiple leaders that form when the terminal bud fails to grow.

Studies indicate that storm breakage, long reputed to be the nemesis of silver maple, is not as severe as once

LEFT: Silver maple (*Acer saccharinum*) is a large, fast-growing tree.

thought if the trees are properly trained and maintained. Individual branches may snap off, but long, destructive tearing injuries and splits are not as common with well-pruned silver maples as they are with many exotic shade trees.

'Northline' is a very hardy selection of silver maple from Canada that grows more slowly than others. 'Silver Queen' is a fruitless form for those who wish to avoid the seed litter problem, and it tends to develop a stronger branching structure with a central leader, as does 'Blair'. Weeping and cutleaf selections, selections with pyramidal or columnar growth, and selections with gold or crinkled leaves are also available. Many are horticultural curiosities with little practical value, but the cutleaf forms ('Wieri', 'Skinneri', 'Beebe', and the newer 'Born's Gracious') are graceful specimens when well grown.

Some of the most exciting horticultural developments involving red maple and silver maple have come from their hybrid, the Freeman maple (***Acer ×freemanii***). This hybrid seems less dependent upon acid soil than red maple. It usually has deeply lobed leaves like silver maple, but cultivars also often develop outstanding fall color like red maple. Freeman maple selections Autumn Fantasy, 'Marmo', 'Firefall', and 'Scarlet Sentinal' have brilliant spring flowers as well as great fall color. 'Armstrong' and 'Scarlet Sentinal' develop fastigiate form, while Autumn Blaze and Celebration have luminous fall color (Celebration is two-toned, red around yellow). 'Marmo' and Celebration, and perhaps some others as well, seem to be seedless. Maple genetics are not neat and precise, and some speculate that Drummond red maple (*A. rubrum* var. *drummondii*) might actually have originated in the wild as a Freeman maple crossed back to red maple.

COMMENTS: Red maple, as a species, includes some of our most intensely colorful and widely adapted landscape trees. Young red maples are preferred by prairie warblers as nesting trees, and the twigs furnish valuable winter food for rabbits, porcupine, deer, and moose.

Silver maple seeds have nostalgic value for those of us whose first introduction to horticulture involved sitting in our sandboxes while magic maple whirlybirds rained down around us, sprouting almost immediately into little trees. I might not have become fascinated by the works of nature at such an early age were it not for watching, growing, and delighting in those maple seeds. Later on in grade school I came to welcome the aerial assault of ripe maple seeds as a harbinger of summer vacation. Why not plant or preserve a silver maple at some appropriate location, such as a child daycare facility or a schoolyard, so that the next generation might have access to the same source of inspiration?

Acer saccharum

SUGAR MAPLE

DESCRIPTION: The standard by which all other trees are measured in fall, sugar maple graces the flag of Canada and the mesic forests of most of eastern North America. It becomes a large, dense, full-crowned tree in open areas but can thrive as a tall, clear-boled, dominant tree in dense shade.

One sugar maple in Norwich, Connecticut, is 93 feet (27.9 m) tall and more than 7 feet (2.1 m) in diameter. In the deep woods many become even taller, though more slender. This slow-growing, strong species, a hard maple (section *Acer*, series *Saccharodendron*), is quite variable but always attractive. It is deservedly popular as a shade tree on any good site and has been designated the state tree of New York, Vermont, West Virginia, and Wisconsin.

LEAVES: The opposite leaves are coarsely toothed, 4 to 7 inches (10 to 17.5 cm) wide and slightly shorter in length, and vary in both thickness and toughness depending upon provenance. Trees originating in benevolent climates tend to grow more quickly, with thinner foliage that is more susceptible to tatter and scorch; while trees from harsher, drier areas tend to grow more slowly, with smaller, tougher foliage. Autumn colors range from gold through orange to carmine and are never disappointing.

FLOWERS AND FRUIT: Sugar maples tend to dominate areas of the forest in which they grow. Their pendulous, pale spring flowers create a soft yellow haze in the leafless woods, which shows to advantage when viewed against the dark bark or a clear blue sky. The winged fruit is not particularly conspicuous but feeds many birds in the fall.

BEST SEASONS: FALL (any sugar maple can outperform almost any other tree for fall color, considering duration and intensity combined). SPRING (the flowers, emerging before the leaves, are fine textured and can light up the woods). SUMMER (a shapely tree that casts a dense, cool shade).

NATIVE AND ADAPTIVE RANGE: Sugar maple dominates mesic forests from northern New Brunswick and southeastern Manitoba down through the southern Appalachians. Provenance is important with this species, but with careful selection it or its close relatives can be grown in almost every climate zone.

Some authorities recognize three ecotypes within this species. Northern trees are very resistant to winter injury but sensitive to drought and leaf damage in warm areas. Those from central latitudes exhibit adequate cold resistance and better drought tolerance, while southern trees resist drought and leaf scorch best but are less winter hardy. The adaptable central tree group also shows increasing toughness but generally decreasing fall brilliance, from east to west, with test trees from parts of Illinois, Missouri, and Iowa performing best over a broad planting range.

Sugar maple should generally be considered hardy north through USDA zone 3, but its southern and western varieties or relatives might be substituted respectively in the South and on the windswept open plains of the Midwest.

CULTURE: Sugar maple demands a reasonably clean atmosphere and moist, well-drained soil. Given those requirements, it is easy to transplant and grow and can be coaxed into moderately fast growth with a little attention to water, mulch, and fertilizer. It thrives in full sun or deep shade and is one of our more tolerant maples to atmospheric ozone. However, it does not respond well to salt, compacted soil, or hot, dry locations.

PROBLEMS: Besides its rather exacting site requirements, sugar maple has suffered from a poorly understood decline disease in some areas. This may be a reaction to road salt, air pollution, and periodic drought, or to localized manifestations of global warming or acid rain. Trees on poor sites, or selections not adapted to local conditions, are susceptible to scorch, sunscald, leaf tatter, and other stresses. Sugar maples are great for most rural or suburban areas, but they seldom like it downtown.

Maple wilt, or *Verticillium* wilt (caused by *V. dahliae* and *V. albo-atrum*), is a systemic, fatal disease that attacks some trees. Maple anthracnose (*Kabatiella apocrypta*) causes conspicuous leaf blotching but is not as serious. Many sugar maples are predisposed to develop narrow

RIGHT: Stately old sugar maples (*Acer saccharum*).

branch crotches that weaken their structure, but their strong, hard wood compensates for this to some degree. In test plantings in Pennsylvania, sugar maple cultivars were not injured by rabbits, though the closely related black maple (*Acer nigrum*) and canyon maple (*A. grandidentatum*) were decimated. See *A. rubrum* for discussion of additional problems.

The dense shade and shallow roots of sugar maple may preclude the establishment of quality turf under its canopy. Where it is locally adapted, sugar maple can dominate the forest through a combination of reproductive success and allelopathy, outcompeting every other tree over the long term.

CULTIVARS: Many sugar maple selections are available in the nursery trade. 'Bonfire' and 'Commemoration' are early-coloring forms selected for good heat tolerance; both have bright red-orange fall color. 'Goldspire', 'Monumentale', 'Endowment', and 'Columnare' develop narrow crown forms. 'Green Mountain' and 'Legacy' are colorful selections recommended for harsh summer climates where resistance to leaf scorch and tatter are necessary. A sugar maple trademarked as Majesty is a fast-growing selection with exceptional cold resistance.

'Caddo' is a seed-propagated geographic selection from outlying groves in Oklahoma. It tends to develop a narrow crown and demonstrates the strongest tolerance to adverse conditions. It colors late in fall, missing much of the peak season when planted further north or east. 'John Pair', named for my old friend from Kansas State University, is an improvement on the type, with early

color rivaling many eastern selections. The trademarked Sweet Shadow is a graceful, fine-textured tree with deeply incised leaves and orange fall color that performs well for us in Illinois. Other selections are available too. Research involving this species is very active, so look for additional selections in the future.

SIMILAR AND RELATED SPECIES: Several other native hard maples are similar to sugar maple. Some taxonomists, mostly those in Europe, combine these with sugar maple as varieties of an umbrella ochlospecies, sometimes called *Acer saccharophorum*, rather than identifying them as separate species. However, they are distinctive when seen together in their native North America, so I will follow the taxonomic splitters who give each one species status, and let the lumpers fuss to their hearts' content.

Black maple (***Acer nigrum***) is the largest mimic of sugar maple, reaching equal size and of equal hardiness. It usually lacks the red fall colors displayed by some sugar maples, but it may perform better at the western edge of the species range and on dry or floodplain sites. Leaves tend to be very large and have drooping tips, and those on vigorous twigs develop conspicuous stipules. 'Green Column' and 'Temple's Upright' are narrowly upright forms.

Canyon maple (***Acer grandidentatum***) is another small hard maple that is native to the Rocky Mountains from Canada south into Mexico. It varies considerably in leaf size, vigor, and coloration and offers good potential for cultivar selection. It seems at least as hardy as the other small relatives of sugar maple and grows well (but slowly) in my USDA zone 5 test site in Illinois. In the wild, trees with access to water produce seeds, while those on higher, drier sites often fail to do so because they develop only male flowers in response to their more stressful environment. Canyon maple is one of the most colorful elements of the desert canyons of the Southwest in fall, where it tolerates very alkaline soils and dry conditions.

Southern sugar maple (***Acer barbatum,*** syn. *A. floridanum*) is a smaller tree that is more tolerant of southern summers but is still relatively winter hardy. It also lacks the brilliant red fall color of sugar maple, turning yellow to rust-colored. Chalk maple (***A. leucoderme***) is a similar but much smaller species of midsouthern latitudes. It often has good red fall color, graceful form, and

LEFT AND TOP RIGHT: Sugar maple (*Acer saccharum*) has outstanding fall color. RIGHT: Sugar maple flowers.

very attractive, chalky bark. Like southern sugar maple, it is hardy north at least into USDA zone 6. A few other obscure species or varieties have been described from the Ozarks and Texas, but they are not considered taxonomically distinct by most botanists. They have a little more or less pubescence, slightly thinner leaves, or somewhat greater or lesser lobing of the leaves, all within the general limits of the species already mentioned. Since they have no discrete horticultural characteristics either, we can ignore them in deference to the taxonomic lumpers.

COMMENTS: Sugar maple is one of those sensitive species expected to have trouble adapting throughout much of the southern portion of its range over the next century, if scientists' predictions about global warming materialize. Nonetheless, at this moment it is actually considered a weed in many commercial forests, where human fire-control activities have allowed it to gain an advantage over the fire-resistant trees preferred for timber purposes.

The source of maple sugar and syrup, and of some of the best fall colors visible anywhere in the world, sugar maple is a superior ornamental shade tree where it can be grown under favorable conditions. Syrup researchers have calculated that a mature maple pumps 5000 gallons (20,000 qt) of sap 450 miles (724 km) through its vascular system! Some of this sap is tapped to become sugar and syrup, but most of it goes on to nourish the tree. In late winter the mildly sweet "sapsicles" that form from broken branches as sap bleeds out and freezes are a tasty treat during a hike in the sugarbush.

LEFT: A cutleaf form of sugar maple (*Acer saccharum*).
BELOW: Canyon maple (*A. grandidentatum*).

Aesculus glabra

OHIO BUCKEYE

DESCRIPTION: The Ohio buckeye is typically a medium-sized tree of rich mesic habitats and stream valleys, seldom emerging fully from the shade of its taller associates. Although this is the state tree of Ohio, where it grows very well, the largest known Ohio buckeye is found across the river in Liberty, Kentucky, standing 144 feet (43.2 m) tall with a trunk more than 3 feet (0.9 m) in diameter. The species seldom reaches such proportions, however, usually growing as a small tree or, on drier sites, a large shrub. It rarely dominates any forest stand, instead existing as a secondary component of many forest types.

Ohio buckeye is representative of the several buckeyes that can grow into medium or large trees. All buckeyes are coarse-branching with opposite, palmately compound leaves, giving them an almost tropical appearance. Most species are unique among our native trees in that they imitate spring woodland wildflowers by leafing out extremely early (thus taking advantage of the sunlight that penetrates the otherwise dormant deciduous forest early in the year), then proceeding into dormancy in late summer as soon as their annual growth increment matures.

LEAVES: The buckeyes are among the first of our native woody plants to green up in spring, and their frost-resistant new leaves herald the end of winter. A hard freeze will cause the expanding new leaves to become limp and droop as though frost-killed, but they usually recover as the temperature rises. The opposite, palmately compound, bright green leaves of Ohio buckeye are typically composed of five leaflets joined at a single point on the leafstalk. They emit an odd odor when crushed, which helps to distinguish this species from the odorless yellow buckeye (*Aesculus flava*, syn. *A. octandra*). Ohio buckeye is subject to scorching during hot, dry summers and is usually among the first native trees to turn color (yellow, orange, or tan) and defoliate at the end of the growing season.

FLOWERS AND FRUIT: All buckeyes are known for their showy flowers, and for the hummingbirds that seek them. The Ohio buckeye has greenish yellow flowers in panicles up to 12 inches (30 cm) tall at the ends of branches. Of those tree species that bloom on the current season's growth, Ohio buckeyes are among the earliest, but the flowers do not expand until after the foliage has developed.

Buckeyes derive their name from the nuts they produce, which are brown with a light eyespot (the point of attachment, called the hilum), resembling the eyes of deer. Buckeye fruit clusters are ornamental early in fall, often remaining on the tree after the leaves have fallen. The purplish brown nuts of Ohio buckeye occur singly or in clusters of two or three, enclosed in bright tan leathery pods or husks armed with scattered weak prickles. They are toxic to humans and cattle but serve as a food source for squirrels.

BEST SEASONS: EARLY SPRING (when they send their bright new leaves out into a dormant deciduous forest) and LATE SPRING (the flowers can show surprisingly well against the backdrop of new foliage). EARLY FALL (for the ripe nuts, and for a shade tree that will drop its leaves early, simplifying cleanup and opening its canopy to the passage of early fall sunlight).

NATIVE AND ADAPTIVE RANGE: Ohio buckeye grows in suitably moist habitats throughout the central United States and is reliably hardy when planted north at least through USDA zone 3 in Minnesota and Canada. It is the most widespread and northerly member of the genus.

CULTURE: Buckeyes are simple to propagate from stratified seed (kept moist but not wet) and can be transplanted easily if moved in early spring while still dormant, or in late summer following natural defoliation. In Illinois I have moved dormant trees up to 6 inches (15 cm) in diameter with hand-dug root balls, and they showed no signs of transplanting stress. The trees prefer decent, moist, well-drained soil and will react to hot, dry conditions by defoliating prematurely unless they are mulched and watered.

PROBLEMS: Ohio buckeye is not affected significantly by disease problems, except for the leaf scorching or blotching that accompanies unfavorable growing conditions or follows infection by the leaf anthracnose fungus *Guignardia aesculi*. The typical late-summer defolia-

tion can be an aesthetic disadvantage, depending upon your viewpoint, and the toxic nuts can cause concerns about poisoning for children, pets, or livestock. As a defense against browsers who would be attracted to its early growth while other trees are still dormant, the foliage is somewhat toxic as well.

Like other members of this genus, and like many other trees, Ohio buckeye is highly susceptible to destruction by the imported Asian longhorned borer beetle (*Anoplophora glabripennis*). A newly discovered leaf miner of unknown origin, the orange-striped *Cameraria ohridella*, is also devastating this and most other buckeye species in much of Europe. It seems likely that this pest will find its way to North America eventually, but we can hope that our European friends find a successful control treatment first.

CULTIVARS: Ohio buckeyes seem to show little variation from tree to tree and therefore have not lent themselves to horticultural selection. I have found a specimen at Starhill Forest with rich, long-lasting purple spring foliage. Tentatively named 'Purple Haze', it remains under observation for possible introduction if its coloration proves to be consistent each year. *Aesculus glabra* var. *nana* is an interesting natural dwarf that remains a

LEFT: A mature Ohio buckeye (*Aesculus glabra*).
BELOW: The upright flowers of Ohio buckeye.

low shrub and features bristly little seedpods and marble-sized nuts. There are several hybrids involving Ohio buckeye as one of two (or more) progenitors, and at least one of them—*A.* 'Autumn Splendor', with red fall color—is available at some nurseries.

SIMILAR AND RELATED SPECIES: Yellow buckeye (***Aesculus flava***) resembles Ohio buckeye but is larger in almost every feature. It has a more restricted southeastern range but can be planted successfully almost anywhere Ohio buckeye grows. It is a dominant canopy tree in some cove hardwood forest areas of the eastern mountains, where individual trees can exceed 5 feet (1.5 m) in diameter. Its fruit husks are smooth, and its flowers are often a brighter yellow than those of Ohio buckeye, becoming a significant ornamental feature on open-grown landscape trees that have retained their lower branches. Its leaves are reportedly more resistant to anthracnose than those of most other large buckeye species. Texas buckeye (***A. arguta***) is a smaller version of Ohio buckeye (sometimes listed as a variety) and is better adapted to hot, dry conditions. It usually has seven leaflets instead of five.

Most of these species hybridize readily, and reliable identification can be difficult. There are additional species in California, Europe, and Asia. European horsechestnut (***Aesculus hippocastanum***) is the one most commonly seen in cultivation. Unlike our native species, it has very large clusters of white flowers.

COMMENTS: The toxic substance in buckeye nuts is aesculin, and it makes them inedible to humans. At one time Native Americans boiled and leached the aesculin from the nuts, which they called *hetuck* (meaning "buckeye"), to make them edible when acorns or other preferred food staples were scarce. Crushed raw buckeyes were also used to poison fish. The smooth nuts are pleasant to handle, and "lucky buckeyes" travel in the pockets of many schoolchildren each fall. They have also been used to make a library paste meant to repel bookworms (hopefully not the two-legged kind).

In England the fruits of horsechestnuts are called conkers due to their propensity to conk the head of anyone who dares to pass under them as they ripen. Of course, such conking is sometimes playfully augmented by children who gather handfuls of the nuts and hide behind the massive trunks of old trees to ambush unsuspecting friends.

Aesculus pavia
RED BUCKEYE

DESCRIPTION: Red buckeye is a small tree or large shrub that grows under the shade of taller trees in rich woodland areas. It and its close relatives (other small buckeyes) are widespread throughout the southeastern United States and can dominate the understory on favorable sites. The largest recorded specimen of red buckeye, perhaps a hybrid, is located in Kalamazoo County, Michigan, well beyond its natural range. It is 64 feet (19.2 m) tall with a diameter of 29 inches (72.5 cm). In general, any specimen more than 25 feet (7.5 m) tall or 1 foot (30 cm) thick is a huge tree for this species.

LEAVES: Red buckeye leaves are dark, lustrous, and early to emerge in spring. All buckeyes have similar, distinctive, opposite, compound foliage that develops early in the season and that, with the exception of bottlebrush buckeye (*Aesculus parviflora*), drops early in fall. As a defense mechanism against hungry browsers searching for the first green foliage of spring, buckeye leaves are toxic when ingested.

FLOWERS AND FRUIT: The variable carmine flower panicles of this species rank among the most beautiful of any temperate-zone tree. On specimens that have been grown in open, well-lit areas and that have developed a full, dense crown, the blooming period is almost surrealistic in its beauty. Plant breeders are attempting to incorporate the superior color of red buckeye flowers into other buckeye species through hybridization. The nuts are similar to those of Ohio buckeye (*Aesculus glabra*) but are orange-brown and encased in smooth husks. Fall basket displays featuring the nuts of both species together are beautiful.

BEST SEASONS: LATE SPRING (during the spectacular blooming period). EARLY SPRING (when the fresh new leaves emerge long before those of other associated deciduous trees).

NATIVE AND ADAPTIVE RANGE: Red buckeye ranges throughout the southeastern United States from North Carolina through eastern Texas and north to Illinois. It has been planted with considerable success much further north and should be rated hardy into USDA zone 4.

CULTURE: Grow this species from stratified seed that has been stored just above freezing in a medium that has been kept slightly moist but never wet, and give it good, rich soil for best results. Transplant it very early in spring, taking care to avoid unnecessary damage to its fleshy root system. It thrives in heavy shade but becomes more dense in full sun. Plants growing in sunny areas should be mulched and watered as necessary to maintain a cool, moist root zone.

PROBLEMS: Red buckeye has no serious pests, although squirrels will occasionally strip sections of bark and girdle branches. As long as the recommended habitat requirements are met and the habitual but harmless early defoliation can be tolerated, this small tree is one of our most trouble-free species. Toxicity characteristics similar to those exhibited by other buckeyes should be considered during the landscape design process, to minimize risk to children and pets.

CULTIVARS: Naturally compact and dwarf forms or varieties of red buckeye and the yellow-flowering *Aesculus pavia* var. *flavescens* are offered by some nurseries. Sufficient variation exists within the species to support cultivar selection, but no true cultivars are commonly available in the nursery trade. Red buckeye and its close relatives are used as parents for some terrific hybrid buckeyes that incorporate the red flower color with the growth habits of larger species.

SIMILAR AND RELATED SPECIES: Differentiation of the small buckeye species can be confusing. Some authorities do not recognize the particolored buckeye (***Aesculus discolor***) as a distinct species. It is usually a shrub, with large panicles of flowers that are sometimes two-toned, red and yellow. Several other nearly identical taxa are occasionally recognized by various authorities, under various names, including the splendid ***A. splendens.*** A hybrid with the European horsechestnut (*A. hippocastanum*) is the popular red-flowering ruby horsechestnut (***A. ×carnea***), which has several named selections.

Painted buckeye (***Aesculus sylvatica***) is a southeastern

RIGHT: A beautiful specimen of red buckeye (*Aesculus pavia*).

species with yellow flowers that often appear to be painted with red. 'Autumn Splendor' is a cultivar that originated from open-pollinated seed of painted buckeye, but it has several generations of hybrids in its ancestry and looks very little like that species now. It was selected as a seedling from the Morton Arboretum, where many different buckeye species are planted together and can cross-pollinate (to the delight of adventuresome horticulturists and to the dismay of fuddy-duddy taxonomists).

The other most significant and distinct small buckeye is the bottlebrush buckeye (**Aesculus parviflora**). It has very tall panicles of feathery, snow-white flowers and blooms in the heat of early summer long after the other eastern buckeyes have finished. It usually remains a shrub, spreading into mounded clonal thickets over time, but occasionally some of its stems reach tree size. One tree in the Blue Ridge Mountains at Cashiers, North Carolina, is 20 feet (6 m) tall.

Bottlebrush buckeye is unique among the hardy buckeyes in its ability to retain its foliage in good condition into fall, and it develops a glowing yellow fall color. Its natural range is confined to Alabama and adjacent areas, but it can be grown northward through USDA zone 4. 'Rogers', a selection introduced by an old friend,

Professor Joe McDaniel at the University of Illinois, blooms even later than the species.

COMMENTS: The small buckeye trees, along with their larger relatives (see *Aesculus glabra*), are some of our most attractive woody plants when in bloom. Because of their early foliage, they are also among our most welcome harbingers of spring. They are attractive to hummingbirds and to a broad array of butterflies, who add much to the dynamic landscape. Their fruit, however, is probably their most memorable attribute, and is very useful for grabbing the attention of children being introduced to the wonders of nature.

BELOW: Red buckeye (*Aesculus pavia*) is one of our earliest native trees to leaf out in spring. RIGHT: A cluster of red buckeye fruits. BELOW RIGHT: Bottlebrush buckeye (*A. parviflora*) flowers.

Amelanchier arborea

DOWNY SERVICEBERRY

DESCRIPTION: Serviceberries (*Amelanchier*) are small ornamental trees and shrubs that bloom in clouds of white in early spring woods. I have chosen to describe the downy serviceberry, one of the most tree-like, as an example of this ornamental but taxonomically confusing genus. Other species are very similar, differing mostly in size and in their tendency to form clumps. Most serviceberries will hybridize, and their reproductive variability can make positive identification of a particular plant very tricky.

While many serviceberry species and hybrids are low, suckering shrubs, several become attractive small trees. A few even reach up into the forest canopy, such as a downy serviceberry in Burkes Garden, Virginia, that is 60 feet (18 m) tall and nearly 3 feet (0.9 m) in diameter. The closely related smooth serviceberry (*Amelanchier laevis*) can grow even taller but is not as thick. I have seen smooth serviceberries in the Finger Lakes area of New York that were 70 feet (21 m) in height. The U.S. national champion is half as tall but broader, with a trunk that is 28 inches (70 cm) in diameter. Serviceberries more typically grow as understory trees but reach their best development in sunny areas on bluff ledges or in clearings where their flowering branches are more dense and their smooth, reflective bark shows up well.

LEAVES: Serviceberry leaves resemble those of their close relative, the apple. True to their name, downy serviceberry leaves usually emerge downy on the lower surface, while smooth serviceberry leaves are always smooth. Fall color seems to vary within each species. Some authorities hold that smooth serviceberry has the best fall color, ranging from orange to purple. Among the plants in my collection in Illinois, downy serviceberry develops a wine-red color, while most other species turn yellow or light orange. Local soil conditions might influence fall colors in the serviceberries, as they do with some other trees.

FLOWERS AND FRUIT: Once again, as with fall colors, the authorities disagree. One species reportedly blooms before leafing out, while another blooms after, but authorities dispute which is which. The eight species of serviceberry I grow all bloom within one week, just as the leaf buds begin to break open. Downy serviceberry is among the earliest.

Serviceberry flowers are generally a spectacular clear white but are occasionally light pink. They hang in elegant clusters from the branches but are at their peak for only a few days, fading just as redbud (*Cercis canadensis*) steps forward to change the predominant color of the woods from white to lavender. The flowers of smooth serviceberry and its hybrids tend to be larger than those of most other species.

The purple fruits are small pomes, like miniature apples, and there is no disagreement about them: smooth serviceberries taste great; downy serviceberries are less filling. Many forms of wildlife love serviceberry fruits, more bird species seeming to prefer the drier fruits of downy serviceberry (which we might hope will leave more of the juicy fruits of smooth serviceberries for us to eat).

BEST SEASONS: EARLY SPRING (for those few days when the flowers dominate the landscape). FALL (most serviceberries develop good fall color, whether it is purple, orange, red, or yellow) or SUMMER (for the fruit). WINTER (the smooth gray bark and artistic branching patterns enhance the winter landscape and show up well when sunlit from the side against a dark or evergreen background).

NATIVE AND ADAPTIVE RANGE: Downy serviceberry is native throughout much of our area, from the Gulf Coast north to Thunder Bay in Ontario and Lake St. John in Quebec, and is reliably hardy through USDA zone 4. Smooth serviceberry is nearly as widespread, with its natural range shifted slightly to the north, and is equally hardy. Several other species occasionally reach tree size; these have more restricted natural ranges but are nearly equal in hardiness.

CULTURE: All serviceberries prefer porous soil but will tolerate a wide variety of growing conditions and thrive in full sun to fairly dense shade. They can be propagated from seed or by dividing the clumping types. In the wild, downy serviceberry generally occupies drier sites than smooth serviceberry. Serviceberries are so easy to graft

that some cultivars come to the market on the roots of a different plant, such as *Crataegus* or *Sorbus*.

PROBLEMS: Serviceberries suffer from many of the same insects and diseases that affect orchard trees, especially trunk borers and leaf rusts. They are quite susceptible to cedar-apple rust (*Gymnosporangium juniperae-virginianae*) and are favorite targets of many defoliating insects, especially Gypsy moth (*Lymantria dispar*). Rabbits seem to prefer serviceberries above almost any other woody browse and destroy many seedlings and small trees. Compacted soils, salt toxicity, fireblight (*Erwinia amylovora*), and other insect and disease problems can also affect this genus.

Perhaps the main problem, though, is taxonomic—you seldom get what you ask for when you request a particular species of serviceberry. This problem arises because their identification can be so confusing, because their names are used interchangeably in the trade, and because they hybridize so readily. Of course, named cultivars seldom have this problem, but it really doesn't matter much anyway as long as you find one with the desired growth form: they all are very ornamental.

CULTIVARS: Regardless of the confusion with species, most cultivars are consistent and predictable. Many of the best have been selected from the apple serviceberry (*Amelanchier* ×*grandiflora*), sometimes confused with *A.* ×*lamarckii*, which is a different hybrid involving *A. canadensis* as one parent. Apple serviceberry is a very ornamental natural cross between downy and smooth serviceberries. It has large ornamental flowers and usually has its peak blooming period just prior to smooth serviceberry. The erect tree habit of both this hybrid and its parent species makes them appropriate for a smaller space than some of the more sprawling, suckering species. 'Autumn Brilliance', 'Cole's Select', 'Forest Prince', 'Princess Diana', 'Robin Hill', and 'Rubescens' seem to have been selected from apple serviceberry. I have been unable to confirm the species origin of 'Robin Hill Pink', a tree-sized selection with light pink flowers, but I suspect it might be a synonym or sister selection of 'Robin Hill', which likewise has pale pink flowers.

'Spring Glory' and 'Tradition' were reportedly selected from thicket serviceberry (*Amelanchier canadensis*), although they behave more like smooth serviceberry

LEFT: Blooming serviceberries (*Amelanchier*) brighten the spring landscape. TOP RIGHT: Flowers of downy serviceberry (*A. arborea*). RIGHT: Fall color of downy serviceberry.

selections. 'Strata' is a superb apple serviceberry shown to me by Professor Ed Hasselkus, a serviceberry expert from the University of Wisconsin. It displays the superior blooming and stratified, layered branching typical of this hybrid at its finest.

The Agriculture Canada Research Station at Kentville, Nova Scotia, introduced *Amelanchier laevis* 'R. J. Hilton', a smooth serviceberry from eastern Canada. It is a prolific bloomer, and its fruits are even sweeter than is typical for the species. 'Majestic', another smooth serviceberry, becomes quite tall and seems to display more resistance to foliage diseases than some others. 'Snowcloud', which has thick, leathery leaves that give outstanding red fall color, and 'Cumulus', which looks like a white cloud when in bloom, are also tree forms of smooth serviceberry with straight trunks and uniform crowns.

SIMILAR AND RELATED SPECIES: Several species besides downy serviceberry, smooth serviceberry (*Amelan-*

chier laevis), and apple serviceberry (*A.* ×*grandiflora*) occasionally reach tree size or are confused with those that do. Thicket serviceberry (*A. canadensis*), frequently confused in the nursery trade with downy serviceberry, usually remains a large, suckering shrub and is limited to an East Coast natural range. Others like *A. bartramiana, A. interior, A. neglecta, A. sanguinea,* and *A. spicata* grow as large shrubs or small trees in portions of our area. Running shadbush (*A. stolonifera*) is a low, spreading species popular in landscape usage.

'Regent' is a cultivar of the shrubby western Saskatoon serviceberry (*Amelanchier alnifolia*), as is the seed germplasm selection 'Newport', introduced by the USDA for habitats too cold and wet to support other selections. Another common western shrubby species that sometimes makes a nice small tree is *A. utahensis.* All serviceberries require similar conditions to perform well: decent soil, good drainage, air circulation to discourage leaf diseases, and occasional watering during droughts to reduce stress and resultant borer infestations.

COMMENTS: Some folks prefer the eastern name "shadbush," which alludes to the tendency for these plants to bloom at the same time the shad run in spring. "Serviceberry" was conferred by pioneers heading west, in reference to the correlation between the plant's blooming time and the ground having thawed enough to be dug for funeral services for those poor souls who perished sometime during the hard winter. Either way, people seem to take notice when these trees are in bloom.

Despite the confusion with their names and identities, most serviceberries make fine plants for ornamental and wildlife purposes. A well-grown serviceberry can become the focal point of the landscape during the peak of its spring bloom or autumn color. The fruits of smooth serviceberry and some shrubby species (particularly *Amelanchier stolonifera*) are attractive and delicious. This was known very well by early pioneers, and by Native Americans, who planted serviceberries and used them in combination with dried meat to flavor pemmican. Serviceberries also furnish valuable food for nesting birds, deer, bears, and many other animals, and seem to make appealing snacks for my dogs and pet goose, who pick them deftly from the lower branches.

LEFT: Saskatoon serviceberry (*Amelanchier alnifolia*).
TOP RIGHT: *A. laevis* 'Cumulus' in bloom. RIGHT: *A. laevis* 'Cumulus' showing fall color.

Aralia spinosa

ARALIA

DESCRIPTION: Aralia, or devil's walking-stick, has a split personality. During the growing season its large, doubly compound leaves, which extend in horizontal tiers from the erect stems, present a fine-textured appearance like that of certain palm trees. The leaves and their stalks fall when the tree goes into winter dormancy, leaving a small cluster of naked, coarse, sparsely branched stems. This species reproduces vegetatively from occasional root suckers and will form clonal clumps or thickets if this tendency is not discouraged.

The potential for ultimate size is limited by a thick, soft pith that facilitates rapid early growth but affects structural strength. Aralia is never a large tree and frequently remains a tall shrub. The largest specimen on record grows at Yorktown, Virginia, and stands about 33 feet (9.9 m) tall with a stem diameter of 8 inches (20 cm). Young stems have almost no taper, but as they mature and start to branch they begin to taper quickly. Aralia usually grows as a prickly, clump-forming understory or fence-row tree, with several erect stems about 15 feet (4.5 m) tall.

LEAVES: The doubly pinnate leaves are arranged horizontally, parasol-like, around the top of each stem or limb. They are the largest leaves of any native tree in our region, sometimes extending out more than 4 feet (1.2 m) in all directions from the coarse stems. They turn yellow or purple-red in fall and set off the dark fruit clusters nicely. The leafstalks are prickly and uncomfortable if brushed against but are not really hazardous.

FLOWERS AND FRUIT: The white flower panicles of aralia perch above the spreading platform of foliage and can exceed 2 feet (60 cm) in height. They are not very effective when seen from below because they are hidden by leaves; however, when viewed from the side, or especially from above, as from a balcony or second-story window, they form a long-lasting, lacy white crown. The late-summer flowering period of this plant makes it especially desirable in landscapes, giving bright color during those sultry days when few woody plants are in bloom.

The fruit clusters that follow are equally impressive and are a good food source for birds beginning their fall migration. Even after the purple-black fruits are eaten, or have fallen, their red stalks persist for several more weeks, continuing the changeable color display.

BEST SEASONS: LATE SUMMER (the huge, handsome flower clusters arrive at a dull time of year when they are especially valuable). FALL (the fruits and their stalks are very attractive, and the fall color of the leaves can be nice as well). SUMMER (the tropical, umbrella form of the tree is graceful if placed carefully in the landscape). WINTER (but only if the dramatic, leggy, naked stems serve a useful design function in the landscape—the effect requires careful planning).

NATIVE AND ADAPTIVE RANGE: Aralia grows in woodlands and borders throughout the southeastern United States, north to southern Illinois and central New York. It is hardy north through USDA zone 4 as a small tree and perhaps further north if occasional winter dieback and resprouting are acceptable.

CULTURE: This plant is easy to establish from divisions or root cuttings in almost any soil. It does well in sun or shade and can tolerate drought, but it becomes more vigorous with ample moisture. Stem prickles can be rubbed off using leather welders' gloves, without damage to the plant, if they present an inconvenience.

PROBLEMS: In general aralia is a trouble-free species. Surprisingly, deer like to browse the new growth of this prickly tree, causing the growing tips to branch. This may or may not be considered a problem, depending upon the landscape design intent. Occasionally a stem will exhibit some winter tip dieback for reasons that are not always apparent, but it will resprout from below the point of dieback.

The biggest problems with this species are caused by the sprouting tendency of its roots, which can turn a docile small tree into a thicket monster within a few years. It can be left to develop as a clump, pruned annually to a small cluster of stems, or planted in an area enclosed by pavement or other containment and allowed to form a thicket like bamboo. Unwanted root sprouts should be pulled by (gloved) hand or cut well below

RIGHT: A fruiting aralia (*Aralia spinosa*) overhangs a lake.

ground when small, since cutting them at ground level only stimulates regrowth. The native species of aralia seems less prone to excessive sprouting than the exotic ones, but it is the prickliest species of all.

CULTIVARS: No selections have been introduced from our native species, although the very similar Chinese and Japanese species have several cultivars available. Most aralias sold by nurseries for outdoor landscaping are the Japanese aralia (*Aralia elata*).

SIMILAR AND RELATED SPECIES: Besides the Asian species, *Aralia spinosa* is closely related to the wild sarsaparilla (**A. nudicaulis**) and the bristly sarsaparilla (**A. hispida**), medicinal plants of the forest floor.

Several small trees not related to this genus are also of interest. Swamp cyrilla (**Cyrilla racemiflora**), also called titi, is a small, tough, semievergreen tree for low spots or land with a high water table. Like aralia, it will grow into thickets if allowed to sucker from the roots but can be kept as a single large shrub or tree by mowing the suckers with the surrounding lawn or occasionally pulling them from a mulched bed. In the wild it is usually found growing in shallow, seasonal southern swamps or around their edges, but it will grow well along ditches and streams and in low swales that remain moist during much of the year. The largest known swamp cyrilla grows in the De Soto National Forest in Mississippi; it is 55 feet (16.5 m) tall and 14 inches (35 cm) in diameter.

The main attraction of this tree is the tremendous number of long, slender, fragrant flower spikes that appear from May through July. They are borne on old wood, beginning just before new growth appears. The most important cultural consideration for swamp cyrilla is that it requires more water than is usual for most upland trees. Like some other wetland plant species, cyrilla uses its tolerance of water to keep competing plants at bay, and so has no need for fast growth; it can be overwhelmed by more vigorous competitors when grown in well-drained soil.

The related buckwheat tree (**Cliftonia monophylla**), also called black cyrilla, is similar, but its smaller clusters of fragrant flowers bloom much earlier, in March and April. It is more fully evergreen, and its range is limited to a coastal strip from Lake Pontchartrain in Louisiana east to around Myrtle Beach, South Carolina.

Hoptree (**Ptelea trifoliata**) is also related to cyrilla. It is an inconspicuous understory shrub or small tree, grow-

TOP LEFT: The fall color display of aralia (*Aralia spinosa*).
LEFT: Purple fruit clusters on an aralia.

ing up to 20 feet (6 m) tall, with trifoliate compound leaves (which are yellow in 'Aurea'). It can be found in scattered locations throughout the eastern half of the United States and west into the canyons of the Southwest, where it can tolerate very alkaline soils. It is only rarely encountered in southern Canada and is officially listed as a vulnerable species in Quebec and Ontario. Hoptree is the hardiest member of the citrus family and in cultivation is reliable north into USDA zone 4. It likes moist soil best and will grow equally well in full sun or dense shade. Its fragrant but inconspicuous flowers develop into interesting winged seeds that resemble giant elm (*Ulmus*) seeds, which germinate well if sown in fall. This species is often functionally dioecious, so not all plants produce fruits.

Several aromatic small trees fit well in a discussion of aralia. The pricklyash (**Zanthoxylum americanum**) is easy to spot in early spring, when its thorny twigs are covered with delicate chartreuse flowers. Its lemon-scented leaves are a favorite food plant of some spectacular butterflies, and female trees bear clusters of small, dark red fruits in late summer. Pricklyash is not a true ash (*Fraxinus*) but is closely related to hoptree and can be found in various habitats across the northern states and southern Canada north to USDA zone 3. It often grows as a clonal shrub like aralia, but I have seen individual stems 20 feet (6 m) tall and 6 inches (15 cm) thick. The larger southern pricklyash (**Z. clava-herculis**) is endemic from the coastal plain in the Southeast west to the black soil prairie region of Texas, and grows only from USDA zone 8 south. It has striking white flowers and great bark texture with stout, triangular, thorny projections like those seen on some tropical trees. Some other pricklyash species are generally shrubby or not hardy in our region. The fruits of all pricklyashes are attractive to birds, who help spread the seeds.

Waxmyrtle (**Myrica cerifera**), also called southern bayberry, is another aromatic species growing up to 40 feet (12 m) tall in the South. It is a fast-growing, erect, symmetrical, fine-textured small tree from the Coastal Plain, hardy north to USDA zone 7 and tolerant of wet or dry conditions and sterile soils. 'Wintergreen' was found in Oklahoma by Logan Calhoun. It was selected from a native stand and is proving to be cold hardy into USDA

zone 5. The related northern bayberry (**M. pensylvanica**) occasionally reaches small tree size as well and can be grown north into USDA zone 3. It becomes a clonal clump and is useful for erosion control. Both bayberries are dioecious, bearing their scented waxy fruits only on female plants. Bayberries survive on sandy, sterile soils but reach small tree size only under more fertile conditions. Fall-planted seeds, cleaned of their waxy coatings, germinate well. 'Wildwood' is a seed germplasm selection bred by the USDA for vigor, hardiness, and insect resistance.

The fragrant, silvery big sagebrush (**Artemisia tridentata**) is more closely related to sunflowers than to our other trees. It is the largest member of its genus—a shrub that wants to be a tree—so it lives in the High Plains, where it can be the biggest fish among the guppies. It tends to dominate much of the 150,000 square miles (388,500 sq. km) of dry grassland on which it grows. In cold desert areas, such as the Great Basin and the open rangeland east of Yellowstone National Park, big sagebrush becomes a picturesque small tree with age. As with bonsai, its character makes it look bigger than it really is, especially compared with the low plants surrounding it. Further west, the U.S. national champion in Washington is 17 feet (5.1 m) tall with an equal spread. It makes a striking landscape specimen in a small yard but must be given good drainage to survive.

COMMENTS: Aralia, like pricklyash, was once known as the toothache-tree. Early settlers rolled pieces of its inner bark into small wads and placed them on sore teeth, biting down to hold them in place, to relieve toothaches. According to those who experienced this, the burning pain produced by the sap prior to the numbing effect was equally effective in making patients forget the toothache. I think I'll take their word for it.

Aralias, both native and exotic, were once very popular in pretentious Victorian landscape designs, due to their unusual appearance in every season. A few venerable clumps still survive around some old houses, occasionally sending up new stems to replace the old ones. Few plants connote the Victorian period in a historic landscape restoration more than aralia, and few impart such unusual diversity to the native landscape as the agglomeration of the other species mentioned with it.

Asimina triloba

PAWPAW

DESCRIPTION: The pawpaw is the nonconformist of its family (Annonaceae). It looks like a tropical tree, and indeed all other members of the Annonaceae are subtropical or tropical in their distribution. Pawpaw, however, is an understory temperate-zone tree of rich woods and high stream terraces. It frequently forms thickets of small stems in its favorite habitats, but it can also be grown in the landscape as a small ornamental tree with one or several stems. Most pawpaw trees are less than 30 feet (9 m) tall, though one specimen in Newton County, Mississippi, measures twice that height, with a trunk 29 inches (72.5 cm) in diameter. The trees that are allowed to send up multiple sprouts from the roots never attain such respectable proportions but are attractive en masse.

LEAVES: One reason pawpaw has such a tropical appearance is because of its foliage. Up to 1 foot (30 cm) long or more and half as wide, the drooping leaves make the pawpaw look like an avocado tree. Fall color is normally a good clear yellow, sometimes brilliant, and the fall-tinted foliage backlit under oaks in the deep woods is very appealing if the tree has escaped damage or drought during the growing season.

FLOWERS AND FRUIT: The three-lobed flowers, which look like inverted red trilliums, give the tree its specific epithet, *triloba*. They mature into a handsome claret-brown color but are not very visible from a distance or for very long because the developing foliage tends to overgrow them visually. They are pollinated by carrion flies and scavenger beetles, so their fragrance cannot be expected to be particularly ingratiating, but it is not noticeable from a distance. This is both good and bad: the tree's smell is not strong enough to be objectionable in the yard, but the odor is so faint that many trees attract very few pollinators, thus limiting fruit production. This is further complicated by the pawpaw's protogynous flowers, which require cross-pollination from other pawpaw trees not part of the same clone. Some extremely dedicated pawpaw growers help their trees attract pollinators by hanging pieces of ripe carrion in the trees.

The yellow, bean-shaped pawpaw fruits ripen into soft, fragrant, custardlike berries, somewhat similar to very ripe bananas in taste and consistency. These are the largest berries produced by any of our native trees, sometimes reaching 6 inches (15 cm) in length, and if pollination is good they develop in clusters like bananas. Each encloses a few large seeds stacked in a row down the middle. These contain an alkaloid drug and are inedible. The fleshy pulp of the fruit, though, can be so tasty that many selections have been made in the past for potential home orchard production.

BEST SEASONS: FALL (the foliage texture and color is eye-catching, and the ripe fruits are consumed quickly by any animal with two or more legs). SPRING (for the emerging new foliage, with the structure of the tree still visible, and for the flowers if they can be viewed closely). SUMMER (for the avocado effect of the leaves).

NATIVE AND ADAPTIVE RANGE: Pawpaw grows in rich soils throughout most of the eastern United States, west into Nebraska and north to the southern Great Lakes and extreme southern Ontario. It can be planted successfully from USDA zone 5 southward.

CULTURE: Pawpaw is one of those clonal grouping trees, like sassafras (*Sassafras albidum*), that are difficult to transplant from the wild because any stems derived from suckers are very deeply rooted. Even true seedlings can be a little tricky to move. Container-grown plants present no problems, though, as long as a suitably moist planting location with rich soil is selected. Pawpaw is easy to propagate from seed, which should be squeezed from the soft fruit pulp and sown in fall. The seeds are epigeal, unlike those of most other large-seeded trees, and produce stout, vigorous seedlings. They should be stored in a cool, moist atmosphere until planting.

Once established, pawpaw requires very little attention, and it grows quickly if mulched well and watered during droughts. It will develop an open crown in dense shade and a more compact, uniform crown in full sun.

RIGHT: A pawpaw (*Asimina triloba*) begins to turn color in early fall.

Decide initially whether you prefer a single stem, a clump, or a grove, and manipulate the tree accordingly. Given the freedom of choice in a favorable site, it will always choose to become a "pawpaw patch."

PROBLEMS: Most complaints about pawpaw concern the messiness of the fruit if it falls on a sidewalk or patio. The occasional suckers that pop up from the root system should be hand-pulled when small if they are unwanted, since mowing or pruning them off simply encourages resprouting from basal buds on the suckers. This tree has very few cultural problems that adequate soil moisture and fertility won't eliminate.

CULTIVARS: I am unaware of any ornamental cultivars currently available in the nursery trade. However, dozens of fruit selections have been made by hobbyists, fruit growers, and researchers over the years, and some of these might be available through local horticultural or permacultural societies. Some of the more popular cultivars among the closely knit groups who grow them are 'Sunflower', 'Overleese', 'Prolific', and 'Wilson'. Cross-pollination among several clones is very helpful in assuring a good fruit set.

SIMILAR AND RELATED SPECIES: One other minor species, the small-fruited pawpaw (*Asimina parviflora*), can be found in the Southeast. It is a smaller version of *A. triloba* in most respects. Several others, all dryland shrubs with thicker leaves, are mostly restricted to subtropical areas of peninsular Florida. *Asimina triloba* is part of a large, tropical family with more than 130 genera, and we are fortunate to have the one species that has been able to adapt to a temperate climate.

Bladdernut (**Staphylea trifolia**) has striped bark, compound, opposite leaves, and inflated, papery seed capsules that cause it to be noticed from up close. At a distance, though, it becomes an inconspicuous understory tree or shrub. It shares many moist woods and stream banks with pawpaw, and although they are not related, they make good companion plantings. A large specimen growing in rich woods may reach 30 feet (9 m) in height, but this species is usually smaller than pawpaw and grows beneath it in the understory. Bladdernut can be found in scattered locations across much of eastern North America, north into USDA zone 3 in Quebec and Ontario. The stonelike seeds rattle in their pods when ripe and should be planted in late summer for germination the following spring.

COMMENTS: Pawpaw is the food plant for the striking zebra swallowtail butterfly, a welcome visitor to any ornamental landscape setting. It is not surprising, though, that few other insects bother this plant. Pawpaw extracts can be used to manufacture potent natural insecticides to control many serious insect pests of agriculture and forestry, including spider mites, Mexican bean beetles, and tent caterpillars. Chemicals called annonaceous acetogenins from these same extracts have also shown promise in anticancer pharmaceutical research at Purdue University.

Pawpaw fruits were a favorite food of Native Americans, and they contain healthy concentrations of vitamins and minerals. Pawpaws helped feed the conquistadores of Hernando de Soto during his discovery of the Mississippi River more than four hundred years ago, and Lewis and Clark subsisted nicely on pawpaws when they ran out of food on their return from their Voyage of Discovery in the fall of 1806.

These banana-, mango-, papaya-like fruits have long been relished and are a taste treat for those who can beat the wildlife to get to them. While less well known in today's market due to problems with shipping and storage, there are entire Web sites devoted to pawpaw cultivation as a food crop for the home orchard or permaculture plantation. The pulp varies from white to yellow and light orange, and most pawpaw enthusiasts prefer the darker fruits, with the portion nearest the seeds being best, as with a watermelon. Many wild mammals eat the fruits whole. The seeds pass through them scarified but undigested, germinating readily the following spring.

LEFT: Pawpaw (*Asimina triloba*) flower.

Betula alleghaniensis

YELLOW BIRCH

DESCRIPTION: I have chosen yellow birch (*Betula alleghaniensis*, syn. *B. lutea*) to illustrate the group of species I'll call the dark-barked northern birches. Unlike other birches, yellow birch is a climax species that is shade tolerant and relatively long lived. It grows larger than any of our other birches, becoming a dominant canopy tree in the cove hardwoods of the Appalachians and the mixed forests of the Great Lakes area. Although much taller individuals can be found, there is a tree in Deer Island, Maine, that is 76 feet (6.9 m) tall and almost 7 feet (2.1 m) thick. Open-grown specimens usually develop a characteristic massive candelabra form, with heavy limbs arching skyward from a short trunk, while forest trees are much taller and more slender, with a dominant single trunk extending well into the canopy.

This species has a silvery yellow, shredded, curly bark that looks like that of some Asian tree lilacs and smells like wintergreen. While not as striking as the white bark of some other birches, yellow birch bark is very handsome. In its preferred cool-climate habitat, this species is relatively resistant to the borer (*Agrilus anxius*) that more readily attacks most exotic white-barked birches.

LEAVES: Yellow birch leaves are 3 to 5 inches (7.5 to 12.5 cm) long, paper thin, and turn a nice yellow in fall. Fall color is especially effective when the leaves, along with the peeling, papery bark, are backlit and viewed against a dark background.

FLOWERS AND FRUIT: All birch catkins are similar, expanding in spring just before the leaves emerge. The staminate catkins are about 3 inches (7.5 cm) long and hang in clusters from the slender twigs like bundles of pale green icicles. Moving with the slightest breeze, they produce a collective visual effect that is delicate and memorable. The pistillate strobiles of yellow birch are shorter and broader than those of our other birches, and the seeds are dispersed by wind through fall and winter.

BEST SEASONS: FALL (the combination of papery bark and yellow leaves brightens the dark forests where this species commonly grows). WINTER (the bark, like that of most birches, is a primary ornamental feature that is most visible and appreciated in the dormant season). SPRING (the catkins add a soft, delicate touch).

NATIVE AND ADAPTIVE RANGE: Yellow birch grows abundantly in the Great Lakes area, eastward through Newfoundland, and south along the Appalachian Mountains, with scattered populations in favorable habitats well outside the primary range. It is adapted to cool climates and moist, well-drained soils up through USDA zone 3.

CULTURE: This is one of the only birches that will do well in semishade. It prefers a cool, moist, well-drained soil, is easy to transplant in early spring, and can be propagated from fresh seed sown on top of loose bare soil in fall (exposure to light enhances germination). Open-grown trees tend to develop massive lower branches and may need corrective pruning while young to establish good limb structure.

PROBLEMS: The northern birches all demand cool, moist soil in summer. They reward inattention to this requirement by falling victim to the bronze birch borer beetle (*Agrilus anxius*). They can be attacked by leaf miners (*Fenusa pusilla*) and other leaf-feeding insects as well, although yellow birch and the related sweet birch (*Betula lenta*) seem more resistant to these and to defoliators like Gypsy moth (*Lymantria dispar*) than other birches. Birches are very susceptible to the Asian longhorned borer beetle (*Anoplophora glabripennis*) and to stem cankers, *Melanconium* dieback, decay organisms, and browsing animals such as deer, moose, porcupines, and rabbits. All birches are extremely sensitive to fires in their wildland habitats, and this is particularly true of yellow birch, to the extent that mature yellow birches are not found in fire-prone areas of the forest.

CULTIVARS: No cultivars of this species are available. This is a good excuse to plant a seedling, knowing it will become a superior tree regardless of its lack of pedigree.

SIMILAR AND RELATED SPECIES: Sweet birch (***Betula lenta***) is a medium-sized tree with rich, dark reddish bark like that of an Asian cherry tree. This is the source of birch beer, a favorite rural libation in some regions. Sweet birch needs more sun than yellow birch but less sun than the white-barked birches and is the most toler-

ant of alkaline soils. This species has perhaps the best fall color of any birch, turning a vibrant gold that is outstanding in combination with its cherry bark color. Like yellow birch, it is intermediate in resistance to the bronze birch borer, depending on its vigor. Sweet birch has an even stronger wintergreen aroma than yellow birch and was once a source of commercial supply for oil of wintergreen.

The roundleaf birch (***Betula uber***) is very closely related to sweet birch. Like yellow birch and sweet birch, it does best with its leaves in half sun but its roots in deep shade. It grows naturally only in a single, isolated location along Cressy Creek in Smyth County, Virginia. In 1978 it became the first tree to be listed as a U.S. federally endangered species; therefore, it cannot be collected or sold without a permit. It was considered extinct until 1975, when a stand of forty-one live trees was discovered. Along with 150 other cooperators worldwide, I am as-

LEFT: Yellow birch (*Betula alleghaniensis*) in the boreal forest of Canada. BELOW: The papery, peeling bark of yellow birch. BELOW RIGHT: Yellow birch seed clusters are short and broad.

sisting under permit with ex situ recovery efforts for this rare species.

Birches are closely related to alders (***Alnus***), a mostly shrubby genus of water-loving species. Alder roots are nodulated with *Frankia* bacteria and are capable of fixing atmospheric nitrogen into the soil, so they are seen frequently in sterile sandbars and old mine tailings where the lack of soil nitrogen stunts most other plants. They also exhibit an unusual form of growth called syllepsis, in which the lateral buds break during their first season. This is occasionally seen on birches also but is uncommon on other temperate trees.

Hazel alder (***Alnus serrulata***) and speckled alder (***A. rugosa***) occasionally reach tree size and look much like small, dark-barked birches with stiff little seed cones. The rare seaside alder (***A. maritima***) is similar and is very interesting to ecologists due to its puzzling natural range. It is found in the wild in only three widely separated locations: the Delmarva Peninsula, southern Oklahoma, and northwestern Georgia. Tests have shown it to be hardy north at least through USDA zone 4, and its wind-disseminated seeds can travel for miles on a stiff breeze, so its restricted natural range remains to be ex-

plained. Some alders were used medicinally by aboriginal Native Americans, so perhaps the seaside alder was distributed in this way.

The giant Mexican alder (*Alnus oblongifolia*) becomes a large canopy tree in canyons of the Southwest. In cul-

tivation it is one of our most rapidly growing trees. It is hardy at least as far north as USDA zone 7 and perhaps zone 6, but its cold hardiness has not yet been fully tested. The largest known specimen, in the Cibola National Forest of New Mexico, is 129 feet (38.7 m) tall and more than 5 feet (1.5 m) in diameter. Mountain alder (*A. tenuifolia*) is a more common species found further north in the mountainous western part of our region. It is usually shrubby, occasionally reaching small tree size. Three other tree-sized alders are found on the Pacific Coast, and additional alder species, mostly exotic, are common in cultivation for ornamental and conservation purposes.

COMMENTS: Yellow birch is the arboreal emblem of Quebec and loves to grow there on old logs and rotting stumps in the cool, mossy forest. As these "nurse logs" gradually decay, the birches are left behind on stilted roots that can be several feet high, so that the trees appear to be walking on legs. Young Canadian children on camping trips have been known to come running back to camp in a panic after having seen their first yellow birch tree "walking" through the dimly lit woods at dusk, seemingly ready to pounce. Far from being an evil monster, the tree is actually the woodsman's friend—its curly bark can be used for kindling even when soaked with rain or fog.

LEFT: A Mexican alder (*Alnus oblongifolia*) in a canyon of the Southwest. BELOW: The leaves of roundleaf birch (*Betula uber*) give this rare tree its name.

Betula nigra
RIVER BIRCH

DESCRIPTION: People living in the southern two-thirds of our area, from about USDA zone 5 south, have found it difficult to grow birch trees because of the bronze birch borer (*Agrilus anxius*), a small metallic beetle that attacks and eventually kills any birch under summer stress. Plant researchers have traveled to Japan, Russia, and China in search of a magic birch tree that can resist this pest. However, the only way a birch can fend off the borer is to be so well adapted to the local climate that hot summer weather will not cause the stress that allows the insect to succeed.

Our native river birch is such a tree. Unlike other birches, this species grows naturally all the way down to Florida and shrugs off summer heat without consequence. It can become almost as large as yellow birch (*Betula alleghaniensis*). One tree in Tennessee is 90 feet (27 m) tall and nearly 5 feet (1.5 m) in diameter, and most river birch trees eventually reach at least two-thirds that size, even on poor sites. This tree develops a pinkish tan peeling bark and a spreading crown of several large ascending limbs that support slightly weeping branches.

LEAVES: River birch leaves are more triangular than those of yellow birch and grow from 2 to 5 inches (5 to 12.5 cm) long. They develop the yellow fall color typical of most birch species, although they are not always as bright or color-saturated.

FLOWERS AND FRUIT: The catkins of this species resemble those of other birches. The tiny seeds grow in strobiles, like those of yellow birch, but ripen in late spring and are dispersed gradually by the wind. In the wild they quickly colonize newly exposed mudflats or sandbars following spring floods, but they cannot establish easily on areas already occupied by other plants.

BEST SEASONS: WINTER (the bark of many individual trees is outstanding and is most visible after leaf abscission). FALL (as the leaves prepare to drop, they turn from an average green to a fairly nice yellow). SPRING (as with other birches, the delicate expanding catkins provide additional landscape interest).

NATIVE AND ADAPTIVE RANGE: This tree is native in wet sites from Minnesota and New Hampshire to Florida and Texas. It is rated hardy north at least through USDA zone 4.

CULTURE: River birch loves water but does not require excess amounts of it. It can survive in low areas that remain flooded for months at a time, but it can also be grown on fairly dry sites once it establishes a deep root system. It is perhaps the only birch that accepts tight clay soils without complaint, as long as those soils are not high enough in pH to trigger iron chlorosis. River birch is easily transplanted and can be propagated from seed sprinkled on the surface of loose soil or from softwood cuttings. Unlike the yellow birch, this species (and most other birches) will not survive in the shade.

PROBLEMS: Various leaf miners and aphids bother river birch (see those listed under *Betula alleghaniensis*), but its freedom from bronze birch borer attacks makes all other insect problems seem inconsequential. Many stressed birch trees produce a cambial chemical called rhododendrol, which is suspected to attract borers, but river birch does not produce this chemical, even under stress. The related birch-alder borer (*Agrilus pensus*) is occasionally found in sublethal quantities in river birch.

River birch is considered very messy. Pollen can be a short-lived nuisance in spring, as it is with most other wind-pollinated trees. Twigs fall all year long with every breeze, and major limbs may come crashing down during ice storms. Under very dry conditions, river birch sheds leaves and twigs in order to conserve limited moisture, a process known as drought-induced cladoptosis; this litter drops continuously during every summer drought unless the tree is planted in a swamp. The shallow roots also make it difficult to grow other plants under a river birch after it is well established.

Still, this species is one of the most adaptable birches, able to survive in a variety of sites. It prefers full sun and acidic soil (below pH 6.5) for best growth and good leaf color. It will be most vigorous with ample water but can survive on relatively dry sites once established.

CULTIVARS: River birch is beginning to yield good selections as more tree researchers realize how uniquely adapted it is, for a birch, to hot summer climates. The interesting new dwarf 'Little King', introduced by Chi-

cagoland Grows, a cultivar-development cooperative, is trademarked as Fox Valley River Birch. (I'm not sure which name will become more common in usage, so I mention both.) It has a compact form and grows only about one-fourth as quickly as other river birches. Another dwarf selection is 'Tecumseh Compact', which grows more as a shrub than a tree. Strongly weeping forms of river birch can also be found occasionally, and one of them is sure to find its way to nurseries before long.

Dura-Heat river birch is a selection from Georgia, where summers can test even the toughest birches. Unfortunately, its actual cultivar name ('BNMTF') is one of those alphabet-soup jokes that discourages the common use of true cultivar names in favor of copyrighted trade names in order to protect patent rights. The original 'Heritage', released by my friend and associate Earl Cully after years of testing, is probably the most impressive river birch cultivar. It has disease-resistant leaves, good form and hardiness, and buff-colored bark that peels in large sheets to reveal an inner bark nearly as white as that

LEFT: River birch (*Betula nigra*) is a water-loving species. BELOW: Bark of river birch. RIGHT: *Betula nigra* 'Heritage'.

of the white-barked birches. 'Heritage' river birch combines many of the aesthetic qualities of paper birch (*Betula papyrifera*)—though no genetic link has been established—in a heat-loving tree with superior cultural adaptability. An improved selection with even whiter bark, possibly a mutation, has been propagated from a supe-

rior individual tree of 'Heritage' by tissue culture and is under production.

SIMILAR AND RELATED SPECIES: The western water birch (**Betula fontinalis**, syn. *B. occidentalis*) is a shrubby species that grows with alders (*Alnus*) along Rocky Mountain streams. The trees that resemble river birch most closely, aesthetically and horticulturally, are all Asian species. Some are equally attractive, but none match river birch for its adaptability to our climate.

COMMENTS: Most birches are known for their beautiful bark, which can dominate any landscape in the dormant season. Whichever species you select, it will be most effective if planted in groupings and clumps that place many replications of that bark at eye level, against a dark background of foliage or shadow. Fortunately, this is the way birches prefer to grow. They seem to enjoy the company of their own kind, providing collective shade for their roots and acting together to modify their microenvironment to suit their needs.

For three decades I have tested twenty-nine species and varieties of birch, both native and exotic, in central Illinois. None have performed better than river birch in our hostile continental climate of hot summers, cold winters, terrible droughts, floods, ice storms, and unpredictable spring and fall freezes.

BELOW: 'Little King' is a compact selection of river birch.

Betula papyrifera
PAPER BIRCH

DESCRIPTION: The most conspicuous and characteristic deciduous tree of the North Woods surely must be the paper birch, also called canoe birch. This extremely cold-hardy transcontinental birch, with its many varieties and geographic races, is the primary white-barked birch that lights up the forest. It is a pioneer of disturbed habitats, reproducing in spectacular, densely packed groves following logging or forest fires. Paper birch is highly sensitive to fire, yet well adapted to it: this tree seeds profusely and, if the top is killed or damaged, develops a basal root collar from which dormant buds send up clusters of new shoots. Many wild trees grow as clumps for this reason, and nature's idea has caught on in the landscape trade as well, with attractive clumps of birch planted in every northeastern town.

Paper birch grows rapidly and becomes one of our largest birches. The U.S. record tree, in Cheboygan County, Michigan, is 93 feet (27.9 m) tall, with a clump of trunks arising from a base almost 6 feet (1.8 m) thick. Most trees seen in forests or residential landscapes, however, are juvenile specimens of much more modest stature, and those that cling to the barren rock of high mountains seldom become more than shrubs.

LEAVES: Much of the considerable geographic variability exhibited within this species is apparent in the leaves. They average 3 inches (7.5 cm) long, are usually hairy below, and are rounded or heart shaped at the base. In fall they turn bright yellow.

FLOWERS AND FRUIT: Birch catkins are similar from species to species, but those of paper birch seem more ornamental due to their background of peeling white bark and the dark twigs from which they are suspended in spring. Unopened male catkins, formed in late summer, stand out from the ends of twigs like gatherings of small brown worms. The minute seeds spread in profusion every year and quickly colonize bare soils, exposed rocky slopes, sandy lakeshores, and peaty bog margins.

BEST SEASONS: WINTER (because of its bark this tree is the king of winter throughout its range, just as sugar maple is the king of autumn). FALL (the yellow foliage partially hides, yet highlights, the white bark). EARLY SPRING (the hanging catkins accent the dark twigs and white branches).

NATIVE AND ADAPTIVE RANGE: Paper birch is the state tree of New Hampshire and the arboreal emblem of Saskatchewan, so its northern-hardy credentials from east to west are beyond question. This tree in its several varieties, and some of its shrubby relatives as well, will grow north nearly to the tree line in northern Canada but will disappear from the woods to the south wherever the average July temperature exceeds 70°F (21°C). Its rated winter hardiness is USDA zone 2.

White-barked birches, especially some related exotic species, are often planted beyond their preferred ranges because of their spectacular bark. They cannot maintain their vigor and insect resistance in areas with hot summer conditions and therefore must be pampered and sprayed faithfully with insecticides to have much chance for long-term survival. While this intensive management and risk may be acceptable to some gardeners or plant collectors, it violates the basic concepts of native tree use that form the premise of this book. By all means, grow the beautiful paper birches if they are adapted to your area; but look for other fine native trees to grow if you live in the Southeast or the lower Midwest.

CULTURE: I have found in provenance trials in Illinois that selecting a source keyed to local climate and soil conditions is critical for success with this variable species in marginal habitats. Paper birches grow easily from seed and can be transplanted with a soil ball in spring without difficulty. Give this tree full sun, but keep the roots cool and moist in a slightly acid soil, and treat the bark with a recommended insecticide to prevent borers unless you live in ideal birch habitat.

PROBLEMS: Paper birch is a favorite browse of deer and moose, which can limit natural reproduction. It can be very sensitive to the bronze birch borer (*Agrilus anxius*) under unfavorable growing conditions, though less so than some of its cousins from Europe and Asia. Paper birches do show considerable borer resistance, however, in cold climates. Stressed birch trees produce rhododendrol, which is suspected of attracting borers. Paper birch

has smaller amounts of the precursor chemical, rhododendrin, in its bark than most other white-barked birches and thus produces less rhododendrol. See *Betula alleghaniensis* for additional discussion of birch problems.

Where paper birch can be grown, no other tree displays more spectacular bark. Although the bark does peel, it does not shed in heavy plates like that of some other trees and is not a major litter problem.

CULTIVARS: Surprisingly few cultivar selections of paper birch are known in the horticultural trade. Perhaps no one has presumed to improve upon the tremendous degree of geographic variation already available as natural varieties. One selection, 'Renaissance Upright', has been developed for its narrow growth habit.

I am trying a selection at Starhill Forest from the Niobrara River of Nebraska. Art Ode, former director of the

Nebraska Statewide Arboretum, provided the seed and believes that this selection may have better resistance to borers. Horticultural selections are much more abundant in the similar but inferior (for North America) European species.

SIMILAR AND RELATED SPECIES: The faster-growing but smaller gray birch (**Betula populifolia**) is abundant on poor, open sites in the North. 'Whitespire', originally thought to be of Asian origin, has been linked to this native species. Several shrub birch species can be found, mostly around bogs and on mountain tops. Birches also hybridize freely, and the paper birch will cross with the shrubby species. Some interesting selections could be expected from such crosses, but none are on the market yet.

Many of the white-barked birches seen dying in suburban landscapes are European species such as **Betula pendula** and **B. pubescens** or Asian species such as **B. ermanii** or **B. platyphylla,** which (despite some claims to the contrary) generally make their best efforts when grown in their native lands. This observation is substantially supported by testing completed by my old friend

LEFT: Paper birch (*Betula papyrifera*) on a lakeshore in Ontario. BELOW: Dark young stems of paper birch peel to reveal the white inner bark after several years. BELOW RIGHT: Catkins of paper birch.

Dr. Frank Santamour Jr. of the U.S. National Arboretum, who was a revered authority among tree experts.

COMMENTS: The bark of paper birch reaches its maximum ornamental value in natural stands, with a dark background of associated pine, spruce, and fir. The species retains many dormant buds at its base as an adaptation to fire. When the top is killed, as happens to birch in even the lightest of fires, these buds spring to life, generating a clump of sprouts that give rise to the natural clump form so often imitated in residential plantings.

This bark was the campfire tinder of early woodsmen and the material of the aboriginal bark canoe, sewn together with larch roots and caulked with balsam resin. It is extremely durable. In fact, I have seen long-dead birch trunks in Canada reduced by decay organisms to hollow shells of pure bark, the wood having vanished a long time before.

The future of the paper birch throughout most of the United States over the next century is uncertain because of global warming. According to predictions, this phenomenon will increase the occurrence of heat waves and drought caused by human-induced escalations in atmospheric concentrations of the greenhouse gases that trap radiant heat. The loss of beautiful trees like paper birch will be one of the early warning signs that the human species has irrevocably fouled its nest.

BELOW AND RIGHT: Paper birch (*Betula papyrifera*) is often found in dense groves.

Carpinus caroliniana
HORNBEAM

DESCRIPTION: Also called blue beech because of its smooth blue-gray bark, hornbeam is a fine-textured, graceful understory tree with strong wood and sinewy fluted stems that give it yet another name: musclewood. Its trunk and major limbs develop a pronounced taper and a spiraling, serpentine growth that can give the tree a bonsai appearance, making it seem older and more venerable than it really is.

Hornbeam typically grows no bigger than a semi-dwarf fruit tree, but some ancient specimens can become medium-sized trees. The U.S. record tree stands in Ulster County, New York; it is 69 feet (20.7 m) tall and more than 2 feet (60 cm) thick at the trunk. In the southern part of its natural range, in southern Mexico and Central America, this giant would be an average specimen. Similar to its namesake, beech (*Fagus grandifolia*), the hornbeam can spread by sending occasional root suckers up at some distance from the parent plant, but most reproduction is from seed.

LEAVES: The paper-thin leaves grow up to 5 inches (12.5 cm) long and about half as wide or less, and have pointed tips and finely toothed margins. The fine texture of the tree is due in part to the leaves and in part to the intricate branches that support them. The claret new foliage that develops in sunlit locations contrasts beautifully with the bright green older leaves.

Most individual trees turn a clear yellow or orange in fall, but some consistently yield a luminous crimson. This variation may be genetic but could be enhanced by environmental factors that affect leaf sugar synthesis and transport. The dried leaves sometimes persist into winter, but not so much as those of some closely related European and Asian hornbeam species.

FLOWERS AND FRUIT: Hornbeam is related to the birches (*Betula*) and has similar staminate catkins in spring as the leaves unfold. The catkins are not spectacular, but they do enhance the overall aspect of the tree. The fruits are tiny winged nuts suspended in small clusters, and they blend in with the foliage. They are particularly favored by ruffed grouse and are sought by finches and wild turkeys as well.

BEST SEASONS: FALL (whether red, orange, or yellow, this tree gives a nice display, especially when the branching structure is silhouetted through a backlit specimen). SPRING (when the flowers and foliage begin to emerge, adding a colorful cast to the tracery of the fine branches). WINTER (the bark, sinewy growth, and graceful structure are best viewed during the dormant season, with low sidelighting against a dark background).

NATIVE AND ADAPTIVE RANGE: Hornbeam spans an incredible range of latitude, from the northeastern shore of Georgian Bay in Ontario across to the vicinity of Quebec City, down through the entire eastern United States to northern Florida and eastern Texas, then extending in the mountains through Mexico and Guatemala to Honduras. Trees selected from northern sources will survive as far north as USDA zone 2, making this one of the most broadly climate-adaptable of all our native trees.

CULTURE: This species is occasionally reported to be difficult to transplant. However, I have moved many medium-sized hornbeams in Indiana and Illinois, from both seedling and sprout origin, with soil and without, in both spring and fall, and never lost one. The major roots are usually shallow and spreading, so digging the tree with a wide, shallow root ball is best. Seed propagation is also easier than some sources suggest. For best germination, plant freshly picked seed (slightly green, if possible) early in fall when the soil is still warm. If you're a little late, just be willing to wait until the second spring for seedlings to emerge. They need a moist seedbed and should not be planted very deeply.

Hornbeam loves shade but will become more dense and uniform in a sunny (but moist) location. Sunny conditions also enhance spring foliage color. The root environment should be kept moist by mulching and by selecting an appropriate planting site. When given moist soil, it is a carefree tree.

PROBLEMS: This tree is notable for its freedom from insect and disease problems. A few minor leaf spot diseases and cankers strike occasionally, but generally they

RIGHT: Hornbeam (*Carpinus caroliniana*) is a small, spreading tree when grown in the open.

are insignificant. A small borer beetle, *Agrilus carpinus*, occasionally attacks stressed trees.

The smooth bark of hornbeam can be blemished by careless use of turf equipment (or by vandals with pocket knives), and the roots are sensitive to soil disturbance. The tree develops narrow branching angles but remains quite resistant to breakage under ice loading due to its small size and strong wood. Soil disturbance, road salt, air pollution, and hot, scorching conditions make this tree unhappy, and it does not recover from large pruning wounds very well.

CULTIVARS: One old columnar selection, 'Ascendens', is listed but not commonly available. Other upright-growing specimens are seen occasionally, suggesting that selections could be made for growth form. Opportunities should also exist for selections based upon provenance and fall color.

SIMILAR AND RELATED SPECIES: *Carpinus caroliniana* is the only native representative of a widespread genus of ornamental American, European, and Asian trees. Susan Wiegrefe, the plant breeder for the Morton Arboretum, is experimenting with hybridization of several of these trees with our native species to develop cultivars that display the best features of the parents and tolerate more severe environmental stresses. The European species, **C. betulus,** becomes larger than *C. caroliniana* and has been more widely planted, particularly in its fastigiate or pyramidal forms. Hornbeams are members of the birch family and are closely related to the similar, stringy-barked ironwood (*Ostrya virginiana*).

COMMENTS: Hornbeam enjoys shady conditions at the bases of north-facing slopes and in the well-drained floodplains of brooks in our region, but I have seen it in the cool, moist cloud forests of mountain peaks in Mexico and Guatemala. This genus has great aesthetic potential for use in landscapes enhanced with directional outdoor landscape lighting ("uplighting") and for locations where the headlights of approaching vehicles highlight the beautiful bark and intricate branching.

The hornbeam is a clean ornamental tree that doesn't have an off-season. It makes an excellent little shade tree for small yards or intimate landscape areas. The many erect branch forks and the dense crowns of open-grown trees make them popular nesting sites for songbirds, who also make good use of the seeds.

TOP LEFT: Spring foliage of hornbeam (*Carpinus caroliniana*). CENTER LEFT: Fall color on a hornbeam. LEFT: The fluted trunk of hornbeam. RIGHT: The uniform crown and fine texture of a young hornbeam.

Carya cordiformis
BITTERNUT HICKORY

DESCRIPTION: Bitternut hickory, or simply bitternut, is one of the so-called pecan hickories (section *Apocarya*), which are distinguished by winter buds that are not covered with overlapping scales. The buds of bitternut are unique in that they are a bright sulfur-yellow, giving the tree its alternate name, yellowbud hickory. This species is, by a narrow margin, the northernmost and most widespread hickory, as well as one of the fastest growing.

Bitternut is also among the largest hickories, frequently exceeding 100 feet (30 m) in height on the rich sites where it prefers to grow. The largest known specimen, at Great Smoky Mountains National Park, is nearly 150 feet (45 m) tall and 4 feet (1.2 m) in diameter. Bitternut typically develops several primary ascending limbs, forming an arching shape. Its bark is tight and relatively smooth, occasionally developing scattered horizontal fissures that resemble the scars inflicted on fence-row trees by old wire.

LEAVES: Bitternut leaves are narrower than those of most other common hickories and are pinnately compound with seven to nine leaflets. They attain a lighter autumn hue than the leaves of other hickories, turning a bright, clear yellow. Bitternut hickories are among the first of our major forest trees to display fall color, and their tall, yellow crowns can be seen from a long distance.

FLOWERS AND FRUIT: The flowers appear as the leaves are reaching full size. The pendent male catkins hang like tinsel from the branches and are visible below the leaves, looking like miniature festoons of moss.

The nuts develop from the smaller, pistillate flower spikes. Unlike most hickory nuts, bitternut hickory nuts seem useful for little else than potent ammunition for young kids' slingshots. Most nuts are too bitter to be of much interest even to squirrels, although they probably serve wildlife as emergency rations when other foods are scarce. Since they have thin husks and shells, any palatable nuts are easy to eat.

BEST SEASONS: FALL (the clear yellow of bitternut combines well with the somber greens and earliest reds of the surrounding hardwood forest). LATE SPRING (the staminate catkins embellish this species, already among the most finely textured hickories). SUMMER and WINTER (a fine tree for lawn or forest in all seasons).

NATIVE AND ADAPTIVE RANGE: Hickories are almost exclusively North American natives, and bitternut is the most common and widespread hickory through most of our region. It grows naturally on mesic sites and bottomlands from central Minnesota and Trois-Rivières, Quebec, down to northern Florida and eastern Texas. It can do well in protected valleys up through USDA zone 3.

CULTURE: Saying that bitternut is one of the easiest hickories to transplant is analogous to claiming that breaking one arm hurts less than breaking both. All hickories are difficult to move and are best established as small seedlings or containerized plants, or by planting seed in the permanent locations desired for the trees. Soak the fresh seeds in water for a couple of days, then plant them in fall and protect the spot from squirrels and mice. Alternatively seeds can be planted in containers if air-pruning pots, root-restricting fabrics, or copper applications are used to produce a branching root system. These container-grown seedlings can then be planted in a nursery bed for a few years and will move relatively easily (for hickories) when it's time to find them a permanent home.

Hickories can be shocked by root disturbance later in life and should not be subjected to construction or soil compaction within their root areas. Bitternut will grow very well with adequate water and fertility, responding better to such care than some of the other hickories, but it can survive under a wide range of growing conditions.

PROBLEMS: Hickories may be stronger, pound for pound, than steel; but the pecan types, including bitternut, are less so than the others. The frame of this species is further weakened by its branching structure, which is frequently divided into several ascending primary limbs.

RIGHT: Bitternut (*Carya cordiformis*) turns a clear yellow in fall at Starhill Forest.

Nonetheless, it remains one of our stronger shade trees in the face of wind or ice storms.

In closely maintained turf areas, the small nuts of bitternut hickory can be a litter problem, usually with no offsetting gastronomic values. Sapsuckers (our only noxious woodpeckers) seem to prefer the sap of bitternut over that of other species and occasionally damage the bark. All hickories are preferred hosts for masses of fall webworms (*Hyphantria cunea*), which are generally more ugly than harmful, due to their late-season activity. In spite of their hard, dense wood, stressed or damaged hickories are attacked and sometimes killed by the painted hickory borer (*Megacyllene caryae*), the hickory bark beetle (*Scolytus quadrispinosus*), and other borers.

CULTIVARS: There are no named cultivars of bitternut hickory, but its large natural range should yield regionally adapted ornamental selections.

SIMILAR AND RELATED SPECIES: Among the other pecan hickories are the water hickory (***Carya aquatica***) and nutmeg hickory (***C. myristicaeformis***), both of which develop shaggier bark than bitternut.

Water hickory is remarkable for its tolerance of seasonally wet soils. It is a swamp-forest tree that not only can withstand protracted flooding during the growing season but can also grow equally well when planted on well-drained sites. A tree of the Mississippi Valley and the Coastal Plain, it grows just as well on dry land at my arboretum in central Illinois. Water hickory and bitter-

nut both hybridize in the wild with pecan, producing trees called bitter pecans.

Nutmeg hickory is an uncommon species with leaves that are attractively whitened underneath. It grows in the United States in scattered relictual stands on upper terraces of river floodplains, along the Red River in Texas, and in a few other isolated locations across the Southeast. Like its relatives, it also grows well in cultivation in central Illinois in my USDA zone 5 climate. Saplings of this species are more tolerant of shade than other hickories. The U.S. national champion nutmeg hickory is almost as tall as the record bitternut, though not as thick. It becomes even larger in the southern part of its range, in Nuevo León, Mexico. The record water hickory is only about 100 feet (30 m) tall but has an immense buttressed trunk more than 6 feet (1.8 m) in diameter.

FAR LEFT: Bitternut hickory (*Carya cordiformis*) is one of our most fine-textured hickories in winter. LEFT: The graceful staminate catkins of bitternut hickory. BELOW: The sulfur-yellow buds of bitternut hickory make it easy to identify in winter. BELOW RIGHT: Water hickory (*C. aquatica*) is a swamp-dwelling relative of bitternut hickory.

COMMENTS: Bitternut and its relatives are among our best forest soil builders due to the mineral content of their leaves. It casts a relatively light, open shade compared with other hickories, allowing turf or ornamental plants to thrive under its canopy.

Bitternut has a reputation, as its name implies, for having bitter nuts. On one occasion I tried to play a joke on my young nephew by picking up some of these nuts, cracking them open with a rock, and pretending to eat them. Monkey see, monkey do, and he followed suit. When he ate a second, and then a third, I became suspicious. As it turned out we had stumbled upon the only sweet-tasting bitternut hickory tree I have ever found. My mischievous little joke had helped us find a great nut tree that we would not have tasted otherwise.

This tree and other hickories also serve as primary hosts for some magnificent and relatively harmless moths, including the beautiful, nocturnal luna moth, several colorful underwing moths, and the scary-sounding little funeral dagger wing. But the most impressive tenant of the hickories is the giant regal moth, with its 6-inch (15-cm) wingspan and its unforgettable larva, the hickory horned devil, our largest North American caterpillar.

Carya illinoinensis
PECAN

DESCRIPTION: The pecan is our largest and most commercially valuable hickory and is the state tree of Texas. Many people who love its tasty nuts don't realize that it is a hickory; in fact it is the closest relative of those hickories with some of the most bitter fruits. Excluding the taste of its nuts, the pecan shares many characteristics with bitternut hickory (*Carya cordiformis*). It is a tree of river bottoms, and in the rich, moist soil of its fertile habitat it grows more quickly than any other hickory. While grafted orchard pecans sometimes stay small, wild trees can be immense.

One very tall pecan I saw a few years ago growing along a rural roadside in Cocke County, Tennessee, was 143 feet (42.9 m) tall with a trunk more than 6 feet (1.8 m) thick. That tree has become the U.S. national champion. Several huge old pecans growing in Maryland and Virginia owe their origins to famous early gardeners like George Washington and Thomas Jefferson. Old trees in open, sunny locations may have spreading limbs that span more than 100 feet (30 m), and even forest-grown trees will form broad crowns of long, arching primary limbs.

LEAVES: Pecan leaves are pinnately compound, as are all hickory leaves, and can have fifteen or more narrow, sickle-shaped leaflets. The foliage has a dark brownish green cast when seen from a distance, so this species is easy to pick out from its bottomland associates. It turns yellow in fall but not as impressively as other hickories.

FLOWERS AND FRUIT: Pecans have catkins similar to other hickories, but the fruits are in a class by themselves. They are so thin-shelled that many kinds can be cracked barehanded, and they yield large kernels of superior nutmeat. Most, if not all, horticultural selections of pecan have been chosen for the size, taste, abundance, hardiness, annual bearing, or ease of shelling of the nuts. Many species of wildlife appreciate them too.

RIGHT: A large pecan (*Carya illinoinensis*) shades a pasture.

BEST SEASONS: FALL (when the tasty nuts ripen). WINTER (the brown, shaggy countenance of the pecan is interesting in the landscape). SUMMER (an old, spreading pecan will offer lots of dappled shade for hot southern backyards).

NATIVE AND ADAPTIVE RANGE: Pecan is restricted in the wild to the valleys of the lower Mississippi and Ohio Rivers and their larger tributaries. It extends along the Mississippi River corridor from the Gulf Coast north through Illinois and reaches westward well into eastern Texas and Oklahoma, bypassing the highlands of the Ozark Plateau. Although not native to many areas east of the Mississippi Valley, it is widely planted throughout the southeastern United States. Provenance is crucial if fruit production is of concern, since northern forms have very small (but sweet) nuts and require a winter chilling period to grow properly, while southern forms require the long southern growing season to mature their crop. As a landscape tree, with no concern about fruit production, it can be planted with relative impunity north through USDA zone 5.

CULTURE: Like bitternut, pecan is one of the easiest hickories to transplant, which isn't saying much. The taproots of seedlings can grow 5 feet (1.5 m) deep in two years, unless cultural techniques such as root pruning or root growth control devices are used. It grows easily from seed planted in fall and can be grafted to propagate good nut-producing individuals. Pecan likes rich, moist soil and can tolerate considerable short-term flooding.

PROBLEMS: In very humid regions, the nuts are sometimes ruined by sprouting while still on the tree, and the scab fungus *Cladosporium caryigenum* sometimes affects the leaves and fruits. Zinc deficiency can be a problem in some pecan orchards. Like all hickories, pecan is affected by various borers, cankers, and decay organisms, but most are secondary problems that are serious only on trees weakened from other causes. See *Carya cordiformis* for additional discussion of hickory problems.

CULTIVARS: The numerous pecan selections available have been chosen almost exclusively for fruiting characteristics. Almost 900 square miles (2331 sq. km) of North America are devoted to cultivation of pecan cultivars. Most commercially sold nuts are harvested from the old

TOP LEFT: Pecan (*Carya illinoinensis*) nuts grow in thin husks. LEFT: Some pecans develop a nice yellow fall color. RIGHT: The U.S. national champion pecan (*Carya illinoinensis*) in Tennessee.

standby, 'Stuart', or the newer 'Schley'. 'Wichita' and 'Hopi' are good cultivars for the famous irrigated pecan orchards of the dry Southwest, where scab disease is not a big problem. 'Mahan' and its improved offspring 'Mohawk' bear huge, long nuts, easily the size of a Vienna sausage. Northern growers frequently plant 'Colby', 'Giles', or 'Major' because their crops mature in a shorter growing season. The USDA selection 'Creek' is said to be very resistant to scab, and 'Kanza', a similar disease-resistant USDA release, will mature commercial grade fruits (albeit small ones) as far north as northern Kansas. 'Pawnee' is a newer selection reported to be widely adaptable in both northern and southern climates.

Pollination of pecan has been studied in depth due to its commercial importance. It and other hickories are affected by dichogamy, which basically means that orchard pecans need cross-pollination from other compatible cultivars for best nut production. For example, 'Kanza' is protogynous and will benefit from pollination by protandrous selections such as 'Pawnee', 'Major', or 'Giles'. Some commercial selections develop into trees of predictable form and vigor and therefore could be useful for horticultural purposes.

SIMILAR AND RELATED SPECIES: See the listings for

LEFT: Pecan (*Carya illinoinensis*) makes a large shade tree and grows faster than most other hickories.

Carya cordiformis. Pecan can cross with other pecan hickories (section *Apocarya*), but to little advantage, producing relatively bitter-fruited hybrids like C. 'Pleas'. The hybrid between water hickory (*C. aquatica*) and pecan is named **C. ×lecontei** and is common in areas where the two parent species grow in adjacent areas. Pecan will also cross with some hard hickories (section *Carya*), producing more tasty "hicans."

COMMENTS: The first pecan cultivar, 'Centennial', was propagated by a Louisiana slave in 1848. Since then more than five hundred additional selections have been made. Many of these are adapted specifically to certain localities where they perform best. In older neighborhoods across the South, pecans are often the principal shade trees. The value of the pecan to wildlife should be a primary consideration in planting or managing trees in a landscape or forest situation.

Giant pecan trees once grew in the flatlands adjacent to the Mississippi River along the border between Missouri and Illinois. My family members who harvested those wild pecans each fall during the Great Depression have recounted how the navigation dams built by the U.S. government in the 1930s raised the water table in the pecan flats, even behind the levees, and slowly drowned those great pecans and other hardwoods. Unfortunately environmental assessments were not required for federal projects in those days, so no one had a forum to speak for the ancient trees.

Carya ovata

SHAGBARK HICKORY

DESCRIPTION: This is the distinctive tree most of us picture when we think of a hickory, with shaggy bark that peels in long, tough curls along its trunk, usually starting about waist height. It is a tall, narrow-crowned tree of moist to relatively dry upland areas. Shagbark hickory is a hard hickory (section *Carya*), with buds covered by overlapping scales. Compared with the pecan hickories (section *Apocarya*), the hard hickories generally maintain a single central stem higher into the crown, with shorter, horizontal side limbs.

Along with bitternut hickory (*Carya cordiformis*), shagbark hickory is one of the northernmost and most widespread hickories. It generally grows slowly, but after many years it can reach a large size. The record specimen is located in the Sumter National Forest in South Carolina and is 153 feet (45.9 m) tall. This U.S. national champion is more than 3 feet (0.9 m) in diameter, which is much more massive than the relatively slender species usually grows. I have counted more than 150 annual growth rings on shagbark hickory stumps less than 18 inches (45 cm) across.

LEAVES: The compound leaves of shagbark hickory usually have five leaflets, each being proportionately wider than those of its frequent associate, the bitternut hickory. The leaflets are about 5 inches (12.5 cm) long, heavy and substantial, and very striking when they first emerge from the expanding pastel buds in spring. Many people mistake these tuliplike leaf buds for blossoms, and they are indeed much superior to the tree's actual flowers in ornamental value. The foliage turns bright gold in fall, relatively early as is typical of the genus. The leaves eventually dry to a warm bronze before falling.

FLOWERS AND FRUIT: The flowers of all hickories, including the shagbark, occur as separate male and female catkins on the same tree. The pistillate catkins develop into the delicious but thick-shelled hickory nuts used for hickory nut cake and hickory bread. They are a favorite food of all types of squirrels and chipmunks, who seem singularly capable of cracking them. With a little help from a nutcracker (or a rock and a brick) they can be enjoyed at bird feeders by cardinals, chickadees, nuthatches, titmice, and many other songbirds, who will delight you by eagerly picking the nutmeats out from the shell fragments.

BEST SEASONS: FALL (shagbark hickory is an erect, golden torch in the early fall woods, and the concurrent nut harvest is valued by humans as well as wildlife). SPRING (the emerging foliage and swelling inner bud scales provide a "blooming" period more splendid than those offered by the actual flowers of many other trees). WINTER (the gray, shaggy bark adds a picturesque texture to the dormant season) and SUMMER (a nice, strong, upright shade tree).

NATIVE AND ADAPTIVE RANGE: Shagbark hickory can be found from southeastern Minnesota eastward to Trois-Rivières, Quebec, and south throughout the eastern United States except for the Coastal Plain and the lower Mississippi Valley. It is dependably hardy from USDA zone 4 south.

CULTURE: Shagbark hickory, like all hard hickories, is among the most difficult of our native trees to transplant. In attempting to dig seedlings only a few feet tall, we invariably encounter taproots that actually seem to increase in diameter with depth, to a point beyond the reach of our spade or our patience. They can be moved if the taproots were undercut during their first growing season or if the deep roots can be severed below the point at which they begin to branch. But until more nurseries start growing the hard hickories in root-controlling containers, it is best to plant hickory nuts in their planned permanent locations in fall, protect them from rodents, and wait for them to grow.

Shagbark hickory is very tolerant of most well-drained soils, but it grows slowly on all but the best of them. Most other hard hickories grow even more slowly, with the exception of shellbark hickory (*Carya laciniosa*).

PROBLEMS: Tough to transplant and slow to grow, shagbark hickory is also sensitive to disturbance once it becomes established. Undamaged trees are quite disease

RIGHT: The golden fall color of shagbark hickory (*Carya ovata*).

resistant, but the hard hickories in general are among the first forest trees to show stress when wooded sites are impacted by hot forest fires or construction. Such weakened trees are frequently attacked by the hickory bark beetle (*Scolytus quadrispinosus*) and more than 180 other insects and mites, most of which are of no consequence.

With their bark plates, leafstalks, and nut husks, shagbark hickories generate considerable quantities of litter. The falling nuts can be hazardous to an unarmored human head, especially when carefully aimed by a spiteful squirrel. This species is a beautiful shade tree when planted or saved in a visible, open setting. Often, though, it is best grown in a pasture, open woods, or landscape border area and kept away from manicured turf, patios, and potentially root-damaging construction zones.

CULTIVARS: Shagbark hickory is sometimes separated into two or more varieties and many geographic races. Selections have been made from some of these for trees with large, sweet, easy-to-crack nuts, but not specifically for landscape use. Most selections are very limited in distribution and are best adapted for regional use, such as 'Wilcox' for Ohio, 'Porter' for Pennsylvania, 'Harold' for Wisconsin, and 'Grainger' for Tennessee. I have selected 'Ben's Big Sweetie' in central Illinois, which has sweet nuts that are about twice the average size.

'Burton' and 'Pixley' are two of several available selections of hican (*Carya illinoinensis* × *C. ovata*). Both have tasty nuts and are adapted to colder climates than pecan. 'Pixley', from Illinois, is also known as an attractive landscape tree. Many other selections can be found locally.

SIMILAR AND RELATED SPECIES: Shellbark hickory (*Carya laciniosa*), also called big shagbark hickory, has a more limited, central distribution than shagbark and is more typically found in bottomland sites or in sites with rich soil. It is almost identical to shagbark but larger in proportion. Intermediate trees are usually thought to be *C. ×dunbarii,* a hybrid of the two species. Its leaves, with their seven or nine leaflets, are the largest of any hickory. Its huge nuts, also the largest, are edible, especially from selections such as 'Keystone' and from hican selections like 'Bergman' and 'Underwood'.

Shellbark hickory bark generally peels in longer, but

TOP LEFT: Shagbark hickory (*Carya ovata*) leaf buds open like beautiful flowers. LEFT: The characteristic shaggy bark of shagbark hickory. RIGHT: A nut and fruit husk of shellbark hickory (*C. laciniosa*). FAR RIGHT: Shellbark hickory becomes a very large tree.

fewer, strips than that of shagbark hickory, and the tree tends to maintain smooth bark farther up its base to at least eye level. As it matures it often develops broadly arching limbs that cover a huge canopy area. The largest known shellbark hickory grows in a woods near Greenup, Kentucky, where it dwarfs all its neighbors. It is 139 feet (41.7 m) tall and more than 4 feet (1.2 m) thick. I have seen many other magnificent specimens nearly this size. Shellbark hickories from northern provenances are hardy through USDA zone 5, but they can be injured by spring frosts. See *Carya tomentosa* for descriptions of other hard hickories.

COMMENTS: Shagbark hickory furnished sap sugar for Native Americans in areas where the sugar maple was not available, and the nuts were boiled to yield cooking oil. Its green wood imparts the familiar "hickory-smoked" flavor to fish and meat dishes, and cured lumber is used for jobs that require the toughest, heaviest, most resilient timber. The rare hickory hairstreak butterfly can be found only where shagbark hickory grows.

This is the great tree whose name was adopted by Andrew "Old Hickory" Jackson, the hickory-tough, battle-hardened seventh president of the United States. He even planted a few shagbarks at the Hermitage, his home near Nashville, Tennessee. It is unfortunate that few others have followed his example, as hickories are notoriously slow to mature and challenging to transplant, and modern folks want "easy" trees. Many of our most magnificent old specimens in wooded neighborhoods are remnants of presettlement vegetation, and as they begin to die out, no one is replacing them. Please plant a hickory—any hickory—for posterity!

Carya tomentosa
MOCKERNUT HICKORY

DESCRIPTION: Excepting shagbark (*Carya ovata*) and shellbark (*C. laciniosa*), the hard hickories (section *Carya*) are a confusing lot, but mockernut hickory is a good representative of the remaining species. This tree is a tall, stately component of dry upland forests. Its dark bark is rough but does not peel like that of shagbark hickory.

Mockernut hickory can survive on some pretty inhospitable sites, where it exhibits somewhat reduced stature and very slow growth, but on good soil it sometimes outgrows shagbark hickory. The largest known specimen grows in Humphreys County, Mississippi, and measures 156 feet (46.8 m) tall and more than 3 feet (0.9 m) in diameter. While this size is exceptional, many others exceed 100 feet (30 m) in height.

LEAVES: The compound leaves of this species are intermediate between those of shagbark and shellbark hickories. They generally have seven leaflets, but occasionally have only five, and are pleasantly aromatic when crushed. As the specific epithet implies, the leafstalks are covered with a fuzzy tomentum. They are very attractive when the buds first begin to swell in spring.

The tree's fall foliage color equals or exceeds that of any other hickory and rivals the best of any native tree with golden fall color, as long as the dry sites where it commonly grows have not been subjected to severe drought that year. Like many other trees, its fall color is diminished by moisture stress. Hickories blend well with their constant companions, the oaks (*Quercus*), by coloring and then defoliating early enough in fall so as not to compete with the late-coloring, often marcescent oaks.

FLOWERS AND FRUIT: Mockernut hickory flowers consist of separate male and female catkins similar to those of other hickories. The nuts resemble those of shagbark hickory but are more rounded, have thinner, more aromatic husks, and generally grow larger. Their increased size, though, mocks those who would gather these nuts for food, because the extra mass is all shell: mockernuts have the toughest nuts in the nut business.

The kernels are usually passably sweet but very small and inextricably entwined within the deep internal convolutions of the thick, rock-hard shell. Their best use might be to crush them between bricks and put the pieces, shells and all, in a bird feeder.

BEST SEASONS: FALL (possibly the best hickory for fall color). SPRING (during budbreak, when the tree looks almost tropical). WINTER (it presents a rugged silhouette) and SUMMER (a strong, stately shade tree).

NATIVE AND ADAPTIVE RANGE: Mockernut hickory is common on upland sites throughout the eastern United States except for the northern Great Lakes area and Maine, and reaches into southern Canada around Lake St. Clair and Niagara Falls. It is very common in the southern portions of this range and along the southern Atlantic Coast, becoming increasingly rare toward the north. This is the hickory commonly associated with oaks (*Quercus*) or pines (*Pinus*) in dry or sandy forests over much of the southeastern United States. It does best when planted in suitable areas within its natural range, which extends north through most of USDA zone 5.

CULTURE: Like other hard hickories, mockernut hickory is a daunting challenge to transplant. It must be grown in the nursery by using root-control techniques or direct-seeded into its permanent location. Husking the seeds for planting is always a pleasure because of the spicy aroma of the husks, a subtle delight of that most spectacular season, autumn.

Mockernut responds to good soil and reasonable moisture but can survive with meager allotments of both. It is not as tolerant of shade as shagbark and shellbark hickories but exhibits stout, vigorous growth as a young sapling on sunny, fertile sites.

PROBLEMS: Like all hickories, this species is sensitive to hot fires in its native woods, especially when small. But hickories resprout readily, and many of the straight, vigorous young stems or stem clumps seen in woods that burn occasionally have grown as sprouts from the root collars of fire-damaged young hickory trees. Mockernut hickory is attacked by most of the same insect pests as shagbark hickory (see *Carya ovata*), and the nuts present

RIGHT: Mockernut hickory (*Carya tomentosa*) develops an erect crown even in open areas.

similar litter problems on patios or in intensively manicured landscapes.

CULTIVARS: No selections are known from this
species, but there is considerable regional variation.

SIMILAR AND RELATED SPECIES: Authorities disagree
on exactly how many other hard hickory species exist.
The variable pignut hickory (**Carya glabra**) has small
leaves and nuts, but the tree can reach considerable size
on good sites. One pignut in Robbinsville, North Carolina, was measured at 190 feet (57 m) tall. Frequently,
though, this tree is stunted by the rigorous ridgetop sites
it seems to favor. The southern *C. glabra* var. *megacarpa*
has larger nuts and is recognized by some authors, while
others separate it into still other varieties. Pignut foliage
rivals that of mockernut in fall, and groves of these trees
punctuated by an occasional companion species with
red foliage are breathtaking.

The closely related sweet pignut hickory (**Carya ovalis**)
has more palatable nuts and shaggier bark than the
pignut. Some authorities suspect it might be a stabilized
cross between pignut and shagbark (*C. ovata*) hickories,
and some others classify it as another variety of pignut:
C. glabra var. *odorata*. Both pignut and sweet pignut oc-

LEFT: Mockernut hickory (*Carya tomentosa*) is a strong,
beautiful shade tree. BELOW: The nuts of mockernut
hickory are tasty but have very thick shells. TOP RIGHT:
Mockernut hickory is a spectacular tree in fall. RIGHT:
Sweet pignut hickory (*C. ovalis*), shown here, has shaggier bark than common pignut hickory (*C. glabra*).

cupy ranges comparable to that of mockernut hickory and are hardy in USDA zone 5.

Black hickory (**Carya texana**) and pale hickory (**C. pallida**) are generally smaller southern species that grow on dry, rocky, or sandy uplands. Black hickory is limited mostly to areas west of the Mississippi River, while pale hickory grows from the Mississippi eastward to the Atlantic Coast. Both will grow in USDA zone 5. Another species, **C. floridana,** is restricted to Florida.

COMMENTS: Mockernut hickory has a rich historical tradition. It was the first hickory encountered by the early European settlers in Virginia and was mentioned in literature dating from the year 1640. Native Americans made a juice from the crushed nuts that they called *pocohicora*, which was later corrupted to *hicoria* (an early scientific name for all hickories) and finally to *carya*. *Carya* may also be traced to *kapva*, an old Greek name for nut trees.

The aesthetic combination of its rich fall color and spicy-scented fruits make this tree a standout species of the harvest season. Each autumn several magnificent old mockernut hickory trees light up the vicinity of Abraham Lincoln's Tomb at Oak Ridge Cemetery in Springfield, Illinois, with their golden foliage.

BELOW: Pignut (*Carya glabra*) is a tough, beautiful hickory that thrives in dry conditions.

Castanea dentata
AMERICAN CHESTNUT

DESCRIPTION: Our great North American chestnut exemplifies a critical concern about importing exotic species. In 1904 Hermann Merkel, a forester working at the Bronx Zoo, noticed a strange new disease infecting some of the chestnut trees lining the zoo's walkways. His concern could not have been more justified, as millions of chestnuts—virtually all those in existence—were killed or reduced to stump sprouts within the next few decades. The disease was the Asian blight fungus (*Cryphonectria parasitica*, formerly *Endothia parasitica*), introduced to North America from Asia on exotic chestnut trees. This alien fungus disease killed the bark and girdled the tree. American chestnut, a magnificent tree with many fine attributes, has been excluded ever since from planting recommendations. However, this may soon change.

Native chestnuts now exist mostly as stump sprouts from fungus-blighted trees, but they once ranked among our largest forest trees. Prior to the deaths of most old patriarch chestnuts decades ago, chestnut trunk diameters of more than 10 feet (3 m) were reported from virgin hardwood cove forests. The largest remaining trees, though, are specimens planted years ago outside the species' natural range. Some of these trees have managed to avoid infection by the blight due to their isolation, and one planted in Grand Traverse, Michigan, is already 110 feet (33 m) tall with a 5-foot (1.5-m) trunk. The current record tree is even farther from the natural range. Found growing among some walnuts in Cicero, Washington, it is 106 feet (31.8 m) tall and more than 6 feet (1.8 m) thick. Open-grown trees such as those are massive and spreading, while forest trees develop long, clear boles. The characteristic bark is smooth on young trees and deeply furrowed on larger ones.

LEAVES: Unlike the leaves of the commonly planted Chinese chestnut (*Castanea mollissima*), those of American chestnut are smooth and narrowly tapered at both ends. They grow to about 9 inches (22.5 cm) long and turn gold in fall.

FLOWERS AND FRUIT: The staminate catkins expand after the leaves, and a grove of blooming chestnuts swaying in the wind looks like a pale green sea with creamy whitecaps. The aroma, however, has been compared to laundry bleach, so chestnut flowers might be best appreciated from a distance. The nuts grow in spiny burs and mature in fall. They usually require cross-pollination due to protogynous blooming, so isolated trees produce many empty burs. However, chestnuts are not periodic bearers like many other nut trees; those that receive adequate pollination produce dependable nut crops almost every year. They also begin to bear nuts when only a few years old, unlike most other nut trees.

BEST SEASONS: FALL (for the gold fall color and the nut harvest). EARLY SUMMER (during the blooming period). WINTER (for the rugged branching pattern and deeply corrugated, spiraling bark on mature trees).

NATIVE AND ADAPTIVE RANGE: American chestnut is native in southern Ontario from Niagara Falls west to the southern tip of Lake Huron and is listed officially as a threatened species by the Canadian government. It ranges southward throughout the mountainous areas of the eastern United States to the southern end of the Appalachians. The best adaptive range, however, is anywhere outside the native range (north through USDA zone 4), since the blight fungus is entrenched throughout this range. This recommendation will change dramatically once the blight is conquered, and that goal is within sight.

CULTURE: Chestnut is among the most adaptable trees, succeeding on almost any well-drained site. Research has shown that chestnut ranks higher than almost any other tree in competitive ability over a broad range of combinations of light and nutrient resource levels, but this species makes its best growth on rich, well-drained, slightly acidic soil in full sun. Nursery-grown trees are not difficult to transplant in early spring, and the seeds are very easy to grow as long as they are not allowed to dehydrate. I obtain nuts each year from two cultivated trees in central Illinois that are planted together and exchange pollen. I have checked other, isolated, trees for burs, but they are empty.

Of course, the limiting factor with chestnut is the fungus, which can survive grudgingly on other trees, like

oaks (*Quercus*), until the next chestnut grows large enough to develop the furrowed bark that expedites infection. Until chestnut blight is overcome, no native chestnut tree is completely safe, even if planted a continent away from its infected native range. Chestnut plantings, for the present, should be located where the potential for their eventual loss to the blight can be tolerated.

LEFT: An American chestnut (*Castanea dentata*) in a home landscape in Illinois, beyond the natural range of the species. BELOW: The ridged bark of American chestnut. BELOW RIGHT: Sprouts develop from a blight-damaged American chestnut in the Appalachians.

PROBLEMS: Eighty years before the appearance of the bark blight, chestnuts growing in low, wet ground were killed by *Phytophthora cinnamomi*, an exotic root-killing fungus. In 1974 yet another exotic chestnut pest was discovered: the chestnut gall wasp (*Dryocosmus kuriphilus*). It is already damaging trees in the southern Appalachian Mountains. Chestnut timber worms (*Melittoma sericeum*) tunnel their way through the trunks of injured or dying trees and produce the figured wood known as wormy chestnut. The main cultural problem with chestnuts in the residential landscape is the bur that encloses the nut: it is covered with vicious spines and will thoroughly discourage a barefoot walk through a chestnut grove in fall.

CULTIVARS: Most chestnut cultivars are selections from Asian species, chiefly the Chinese chestnut (*Castanea mollissima*). A few Asian-American hybrid selections have been named, and they vary widely in their growth form, nut quality, and blight resistance. 'Clapper', 'Sleeping Giant', 'Douglas', and the Dunstan series are among the earliest and best-known hybrids to have shown promise, but these are being left behind by the current backcrossing programs. Once chestnut blight is brought under control, we can begin to select from the pool of disease-resistant trees for growth form, hardiness, and other features.

SIMILAR AND RELATED SPECIES: There are several European and Asian chestnut species, plus three smaller North American chestnuts known as chinkapins. The nearly identical European chestnut (**Castanea sativa**) was traditionally called castaneo in parts of Europe, and the nuts were castaneas—hence the genus name. The most commonly seen species in cultivation in North America is the Chinese chestnut (**C. mollissima**), a smaller, spreading tree planted chiefly for nut crops.

The rare Ozark chinkapin (**Castanea ozarkensis**) reaches about 50 feet (15 m) on good sites in the Ozark Plateau. Allegheny chinkapin (**C. pumila**) usually grows as a shrub, ranging as a scattered understory species throughout the southeastern United States. The largest known specimen, in northeastern Florida, has grown into a tree several stories high, similar to the size of a mature Ozark chinkapin. Both species have smaller nuts than American chestnut, and both were reportedly pre-ferred by aboriginal Native Americans for their even better taste. Florida chinkapin (**C. alnifolia**) is a shrubby species of northern Florida and adjacent areas. All are susceptible to chestnut blight.

Other chestnuts and chinkapins are found in Asia. The European horsechestnut (*Aesculus hippocastanum*) is a buckeye and is not related to the true chestnuts.

COMMENTS: Chestnuts were once the preferred food of wood ducks, ruffed grouse, nuthatches, and many other birds, and a favorite among wild mammals and humans; we all begrudge what has been taken from us by the blight fungus. Yet there is a biological war in progress, and the formerly invincible blight is beginning to stagger under attacks on many fronts.

Even decades after the last chestnut tree in a region dies from bark blight, it remains unsafe to replant chestnuts there because the blight can survive on several oak species, awaiting the return of its favorite host. However, this disease cannot act in contact with the soil, due to antagonistic interactions with the soil bacterium *Bacillus megaterium*, and this is why chestnut roots survive to re-sprout after infection. Mudpacks of soil from around the bases of infected trees have been used with success to treat individual fungus cankers.

Offspring of trees grown from irradiated seed, an old research technique that had been placed on the back burner until recently, are displaying some blight resistance. A few wild trees have also survived, despite the fungus, and progeny testing continues to select for modest levels of natural resistance within those trees and to

identify the genetic combinations responsible for such resistance. The primary group advancing this approach, using pure American chestnut trees in a resistance breeding program, has been the American Chestnut Cooperators' Foundation in Virginia.

Hypovirulence, a condition in which the fungus itself is diseased with a virus, is showing great promise in Europe and has potential for saving North American trees as well. Efforts are underway to find effective methods to encourage the natural spread of this virus, and an artificial form of the virus has reportedly been synthesized in a New Jersey laboratory.

A biochemical peptide compound that could be induced to form within blight-susceptible trees by genetic engineering techniques is showing indications that it can inhibit the blight. Molecular biologists are attempting to introduce the gene that could encode trees with the capability to produce this compound. Others are studying escargot snails (*Helix pomatia*), which eat the

fungus, in an attempt to isolate a microbial protein material that protects the snail from being attacked internally by fungus spores.

Controlled crosses by the American Chestnut Foundation in Vermont, involving successive generations of backcrossing the Asian genes that impart disease resistance into our native trees, are producing resistant trees that are 98 percent *Castanea dentata*. Resistant backcrossed trees that are almost pure *C. dentata* (the third generation of the third-level backcross, called BC3F3) could be available in a few years. It will take longer, of course, to develop the multiple lines of disease-resistant trees necessary to preserve adequate genetic diversity within the entire backcross program, but the progress is exciting.

Combinations of these strategies bring us closer to the day when we can confidently reintroduce the American chestnut to its former range. Most of this fascinating work is being coordinated by several state university research programs and by the American Chestnut Foundation (ACF) and its several regional chapters. I am an ACF member, and I support these efforts and encourage other native tree enthusiasts to join us. At one time the magnificent chestnut was the dominant tree of our eastern forests, and it's coming back.

FAR LEFT: American chestnut (*Castanea dentata*) burs pop open after they fall. LEFT: Fall color of American chestnut . BELOW: Allegheny chinkapin (*C. pumila*) bears small nuts clustered on long stalks.

Catalpa speciosa
NORTHERN CATALPA

DESCRIPTION: Northern, or western, catalpa is the northernmost representative of a genus of trees and shrubs native mostly to the south-central United States and portions of China. Unlike most other species, this catalpa can become an imposing specimen. A slingshot-shaped catalpa on the state capitol grounds in Michigan is 107 feet (32.1 m) tall and about 6.5 feet (2 m) thick, and I have seen many other weathered old monarchs that approach such dimensions.

These trees typically develop massive trunks, supporting uneven crowns of several large, curving, ascending limbs, with few twigs. The wood is decay resistant but brittle, so many catalpa trees tend to become craggy as they enter their second century of life. Neglected old trees become rustic and picturesque, their weathered crowns testifying to the passage of previous wind storms, and would look very much at home towering over Boot Hill on Halloween. However, specimens that have been pruned and maintained with reasonable care make impressive visual statements in parks or rural areas, where their size and texture are appropriate to their surroundings.

LEAVES: Catalpa leaves are heart shaped, 12 inches (30 cm) or more in length, and impart a very coarse texture to the landscape. They are arranged in pairs, or frequently in whorls of three, and are unique in appearance. Fall color generally does not develop; most leaves simply turn brown and drop after the first hard frost.

FLOWERS AND FRUIT: Individual trumpet-shaped white flowers about 2 inches (5 cm) across, with yellow stripes and purple spots inside, develop in large clusters during early summer. The huge flower clusters rival those of any other tree from a distance and are as impressive as orchids when seen up close.

Seedpods, called catalpa beans (but also known as cigars by the foolish children who try to smoke them), follow the flowers. The clusters of 15-inch (37.5-cm) pods frequently remain attached to the tree throughout winter, hanging in visually powerful vertical lines like brown icicles from the thick twigs.

BEST SEASONS: EARLY SUMMER (the flowers are spectacular). WINTER (for the picturesque form and interesting seedpods) and SUMMER (if the large leaves fit the landscape setting).

NATIVE AND ADAPTIVE RANGE: Northern catalpa is surprisingly adaptable for a tree with such a restricted original range. It was limited at one time to a small portion of the bottomlands around the confluences of the Wabash, Ohio, and Mississippi Rivers, down to about Memphis, Tennessee, and north to Lawrence County in southeastern Illinois. A few outlying populations beyond that range were reported, but their exact extent is difficult to determine because this tree has been so successfully established in forestry plantings throughout the eastern and midwestern United States. It is fully hardy when planted in USDA zone 4.

CULTURE: This species can survive under very diverse circumstances, including rich or poor soils, alternate flood and drought conditions, full sun or partial shade, and basic or acidic soils. It can also persist under total neglect, without attention to pruning or other care, and even resists damage from salt spray. Like other adaptable trees, though, it performs much better when properly tended. It grows naturally in the deep, alluvial soils of large river valleys, and providing similar conditions under cultivation will yield surprising dividends. Northern catalpa is very easy to transplant or grow from seed. Seed may be sown without any special treatment or conditioning any time it is found flying from its pods on the wind.

PROBLEMS: With their seedpods, large leaves, and small branches that continuously shed, catalpas are major litter producers that should be located with future yard grooming in mind. If they are to serve as well-formed specimen trees, they may require corrective pruning when young and sanitation pruning when older.

Although relatively disease resistant, some trees do become infected by *Verticillium* wilt. They also serve as hosts for voracious feeding groups of the large, spotted

RIGHT: Northern catalpa (*Catalpa speciosa*) becomes a large and picturesque tree.

caterpillars of catalpa sphinx moth (*Ceratomia catalpae*), and the large leaves can become bronzed from ozone pollution. The wood is brittle, but the coarse branching structure does not accumulate much ice during glaze storms, and therefore catalpas are rated by many researchers among the trees most resistant to ice breakage.

CULTIVARS: Northern catalpa is very consistent in growth habit across its limited natural range. No cultivars are widely available in North America, although one with spotted foliage, 'Pulverulenta', is occasionally seen in Europe. Perhaps, like many other common North American trees, our native catalpa must travel across the pond to be most appreciated. Other catalpa species have yielded more selections.

SIMILAR AND RELATED SPECIES: The southern catalpa (*Catalpa bignonioides*) is a smaller tree with a more southerly natural range. Whoever coined the phrase "Nature doesn't believe in straight lines" might have been inspired by the habit of this character-filled species. More variable than northern catalpa, it has given rise to several cultivars and hybrids. The most distinctive and commonly seen is 'Nana', a densely branching dwarf form that was frequently grafted on a tall stem, or standard, to make the umbrella-tree catalpas that were popular in garish Victorian landscapes. Some cultivars with colored foliage ('Aurea' with chartreuse foliage, 'Aureo-

variegata' with mottled foliage) are popular in areas where summers are not too hot and sunny for the leaves to hold up. Southern catalpa blooms several weeks later than its big brother, which is the easiest way to separate them at a glance, and is nearly as cold hardy (to USDA zone 5). An Asian catalpa species with shallow-lobed leaves, **C. ovata,** can also be seen occasionally in the United States.

Desert-willow (***Chilopsis linearis***), which is not a true willow (*Salix*), is found in the Southwest along the banks of streams and arroyos, and will grow north into USDA zone 7. Though it can become a medium-sized tree, elevating its beautiful flower display as high as a fifth-story window on a sinuously ascending trunk, it is more often seen as a large shrub. Its flowers are much like those of catalpas, but pink, and they are pollinated by the same big, black carpenter bees that hollow out the dead stubs of its old limbs for nests. Its leaves, however, are quite distinct, being as narrow as a pencil. Several cultivars are available, including the dark-flowered tree form 'Bubba', two-toned 'Bicolor', white 'Hope', pink 'Barranco', and purple-flowered 'Amethyst'. The pink-flowered chitalpa (*Catalpa bignonioides* × *Chilopsis linearis*) is fairly common in cultivation in the South.

Catalpas and desert-willows form part of a family of more than one hundred genera of mostly tropical trees and other plants. Many are American, and some, such as the yellow trumpet (***Tecoma stans***), which barely enters our region in southwestern Texas, are among the most beautiful landscape trees planted in warm climates worldwide.

LEFT: The rugged crown of a large northern catalpa (*Catalpa speciosa*). BELOW: A northern catalpa in bloom. RIGHT: A close look at the beautiful flowers of northern catalpa.

COMMENTS: Catalpas have the potential to become, with great age, some of our most picturesque trees, often assuming shapes reminiscent of trolls and gargoyles. One such specimen, planted on a lonely farmstead near Cantral, Illinois, around 1820, was featured in the Belgian book *La Sève du Silence* by photographer Michel Timacheff, highlighting such trees around the world.

Some people in the southern United States grow catalpas solely as fodder for sphinx moth larvae, using the "catalpa worms" as convenient bait. For this reason southern catalpa is sometimes called fishbait tree. An insult to the tree, certainly, and the effects can go beyond that. As the fishermen strike the trees with sticks to shake loose the bait, bark lesions and broken branches are left behind, which can become infected with fungus cankers that could not have invaded undamaged trees.

The trees, which by this time have already lost much of the energy source of their foliage to the caterpillars, must somehow find the strength to restore themselves, year after year, delighting us with their splendid flowers despite how we mistreat them. Anyone who presumes that reverence, or at least respect, for trees must be an innate part of the superior human intellect need only think of the poor "fishbait tree" to revisit reality.

BELOW: A golden selection of southern catalpa (*Catalpa bignonioides*). RIGHT: The colorful flowers of desert-willow (*Chilopsis linearis*). FAR RIGHT: A large desert-willow.

Celtis occidentalis

COMMON HACKBERRY

DESCRIPTION: Common hackberry is one of our most versatile shade trees. It is related to the elms (*Ulmus*) and looks very elmlike in form and foliage. It has attractive bark that develops series of layered, warty bumps or plates over a smooth gray background, with some trees being much smoother than others.

Hackberries on good bottomland soils, such as those of the Midwest prairies, grow quickly and attain large size. Until recently, a tree that was 111 feet (33.3 m) high and more than 6 feet (1.8 m) thick stood in Rock County, Wisconsin. The current record is held by a tree in Mason City, Illinois, just a few minutes from Starhill Forest Arboretum. This specimen is 94 feet (28.2 m) tall and more than 6 feet (1.8 m) in diameter. It has been damaged severely by a prairie storm, but if it falls, several other huge Illinois hackberries are waiting to assume the throne.

Through the rest of their range hackberries are more often seen as medium-size trees growing on less ideal sites. They are very tolerant of rocky ridgetops, high pH soil, drought, air pollution, salt spray, and short-term flooding, but they may grow more slowly under such limitations.

LEAVES: The finely toothed leaves are about 4 inches (10 cm) long with wide, asymmetrical bases, and they taper to a long point. Because they are very scabrous and look much like stinging nettle (*Urtica*) leaves, hackberry is occasionally called nettle-tree. Fall color—a variable greenish yellow—is usually unimpressive.

FLOWERS AND FRUIT: Inconspicuous greenish flowers appear in spring, with both sexes on the same tree. The small drupes that follow the flowers turn orange-brown and finally purplish black as they ripen in late summer, reaching the size of a garden pea. The thin, leathery layer of flesh that surrounds the hard seed has a pleasant raisinlike taste and is relished by birds. Some fruits persist into late winter, providing a food source for many northward-migrating birds unless a greedy flock of cedar waxwings finds them first. The fruits are consumed whole, and the seeds pass through the birds intact or are regurgitated, providing the primary means of seed dispersal and propagation for all hackberry species. Hackberry fruits can also float, drifting on the surface of a swamp or stream to a suitable growing spot.

BEST SEASONS: WINTER (the interesting bark and fine-textured branching are most apparent during the dormant season). SUMMER (a good general-purpose shade tree that hosts many butterflies).

NATIVE AND ADAPTIVE RANGE: Hackberry is one of the few trees that thrives on the Great Plains, from Manitoba to Texas, yet extends across the continent to the Atlantic Coast. It can be grown north into USDA zone 3.

CULTURE: Although this tree will adjust to almost any cultural situation, including roadside salt spray, the best hackberry sites are rich, deep, alluvial soils with neutral to basic pH, adequate moisture, and full sun; such conditions often stimulate very rapid growth and immense size. It is easy to transplant but will take a year or two to recover. Seeds can be germinated easily if stratified or sown outdoors in fall.

PROBLEMS: Many authors refer immediately to the occasional rosetting of small twigs into witches'-brooms (caused by *Eriophid* mites and *Sphaerotheca phytophila* mildew) as the primary problem associated with this tree, but this is usually nothing more than a superficial blemish that can actually provide some winter interest (clipped brooms can make interesting accessories in dry bouquets). Common hackberry is also subject to leaf galls, mistletoes, and mosaics, but nothing really serious. All hackberry species are reported to be strongly allelopathic and may adversely affect the growth of turf and some other plants within their root zones. Several organic acids that leach from the foliage are believed to cause this, so it is probably wise to rake hackberry leaves promptly in fall.

The most important problems I have observed are probably a tendency for forks to split and a susceptibility to decay, which frequently begins following damage from storms, forest fires, or improper pruning. The bark is prone to fire injury and the forking, arching architec-

RIGHT: Common hackberry (*Celtis occidentalis*) develops a muted fall color.

ture of the tree can lead to weak branch unions, characteristics that become more serious due to poor decay resistance. Damaged hackberries don't age gracefully.

CULTIVARS: This variable species should be expected to have many selections available, but few individual trees seem to have a decided advantage over random seedlings, so few potential cultivars have been named. 'Prairie Pride' is one of them, selected from a tree in Illinois. It has dark, tough foliage and develops a strong central stem that resists storm damage. 'Windy City' and a selection trademarked as Chicagoland, also of Illinois and introduced by my friend Roy Klehm, are strong, upright trees with central stems, and I have another potential future cultivar with excurrent form and apparent resistance to witches'-broom under observation at Starhill Forest. The Prairie Farm Rehabilitation Administration of Saskatchewan is screening common hackberry for superior strains to use in shelterbelt plantings in the uncompromising environment of the Northern Plains.

SIMILAR AND RELATED SPECIES: There are more than fifty other hackberry species in the world, and several of the finest for use in the landscape are North American natives. Sugarberry (**Celtis laevigata**) is one that makes an excellent shade tree from USDA zone 5 south. It has smoother bark and narrower leaves than common hackberry and can tolerate extensive flooding and soil compaction. It is at its best on acidic, young, or disturbed soils with no horizon development (stratification) but tolerates many different soil situations. Sugarberry is not seriously bothered by witches'-brooms or some of the leaf galls that attack common hackberry. It seems even more prone, though, to decline from any mechanical damage.

Sugarberry is a predominant tree of the Cumberland Plateau in Tennessee, the Ozark Plateau, the southern Coastal Plain, and down the lower Mississippi River valley. It extends south all the way to the tip of Florida and is found in the eastern part of Texas and Oklahoma, then on into Mexico, where it is called *palo blanco* ("white tree") for its soft white wood and light-colored bark. Its branching pattern is frequently very graceful and sinuous, and its gray bark can be as smooth as that of beech (*Fagus grandifolia*).

One specimen at my arboretum, of southern Illinois provenance, develops the best brilliant yellow fall color

of any tree in my hackberry collection. The record-size sugarberry, in South Carolina, is 81 feet (24.3 m) tall with a massive trunk nearly 8 feet (2.4 m) in diameter. 'All Seasons' is a selection of sugarberry, and 'Magnifica' is thought to have originated from a vigorous hybrid between sugarberry and common hackberry.

European hackberry (**Celtis australis**) is similarly magnificent in southern Europe and is occasionally seen in cultivation here. Its smooth bark resembles that of sugarberry, but its leaves are closer to those of common hackberry. See *C. tenuifolia* for information on the smaller native hackberry species.

COMMENTS: Those who would seek wealth from walnut (*Juglans nigra*) tree farms would do well to look for big, vigorous hackberries. Hackberries and walnuts are cohorts on their favorite soils, along with blue ash (*Fraxinus quadrangulata*), Kentucky coffeetree (*Gymnocladus dioicus*), and chinkapin oak (*Quercus muhlenbergii*); where one grows well, usually the others will too. Yet, like walnut, hackberry will also survive as a scrubby tree on much poorer soils. In the southwestern part of its range in Texas (where its name is often disrespectfully down-

LEFT: Typical form and fine texture of common hackberry (*Celtis occidentalis*). RIGHT: Common hackberry bark has winter appeal.

graded to "hagberry"), this noble species is viewed as a weed that will never amount to much compared with its performance in the heartland. But it survives despite such irreverence.

Hackberries are among the best trees to plant for wildlife. Their persistent fruits are eaten over a long season by many birds and mammals. Wild trees frequently develop cavities at decaying old branch stubs, providing nesting and hibernation sites for many wildlife species, and the narrow limb crotches and numerous spur branches of some species also support many bird nests. Hackberry foliage is a primary larval food source for several popular garden butterflies, including the snout butterfly, question mark, mourning cloak, tawny emperor, and friendly hackberry butterfly, which will often land on a human shoulder to say hello.

TOP LEFT: Sugarberry (*Celtis laevigata*) leaves are narrower and smoother than those of other hackberries. LEFT: This sugarberry at Starhill Forest displays outstanding fall color. BELOW: Sugarberry and other hackberries often develop beautiful, intricate branching.

Celtis tenuifolia

DWARF HACKBERRY

DESCRIPTION: Unlike common hackberry (*Celtis occidentalis*), to which it is very closely related, dwarf hackberry is quite content to remain small and inconspicuous. The Illinois State champion, which grows at Starhill Forest, is less than 30 feet (9 m) tall and wouldn't even be that large if I had not rescued it as a seed thirty years ago from the stark habitat of its parents. Planted on decent soil and given nothing more than a smile every morning, it has developed into an outstanding, intricately branched little tree with character to spare. The record-size specimen for North America is only a few inches larger.

LEAVES: The rough, finely toothed leaves are similar to those of the larger hackberry species but shorter, about 3 inches (7.5 cm) long. Fall color can be a bright yellow, showing to advantage when bathed in sidelighting against a dark building or background of conifers.

FLOWERS AND FRUIT: The flowers are inconspicuous, like those of common hackberry. Fruits are a little larger and appear as attractive orange globes for several weeks in fall before turning dark and clinging into winter. They are attractive to birds and are usually eaten before they drop, though some persist into late winter. As with other hackberry species, birds consume the fruits whole and pass the seeds intact to grow wherever they land.

BEST SEASONS: WINTER (the intricate branching structure is fascinating, especially up close and covered with hoarfrost on a cold morning). FALL (nice bright yellow leaf color developing after the orange fruits).

NATIVE AND ADAPTIVE RANGE: Dwarf hackberry has a spotty natural range due to its habitat requirements. It is concentrated in the Piedmont, the Cumberland Plateau, and the Ozark Plateau, with outlier populations ranging from a few rare stands in southern Ontario to Florida and west to Nebraska and eastern Texas. It can be grown north to USDA zone 4.

CULTURE: This tough little species will adjust to almost any reasonable cultural situation as long as it has full sun and good drainage. As we have seen with my state champion tree, better soils grow happier trees. It is easy to transplant and easy to grow from stratified or fall-planted seed. In the wild it will not survive competition from larger, more vigorous trees on good sites, so it is limited to escarpments and barrens where nothing else will contest its place in the sun.

PROBLEMS: Dwarf hackberry develops sharp spur branches that can be hazardous if exposed at eye level next to a sidewalk or patio. Conversely, however, these intricate spur branches clothing the trunk are one of the features that give this tree so much visual pop up close. See *Celtis occidentalis* for discussion of other hackberry problems.

CULTIVARS: Dwarf hackberry is little known in cultivation, so it is not surprising to find no cultivars listed. If no one steps forward to offer one, perhaps someday I'll introduce my Illinois champion.

SIMILAR AND RELATED SPECIES: Additional hackberry species can be found in the southwestern United States and Mexico. Netleaf hackberry (**Celtis reticulata,** syn. *C. douglasii*) is a tough little western tree with conspicuous netlike veins on the lower surface, occasionally seen in cultivation in the East, north into USDA zone 5. In its native haunts—rocky slopes in nearly treeless shortgrass prairies of the High Plains, and canyons of mountains and plateaus from Hell's Canyon in the Northwest down into central Mexico—it looks much like dwarf hackberry does back East, and occupies a similar ecological position. However, it is believed to be more closely related to sugarberry (*C. laevigata*) than to common or dwarf hackberry and is sometimes listed as a variety of that larger species. Its thick leaves are impervious to drought, but trees under cultivation on irrigated sites grow much more vigorously and sometimes develop an attractive, weeping habit.

Lindheimer hackberry (**Celtis lindheimeri**) is nearly identical but has fuzzy gray hairs on the undersides of its leaves that give it a shimmery appearance in the wind. Its natural range is confined to a small local population in Texas and a few more in Mexico, but it will grow in cultivation north to USDA zone 5.

The shrubby spiny hackberry (**Celtis pallida**) grows on even rougher, desert sites in southern Texas and Mexico, where it provides valuable wildlife cover. It has evolved

131

paired spines at each node to discourage browsing animals, and its tiny semievergreen leaves are very resistant to the effects of heat and drought. Its sweet, protein-rich fruits are a luminous orange and highly sought by wildlife. ***Celtis spinosa*** is similar, and most authors consider it to be a synonym. Many more hackberry kin are found in Central America.

COMMENTS: Dwarf hackberry is a compact tree of dry cliffs and stony ridges that makes a beautiful, picturesque specimen for the small yard or terrace. It looks like

LEFT: A mature dwarf hackberry (*Celtis tenuifolia*) at Starhill Forest. BELOW: The dense crown of dwarf hackberry is excellent habitat for nesting birds. RIGHT: The decorative orange fruits of dwarf hackberry.

a miniature replica of common hackberry. This species should be more adaptable than most trees to raised planters, given its stressful natural habitat and moderate growth rate under cultivation.

All of the smaller hackberries are great for wildlife. The fruits are eaten during fall migration and winter by many birds and mammals, and the interwoven twigs offer protective nesting territory. The leaves are a food source for many garden butterflies. They are also good food for the soul, appreciated on long hikes in the rough terrain of rock ledges, escarpments, talus piles, and desert canyons where they survive everything that nature tosses their way.

BELOW: Netleaf hackberry (*Celtis reticulata*) is a small drought-resistant southwestern tree.

Cercis canadensis

REDBUD

DESCRIPTION: Redbud has neither red buds nor red flowers, but it is nonetheless one of our most outstanding ornamental trees. Its flowers emerge during a time of year when lesser beauty would be lost amid the spectacle of the season, yet it dominates the landscape while in full bloom. Its arching branches are covered with pretty rose-pink blossoms in early spring, as colorful as those of any Asian flowering tree.

Redbuds always remain relatively small. The two largest trees on record grow in Nashville, Tennessee, and Roanoke County, Virginia, and both are about 40 feet (12 m) in height and 3 feet (0.9 m) in diameter. Often this species will develop as a clump, becoming little more than a large shrub, but old specimens develop that certain bonsai quality that makes them look larger and more ancient than they really are.

LEAVES: The smooth, heart-shaped leaves of redbud can grow up to 6 inches (15 cm) long and wide, with those from harsher climates in the southwestern portion of its natural range being proportionately smaller, thicker, and glossier. They emerge reddish, turning green as they expand. The flower pigmentation seems to be expressed in the leaves as well, since those that don't exhibit much reddish spring leaf color can have pale pink or even white flowers. Others have even redder spring leaves than normal, with the color persisting into summer in 'Forest Pansy'. Fall color is usually a nice, though not brilliant, yellow.

FLOWERS AND FRUIT: At their prime, the rose-pink flowers of redbud are the most impressive visual sensation of the woods, reaching their peak between the very early whites of serviceberry (*Amelanchier*) and wild plum (*Prunus americana*) and the overlapping, subsequent white of flowering dogwood (*Cornus florida*). Were it not for the pealike blooms of redbud, we would have a nearly unbroken sequence of white in the early spring deciduous forest. Redbuds hold forth especially on overcast days, when the white flowers of other trees fade into the bleak background sky.

Occasionally, though, a white-flowered redbud (*Cercis canadensis* var. *alba*) can be seen, usually blooming a few days later than its rosy cousins, and its graceful, arching form sets it apart from other white-blooming trees. It should probably be classified as a form instead of a variety and should be propagated by grafting, because I have not found it to come true from seed. The flowers of all redbuds are unusual in not being restricted to the one-year twigs or spur branches; flower buds push through the bark of all but the very oldest and largest limbs. The dry brown seedpods develop in clusters and persist through the winter months.

BEST SEASONS: EARLY SPRING (for the flower display). WINTER (the arching limbs with clinging seedpods add interest).

NATIVE AND ADAPTIVE RANGE: Despite its specific epithet, *canadensis*, redbud is a rare tree in Canada. I have found isolated specimens near Point Pelee, the southernmost contiguous land area of Canada, and a few have been reported on Pelee Island in Lake Erie and around Lake St. Clair. The breadth of its range to the south, however, is most impressive. It is common from Iowa and Pennsylvania southward throughout the eastern United States and westward into the Great Plains, where it has been named the state tree of Oklahoma.

This tree is notorious for varying in hardiness with provenance, and it has served as the textbook example to illustrate geographically linked winter hardiness for countless horticulture students. It is very important to select landscape trees that are adapted to local climate conditions. I have a very hardy selection growing at Starhill Forest, from seed collected at the northwestern limit of the species' range along the Iowa River. The Minnesota Landscape Arboretum near Minneapolis, in the northern part of USDA zone 4, also has some potentially hardy seedlings in trial plantings.

CULTURE: Redbud needs well-drained soil yet can tolerate the short-term flooding that occurs along small streams. The tree does equally well in acidic or basic soil types. It grows well in fairly dense shade but becomes more dense and blooms more heavily in sunny locations as long as it has adequate moisture. Seedlings frequently volunteer into landscaped areas around mature trees, and these can be moved easily when very small. Larger

plants, however, develop a coarse and extensive root system that makes them trickier to transplant.

PROBLEMS: Redbuds have three primary health problems: stem cankers caused by pathogens such as *Botryosphaeria dothidia* and *B. ribis*, *Verticillium* wilt, and extreme sensitivity to phenoxy herbicides like 2,4-D. Each problem can be serious, but most redbuds are never affected by them. The cankers, in particular, only become a problem on stressed trees. Redbud can also be bothered by leaf maladies such as anthracnose (*Mycosphaerella cerci-*

LEFT: A large redbud (*Cercis canadensis*) begins to turn color in fall. RIGHT: Redbud flowers. BELOW: Old redbuds can add character as well as color to the landscape.

dicola), and its arching form makes it somewhat prone to damage from ice storms. This weakness becomes more pronounced in the presence of several borer species that frequently attack the wood of old redbuds. Volunteer seedlings, so welcome in naturalized situations, can be a minor nuisance in manicured landscapes.

CULTIVARS: White-flowered redbud (*Cercis canadensis* var. *alba*) has yielded at least one selection, 'Royal White', with larger flowers and more compact form. It was found growing in Scott County, Illinois, by Professor Joe Mc-Daniel. White-flowering redbuds, or "whitebuds," don't often come true from seed, but sometimes they can be screened for future blossom color as young seedlings by observing the hue of their new leaves.

At the other end of the color scale, *Cercis canadensis* 'Forest Pansy' is a selection that has darker flowers than the type and that retains its reddish leaf color even after the leaves mature. It is one of the most refined red-leaved trees, but any tree with such unnatural foliage color can be difficult to place in most landscapes without appearing contrived or gaudy. It does present an acceptable native alternative to Asian maples and European beech, wherever tasteful colored foliage truly is appropriate. 'Silver Cloud' is a variegated selection, again useful for those limited situations where colored summer foliage is acceptable. Neither selection seems to be as robust under adverse conditions as are local wild trees.

'Pinkbud' and 'Withers Pink Charm' both have flowers that are true pink, without the rose-colored pigment. This makes them easier to place among other flowering plants in a landscape design. 'Flame' is a double-pink selection, and 'Appalachia' is magenta like some of the southwestern redbud selections. 'Lavender Twist' (sometimes called 'Covey') is a vigorous weeping cultivar from New York.

SIMILAR AND RELATED SPECIES: Redbuds from Texas and the Mexican mountains have very small, glossy leaves and compact form. Selections are being introduced from these provenances for cultivation in south-

LEFT: Redbud (*Cercis canadensis*) flowers add a unique color to the white flowers of dogwoods (*Cornus*) and other flowering trees. BELOW: A white-flowering selection of redbud.

ern regions, perhaps north through USDA zone 7. They include ***Cercis canadensis* var. *mexicana*** and ***C. canadensis* var. *texensis*,** as well as the related ***C. reniformis*** (considered a synonym of variety *texensis* by some authorities) and its selections 'Oklahoma', 'Texas White', and the weeping 'Traveller'. Redbud species from California (***C. occidentalis***), Europe (***C. siliquastrum***), and Asia (***C. chinensis***) are seen here in cultivation where they are hardy.

COMMENTS: Redbud blossoms are harvested for food in some parts of Mexico and were used in salads by early settlers in North Carolina. The flowers are visited for nectar by a broad spectrum of early-season butterflies, and the petals are the primary food source for the larvae of one of our unusual spring ephemeral butterflies, Henry's elfin. This interesting little "flutter-by" is seen only when redbuds are blooming.

LEFT: Fall color on *Cercis canadensis* 'Forest Pansy'.
BELOW: 'Forest Pansy' features colorful foliage.

Chionanthus virginicus
FRINGE TREE

DESCRIPTION: The genus name *Chionanthus* ("snow flower") suggests the appeal for which the small fringe tree is famous. Old fringe trees typically form irregular, spreading crowns supported by clumps of stems. Essentially they are shrubs that just don't know when to stop growing. They can be grown easily as single-stem trees, too: unlike true shrubs, their dominant stems persist and are not replaced over time by younger ones.

A fringe tree at Mount Vernon, Virginia, near George Washington's former home in Fairfax County, is 32 feet (9.6 m) tall with a trunk 17 inches (42.5 cm) across. Even taller specimens have been observed in moist areas of open woods, reaching for the shafts of light that penetrate the taller crowns of adjacent trees. However, fringe trees grown in semishade seldom achieve stem diameters even half as large as the tree at Mount Vernon.

LEAVES: The thick, opposite leaves grow 5 to 9 inches (12.5 to 22.5 cm) long, with a dark green, waxy appearance. They emerge very late in spring, barely in time to serve as a foil for the fully developed flowers, and turn dull yellow in fall, dropping early. The heavy leaves and thick twigs give small fringe trees a strong, coarse texture when not in bloom.

FLOWERS AND FRUIT: Fringe tree begins flowering when very young. The fragrant late-spring blossoms signal the closure of spring and the onset of summer. They are wispy and cloudlike, pure white, and brilliant when viewed against the dark foliage in the low, warm sidelighting of the rising sun.

Fringe trees are substantially dioecious. The male plants are more impressive in bloom, but the females bear the blue, datelike fruits that are so attractive to wildlife.

BEST SEASONS: LATE SPRING (for the flower display). EARLY FALL (when the fruits ripen).

NATIVE AND ADAPTIVE RANGE: Fringe trees can be found scattered in moist wooded areas, swamp borders, and occasionally on higher ground from eastern Texas and southern Missouri eastward to the Atlantic Coast and north to Ohio and Pennsylvania. The reason for the northern limit of this natural range is one of those mysteries of the plant world, since these little trees thrive under cultivation well into USDA zone 4 in southern Quebec and Ontario.

CULTURE: Transplant fringe trees with a soil ball of sufficient size to protect its coarse root system. It prefers loose, sandy soils, but it can be grown in silty clay and can tolerate urban conditions. Trees are found in open shade in the wild, but they do better in full sun. Although they can be grafted onto understock of the closely related ash (*Fraxinus*), they are much easier to grow from seed if you don't mind taking your chances about gender. Plantings grown for fruit production should consist of enough seedlings to assure inclusion of both male and female plants. The seed sometimes remains dormant until the second spring following planting.

PROBLEMS: Given a suitable site and protection from excessive deer browsing, this is among the most trouble-free small trees. I have never seen one nibbled by insects. Fringe tree is very sensitive to allelopathy from some trees in the walnut family and should probably not be planted near walnuts (*Juglans*) or hickories (*Carya*).

CULTIVARS: I have found no cultivars listed for this species. Natural variation is significant enough that some authors recognize several natural botanical varieties. These include forms with narrow leaves, broad leaves, and pubescent leaves, none of which is sufficiently distinct for ornamental purposes to merit individual treatment. Gender-specific cultivars would be a welcome addition to the plant palette.

SIMILAR AND RELATED SPECIES: A rare shrubby species known as pygmy fringe tree (**Chionanthus pygmaeus**) grows in one area of Florida. It is an endangered species, protected under law, and cannot be collected or sold without a permit. The Chinese fringe tree (**C. retusus**) is often seen in cultivation in the warmer parts of our region. It is similar to our native species but has smaller flower clusters and more interesting bark.

Devilwood (**Osmanthus americanus**) is another olive relative, found in wet areas and moist, rich woods along the Atlantic and Gulf Coasts. It has smooth gray bark, leathery evergreen foliage, and wonderfully fragrant white flowers in spring. Most of us are more familiar with its Asian relatives, but this native southeastern species is much hardier, north at least through USDA zone 6. It can grow nearly 50 feet (15 m) tall and up to 1 foot (30 cm) in diameter in the warmest parts of its range but remains a large shrub when planted in the North. Devilwood will grow in sun or shade and on acidic or alkaline soil, but it is not easy to propagate unless you use cuttings or are willing to wait a couple of years for its seeds to wake up and sprout. Its evergreen foliage and fragrant white flowers would be a plus in many landscapes, if only devilwood were more available in the nursery trade.

COMMENTS: Fringe tree fruits are among the favorite foods of wild turkeys and many other birds. Tea made from the boiled bark holds an esteemed place in traditional medicine as a tonic and a topical treatment for skin irritations. But the ornamental value of the fleecy flowers preempts such utilitarian values. This tree looks stunning, almost ethereal, when seen at peak bloom at night, illuminated by a full moon. And in the developed

landscape of your home, car headlights scanning around the edges of a driveway as you arrive home at night work just as well.

LEFT: A fringe tree (*Chionanthus virginicus*) beginning to bloom. BELOW: Fruits developing on a female fringe tree. BOTTOM: Fringe tree flowers. RIGHT: Fringe tree foliage.

Cladrastis kentukea

YELLOWWOOD

DESCRIPTION: Yellowwood (*Cladrastis kentukea*, syn. *C. lutea*) brings together the smooth, gray bark of beech (*Fagus grandifolia*), the vaselike form of elm (*Ulmus americana*), and the snow-white flowers of locust (*Robinia pseudoacacia*) in a single, handsome ornamental tree. It usually forks repeatedly into a spreading outline in cultivation or on open hillsides exposed to full sunlight, but it maintains a single tall stem and a much narrower form under dense forest conditions. Yellowwood is a medium-sized tree, occurring as a subcanopy component of Ozark and Appalachian cove forests and limestone ridge areas.

The largest known specimen, a stout but declining old tree growing along the edge of Spring Grove Cemetery in Cincinnati, Ohio, is more than 7 feet (2.1 m) in diameter but only 72 feet (21.6 m) tall due to storm damage in its upper canopy. Most yellowwoods are more slender, few ever approaching the girth of this old giant. Many of the finest specimens are cultivated trees planted in sheltered locations. Several beautiful specimens grow on university campuses in the Midwest, planted decades ago by wise horticulture professors who appreciated these refined trees.

LEAVES: The leaves are pinnately compound, usually with about seven leaflets, each about 4 inches (10 cm) long and half as wide. Because the leafstalks cover the buds, some people unfamiliar with this tree find it tricky to determine just where the compound leaf stops and the twig begins. Fall color can be a clear yellow but sometimes tends toward a warm gold-orange and always contrasts handsomely with the smooth gray bark.

FLOWERS AND FRUIT: Yellowwood doesn't bloom every year, but when it does it is spectacular. Fragrant, white, pealike flowers hang from the twigs in late spring in chains more than 12 inches (30 cm) long, densely covering the tree. The small dry pods that follow the flowers ripen in fall and persist into winter.

BEST SEASONS: LATE SPRING (during the blooming period). WINTER (when the smooth bark and elegant branching pattern show to best advantage, especially in a morning sunbeam against the backdrop of an approaching stormy sky). FALL (for those individual trees that develop the best foliage color) and SUMMER (a pleasant, graceful shade tree).

NATIVE AND ADAPTIVE RANGE: This tree is confined to isolated locations across the southeastern United States and is not common except in a few localities. Groups of wild trees I have observed growing at the edge of the natural range are declining and disappearing, so the range seems to be shrinking. Yet under cultivation yellowwood is hardy and healthy throughout the eastern United States, north from Minnesota across to Maine and into southern Canada to USDA zone 3.

CULTURE: Yellowwood is normally recommended for sunny areas, where its crown becomes full and dense, but it is also very happy, and quite stunning, when naturalized into the north-facing slope of a forest setting. It can be transplanted easily in spring with a soil ball and grows readily from stratified seed or softwood cuttings. The pH of the soil is not critical, but the tree should have good drainage. Corrective pruning is important when the tree is young in order to eliminate weak branch forks (*Cladrastis* means "brittle branch"), and this should be done late during the growing season rather than in spring to minimize excessive sap flow from the cut surface.

PROBLEMS: Yellowwood grows relatively slowly and takes a long time to reach blooming age. Although its wood is strong, it splits easily, and the branching structure can be very weak without early training, thus inviting storm damage and the decay organisms that invariably follow breakage. This species is also susceptible to *Verticillium* wilt, *Phyllactina corylea* mildew, root decay from *Polyporus spraguei* fungus, and cankers caused by *Botryosphaeria dothidea*. In portions of its natural range, wild populations of this tree are declining from one or more of these diseases, but specimens under cultivation in the same areas seem to be unaffected. The thin bark is easily damaged and sometimes attracts the same lovestruck vandals who tend to carve on beeches.

CULTIVARS: 'Rosea' (syn. 'Perkins Pink') is a pink-flow-

RIGHT: A large yellowwood (*Cladrastis kentukea*) in summer.

144

ering yellowwood that has been propagated by seed from a single tree in Massachusetts. Its status as a cultivar versus a natural variety remains a discussion topic among botanists. The seedlings are being tested by several cooperating researchers hopeful of finding one with even deeper pink flowers. 'Sweet Shade' has extra large white flower clusters. Considering the wide separation of wild populations of this species, it seems very likely that some additional distinct forms have evolved and could be propagated.

SIMILAR AND RELATED SPECIES: We have only one yellowwood species in North America. Others can be found in Asia, a couple of which (**Cladrastis platycarpa** from Japan, **C. sinensis** from China) are occasionally grown here in cultivation. Yellowwood is a member of the vast legume family, along with many other beautiful flowering trees and shrubs.

COMMENTS: The root bark of yellowwood was a primary dye ingredient for early settlers in the southern Ap-

palachians, and the wood was prized for gunstocks. Fortunately for the preservation of this rare tree, these commercial uses are no longer important and the chief value is ornamental.

Yellowwood is so uncommon in the wild that on one occasion when I happened upon a mature wild specimen in full bloom, the experience was a combination of aesthetic appreciation and a highly satisfying feeling of discovery. This certainly must have been the reaction of botanist André Michaux, even in winter, when he first discovered the species in 1796 and returned later to propagate it. By 1812 it was already growing in the gardens of Europe, where it remains a prized species.

FAR LEFT: The typical deliquescent branching structure of yellowwood (*Cladrastis kentukea*). BELOW LEFT: Fall color of yellowwood. BOTTOM LEFT: Yellowwood bark is smooth and often covered with attractive lichens. Photo by Jim Wilson. BELOW: Yellowwood flowers.

Cornus drummondii

ROUGHLEAF DOGWOOD

DESCRIPTION: Several shrubby dogwood species become small trees in portions of eastern North America, and roughleaf dogwood (*Cornus drummondii*, syn. *C. asperifolia*) is probably the most resilient of the lot. It is a clumping shrub or small tree of the prairie border, existing on that harsh ecological fringe where most woody plants yield to the herbaceous flora of the plains. Exceptional treelike specimens were seldom found in such habitats originally, due to the periodic fires that kept the prairies free from most woody competition. Roughleaf dogwoods and a few other hardy woody plants persisted by sprouting from unburned roots, growing in thickets until the next fire pruned them back again.

But prairie fires are mostly a thing of the past, and roughleaf dogwoods can rise above their shrubby nature to become attractive small trees. One tree in Bolivar City, Mississippi, is 43 feet (12.9 m) tall with a 5-inch (12.5-cm) stem. I frequently see this species as a small tree in its old haunts at the edges of former prairie areas, wherever its central-stem growth has not been stunted by suckering from the roots.

LEAVES: The leaves of most small dogwoods are similar, arranged in pairs and up to about 4 inches (10 cm) long, with veins that curve at their ends to parallel the margin. As the common name implies, leaves of this species are rough to the touch. They turn a deep purplish red in early fall, with the timing somewhat dependent on the degree of drought stress the tree has experienced that year.

FLOWERS AND FRUIT: The tiny white flowers of all small dogwood species are displayed in clusters, but without the colorful bracts that surround those of some larger species. The flat-topped flower clusters of this species are among the largest and can be quite showy when seen from above against the backdrop of newly expanded foliage.

The white fruits of roughleaf dogwood, with their bright red stalks, tend to be even more attractive because they mature as the leaves are developing their fall color. Dogwood fruits generally cling to the trees until harvested by hungry birds, and these trees and shrubs are recognized widely as some of our most valuable wildlife plants. Among the colorful birds most attracted to this tree are bluebirds, cardinals, kingbirds, and several woodpeckers.

BEST SEASONS: FALL (for the combination of red foliage and white fruit). LATE SPRING (during the blooming period).

NATIVE AND ADAPTIVE RANGE: Roughleaf dogwood grows naturally from southernmost Ontario west to South Dakota and south into Texas, Louisiana, and Mississippi. It is reliably hardy north into USDA zone 4.

CULTURE: This species does well on open, dry sites, while most other small dogwoods prefer more moisture. All are easy to transplant and can tolerate a wide range of soil textures. They can be propagated by seed sown early in fall, before the soil cools down.

PROBLEMS: Although resistant to Gypsy moth (*Lymantria dispar*), most dogwoods can be stripped of foliage within a few days by the dogwood sawfly (*Macremphytus tarsatus*), which should be controlled promptly if encountered in ornamental plantings. Dogwoods can also be afflicted with borers, stem cankers, scale insects, and twig blights. Most of these problems are isolated or do not become serious if the trees are kept in vigorous condition.

The small dogwoods, including roughleaf dogwood, are given to clumping into thickets. They may be allowed to do so naturally or may be maintained as trees or solitary shrubs by removing the surplus shoots.

CULTIVARS: A few variegated selections of this and similar species have been cultivated. Often such curious foliage color patterns are due to virus mosaics, but the virus seems harmless and the visual effect can be interesting in the right setting. Some other small dogwood species have yielded cultivars with brilliant red or yellow winter bark, but the best color is maintained only on the vigorous young shoots of those plants pruned as shrubs.

SIMILAR AND RELATED SPECIES: There are many

TOP RIGHT: Flowers on roughleaf dogwood (*Cornus drummondii*). RIGHT: Fruits on roughleaf dogwood.

small dogwoods. Their identification can be very confusing, and their taxonomy and nomenclature are widely disputed. Many are identical, except for minor taxonomic distinctions irrelevant to their landscape utility. Gray dogwood (**Cornus racemosa**) is a tough upland species similar to roughleaf dogwood but with smoother leaves and smaller, more pyramidal flower clusters. Willow dogwood (**C. amomum**), stiff dogwood (**C. foemina**), and silky dogwood (**C. obliqua**) are usually shrubby, have blue-tinted fruits, and prefer wetter sites, along with the grex of extremely cold-hardy redosier dogwoods such as **C. sericea.**

BELOW: A mature pagoda dogwood (*Cornus alternifolia*). RIGHT: Redtwig dogwood (*C. stolonifera*) in bloom.

The USDA has evaluated several shrubby dogwoods for conservation use. In 1982 *Cornus obliqua* 'Indigo' was released, originating from Michigan, followed in 1988 by *C. sericea* 'Ruby' from New York. 'Indigo' is recommended for conservation planting throughout the eastern United States, while 'Ruby' does best in New England. Dale Herman at North Dakota State University named a selection of gray dogwood 'Snow Mantle' for its heavy flowering and fruiting. It reaches about 15 feet (4.5 m) in height, and if Dale can grow it in the severe climate of North Dakota you can probably grow it wherever you live too.

Pagoda dogwood (**Cornus alternifolia**) is a small tree that is unique among the native dogwoods because of its alternate leaf arrangement. It develops a sympodial habit similar to that of sassafras (*Sassafras albidum*) due to proleptic growth. Spreading lateral twigs that grow from current-season lateral buds impart a pagoda-like, layered branching structure.

Pagoda dogwood is occasionally subject to *Cryptodiaporthe corni* canker, a host-specific twig disease that seems to affect only this species. But it is very winter hardy, growing in woodlands from southern Manitoba across to the island of Newfoundland and southward in mesic habitats throughout the southeastern United States. It does not do well in hot, sunny exposures but thrives in any cool, moist location with afternoon shade, north through USDA zone 4.

I have encountered some beautiful pagoda dogwoods along the Finger Lakes hiking trail in New York but none quite as large as the U.S. national champion tree in New Jersey, which is 49 feet (14.7 m) tall and more than 1 foot (30 cm) in diameter. 'Argentea' is a variegated selection that never gets nearly so large. In the wild, pagoda dogwood thrives where many understory trees could not exist, beneath the dense canopies of three of the shadiest characters in the forest: *Acer saccharum*, *Fagus grandifolia*, and *Tilia americana*.

Garrya wrightii is the only species of silktassel (*Garrya*), or grayleaf dogwood, that can become a small tree in our region. It is confined to western Texas and southern New Mexico. Silktassels are in the same family as dogwoods but are not true dogwoods, and some botanists even assign them to another family. (I like to call such discussions "family disputes"; they are common whenever serious taxonomists assemble, with their little hand lenses dangling from cords around their necks like gang colors.) The largest known silktassel tree is 22 feet (6.6 m) tall. When silktassels do grow large enough to become trees, the hard, strong wood is similar to that of true dogwoods.

COMMENTS: Many small dogwoods are cultivated as ornamental shrubs by pruning out old stems. The vigorous shoots that resprout can develop intense bark coloration on some species, providing the dominant ornamental feature in a winter landscape. Dogwood fruits feed a large variety of birds in fall and winter, and their foliage is host to several interesting insects. Among these are the buttercup moth and the friendly probole moth, a most inquisitive and sociable garden animal.

Cornus florida
FLOWERING DOGWOOD

DESCRIPTION: The king of spring in the eastern United States and southern Ontario, flowering dogwood may be the most spectacular flowering tree native to our region. It grows slowly into a multilayered pagoda of color, its symmetrical branching pattern providing a sympodial crown of horizontal tiers similar to that of pagoda dogwood (*Cornus alternifolia*). Understory dogwood trees can reach 40 feet (12 m) or so into the forest canopy, with supple, wispy stems. But the shorter trees at the woodland edge, exposed to sunlight, develop the compact crowns that show their dense blossoms to such advantage along rural roadsides. The largest known flowering dogwood is an old tree in North Carolina that stands 31 feet (9.3 m) tall with a trunk about 3 feet (0.9 m) thick. In general flowering dogwoods more than 1 foot (30 cm) in diameter are considered large specimens.

LEAVES: The opposite leaves of this species resemble those of other dogwoods but can grow up to 6 inches (15 cm) long on vigorous young shoots. If its flowers were not so impressive, this tree would be more famous for its radiant red fall color. Leaf litter from flowering dogwood liberates calcium, enriching the topsoil for associated plants.

FLOWERS AND FRUIT: The small flower clusters are surrounded by four leafy bracts that turn white as they expand, enhancing the blooms in the same way the pink sepals enhance the flowers of pinckneya (*Pinckneya bracteata*). The bracts initially emerge greenish white, sometimes showing a pinkish touch when partially expanded. They become visually effective when they reach a span of about 2 inches (5 cm), and attain their full brilliance a couple of weeks later at almost double that size. On some popular selections the color can be pink or red. The long blooming period overlaps the end of that of redbud (*Cercis canadensis*), and the two species commonly grow together in similar habitats throughout their sympatric range, combining in an annual springtime spectacle that, once seen, is never forgotten.

The small clusters of fruit are glossy and bright red, adding sparkling highlights to the rich red fall foliage. Some fruits persist after the leaves have fallen, unless migrating birds find them first, and are an important food for overwintering birds, especially bluebirds, in the South.

BEST SEASONS: SPRING (during the blooming period). FALL (the colored foliage and fruit are nearly as impressive as the flowers). WINTER (for the violet-tinted, layered branches, punctuated by reflected points of light from the turban-shaped flower buds).

NATIVE AND ADAPTIVE RANGE: Flowering dogwood can be found from Toronto south to the Gulf Coast and from southern Maine to eastern Texas. It has been named the state tree of both Virginia and Missouri, and the state flower of North Carolina. This broad range can be misleading, though, because flowering dogwood is a classic example of the influence of provenance. Individual trees may not be reliably hardy or may not bloom well if transplanted very far in any direction from their ancestral home region. Always try to acquire dogwood planting stock grown from a lineage adapted to your local climate and soil. With this caution in mind, flowering dogwood is rated hardy north through USDA zone 5.

CULTURE: This tree grows readily from seed but is not very easy to transplant. Seeds must be planted in late summer or early fall while the soil is still warm, or they will likely take two years to sprout. Move flowering dogwood with a soil ball in early spring, and be sure to set it a little high in the planting hole.

Although wild dogwoods seem to survive in some pretty exposed locations, they do best under cultivation when given a birch-type setting: leaves in the sun, roots in the cool shade. A breezy location will add some motion to the flowers and discourage the anthracnose disease *Discula destructiva*. Trees in fairly deep shade thrive but become leggy and do not bloom as profusely. Avoid compacted or alkaline soils and poorly drained sites, and never plant a dogwood deeper than it grew in the nursery.

PROBLEMS: The red-tinted cultivars are generally not as hardy or as vigorous as most white-blooming forms, and they must be grafted since their seedlings usually

RIGHT: Fall color of flowering dogwood (*Cornus florida*).

revert to white unless pollinated by another red tree. Many minor leaf diseases and insects attack flowering dogwood, most of them succeeding in direct proportion to the overall stress level resulting from drought, poor planting, or abuse. Despite its reputation as a delicate tree, however, flowering dogwood is not much affected by city smog, and it seems impervious to the notorious Gypsy moth (*Lymantria dispar*). Dogwood borer (*Synanthedon scitula*) is a clearwing moth that resembles a slender bee and is attracted to weakened trees, pruning cuts, and sunscald-damaged bark areas. The wasp that causes horned oak galls on *Quercus* species also provides habitat for these borers, which can live in the oak galls as an alternative host.

Dogwood anthracnose is a recently described disease that first became a problem around 1980. Although it is

LEFT: A pink cultivar of flowering dogwood (*Cornus florida*). BELOW: Flowering dogwood flower detail. BOTTOM: Fall color of flowering dogwood .

very destructive in some high-elevation forests in the southeastern United States, concerns about it becoming the next chestnut blight or Dutch elm disease are dismissed by most pathologists. Vigorous, well-maintained trees in sunny areas with good air circulation and proper soil moisture are rarely killed. The disease apparently cannot survive in hot summer temperatures and cannot spread on dry foliage. However, new trees should be purchased from disease-free nurseries and never transplanted from infected forest areas.

CULTIVARS: Many selections of flowering dogwood have been recorded since the species was first discovered more than three hundred years ago. In one case, a single

healthy flowering dogwood tree was found in the middle of a grove decimated by anthracnose in Catoctin Mountain Park, Maryland, and that tree was the progenitor of the disease-resistant 'Appalachian Spring' bred by the University of Tennessee. Most other cultivars are divided into groups based on certain characteristics: large flowers, pink flowers, red flowers, fragrant flowers, double flowers, heavy blooming, variegated leaves, dwarf form, or weeping form. Most of these originated from plants in the southern portion of the species' range and should be used with caution in colder climates.

Of particular interest to many people in the North are selections made for winter hardiness. 'Ozark Spring', introduced by my late friend John Pair in Kansas, is one such plant, and 'New Hampshire' from Atkinson, New Hampshire, is another. More commonly available selections include 'Cherokee Princess', 'Cloud Nine', and 'White Cloud', all with white flowers. 'Cherokee Chief', 'Royal Red', and variety *rubra* have pink or red flowers, and 'Rainbow' and 'Welchii' have multicolored foliage.

I have tested variety *urbiniana* in Illinois, grown from seed I collected in the mountains of Nuevo León, Mexico. The flowers of this form are unique in that the bracts remain connected at the ends, giving the appearance of Chinese lanterns. It is not fully hardy in Illinois but grows well in milder areas. Breeding programs using this high-elevation dogwood variety could add much to the diversity of the species in cultivation.

Some of the newest dogwood selections on the market are hybrids with other large-bracted dogwood species. 'Eddie's White Wonder' was derived from a cross with Pacific dogwood (*Cornus nuttallii*). Crosses with the Chinese *C. kousa* have yielded 'Stardust', 'Galaxy', 'Aurora', 'Constellation', 'Ruth Ellen', and 'Stellar Pink'. These selections do have some "native blood" and incorporate some of the best qualities of each parent, but they are not native, nor even natural, in the truest sense.

SIMILAR AND RELATED SPECIES: Flowering dogwood is closely related to roughleaf dogwood and its related species (see *Cornus drummondii*), and even to the tiny groundcover bunchberry (**C. canadensis**). It is most similar, however, to the giant Pacific dogwood of western North America and to the Asian kousa dogwood.

COMMENTS: This ornamental tree has been admired by horticultural writers ever since the publication of

TOP LEFT: Pink flowering dogwood (*Cornus florida*) detail. LEFT: Fruits on flowering dogwood. RIGHT: Fruits and fall color on flowering dogwood.

John Ray's *Historia plantarum* (1686–1704). About a century later, in 1791, the famous naturalist William Bartram noted an exceptional grove of "dog-woods" that "continued nine or ten miles unaltered," writing at length of its beauty in his *Travels* (Van Doren 1928).

During that same period George Washington and Thomas Jefferson were initiating a landscaping trend, planting flowering dogwoods at Mount Vernon and Monticello, respectively. While such scattered landscape specimens can be magnificent, I can't help but try to envision hiking for hours through what must have been the unparalleled spectacle of Bartram's "dog-woods" in peak bloom.

Cotinus obovatus

SMOKETREE

DESCRIPTION: Smoketree (*Cotinus obovatus*, syn. *C. americanus*) has a whitened inner bark that turns orange when peeled. This bark, and the yellow wood, were early sources of natural dyes. Today, however, smoketree has much more value as a fine ornamental tree.

Only two species of smoketree are known. One, *Cotinus coggygria*, is a large shrub from Europe and China, and its purple-leaved form is seen frequently in cultivation. But the other smoketree, our rare North American species, is the superior plant. It becomes a small tree, sometimes with multiple stems that originate as sprouts from cut stumps. If allowed to grow in its own style, undamaged by storms or careless pruning, it becomes a striking specimen.

As is the case with many garden trees that come from difficult growing situations in their natural habitat, this species seems happier in cultivation than in the wild. Most smoketrees that grow on the calcareous highlands of the Edwards Plateau in Texas are shrubby, while those in other parts of the range become small trees; but those in well-drained, fertile soil in landscapes are vigorous and reach the largest size.

LEAVES: The leaves of our native smoketree grow nearly twice as large as those of its Asian cousin. They are nearly round and average about 4 inches (10 cm) long. Smoketree is related to sumacs (*Rhus*) and is one of the few trees that can equal their fall color. The brilliant orange autumn leaves of the two smoketrees that grow at the base of the hill below Abraham Lincoln's tomb in Springfield, Illinois, glow like beacons in the setting sun each October, welcoming visitors who approach the tomb from the west entrance to the cemetery.

FLOWERS AND FRUIT: The misty flower sprays of our native smoketree are smaller than those of the exotic species. These sprays are responsible for the common name of the genus, resembling as they do puffs of gunsmoke emerging from the ends of the branches. As with sumacs, smoketrees are dioecious. Male trees have larger, showier flower clusters, up to about 6 inches (15 cm) long.

The best attribute of the flowers is not their beauty alone but that they develop in late spring and remain attractive, as fruit panicles, into fall. The actual seeds are tiny, inconspicuous, and sparse, with many panicles having no seeds at all, but they are a choice food among native finches.

BEST SEASONS: FALL (this fiery yellow-orange plant, seen backlit against a dark background of ledge rock or evergreens, is unsurpassed). SPRING and SUMMER (for the smoke effect of the panicles, which can be especially striking when displayed against a tall wall of a white house or backlit in front of a shadowy background).

NATIVE AND ADAPTIVE RANGE: Smoketree occurs in isolated stands on limestone soils in Alabama, Arkansas, and Texas, with a few scattered trees ranging north to Kentucky and Missouri. It grows vigorously under cultivation well beyond its natural range, north at least through USDA zone 5.

CULTURE: Most suggestions for growing the Asian species apply equally to our own, such as providing a sunny exposure in neutral to alkaline soil. Smoketree is easy to transplant, but propagation from seed can be frustrating because so few seeds are formed and they take a long time (perhaps several years, without treatment) to germinate. Most commercial production is done from cuttings. Smoketree sprouts readily from the stump and may be grown as a shrub, if desired, by periodically cutting out old stems. However, the species is so impressive as a small tree that such renewal pruning might be better reserved for the exotic Asian smokebush.

PROBLEMS: This tree can basically be planted and forgotten. It thrives on neglect once established and requires no attention to insect or disease control so long as it is planted in a well-drained soil where *Verticillium* wilt and root decay fungi are unlikely to bother it. Its worst weakness may be that it shares the brittle wood so typical of other members of its family, resulting in occasional storm damage. If stems are broken they may be pruned back to a crotch or cut back to the ground and allowed to start over, which they will do with aplomb.

CULTIVARS: Several smoketree cultivars can be found in nurseries, but almost every one is a selection of the

RIGHT: A young smoketree (*Cotinus obovatus*) in fall.

Asian species. 'Red Leaf' is described by some authors as a native selection with very good fall color, and 'Grace' is a vigorous wine-colored hybrid cultivar originating as a cross with *Cotinus coggygria* 'Velvet Cloak'.

With the range of smoketree being so scattered, literally skipping over entire states, it would seem logical that distinct wild forms could be located. A few nurseries in the southeastern United States are considering this possibility, and I expect to see more selections marketed in the future. If these selections really are improvements over the species, they will be special indeed.

SIMILAR AND RELATED SPECIES: *Cotinus coggygria*, the Asian or European smokebush, is the only other

member of the genus. Its cultivars are very common in the landscape trade. Some maintain a raucous purple leaf color throughout the growing season, making them a challenge to place in any discreet noncommercial landscape. Unfortunately too many people accept this challenge and fail. Even the most refined purple trees require special siting and restrained use or they quickly become gaudy.   The Texas pistache (***Pistachia texana***) is a rare desert tree found in the wild in only a few counties in southern Texas. The primary known population of this tree (the Hinojose Spring population) was destroyed by construction of the Amistad reservoir decades ago, but a few nurseries in the Southwest are propagating it from the remaining stands and making it available for planting in the hot climate areas where it is adapted. It is interesting not only for its fine-textured, pinnately compound evergreen foliage and bright red fruits (on female plants) but also as a collectors' item for rare plant hobbyists and as our only native representative of the genus that includes the edible pistachio (***P. vera***). This same interesting plant family also includes many tropical trees of commercial or ethnobotanical interest, such as mango (***Mangifera indica***), cashew (***Anacardium occidentale***), and pepper trees (***Schinus***). See *Rhus typhina* for additional information.

COMMENTS: For several decades I admired a particularly fine old smoketree growing inconspicuously in a residential yard near the Purdue University campus in West Lafayette, Indiana, many miles from its natural range. When I heard via the alumni newsletter that Purdue planned to remove it in 2000 for construction of a new building, I spread the word. Tree lovers from around the world contacted Purdue to explain the unique significance of the tree and to ask the university to transplant it out of harm's way instead of destroying it. To its credit, the university agreed.

This national treasure is the largest smoketree known anywhere. It stands nearly 40 feet (12 m) tall with a trunk 30 inches (75 cm) thick, and it was moved to an open area at the south edge of campus with a root ball as big as a small backyard. As luck would have it, shortly after the move a windstorm came along and tipped it over. Undaunted, Purdue arborist and tree hero Tim Detzner brought in the necessary equipment to right it, and restaked it into place with steel cables, where it can still be seen.

TOP LEFT: Fruits and foliage on smoketree (*Cotinus obovatus*). LEFT: The brilliant fall foliage of smoketree.

Crataegus mollis
RED HAWTHORN

DESCRIPTION: If I attempted to discuss every hawthorn, or haw, in North America this book would need another full volume. Canada can claim at least twenty-five hawthorn species, and some botanists suggest that perhaps several hundred more can be found in the United States. However, the hawthorn most often encountered over the broadest part of our range, and the easiest to identify, is the red hawthorn, also called red haw. It is a tough little flowering tree with a short ashen-gray trunk and a dense crown of spreading thorny branches.

Red haw is among the largest hawthorns. One tree in Grosse Ile, Michigan, is 52 feet (15.6 m) tall and has a trunk 33 inches (82.5 cm) in diameter. Still, most red haws, and most hawthorns in general, seldom exceed 30 feet (9 m) in height or 18 inches (45 cm) in diameter. They become very picturesque as they approach such dimensions.

LEAVES: Red haw is also known as downy haw because of its fuzzy leaves. For hawthorn leaves, they are large, reaching up to 6 inches (15 cm) in length. Most hawthorns are susceptible to a number of leaf diseases, and red haw may be the most prone of all to early defoliation from leaf blight (*Fabraea thuemenii*), scab (*Venturia inaequalis*), and several rusts (*Gymnosporangium*). Its fall color is usually aborted when the leaves drop in late summer due to these infections. Little harm is done, however, since the leaves have done most of their work for the year by then, and since this particular species is not known for great fall foliage color.

FLOWERS AND FRUIT: Hawthorns are attractive in bloom. The native species have clusters of white blossoms that develop in spring, and red haw is among the earliest to bloom. The fruits of this species, known to schoolchildren as thornapples, are also the first to ripen, dropping to the ground as school begins each fall. But before these little apples drop, the leaf diseases that plague red haw sometimes do us an indirect favor by removing the foliage, thereby exposing the bright scarlet fruit display to full advantage. The fruits are edible, as most children soon discover, but they are not especially sought by wildlife until long after they have fallen, when they soften and ruffed grouse forage for them.

BEST SEASONS: SPRING (during the blooming period). LATE SUMMER (when the fruit ripens). WINTER (most hawthorns are interesting in the dormant season, with their dense, intricate branching, and many have reflective gray bark).

NATIVE AND ADAPTIVE RANGE: This species is found from southeastern North Dakota eastward through southern Ontario to Nova Scotia, and southwest to northwestern Alabama and eastern Texas. It is the state flower of Kentucky but is probably more commonly seen in a belt from Texas through Arkansas and southern Missouri, and in wooded bottomlands from Mississippi to Ohio and Pennsylvania. It also grows in the Midwest savanna understory and along the prairie border and is fully hardy in USDA zone 4.

CULTURE: Hawthorns survive under circumstances that foil most other, "upscale" flowering trees. They are indifferent to soil conditions and road salt, tolerate full sun or considerable shade, resist drought, and will often endure wetter conditions than most other trees in their family. Hawthorns were among the trees most recommended for water-conservation landscape use during the first Prairieland Xeriscaping Conference at the University of Saskatchewan. They are not as easy to transplant as their close relatives, the crabapples (*Malus*), but are not particularly difficult either. Seed should be planted in fall and may not germinate until the second year.

PROBLEMS: If this species is expected to have any leaves left by autumn, it must be sprayed with an orchard fungicide. It can survive just fine without such treatment, however, and as mentioned, early leaf abscission enhances the fruit display. One of the primary leaf diseases, cedar-hawthorn rust (*Gymnosporangium globosum*), is not a serious problem except where junipers (*Juniperus*), the alternate host of the disease, grow within a few city blocks of the red haw. All hawthorns are defoliated quickly during outbreaks of Gypsy moth (*Lymantria dispar*), and like many members of their family, they are susceptible (in varying degrees, depending upon the species) to bacterial fireblight (*Erwinia amylovora*).

The other serious problems with red haw are caused by the tree itself. It has long, sharp thorns that are very hazardous at eye level, and careful attention to the planting location is required for safety. In early autumn the abundant fallen fruits can coat paved areas with a slippery red squish, again suggesting that this tree be located away from the paths of human ramblings.

CULTIVARS: Several hawthorn cultivars are common in the nursery trade, but none are derived from red haw.

SIMILAR AND RELATED SPECIES: Authorities differ on the number of true, distinct hawthorn species, with estimates ranging from about two hundred to twelve hundred. My friend Ron Lance, a dedicated student of this wonderful genus, has made some fascinating observations about its complexity. He has grown about one hundred taxa from seed and found that nearly every taxon, whether a true species or a putative hybrid, will come true from seed very often with no sign of F_2 segregation (reversion to the characteristics of different ancestral parent species). This happens even in trees mixed with other taxa growing in proximity and presumably available as pollinators.

The extent of apomixis thus seems more pronounced in *Crataegus* than is commonly realized. This might be one reason why so many supposed species of hawthorn have been described; even though some might have been named from only one specimen, the trees "came true" from seed due to apomixis, and so were thought to be true species. Many hawthorns can cross if weather conditions and the very narrow window of pollination timing are exactly right, yielding occasional true hybrid progeny. And many intermediate forms, presumed for decades to be valid species, may be descended from hybrid offspring resulting from such occasional crosses, reproducing faithfully like good species via generations of apomixis.

Hawthorns are in the rose family, together with many of our most popular ornamental and orchard trees. Many native hawthorns are superior plants for ornamental and conservation use, and most reach about the same ultimate size. A few of the most common, and most decorative, hawthorns are discussed here.

A hardy northern species, Arnold hawthorn (***Crataegus arnoldiana***), has very large edible fruits and has provided the USDA seed-propagated 'Homestead', used in permaculture plantations. 'Homestead' originated at the

LEFT: The late summer fruit display of red hawthorn (*Crataegus mollis*).

Agriculture Canada Experiment Station in Morden, Manitoba, and is rated hardy north through USDA zone 3. It has pale yellow flowers and bright red fruits that ripen early like those of red haw. There is some taxonomic debate regarding the separation of Arnold hawthorn and red hawthorn as distinct species, based mostly upon the number of stamens in the flowers.

Frosted hawthorn (**Crataegus pruinosa**) also resembles a small red haw except for its glabrous, waxy foliage that is a deep blue-green in summer. Its purplish fruits grow almost as large as those of red haw. Frosted haw is commonly encountered in thickets from Newfoundland southwest to eastern Oklahoma.

Washington hawthorn (**Crataegus phaenopyrum**) is an upright-growing, densely thorny species. Its small glossy leaves show good red fall color, and the small bright fruits persist through most of the winter until eaten by

LEFT: A red hawthorn (*Crataegus mollis*) blooming at Starhill Forest. BELOW: Flower clusters on red hawthorn. RIGHT: Typical thorns on red hawthorn.

hungry wildlife. This hawthorn grows in scattered locations from southern Illinois to the Gulf Coast, but is hardy north through USDA zone 4 in southern Canada. Seedling selections have been made for more columnar growth, making them useful in narrow planting areas. This species seems very resistant to the leaf diseases that attack some hawthorns.

Cockspur hawthorn (*Crataegus crus-galli*) develops a spreading, flattened crown of long, layered limbs that sometimes sweep the ground on mature specimens. Its narrow, glossy leaves turn orange to red in fall, and its dull red fruits persist into early winter. This tree has some of the longest thorns of any hawthorn, but a thornless version, *C. crus-galli* var. *inermis*, is available. Cockspur haw has a broad natural range, from the Florida Panhandle up to Montreal, and can be grown north through USDA zone 3. *Crataegus crus-galli* 'Crusader' is also thornless (an interesting name, I think, for a "swordless" cultivar). The heavily fruiting *C.* 'Vaughn' is reportedly a cockspur hybrid with Washington haw but seems to have derived most of its characteristics from that other species, so the cockspur parentage could be questionable. The colorful *C.* ×*lavallei* is also a descendent of cockspur haw.

The similar dotted hawthorn (*Crataegus punctata*) is a floriferous species with densely branching, marble-sized red fruits and vein-patterned small leaves. This hardy tree can be found growing north into southern Newfoundland. The Secrest Arboretum has introduced a hybrid selection, 'Ohio Pioneer', that is substantially thornless and quite ornamental. The cerro hawthorn (*C. erythropoda*) is found along high-elevation streams throughout most of the Rocky Mountains. It resembles the dotted hawthorn of the East but has thorns nearly as long as those of cockspur haw.

Green hawthorn (*Crataegus viridis*) is a species of broad southern river bottomlands and coastal plains, known primarily by its Indiana cultivar, 'Winter King'. Among a genus of outstanding ornamental fruiting trees, this might be the most impressive. It doesn't bear heavily every year, but in good years no winter display of any other tree is more brilliant. The fruits are persistent and retain their substance and color until early spring unless discovered by flocks of hungry cedar waxwings. Green hawthorn can be grown north into USDA zone 4.

TOP LEFT: Fall color of Washington hawthorn (*Crataegus phaenopyrum*). LEFT: Bark of green hawthorn (*C. viridis*). RIGHT: Washington hawthorn in fruit.

Crataegus rivularis is the river hawthorn of the Southwest and can be considered the western counterpart of green hawthorn both in appearance and ecology. The widespread, western black hawthorn (**C. douglasii**) has been combined with river hawthorn by some taxonomists.

Fleshy hawthorn (**Crataegus succulenta**) is a species with glossy leaves, a profusion of edible fruit nearly as big as wild crabapples (*Malus*), and waxy blossoms that look like porcelain. It is not as common in cultivation for ornamental purposes as its merit would indicate, but it is important in permaculture plantings both in North America and abroad. Fleshy hawthorn has a wide northerly natural distribution, ranging from the southeastern corner of Saskatchewan and southern Manitoba east through southern Quebec to Cape Breton Island, and extending south to Tennessee and North Carolina.

'Toba' is a hybrid of this species with the European *C. laevigata* 'Paul's Scarlet'. **Crataegus macracantha** is the western analog of fleshy hawthorn and is found in the Rocky Mountains from Colorado north into Canada.

May haw (**Crataegus aestivalis**) is a popular ornamental tree in the southeastern United States. In the wild it grows throughout the lower Coastal Plain, from North Carolina southward, in seasonal swamps, borrow pits, or ditches that dry up in late summer. The western counterpart of May haw, **C. opaca,** is used for similar purposes in Louisiana and Texas. Horticultural selections from either species, or hybrids such as 'Big Red' (from Mississippi), 'Super Berry' (from Texas), and 'Lindsey' (from Georgia), can be grown in regular garden soil, with mulching to retard evaporation. Some of my friends gather wild May haw fruits in swamps, where the trees grow about 15 feet (4.5 m) high, by skimming the water surface for them like cranberries. May haw jelly and wine are highly regarded.

Another small southern species, parsley hawthorn (**Crataegus marshallii**), shares the general flower and fruit qualities of other hawthorns but might have the most ornamental foliage of all. The leaves are deeply dissected, having a visual texture that resembles garden parsley. The very tiny red fruits also contribute to the fine texture of this tree. Parsley hawthorn grows in low woods and wet areas but is adaptable to average garden soil.

Many hawthorns seen in cultivation are cultivars of a European species. Both the European hawthorn (**Crataegus monogyna**) and the English May hawthorn (**C. laevigata,** syn. *C. oxyacantha*) are well represented in ornamental horticulture.

COMMENTS: Hawthorns are known to have been planted for fruit by Native Americans and are assumed to provide valuable wildlife food. Many animals do snack on them, especially during winter when other food is scarce, but these trees are more valuable to wildlife for nesting and roosting cover. The dense thorny branches and the trees' frequent habit of growing in thickets and fence rows rank hawthorns among the most useful of all woody plants for wildlife habitat.

LEFT: Fruit clusters on cockspur hawthorn (*Crataegus crus-galli*).

Diospyros virginiana
PERSIMMON

DESCRIPTION: Most people know persimmon as a shrubby tree of old fields and fence lines. It commonly associates with sassafras (*Sassafras albidum*) and sumacs (*Rhus*) in such habitats and, like them, forms thickets by sending up root suckers. Persimmon responds well to good soil and moisture, and in bottomland forests it can become a large tree. Specimens more than 120 feet (36 m) tall and 3 feet (0.9 m) in diameter are known from nearly every southeastern state. U.S. national cochampions of such size exist in Georgia, Missouri, Mississippi, South Carolina, and Arkansas.

Persimmon is an attractive, long-lived tree when well grown. It is symmetrical in youth and develops a picturesque, wild branching pattern and dark, charcoal-checkered bark with maturity. A member of the ebony family, its hard black heartwood closely resembles that of its tropical cousins and is so heavy that it sinks in water.

LEAVES: Persimmon leaves emerge late in spring, eventually reaching up to 6 inches (15 cm) in length. They tend to hang from the twigs when mature, giving the tree a soft appearance much like that of pawpaw (*Asimina triloba*). Fall foliage color is variable; individual trees can be quite impressive in shades of gold, orange, or purple, while others are comparatively drab.

FLOWERS AND FRUIT: This is a dioecious species, with staminate trees bearing small flowers in clusters of three and pistillate trees having slightly larger, solitary flowers up to three-quarters of an inch (1.9 cm) across. Flowers are yellowish white, bell shaped, and powerfully fragrant, with excellent nectar for honeybees.

The 1-inch (2.5-cm) orange fruits give the genus its name, *Diospyros* being interpreted as "God's pear" (or "God's fire" if the fruits are eaten before fully ripe—either translation is quite defensible). Many species of wildlife eat ripe persimmons in the late fall when they sweeten up after a hard frost. It's not the frost that does it directly but the passage of sufficient time, as marked by the frost date. The fruits can also be made into pudding, bread, brandy, and preserves. After the leaves drop in fall the clinging orange balls on female trees stand out like Christmas ornaments until they are removed by wildlife or by the cold winds that herald the coming of winter. Mockingbirds are especially fond of them, and wild turkeys pick them from the ground as they fall.

BEST SEASONS: FALL (especially if the tree has good fall color or is a female loaded with fruit). WINTER (for the alligator bark and picturesque branching habit).

NATIVE AND ADAPTIVE RANGE: Persimmon can be found at low elevations from southern Connecticut to eastern Kansas and south to the Gulf Coast. Under cultivation it does well north at least through USDA zone 5.

CULTURE: This is among the most difficult native trees to transplant successfully in large sizes due to its coarse, deep root system. Once established, though, that same root system gives it an ironclad survival rate. It is quite adaptable, tolerating dry sites, sterile soils, flooding, heat, drought, shade, wind, and almost any other stress factors that might combine to overwhelm a weaker species. But it grows best in rich, organic soils with abundant moisture and full sun.

Persimmon seeds germinate easily, but the hardy seedlings grow slowly unless given ideal conditions. They survive neglect but reward attention, especially regarding fertility and moisture, and are tolerant of shade but grow more quickly in the sun. Wild trees sprout freely from the roots if damaged by fire or if the roots are cut by the soil disturbance associated with tillage of adjacent farm fields (hence their ability to form clonal thickets along fence lines, and our ability to propagate trees of known gender from root cuttings). Persimmon trees are good soil builders and are deep rooted; the males make excellent lawn trees where quality turf is desired.

PROBLEMS: Female trees should not be located where their overripe fallen fruits will constitute a litter problem. Persimmon trees are usually trouble-free except for possible infection by persimmon wilt (*Cephalosporium diospyri*), a systemic disease that has killed many wild trees in Tennessee. I have seen entire fence lines of persimmon pruned back annually by a twig-girdling insect, *Oncideres cingulata*, but the trees seem to recover with no loss of vigor. Raking and burning the fallen twigs, which harbor the eggs of the next generation of girdlers, will control this pest.

CULTIVARS: Seedless forms of *Diospyros virginiana* are known, and many tasty selections have been made since Captain John Smith of Jamestown first sampled the fruit almost four hundred years ago. Among the favo-.rites for table fare are 'Craggs', 'Florence', 'Garretson', 'Meader', 'Morris Burton', 'Penland', 'Pieper', and 'Wabash'. Many of these were derived from 'Early Golden', found about two hundred years ago in Illinois.

'John Rick', one of the best, began as a seedling planted by my old friend Joe McDaniel of the University of Illinois, grown from seed taken from the older 'Killen'. Joe gave me a few seeds in 1972 from his favorite 'Woolbright', which was selected for superior red fall foliage color. The two resulting male seedlings have performed brilliantly each fall, but one turns violet while the other turns bright gold. Fall color is difficult to predict, even from superior parent stock, unless trees are asexually propagated and grown on similar soils. For ornamental purposes where fruit litter is unwanted, either of these male 'Woolbright' offspring would be worthy of further study. I expect to see other male selections become available in the trade as nurseries learn how to transplant specimen-sized persimmon trees and as the public becomes increasingly aware of their ornamental qualities and resiliency under stress.

SIMILAR AND RELATED SPECIES: The chapote (***Diospyros texana***), also called Texas persimmon, is a small tree found from central Texas south into Mexico. It is unlike the eastern species in having black fruit, much smaller leaves, and gorgeous smooth gray bark that looks strikingly similar to that of the exotic crape myrtle (*Lagerstroemia indica*). Its small leaves curl under at the margins, and the edible fruit that forms on female trees ripens to a purplish black. The largest known specimen is in Uvalde, Texas. It is only 26 feet (7.8 m) tall but nearly 2 feet (60 cm) in diameter.

Two Asian persimmons are seen occasionally in cultivation where winters are mild. The Chinese ***Diospyros lotus*** has very small fruits and is used mostly as rootstock for grafting the other. The Japanese ***D. kaki*** has fruits the size of a tangerine and is grown for fruit production in Europe and Asia. The tropical ***D. ebenum*** from India is the primary species used for ebony timber.

COMMENTS: Persimmon is one of our most diversely

LEFT: Persimmon (*Diospyros virginiana*) in fall color. TOP RIGHT: Flowers on a male persimmon. CENTER RIGHT: Early fall coloring on a persimmon. RIGHT: Ripe persimmon fruits.

useful trees, with benefits beyond its obvious value in the landscape and as food for wildlife and humans. Native Americans relied upon the bark as a cure for fevers and upon the roots as a treatment for dropsy. The rock-hard wood has been used for many specialty articles such as golf clubs and loom shuttles. Persimmon trees also attract two spectacular garden moths: the regal moth, which can be 6 inches (15 cm) across, and the ethereal, swallow-tailed luna moth, which flies in the night like a green ghost.

BELOW: A mature persimmon (*Diospyros virginiana*).

Euonymus atropurpureus

WAHOO

DESCRIPTION: Many people are familiar with the introduced winged burning-bush (*Euonymus alatus*), which has escaped from cultivation to become a serious weed species in some natural forest areas. Some also know of the exotic winter-creeper (*E. fortunei*), which can overtop trees and crowd out native wildflowers. Few are aware, however, of the several attractive native species of *Euonymus*, one of which can become an appealing small tree.

The wahoo, or strawberry-tree, is an understory species of rich woods and stream valleys throughout most of eastern North America. It sprouts from the roots and commonly forms loose clonal thickets under favorable conditions in shady forests, but it can become a dense, symmetrical, flat-topped small tree under cultivation in open areas. The largest known wahoo tree grows in Michigan, standing 32 feet (9.6 m) tall with a stem 7 inches (17.5 cm) in diameter.

LEAVES: All *Euonymus* leaves are arranged in pairs along the twigs. Those of our native wahoo become larger than most, reaching 5 inches (12.5 cm) or more in length. They seem as one with the fresh lime-colored twigs, looking as though molded from the same green plastic in a single pour. The red fall color of this species is similar to that of the exotic winged burning-bush but free of the clashing magenta overtones that can make winged burning-bush so difficult to place in the landscape.

FLOWERS AND FRUIT: Wahoo flowers hang in branching clusters from the new twigs in early summer. They are mostly hidden by leaves but add a fine texture and can be visually effective when the canopy is viewed from below, as on a patio specimen. Each tiny purple flower has four petals and develops into the four-parted fruit that is the best ornamental feature of this plant.

In late summer the fruit capsules gradually color to white, then to rosy pink. Later they split open to expose shiny red-skinned seeds similar to those of magnolias. Wahoo usually fruits annually, and some individuals bear very heavily. The seeds are released gradually through fall and early winter, remaining ornamental for an extended period because birds such as bluebirds and mockingbirds use them only sparingly for emergency rations when their preferred foods are unavailable. Lasting well into the new year, wahoo ranks alongside deciduous hollies (*Ilex*) at the top of the winter color display.

BEST SEASONS: FALL (for the dependable, long-lasting fruit display and red foliage). WINTER (for the remnant fruits and bright green twigs).

NATIVE AND ADAPTIVE RANGE: Wahoo can be found in mesic woodlands from Toronto south to northern Tennessee and west to central Kansas, with outlying groups extending into southeastern North Dakota, central Texas, and near Florida. It seems most at home in the Midwest and can be grown under cultivation north into USDA zone 3.

CULTURE: Wahoo is among our most shade-tolerant woody plants, yet it grows well and becomes an attractive dense specimen in full sun. It prefers a rich forest soil but has no special drainage or pH requirements as long as sufficient moisture is present during the growing season. Its dense, shallow mass of roots makes it very easy to transplant during the dormant season.

PROBLEMS: Wahoo is not immune to the Asian scale insect (*Unaspis euonymi*) that plagues other members of the genus. It is also a highly preferred browse species for deer and rabbits and should be protected from them until it outgrows their reach. The seeds are reportedly poisonous to humans but are eaten by wildlife. Wahoo is one of the few native understory trees that can tolerate high levels of ozone pollution without sustaining foliar damage.

Occasional root suckers may be pulled by the gardener as they occur (or they may be mowed down by rabbits) if a single-stemmed tree is desired, or the plant may be allowed to form a clump. Suckering seems to be less prevalent on wahoos grown as specimen trees in open settings than on those growing in the forest understory.

CULTIVARS: No cultivars are listed for this species. Selections should probably be made for fall color and for superior fruit displays, since these characteristics seem to vary from tree to tree.

SIMILAR AND RELATED SPECIES: Other North American *Euonymus* species, such as **E. americanus,** are low or

running shrubs. There are Asian and European species that develop into small trees similar to wahoo, and many popular horticultural selections have been derived from some of the exotic species. Chief among them are ***E. yeddoensis, E. hamiltonianus,*** and ***E. europaeus.*** All are attractive small trees with nice fruit displays, but they can become invasive, and none is more colorful than our own native species.

COMMENTS: For a horticulturist, the root system of wahoo is a joy to behold. A small specimen, dug from silty forest soil and plunged into a bucket or nearby brook to flush the roots clean, reveals a fine, luxuriant, fibrous white root mass that any plant propagator would admire.

The pink-popcorn fruit capsules of wahoo, reminiscent of bittersweet (*Celastrus*), are distinctive in fall and sufficient reason to give this small tree a place in the ornamental landscape. They are especially effective after the leaves have fallen, and are useful in cut floral displays. Wahoo and witch hazel (*Hamamelis virginiana*) make good companion plants: the combination of yellow flowers and red-popcorn fruit in late fall makes a great Thanksgiving display, beginning with the Canadian Thanksgiving in early October and lasting through the late November Thanksgiving celebrated in the United States.

LEFT: A fruiting wahoo (*Euonymus atropurpureus*) at Starhill Forest. BELOW: Wahoo fruits cling through much of winter. TOP RIGHT: Wahoo in fall color. RIGHT: Flowers of wahoo.

Fagus grandifolia
BEECH

DESCRIPTION: Due to the combination of its expansive range and distinctive appearance, the gray-barked beech is among the most familiar forest trees of eastern North America. Beech associates and competes with sugar maple (*Acer saccharum*) over a vast range for top honors as the climax species of the hardwood forest. Both trees are very tolerant of shade and can develop under the canopies of other trees, but they differ in their reproductive strategies.

Maple produces great quantities of seedlings, some of which invariably survive. Beech, though, cannot be so dependent upon seedlings, since most of its seeds are eaten by wildlife. Consequently, once it becomes established it develops occasional suckers from its vast system of surface roots. Many supposed beech "seedlings" in the forest are interconnected by such a root system, thus possessing a significant competitive advantage over true seedlings and enabling the tree to dominate drier sites than the maple. Entire beech groves have grown from the roots of a single tree.

Beech becomes a large, fine-textured tree with a dense canopy and graceful, spreading form. It is highly phototropic, responding to shade patterns by leaning toward the strongest light. The U.S. national champion is located in the northeastern corner of Ohio and measures 130 feet (39 m) tall with a trunk nearly 6 feet (1.8 m) thick. Equally impressive specimens might be found in Canada, considering the large Canadian range of the species.

LEAVES: Bright new beech leaves emerging from the long-pointed buds, seen against the background of smooth gray bark, are a sight not soon forgotten. The leaves expand to 5 inches (12.5 cm) in length and remain attractive throughout the growing season. In fall they turn yellow, then golden bronze. Beeches are marcescent, as are a number of the closely related oaks (*Quercus*), with many leaves clinging each winter, bleaching in the sun, and rattling in the cold wind.

FLOWERS AND FRUIT: Staminate flowers hang from long stalks in marble-sized round clusters, while pistillate flowers are arranged in pairs on shorter stalks at the ends of branches. They develop into triangular beechnuts paired in heart-shaped burs, which have been documented as a primary food source for more than thirty wildlife species, such as wild turkeys and squirrels. When in season, beechnuts can make up 50 percent of the food of black bears.

In an earlier time in North America, beechnuts were relied upon almost exclusively each fall by huge flocks of passenger pigeons, which became extinct when the last one died around 1914. These enormous feeding flocks have been described as one of the most impressive sights in nature, akin to an approaching storm. Because of their senseless destruction by humans, we can never see them again.

BEST SEASONS: EARLY SPRING (when the long sharp buds expand and fresh new leaves emerge, a spectacular green, after a long hard winter). WINTER (for the silvery smooth bark and intricate twig structure, most visible in the dormant season, accented by marcescent leaves). FALL (the yellow fall foliage color is modest when compared with adjacent maples and certain oaks, but the combination of leaves and bark is quietly elegant). SUMMER (a stately tree that casts a cool but luminous shade).

NATIVE AND ADAPTIVE RANGE: Beech can be found in rich, mesic forests from Sudbury, Ontario, Cape Breton Island, and Quebec City down throughout the eastern United States to northern Florida and eastern Texas. As with many other trees with such a broad range, local seed sources usually produce the trees best adapted to local conditions. Northern beech ecotypes can be grown north to USDA zone 3.

CULTURE: This tree should be preserved in natural forest settings or planted in mesic sites where it can be left alone. It has an undeserved reputation as being difficult to transplant, probably because many people have tried to collect wild "seedlings" that were actually root suckers, or because it will not survive if planted too deeply. I have moved wild trees of seedling origin, and even a few small root sprouts, with no problem. Nurs-

RIGHT: The smooth bark of beech (*Fagus grandifolia*) is conspicuous in the forest.

ery-grown specimens can be transplanted in large sizes, and beech can be grown easily from seed (which must be protected from rodents and birds throughout the first growing season) or by rooting layers from low branches.

PROBLEMS: The most immediate concern with beech is a serious bark-fungus disease, *Nectria coccinea* var. *faginata*. The fungus seems to be fatal most often when it invades susceptible trees following attacks by another pest, the beech scale insect (*Cryptococcus fagisuga*), which was introduced into Nova Scotia from Europe around 1890. Researchers hope that the disease will run its course and that the most resistant trees will survive to contribute their genes to future beech forests. Another common pest peculiar to beech is the woolly beech aphid (*Phyllaphis fagi*). This insect does not kill the tree but litters the ground (or patio) below with a sticky honeydew.

Beech is also intolerant of severe drought, soil compaction, and poor soil drainage. Newly planted trees (or those recently exposed by adjacent clearing) are prone to sunscald damage. Beech trees in the forest are killed easily by fires, and damaged trees are very prone to decay.

Shallow surface roots make it difficult to establish and maintain turf under beech; turf competition and mower-inflicted injury can, in turn, have adverse effects on the vigor of the tree. The best solution, for your mower and your beech tree, is to accumulate a natural duff or mulch under the canopy and allow the lower limbs to sweep the ground or encourage native wildflowers to fill in beneath.

CULTIVARS: The European beech (*Fagus sylvatica*) has given rise to more horticultural selections than almost any other forest tree, but not so with our native species. Two beech selections from Indiana, 'Abrams' and 'Abundance', were made in 1926 for nut quality, and another, 'Jenner', was added more recently from New York.

There are natural geographic races, known locally as red beech, gray beech, and white beech, and some authorities recognize a variety or two. We have not yet seen the dawn of cultivar development in native beech. Perhaps this is because any seedling beech can always be counted upon to produce a tree of consistently high ornamental value, or perhaps it is because our native species is more demanding of its site than most trees, including even its European cousin. It could simply be that the European beech was tinkered with for centuries

LEFT: The beautiful form of an open-grown beech (*Fagus grandifolia*).

before our native tree was discovered, and no need has been perceived for more beech cultivars.

SIMILAR AND RELATED SPECIES: There are about ten species of beech worldwide, all in the Northern Hemisphere. Perhaps four species (our native tree and the common European species in all its forms and cultivars, plus the Asian *Fagus crenata* and *F. orientalis*) are hardy in much of eastern North America. Of these, the most commonly seen by far is European beech. *Fagus sylvatica* is slightly more drought tolerant than *F. grandifolia*, while our native species is more cold hardy and could be viewed by some as having smoother, more attractive bark. *Fagus ×moesiaca,* a natural hybrid of European and Asian species, is also seen occasionally. All these species can become very confusing as one begins to compare the countless cultivars of *F. sylvatica*. The small-leaved beech trees of the Southern Hemisphere actually belong to **Nothofagus,** a related genus, and some are cultivated in mild areas of North America.

COMMENTS: Two of the more interesting organisms associated with beech are the early hairstreak, a small,

LEFT: Beech (*Fagus grandifolia*) clings to much of its foliage throughout the winter. BELOW: Feathery new growth on a beech in spring. BOTTOM: Fall color of beech. RIGHT: Fruits on a beech.

quick, brown-over-blue butterfly, and beechdrops (*Epifagus virginiana*), a parasitic plant that grows beneath beech canopies. Beech bark, especially where it is naturally sculpted around unions where low limbs join the stem, is a tactile as well as visual masterpiece that should be part of all sightless interpretive trails. Old trees beneath a gray winter sky seem cast from molten pewter.

Beech bark has been used as writing paper for centuries. The word "book" comes from the Anglo-Saxon *boc* ("letter"), which derives from *beece* ("beech"). Everyone interested in woods lore has probably heard about "D. Boone cilled a bar" being carved on the smooth bark of beech trees wherever the famous explorer had a successful bear hunt. The trunk of the last of Daniel Boone's defiled beeches can still be seen in a museum in Louisville, Kentucky. Unfortunately, this least admirable trait of Boone's seems to be the one people most imitate, and it is increasingly difficult to find elegant old beech trees with smooth, lichen-mottled bark not disfigured by some thoughtless person's knife.

Beech cannot be grown outside its undisturbed natural habitat without careful attention to its precise requirements, but it is a prize well worth the cost for those who want to grow or preserve one of the world's most beautiful trees. It can also serve as the "canary in the coal mine" for those who hope to build their houses in the forest without damaging the surrounding trees. When the beech in your wooded lot starts to die, you will know that your construction activity was not as benign as you had hoped, and that your other trees may die as well.

This species is projected by many scientists to be a significant future victim of environmental degradation in the United States, based upon current predictions of global warming and measurements of acid precipitation (the unnatural aluminum concentrations in soils affected by acid rain inhibit calcium uptake in beech). While global warming may not kill trees in managed landscape settings or in the coolest forest ravines, the warming, drying effect of greenhouse gases produced in abnormal concentrations may eliminate most beeches in many of our forests over the next century. We should all work together to minimize such trends wherever possible—for the noble beech and for our own species as well.

Forestiera acuminata

SWAMP PRIVET

DESCRIPTION: The wild privets are well represented by swamp privet, the hardiest member of the genus. They are an obscure collection of small trees and shrubs, almost unknown in cultivation except where they have been transplanted from nearby wild stands or planted in the special gardens of plant collectors. Generally shrubby in the wild, with stiff branches that emerge at a right angle to the trunk or limbs, swamp privet can be grown as a small tree. The largest known specimen, found growing in Richland County, South Carolina, is 42 feet (12.6 m) tall with a main stem that is 10 inches (25 cm) thick. Larger individuals probably exist back in some inaccessible bayou never seen by human eyes.

Swamp privet is related to the olives (*Olea*), and a mature specimen looks similar to an olive tree. It has smooth gray bark on all but the largest stems, stone fruits about the size and shape of a wild European olive, small opposite leaves, and a picturesque crown. Unlike olive, though, it shares a special ability with buttonbush (*Cephalanthus occidentalis*) and water tupelo (*Nyssa aquatica*) to survive in swampy soils that can be submerged for nearly the entire growing season.

LEAVES: The leaves are arranged in pairs on bright green new twigs, which contrast with the gray bark of the older branches. They are very smooth and generally do not exceed about 3 inches (7.5 cm) in length by less than half as wide. In fall they drop without showing any significant color.

FLOWERS AND FRUIT: The swamp privet is usually dioecious, but occasionally some fruits can be found on predominantly male plants. The flowers emerge without petals in early spring, before the leaves, and the staminate flowers are one of the best-kept secrets of ornamental horticulture. The plants become a mass of pale yellow, similar to the effect of male spicebush (*Lindera benzoin*) in bloom, subtly illuminating the most dismal of swamps.

Female trees bear purple, olivelike drupes that ripen in early summer and fill an important summer food need for waterfowl and songbirds. They are lightly textured and reach the size and consistency of raisins.

BEST SEASONS: EARLY SPRING (during the blooming period, especially for staminate trees). WINTER (for the smooth bark and the branching character of large, well-grown specimens). SUMMER (for the colorful fruits on pistillate trees).

NATIVE AND ADAPTIVE RANGE: Swamp privet is essentially an inhabitant of low ground in the lower Mississippi Valley, with outlying populations occurring eastward to South Carolina and westward to central Texas and eastern Kansas. It reaches up the Mississippi and Illinois Rivers into central Illinois and up the Wabash River into southwestern Indiana. This species is so rarely seen in cultivation that its full hardiness is probably unknown, but I grow it in central Illinois in USDA zone 5.

CULTURE: Swamp privet is not a very demanding species, but it does best in rich, moist soil. It is very useful for wet situations where almost no other small tree can survive, and part of its natural competitive edge centers upon its ability to grow where most potential competitors would drown. It is tolerant of shade but, like many other species, forms a more dense, uniform crown in full sun.

Fresh ripe fruits may be sown intact as soon as they mature, and will germinate within days. The resulting seedlings should be given fertile soil and plenty of sunlight and water to help them grow large enough to withstand their first winter. Trees of known gender can be propagated by layering their lower branches. In this way, fruiting females and the more attractively blooming males can be planted together for optimum fruit production for wildlife, or a purely ornamental planting can be limited to males only. Prune young trees to form the desired limb structure and eliminate any parallel, ascending limbs.

PROBLEMS: Predictably, swamp privet is not fond of drought, but it does not demand soggy conditions ei-

RIGHT: Swamp privet (*Forestiera acuminata*) thrives in wet sites.

ther. It develops short, stiff, heavy spur shoots on lateral branches, like those found on crabapples (*Malus*), but is not truly thorny. Fruits can be messy if they fall on pavement before the birds can pick them, so plant pistillate trees where they are underlain by turf or mulch.

I have found damage from the ash-lilac borer (*Podosesia syringae* var. *fraxini*) on this species, which seems logical since ash trees (*Fraxinus*) are close relatives of swamp privet. Deer and rabbits can damage young plants by browsing, and wild plants are sometimes tilted or nearly smothered by heavy flooding and siltation along river banks.

CULTIVARS: No cultivars are listed for any wild privet species.

SIMILAR AND RELATED SPECIES: Several similar species are restricted to extreme southern portions of the United States and parts of Mexico. Florida privet (**Forestiera segregata**) is a species from the coastal plain that extends north only to the Savannah River in Georgia. Narrow-leaved privet (**F. angustifolia**) is a salt-tolerant, dryland, evergreen species of southern Texas and eastern Mexico, and desert-olive (**F. phillyreoides**) is found only in dry, rocky areas in southern Arizona and western Mexico. The rare netleaf desert-olive (**F. reticulata**) is confined to a few isolated locales in southwestern Texas. Cruzilla (**F. pubescens**) is a broader-leaved species that can be found in widely scattered locations across the South and Southwest.

Some authorities follow a different taxonomy, alternatively recognizing a different species, ***Forestiera neomexicana,*** as desert-olive and adding ***F. ligustrina*** as a distinct southeastern species. Of all these related taxa, the species known generally in horticulture as *F. neomexicana* seems to be the hardiest, surviving for me in USDA zone 5. The other closest familiar native relatives of the swamp privet are fringe trees (*Chionanthus*), devilwoods (*Osmanthus*), and ashes (*Fraxinus*). The introduced, and frequently invasive, common privets (*Ligustrum*) are also related, as are lilacs (*Syringa*).

COMMENTS: Sometimes gardeners and conservationists wisely accept the biological premise that diversity within communities of native species is healthy for its own sake, and that rare or unusual plants frequently have ecological merits that escape casual notice. Swamp privet is worthy of consideration on that basis, if for no other reason. I believe, in addition, that the early flower display of this tree, and its ability to thrive on flood-exposed river banks and in wet sites that would be fatal to most other trees, merit its wider use in specialty landscapes and its appreciation in the wild wetland forests it calls home.

LEFT: A dense specimen of swamp privet (*Forestiera acuminata*). BELOW: The opposite leaves and twigs of swamp privet. RIGHT: Fruits developing on a female swamp privet. BOTTOM RIGHT: Early yellow flowers on a male swamp privet.

Fraxinus americana
WHITE ASH

DESCRIPTION: The ashes are among the most common and widespread of our native forest trees, and white ash is our largest and most impressive species. It shows strong apical dominance that encourages the development of a straight central stem, whether grown in an open field or under the dense competition of a cove hardwood forest. With great age, however, it will increase in spread as far as its neighbors will permit.

The largest, though certainly not the tallest, known white ash grows next to a restaurant in Palisades, New York. It stands 95 feet (28.5 m) tall with a massive trunk more than 8 feet (2.4 m) in diameter, located next to the road with its root flare surrounded by a low retaining wall. Forest-grown white ash trees can become half again as tall but are seldom more than half as thick as this stout old witness to the Revolutionary War.

Though many ash species prefer wet soil, white ash is a tree of mesic uplands and the well-drained valleys of small streams. It tolerates short-term flooding in order to gain access to the mineral-rich sediments deposited by flash floods, and it makes its best growth under such nutrient-rich conditions.

LEAVES: Most native ash leaves are similar. White ash develops opposite, pinnately compound leaves composed of about seven leaflets, arranged in pairs along the twigs. The leaflets each measure 2 to 5 inches (5 to 12.5 cm) long by slightly less than half as wide. They are held on petiolules and are whitened underneath. Fall color is variable, depending on genetics and perhaps soil acidity, but always impressive and always early, whether it's the gold that predominates in some southern trees or the orange-purple so prevalent in the North.

FLOWERS AND FRUIT: Ashes are dioecious. Male trees bloom annually, with clustered purplish bronze flowers appearing in early spring. The male flowers are only mildly interesting, but they become more conspicuous when infected with the flower gall mite (*Eriophyes fraxinoflora*).

Most female trees bloom heavily, or at least set major seed crops, only once every several years. The female flowers have reddish purple pistils that develop into loose clusters of greenish yellow winged seeds. On *Fraxinus americana* f. *iodocarpa* the red color is retained as the seeds expand. This form was found originally in Maine in 1911 and was described by Merritt Fernald. It is very striking in summer as the fruits mature, offering good reason to plant female trees, which are otherwise avoided during cultivar selection because of the fruit litter. The ripe seeds are tan winged samaras about 2 inches (5 cm) long and are a favorite food of grosbeaks and finches.

BEST SEASONS: FALL (white ash generally has the best fall color of any ash, especially on those trees that turn an iridescent orange-violet, and it is among the first of our large trees to color). LATE SPRING (for those select female trees that have colorful immature fruit).

NATIVE AND ADAPTIVE RANGE: White ash occupies favorable sites over an extensive range, from Cape Breton Island westward well north of Quebec City to the eastern end of Lake Superior, and south through almost the entire area of the United States east of a line from around Omaha to Dallas. It misses only southern Florida and the coastal plains of the adjacent southeastern states. Trees of properly selected provenance are hardy under cultivation throughout the East up to USDA zone 3.

CULTURE: This species does well under a wide range of moderate conditions but will not tolerate extremes. It is easy to transplant when dormant and can be propagated from seed or by budding selected trees onto seedlings. White ash is tolerant of city smog pollution. Wild trees are shade tolerant when young but must be released from competition if they are to develop properly.

PROBLEMS: The most critical insect problems on white ash are the ash-lilac borer (*Podosesia syringae* var. *fraxini*), which also attacks swamp privet (*Forestiera acuminata*) and related plants, and to a lesser extent the banded ash borer (*P. aureocincta*). Ash trees are less likely to be damaged by these borers if they are otherwise healthy and vigorous, but borers can become a serious concern on weak specimens. The adult ash-lilac borer

RIGHT: A large white ash (*Fraxinus americana*) in fall color.

moths, which actually look like small wasps, are active during morning, and their populations may be monitored with inexpensive pheromone traps to determine when (and if) spraying is needed. Oystershell scale insects (*Lepidosaphes ulmi*) can also be serious pests on ash. All ashes are very resistant to Gypsy moth (*Lymantria dispar*), which defoliates so many other trees, but are extremely attractive to the deadly Asian longhorned borer beetle (*Anoplophora glabripennis*).

Another introduced borer beetle, the metalic-green emerald ash borer (*Agrilus planipennis*), recently entered North America in southern Michigan and adjacent areas of Ontario from Asia, where it reportedly attacks both ashes and elms (*Ulmus*). This buprestid beetle is known to feed on ash bark and sapwood and, like the longhorned borer, probably arrived on the continent as larvae or pupae in shipping pallets. Both of these introduced borer beetles have the potential to devastate white ash and other native ash trees.

LEFT: Fall color on a young white ash (*Fraxinus americana*). BELOW: Fruit clusters on a female white ash. RIGHT: The fissured bark of white ash.

Ash yellows is a poorly understood, frequently fatal disease caused by a phytoplasma. It results in growth reduction, dieback, multiple leaders (loss of apical dominance), and congested witches'-brooms of sprouts on the trunk. It may be transmitted by insect vectors or by dodder, a parasitic vine. Ash trees are also disfigured by anthracnose (*Gnomoniella fraxini* or *Apiognomonia veneta*) in years with wet spring weather, but the disease is not a serious threat to the health of the tree. Peak fall color is occasionally aborted due to premature defoliation by leaf spot (*Mycosphaerella effigurata* or *M. fraxinicola*). Some ash trees decline for unknown or multiple causes, lumped together as a syndrome called ash decline. Most of these cases originate with trees weakened by root damage or borers.

Seed litter can be a problem in developed areas, and heavy seed crops probably weaken female trees, predisposing them to insect and disease damage. Individuals that develop codominant stems with narrow forks can be subject to ice damage, but white ash is generally considered a strong tree.

CULTIVARS: White ash selections have been made for seedlessness (male trees) and superior fall color. 'Autumn

Applause' and 'Autumn Purple' are among the most popular cultivars. 'Chicago Regal', 'Elk Grove', 'Autumn Blaze', 'Fall Festival', and 'Royal Purple' are excellent selections with outstanding color. 'Rosehill' and 'Champaign County' are more adapted to southern areas, while 'Manitoo', 'Empire', and 'Skyline' are upright forms with strong central leaders.

SIMILAR AND RELATED SPECIES: There are more than a dozen ash species in North America. The one most likely to be confused with white ash is Biltmore ash (**Fraxinus biltmoreana**), which is considered a variety of white ash by some authorities, rather than a species. European ash (**F. excelsior**) and some of its cultivars are widely cultivated. See *F. pennsylvanica* and *F. quadrangulata* for additional information.

COMMENTS: White ash is intermediate in tolerance to nearly every growing condition. It does well under a wide range of average circumstances but poorly on extreme sites, so it is an excellent choice for the average landscape. Many people think of white ash in terms of the baseball bats made from its sapwood, but I prefer to admire the tree as a living organism rather than a dead stick. It is among our fastest-growing strong-wooded shade trees, and it has outstanding early fall color. Planting white ash with hickories (*Carya*) and oaks (*Quercus*) will result in a continuous fall color season that runs from purple to gold and red, lasting for more than a month. It also casts a bright, inviting shade because of the light color of the undersides of its leaves, and it is a choice host for the tiger swallowtail butterfly.

LEFT: The striking fruits of *Fraxinus americana* f. *iodocarpa*, a rare, red-fruiting white ash.

Fraxinus pennsylvanica

GREEN ASH

DESCRIPTION: While white ash (*Fraxinus americana*) may be the most impressive member of the genus, green ash is certainly the most widespread and most adaptable. It is a variable species, which is to be expected for a tree with such an expansive geographic range and wide habitat tolerance.

Green ash is probably the most commonly seen native ash species, both in the wild (in bottomland forests and along prairie streams) and in cultivation. Open-grown trees develop into a candelabra of massive limbs, exhibiting less apical dominance than white ash, and can reach impressive proportions in favorable habitats if their weak limb structures do not cause them to fall apart from the impacts of ice or wind. The U.S. national champion, located at a country crossroads in Cass County, Michigan, is 131 feet (39.3 m) tall and has a trunk more than 6 feet (1.8 m) in diameter. The species has an extensive Canadian range as well, so there may be even larger green ashes in Canada.

LEAVES: Opposite and pinnately compound, green ash leaves generally resemble white ash leaves in size and shape, but the leaflets are usually narrower and their stalks are slightly winged. Green ash leaves are uniformly green on both sides during the growing season, turning bright yellow in fall.

FLOWERS AND FRUIT: Like most ash species, this tree is fully dioecious. The flowers and fruits resemble those of white ash. Female trees are prolific annual seeders, providing much food for wildlife and much litter in the domestic landscape.

BEST SEASONS: FALL (for the bright foliage color). SUMMER (for the welcome shade in some of the savage climates this tree calls home).

NATIVE AND ADAPTIVE RANGE: Green ash is successful over a broad and challenging range, essentially equaling that of white ash but expanding northeast through the Gaspe Peninsula and around Lake St. John in Quebec, northwest to central Alberta, and west to central Wyoming. Over much of this expansive range it is one of the only deciduous trees tough enough to survive. Selected trees are reliably hardy north to USDA zone 2.

CULTURE: The term "culture" seems almost oxymoronic when used in the same sentence with "green ash." As long as the tree is planted green side up, it seems capable of surviving. It will tolerate flooding for months at a time in its natural habitat and can survive on top of the toxic gob piles of abandoned mines, along heavily salted roads, and even in the sterile, parched ballast found along recreational trails constructed on old railroad rights of way. Still, like other trees with reputations for coyote-like toughness, this species responds noticeably to good treatment.

Moist, fertile soil will stimulate the amazingly fast growth that green ash is capable of producing. Careful attention to proper pruning during its early years will minimize the poor form and weak branch unions for which it is notorious. Selections of locally adapted provenance will be less affected by injury from drought, cold, heat, and other factors than will unadapted ecotypes. These can be grown easily from seed, collected fresh and sown outdoors promptly in early fall.

PROBLEMS: Green ash is subject to the same insect and disease problems as white ash (see *Fraxinus americana*). It may be the most susceptible North American species to ash anthracnose (*Gnomoniella fraxini*), but this problem seldom causes serious damage to the tree's health. The banded ash borer (*Podsesia aureocincta*) is especially fond of green ash, and research is underway into using parasitic nematodes to control this pest in nursery production fields. Green ash is so resistant to Gypsy moth (*Lymantria dispar*) that scientists in Wisconsin are trying to develop a Gypsy moth repellant from chemical extracts of this tree.

While green ash is less influenced by marginal environmental conditions than white ash, its characteristic poor form makes it prone to structural damage from wind and ice. This should be prevented by proper pruning while the young tree is developing its primary limb structure. In particular, the vigorous side branches should be thinned and headed back to reduce their dominance. This will prevent them from ever becoming as large as the leader and ensure that several of them don't join the trunk at one point. Female trees can generate consider-

able seed litter, so males should be planted in areas where the seeds from female trees would be unwelcome.

CULTIVARS: There is a standard caution that any cultivar you plant should be from a geographic provenance adapted to your local area, and that you should not create a large monoculture consisting of a single cultivar in any landscape area. Planting random seedlings of local provenance helps to maintain biological diversity and perpetuate locally evolved ecotypes. That said, green ash nonetheless serves as the perfect model to illustrate the potential advantages of cultivars over random seedlings. Many named selections exist, and some are so superior to average seedlings that they look like different species.

'Marshall Seedless', introduced in 1946, was one of the first modern tree cultivars, and it remains popular. 'Aerial' is a columnar selection derived from a witches'-broom found in Wisconsin. 'Leprechaun' is a dwarf se-

lection that matures at less than half the normal size, often grafted high on seedling understock to raise the shrubby crown above eye level. 'Bergeson', 'Dakota Centennial', 'Emerald', 'King Richard', 'Newport', 'Prairie Spire', 'Robinhood', 'Sherwood Glen', and 'Summit' are among the many highly recommended male selections. Each of these cultivars develops a stronger branch structure than the average green ash, and most have attractive foliage and good vigor.

'Cimmaron', 'Urbanite', and Skyward are also listed as improved new selections of green ash, but they display foliage characteristics, reddish fall color, and improved branching habits that suggest they might have been derived from hybrids. 'Patmore' originated in Manitoba and may be the hardiest selection for northern regions, along with the narrower 'Prairie Spire' from North Dakota. The Prairie Farm Rehabilitation Administration of Canada has tested other green ash selections for windbreak use at their research station near Indianhead, Saskatchewan, since 1985; and the USDA is also testing provenance selections of green ash.

LEFT: An old green ash (*Fraxinus pennsylvanica*) displays fall color. BELOW: Green ash develops a spreading branching habit with heavy limbs.

SIMILAR AND RELATED SPECIES: Most authorities incorporate red ash under the taxonomic umbrella of green ash, formerly considered a glabrous variety (*subintegerrima*) of red ash. The U.S. national champion red ash is among several champion trees being propagated as cultivars.

Pumpkin ash (***Fraxinus tomentosa,*** syn. *F. profunda*) is a hexaploid intermediate between red ash and white ash, and possibly originated as a stabilized hybrid between the diploid green (red) ash and the tetraploid white ash. It has a spotty distribution, found mostly in wetland areas of the Atlantic Coastal Plain and Ohio and Mississippi River valleys, and can be grown through USDA zone 5. It can become huge in suitable habitat—the record tree, in southeastern Missouri, is 133 feet (39.9 m) tall—and in swampy sites it develops a broadly tapered basal buttress.

Pop ash (***Fraxinus caroliniana***) is a similar swamp tree, more southerly in distribution and much smaller in stature. Black ash (***F. nigra***) is usually a small, slender tree but can exceed 100 feet (30 m) on good sites. It occupies the same type of wetland habitat in the boreal forests of the northern United States and Canada, surviving even in peat bogs. *Fraxinus nigra* 'Fallgold' is a superior male selection with long-lasting fall color, introduced by the Morden Experimental Station in Manitoba. Black ash is being used in experimental crosses with a Manchurian ash species to develop hybrid cultivars suited to the northern Canadian plains.

COMMENTS: Green ash could be considered the junkyard dog of the genus. Left to its own devices it is a survivor, but not much more. But when taken into cultivation, selectively propagated, and properly groomed, it becomes a respectable shade tree for refined landscapes.

We have all been fascinated by the story of Lewis and Clark and the Voyage of Discovery undertaken from 1804 to 1806. Green ash is likely to have been the most satisfactory firewood available to them, as well as to the nomadic Native Americans they encountered over much of the upper Missouri River valley. It has the capacity to burn well without being seasoned, unlike its juicy prairie associates, cottonwood (*Populus*) and Manitoba maple (*Acer negundo*). Had it not been for green ash, those famous explorers may not have survived their first winter on the Great Plains.

TOP LEFT: Female green ash trees (*Fraxinus pennsylvanica*) produce heavy seed crops. LEFT: Pop ash (*F. caroliniana*) is a familiar tree of southern swamps.

Fraxinus quadrangulata
BLUE ASH

DESCRIPTION: Blue ash is a medium to large tree, upright in habit, with attractive light gray bark. It has wings or lines on its twigs that give the twigs a square cross section, and it is unique among the hardy eastern ash species for its exceptional tolerance of alkaline soil. This makes it very desirable for planting in prairie areas. Blue ash and bluegrass mix well, so the racehorse region of Kentucky is also prime blue ash country. The largest known specimen occurs there, standing 86 feet (25.8 m) tall with a trunk nearly 5 feet (1.5 m) thick.

This tree is usually common wherever it is found at all. In general these populations are isolated and restricted to the soil associations where it competes the best. It thrives in moist or dry soil as long as it is rich, deep, and alkaline.

LEAVES: This ash has glossy, pinnately compound leaves up to about 12 inches (30 cm) long, with seven to eleven leaflets that are narrower and finer in texture than those of most other species. They are blue-green in color, turning bright yellow in fall.

FLOWERS AND FRUIT: Like most ash trees, blue ash is dioecious. While some sources report otherwise, I have seen no monoecious trees during several decades of observing this species. The flowers and fruits are similar to those of white ash, but the seeds have much broader wings.

BEST SEASONS: FALL (for the clear yellow color). SUMMER (for the welcome shade of its blue-green foliage). WINTER (for its nice gray bark and the interesting square detail of its twigs).

NATIVE AND ADAPTIVE RANGE: Blue ash is found in high pH soils from western Ohio and northwestern Georgia west into eastern Kansas and Oklahoma. Its northern limit extends throughout Illinois and Indiana, with outlier populations in southern Michigan and extreme southern Ontario. In Canada it is listed as a threatened species. It performs well in cultivation north into USDA zone 4.

CULTURE: This tree tolerates severe drought once established and thrives in soil too alkaline to support most other eastern forest trees. It is frequently found in groves with chinkapin oak (*Quercus muhlenbergii*), hackberry (*Celtis occidentalis*), black walnut (*Juglans nigra*), Kentucky coffeetree (*Gymnocladus dioicus*), and other calciphiles. It transplants easily, like most ash species, and can be grown from fresh seed sown early in fall while the soil is still warm and allowed to stratify naturally over the coming winter. Given rich soil and adequate water, it grows very rapidly. Vigorous young trees grown in full sun develop the most pronounced square twigs and the brightest fall color.

PROBLEMS: Blue ash is subject to most of the same insect and disease problems as white ash (see *Fraxinus americana*) and the other ashes with the exception that it is the most resistant species to ash anthracnose (*Gnomoniella fraxini*). Its limb structure is usually well formed and does not develop the weak crotches and heavy, spreading limbs for which green ash (*F. pennsylvanica*) is notorious.

CULTIVARS: My late friend Joe McDaniel from the University of Illinois selected *Fraxinus quadrangulata* 'Urbana' as a superior tree with whitened bark from an old cultivated specimen he first showed me in 1970, growing near the campus. Almost any random seedling makes a fine specimen.

SIMILAR AND RELATED SPECIES: Lowell ash (***Fraxinus lowellii***) is another species with unusual square twigs. It is an obscure ash, found only in one or two desert canyons in the Southwest, and its adaptability to cultivation remains untested. It is sometimes considered a variety of the single-leaf ash (***F. anomala***), found in the southern Rocky Mountains. Single-leaf ash also has somewhat four-sided twigs, though not as pronounced as those of blue ash. It is our only native ash without compound leaves.

Several other western ash species share the drought tolerance of blue ash, but most are much smaller trees. Velvet ash (***Fraxinus velutina***) is the largest and most often encountered. In the wild it is common in mountain canyons throughout the Southwest. The largest known specimen, found west of our region, in Arizona, is 90 feet (27 m) tall and 5 feet (1.5 m) in diameter. It is

frequently seen in cultivation (often as 'Modesto') north to USDA zone 6. It is a tough, resilient tree with feltlike leaves but suffers its share of borer damage when planted in parking lots and other stressful situations outside its native streamside habitat. Texas ash (***F. texensis***) is similar and is also hardy to USDA zone 6. It has very bright orange or purple fall color and has reportedly grown as tall as 72 feet (21.6 m) in Bandera County, Texas. It is endemic to isolated populations in central Texas and southern Oklahoma. Both velvet ash and Texas ash are very closely related to white ash.

Mexican ash (***Fraxinus berlandieriana***), also called Arizona ash, barely enters our region from Mexico, along the Rio Grande and Gulf Coast. It is widely planted in southern Texas and likely to be seen there in cultivation north through USDA zone 7. Though Mexican ash is

usually a small tree, one specimen in Cameron County, Texas, has reached 65 feet (19.5 m) in height with a massive trunk more than 6 feet (1.8 m) thick. Gregg ash (***F. greggii***) shares the tolerance of blue ash for alkaline soils and seems unique among ashes in its ability to root easily from cuttings. It is a small semievergreen tree found in the wild only in the Rio Grande Valley east of Big Bend

LEFT: Tall, stately form and light-colored bark make blue ash (*Fraxinus quadrangulata*) an attractive tree. BELOW: Seed clusters on a female blue ash. RIGHT: Blue ash is one of our few trees with square twigs.

and on south into Mexico, but it is rated hardy north to USDA zone 7 under cultivation.

Flowering ash (**Fraxinus cuspidata**) is unique among our native ashes. Its fragrant white flowers, similar to those of the related fringe tree (**Chionanthus virginicus**), make the whole tree look covered with snow. Texas tree guru Benny Simpson chose this small species for the cover of his *Field Guide to Texas Trees* (1988), and I know he was as impressed with it as I am. It will grow on most soils, thrives on desert heat, and is hardy north through USDA zone 7.

COMMENTS: Blue ash enjoys its association with the color blue so much that its leaves and bark show a blue tint and even its sap turns blue when exposed to air. Pioneers once used the inner bark to make blue dye. If its square twigs were not so unusual and conspicuous, perhaps it might have been named something like *Fraxinus caerulea* instead of *F. quadrangulata*. Its hard wood is 15 percent more dense than that of green ash (*F. pennsylvanica*) and even heavier than Rocky Mountain maple (*Acer glabrum*) or red oak (*Quercus rubra*). This density, coupled with its better form, is probably what makes blue ash a much stronger tree than green ash.

LEFT: A blue ash (*Fraxinus quadrangulata*) shows its typical branching structure in winter. BELOW: Velvet ash (*Fraxinus velutina*) grows along streams in the Southwest.

Gleditsia triacanthos
HONEYLOCUST

DESCRIPTION: Honeylocust is among our most adaptable and graceful trees, and its cultivars have been popular as street trees for several decades. There is, however, a critical distinction to be made between the typical wild form of this species and its cultivars. While most cultivars are seedless and virtually all are thornless, many wild honeylocusts possess seedpods and thorns. The seedpods are merely inconvenient, presenting a litter problem in the landscape, but the long, needle-sharp trident thorns are the most deadly weapons carried by any temperate-zone tree, capable of puncturing shoes, tractor tires, and anything else without armor plating. The thorns emerge on new twigs with the leaves, but even larger ones up to almost 2 feet (60 cm) long, with multiple points, sprout annually in red clusters directly from the lower trunk, forming downward-pointing pickets that convincingly discourage tree climbers. Old thorns turn brown, then weather to gray, but persist for decades.

The arching form and fernlike foliage of honeylocust would make it seem at home with the acacias of tropical Africa, to which it is related. But in the temperate forests of North America it has no aesthetic equivalent. The loftiest specimens usually grow in floodplain forests, with one in Wayne County, Michigan, standing 115 feet (34.5 m) tall above a trunk nearly 6 feet (1.8 m) through.

LEAVES: The feathery compound leaves of this species and its close relatives are unlike those of any other native tree. The slender leaflets are about 1 inch (2.5 cm) long and are usually pinnately compound on old trees but bipinnately compound on vigorous young trees. They turn a clear yellow in fall.

FLOWERS AND FRUIT: Staminate and pistillate flowers generally develop separately but on the same tree and are not conspicuous. Seedless trees can be grown by grafting or rooting branches that bear only male flowers, even though other branches on the same tree might bear female flowers. Pistillate flowers grow into curved brown legume pods sometimes 18 inches (45 cm) in length, with hard seeds embedded in a sweet, sticky matrix that is eaten by foxes, squirrels, and livestock.

BEST SEASONS: SUMMER (the feathery grace and filtered shade of this tree are unique in our area). FALL (the yellow color of some selections shows well against the dark bark, and the maturing pods of fruitful forms are colorful, conspicuous, and attractive). WINTER (for wild trees with thorns and seedpods, which combine to make a riveting, bristly silhouette).

NATIVE AND ADAPTIVE RANGE: Honeylocust is commonly found from central Pennsylvania and southeastern South Dakota down to New Orleans and Dallas. I have seen outlying natural populations near London, Ontario, and in the Sierra Chiquita mountains in Tamaulipas, Mexico. Provenance is critical with such a wide-ranging species, especially one with the broad genetic variation of honeylocust; Mexican seed should not be planted in Canada, just as Canadian seed should not be planted in Mexico. But with proper attention to seed source, honeylocust can be grown in suitable sites throughout our area north into USDA zone 3.

CULTURE: Honeylocust grows well under a variety of conditions but prefers moist, deep, well-drained soil. It must have full sun but is remarkably tolerant of urban conditions, alkaline soil, drought, road salt, heat, and compacted soils. On marginal sites at the edge of its range, this species sometimes remains a large shrub.

Thorny wild trees are obviously impervious to grazing animals (as well as to climbing children). They are frequently the first trees to appear in an overgrazed pasture, spread by horses and cattle that eat the fallen pods but pass the seeds intact. Under heavy browsing pressure, nature selects the most forbiddingly thorny seedlings to survive, and an old pasture full of such trees becomes impenetrable.

It is very easy to transplant honeylocust at any size, and it can be propagated from seed (thornless forms come true about 50 percent of the time) or by grafting (use scionwood from a male branch of a thornless tree). It casts a light shade amenable to turf growth and does not deplete the soil, so it is generally a desirable lawn

RIGHT: Honeylocust (*Gleditsia triacanthos*) usually develops a nice fall color.

tree, but it sometimes forms knobby surface roots that can interfere with mowing or fracture pavement.

PROBLEMS: Thorny trees, and to a lesser extent seed-bearing trees, may be inappropriate for domestic landscapes, although they can be picturesque in rural settings where these traits do not constitute a problem. Mature trees can be trimmed of their lower trunk thorns annually if they pose a hazard. This is most easily and safely done in early summer, before the supple new thorns harden into weapons-grade devices of mass destruction. Many cultivars have been selected to eliminate these concerns.

Honeylocust is resistant to many of our most troublesome defoliating insects, including Gypsy moth (*Lymantria dispar*), but the mimosa webworm (*Homadaula anisocentra*) is a serious pest in the South, sometimes stripping away almost every morsel of foliage. Spider mites (*Platytetranychus multidigituli*) sometimes cause serious damage in dry years, and the fungus canker *Thyronectria austro-americana* is a problem on some trees. The same fungus causes a vascular wilt disease in the related Japanese honeylocust (*Gleditsia japonica*), which is occasionally seen in cultivation. Knot galls caused by *Pseudomonas* bacteria should be removed before they become systemic and kill the tree.

CULTIVARS: Honeylocust trees vary in the size and

BELOW: Honeylocust (*Gleditsia triacanthos*) is a popular shade tree in North America. RIGHT: The open, spreading form of honeylocust shows well in winter.

number of their thorns, and cultivars selected from thornless trees make safe and desirable lawn trees. The tall, elmlike 'Moraine' was the first popular selection, patented in 1949, and remains one of the best. It became popular during the initial Dutch elm disease epidemic of the 1960s as a replacement for dying American elms (*Ulmus americana*). 'Shademaster' (another old, reliable, elmlike selection), 'Emerald Lace', 'Fairview', 'Summer Lace', 'True-Shade', 'Majestic', and a honeylocust trademarked as Perfection are among the other most popular selections. 'Sunburst' has early yellow foliage but is not as vigorous as some others, and 'Spectrum' is a newer selection with yellow tips. 'Rubylace' has attractive red young foliage but poor branching structure.

'Maxwell' is an artistic, picturesque tree that is very

cold hardy, and 'Northern Acclaim' is a new cultivar selected by Dale Herman at North Dakota State University for its exceptional cold hardiness. 'Green Glory' and 'Skyline' are large, well-formed trees with good central leaders. 'Halka' is a strong, vigorous tree but is not completely seedless. 'Imperial' is a small, compact tree that also bears a few seeds. 'Bujotii' is a weeping form, and 'Elegantissima' is compact. 'Millwood', offered by my friend Ken Asmus at his nursery in Michigan, is a heavily fruiting form selected for production of especially sweet pods for livestock feed.

SIMILAR AND RELATED SPECIES: Water locust (***Gleditsia aquatica***) is a smaller, swamp-loving species. It has smaller leaves that are not bipinnate, with miniature seedpods and shorter, though even more numerous,

thorns. The two species occasionally interbreed, forming Texas honeylocust (**G. ×texana**). Water locust offers little advantage over honeylocust except as a source of genetic diversity, but it would make a formidable hedge plant.

At least ten other species of honeylocust occur in other parts of the world. Some are hardy in North America, but few are commonly seen. They all look very much like *Gleditsia triacanthos*.

COMMENTS: Honeylocust has been so popular in recent decades that many people have grown bored with it. This is unfortunate because it remains an attractive, adaptable shade tree. It attracts many colorful butterflies including the silver-spotted skipper, the iridescent honeylocust moth, the moon-lined moth, and the tiny orange-wing.

The huge, branched thorns of wild trees are used by shrikes to hold their prey and by unknown, ungodly spirits to puncture car tires. New thorns formed on the trunk each year are bloody red, as if in warning. Many campers have undoubtedly dreamt of being chased by a formidable predator of some kind, with the only possible escape being to climb a thorny locust tree.

The ripening seedpods add additional color and, later, winter interest, as they rattle and clack in the wind. Many of the honeylocusts I have seen planted in the parks of Europe appear to have been derived from a type with seedpods that develop a striking racing stripe down their back edge as they ripen. These pods add greatly to the aesthetic value of the tree in areas where the litter is not a concern, something our European friends seem to have learned to appreciate much more quickly than we have. The large pods probably evolved to attract large prehistoric mammals like mastodons, which could eat them whole and distribute the seed. Beasts of the Ice Age are gone now, of course, but the honeylocust seems perfectly capable of perpetuating itself through livestock.

BELOW: The decorative but messy seedpods of honeylocust (*Gleditsia triacanthos*). RIGHT: Honeylocusts may be either thorny or thornless.

Gordonia lasianthus

LOBLOLLY-BAY

DESCRIPTION: Loblolly-bay is a splendid, slender, flowering tree with evergreen leaves. Its ultimate size depends upon soil moisture. It usually grows rather slowly, but it can reach well into the forest canopy on favorable soils when crowded by surrounding trees. The largest loblolly-bay on record, in the Ocala National Forest in Florida, is 94 feet (28.2 m) tall with a 30-inch (75-cm) trunk. Smaller—but striking—specimens, clothed to the base with leaves and flowers, grow on swamp hummocks and shoreline areas around the eastern edge of Okefenokee National Wildlife Refuge in southern Georgia.

LEAVES: The evergreen leaves are leathery and deep green, around 5 inches (12.5 cm) long by less than half as wide. The upper surfaces are textured with indented veins. At the northern limit of its range, loblolly-bay becomes partially deciduous, like sweetbay (*Magnolia virginiana*), which it resembles and with which it often grows.

FLOWERS AND FRUIT: Loblolly-bay bears silky white flowers much like those of its close relatives, the camellias. They reach 3 inches (7.5 cm) across and are very fragrant. The flowers occur singly in leaf axils but are concentrated at the branch tips, giving the appearance of clusters. The individual cup-shaped flowers on each twig open one at a time, thus prolonging the attractive blooming period from late spring throughout the following summer.

The woody fruits that follow are shaped like little green tulips with sharp-pointed divisions. They turn brown in fall and split open gradually throughout the winter to release small winged seeds.

BEST SEASONS: SUMMER (as the fat, erect flower buds swell and open progressively through each cluster). WINTER (the evergreen foliage is especially handsome on windy days, when the pale undersides turn up, and the trees are very conspicuous after nearby deciduous trees drop their own leaves).

NATIVE AND ADAPTIVE RANGE: Loblolly-bay is a southern coastal tree of swamps, bays, and bayous. It ranges from southern Mississippi around the southeastern fringe of the United States up to Albemarle Sound in North Carolina, extending inland as far as Augusta, Georgia. It is hardier than most broadleaved evergreen trees and can be grown in protected areas with suitable soil north partway into USDA zone 7.

CULTURE: For a swamp tree, loblolly-bay is surprisingly tolerant of dry, sandy soil, in which it sometimes grows in the wild as a large shrub. It does best under cultivation in full sun where ample moisture is available. A high water table with occasional standing water suits it just fine, and acidic, sandy soil with a high organic content is the substrate of choice in the wild.

Few gardeners have wetland habitats in their home landscapes, but loblolly-bay can be grown under mesic conditions if mulched heavily with pulverized pine bark and watered during dry spells. It should be protected from wind exposure and direct sun during winter along its northern limits. In order to keep its evergreen leaves from dehydrating in cold climates, it might be planted over a warm utility tunnel or adjacent to a heated basement, where the soil around its roots will not freeze.

This tree is not particularly easy to transplant, but new plants may be propagated from seed or, with luck, from softwood cuttings. Gather seedpods in late summer, when the capsules show signs of splitting down the sutures. Dry the capsules in a paper bag until they open, and then immediately sow the seeds outdoors in sandy potting soil. Some seedlings will begin to emerge by warm weather the following year, and the remaining seeds will sprout a year or more later. Small container-grown plants are easy to establish if watered frequently the first year, and stump sprouts will develop readily to replace cut or broken stems.

PROBLEMS: Loblolly-bay has few insect or disease problems, but it can be finicky and short lived under cultivation unless its natural habitat conditions are closely duplicated. On upland sites it is sometimes killed by root nematodes. Its leaves can become scorched and discolored if it is planted in full sun without adequate mulch to keep the roots cool and moist. Prior to planting, amend clay soils throughout the planting area with generous amounts of gritty sand, pine bark, and sphagnum

peat moss to prevent root problems. The most significant limitation of loblolly-bay in the North is its lack of winter hardiness, but it will nonetheless grow further north than many other broadleaved evergreen trees.

CULTIVARS: No cultivars of this species are recorded. It seems to vary in size and shape due more to habitat conditions than to genetic makeup. I suspect that provenance might influence winter hardiness, as is the case with sweetbay (*Magnolia virginiana*) and other similar southern trees.

SIMILAR AND RELATED SPECIES: There are about

LEFT: Loblolly-bay (*Gordonia lasianthus*) becomes a tall, pyramidal tree at maturity. Photo by Jim Wilson. BELOW: A grove of mature loblolly-bay. Photo by Ron Lance. RIGHT: The beautiful flower of loblolly-bay. Photo by Jim Wilson.

thirty more species of *Gordonia* in Asia. Loblolly-bay has been upstaged in North American nurseries by its closest relative, the deciduous Franklin-tree (**Franklinia alatamaha**), which has a fascinating history. It became extinct in the wild shortly after it was brought into cultivation by William Bartram in the 1770s. The only known wild population, near Fort Barrington along the Altamaha River in Georgia, was never rediscovered after 1803 and is presumed to have been extirpated. A worldwide survey conducted in 1999 identified 2046 surviving Franklin-trees, all descended from the original Bartram collection. It does not grow as large as loblolly-bay and is not evergreen, but it has similar flowers, good fall color, and can be grown north through USDA zone 6 or, in protected areas, zone 5. Seeds germinate readily when extracted from the accordion-folded pods and planted in fall.

Franklin-tree is an irregularly shaped small tree with sympodial branching reminiscent of sassafras (*Sassafras albidum*). When in bloom it can be the focus of the landscape, but during the rest of the year it melts into the background (so much so that if there really are any plants left hiding out in the wild they might easily go unnoticed). It likes the same sandy, organic soil conditions as loblolly-bay, with the exception that it must have perfect drainage. Hybrids of the two species have been produced, and such work might lead to cultivar development for improved hardiness or other horticultural qualities.

Franklin-tree doesn't seem to survive on old cotton land. Its disappearance from its native habitat began at about the same time that cotton cultivation was introduced to the Altamaha Valley region, where this obscure tree was discovered and last seen in the wild. Some people thus speculate, reasonably in my view, that cotton may be a host or carrier species for some fungus or virus disease that is fatal to *Franklinia*. If that disease could be identified and treated, perhaps *Franklinia* might once again reclaim some of its former habitat; but unlike some large tree species of commercial importance for timber or nut production, there is no economic incentive for anyone to explore such research on behalf of the little Franklin-tree.

The largest known Franklin-tree can be seen in Wyndmoor, Montgomery County, Pennsylvania, far north of its historic range. It is a sprawling tree 37 feet (11.1 m) tall and about 2 feet (60 cm) in diameter below the fork at its base.

Stewartias are similar and also related, as are the Asian gardenias and camellias. There are two shrubby native stewartias, the mountain stewartia (**Stewartia ovata**), which can become a small tree and is hardy to USDA zone 5, and the silky stewartia (**S. malacodendron**), which is not much hardier than loblolly-bay. A closely related Asian tree, **Camellia sinensis,** is a commercial source of tea.

COMMENTS: Loblolly-bay frequently grows with swamp cyrilla (*Cyrilla racemiflora*) and pond pine (*Pinus serotina*) in or near water, and with sweetbay (*Magnolia virginiana*) on slightly higher moist soils. Seed could be gathered in such areas, but I don't recommend trying to collect seedlings from wild populations, as seedlings of this tree can be found at specialty nurseries.

If you are too impatient to begin with such small plants or with seed, or if your thumbs are not sufficiently green to satisfy loblolly-bay's rather precise growing requirements, you would do well to visit it in its native habitat or in a botanical garden. The trip will be a memorable experience if you appreciate beautiful trees. And if you live too far north of this southern swamp delicacy, you can always check out the beautiful and historic Franklin-tree.

LEFT: Silky stewartia (*Stewartia malacodendron*) has flowers similar to those of loblolly-bay (*Gordonia lasianthus*). Photo by Ron Lance.

Gymnocladus dioicus
KENTUCKY COFFEETREE

DESCRIPTION: This tree has a wide range, but nowhere is it common. It has been designated the state tree of Kentucky more because of its common name than because of any supposed predominance in the local landscape, although it does reach its best growth there. Still, the U.S. national champion tree is in Lake County, Ohio. It is 92 feet (27.6 m) tall and more than 5 feet (1.5 m) thick. Apparently hedging their bets, Kentuckians also claim tuliptree (*Liriodendron tulipifera*) as their state tree.

Kentucky coffeetrees occur most often as widely dispersed individuals or in small clonal groups with all individuals connected as sprouts from a common root system. They can be found occasionally on rocky hillsides and coves or in limestone woods with blue ash (*Fraxinus quadrangulata*), but are more commonly seen scattered in river valleys and floodplain terraces.

LEAVES: The leaves are bipinnate, with leaflets arranged like feathers on branched rachises. While the leaflets seldom exceed 2 inches (5 cm), a complete compound leaf assembly can grow to 36 inches (90 cm), giving the tree a ferny demeanor when in full foliage. Leaves of this tree are among the very last to emerge in spring, and therefore they avoid spring frosts. Their absence in early spring allows the warming sun to reach wildflowers or turf on the ground below. Even when fully developed, Kentucky coffeetree leaves cast a very light shade. They emerge reddish, fade to green as they enlarge, and normally turn a nice yellow early in fall. Some trees develop scarlet rachises that cling longer than the leaflets and offer a two-stage color effect.

FLOWERS AND FRUIT: Kentucky coffeetree is typically dioecious. Where clonal groves have developed, an entire grove will be the same gender. The flowers occur in long terminal clusters in late spring. The clusters, or panicles, of male trees are about 3 inches (7.5 cm) long, but those on female trees reach nearly 12 inches (30 cm) in length and become pleasantly fragrant as they open.

The flowers are not conspicuous because they become lost amid the fine texture of the new foliage.

Female trees bear the seedpods (although not every year) that mark them as members of the legume family. Some pods will already be forming while flowers on the same panicles are still blooming. The pods become stouter, but shorter and straighter, than those of honeylocust (*Gleditsia triacanthos*). They are heavy and hard, almost woody, and filled with a gooey pulp surrounding several smooth, stony, marble-sized seeds.

Many pods persist through winter, adding interest to the dormant landscape. The seeds have been roasted as a coffee substitute, hence the name, but they contain cytisine and are toxic when raw. Animals must sense this, or perhaps they are thwarted by the hard seed coat, since none seem to feast on Kentucky coffee beans.

BEST SEASONS: FALL (when the gray bark, yellow leaflets, red leafstalks, and dark purple fruit are visible together). WINTER (with snow dusting the coarse, dramatic branching and shaggy bark, and pods clinging on female trees). SPRING (when the pinkish new leaves begin to emerge) and SUMMER (as the fine-textured foliage converts the heavy-twigged tree to a ferny appearance).

NATIVE AND ADAPTIVE RANGE: Isolated wild populations of Kentucky coffeetree can be found in the vicinity of Lake St. Clair in southern Ontario, where it is listed by the Canadian government as a threatened species. From there it ranges westward to the upper Mississippi River valley in southern Minnesota and the Missouri River valley in southeastern South Dakota, through northern Oklahoma and down the Ohio and lower Mississippi Rivers to central Arkansas. It can be found locally in the Finger Lakes area of New York and in Pennsylvania, West Virginia, and Tennessee, and it has spread from cultivation elsewhere. It does nicely under cultivation in USDA zone 3, and healthy planted trees can be found in Ottawa.

CULTURE: Kentucky coffeetree can be tricky to transplant, and establishes slowly. The root system is deep and sometimes seems as coarse as the branches. Many wild saplings originated as root suckers and are harder than seed-grown trees to dig. Scarified seed will start easily, and trees of known gender can be propagated from suckers or root cuttings.

Young trees remain almost devoid of branching until they reach nearly the diameter of a baseball bat, and it takes a little faith in the future to believe that such an ungainly sapling will ever amount to much. But with sufficient sunlight, ample moisture, and a deep, rich alluvial soil, such faith will eventually be rewarded with a vigorous, well-formed tree.

PROBLEMS: Once established, Kentucky coffeetree is bothered little by heat, cold, road salt, insects, disease, or drought. Though it is rather slow growing, it is not strong wooded; and yet its branching is so coarse that it escapes damage from ice accumulation because the ice has so little surface area to cling to. It likes full sun and is more tolerant of alkaline soils than many trees, though less tolerant of acidic ones.

Its light, filtered shade encourages healthy turf under its canopy. Occasional root suckers in lawn areas should be pulled, and trees in manicured lawns should be expected to require repeated raking to gather the leaflets, stalks, and pods, all of which fall at different times.

CULTIVARS: Kentucky coffeetree selections should be made for trees with superior growth rate, form, fall color, and known gender. 'Stately Manor' is a hardy male selection with a narrow, upright habit propagated from a cultivated tree in Minnesota. 'Espresso' is a broadly spreading male clone. Chicagoland Grows is evaluating at least one other potential male cultivar, and a variegated selection can be found growing at Kew Gardens in England.

SIMILAR AND RELATED SPECIES: One other *Gymnocladus* species grows in China. False indigo (***Amorpha fruticosa***) is another woody legume, at the opposite end of the tree-size scale. Forming an open, tall shrub in the wild, it occasionally reaches treelike proportions. It grows in stream valleys and exposed sites throughout the eastern United States from Minnesota south and east and is hardy north into USDA zone 4. Its spicy-smelling compound leaves and unusual spikes of purple and orange flowers give it up-close appeal in the landscape. Ornamental cultivars include the white-flowered 'Albiflora' and the blue-flowered 'Coerulea', as well as 'Crispa', 'Dark Lance', 'Lewisii', and 'Pendula'. False indigo thrives in almost any soil, even in sterile quarries

LEFT: Fall color on an old Kentucky coffeetree (*Gymnocladus dioicus*). TOP RIGHT: Heavy fruit pods developing on a female Kentucky coffeetree. RIGHT: The red rachis color of Kentucky coffeetree often holds after the yellow leaflets fall.

and strip-mined lands, but needs full sunlight and judicious pruning to develop into an attractive specimen. It grows easily and quickly from seed and volunteers freely if soil conditions are to its liking.

Kentucky coffeetree is also related to woody legumes such as the locusts (*Gleditsia* and *Robinia*), redbuds (*Cercis*), and mesquites (*Prosopis*).

COMMENTS: The satin-smooth seeds of this tree make wonderful lucky charms or worry stones to carry in your pocket. They are smaller and much more durable than "lucky buckeyes" (*Aesculus* nuts), which traditionally assume such a role, but are equally toxic if eaten. They have also served successive generations as superior slingshot ammunition, for children so inclined, and can be drilled and strung as beads that cluck like stones as they bounce against one another.

A magnificent old Kentucky coffeetree specimen still grows in Chancellorsville, Virginia, at the site where it shaded the grave of General Thomas "Stonewall" Jackson's amputated arm, buried there following a battle in 1863. Four others, planted by George Washington, can be seen at his former homesite in Alexandria, Virginia.

There is cause to wonder about the widely scattered populations of this species. Kentucky coffeetree is not dying out from portions of its range, yet it has jumped entire states in seeking islands of preferred habitat. The seeds do not seem to be sought and spread afar by birds, nor can they be carried by wind, so how has this tree spread in such a checkerboard pattern? And will it someday fill the gaps it has missed?

We could speculate that gomphotheres, the giant mammals that became extinct at the end of the last ice age some ten thousand years ago, fed upon the sweet pods, swallowing them whole and later depositing the hard seeds intact into new areas during their migrations. Or we might choose to believe that Native Americans, themselves fond of the pulp in the pods, carried the

durable seeds to new locations, thus conjuring up visions of a prehistoric "Johnny Coffeeseed." Many seemingly natural groves of this tree in the northeastern part of its range are actually associated with known prehistoric village sites.

If such were the vectors upon which it originally depended, Kentucky coffeetree now seems doomed to maintain its checkerboard existence in the wild. Perhaps the island effect of its patchy distribution, which prohibits genetic exchange between distant populations, will cause it to evolve into regionally adapted forms or subspecies, further enriching its diversity and usefulness for horticultural purposes.

LEFT: The picturesque branching of a mature Kentucky coffeetree (*Gymnocladus dioicus*). RIGHT: Flower spikes on a false indigo (*Amorpha fruticosa*) at Starhill Forest.

Halesia tetraptera

SILVERBELL

DESCRIPTION: Silverbell (*Halesia tetraptera*, syn. *H. carolina*) is not a common tree but is normally found in abundance in the localities where it grows. It exists in several forms, varieties, or species, depending upon the taxonomic authority consulted, ranging from large shrubs to slim trees that reach well into the forest canopy.

It makes its best growth in cove forests and moist slopes of the southern Appalachians. The biggest of many large specimens in the Great Smoky Mountains in Tennessee is 110 feet (33 m) tall and more than 4 feet (1.2 m) in diameter. Even trees of this size retain the attractive bark pattern—whitened furrows between gray-brown plates—characteristic of the genus.

LEAVES: Silverbell leaves may grow as much as 6 inches (15 cm) in length by about half as wide. They are usually free from insect damage and maintain a bright green color until late summer, when they fade to yellow or, in drought years, fall without noticeable coloration.

FLOWERS AND FRUIT: The flowers are sensational, usually reaching their peak bloom around Arbor Day, when we all should be thinking about trees anyway. They are a pure snow-white, sometimes with a touch of pink, up to 1 inch (2.5 cm) long, and hang like bells in clusters from the twigs. Flowers of all *Halesia* species and forms are similar. The fruits are slender, winged drupes up to 2 inches (5 cm) long. Those of *H. tetraptera* and its forms have four wings, while those of the related two-winged silverbell (*H. diptera*) have only two. The tan fruits are not used significantly by wildlife, although some rodents will gnaw through them, but they make an interesting fall display.

BEST SEASONS: SPRING (the flower display is the primary aesthetic feature of this tree). WINTER (for the striped bark and, in early winter, the clinging fruit).

NATIVE AND ADAPTIVE RANGE: The typical form, known as Carolina silverbell, has a spotty range centering upon the southern Appalachians. Outlying populations occur in the Ozark Plateau of Missouri, Arkansas, and Oklahoma, the Shawnee Hills of southern Illinois, and scattered locations north, east, and south of the primary range, from the Ohio River valley to northern Florida.

The two-winged silverbell (*Halesia diptera*) is confined to the Gulf Coastal Plain, and the impressive mountain form, sometimes separated taxonomically as *H. monticola*, is more narrowly restricted to the higher mountains of Tennessee and North Carolina. All silverbells are adaptable under cultivation far beyond their natural range, and *H. tetraptera* and *H. monticola* are fully hardy in USDA zone 5.

CULTURE: Silverbells are tolerant of most moderate conditions, and of sun or shade, but are sensitive to drought, salt, and alkaline soil. They grow moderately quickly and do best in a moist organic loam, with their roots in the cool shade and their leaves exposed to partial or full sun. They are not subject to serious insect or disease problems, but some of the outlying natural populations show the effects of environmental stress, so the natural range may be shrinking.

They are easy to transplant and can be grown readily from seed as long as you don't mind stratifying it or waiting two years for it to sprout. Seedlings frequently volunteer into mulched planting beds under favorable growing conditions, and collecting them can provide a head start for the propagator. Young trees also sprout promptly from the stump if cut, and these sprouts can be stool-layered to propagate more trees.

PROBLEMS: The wood is somewhat brittle, but I have not noticed many trees with major storm damage. Insects and diseases seem to avoid silverbells.

CULTIVARS: The dwarf form 'Meehanii', reportedly even more striking in bloom than the species, is available from a few nurseries. 'Wedding Bells' is a recent introduction from the University of Connecticut with extra large flowers. There are several pink-flowering selections, collectively listed as *H. tetraptera* var. *rosea* or *H. tetraptera* 'Rosea'.

SIMILAR AND RELATED SPECIES: I have been very impressed with **Halesia monticola**, considered a variety by many authorities. Known as the mountain silverbell, it is

RIGHT: The U.S. national champion two-winged silverbell (*Halesia diptera*).

larger, more erect, and more dramatic in all aspects than any other *Halesia* species or variety. I have grown *H. monticola* var. *vestita* from seed collected at the Washington Park Arboretum in Seattle, and I am delighted with the vigor, erect stature, and large flowers of this selection. Occasional pink-flowered forms, such as *H. monticola* 'Arnold Pink' from the Arnold Arboretum, are also seen.

The smaller two-winged silverbell (***Halesia diptera***) has fruits with two broad wings instead of four narrow ones. It has a reputation for being more sparse of bloom, with the exception of variety *magniflora*, which is vigorous, heavy blooming, and more tolerant of dry sites than other silverbells. The U.S. national champion two-winged silverbell, in Cincinnati's Spring Grove Cemetery Arboretum, is a fine tree standing 42 feet (12.6 m) tall with a double stem. Another small species, **H. parviflora**, is confined to the Gulf Coastal Plain, and an additional species is found in China.

Snowbells (***Styrax***) are shrubby relatives of the silverbells. The most common native species is **S. americanus**, a large shrub of rich woods and swamps. **S. grandifolius** is a more robust version, and **S. japonicus** is one of several small Asian trees found commonly in cultivation in mild climates.

COMMENTS: Blooming silverbell groves that overhang mountain roads provide quite a spring spectacle. I have often felt compelled to turn into every overlook parking area along the Blue Ridge Parkway during the silverbell bloom to observe the drifts of white flowers that cover the wooded slopes like snow. Few trees match the beauty of these trees at peak bloom.

Silverbells are distributed widely by nurseries for lawn trees, but they need mulching to thrive and maintain good foliage color during dry weather. Where summer moisture is adequate, creative landscape design might place this tree in a position where its flowers will be viewed from below (just above eye level) and over a lawn, so that the spent flowers, which fall intact and lodge in the turf facing up, provide a second show at ground level.

Silverbell was a favorite of the famous naturalist-landscape architect Jens Jensen, who established a grove of them in the Abraham Lincoln Memorial Garden in Lincoln's hometown of Springfield, Illinois, during the 1930s. This large, lakeside natural garden is Jensen's most famous design. He would undoubtedly be delighted if he were able to hike through it now and see how prolifically those original silverbell plants have reproduced, even though the soil and climate are not ideal for the species.

TOP LEFT: The bell-shaped flowers of a slightly pink silverbell (*Halesia tetraptera*). LEFT: Silverbell bark displays light-colored stripes as it expands with growth.

Hamamelis virginiana

WITCH HAZEL

DESCRIPTION: Witch hazel is not a true hazel (*Corylus*), and it's certainly not a witch. It is a superior ornamental species that inhabits stream banks and the moist understories of open, rocky, or sandy mesic forests. Witch hazel usually brings to mind the term "shrub," yet this species can be more of a tree than many of the exotic small ornamentals sold as trees by nurseries. It does develop a multiple-stemmed structure, but the primary stems continue to mature into a clump of small tree trunks over time.

If you look out a second-story window at yellow flowers held at eye level by tall witch hazels with stems nearly 6 inches (15 cm) in diameter, "tree" certainly seems to be the correct call. If there is any doubt, you need only visit the U.S. national champion witch hazel in Bedford, Virginia, which stands 35 feet (10.5 m) tall with a trunk 16 inches (40 cm) in diameter.

LEAVES: The leaves of witch hazel emerge with a reddish tinge, especially when exposed to full sun, turning lettuce-green as they mature. They can reach 6 inches (15 cm) in length but are usually shorter, become more than half as broad, and have scalloped margins. The leaves on my trees are thinly traced with a hairline edge of lighter green that outlines each leaf against the darker body of the one behind it. Witch hazel leaves maintain a thick, rich, almost succulent consistency into fall, when they turn gold. They may or may not drop before the tree comes into peak bloom in fall.

FLOWERS AND FRUIT: No other hardy woody plant, native or exotic, can match the flower display of witch hazel, and this is because of its timing. In fall, after the leaves have colored and are beginning to drop, spicy-scented flowers up to nearly 1 inch (2.5 cm) across appear like glowing four-legged spiders climbing up and down the twigs. Some trees bloom early, and their flowers are mostly hidden among the leaves; but many flower later or drop their leaves earlier. These latter types provide the best floral display, which is also the last of the season, continuing even as snow starts to fly across the North. When seen against a dark backdrop or a bright blue sky, the flowers are an effective postponement of the inevitable winter. On very cold days they simply curl and hide, flaring open again when it warms up. They make a great combination with the ripe fruits of wahoo (*Euonymus atropurpureus*) or a deciduous holly (*Ilex*).

The fruits are small pods, and the ones from the previous year ripen just as the current year's flowers open. The pods explode open to scatter their little black seeds, and if you step too close to sniff the fragrant blooms you may get shot by the seeds, which are about the size of BBs. They are ejected with considerable force, sometimes landing several yards away. Keeping this in mind, remove the seedpods if you want to harvest blooming branches for an indoor display.

BEST SEASONS: EARLY FALL (for the foliage color) and LATE FALL (for the flowers, which will bloom right through a Thanksgiving blizzard).

NATIVE AND ADAPTIVE RANGE: Witch hazel grows in suitable habitats from Nova Scotia and Quebec City west through southern Ontario, lower Michigan, and the southern half of Wisconsin, then south through the eastern states to Florida and west into Texas. It is hardy north into USDA zone 3.

CULTURE: Witch hazel naturally selects shady sites in the wild but will only become a full, symmetrical specimen in full sun. Without shade it needs some protection from severe drought and heat. It can be slow to recover from transplanting when moved in large sizes and is best handled as a small field-grown or container-grown plant. Selected types can be propagated by layering or rooted from cuttings, although it takes a pretty green thumb.

Gather the seedpods in the fall before they open and place them in a closed paper bag until they pop and the seeds fly out. (This can sound a little like microwave popcorn if you happen to hear one pop.) Seeds should be sown outdoors in fall and may take either one or two years to germinate.

PROBLEMS: In areas prone to infestation by Gypsy moth (*Lymantria dispar*), witch hazels are among the first plants to be defoliated. Elsewhere, as long as they are planted where they can avoid severe drought, heat reflection, and sunscald, they have few serious problems. They are an alternate host for birch gall aphids (*Horma-*

phis hamamelidis and *H. cornu*), which make galls on the leaves and then send forth a second generation to feed on birch trees (*Betula*), but this is more of a curiosity than a problem.

CULTIVARS: Flowering qualities such as size, color, density, and seasonal timing are quite variable. Nearly every horticulturist who has studied witch hazel recommends that superior selections be propagated and marketed, yet nobody seems willing to start. The red-flowering 'Rubescens' is listed in the literature, and geographic varieties or races are separated by some taxonomists. Some southern forms tend to be marcescent. The most ornamental northern specimens hold their blooms long after the leaves have fallen. Such special trees can be found occasionally in horticultural collections, including my own at Starhill Forest.

SIMILAR AND RELATED SPECIES: The large-leaved

LEFT: A witch hazel (*Hamamelis virginiana*) blooming in its natural habitat. BELOW: The spiderlike flowers of witch hazel.

witch hazel (**Hamamelis macrophylla**) is essentially a robust southern cousin of our common species and is considered by some experts to be a variety. There is reportedly a white-flowering species from northern Mexico, **H. mexicana,** that blooms in summer, but I have not seen it.

Ozark witch hazel (**Hamamelis vernalis**), also called vernal witch hazel, frequently grows on the banks of small streams, where its pliable wood springs back easily after being flattened by flash floods. It blooms in late winter with the more commonly cultivated Asian species and their hybrids. It is usually more shrubby than tree-like, but I have one in our collection that is approaching 18 feet (5.4 m) tall and I have seen a few in the Ozarks with substantial trunks. There are at least a dozen named selections of Ozark witch hazel, including 'Autumn Embers', 'Carnea', 'Christmas Cheer', 'Red Imp', and 'Sandra', many of which have abundant flowers of varying shades of yellow and orange. Because this smaller species blooms in late winter after the leaves are gone, phenology is not such a concern in making selections. The Ozark witch hazel in our arboretum has darker foli-

age without the pale outline or the red tint on new leaves. It is more restricted in range than our common native species, growing naturally only in the Ozark Plateau of Missouri and Arkansas, but is widely cultivated and nearly as hardy. It is also reportedly more tolerant of alkaline soil and easier to root from cuttings.

Japanese witch hazel (**Hamamelis japonica**) and Chinese witch hazel (**H. mollis**) are seen more commonly in cultivation, as are many hybrid selections.

COMMENTS: Witch hazel has a rich ethnobotanical heritage as a medicinal plant. It has been used as a treatment for eye irritations, a wound dressing, and even an aftershave. The name "witch" supposedly grew out of the old English *wych*, meaning "pliable," and this description does fit the species. However, a forked stem of witch hazel, one that grows erect with one branch pointed north and the other south, is also a traditional tool for divining, or witching, water wells. Few people admit to taking this procedure seriously, yet many testify to the uncanny luck of a dowser who walked their property and advised sinking a well in a particular spot, with good results.

Those who live in cities, where water simply flows from the tap, may never know the throbbing, irresistible pull of a good witching stick when it is passed over hidden intersecting veins of groundwater. The eerie pull of the stick, which seems to come to life in the hands, cannot be ignored if the dowser happens to have "the gift."

Of course, I don't personally believe in such a phenomenon. Certainly not . . .

TOP LEFT: Foliage of Ozark witch hazel (*Hamamelis vernalis*). LEFT: Flowers and fruits of Ozark witch hazel.

Ilex opaca

AMERICAN HOLLY

DESCRIPTION: Many people who admire sprigs of holly during winter are not aware that these exotic-looking holiday decorations come from a fine native tree species. American holly is a deep-woods understory or midstory tree in the southeastern United States, and the state tree of Delaware. Seen often as a lawn specimen, holly is more at home in moist, open woodlands. Wild specimens typically respond to their shady environment by becoming loose and irregular in form, while cultivated trees in full sun are densely symmetrical. American holly is one of about twenty native hollies, and it's the largest. The U.S. national champion in Chambers County, Alabama, is 76 feet (22.8 m) tall and has a smooth gray trunk more than 3 feet (0.9 m) thick.

LEAVES: The leaves of American holly, though not of all hollies, are fully evergreen. They reach about 3 inches (7.5 cm) in length and are thick and stiff with sharply pointed teeth along the margins. New growth finally pushes off the old leaves in spring.

FLOWERS AND FRUIT: Hollies are dioecious, requiring both male and female plants to produce fruit. The flowers develop in the leaf axils, those on staminate trees being clustered and those on pistillate trees usually being solitary, with neither being very conspicuous. Holly fruits can be the visual focus of the landscape for extended periods in fall and winter. The pea-sized drupes, or holly berries, are borne in great quantities and can be bright red, dark orange, or occasionally yellow. After a hard freeze they become choice winter foods of bluebirds, robins, mockingbirds, cedar waxwings, and many other birds.

BEST SEASONS: FALL and WINTER (when fruits are present on female trees, and for the smooth gray bark). ALL YEAR (if the evergreen foliage is maintained in healthy condition).

NATIVE AND ADAPTIVE RANGE: American holly can be seen in isolated populations around Long Island Sound, south to central Florida, and southwest to east-ern Texas. Hardy selections of American holly will survive north to USDA zone 5. Different cultivars, however, will show considerable variation in hardiness, and locally adapted individuals should be selected when possible.

CULTURE: Most hollies like moist soil, and American holly needs some winter protection for its foliage when planted north of its natural range. Holly can be grown from seeds, but they take two or more years to germinate and grow frustratingly slowly. To gain a head start, try transplanting the volunteer seedlings that can usually be found in the mulch under fruiting American holly females. Rooting American holly from cuttings and layering low branches are the only sure ways to guarantee the desired mix of male and female trees.

PROBLEMS: American holly is frequently planted in areas beyond its adaptive range, where it experiences periodic winter damage. Foliar diseases and the holly leaf miner (*Phytomyza ilicis*) can disfigure the leaves of ornamental specimens. Scale insects of various species damage it as well, and American holly is very slow growing.

Since most hollies are planted for their fruit display, it can be disappointing if the proper mix of compatible male and female plants is not present to ensure fruit set. Seedlings should be planted in large quantities, or cuttings of known sex and similar blooming time obtained, in order to produce the desired result. They don't need to be too close to one another, though, because bees adore holly flowers and will bring pollen from a considerable distance. An old American holly growing at Jim Wilson's Savory Farm in South Carolina is very fruitful without having a staminate tree anywhere within sight.

CULTIVARS: Various sources list from one hundred to more than one thousand American holly cultivars. Many are nearly identical, and it would be impractical to describe them all here, but a few examples are worth mention.

'Amy', 'Cardinal', 'Dauber', 'MacDonald', 'Merry Christmas', and 'Old Heavyberry' (I've always liked that name) are vigorous females with red fruit and are reportedly hardier in the North than most. 'Croonenberg' is slightly monoecious and therefore self-fruitful, making it a good option if you don't have room for a separate male tree. 'Fruitland Nursery', 'Canary', and 'Goldie' are selections from the yellow-fruited *Ilex opaca* f. *xanthocarpa*. For pol-

lination, some attractive male selections include 'Isaiah' and 'Jersey Knight'. One popular large-leaved selection for southern areas, 'Savannah', is a hybrid with another native holly, dahoon (*I. cassine*).

SIMILAR AND RELATED SPECIES: A few other native hollies are hardy tree species. Chief among them is possum haw (**Ilex decidua**), also called deciduous holly, a stiff little clumping tree with sharp spur branches and striking gray bark. In the Congaree Swamp of South Carolina, one possum haw reaches 42 feet (12.6 m) in height

LEFT: An ancient American holly (*Ilex opaca*) at the home of President Andrew Jackson. BELOW: An American holly pruned to an open branching structure. RIGHT: Fruits on a female American holly.

with its largest stem 1 foot (30 cm) in diameter. Winter-berry (*I. verticillata*) is a similar species that can become a small tree, especially in the southern part of its range. Specimens up to 20 feet (6 m) can be found in Shenan-doah National Park. Possum haw and winterberry are quite comfortable in the understories of swamp forests and tolerate poorly drained, flooded sites as easily as they do a good garden soil.

The deciduous hollies are usually trouble free, al-though winterberry foliage can be affected by mildew. The fruits of possum haw and winterberry are even showier than those of American holly because they are more highly visible among yellow leaves in fall or massed on bare gray branches in winter. Possum haw covers the same general range as American holly but extends north-west along streams of the Ozark Plateau and up the Mis-sissippi River and its tributaries to southern Indiana, Illinois, and the southern tip of Iowa. Winterberry, the hardiest tree holly, ranges north to upper Michigan, the Ottawa River in Ontario, and northeast to the island of Newfoundland. Possum haw is hardy in USDA zone 4, and winterberry to USDA zone 3.

Possum haw has yielded several good cultivars, mostly selected for ornamental fruit. They include 'Reed', 'Sun-dance', 'Warren Red', 'Council Fire', and the yellow-fruited 'Byers Golden'. Winterberry selections include 'Afterglow', 'Cacapon', 'Fairfax', 'Late Red', 'Red Sprite', 'Shaver', 'Sunset', 'Winter Red', and 'Winter Gold'. Of these, the last three are most likely to develop into tree form. The larger-growing selections of winterberry are

generally selected from the southern part of its range, but they are still hardier than other hollies. Mountain holly (*Ilex montana*) is an upland Appalachian species nearly identical to winterberry. It grows about twice as large, approaching the size of possum haw.

Dahoon (*Ilex cassine*) and yaupon (*I. vomitoria*) are small coastal evergreen trees of the southeastern United States (I've never liked the specific epithet for yaupon, though it's true Native Americans used it as an emetic). Both have tiny fine-textured leaves and are adaptable species but, like most native hollies, are not hardy north. Gallberry (*I. coriacea*) is another Coastal Plain species. It features larger, evergreen foliage, glossy black fruit, and is hardy to about USDA zone 7. Inkberry (*I. glabra*) is a very hardy evergreen holly, but it remains a shrub. Sev-eral European and Asian species and their hybrids are popular as ornamental plants, including *I. aquifolium, I. cornuta, I. crenata,* and *I. rotunda.*

Nemopanthus mucronatus, the so-called mountain-holly, is closely related but placed in a different genus. It remains a large, erect shrub and functions much as a true holly in the landscape. The red berries hang from long, pendent pedicels on female plants. Seedlings flower in as little as two years from seed, so gender sepa-ration can be done at that stage before consigning the plants to their permanent positions in the landscape. Mountain-holly can be found in bogs and other wet places and is hardy to USDA zone 4.

COMMENTS: We are all so accustomed to thinking about the leaves and fruit of holly that we sometimes forget about its bark. An old American holly, free of the lower limbs that frequently skirt its base, exhibits a smooth, convoluted, lichen-adorned stem and abrupt root flare that resemble the foot and toes of a giant ele-phant. This engaging character does not develop over-night but takes many decades, and a big holly is one of the few trees that is usually older than it looks.

The slow-growing American holly, like some of our finest oaks, is an investment in the future. George Wash-ington certainly thought so, for his records show that his failed attempts to transplant wild trees led him to germinate seedlings, which gave rise to the holly grove in the South Semicircle at Mount Vernon. Andrew Jackson thought so too, and his original plantings can still be seen in front of the Hermitage near Nashville.

LEFT: Fruits begin to color in late summer on winterberry (*Ilex verticillata*).

Juglans nigra

BLACK WALNUT

DESCRIPTION: Our most valuable native hardwood lumber comes from one of our most interesting and resilient trees. Black walnut is a tall, strong forest tree of well-drained bottomlands but is seen just as often as a picturesque, weathered survivor in overgrazed pastures or sterile, eroded old fields. Everywhere it grows, humans and squirrels compete for its valuable nut crop, and mature trees in the back forty must be guarded with vigilance against log poachers.

It is rare to see massive old-growth walnuts in their native habitat, with straight trunks clear of limbs for their first 80 feet (24 m), such as those along Sugar Creek in Turkey Run State Park, Indiana. Most old giants in national forests or on private land have already been harvested for their valuable wood. In fact, the largest known black walnut is a planted tree on Sauvie Island, Oregon, more than 1000 miles (1600 km) from its ancestral home. Measured in 1991 at 130 feet (39 m) in height, it is a sprawling, low-limbed tree with a trunk that is 7.4 feet (2.25 m) in diameter. It is probably still alive because its trunk is too short to make a good sawlog.

LEAVES: The highly aromatic, pinnately compound leaves of all our native walnut species look similar, emerge very late in spring, and drop early in fall. Those of black walnut are up to 2 feet (60 cm) long, with paired leaflets and no terminal leaflet. They can turn a good clear yellow early in fall, contrasting nicely with the dark bark, but many trees are defoliated by insects or leaf blights before this happens.

FLOWERS AND FRUIT: Walnuts are close relatives of hickories (*Carya*), and their flower structures are nearly identical. Staminate catkins are produced in hanging clusters, like green tinsel; pistillate flowers occur singly or in small groups at the ends of twigs.

The fruits ripen in late summer, but many don't fall until after the first autumn frost. They are among the largest of our native nut-tree fruits; before husking, they occasionally exceed the size of tangerines. The nuts are predictably variable from tree to tree in size, shape, and quality. Lester Cox of Carlinville, Illinois, who has gathered walnuts on his property for years, can examine a nut, tell you which tree it came from, and accurately predict the quality and oil content of each nut based upon the historic performance of that tree.

BEST SEASONS: FALL (for the nut harvest and for the good yellow fall color on disease-resistant specimens). SUMMER (for the open shade and for the aromatic, fernlike foliage).

NATIVE AND ADAPTIVE RANGE: Black walnut grows in scattered groves along the St. Lawrence River, southwest through southern Ontario, and westward to eastern South Dakota, then south throughout most of the eastern United States except for southern coastal areas.

This tree's performance is closely tied to provenance, and seed sources from local areas or from up to 100 to 200 miles (161 to 322 km) south are recommended. Seeds from more southern sources, when moved north, grow more each year than those from local stock, but the trees are less hardy and more likely to die back in severe winters. Locally adapted black walnut is hardy through most of USDA zone 4.

CULTURE: Black walnut is a tough tree that survives with abuse but thrives with proper care. Such care includes full sun and a good, fertile, moist, well-drained soil (limed if too acidic). Black walnut can grow surprisingly quickly under such conditions. It will propagate readily from fall-planted seed, which must be protected from squirrels for the entire first year, and selected trees can be grafted or budded.

Care should be taken to minimize pruning wounds that might serve as entry points for disease, but black walnut is resistant to damage from storms, drought, alkaline soil, and atmospheric ozone. Its deep roots, the long, leafless dormancy period from early fall to late spring, and the light shade cast even in summer promote strong turfgrass growth under its canopy. All native walnut species develop long taproots and can be tough to transplant unless they have been undercut in the nursery.

PROBLEMS: Walnut foliage can be subject to heavy attack by the walnut caterpillar (*Datana integerrima*) and the related yellowneck caterpillar (*D. ministra*). These moth larvae feed in groups and arch into a fearsome bluff when disturbed. Target canker (*Nectria galligena*) is

destructive to damaged or weakened trees. The most noticeable disease on some black walnuts is anthracnose, caused by *Gnomonia leptostyla*. Trees vary in resistance to this leaf spot fungus, which harmlessly but conspicuously defoliates the most susceptible victims in late summer. Many other leaf diseases affect these trees to a lesser extent.

All walnut species and many close relatives manufacture an allelopathic substance called juglone, and none are more potent than black walnut. When the roots of juglone-sensitive plants (including other walnut seedlings) contact walnut roots, they can be stunted or killed. Turfgrasses, most ferns, conifers such as hemlocks (*Tsuga*) and junipers (*Juniperus*), and ornamental shrubs like boxwoods (*Buxus*) and *Viburnum* species are not usually harmed by juglone. Most of the usual forest tree associates like oaks (*Quercus*), maples (*Acer*), hickories (*Carya*), hackberries (*Celtis*), ashes (*Fraxinus*), and beeches (*Fagus grandifolia*) are also not severely affected. But juglone is potent against some garden vegetables, apples (*Malus*) and their relatives, fringe trees (*Chionanthus*), birches (*Betula*), azaleas (*Rhododendron*), and pines (*Pinus*).

The falling nuts of black walnut can injure the objects or people they land on, and the stain released by their husks is practically impossible to remove from patios. They can also cause litter and mowing problems in closely maintained lawn areas, along with the leaflets and stiff leaf rachises that begin to drop in late summer or early fall.

CULTIVARS: For many years I have admired the lacy, ornamental, slow-growing 'Laciniata' at the Morton Arboretum near Chicago. Most other black walnut selections have been directed toward timber or fruit production, and many exist. 'Lambs Curly' was chosen not for its fast growth or straightness but for its crooked, curly grain, which is so valuable in the specialty wood trade.

The Northern Nut Growers Association has worked for decades to identify superior trees for nut production throughout the range of the species. Among the best are 'Cochrane' from Wisconsin, 'Edras' and 'Grundy' from Iowa, 'Hare' from Illinois, 'Schreiber' from Indiana, 'Bowser' from Ohio, 'Harney' and 'Victoria' from Kentucky, 'Norris' from Tennessee, and 'Monterey', 'Pinecrest', 'Thomas', and 'Vandersloot' from Pennsylvania. Although the large-fruited 'Thomas' is most frequently

LEFT: A mature black walnut (*Juglans nigra*) shades a home. RIGHT: The spreading form of an ancient, open-grown black walnut.

offered by nurseries, 'Pinecrest' and 'Vandersloot' reportedly bear even larger nuts. I have selected two more in central Illinois with orange-sized fruits that we use for superior seed sources, but it hardly seems necessary to introduce more walnut selections as cultivars.

SIMILAR AND RELATED SPECIES: Butternut (***Juglans cinerea***), our other relatively common walnut species, is usually a smaller tree. Butternut leaves are complete with a terminal leaflet, unlike those of black walnut. The U.S. national champion grows in a sylvan setting in Chester, Connecticut. It is an exceptional example, standing 78 feet (23.4 m) tall with a trunk nearly 7 feet (2.1 m) thick. The distribution of butternut is more northerly than other native species, but nowhere is it common. It extends north to Quebec City and southern New Brunswick, and many of the finest specimens I have seen have been in Canada. Butternut is hardy in USDA zone 3. It is more particular about soil than black walnut and will not succeed on a poor or dry site, though it tolerates rocky soil. Nut crops can be sporadic due to the sensitivity of the pistillate flowers to frost, even when the staminate catkins develop normally.

Butternut blight is a fatal disease caused by a fungus named *Sirococcus clavigignenti-juglandacearum*, which forms cankers later invaded by another fungus, *Melanconis juglandis*. These organisms are as difficult to cure as they are

to pronounce, and eventually the tree dies. This disease is spreading throughout the natural range of butternut, even into Ontario, and the tree may be on the road to extinction unless a cure is found.

Of the four other walnuts native to North America, two can be grown in the warmer portions of our area: Arizona walnut (***Juglans major***), from Arizona and western New Mexico, and nogalito (***J. microcarpa***), or little walnut, from Oklahoma, Texas, and New Mexico. They make beautiful specimens in desert canyons of the Southwest and are very tolerant of alkaline soils. Both may be grown at least as far north as USDA zone 6 under the right soil conditions, and they have very small fruits that are much less painful when landing on your head. The record Arizona walnut is 73 feet (21.9 m) tall and nearly 6 feet (1.8 m) thick. Nogalito is smaller, with a U.S. national champion in Texas that is 50 feet (15 m) tall and slightly more than 4 feet (1.2 m) in diameter. It is particularly fine in texture for a walnut and is useful in small landscapes that might not have room for a larger walnut species. The other two native North American walnut species are confined to California.

About fourteen additional species are found in other parts of the world, including some commercially productive nut-orchard species. Of these, by far the most well known is Persian walnut (***Juglans regia***), also known as European walnut, sold in stores and grown in parts of North America for nut production.

COMMENTS: Black walnut is a preferred host of the beautiful luna moth and the immense regal moth (including its awe-inspiring larva, the hickory horned devil), which can be 6 inches (15 cm) across. Once seen, neither can be forgotten. Black walnut also hosts the larva of the walnut sphinx moth, unusual for the squeaking sound it makes. Nutmeats of black walnut and butternut are used commercially for oil and flavoring, and on the farm for walnut bread and other delights. Birds pick through the debris left behind when humans shell out walnuts, but they are unable to crack whole walnuts without help. The shells are extremely hard, so squirrels and chipmunks seem unique among wildlife in being able to gnaw through them.

Some creative uses have been devised for walnut. Dried walnut leaves can be mixed with straw as a flea repellent in animal bedding. Ground walnut shells have been used as specialty abrasives in sandblasters to polish metals. Some orchardists who grow Persian walnuts commercially graft them high on black walnut understocks; when production peaks out and the trees are removed, each tree has developed a high-quality, marketable black walnut veneer log at its base.

Butternuts are so tasty that Native Americans planted them for a food source. One tree that was probably planted for this purpose, a state champion in Poughkeepsie, New York, was rescued from destruction in 2001 by a heroic effort of the Forbus Butternut Association, a neighborhood association of concerned citizens. They raised enough money to buy the vacant city block, where the tree had lived for centuries, from the developer who planned to remove it for construction of a subdivision.

On a much broader scale, the U.S. Forest Service is leading an interagency effort to solve the butternut blight problem through research and identification of resistant trees. If you know of mature, healthy butternut trees in an area where butternut blight is established, you can help by reporting their location to the Forest Service or to your state or provincial natural resource agency for possible use in resistance-selection breeding programs.

LEFT: A vigorous young black walnut (*Juglans nigra*). TOP RIGHT: The staminate catkins of black walnut. RIGHT: Black walnut fruits are tasty and aromatic but messy.

Juniperus virginiana
REDCEDAR

DESCRIPTION: Redcedar is actually a juniper, not a true cedar. It is one of our most adaptable conifers and occupies a larger and more diverse natural range than any other coniferous tree in eastern North America. Redcedar commonly grows on rocky ridges, in hill prairies, and in open, dry woods and seeds prolifically into abandoned pastures and along fence lines. Stunted, gnarly specimens many centuries old can be found clinging to rocky cliffs in the scorching summer sun of the Ozark Mountains, growing less than 1 inch (2.5 cm) per year and looking much like the ancient bristlecone pines (*Pinus longaeva*) of Nevada. Yet on very favorable sites the same species grows moderately quickly into a conical tree 100 feet (30 m) high. The largest known redcedar is not nearly so tall—only 57 feet (17.1 m)—but it has a trunk 5.6 feet (1.7 m) in diameter and a broadly spreading crown that shades a large portion of the Lone Hill Cemetery in Coffee County, Georgia. There are many geographic races or forms of redcedar, each with a localized advantage, such as northern forms with branches that shed snow without breakage.

LEAVES: The aromatic evergreen needles of vigorous young redcedars are sharp and prickly to the touch, providing some defense against browsing animals. As the trees grow above the reach of browsers, the needles change into a more efficient, water-conserving scale form, smooth like the mature foliage of arborvitae (*Thuja*). Some trees remain green throughout the winter, while others develop a bronze or purple cast. The foliage patterns of some trees are erect, others are clumpy, and still others droop at the tips.

CONES AND SEEDS: Like many junipers, redcedar is dioecious. The trees shed their pollen in late spring, with females showing a reddish tint and males staying yellow-green. The strobili are not conspicuous in the landscape.

In late summer, female trees bear small, blue, modified cones casually called juniper-berries, holding them through most of the winter or until they are eaten by birds. Unlike some junipers, redcedar matures its seed in one year. The juniper-berries are metallic blue, reaching perhaps a quarter of an inch (0.6 cm) in diameter. The trees don't bear heavily every year, but a redcedar with a bumper crop appears to be covered with bright blue frost.

BEST SEASONS: WINTER (most conifers are trees of winter, and fruiting female redcedars are particularly colorful in an otherwise bland winter landscape). LATE SPRING (for the telial spore horns of rust galls, which are as bright as orange Christmas lights and, although a health menace to some alternate-host trees, are relatively harmless to redcedar). ALL YEAR (for picturesque old trees or selections with dramatic form).

NATIVE AND ADAPTIVE RANGE: Various races and ecotypes of redcedar can be found from the Ottawa River and the Georgian Bay area of Lake Huron down through southern Ontario, east to Maine, west to the Dakotas, and south to the Gulf Coastal Plain. It is hardy in cultivation from at least USDA zone 3 south, although studies by the U.S. Forest Service recommend collecting seed from areas within about one degree latitude south of the planting site for best survival and growth.

CULTURE: Extremes of heat, drought, wind, cold, and soil are not significant to this tree. It cannot tolerate dense shade or swampy sites and avoids very alkaline conditions in the wild. Beautiful old specimens with fluted trunks and tufted foliage, reminiscent of miniature sequoias, can be seen in cemeteries, pastures, river bluffs, and parks on almost every soil type imaginable, wherever the competition of less stalwart but faster-growing tree species has been kept in check.

Seed germinates slowly, sometimes not until the second year after planting unless elaborate stratification and scarification practices are followed. Soaking the seeds for a couple of days prior to planting seems to help, and planting them immediately upon harvest is essential for prompt germination. Selected forms are rooted from cuttings. Where redcedar has invaded old fields or fence lines, it is normally so abundant that wild-collection of seedlings can be desirable to thin the stand.

RIGHT: A female redcedar (*Juniperus virginiana*) loaded with blue fruits.

Such volunteers are best relocated when fairly small, due to the deep root systems they generate.

PROBLEMS: Wild redcedars in prairie areas and pastures are extremely sensitive to fire. Redcedar is also an alternate host for several rust diseases, including cedar-hawthorn rust (*Gymnosporangium globosum*), cedar-apple rust (*G. juniperi-virginianae*), and cedar-quince rust (*G. clavipes*), which affect fruit orchards and certain ornamental trees in the rose family. Rust-resistant varieties of these species should be used near groves of redcedar, for their own sake, since the rusts do not seriously damage the redcedar. Needle blight (*Phomopsis juniperovora*) attacks this and most other junipers.

The primary insect pests are bagworms (*Thyridopterix ephemeraeformis*) and (not a true insect) spruce spider mites (*Oligonychus ununguis*). Several borers may attack this tree, especially if it is weakened by stress, and various sawflies, scales, and root weevils cause occasional damage. Deer also mutilate young saplings.

It can be difficult to grow other plants beneath large redcedars because of their competitive root systems and the deep duff of decay-resistant needles. Redcedars, like most junipers, should not be pampered with too much artificial irrigation or they are likely to suffer a reduction in root development and might topple in a windy, wet spring.

CULTIVARS: Redcedar has given rise to many selections, of both tree and shrub form. Among the most popular and useful tree forms are 'Burkii', a pyramidal male with a blue foliage tint; 'Canaertii', a picturesque, tufted female form; 'Emerald Sentinel', a narrow pyramidal form; 'Hillii', a compact columnar selection with purple winter color; 'Pendula', with drooping foliage; and 'Skyrocket', a narrow, spire-shaped, silvery blue accent plant that might be a hybrid with the closely related Rocky Mountain juniper (*Juniperus scopulorum*).

Three promising new selections are very resistant to *Phomopsis juniperovora* needle blight and other foliage diseases. 'Taylor' is a columnar form that was discovered in rural Nebraska; the ortet is around 35 feet (10.5 m) tall and only 6 feet (1.8 m) wide. 'Sunshine Silver' is a broader, pyramidal form with silver-blue foliage that retains good color through the winter, and 'Hydro Green' is similar but has deep green foliage through the winter months.

LEFT: Many old redcedars (*Juniperus virginiana*) can be found in cemeteries. TOP RIGHT: Fruits forming on a female redcedar. RIGHT: A vigorous young redcedar.

The USDA began testing 307 selections of redcedar in 1986 and should release the winners for commercial use in 2005. An impressive collection of redcedar selections may be viewed at the North Carolina State University Arboretum at Raleigh.

SIMILAR AND RELATED SPECIES: The shrubby common juniper (*Juniperus communis*), a variable circumpolar species that grows throughout much of our region and most of the Northern Hemisphere, is closely related to redcedar and may hybridize with it. One of its upright cultivars, 'Schneverdinger Goldmachangel', is interesting if for no other reason than for its name, derived from a drink. I was introduced to this plant by Dick van Hoey Smith, who used all the throaty Dutch force he could muster to pronounce it, slowly and repeatedly, to my bemusement and delight. A few other cultivars and hybrids may also assume tree form.

Southern redcedar (*Juniperus silicicola*) is a southern coastal wetland tree hardy to USDA zone 7, and it is also closely related to redcedar. *Juniperus horizontalis* is a creeping groundcover native to many of the same northern habitats as common juniper.

Other junipers native to our region are mostly found in the West. Rocky Mountain juniper (*Juniperus scopulorum*) can be found at elevations from 5000 to 8000 feet (1500 to 2400 m) throughout the Rocky Mountains, Black Hills, and many outlying habitats from western Canada south through New Mexico. It is the western counterpart of redcedar and is nearly identical except that it has larger fruits that take two years to ripen instead of one. Cultivars are planted frequently in the East. It is rated hardy north to USDA zone 3. The largest known specimen is the focal point of an overlook in the Cache National Forest in Utah. It is a massive, grotesquely scenic tree with a tiny crown of live foliage atop a mostly dead base, standing 40 feet (12 m) tall with a gnarly, ancient trunk more than 6 feet (1.8 m) thick.

Alligator juniper (*Juniperus deppeana*) can also become massive (for a juniper) and picturesque after several centuries, and can live for several more centuries beyond that. It is limited in the wild to the southern Rocky Mountains, western Texas, and Mexico at elevations from 4000 to 8000 feet (1200 to 2400 m). The foliage of juvenile plants (especially variety *pachyphlaea* and its cultivar 'Silver') can be a beautiful blue, totally unlike the green foliage of very old trees, and the checkered bark of all alligator junipers is rife with character. Large fruits with up to four seeds, which take two years to ripen, add appeal to female trees. This juniper is probably not reliably hardy north of USDA zone 7, but it is a beautiful species worth testing in zone 6.

Ashe juniper (*Juniperus ashei*), a smaller, bushy tree with shreddy bark and blue fruits, enters eastern North America in the Ozark Plateau but is more prominent in central Texas and south into Mexico. The twigs often have a graceful, semiweeping habit. It thrives best on thin, alkaline clay soil and will survive north into USDA zone 6. A tough, resilient little tree in its natural habitat, Ashe juniper also increases in abundance on rangeland following abusive overgrazing by livestock. Fur-

LEFT: Alligator juniper (*Juniperus deppeana*) adds much to the landscape character of the Southwest.
RIGHT: A huge alligator juniper, many centuries old.

thermore, it is a vital component of the habitat for the golden-cheeked warbler, an endangered species that uses small slivers of the juniper's shedding bark for nest building. Thus, ranchers who abuse their land occasionally initiate a beneficial offsetting environmental change that was never intended.

Utah juniper (*Juniperus osteosperma*) is the primary component of the vast pinyon-juniper habitat throughout much of the Great Basin and the High Plains, and grows north all the way into southern Montana, which gives it a hardiness rating of at least USDA zone 4. It's a low, bushy tree but a tree nonetheless, again with shreddy bark but usually a single trunk at the base. Its foliage could have been the inspiration for the military camouflage color called olive-drab. Utah juniper has fruits at least half an inch (1.25 cm) in diameter, enclosing several seeds.

The similar single-seed juniper (*Juniperus monosperma*) has much smaller fruits than those of Utah juniper, with only one seed, and is often more shrubby without a well-defined central trunk, although it can grow just as large. It is limited to the southwestern edge of our region, mostly New Mexico and beyond into Arizona, but can also be found in the Texas Panhandle in USDA zone 6. Redberry juniper (*J. erythrocarpa*), nearly identical except for the redder fruits, was not distinguished from single-seed juniper and placed in a separate species until 1936. It is rated to USDA zone 7, and unlike many western junipers it is best adapted to acid soils.

Pinchot's juniper (*Juniperus pinchottii*) and rose-fruited juniper (*J. coahuilensis*) are similar low-elevation species found in the foothill grasslands of the Southwest. They are closely related to single-seed juniper and difficult to tell apart without fruit. Pinchot's juniper is found primarily in western Texas, north barely into USDA zone 6 in the Panhandle and southwestern Oklahoma, and west into southeastern New Mexico. Rose-fruited juniper has gorgeous red fruits that can give a pistillate tree a rosy glow. It extends across southern New Mexico into Arizona.

Weeping juniper (*Juniperus flacida*) barely enters our region from Mexico, occurring in the wild only at high elevations in Big Bend National Park; but it is often encountered in hot Texas towns as a cultivated landscape tree due to its graceful weeping habit. Despite its primarily Mexican range, this species is hardy under cultivation north at least through USDA zone 7.

Approximately fifty additional juniper species can be found worldwide. Some, such as *Juniperus chinensis* and its many cultivars, are very common in cultivation.

COMMENTS: The first aroma many of us can recall from childhood is the wonderful smell of the cedar chest or cedar-lined closet where our baby blankets were kept naturally moth-free. The wood is equally resistant to decay organisms, so many young redcedar trees are harvested for fence posts.

Redcedar is also among our most valuable wildlife trees. Cedar waxwings earned their name from their preference for the fruit of this plant, and more than forty other wildlife species depend heavily upon it for food. Fence-sitting birds have deposited redcedar seeds along nearly every fence within its range. The birds also seem to aid in transmitting the rust diseases to fruit trees, since redcedar seedlings are frequently found in orchards, providing evidence of bird travel between the two plant types. The dense foliage furnishes protective cover and nesting sites for many birds, and hosts the iridescent olive hairstreak butterfly.

On a less noble note, redcedar fruits are also used to make gin. Oh, well.

Larix laricina

TAMARACK

DESCRIPTION: Tamarack is one of three native North American larch species, and the only one found east of the Rocky Mountains. The larches are conifers closely related to pines (*Pinus*), firs (*Abies*), and spruces (*Picea*), but are unique among them in being deciduous, like baldcypress (*Taxodium distichum*). Tamarack is perhaps the most cold hardy of any native tree and, pound for pound, has some of the strongest wood among conifers.

It grows in extremes of cold and wet and seldom attains great size under such conditions. On good sites, though, it becomes a tall and picturesque specimen. One venerable monster that supports a rope swing in Coventry, Connecticut, is only 62 feet (18.6 m) tall but has a trunk more than 4 feet (1.2 m) in diameter. Larger individuals could probably be located in remote areas across the breadth of Canada, especially in the prime tamarack habitat around Lake Winnipeg in Manitoba.

LEAVES: Unlike most conifers, tamarack provides colorful seasonal variation in the landscape. Bright lime-green needles gradually emerge in tufts in spring, showing well when seen against a backdrop of the dark evergreen foliage of pine or spruce. They slowly mature at about 1 inch (2.5 cm) long, remaining in circular patterns on spur branches along the previous season's growth but developing singly along the new twigs, which begin to elongate only after the initial flush of tuft-needles has expanded.

In late fall, which passes unnoticed by other conifers, tamaracks become golden searchlights over the muskegs and bogs of the North. Seen with the dark green of spruce (*Picea*), the white of birch bark (*Betula papyrifera*), and the crimson of cranberry (*Vaccinium*), near the blue water of a clear pond, with the dynamic overhead ascent of migrating geese and a light dusting of fresh snow, they are unforgettable. Few other conifers provide any fall color, and those that do generally turn more somber tones of russet; among them, the larches are without parallel.

CONES AND SEEDS: Tamarack bears separate staminate and pistillate strobili on the same tree. They are small, inconspicuous, and visually overwhelmed by the spectacle of the emerging foliage. Male strobili are yellow-green, and females are a soft red.

Tamarack cones are among the smallest of any member of the genus—or of any other conifers, either—and rarely grow much more than half an inch (1.25 cm) long. Young cones emerge from a basal whorl of short needles and are pleasantly waxy, looking (but not tasting) like some type of cruciferous vegetable. They mature to a warm brown, gradually fading to gray-brown as they continue to cling to their short spur branches for two or three years.

BEST SEASONS: FALL (the yellow needles, even during those years when their color is straw-tinted by cold or drought, add sparkle to any boreal forest). SPRING (the fresh green of new needles, emerging early from a bare coniferous tree, is the essence of the awakening season).

NATIVE AND ADAPTIVE RANGE: Tamarack forms our northernmost line of tree growth, from northern Newfoundland and Ungava Bay in Quebec across James Bay and the central provinces to the southern end of Great Bear Lake, and on to the Arctic Circle in central Alaska. From there it follows suitable habitat south through the Great Lakes area and eastward down to Pennsylvania and New Jersey.

This is one of those few trees whose hardiness under cultivation is expressed more appropriately in terms of its southern (not northern) limit, which is variable depending upon available soil moisture and summer heat intensity. Wild trees are known to survive temperatures at least as low as –79°F (–62°C) without harm, so cold is of no concern. They also experience short periods of summer heat where temperatures exceed 100°F (38°C). Thus, under ideal moisture conditions, tamarack can be grown south through much of USDA zone 6, especially if a cool breeze from a nearby lake or evaporation from a saturated sphagnum bog moderates the most extreme summer temperatures.

CULTURE: This tree requires moisture and cool temperatures. It also needs acidic soil and full sun. Long, cool summer days at high latitudes are ideal. Tamarack often grows slowly in the wild, due to its stressful envi-

ronment, but can shoot up nicely under cultivation. It has a shallow, compact root system, so a nursery-grown specimen can be transplanted with no difficulty when dormant, or it can be grown from seed sown in fall. It will do well in any moist acidic soil, from sand to clay, but prefers a mulched organic loam. It casts a very light shade and may be underplanted successfully with acid-soil wildflowers and shrubs.

PROBLEMS: Native stands of tamarack can be damaged severely by porcupines and deer. The trees are shallow rooted, especially on wet sites, and may be subject to windthrow. Shade and drought are probably the primary limiting factors to successful larch culture in the managed landscape.

The larch casebearer (*Coleophora laricella*) is a serious pest introduced from Europe. It is a tiny insect that lives inside a hollowed-out needle, which it carries on its back as it feeds on other needles. Larch sawfly (*Pristiphora erichsonii*) can also be a troublesome defoliator, as can Gypsy moth (*Lymantria dispar*). The importation of unprocessed larch timber from Siberia should be monitored closely, or more exotic borers and other serious pests might be introduced into North America.

CULTIVARS: Tamarack seems to be a very homogenous species, considering the extent of its natural range and the variability of habitat conditions under which it thrives. A few obscure selections for blue or yellow leaf coloration have been made in the past, but none are common in cultivation.

SIMILAR AND RELATED SPECIES: Two other beautiful larch species, western larch (**Larix occidentalis**) and the smaller subalpine larch (**L. lyallii**), are found at high elevations in the northern mountains of western North America. Of these two, western larch seems more adaptable to cultivation at lower elevations. It becomes a very large tree in its native habitat, approaching 200 feet (60 m) in height, and the record-sized tree has a trunk 7 feet (2.1 m) thick. European larch (**L. decidua**) and Japanese larch (**L. kaempferi**) are commonly grown in North America as ornamental trees. The related golden-larch (**Pseudolarix amabilis**) from China is also seen occasionally in cultivation.

COMMENTS: Irregular horizontal layers of branches and a rough excurrent form can make the deciduous tamarack look like a dead evergreen in winter. But it more than compensates during the rest of the year with

LEFT: A natural grove of tamarack (*Larix laricina*) at the edge of a northern bog.

its colorful foliage and seasonal variation, working a double shift on long summer days. This deciduous characteristic makes tamarack nearly immune to winter salt spray from road deicing, which severely damages many other conifers planted along highways.

The seeds of larches are a favorite food of crossbills, and the buds are eaten by spruce grouse. Many other birds also value these trees for nesting sites, and the western larch in particular is a prime timber species. While many of us know about the historical use of birch-bark canoes by some Native Americans, most are unaware that tamarack root strips were used to sew the craft together.

The famous early American landscape gardener Andrew Jackson Downing recognized as early as 1849, in *A Treatise on the Theory and Practice of Landscape Gardening*, that the flexible tamarack had an "expression of boldness and picturesqueness peculiar to itself." It is indeed an expressive tree, and I agree with him that it should be used with greater frequency "to give spirit to a group of other trees, to strengthen the already picturesque character of a scene, or to give life and variety to one naturally tame and uninteresting."

Very well said, Mr. Downing, and still true.

LEFT: The open crown of tamarack (*Larix laricina*) casts a very light shade. BELOW: Cones and tufted needles on tamarack. BELOW RIGHT: Tamarack turns yellow in fall and drops its needles by winter.

Leitneria floridana
CORKWOOD

DESCRIPTION: One of the distinct pleasures of writing a reference book about plants lies in the occasional opportunity to include and promote the unusual. Corkwood is such a pleasure.

Corkwood is aptly named. It has the lightest wood of any tree in North America, weighing less than half as much as cottonwood and less than a third as much as oak. The tree forms thickets in a few scattered, sandy or peaty wet areas in the southern United States, and grows nowhere else in the wild. Although not yet formally classified as a federally endangered species, this tree is rare enough that nature preserves have been set aside specifically in order to safeguard it from regional extinction.

Corkwood forms clonal colonies in the wild and in cultivation. Specimens standing 25 feet (7.5 m) tall have been found in the past, but currently none that large are known. The U.S. national cochampions in Waccasassa Bay State Preserve, Florida, are only 15 feet (4.5 m) tall. Several of the largest specimens in Missouri, which has the northernmost (and some of the best) stands of this rare species, are dying from competition from other species. Yet this unusual tree, with such a tenuous hold on its niche in the wild, has much to recommend it for the landscape.

LEAVES: Corkwood leaves emerge leathery and woolly in spring, with rugose surfaces, and eventually reach almost 6 inches (15 cm) in length by less than half as wide. They are the primary aesthetic attraction for this species, looking like they must belong to some exotic, tropical evergreen tree. But corkwood is quite at home in our temperate climate and fully, if tardily, deciduous in autumn. Some leaves turn a pleasant yellow before dropping, while others on the same tree might remain green until they are blitzed by a hard freeze.

FLOWERS AND FRUIT: Corkwood is fully dioecious, so each plant or clonal group of plants is either male or female. They bloom in very early spring before the leaves emerge, developing erect brown catkins on the twigs of the previous year. Pistillate catkins are looser and slightly larger than those of staminate plants, reaching about 1 inch (2.5 cm) in length.

Fruits are produced only on female plants that have been pollinated, and usually only on trees growing in the wild or in ideal garden habitat. They reach three-quarters of an inch (1.9 cm) in length and are conspicuously laced with surface veins, forming small yellowish brown clusters in summer. The fruits are timed to fall with the frequent flood waters of the plant's natural habitat, and they float to their new homes, where they promptly germinate on bare wet sand or muck.

BEST SEASONS: SUMMER (for the lush foliage). LATE FALL (for the green-and-yellow effect). LATE WINTER (for the flowers on male plants, which look like small pine cones, and for the interesting architecture of the plant).

NATIVE AND ADAPTIVE RANGE: Corkwood is so limited in distribution that if you really tried you almost could know every tree, like Davy Crockett. It occurs in small, isolated groves in southern Missouri, eastern Arkansas, eastern Texas, northern Florida, and southern Georgia. Most landscape reference books don't even acknowledge its existence, and the few that do generally rate it hardy north to USDA zone 6, probably based upon its natural range rather than first-hand experience cultivating it. I have grown clones of Missouri provenance easily in USDA zone 5, and it does well in northern Illinois as well, nearly to zone 4.

CULTURE: Corkwood requires full sun, control of competition, and reasonable moisture, but little else. It is not bothered by insects, diseases, or gross inattention. Under cultivation it is amenable to almost any soil and does not seem to need the swampy conditions of its native habitat. Perhaps, like many wetland trees, corkwood uses soggy soil to keep competitors at bay or to facilitate the establishment of its seedlings, because such species almost all do very well under cultivation in ordinary garden soil.

PROBLEMS: This species forms thickets and can become frustrating if your landscape design calls for a single-stemmed tree. It reaches its best ornamental potential, though, when left to its own devices and allowed to

RIGHT: A clonal corkwood (*Leitneria floridana*) clump.

clump, and this eliminates the only maintenance (pulling sprouts) accompanying its cultivation.

CULTIVARS: No named selections of corkwood are known in cultivation. In fact the species itself is barely known in cultivation. Since corkwoods are so easy to propagate asexually from root cuttings or sprouts, it is a simple task to select at least for male or female plants. Once you find a garden-club friend or local botanic garden with a corkwood, all you have to do is ask.

SIMILAR AND RELATED SPECIES: Corkwood is the only species in the genus *Leitneria*, and *Leitneria* is the only genus in the family Leitneriaceae. You would expect the tree to have a few tropical or Asian relatives, but in fact it is a true loner of the plant kingdom. The closest it comes to being related to anything is a very distant affiliation with willows (*Salix*) and bayberries (*Myrica*). Still, there are three obscure little unrelated trees that fit well in a discussion of corkwood.

Though leatherwood (***Dirca palustris***) never really attains tree size, it maintains a single trunk and seems to try so hard to look like a small tree that I have to include it. Forester Greg Hoss has studied leatherwood specimens in Missouri and believes that those with stems 2 inches (5 cm) in diameter could be more than a century old. This plant is the aesthetic equivalent of a tree for small gardens. It makes an intriguing landscape plant because of its rubbery twigs, which can be tied into knots without breaking, and because of its very early blooming period, which arrives just after that of Ozark witch hazel (*Hamamelis vernalis*). Leatherwood inhabits cool ravines and moist, well-drained woods north into USDA zone 4. It blooms in very early spring and can be grown from seed sown in fall. It is one of our few small trees that seem nearly immune to deer damage.

At the other end of the deer-damage spectrum is horse-sugar (***Symplocos tinctoria***), also known (at least to deer) as sweetleaf, an understory tree of southern swamp borders. It is useful under cultivation north into USDA zone 7 and develops an open, irregular limb framework that becomes picturesque with increasing age. Fragrant yellow-orange flowers are produced in large clusters in spring after the semievergreen leaves have dropped to expose the branches. Horse-sugar can grow to 50 feet (15 m) or more in good soil. Seeds should be extracted from the orange fruits and planted in late summer as soon as they ripen. Be sure to protect seedlings and young trees from browsing animals.

For very dry or alkaline sites on the High Plains, consider one of Lewis and Clark's discoveries, silver buffaloberry (**Shepherdia argentea**). This plant resembles and is related to the silver-leaved oleasters (*Elaeagnus*) of Asia but has opposite leaves and is not so invasive. It makes a small, bushy, thorny tree with great wildlife value, seems immune to wind, and is hardy throughout the Great Plains from USDA zone 2 southward. Like corkwood, it is also dioecious and requires plants of both genders for fruit production.

COMMENTS: Corkwood is fun to grow, if only for a supply of wood from its surplus stems. It is the nearest thing to balsa wood that can be obtained from any temperate-zone tree and makes great fishing bobbers and carving material. The tree itself is a charming ornamental and so easy of culture that there really seems to be no good reason not to try it, if you can find it.

It is interesting to note that species such as corkwood, baldcypress (*Taxodium distichum*), and water tupelo (*Nyssa aquatica*) exhibit much greater winter hardiness and accept drier soils under cultivation than their natural ranges and habitats would seem to indicate. This might suggest that they are confined in nature to southern wet-

lands only by the winter ice of more northerly wetland habitats and by the competition of other, less flood-tolerant species on higher ground, or that their seedlings are unable to establish except under a southern swamp environment. Many such tree species are able to thrive if planted and tended in situations where they would be unable to establish naturally from seed.

TOP LEFT: The richly textured foliage of corkwood (*Leitneria floridana*). LEFT: Staminate catkins on a male corkwood. BELOW: Developing fruits on a female corkwood. RIGHT: The smooth bark of a young horse-sugar (*Symplocos tinctoria*). Photo by Ron Lance.

Liquidambar styraciflua
SWEETGUM

DESCRIPTION: Looking in winter like a conifer bare of foliage, a young sweetgum develops a distinctive, excurrent conical form with a central stem extending unforked to the pointed tip. As the tree matures it loses this characteristic architecture and begins to blend in with the oaks (*Quercus*) and other deciduous trees in the vicinity. This change in form results from sweetgum's tendency to begin to fork at about half its ultimate height, causing one of the most sudden and dramatic architectural transformations from juvenile to adult form visible anywhere in our native forests. Many people have seen only the juvenile trees in urban landscapes and might be incredulous if shown an old-growth sweetgum swamp.

Bottomland woods are home to this tree, but it is almost as comfortable in old, disturbed upland fields and grows in the lower Appalachian Mountains up to about 3000 feet (900 m) above sea level. It also extends south into Mexico and Central America, where it truly becomes a mountain tree. The most massive specimens, though, are found in deep, well-drained bottomland soils of the southeastern United States. The largest known sweetgum stands 136 feet (40.8 m) high in Craven County, North Carolina, on a base more than 7 feet (2.1 m) thick above the root buttress. It is a magnificent tree, but many old sweetgums came close to such dimensions before the great virgin forest of North America was logged.

LEAVES: Sweetgum leaves are like maple (*Acer*) leaves in that both are palmately lobed and both color magnificently in fall, turning various shades of gold, red, pink, and purple, often on the same tree. Unlike maples, though, sweetgum bears its lustrous leaves arranged alternately along the twigs, and the leaves are pleasantly fragrant when scraped. They can grow up to 7 inches (17.5 cm) across on vigorous shoots. The fall color of this species will develop even without cold temperatures, so sweetgum is a favorite tree for planting in California and other warm-climate areas.

FLOWERS AND FRUIT: The conspicuous flowers are greenish, emerging just prior to the foliage, which then tends to camouflage them. Pistillate flowers develop in spherical clusters, while the more prominent staminate flowers occur in upright clusters and expand early enough to have some ornamental value before being concealed by the leaves.

The fruits, conversely, are among the most conspicuous (and notorious) of any native North American trees. Woody seed capsules (called gum-balls) develop from the female flower clusters, reaching a little more than 1 inch (2.5 cm) in diameter. They hang by the thousands from the dormant branches through much of winter, gradually falling after releasing their small seeds to the wind. When they land in a lawn area they refuse to decompose, and their hornlike projections cling to the turf like Velcro, jamming reel-type mowers and creating a severe maintenance headache in closely maintained lawns. While they remain attached to the tree, however, swinging from their flexible stalks, they enhance its ornamental value immensely, and many are collected and painted for holiday ornaments.

BEST SEASONS: MID FALL (for the colorful foliage) and LATE FALL (for the attractive fruit capsules). SUMMER (for the glossy, leathery leaves) and WINTER (for the gray bark, corky winged twigs, gum-balls, and symmetrical outline, most visible during the dormant season).

NATIVE AND ADAPTIVE RANGE: Sweetgum can be found, often in pure stands on good sites, from southern Illinois east to Long Island and south throughout the southeastern United States to eastern Texas and central Florida, skipping only the higher mountains. It then reappears in the Sierra Madre and in high elevations in Central America. Fossils of sweetgum have been found in Siberia, Greenland, and Switzerland, indicating an even more extensive range prior to the Ice Age, which reduced the flora of Europe to a small fraction of what it once was.

Although geographic races are not recognized, this species is a good example of the effects of provenance. Trees from comparable hardiness zones should be se-

RIGHT: Sweetgums (*Liquidambar styraciflua*) develop variable but striking fall color.

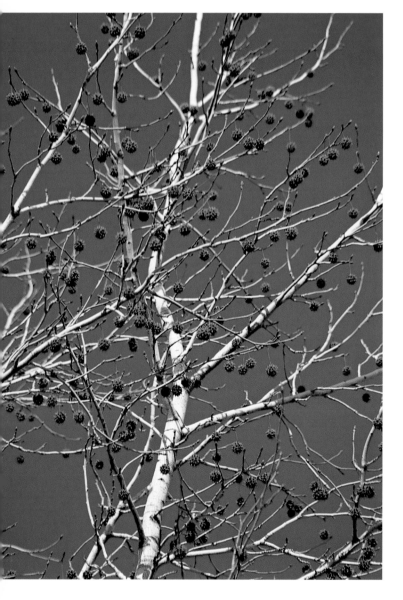

lected for optimum vigor and hardiness under local conditions. With this caution in mind, sweetgum can be considered hardy north through USDA zone 5.

CULTURE: This tree is adaptable to a variety of conditions, preferring deep, moist, acidic soil and full sun. It grows rapidly when given such a situation but more slowly on dry sites or in less ideal soil. It is a little tricky to transplant because of its coarse root system, but root-pruned or container-grown trees from nurseries establish readily. The tiny seeds germinate freely if stratified and surface-sown in spring (or if they land in a nicely tilled flowerbed), but they must be collected early in fall before the gum-balls open and release them to the wind.

PROBLEMS: Trees in natural stands are very susceptible to fire injury, and many planted specimens suffer from animal browsing. Sweetgums from southern origins are damaged by late spring freezes and winter cold in the North, and the species is generally sensitive to ozone pollution. Although it is a favorite target of the Gypsy moth (*Lymantria dispar*), most other insects and diseases seldom attack it.

Culturally, sweetgum can become chlorotic on soils that are not sufficiently acidic, and drought-stressed on those that are shallow or excessively well drained. Its gum-balls can be a litter problem of major concern if the tree is planted in an area where they cannot be allowed to remain where they fall, but this is more a matter of improper planting design than one of a flawed tree. In places where gum-balls simply cannot be tolerated but

TOP LEFT: The staminate flowers of sweetgum (*Liquidambar styraciflua*). LEFT: Many sweetgum fruit balls cling all winter. BELOW: Sweetgum leaves in fall. RIGHT: 'Rotundiloba' is a fruitless selection.

existing trees are too valuable to be removed, there are chemical sprays that can be used each year to arrest the fruit development.

The extensive root system, some of which invariably expands above the surface of the ground, needs a lot of room and protection from damage caused by mowers set too low. The combination of surface roots and gum-ball litter should encourage the conversion of turf to a mulch bed under this species, which then becomes a wonderful seedbed for volunteer gum seedlings.

CULTIVARS: 'Variegata' has yellow-speckled leaves, and 'Silver King' has large white patches. Both are popular in Europe. Northern gardeners may choose 'Moraine' or a variegated form trademarked as Gold Dust, both hardy selections with good fall color. Southern gardeners might also consider 'Burgundy', 'Festival', or 'Palo Alto' where brilliant fall color is needed. 'Emerald Sentinel' is an erect form with great foliage in both summer and fall and is reported to bear fewer fruits than the average gum tree. The upright 'Obtusiloba' and 'Rotundiloba', which may be synonyms, were the first selections made solely for reduced fruit production. They were discovered in North Carolina in 1930 and propagated for their unusual leaves, but were little known until the 1970s, when it was finally realized they were essentially fruitless.

'Worplesdon' was selected in England for its fall color and doubly lobed leaves. Subsequently a shrubby variegated sport of this selection was found in a tissue culture lab, and that form has been introduced into the trade as well. Several nurseries are also testing selections for corky bark. Among the first to reach the market was 'Cherokee', a hardy northern selection from Illinois. 'Gumball' is a novelty form, propagated for its dwarf, globose, shrubby growth pattern. Other cultivars exist, but many people prefer to select vigorous seedling trees of known local provenance for best performance. Although not as predictable as the cultivars, they are seldom disappointing. Pick one out in fall, when its color tendencies are revealed.

SIMILAR AND RELATED SPECIES: There are two Asian species (**Liquidambar formosana** and **L. orientalis**) that might be encountered under cultivation in the South, but neither is as hardy as, or aesthetically superior to, our native species. Sweetgum is more closely related to witch hazels (*Hamamelis*) than to any other native North American trees.

COMMENTS: Sweetgum was among the first trees of the Western Hemisphere to be documented in history. The Aztecs called it *xochiocotzoquahuitl* (say that three times fast without tripping over your tongue), and the Aztec emperor Montezuma smoked a medicinal concoction of it with the explorer Hernando Cortés in 1519, one year before the bloody Spanish conquest of the Aztec empire. The species was given its modern common name, which is certainly easier to pronounce, from the taste of the gummy resin that coats fire scars and other wounds.

The vast quantities of tiny seeds produced by sweetgum are a favorite food source for small birds such as finches and are carried far by the wind, enabling the tree to succeed as a pioneer species both on abandoned fields and floodplains. The foliage serves as a preferred host for larvae of the beautiful luna moth, and the much-despised gum-balls have a beneficial use in the flower garden as a long-lasting mulch that repels any cats seeking an outdoor litter box.

Liriodendron tulipifera
TULIPTREE

DESCRIPTION: There is something special about tuliptree, also known as yellow-poplar over much of its range. In the old-growth Cathedral forests encountered by early settlers, tuliptrees were the Corinthian columns. Massive, straight, and plumb, supporting a crown of foliage often barely visible above the crowns of its lesser neighbors, a great tuliptree might be 200 feet (60 m) tall. No other broadleaved trees grew so tall in eastern North America, and only the most exceptional white pines (*Pinus strobus*) were their equals.

Some of these patriarchs still exist, but so few that it might be possible to become acquainted with each one. The current king among these kings is located in Bedford, Virginia. It is only 111 feet (33.3 m) to the tip of its broken top, which is not exceptional for this species, but its crown is supported by a base 10 feet (3 m) thick. The most impressive tuliptree grove, though, surely must be the one above Little Santeetlah Creek in Joyce Kilmer Memorial Forest, which boasts dozens of straight, massive trees much taller than the U.S. national champion, with trunks as thick as upended minivans. Located in the Nantahala National Forest at the western end of North Carolina, this remnant of our natural heritage provides an inspirational window to our past.

LEAVES: Many people who have not seen the flowers of this species believe it was named for the tulip-shaped silhouette of the leaves. Each leaf develops a truncated outline with four or occasionally six lobes, and the blade reaches about 5 inches (12.5 cm) in width and length, quivering at the end of an equally long petiole. The leaves are waxy and smooth and are fascinating to watch unfold in spring. They seem impervious to insect damage and retain their clean appearance through the summer. Fall color is a dependably bright, saturated yellow. The long, slender petioles cause the leaves to hang from the duck-bill-budded twigs and quiver in the breeze like those of true poplars (*Populus*), which might account for this tree's other common name.

FLOWERS AND FRUIT: The flowers are the size and shape of common garden tulips, with two-toned orange and yellow petals around pale orange anthers, all surrounding a central cone-cluster of pistils. They bloom in May after the first leaves have expanded and must be seen from above to be fully visible. People who don't have second-story windows or balconies adjacent to their tuliptrees sometimes miss one of the best floral displays of the late spring garden. Tuliptree flowers are attractive to bees and make a gourmet honey.

The green, lemon-scented central cone matures into a tan woody cluster of winged seeds. The seeds gradually break away in the winter wind, leaving behind only the woody core by spring, but while they remain intact the fruits provide visual interest in early winter.

BEST SEASONS: FALL (the bright color and large size of this tree make it a prominent feature of the fall landscape). SPRING (if the spectacular flowers were not partially concealed from below by the foliage, spring might rate the best season of all). SUMMER (for the bright, clean foliage) and WINTER (for the persistent fruit).

NATIVE AND ADAPTIVE RANGE: Tuliptree covers a broad area from Grand Rapids, Michigan, through Hamilton, Ontario, and Burlington, Vermont, down to the Gulf of Mexico. Within this range it selects growing positions, relative to altitude and moisture, which reflect its need for moderate, mesic conditions. As with some other trees with such a wide degree of adaptability, provenance plays an important part in its success, and relatively local seed sources are best for areas near the northern or southern limits of its natural range. Northern ecotypes are hardy through USDA zone 5.

CULTURE: Tuliptree needs many things to do well; but when it has them, it does very, very well. It is a mesic species and likes deep, rich, well-drained soil, with uniform rainfall (or supplemental irrigation) throughout the growing season. Although late-season droughts affect its growth less than dry springs, dry summer weather causes physiological problems like sunscald and early leaf abscission. This tree needs a productive setting with good moisture, good drainage, sun on the leaves, and

RIGHT: Tuliptrees (*Liriodendron tulipifera*) are usually the tallest trees in the forest.

shade on the roots. Given such a site, tuliptree becomes one of our fastest-growing and most magnificent trees.

When transplanting this species, select a large, open area with sufficient room for it to grow and sufficient soil mass to support its root system. It can be a little tricky to transplant because of its fragile, fleshy roots and juvenile taproot, so move it with a soil ball in early spring, the same way you would with a magnolia. Seed germinates readily if sown in fall, but expect only about 10 percent of the seed to be viable.

PROBLEMS: Tuliptree is remarkably free from most insect and disease pests. In areas where Gypsy moths (*Lymantria dispar*) have denuded entire forests for miles in every direction, the tall islands of green that remain unscathed are invariably tuliptrees. The scale insect *Toumeyella liriodendri* is troublesome on stressed trees. Whether it causes the stress or is successful because of it is open to debate.

Tuliptree is quite susceptible to *Verticillium* wilt (caused by *V. dahliae* and *V. albo-atrum*) and to environmental problems such as air pollution, ice storms, drought, spring frosts, soil compaction, road salt, sapsucker pecks, animal browsing, antler rubbing by deer, and, while still young, sunscald and fire. I have seen many unhappy tuliptrees in urban settings. Due to their immense mature size, these trees also become exposed targets for wind and lightning, and trees thus damaged are prone to decay from *Polyporus versicolor* and many other fungus species.

CULTIVARS: Tuliptree is not known for its cultivars, but a few do exist. Several variegated forms are known, and botanical gardens sometimes grow the globe-shaped 'Compactum' or the narrow 'Fastigiatum'. Most of the finest cultivar specimens are found in Europe, where they originated from plants introduced from North America as early as 1637. The famous Arboretum Trompenburg in Holland has huge specimens of some of the variegated cultivars, including a great 'Medio-pictum'. A few forms with abnormal foliage shape are listed in horticultural literature. In general these selections offer little advantage over the species type, but they are interesting as curiosities.

Some of the finest tuliptrees in the world grow in Union County, Illinois. The USDA has released a seed germplasm selection from there ('Union') for reforestation and ornamental use, and I have three beautiful trees propagated from that same provenance planted at Starhill Forest.

SIMILAR AND RELATED SPECIES: There is one other tuliptree, ***Liriodendron chinense*** of China. It is a smaller tree with deeply lobed leaves and is not as hardy as our native species (though I am having success with it in Illinois).

LEFT: Old-growth tuliptrees (*Liriodendron tulipifera*) in the Joyce Kilmer Forest. RIGHT: The bright fall color of tuliptree.

The genus *Liriodendron* is closely allied with **Magnolia.** The anise trees, yellow anise (**Illicium parviflorum**) and Florida anise (**I. floridanum**), are our only other native trees from the magnolia family. They are beautiful small understory trees of the Deep South that perform well only as far north as USDA zone 7. These licorice-scented plants are small broadleaved evergreen trees with gorgeous foliage. Florida anise, probably the hardier of the two, grows naturally north into USDA zone 7 and might survive as a deciduous tree in part of zone 6. Yellow anise is more common in cultivation, often used as a hedge plant in coastal areas subject to salty ocean spray, which would kill more sensitive plants.

Both anise species prefer shady sites with wet, sandy soil and have hanging flowers best appreciated from below. Like other shade plants, they can suffer photooxidative bleaching in full sun on a hot site, an effect similar to sunburn in humans but with a loss of chlorophyll, which causes whitened leaves. Both are good to plant near a walkway, as they emit a characteristic fragrance when brushed. Seeds are expelled explosively from the ripe pods and germinate very readily, so small volunteer seedlings may be transplanted to desired locations.

BELOW: Tuliptree (*Liriodendron tulipifera*) flowers resemble their namesake. BELOW RIGHT: Tuliptree fruits.

COMMENTS: Tuliptree is the state tree of Indiana, Tennessee, Kentucky, and North Carolina (although the last two have also claimed other species: *Gymnocladus* for Kentucky, unspecified southern pines for North Carolina). It is a favorite nest tree for many birds, and the flowers are a choice nectar source for hummingbirds. The tiger swallowtail butterfly uses this species, and old trees sometimes develop cavities large enough to be used as winter denning sites for bears, thereby serving an important ecological function where caves and other alternative den sites are scarce.

This tree's notoriety seems to spring from its size and history. Daniel Boone reportedly constructed a 60-foot (18-m) pirogue from a single hollowed-out tuliptree log, used by his entire family to journey down the Ohio River from his Kentucky home to the western frontier. Some of the largest tuliptrees in cultivation in the East owe their origins directly to George Washington or Thomas Jefferson, including original specimens planted by both men that still grow at Mount Vernon and Monticello. The largest one at Mount Vernon, planted by Washington in 1785, was designated the estate's official bicentennial tree. It has been pollinated artificially to produce bumper crops of seed for the national Famous and Historic Trees program of American Forests.

Maclura pomifera

OSAGE-ORANGE

DESCRIPTION: In the Midwest, gnarly Osage-oranges, or hedge-apples, are frequent components of field borders and pastures. They are not true oranges (*Citrus*) or true apples (*Malus*), but they do make the toughest hedges in the hedge business. Throughout much of the South they are called *bois d'arc* ("tree of the bow"), so named when early French explorers learned that Native Americans preferred the tough wood for bows. For decades I have admired their artistic form and tenacity. I don't admire all of them, mind you, just the exceptional trees that seem to stand out from the rest.

The species displays considerable genetic variation, and some individuals are just as promising for landscape use now as their ancestors were for hedgerows more than a century ago. Those early, trimmed hedgerows, grown from seed collected in the species' restricted natural range, helped protect adjoining crop fields from wandering livestock. Later, as they were allowed to grow taller, they slowed the wind and helped preserve the land from the effects of the Dust Bowl.

Osage-orange is generally a medium-sized tree, becoming stout and artistic with age. The U.S. national champion at Red Hill, the home of Patrick Henry in Charlotte County, Virginia, is 60 feet (18 m) tall with a branch spread of 85 feet (25.5 m) and a short trunk more than 8 feet (2.4 m) in diameter. It is much larger than any original tree remaining in the species' inhospitable natural habitat, reflecting the value of a favorable site and horticultural attention. Local legend says Henry often sat under this great tree, and it certainly looks old enough, but in fact the species was not introduced into cultivation until a few years after the old patriot died in 1799. So much for oral histories.

LEAVES: Osage-orange leaves appear citruslike, long-pointed, smooth, and glossy, reaching about 5 inches (12.5 cm) long by half as wide. They emerge very late, avoiding spring frosts and allowing the early spring sun to warm the cold ground (or house) below. Fall color is a rich, deep yellow.

FLOWERS AND FRUIT: This species is fully dioecious. The inconspicuous flowers emerge with the leaves and are of no great consequence unless you are attempting to identify the gender of your tree. Such matters can be very important because female trees produce pebbly, grapefruit-sized, chartreuse hedge-apples that can fall with sufficient force to dent the roof of a car or send an unwary pedestrian to the hospital. They are filled with the tree's sticky white sap, and their resemblance to large oranges is superficial only. While these fruits constitute a hazard and a litter problem in managed landscape areas, they are ornamental after the leaves drop in fall, and they seem to inspire much interest among the uninitiated.

Folklore holds that the fruits are repellent to roaches, but I suspect they are most effective in this regard if they happen to fall directly on the roach. Female trees should be relegated to agricultural landscapes or to large, mulched borders, where the fruit display may be appreciated from a distance, then harvested for a roach test or left to feed the local squirrels, who will tear the fruit apart over the ensuing winter to retrieve every seed. Finches, grosbeaks, and crossbills also eat the seeds, and deer, goats, and horses occasionally dig the fruits out from under snow if they are hungry enough.

BEST SEASONS: FALL (the foliage color ranks among the best available, and female trees offer fruit displayed to best advantage after the leaves drop). WINTER (for the dark orange and gray rugged bark, especially on trees that have developed artistic form) and SUMMER (for the glossy foliage).

NATIVE AND ADAPTIVE RANGE: Osage-orange was originally found only in a small area of Texas and adjacent Oklahoma, where it had been driven by ancient glaciers. This range limitation is meaningless today, however, as hedgerow plantings of the past century have helped the tree reclaim much of its prehistoric range in the central and eastern United States. Its limits are still tested as it integrates into the agrarian landscapes of the Corn Belt, but it can be grown, under suitable conditions, north at least through USDA zone 5.

CULTURE: This tree may experience dieback if transplanted carelessly. Move it with a soil ball in spring as the buds barely begin to show signs of life. It thrives in most soils, including tight clay, compacted urban subsoil, and

floodplain sand, and is not fussy about pH. Seeds grow readily; the ripe fruits may be chopped into pieces and planted in fall like seed-potatoes, or allowed to soften in the hard freezes of early winter, whereupon the seeds can be picked from the sticky mess of pulp (about three hundred per fruit). If fruits are left outside all winter and squirrels don't find them, seedlings can be plucked and potted up the following spring as they emerge from the decaying pulp. Selected trees can be grown asexually from softwood cuttings or root cuttings.

Osage-orange is like a spirited horse, becoming valuable only with an investment of some effort. It retains all its dead branches until you remove them, and the tangles of hard wood (and thorns on many wild trees) can test your resolve. It can be nondescript and unruly, and like the wild mustang, it is easiest to urge it to follow the general direction it already wants to go, with just a slight touch here and there to keep it under control. Such touches should include removal of dead wood, vertical epicormic sprouts, and the occasional suckers that spring from the brilliant orange roots, but you need not be very attentive to the structural pruning and training that can be so important with weaker-wooded trees. Osage-orange doesn't break or rot, so don't worry too much about narrow crotch angles or large pruning scars.

This species may serve best when selected mature trees are allowed to remain on a building site. Magnificent seventy-five-year-old specimens shade our residence in Illinois. Many older trees are relatively thornless, and their gender can be determined from the flowers if they are old enough to bloom. Sex determination can be guessed at during winter, too, by looking for fruit remnants and by observing the crown structure with a practiced eye: male trees are often more upright than females.

These tough, windfirm trees are safe to keep around houses and are more tolerant of the impacts of nearby construction than most other trees. Of course, good care pays dividends. Having proven their mettle as windbreak trees in the drought-stricken Great Plains, these trees are equally at home as the picturesque visual focal points in residential landscapes. Osage-orange is a wind-resistant, drought-resistant, disease- and insect-resistant, pollution- and salt-resistant, everything-resistant survivor with considerable aesthetic potential. It need only be tamed.

PROBLEMS: This species does have its drawbacks, and

LEFT: A large Osage-orange (*Maclura pomifera*) at Starhill Forest.

they can be serious. Most juvenile individuals and sprouts are armed with vicious thorns, strong and sharp enough to puncture a tire. Some trees, though, particularly older ones, are nearly or completely thornless. Females bear the attractive but messy fruits, which can weigh up to 3 pounds (1.4 kg) and cause a severe headache upon impact when they fall. On a calm, sunny late-fall morning following a hard freeze, I once watched a single female tree drop several hundred fruit in less than an hour, pulverizing a trash can and everything else beneath it.

If this tree is cut, and the stump left untreated, the root system will send forth a profusion of thorny sprouts. And, in spite of your best pruning and staking efforts, some trees seem genetically programmed to develop a ragtag branching pattern instead of a more graceful form.

CULTIVARS: My old friend John Pair of Kansas State University was in the forefront of cultivar testing with Osage-orange, and promoted several excellent forms chosen for their lack of thorns or fruit. Among these are 'Altamont', an upright male selection from Illinois; 'Park', from a superior tree found in Ottawa, Kansas; 'Pawhuska', another release from Kansas stock, named for Chief Pawhuska of the Osage Nation; and 'Wichita', from a spreading tree found south of Wichita, Kansas.

John's favorite was the upright-growing male 'Whiteshield', found by John Flick in Oklahoma at Whiteshield

Creek (named after a Cheyenne chief) and developed as a cultivar by Steve and Sherry Bieberich. The Morton Arboretum has a nice tree under observation named 'Double-O' (for "Osage-orange"), but as yet it is not as completely thornless as others. There is also a 'Triple-O' in the evaluation program, in addition to 'Denmark', 'Smolan Graham', 'K-2', 'Cambell', 'Quaker', and 'Whatcheer'.

Kansas State is testing some of my own selections for potential introduction as well. Two of the most intriguing have the temporary experimental names Beta (a majestic, thornless male tree shaped like an American elm) and Delta (a thornless female with graceful, picturesque, horizontal branching and cantaloupe-sized fruit). Delta is potentially useful for special ornamental and wildlife applications where massive fruits and artistic form are desired. I am giving it the cultivar name 'Cannonball' and have released it for specialty use (as the only selected

LEFT: The rugged form of Osage-orange (*Maclura pomifera*). BELOW: A heavy fruit crop on a female Osage-orange. RIGHT: Bark of Osage-orange.

superior female cultivar) in Europe. Beta will await further comparison with the many other male clones under study at the university.

SIMILAR AND RELATED SPECIES: *Maclura* is a monotypic genus but is closely related to the smaller but very similar Chinese ***Cudrania tricuspidata,*** with which it can be crossed to produce an unusual bigeneric hybrid. It is in the same family as the mulberries (*Morus*).

COMMENTS: Osage-orange is home to the Hagen sphinx, a large, host-specific moth. The tree is also very valuable for wildlife habitat in general, and it is a biological tragedy to see so many old hedgerows bulldozed in the Midwest to make room for an extra few rows of corn. Its bright yellow heartwood is the heaviest of any of our native woods, and the most decay resistant, due to the natural fungicide 2,3,4,5-tetrahydroxystilbene, which is concentrated in the wood. I sometimes hear old farmers claim that you can place a rock on top of a hedge post, and the rock will rot before the post does. That may be a little much, but I do have fence posts made from untreated Osage-orange that have remained solid since 1930, outlasting later ones made from treated pine. The wood burns with nearly the heat value of coal, generating an endless shower of sparks, and will warp or crack a wood-burning stove if carelessly burned.

Lewis and Clark discovered this species growing in St. Louis at the start of their expedition, and sent it back to President Jefferson in May of 1804. The fruit, Lewis said, "had an exquisite odour and was the size of the largest orange, of a globular form and a fine orange colour." It

was the first of many new plants to be introduced by these great explorers. Jefferson shared the tree with his friend George Washington, and it can still be seen at Washington's River Farm, now the headquarters of the American Horticulture Society. Of course, it has grown a little since 1804.

A few decades later Osage-orange became the plant of choice for living fences as the Great Plains evolved from open range to farming. During the Civil War, when its Confederate natural habitat was off limits to Yankees as a seed source, bushels of fruits brought big money. Not much later, beginning in 1874, the hedges were allowed to grow up and the trunks were used as posts to attach that newfangled invention, barbed wire, which some believe was inspired by the thorny twigs of this tree. Interestingly, Osage-orange posts are so decay resistant that they remain standing after the wire rusts away.

Most remaining old trees are no longer trimmed or hedged, except for historic restorations. However, one famous old male tree near Bondville, Illinois, has been trimmed several times every year since the early 1900s by Neimiah Jacobs and his descendants. This trimming cycle was not begun for hedge purposes but to save the tree from removal when the first overhead utility lines were installed in the area prior to the Great Depression. Its dense crown can still be seen (under the wires) along the north side of Illinois Route 10, west of Champaign.

The fossil record of Osage-orange makes for fascinating speculation. Native as far north as Minnesota and southern Ontario during the Sangamon interglacial period of 100,000 years ago, Osage-orange, like every other species, was driven south by the Pleistocene glaciers. The large heavy fruits of this tree probably fed the gomphotheres, who would have consumed them whole or in large pieces and passed the seeds intact along their migration routes. But these magnificent animals were hunted to extinction by humans at the close of the last ice age, and Osage-orange thus lost its vectors—the means by which it could move its seed and reclaim its former territory when the ice retreated. It had to wait for humans, the very species that had eliminated those vectors, to find it valuable as a hedge and become the new vectors. This we have done, with great success, during the past 150 years.

LEFT: Squirrels open Osage-orange (*Maclura pomifera*) fruits to eat the seeds.

Magnolia acuminata

CUCUMBERTREE

DESCRIPTION: Many people think of magnolias only as Asian flowering shrubs, but several magnolia tree species are native to North America. The largest and hardiest is the cucumbertree. It becomes a canopy tree in mesic forests, looking more like a large timber tree than a cousin of the dainty, pastel-flowering hybrid Asian magnolias. It prefers mesic conditions similar to those frequented by its other cousin, tuliptree (*Liriodendron*), but tolerates more shade.

The only native magnolia of Canada, cucumbertree is listed as an endangered species there, being found only in a few stream valleys and protected slopes near Lake Erie. Its ultimate size at this northern limit of its natural range is restricted to about half of what it can attain in the cove forests of the southern Appalachians. The largest specimen is a planted tree located in Waukon, Iowa. It is a respectable 75 feet (22.5 m) tall, which is not particularly large, but it has a trunk nearly 8 feet (2.4 m) thick. This particular tree has attained such a large diameter by growing free from the normal competition of its forested habitat. Only an open-grown specimen like this can develop the massive lower limbs that build such trunk caliper.

LEAVES: Cucumbertree leaves look much like those of pawpaw (*Asimina triloba*). They reach approximately 8 inches (20 cm) in length and develop acuminate points at their tips that give the tree its specific epithet. Fall color can be pale yellow or a warm, bright tan, but the leaves are sometimes blasted by frost before any significant color develops.

FLOWERS AND FRUIT: The magnolias are known for their flowers, but those of this species are comparatively modest. They are greenish yellow, with some trees showing more yellow than others, and grow to about 3 inches (7.5 cm) across. They would be much more conspicuous if they emerged before the foliage, but they don't. Several ornamental hybrid cultivars have incorporated the hardiness and yellow flower color of this species with the flower size and timing of Asian species.

The aromatic fruit follicles that develop from the flower core resemble small cucumbers when green. Later they turn deep red and the compartments split open to expose the bright orange-coated seeds, which hang from threads as they fall free. Pollination is often incomplete, perhaps due to a lack of the necessary beetle pollinators, and the little cucumbers become lumpy and asymmetrical as some seeds develop while others don't. Many fruits fall to the ground with their seeds still enclosed, where they are foraged by towhees and other ground-feeding birds, as well as small mammals.

BEST SEASONS: FALL (for the fruits with their red seeds, and for the occasionally nice leaf color). SUMMER (an attractive shade tree with clean foliage) and SPRING (the flowers are attractive when viewed close at hand).

NATIVE AND ADAPTIVE RANGE: Cucumbertree can be found from southern Ontario and western New York southwest through the mountains of the eastern United States, with outlying populations in suitable habitats to the south and west as far as the Gulf Coastal Plain and eastern Oklahoma. Under cultivation it is hardy north into USDA zone 4.

CULTURE: Most of our native deciduous magnolias require deep, moist, well-drained soil and protection from extreme wind and heat. They will accept partial shade and any moderate pH but will not take wet soil or drought conditions. They are tricky to transplant due to their coarse, fleshy root system and should be planted shallow and moved in the early spring with a good soil ball, just like the commonly cultivated Asian species. This magnolia grows rapidly once established in a suitable site.

The seeds germinate readily if removed from the fruit, cleaned of their colorful soft coating, and planted in fall. Cleaning magnolia seed for planting can be a messy job, thoroughly redeemed by the citruslike aroma of the brightly colored seed coats. But the real reward comes the following June when, after waiting so long and becoming convinced the seed will never sprout, you finally see the little magnolia trees bursting out of the soil.

PROBLEMS: All magnolias are brittle and sometimes show a reluctance to heal wounds or pruning cuts. Cucumbertree is less prone to storm damage than other species, but it should be trained into a strong branching

pattern while young. This usually takes little effort, because the tree's growth habit is naturally strong and uniform. Unwanted limbs should be removed while still small, if possible. Most of our native magnolias, including cucumbertree, are more sensitive to ground fires than most associated species and are frequently the targets of pecking sapsuckers.

CULTIVARS: Only two cultivars are widely grown: 'Variegata', with white-speckled leaves, and 'Golden Glow', with yellow flowers. Cucumbertree and its close relative yellow cucumbertree (*Magnolia cordata*) have been very useful in breeding programs using Asian species. 'But-

LEFT: A mature cucumbertree (*Magnolia acuminata*) in winter. BELOW: Fall color on a large cucumbertree.

terflies', 'Elizabeth', 'Evamaria', 'Ivory Chalice', and 'Yellow Bird' are among the most promising offspring of such programs.

SIMILAR AND RELATED SPECIES: Of some eighty magnolia species worldwide, about half a dozen are deciduous species native to the southeastern United States, and all of these have horticultural merit. **Magnolia cordata,** which may be a variety instead of a distinct species, is most closely allied to the cucumbertree and is most often seen in hybridization programs. It is a smaller tree with larger, showier flowers. 'Peirce's Park' is a selection from this taxon.

Umbrella magnolia (**Magnolia tripetala**) is also seen occasionally in cultivation. This unique plant resembles a small version of cucumbertree with immense 15-inch

(37.5-cm) leaves, large creamy flowers, and fruits up to 8 inches (20 cm) long, looking like a relict from the prehistoric tropical jungles of Jurassic Park. Magnolias are indeed very primitive trees, but they have evolved to explore habitats far removed from their tropical origins. This one is nearly as hardy as cucumbertree if given a protected location where its leaves will not be torn apart by wind or scorched by hot sun. There is at least one cultivar floating around the nursery trade: 'Urbana', selected from cultivated plants in Illinois.

Fraser magnolia (**Magnolia fraseri**) is a small, fragrant, basal-branching tree of the southern Appalachians. Sometimes called earleaf magnolia, it has narrow, auriculate-lobed leaves and white flowers. *Magnolia fraseri* var. *pyramidata*, which is often considered a distinct species, extends southward into the Gulf Coastal Plain.

Another species with auriculate-lobed leaves is the bigleaf magnolia (**Magnolia macrophylla**). Its leaves exceed even those of the umbrella magnolia, sometimes reaching nearly 3 feet (0.9 m) in length, and a young specimen with a single stem capped with a ring of such foliage gives the visual impression of a banana plant. With such a tree you really don't need a rake; the leaves are so big and so few in number that you can just pick them up by hand. This is a very attractive species with huge 8-inch (20-cm) fragrant white flowers, but it needs a totally protected site and careful design placement because of its huge, fragile leaves. Named cultivars include 'Sara Gladney' and 'Whopper'. Bigleaf magnolia is very

rare and widely scattered in the wild; few people have seen it except in cultivation.

The southern **Magnolia ashei** (syn. *M. macrophylla* var. *ashei*) has slightly smaller flowers and leaves. It grows into a compact, shrubby tree and starts producing its huge, fragrant flowers when only three or four years old.

All of these trees are fully deciduous and surprisingly hardy north of their native haunts. I grow every one in USDA zone 5 at Starhill Forest, and some can be seen still further north. Southern magnolia (*Magnolia grandiflora*) and sweetbay (*M. virginiana*) are evergreen or semievergreen species.

COMMENTS: Old cucumbertrees are occasionally seen in northern residential landscapes, where they sometimes arrived by accident. This species has been popular as a grafting understock for tender hybrid magnolias that are not reliably hardy north. When the grafted scion is killed by a hard winter, the hardy cucumbertree root sends up a sprout of its own. Years later an inattentive gardener may wonder how his or her delicate grafted magnolia grew into such a magnificent tree without any of the anticipated pink flowers.

LEFT: Foliage and fruits of cucumbertree (*Magnolia acuminata*). BELOW: The beautiful flower of bigleaf magnolia (*Magnolia macrophylla*). RIGHT: Bigleaf magnolia needs a protected location where its leaves will not be torn by wind.

Magnolia grandiflora

SOUTHERN MAGNOLIA

DESCRIPTION: Among the most envied landscape trees at Jim Wilson's house at Savory Farm in South Carolina is the perfect specimen of evergreen southern magnolia, also known as bull bay. Nearly every southern town has at least one such specimen, and its owner's residence is usually described as "the house with the beautiful magnolia tree." But southern magnolia grows in the forest too, where it is transformed from a leafy specimen plant, branched to the ground, into a canopy tree with a tall, straight trunk clear of limbs for half its height. Of all the magnolias, this is the species most often harvested for sawtimber.

Southern magnolia is the state tree of Mississippi, and the largest individual known grows in Jones County, standing 98 feet (29.4 m) tall with a trunk more than 7 feet (2.1 m) in diameter. This tree is usually found growing with beech (*Fagus grandifolia*), gum (*Liquidambar styraciflua*), oak (*Quercus*), and other forest trees in sandy, fertile, well-drained soil around the fringes of wet areas. While it is very adaptable under cultivation, most of its entire natural range lies within 200 feet (60 m) of sea level.

LEAVES: The leaves are thick, shiny, and stiff, creased along the midrib, growing up to 10 inches (25 cm) long. They are the darkest green, with tomentose undersides that vary from pale green to rusty red. This species is fully evergreen, and the leaves are retained for two years under most conditions. They will bronze, blotch, and burn in severe winters at the northern limits of cultivation, but most still cling at least until they are replaced by new foliage in spring. Old dead leaves are almost woody, like miniature brown canoes skimming the forest floor below.

FLOWERS AND FRUIT: This is one of the showiest magnolias, for both flowers and fruit. The white, waxy flowers are up to 1 foot (30 cm) across and powerfully fragrant. They are borne on the ends of nearly every twig on mature trees in late spring, and a few continue to open through summer, each lasting for only a day or two once fully open. The conelike fruits that follow are heavy and symmetrical, with a crimson-velvet surface. The individual seed compartments split open to reveal bright flame-red seeds in each seam.

BEST SEASONS: SPRING (for the appearance and fragrance of the primary blooming period). FALL (for the ripening fruit). ALL YEAR (for the deep shade and evergreen foliage).

NATIVE AND ADAPTIVE RANGE: Southern magnolia is found in mixed stands along the coastal plains from North Carolina to eastern Texas. Its seedlings are extremely sensitive to frost, which is the primary reason its natural range is so limited. Some selections (mostly of the type with reddish tomentose leaves, called brownbacks) are being tested as far north as USDA zone 5. '24-Below', an experimental plant I received from Mike Stansberry, a plantsman in Knoxville, Tennessee, is the only selection I have tested that has endured several winters as far north as central Illinois. Most selections are reliably hardy north only through USDA zone 7 or barely into USDA zone 6. The species should remain there for general landscaping purposes unless it is to be grown experimentally, but it can be grown further north as a foliage shrub, cut back to the ground after every hard winter.

CULTURE: Because it is evergreen, this tree must be container grown or transplanted with a soil ball, preferably in early spring except in the Deep South. Young transplanted trees must be watered during dry spells until they are well established. Southern magnolia likes a deep, rich, acidic, gritty soil with good drainage. Partial shade is acceptable, and winter shade is preferred in northern areas where the ground freezes, immobilizing the extra soil moisture needed by sunlit leaves. The most dense form and flowering occurs in full sun. Southern magnolia seeds germinate more quickly than those of some deciduous magnolias, and clean seed can be sprouted without a winter cold period.

PROBLEMS: This magnolia seems to drop old leaves almost continuously and casts shade as dark as a coal mine, so quality turf maintenance beneath its canopy is

RIGHT: A southern magnolia (*Magnolia grandiflora*) in the understory of a Coastal Plain forest.

impossible. It is best grown in a mulched border with its lower branches left intact to blanket the ground. The leaves are very heavy and shed only from the internal parts of the crown where the wind seldom reaches, usually falling straight down to form a natural mulch. This should be encouraged, since nothing will grow under this tree. Stray fallen leaves should be chopped with a rotary mower and blown back under the branches to avoid continuous removal of the minerals recycled in the leaf litter.

Specimens grown under severe winter conditions, especially in full sun, develop sunscald and foliage damage that will destroy their ornamental value, if not kill

them. Otherwise this tree seems immune to insect and disease problems, and its waxy leaves make it resistant to salt spray and urban air pollution, unlike most magnolias. Once established, it is also the most drought resistant of the magnolias.

CULTIVARS: More than one hundred southern magnolia selections have been made for superior flowers, foliage, growth rate, or other merits. 'Little Gem' is a reblooming compact form from Steed's Nursery in North Carolina, and 'Overton' is even smaller, growing to only about 24 feet (7.2 m) tall. Majestic Beauty magnolia is another popular selection, from Monrovia Nursery in California. These are all very ornamental but also very tender and useful only for the South. The narrowly upright 'Hasse', 'Alta', and 'DD Blanchard' may be somewhat hardier, surviving some tests in USDA zone 6.

The current trend is to select for increased winter hardiness, and several promising cultivars are becoming available for gardeners in the upper South. 'Edith Bogue' is an award-winning tree suitable for such areas and has been the winner of laboratory testing for hardiness. 'Bracken's Brown Beauty', 'Tulsa', and 'Russet' are recent selections that have shown similar hardiness in early testing. 'Victoria' is another hardy type, one of the few hardy green-back forms, without rusty-colored tomentose leaves. All of these are worth trying in USDA zone 6 or perhaps even zone 5 in protected sites.

Many other new selections show promise, including the one from Knoxville that I am testing and another found by Matt Vehr at Spring Grove Cemetery in Cincinnati. Nevertheless, the basic principle remains that, for excellent performance over the long haul, the term "native" for this species usually means south of USDA zone 6.

SIMILAR AND RELATED SPECIES: Northern gardeners who covet a semievergreen magnolia and southern gardeners who seek a refined, graceful, small evergreen tree without the gaudier qualities of southern magnolia should consider sweetbay (***Magnolia virginiana***). It is more diminutive in all respects. Unlike southern magnolia, its leaves have silvery undersides that flash in the wind, and it has the ability to shed its foliage during se-

TOP LEFT: Each of the spectacular flowers of southern magnolia (*Magnolia grandiflora*) are at their best for only one day. LEFT: The decorative, long-lasting fruits of southern magnolia. TOP RIGHT: Brown-back southern magnolias have attractive tan indumentum on the leaf undersides. RIGHT: The northern, spreading, deciduous form of sweetbay (*M. virginiana*).

vere winters before physiological drought causes damage to the woody tissue. The evergreen *M. virginiana* var. *australis* is more erect and less hardy than the shrubbier, deciduous form.

When northern-provenance plants are selected, sweetbay is at least a full zone hardier than the hardiest southern magnolia cultivars. It is our most fragrant and flood-tolerant magnolia, and it does fine in any average garden soil that is not too alkaline. Several cultivars are available or under development, including 'Ludiviciana' from Louisiana, 'Silver Sword' from Tennessee (a selection by Plato Touliatos's nursery in Memphis), 'Santa Rosa' from Florida, and 'Willowleaf Bay' from Alabama. 'Timeless Beauty' originated from a rare cross between southern magnolia and sweetbay. I am most honored, how-

ever, to recommend 'Jim Wilson', selected and named for my friend Jim by another friend, Earl Cully, from a hardy specimen growing at Earl's nursery in Illinois. Trademarked as Moonglow magnolia, it is unusual in that it displays the upright growth and evergreen tendencies of *Magnolia virginiana* var. *australis* but is hardy in USDA zone 5.

COMMENTS: Milky Way Farm in southern Tennessee is famous for its creator (the founder of the Mars Candy Company), its champion livestock, its stone mansion, and its unparalleled collection of unique stone barns. But tree lovers are most impressed with its southern magnolias—the largest private grove of this tree ever planted in North America.

Further west, in Washington State Park, Arkansas, grows a venerable old specimen called the Jones Magnolia, named for two men named Jones who were born near the tree in 1839, the year it was planted. One Jones would become senator of Arkansas, the other the governor. The tree was placed just east of the inn where Sam Houston,

William Travis, and others had met four years earlier to plan the independence of Texas, and a short distance south of the blacksmith shop where James Black and Jim Bowie made the first bowie knife. Bowie and Travis died with Davy Crockett at the Alamo in 1836, but Houston went on to become the first president of the independent Republic of Texas and lived to see the Jones Magnolia reach its twenty-fourth year. The commemorative tree is now almost 5 feet (1.5 m) in diameter.

Southern magnolia might rank second only to certain oaks in the number of such events and legends with which it has become associated in the South. It is a handsome, long-lived, commanding tree, appropriate and worthy to consecrate history. It is also among the most popular American trees planted in southern Europe and even China.

BELOW LEFT: The creamy flower of sweetbay (*Magnolia virginiana*). BELOW: Seeds emerge from a sweetbay.

Malus ioensis

PRAIRIE CRAB

DESCRIPTION: In the savannas and borders of the prairie that once dominated so much of the heart of North America, one of the most beautiful and useful small trees was the prairie crab (*Malus ioensis*, syn. *Pyrus ioensis*). It is a miniature apple tree, or crabapple, and its fruit is sought by myriad species of wildlife, just as it was by early settlers in the days before Johnny Appleseed brought domesticated apples to the frontier. Prairie crab's prairie-fire heritage has encouraged it to evolve into a cloning species that sprouts additional trees from the roots after fire kills the top (it frequently sprouts in the absence of fire as well). When grown as a single specimen, it grows much larger than it does when allowed to clump. The U.S. national champion prairie crab, located in Oakland County, Michigan, is nearly 50 feet (15 m) tall with a trunk 1 foot (30 cm) in diameter.

LEAVES: The leaves of all our native crabapples look much like those of cultivated apples. Prairie crab leaves are the largest, up to 4 inches (10 cm) long, and are frequently shallow-lobed. They emerge red in early spring and are quite attractive as they highlight the intricate tracery of twigs against the colorful scaly bark. Vigorous trees that escape premature defoliation from fungus diseases can develop a glowing orange-red fall color.

FLOWERS AND FRUIT: Crabapples, whether native or exotic, are spectacular in bloom. Our native species have fragrant light pink flowers that resemble wild roses, growing in clusters that cover the trees in spring. Those of the prairie crab are the largest, sometimes up to 2 inches (5 cm) across. This species blooms later than most exotic cultivated ornamental crabapples; in my own crabapple collection in central Illinois, prairie crab blooms about the same time as the late-blooming toringo crab (*Malus sieboldii*). The attractive flower buds are deep pink to red before they open, and the flowers on some trees fade to nearly white as they expand. The combination of buds and flowers gives the tree the appeal of a peppermint stick.

The fruits are not ornamental by crabapple standards but do add landscape interest in fall after the leaves drop. They can grow almost as big as golf balls, though they are often only half that large, and they remain pale green until they fall or are eaten by wildlife or gathered by humans.

BEST SEASONS: SPRING (the flowers rival those of many of the most admired exotic species and hybrids). FALL (for the fruit and the leaf color, but only if the tree has not been disfigured by leaf-fungus diseases). WINTER (for the silvery reddish bark and the intricate twig patterns that cast fascinating shadows on the snow).

NATIVE AND ADAPTIVE RANGE: Our native crabapple species are nearly allopatric, but together they cover a large territory. Prairie crab is the common midwestern species, growing from Minnesota and Wisconsin south through Illinois and Missouri to scattered locations in Louisiana and Texas. It is hardy through USDA zone 4.

CULTURE: Native crabapples thrive anywhere their exotic relatives do, and they have similar limitations as well. They transplant fairly easily and are simple to grow from seed picked from the fruit and sown in fall or early winter.

PROBLEMS: The native crabapples are notorious for their severe susceptibility to every foliage disease known to affect the genus. Apple scab (*Venturia inaequalis*) is the most serious and frequently defoliates them by late summer. Several leaf rusts (*Gymnosporangium*) are common defoliators, but each following spring the crabapples leaf out again without any perceptible loss of vigor.

Crabs will not tolerate poor drainage, and become scraggly in shade. They tend to form clonal thickets that become productive but impregnable wildlife habitat; periodic attention is required to keep the occasional suckers pulled if a single specimen is desired. The large fruits of native crabapples will cause a litter problem if the trees are planted near pavement or in manicured lawns, and the sharp spur branches can be hazardous near sidewalks or other areas where accidental contact is likely.

Unthrifty or stressed trees are prone to suffer attack from borers such as the round-headed apple borer (*Saperda candida*), which occasionally inflicts enough mechanical damage at the base of a tree to induce wind breakage. Rabbits and deer also cut or girdle many young crabapples in winter. This is not a problem for

trees in wildlife plantings or natural thickets, since they simply send up new stems from the root system, but it can be a cause for concern with specimen trees.

CULTIVARS: Native crabapples are generally used for naturalizing or preserved in place as existing wild trees. Since so much attention has been given to selecting and breeding disease-resistant hybrids of exotic crabapples for domestic landscape use, the cultivars of our native species receive little notice. There are several, however, that have been propagated for their superior ornamental qualities. 'Plena' is an inclusive name that encompasses the old form 'Bechtel' and the improved selections 'Nova', 'Fimbriata', 'Fiore's Improved Bechtel', 'Klehm's Improved Bechtel', and 'Brandywine', all prairie crab cultivars with double flowers. 'Nevis' and 'Boone Park' are single-flowered selections. Greg Morgenson of Lincoln Oakes Nursery in North Dakota is assembling a collec-

LEFT: Prairie crab (*Malus ioensis*) in bloom. BELOW: Prairie crab in its native environment.

tion of native crabapples that should result in some very hardy selections.

SIMILAR AND RELATED SPECIES: Other native crabapple species include sweet crab (***Malus coronaria***), southern crab (***M. angustifolia***), and western crab (***M. diversifolia***). Sweet crab dominates the northeastern part of the crab territory, from Michigan, southern Ontario, and New York south through Indiana and Ohio to scattered locations in the southern Appalachians. Southern crab begins to dominate where sweet crab fades out, extending its range southward to the Gulf Coast. In the West the crab niche is filled by western crab. Each species also occurs in small areas within the range of one or more of the others.

Under cultivation sweet crabs are perfectly hardy north into USDA zone 4, while southern crab and western crab can perform well as far north as portions of USDA zone 5. Generally each species is best when used in its own home territory. The U.S. national champion sweet crab grows in Hampstead, Virginia, and stands 37

feet (11.1 m) tall, while the biggest southern crab is in Swannanoa, North Carolina, and is about the same size. Both have trunks twice as large as that of the largest prairie crab. The leaves of southern crab, also known as narrow-leaved crab, are only about half as large as those of prairie crab and are seldom lobed. I have found no size records for western crab. Some taxonomists separate a few varieties and probable hybrids into additional species in the southeastern United States. The differences even among the primary species are so obscure that further splitting of the genus would accomplish little from a horticultural standpoint.

'Big O', from the USDA, is a seed germplasm selection of sweet crab from Georgia that is resistant to rust diseases. 'Charlottae' and 'Nieuwlandiana' are two selections with semidouble flowers; 'Elk River' has fully double flowers. 'Callaway' is a southern crab selection from Callaway Gardens in Pine Mountain, Georgia. 'Prince Georges' has large double flowers and is reportedly a hybrid of prairie crab and southern crab. Other hybrid selections involving crosses of native and exotic crabapples are available from some nurseries.

COMMENTS: There are more than five hundred crabapple cultivars on the market, derived from about thirty-five species, and hundreds of selections of edible apple species and hybrids exist. Technically a crabapple tree is just an apple tree with fruit that remains smaller than about 2 inches (5 cm) across, since there is no real taxonomic distinction between the two types. It is also worth noting that the historic name of the genus was *Pyrus*, which now applies only to the true pears but which once included such trees as apples and mountain-ash (*Sorbus*).

Crabapple thickets provide valuable wildlife habitat, protecting nests from predators and offering shelter to many species. The fruits of wild crabapples are sought by many mammals and large birds, especially ground feeders that find them under the snow in winter when other food is scarce. Wild crabs also host the short-lined chocolate moth, a gentle and benign relative of the blood-sucking "vampire moth" of the Malay Peninsula.

BELOW: Prairie crab (*Malus ioensis*) fruits are valuable for wildlife. BELOW RIGHT: The pink flowers of prairie crab.

Morus rubra

RED MULBERRY

DESCRIPTION: Unlike its weedy exotic cousins, which neither receive nor deserve much respect in horticultural circles, our native mulberry is a handsome, unaggressive forest tree. It inhabits rich, fertile, mesic forest soils, rather than the sidewalk cracks favored by the exotic species, and becomes a vase-shaped spreading shade tree in the open, reminiscent of a small American elm (*Ulmus americana*).

Seldom emerging to the top of the forest canopy in the wild, red mulberry is content to remain in the midstory under the shade of its tallest neighbors, where its large round leaves capture the occasional rays of sunlight that sneak through. The former U.S. national champion at Tower Hill in Illinois had a trunk nearly 7 feet (2.1 m) thick. It was once part of the old Craddick homestead located there and later served as the landmark for the town grade school. It was removed around 2002 by community officials who placed more value upon the sidewalk it was displacing than they did upon the champion tree. The current champion red mulberry is found in Tennessee. It is 52 feet (15.6 m) tall with an equal spread and a trunk that is 8 feet (2.4 m) thick.

LEAVES: Red mulberry has larger, hairier leaves than most exotic mulberries. In the deep shade of the species' native forest habitats, the leaves can grow more than 8 inches (20 cm) long by almost as broad, making this tree easy to identify from a distance. It is commonly cultivated west of its natural range, and though it thrives in this region, the leaves become much waxier and smaller, presumably due to the dry climate. Having seen red mulberries in both the East and West, it is a little difficult for us to accept they are the same species. The leaves are occasionally lobed like those of the Asian white mulberry (*Morus alba*), especially on vigorous sprouts, but more often resemble the unlobed leaves of lindens (*Tilia*). The strong golden fall color of some red mulberry trees ranks with that of hickories (*Carya*).

FLOWERS AND FRUIT: Mulberry is usually, but not always, dioecious. Sometimes individual branches on the same tree are either male or female, like those of honeylocust (*Gleditsia triacanthos*), and there have been a few reports of trees that seem to change their gender from year to year. The green staminate flowers grow in clusters up to 2 inches (5 cm) long, while the pistillate flower clusters are about half as large.

The flowers appear with the leaves in spring and are not very conspicuous, but the dark red fruits that follow on female trees are attractive and blandly sweet. These cylindrical clusters of individual drupes, similar to blackberries, are longer and narrower than those of white mulberry and generally ripen slightly later. Individual fruits mature at different times over several weeks, prolonging the availability of this favorite food for more than thirty species of nesting songbirds and mammals.

BEST SEASONS: FALL (the huge golden leaves of a deep-forest red mulberry, backlit along a dark, wooded stream bank, can dominate the visual scene). SUMMER (for the foliage texture and, where they don't create a litter problem, the tasty fruit).

NATIVE AND ADAPTIVE RANGE: Red mulberry is never a dominant species, but it can be found as an indicator of good soils over an extensive range of latitude. It occurs as a rare species (listed as threatened by the Canadian government) in southern Ontario and from there extends without a break southward throughout the eastern United States to southern Florida and over to Bermuda. Its western natural limit runs from southern Minnesota to the Pecos River valley of western Texas, where its range overlaps that of the smaller Texas mulberry (*Morus microphylla*); then it extends northeast through southern Pennsylvania to the Hudson River in New York and sporadically beyond. While provenance is certain to play a role in the local adaptability of such a wide-ranging tree, it can definitely be grown throughout eastern North America north into USDA zone 4.

CULTURE: Red mulberry can tolerate full sun under mesic conditions or will grow in the dense shade of taller trees. While not as immune to drought and poor soil as some exotic mulberries, it will persist under some really trying conditions. It grows slowly unless given ample moisture throughout the summer, in which case its

growth rate increases dramatically. This tree also responds well to high fertility and is very resistant to damage from air pollution and decay.

All mulberries are easy to transplant and can be grown from seed sown in late summer or fall. The fruits should be fermented for a few days and squeezed through a strainer to remove the seeds from the juice and pulp for storage, but intact fruits can be sown outside without cleaning. Cuttings of selected male or female trees can be rooted in summer.

PROBLEMS: The predominant problem with mulber-

LEFT: Fall color of red mulberry (*Morus rubra*). BELOW: A large red mulberry.

ries is the mess birds make when they eat the fruit from female trees and then roost above a patio or car. This is the cost associated with using this tree to attract so many songbirds, and for some people it is too high a price to pay. Where roosting birds do not pose this problem, the fruits are advantageous.

Red mulberry is subject to some minor leaf mildews, notably *Mycosphaerella mori* and *Phyllactinia guttata*, but they do no serious damage. It does not seem very susceptible to the notorious twig blight (*Fusarium lateritium*), which causes brooming on white mulberry, and despite its usefulness as fodder for commercial silkworms, it is seldom attacked by defoliating insects such as Gypsy moth (*Lymantria dispar*). Trees in the South can

be damaged by the mulberry borer (*Dorcaschema wildii*), but in general red mulberry has fewer problems than its exotic relatives if given a decent site.

CULTIVARS: Mulberry cultivars available at nurseries can all be traced back to exotic species. Unfortunately, our native red mulberry is seldom available for purchase even as seedling stock and must be sought with some measure of determination or propagated at home from seed or cuttings.

SIMILAR AND RELATED SPECIES: Of perhaps ten or twelve mulberry species, only two are native to North America: red mulberry and the smaller but similar Texas mulberry (**Morus microphylla**). The latter grows in Texas, Arizona, and Mexico, where it provides valuable food for wildlife. It has adapted to the hot, dry climate in which it lives by producing very small, tough leaves and remaining a smaller tree than its eastern cousin. The Asian white mulberry (**M. alba**) and the cultivated black mulberry (**M. nigra**) are frequently seen around farmsteads and in urban settings. Both are adapted to poorer soils and harsher habitats than red mulberry.

Mulberries are related to Osage-orange (*Maclura pomifera*) and to several tropical food-producing trees, including breadfruit (**Arctocarpus communis**), the plant Captain Bligh had been transporting during the famous voyage of the *Bounty*, ending in the 1788 mutiny led by Fletcher Christian.

COMMENTS: Most people either love or hate mulberries because of the fruit. In *The Trees of America* (1846), early American tree expert Daniel Jay Browne reported that red mulberry had been cultivated in Europe for well over a century for its fruit and potentially for silkworm food. John Clarke (1839), superintendent of the Morodendron Silk Company of Philadelphia, recorded that red mulberry from Missouri yielded a silk "stronger and finer than that of France," although unfortunately for him the silkworms seemed to prefer the smoother leaves of white mulberry.

The picky taste of silkworms eventually caused the silk industry to abandon the tough red mulberry, but the tree had other values that were equally important to early Americans. Its fibrous bast was woven into blankets by the Choctaw and into ropes to refit the ships of Hernando de Soto in 1540. This makes sense since mulberries are in the same plant family as hemp (*Cannabis sativa*), the natural fiber of preference worldwide for ropemaking. Mulberries are also closely allied to members of *Broussonetia*, the trees that furnish bast for the Polynesian tapa that Samoan people decorate ceremonially with dyes made from their volcanic soil.

LEFT: The tasty fruit of red mulberry (*Morus rubra*).
BELOW: Red mulberry leaves in late fall.

Nyssa sylvatica

BLACK GUM

DESCRIPTION: Architecturally, young black gum presents one of the most refined silhouettes of any tree, resembling a fine-textured, youthful pin oak (*Quercus palustris*). It has reflective, pewter-colored bark on its twigs and small limbs, which catch the sunlight on typical specimens with perfectly horizontal branching habits. This can make the tree glisten as though covered with ice on a sunny winter day. Other trees have limbs that arch downward gracefully, or even weep.

This species has several close relatives; each is known respectively within its home range as tupelo. Its etymology derives from a Creek Indian word meaning "swamp tree" or, according to some, from the Greek name of a mythological water nymph. The species called black gum—or sour gum, to distinguish it from the unrelated sweetgum (*Liquidambar styraciflua*)—is an adaptable tree of both upland and bottomland forests, while the other species and varieties are limited to wetland habitats.

Black gum can become a large specimen after many years, although the oldest trees tend to shrink in size due to storm damage and top dieback. The U.S. national champion black gum is located in Wood County, Texas. When measured in 2000 it stood 110 feet (33 m) tall with a trunk more than 6 feet (1.8 m) in diameter. That year was important for this species in another way as well: black gum was named Tree of the Year by the International Dendrology Society.

LEAVES: The leaves are so smooth, waxy, and glossy that they seem to plead "Touch me!" when viewed up close. Except on vigorous sprouts, most leaves reach only about 4 inches (10 cm) in length by less than half as wide. They are very dark (as is the alligator-skin bark on old trees), hence the tree's common name. Foliage is arranged in horizontal layers that reinforce the layered appearance of the horizontal branches.

Black gum is famous for the intensity of its crimson fall color, but this varies somewhat from tree to tree. If you intend to purchase a black gum specifically for this purpose, visit your local nursery in fall to pick out the most brilliant tree of the bunch. In general, though, even the worst one will not be disappointing.

FLOWERS AND FRUIT: Although I have a black gum next to my garage and see it every day, I never notice the flowers until honeybees attract my attention to them. If you search for them, they can be found in tiny axillary clusters as the leaves are expanding to full size. Black gum is usually dioecious. The fruits that appear on female trees grow to about the size of navy beans and turn dark blue in fall, just as the leaves begin to turn red, hanging in small clusters or pairs. They are a favorite food of many birds, so they don't last long.

BEST SEASONS: FALL (few trees can match the lustrous red fall color, ornamented with blue fruits on female trees). SUMMER (for the shiny foliage, which seems immune to the ravages of summer that tatter and tarnish the leaves of many other trees). WINTER (for the strong framework, fine texture, and silvery bark of young trees).

NATIVE AND ADAPTIVE RANGE: Black gum is similar to red maple (*Acer rubrum*) in that it grows in very wet areas yet sometimes on dry rocky uplands as well. It ranges from Sarnia and Hamilton in Ontario across to southern Maine, down through the eastern United States into Florida, west to Texas, and sporadically far to the south in central and southern Mexico. This immense range, coupled with its fondness for upland as well as lowland sites, makes it one of our most variable and adaptable native trees.

Specimens of local provenance should be used when planting this species; as an extreme example, trees originating from tropical Mexico are unlikely to thrive in the different climate and photoperiod of Canada. By using locally adapted sources, black gum can be grown in every USDA zone from 11 up to the warmest parts of zone 3.

CULTURE: Black gum is a slow grower that does best on moist, acid soil, but it is adaptable to many different soil types and climate extremes. I have seen gnarly little black gum shrubs growing on desolate rock outcrops in Alabama, and tall, magnificent black gum trees in the fertile river bottoms visible downslope from the same site. Once well established in any soil, black gum is resistant to both drought and short-term flooding, and the tough wood of healthy young trees remains firm

against the forces of wind and ice. The glossy, waxy leaves are also resistant to salt spray.

This species can be propagated from seed sown in fall. The easiest and most pleasant way to clean the seeds is to eat the tasty pulp and spit out the stones, but the whole fruits may be planted. In the most southern areas of its range, where soil temperatures might not become cold enough to stimulate germination the first year, the seed should be stratified over winter to break dormancy, then sown outdoors or in containers the following spring to ensure prompt germination.

Black gum is very difficult to transplant from the wild or as a field-grown tree. Mechanical transplanting machines that dig a deep, pointed root ball should be used for landscape-size nursery specimens that have not been undercut or grown in a root-control bag. Small trees should be grown in containers designed for self-pruning of the root system, in order to minimize taproot development and subsequent root girdling. Move black gum in early spring to expedite healing of its fleshy, sensitive roots.

PROBLEMS: This tree can become stag-headed with advancing age. Saplings occasionally develop secondary leaders, which should be removed immediately because they are highly orthotropic and will form weak crotches if left in place. Some black gums in parts of the Appalachians have begun to develop cankers and leaf spotting similar to those inflicted on flowering dogwood (*Cornus florida*) by anthracnose (*Discula destructiva*). Affected trees exhibit branch dieback, and some die. This

decline is happening in the same areas where dogwood anthracnose damage is most concentrated. Black gum and dogwood are related closely enough to have been formerly classified in the same plant family, so there may be a connection. On the other hand, some black gums in New Hampshire have been found to be among the oldest of all living trees in eastern North America.

My trees are occasionally attacked by leaf-eating caterpillars such as the forest tent caterpillar (*Malacosoma disstria*). The tupelo leaf miner (*Antispila nyssaefoliella*), a shield-bearing insect, can cut disfiguring holes in the leaves. The primary problem with this otherwise carefree tree, however, is the difficulty involved with transplantation. By using techniques such as those used for growing and moving other taprooted species, the difficulty can be overcome, and black gum is worth the effort.

CULTIVARS: There are few cultivars readily available for black gum, nor for any other members of the genus. 'Sheffield Park' was selected long ago from a tree planted in England. 'Autumn Cascade' is a more recent selection from one of the weeping forms, found in a nursery in Australia, and 'Bernheim Select' is a superior tree from the Bernheim Arboretum in Kentucky. Several more cultivars have been advanced recently by various arboreta and nurseries in Europe, where beautiful American trees seem to receive so much more appreciation than they do in their native land. Provenance is very important and should be considered before purchasing a black gum tree.

SIMILAR AND RELATED SPECIES: There are ten other *Nyssa* species worldwide. Swamp tupelo (***N. biflora***), considered a variety of black gum by some authorities, is a narrow-leaved form restricted to swampy areas in the South. Another shrubby, suckering relative, Ogeechee

LEFT: Black gum (*Nyssa sylvatica*) is one of our most colorful trees in fall. BELOW: Flowers on a female black gum. BELOW RIGHT: Black gum fruits and fall color.

tupelo (**N. ogeche**), is confined to swamps in the coastal plains of Georgia and adjacent South Carolina and Florida. The largest known Ogeechee tupelo is located in a swamp in the Apalachicola National Forest of Florida and is nearly 5 feet (1.5 m) in diameter. Its lumpy trunk looks like a giant cottonmouth that just swallowed a family of beavers. This species' chief value is its large, edible fruit, used locally as substitutes for limes. It develops a more uniform, round-headed appearance under cultivation than it does in the wild, looking much like an orchard tree, and a few specimens have good red fall color.

The other major North American species is water tupelo (**Nyssa aquatica**), also called cotton gum for its

LEFT: A weeping selection of black gum (*Nyssa sylvatica*).
BELOW: Water tupelo (*N. aquatica*) in its native habitat.

cottony new growth. It ranks with baldcypress (*Taxodium distichum*) as the most flood-tolerant large tree in temperate North America. The cypress generally does better under shallow, nearly permanent inundation, while the tupelo dominates in areas subject to deeper, periodic inundation, but the two can often be seen growing side by side. Water tupelo moves air to its flooded roots through a porous wood structure, which makes the wood so light that it is used for fishing floats. Once established (often from a seedling on a mudflat or floating log) it can grow with its base continuously submerged, but it will do fine

on a moist upland site if planted. Its fruits will drift along, nose down, on the water surface until they land on a log or mudflat, where the seed germinates.

Water tupelo is a coarse tree with larger leaves and fruit and a more irregular form than black gum. It is even less tolerant of shade, and turns yellow in fall instead of red. This species becomes huge: the record tree in Southampton County, Virginia, is 105 feet (31.5 m) tall with a trunk 9 feet (2.7 m) thick above the basal buttress. It is hardy on well-drained sites (where winter ice cannot girdle it as it could in a flooded swamp) north to USDA zone 5.

COMMENTS: The tupelos include some of our best trees for honey nectar. Tupelo honey is sold by apiarists throughout the South. Fire-damaged cotton gum typically decays from the inside out, remaining solid around the perimeter, and hollow cotton gum logs were used for drainage culverts during cypress logging operations years ago. The common names of the various tupelo species are used interchangeably in their home regions, so it pays to know the scientific name of the tree you wish to buy from your local nursery. Make sure the nursery knows the difference too.

Black gum is well known among birders as a primary food source for robins during fall migration (a phenomenon documented as early as 1812), and the acidic, floating fruits of the aquatic species are an important food source for ducks. Rodents gnaw the stony seeds and have done so since prehistoric times, according to fossil evidence. Black gum is also the food plant of the Hebrew moth, a handsome black-and-white moth of the noctuid family. The interesting moths of this family have developed the special ability to detect the sonar of predatory bats and will take evasive action when bats "lock radar" on them.

LEFT: Fruits of water tupelo (*Nyssa aquatica*).

Ostrya virginiana
IRONWOOD

DESCRIPTION: In many ways ironwood can be considered the upland analog of hornbeam (*Carpinus caroliniana*). It is often called hop-hornbeam (for the hoplike fruits reminiscent of the hop vine, *Humulus lupulus*), just as the true hornbeam is frequently labeled ironwood. Both trees have some of the hardest wood around, and they have so much else in common that it becomes easier to review their differences than their similarities.

Ironwood is a small understory tree of well-drained deciduous forests. It loves hilly ground and is typically found up the slope from the valley floors occupied by hornbeam. Its spiral-patterned reddish bark is shreddy on large stems and limbs, most unlike the smooth gray bark of hornbeam, but young broomhandle-size trees have smooth bark and look remarkably like sweet birch (*Betula lenta*) saplings at all seasons. Ironwood also grows a little more erect than hornbeam, with a strong central leader (though old open-grown trees spread broadly), and it usually becomes slightly larger. The U.S. national champion, near Grand Traverse, Michigan, is 74 feet (22.2 m) tall with a trunk that is 3 feet (0.9 m) thick.

LEAVES: Ironwood leaves are oval-pointed, paper-thin, and feel like felt to the touch. The leaves are not uniform in size; those on the ends of shaded lower branches can reach 6 inches (15 cm) in length, while those farther back on the twigs or higher in the crown remain much smaller. Like hornbeam leaves, they sometimes emerge with an ephemeral red tint. The mild yellow fall color of this species is enhanced by its contrast against the dark bark, and many trees are marcescent.

FLOWERS AND FRUIT: The flowers are not conspicuous in spring, when the leaves are unfolding, but the unopened staminate catkins are visible in winter and add even more detail interest to this fine-textured tree. The fruit strobiles that develop in summer are visually effective into fall, reaching about 2 inches (5 cm) long. They are pale green, tightly bunched clusters of inflated papery capsules, each enclosing a small nut. Ground-dwelling forest birds such as grouse and turkey feed on them as they fall.

BEST SEASONS: FALL (for the fruits and dependable yellow color). ALL YEAR (for its classy fine-textured demeanor).

NATIVE AND ADAPTIVE RANGE: The immense natural range of ironwood is nearly identical to that of hornbeam. It extends even further northeast, to Chaluer Bay in New Brunswick, and further northwest, to Winnipeg, and is absent only from the southern Atlantic Coastal Plain in the eastern United States. Like hornbeam, it also occurs in Mexico and Central America. Trees of locally adapted provenance can be grown north into USDA zone 3.

CULTURE: This is one species that really does thrive on neglect. Although it won't tolerate flooding, it is not sensitive to drought and seems impervious to the predominant tree-testing forces of nature: soil and temperature variations, most insects and diseases, and wind. Ironwood always seems to make the top-ten lists for trees likely to emerge unscathed from ice storms. It does well in full sun, where it becomes more broad than tall, or in shade, where it retains its pyramidal juvenile form.

Ironwood can be tricky to transplant, but I have moved young trees up to 10 feet (3 m) tall in spring, even bare-root (not recommended), with good success. The seeds have a physiological dormancy that delays germination. They are best picked when slightly green and should be planted outdoors early in fall when the soil is still warm, or treated with a warm-cold moist stratification sequence.

PROBLEMS: Ironwood's primary limitations are slow growth and difficulty with transplantation, but both can be overcome significantly with appropriate horticultural techniques. It responds well to a combination of mulch, moderate irrigation, fertilizer, and increased sunlight and will grow reasonably quickly under ideal conditions once it is well established. Its deep taproot can be undercut in the nursery to produce a root structure more amenable to future relocation, or it can be grown in containers or root-control bags.

This species is notoriously sensitive to salt, whether from ocean spray or salted winter roads. It is one of the first trees in any woods to be defoliated by outbreaks of

Gypsy moth (*Lymantria dispar*) but is not insect-prone in general. Stressed trees may fall victim to the two-lined chestnut borer (*Agrilus bilineatus*), the scourge of newly transplanted trees of many species. The harmless-looking fruit clusters can cause itchy fingers when the seeds are extracted by hand for planting, so rubber gloves might be advisable if you have sensitive skin.

CULTIVARS: No ironwood selections have been marketed. Presumably its overall high quality, but absence of spectacular ornamental features, has caused any

superior individuals to go unnoticed. Its transplantation and propagation problems might discourage researchers from tinkering with it and keep nurseries from growing it.

SIMILAR AND RELATED SPECIES: There are several *Ostrya* species native to various parts of the Americas, Europe, and Asia, and their differences are subtle at best. Knowlton ironwood (**O. knowltonii**) is a smaller species with a very restricted natural range in canyons of the southwestern United States, from the Guadalupe Mountains of Texas and New Mexico westward. It is hardy into USDA zone 6, and I am testing it in zone 5. The largest known specimen is 44 feet (13.2 m) tall with a slender trunk about 1 foot (30 cm) in diameter. **Ostrya chisosensis** is an even rarer little tree, known only from the botanically rich Chisos Mountains of western Texas, and is probably hardy to USDA zone 7. Ironwood is in the birch family and is closely related to hornbeam (*Carpinus caroliniana*), with which it should be compared.

COMMENTS: Sometimes quality is difficult to come by, but opportunity will break the door down. While this tree can be frustrating to grow from seed, difficult to transplant, and unavailable at many nurseries, it is frequently found growing wild in the understory of undeveloped wooded lots. Instead of bulldozing every small

LEFT: Fall color of ironwood (*Ostrya virginiana*).
BELOW: The spreading form of an old ironwood.

tree (a process that is likely to kill some of the large ones as well), we should consider understory species like ironwood a gift from nature and retain them where possible.

One of the great temptations to be overcome in residential landscape design is the overuse of ornate focus species that, used in combination, can turn the scene into a visually discordant disaster. A purple-leaved something here, a yellow-leaved something there, a weeping or contorted something in the corner, a gaudy yard orna-ment in the middle, and suddenly we have a typical cluttered landscape. Every piece of art needs a focus and a harmonious background. The trouble-free ironwood provides such a background, with finesse.

BELOW: Flower catkins on ironwood (*Ostrya virginiana*) in late winter. BOTTOM LEFT: Fall color and fruits of ironwood. BOTTOM RIGHT: Ironwood bark becomes rough and shreddy with age.

Oxydendrum arboreum
SOURWOOD

DESCRIPTION: This is a medium-sized tree of outstanding ornamental value in every season. It can be found in the forest understory or along roadsides and in clearings, and within its natural range it adapts to a wide variety of habitat types. Sourwood is most often seen neighboring oaks (*Quercus*) on some of the better soils of slopes just uphill from wet bottomlands. It does not compete as well on the poor, disturbed soils inhabited by opportunistic successional trees such as persimmon (*Diospyros virginiana*) and sumac (*Rhus*), where grazing and cropping have depleted the land.

Open-grown trees are pyramidal and frequently branched to the ground, while those in forested areas develop straight, limbless trunks and can become surprisingly tall. They thrive along road cuts that are protected from hot afternoon sun, where they defy slash-and-burn road maintenance crews by sprouting enthusiastically from cut stumps. Some of these vigorous, sprout-formed trees are more colorful in fall than any other tree, and their roadside locations make them highly visible.

I have seen sourwoods along the Roanoke River in Virginia that formed part of the forest canopy, as tall as the adjacent oaks. The largest known specimen in North America, located in that area, is 95 feet (28.5 m) tall and has a trunk more than 3 feet (0.9 m) in diameter. Jim Wilson once saw a planted specimen near the city center of Hamilton, New Zealand, that was even larger. Halfway around the world from its native range, this great, spreading tree resembled a mature oak; only close inspection revealed its identity.

LEAVES: The silky smooth deciduous leaves resemble those of black cherry (*Prunus serotina*) and attain an average length of 5 inches (12.5 cm). Thirsty hikers in the Appalachians seek the twigs and leaves for a chew or a brew, just as those in the Midwest seek sassafras (*Sassafras albidum*). In sunny areas sourwood twigs are reddish, but on shaded branches they match the rich green color of the leaves in summer, so much so that it is easy to assume, incorrectly, that the twigs are part of a compound leaf structure. Early in fall the brilliant crimson or purple-red leaves stand apart from everything else in the woods.

No other tree colors up earlier in the forests of the South. Tourists along the Blue Ridge Parkway in early October fall in love with this species, and many try (unsuccessfully) to take starts of it back home to the North and Midwest. Sourwood and black gum (*Nyssa sylvatica*) planted in combination make a great one-two punch with their fall color.

FLOWERS AND FRUIT: Turn a lily-of-the-valley upside-down, hang it with hundreds more from the end of every twig in early summer, and you will have a sourwood tree in full bloom. The drooping panicles of upturned white bells, seen against the pea-green foliage, constitute one of the finest floral displays available. The flowers are very attractive to honeybees as well, and sourwood honey is considered a delicacy.

The clusters of pale yellow fruit capsules that follow, highlighted against the spectacular color of the foliage, are nearly as impressive. They darken and cling through the winter, long after the tenacious red leaves have finally fallen.

BEST SEASONS: EARLY SUMMER (for the blooming period, which reaches its peak after most spring-flowering trees have faded). FALL (for the long-lasting fall color display). WINTER (the persistent fruits emphasize the picturesque winter outline of the branches).

NATIVE AND ADAPTIVE RANGE: Sourwood is primarily a tree of the hill country, ranging from southern Pennsylvania and Ohio south to the Gulf Coastal Plain, west to the Mississippi Valley, and east to the Atlantic Coast along streams and bluffs. Scattered populations can be found in southern Indiana and west to eastern Texas. Some authorities list it as hardy north to USDA zone 4, but I have found it to be marginal even in zone 5.

CULTURE: Sourwood is in the heath family. Like some of its relatives, which include *Rhododendron* species and mountain laurel (*Kalmia latifolia*), this plant needs good drainage, acid soil, and protection from climate extremes. Either full sun or partial shade will do, and fairly dry soils are not a problem. This is a difficult tree to

transplant, so move it as a small container plant in spring. The minute seeds are difficult to handle and should be sown under mist on the surface of a finely sifted seedbed.

PROBLEMS: Sourwood is slow growing and sensitive to air pollution, poor drainage, root disturbance, and soil compaction. It often does poorly on exposed sites beyond its natural range and needs a gritty, woodsy soil and the attention of a substantially green thumb. If its site requirements can be met, it is generally free from insects and diseases.

CULTIVARS: Surprisingly, no cultivars of this outstandingly ornamental tree are available, possibly due to difficulties in propagation and culture. These same difficulties have kept it out of many landscapes in the South, where it is best adapted. Container-grown sourwood trees and small "liner" plants are sometimes available from nurseries specializing in native trees, but there never seem to be enough to meet the demand. Research-

ers are refining laboratory methods for micropropagation from shoot tips, so we should expect to see some sourwood cultivars in the future.

SIMILAR AND RELATED SPECIES: Though *Oxydendrum* is a monotypic genus, sourwood does have many cousins in the plant world. Georgia plume (**Elliottia racemosa**) is another ericaceous tree and is quite similar. It features beautiful, long, terminal spikes of white flowers in early summer. It has a very restricted natural range, being found only in a few isolated localities in Georgia, where it is listed as an endangered species. Under cultivation it is successful in arboreta located as far north as USDA zone 6. Propagation can be difficult. Sow the seeds on the moist surface of a peat bed, in full light, or purchase a nursery-grown plant.

Mountain laurel (**Kalmia latifolia**) is a prized woody ornamental flowering plant. It becomes a small tree up to 25 feet (7.5 m) tall on ideal sites in mesophytic cove forests. Wild plants typically bloom white or light pink, but many horticultural selections are available with colored flowers. Mountain laurel is among our hardiest broadleaved evergreens and can be grown successfully

LEFT: A mature sourwood (*Oxydendrum arboreum*) in fall color. BELOW: The brilliant fall color of sourwood.

north into USDA zone 5 on protected slopes. Propagation can be difficult, as with Georgia plume. Sow the tiny seeds on the moist surface of a peat bed, in full light, or purchase a plant from a nursery.

Rosebay rhododendron (***Rhododendron maximum***) is the primary tree-sized rhododendron from the Southeast. It forms dense stands along mountain streams and can reach more than 20 feet (6 m) in height. It can be grown with protection in USDA zone 5. Catawba rhododendron (***R. catawbiense***) is slightly smaller and hardier, being native to higher elevations and reliable in USDA zone 5. Both of these evergreens are among the most spectacular of all flowering plants, native or exotic, and are used as parents in hybrid cultivar development. They are also difficult to raise from seed but are available for purchase as container-grown stock.

Farkleberry (***Vaccinium arboreum***) is our largest native blueberry species. It grows from a shrub into a tree only after many decades, especially on the acidic, rocky bluffs where it thrives better than almost any other woody plant. Seldom reaching more than 20 feet (6 m) tall, it often has the grizzled appearance of a bonsai. Farkleberry is a southern tree that displays fine red color in fall and has attractive peeling bark. In many books it is reported to be hardy north only into USDA zone 7, but I have seen it doing just fine in the wild at the south edge of zone 5. Seed can be sown into a sandy-peaty bed in fall, but this slow-growing species may serve best when preserved in existing natural stands.

Texas madrone (***Arbutus xalapensis,*** syn. *A. texana*), an-

other gorgeous ericaceous tree, is the native madrone species of the Southwest. It is one of the most beautiful and most finicky trees, requiring sunny, gravelly sites and other cultural conditions that rank among the best secrets of horticulture. It is nearly impossible to transplant, and I have never tried to propagate it. Some people exploit the species' natural tendency to sprout after forest fires by putting the fruits into a paper envelope, burning it, and planting the charred seeds.

COMMENTS: Few trees, native or not, can match sourwood's combination of early and intense fall color, extravagant blossoms followed by equally showy bracts and seedpods, and shiny deep green summer foliage. This is a premier landscape plant wherever it is native and well adapted, and it fully deserves all the praise it is accorded by those who know it well.

Many of our native tree species are endemic to North America, occurring nowhere else in the world except as planted specimens. Generally, though, they have close relatives living in Asia or Europe. *Oxydendrum* joins the likes of *Leitneria*, *Maclura*, and *Robinia* as one of our few endemic genera. There is only one species of sourwood, and it can be found growing wild only in the eastern United States.

BELOW: Sourwood (*Oxydendrum arboreum*) flowers.
RIGHT: Texas madrone (*Arbutus xalapensis*) is unsurpassed for beautiful bark.

Picea glauca
WHITE SPRUCE

DESCRIPTION: Fossil pollen extracted from ancient bogs tells a fascinating story about the prehistory of our continent. Ten thousand years ago, before the North American landscape had warmed up from the last ice age, most of the deciduous forests we now see were spruce tundra. And the dominant tree found there, sheltering the giant sloths and mastodons from icy winds, was white spruce. Now this landscape has retreated to the northern edge of the United States and much of Canada, where white spruce remains the dominant tree of the Great Boreal Forest, one of the largest biomes on Earth.

On a good site, white spruce is typically a fast-growing, spire-shaped conifer. Even under extreme winter climate conditions it frequently exceeds 100 feet (30 m) in height. The largest known U.S. specimen is located near the United States–Canada border, in Koochiching County, Minnesota. It stands 130 feet (39 m) tall and has a long, straight trunk more than 3 feet (0.9 m) thick.

LEAVES: Spruces have pointed, evergreen needles that are square in cross section and less than 1 inch (2.5 cm) long. The malodorous needles have a waxy coating, giving the tree a frosted appearance that varies from tree to tree.

CONES AND SEEDS: This tree forms small, conelike, reddish or purplish strobili. The female strobili grow into papery-woody cones up to 2 inches (5 cm) long. The cones blend into the foliage background and are not particularly noticeable until they mature and turn brown.

BEST SEASONS: WINTER (for the fine-textured, evergreen foliage and conical form). FALL (the dark needles contrast beautifully with the fall colors of deciduous trees). SPRING and SUMMER (as a dark, pyramidal visual accent).

NATIVE AND ADAPTIVE RANGE: White spruce extends north to the utmost limits of tree growth in northern Canada and Alaska. It is the dominant canopy tree over much of its natural range, which in greater part lies to the north of most of the more populous regions of Canada, descending southward into the contiguous United States only in the Great Lakes region, northern New England, and to a limited extent the northern Rocky Mountains in Montana and the Black Hills of South Dakota and Wyoming.

Under cultivation it will grow from the northern limits of tree growth in USDA zone 2 south into USDA zone 6. Summer swelter, rather than any test that winter has to offer, is its limiting climatic factor.

CULTURE: White spruce is somewhat drought resistant for a spruce and can be grown on almost any reasonable planting site. It tolerates wind, cold, and sun or shade. It is actually one of the toughest conifers available—most unusual for a spruce—and does well even in windbreaks on the Great Plains. There are several geographic races or varieties, and the western ones are better adapted to western and southern climates than the typical form of the Northeast and North. All varieties tolerate a wide range of soil types.

Our native spruces are all resistant to damage from snow loads and other winter hazards. They are easy to transplant with a soil ball in early fall or spring, and the seeds germinate so easily that they are frequently used in sampler packets to encourage young children to plant trees.

PROBLEMS: Spruces are frequently damaged or killed by salt spray, root rot, air pollution, insects, and fire, and their wood decays rapidly following injury. Watch for several major insect and mite pests, especially spruce budworms (*Choristoneura fumiferana*), European spruce sawflies (*Diprion hercyniae*), gall adelgids (*Adelges lariciatus*, *A. abietis*, and *A. laricis*), spider mites (*Oligonychus ununguis*), and bagworms (*Thyridopteryx ephemeraeformis*).

Birds like to land on the growing tips of spruces. I have seen birds repeatedly break off the succulent new leaders of their favorite spruce perches in campgrounds, where they wait for handouts, deforming the trees into flat-topped shapes. The antlers of rutting male deer are the worst nightmare for a spruce tree in the first several decades of its life.

CULTIVARS: There are several varieties and many cultivars of white spruce. The Black Hills spruce (*Picea glauca* var. *densata*) is a tough, drought-resistant, slow-growing tree that survives on difficult sites and develops

a very dense crown. It has been designated the state tree of South Dakota, and it is a popular landscape selection.

'Sander's Blue' is a white spruce cultivar with slate-blue needles. 'Pendula', a naturally graceful tree with a straight trunk, and 'Coerulea' are attractive silvery blue selections with pendulous branches. Picturesque natural bonsai specimens of Alberta spruce (*P. glauca* var. *albertiana*), the western variety, grow extremely slowly at the edge of the tundra. Its dwarf form, 'Conica', commonly seen in rock gardens and dwarf conifer collections, has given rise, through mutations, to dwarf selections such as 'Daisy's White'.

SIMILAR AND RELATED SPECIES: All three closely related spruce species native to eastern and northern North America have colorful names, including white spruce, red spruce (**Picea rubens**), and black spruce (**P. mariana**). Collectively they are among our most cold-hardy trees and are also among the most useful nesting sites for many birds. Black spruce needles are shorter than those of white spruce, darker in color, and more tightly packed on the dense, dark twigs of old trees, which makes a mature grove of black spruce look almost black when seen against winter snow. Red spruce needles are more yellow-green, and the twigs, buds, and cones are reddish.

Black spruce is typically a long-lived tree of infertile, acidic northern bogs. It grows extremely slowly to about half the size of white spruce and shares a nearly identical natural range except for its absence from the Black Hills. It is the arboreal emblem of Newfoundland. Under cultivation on decent soils, its growth rate is similar to that of some of the slower western forms of white spruce. It develops a narrow, irregular crown with a dense top. Black spruce will perform satisfactorily under mesic conditions but is not genetically equipped to handle the combination of heat and drought. Most of its cultivars are dwarf forms that emphasize, to an extreme, the naturally slow and compact growth of this species. Black spruce also has some variegated, weeping, and prostrate selections, but none are available at nurseries other than those specializing in unusual conifers.

LEFT: White spruce (*Picea glauca*) is a common sight in much of Canada. BELOW: The dense needle arrangement of white spruce. RIGHT: Alberta spruce (*P. glauca* var. *albertiana*) is the northwestern mountain form of white spruce.

Red spruce is the predominant spruce of Nova Scotia, New Brunswick, southern Quebec, and New England. It follows the subalpine zones of mountains southward into North Carolina and Tennessee. A more broadly pyramidal tree of the eastern mountains, it reaches its most impressive dimensions near the southern end of its natural range, in the Great Smoky Mountains. The only tree-sized cultivar I know of is a misshapen, unbranched mutant, 'Virgata', found only at botanic gardens and in the yards of conifer collectors.

Very cold hardy in the East, red spruce is unhappy when planted in the desiccating winds of the Great Plains. It is another long-lived species in the absence of insect or disease problems and grows nearly as slowly as black spruce. The largest specimen, in Great Smoky Mountains National Park, is about the same height as the record white spruce but half again as big in diameter. Red spruce is the arboreal emblem of Nova Scotia. It is also the preferred host for a symbiotic mycorrhizal fungus, *Elaphomyces granulatus*, which produces the truffles that are the primary diet for the endangered northern flying squirrel (*Glaucomys sabrinus*).

Several other spruces are major components of the forests of western North America, particularly the ubiquitous Engelmann spruce (**Picea engelmannii**) of the Rocky Mountains and the less common but frequently cultivated Colorado spruce (**P. pungens**), or blue spruce, state tree of both Colorado and Utah. Glaucous forms of Colorado spruce add yet another color to the spruce family. Both of these Rocky Mountain species are hardy through USDA zone 3 and can be grown well beyond their natural ranges. They prefer neutral to acid, well-drained soils, and Colorado spruce in particular is more tolerant of drought but less tolerant of shade than the eastern species.

Colorado spruce is the progenitor of most of our native spruce cultivars. In addition to many dwarf selec-

LEFT: Engelmann spruce (*Picea engelmannii*) is closely related to white spruce and is common in the Rocky Mountains. BELOW: Red spruce (*P. rubens*) is our eastern mountain spruce species.

tions that are not trees there are popular steely blue selections like 'Koster', 'Hoopsii', 'Thomsen', 'Idaho Select', 'Bakeri', 'Continental', the stout 'Fat Albert', and the narrow-crowned 'Moerheim'. 'Sunshine', 'Walnut Glen', and 'Aurea' have gold needles, while 'Fastigiata' and 'Iseli Foxtail' develop a narrow, columnar habit.

Our native spruces are known to hybridize with one another and with exotic spruce species. Our hardy old friend from Alaska, Alberta spruce (*Picea glauca* var. *albertiana*), might actually be a stabilized cross of white spruce with Engelmann spruce. There is no sharp distinction between the two species, and they intergrade where their ranges overlap. Engelmann spruce, in turn, crosses with Colorado spruce in the Rocky Mountains. Red spruce and black spruce hybrids can be found in the wild as well, growing together in eastern Canada.

The giant Sitka spruce (**Picea sitchensis**) is restricted to the Pacific Coast and does not grow well in our region. European spruce (**P. abies**), also called Norway spruce, is very common in cultivation throughout much of eastern North America. About fifty other spruce species grow in various regions throughout the Northern Hemisphere.

COMMENTS: White spruce is the arboreal emblem of

LEFT: Black spruce (*Picea mariana*) is a wetland tree of the North. BELOW: The popular Colorado spruce (*P. pungens*).

Manitoba. If that does not convince you of its mettle, let me tell you about the time I climbed a steep glacial outwash slope in central Alaska to photograph an eagle nest. The wind was so strong that palm-sized flat cobbles rattled across the slope in saltation, and the handholds I used to keep from blowing away were the weather-beaten trunks of stunted centuries-old white spruce. I was unable to hold steady enough to photograph that nest, but I came away with an indelible impression of the tree that can survive in such a spot.

Still not tough enough for you? Then consider black spruce. In the wilds of the far North, black spruce replaces white spruce wherever needle litter accumulates sufficiently between ground fires to insulate the soil and allow permafrost to develop. It thus grows in soils that never drain because they never fully thaw. Red spruce is cold hardy too, but southern high-elevation forests of red spruce are following the ominous pattern of *Waldsterben* ("forest death"), which has caused so much concern in Europe. This species is dying over much of its southern subalpine range, probably due to a tragic combination of acidic precipitation, climate warming, and exotic insects, all human-generated problems. Along with the associated Fraser fir (*Abies fraseri*), it is becoming an arboricultural poster child for conservation groups concerned with reversing the environmental degradation affecting our planet.

A century ago red spruce was more endangered by logging than by pollution and was the subject of a study conducted by a young forester in the undeveloped wilds of the western Adirondacks, at Nehasne Lake. The forester sampled the biology of a 40,000-acre (16,187-ha) private timber holding and made recommendations for sustained-yield management of the red spruce. He published the results of his work in 1898 in an unassuming little book called *The Adirondack Spruce*.

Today the Nehasne Lake study site remains a blank space on the map—remote, undeveloped, mostly unknown except to its few local residents—and *The Adirondack Spruce* is an obscure item for collectors of antiquarian natural history books. The bright young forester who completed the study is remembered more for his later accomplishments, as the acknowledged founder of modern forestry in North America, at Biltmore, North Carolina, and as the first (and certainly the most famous) chief of the U.S. Forest Service, created by his friend President Theodore Roosevelt.

The forester's name was Gifford Pinchot.

Pinckneya bracteata

PINCKNEYA

DESCRIPTION: When in full color, *Pinckneya bracteata* (syn. *P. pubens*) can cause traffic jams. No gardener can see one without burning to know its name. A few years ago Jim Wilson planted two small container-grown pinckneyas at his Savory Farm in South Carolina, and throughout the month of June they reward him with pink flower clusters about 5 inches (12.5 cm) across. They provide an astonishing color display, even while very young. Pinckneya is a stiff little tree that looks like an overgrown houseplant, sparsely clothed with rather large, coarse leaves concentrated at the ends of the branches. It often occurs as a cluster of upright stems sprouting from the base.

Some very large pinckneyas were planted at Callaway Gardens in Pine Mountain, Georgia, more than twenty-five years ago. They quickly reached 20 feet (6 m) in height. Knowing the trees needed moist soil, Fred Galle (then director of horticulture) planted them near the bases of the earthen dams that retain Callaway's artificial lakes. They flourished in this spot, where they were also protected from the hot afternoon sun.

The current U.S. national champion is reported from Marion County, Florida. It stands 21 feet (6.3 m) tall but has a slender trunk only 3 inches (7.5 cm) in diameter. Pinckneya is such a fast-growing and short-lived tree that such records are temporary at best, but this indicates the tree's potential growth.

LEAVES: Pinckneya leaves are wide, thick and soft, pointed at both ends, and about 5 inches (12.5 cm) long. They have wrinkled surfaces and are rough to the touch. The foliage may turn yellow for a few days before dropping in autumn but usually shows little or no fall color.

FLOWERS AND FRUIT: The greenish white flower petals are small and inconspicuous but are surrounded by prominent, irregular sepals that appear rather tousled. These sepals are the most noticeable part of the calyx, both for humans and for hummingbirds, and vary from creamy white to pink and rose to red, creating an effect not unlike that of poinsettia. They are borne in late spring on new growth at the tips of the plump, furry twigs. The clustered, round, pale yellow fruit capsules that follow are about 1 inch (2.5 cm) across and seamed at the center. They turn reddish brown as they split in half to release the flat seeds.

BEST SEASONS: LATE SPRING (or early summer north of its natural range, when the large flower clusters appear). SUMMER (for the tropical effect of the foliage).

NATIVE AND ADAPTIVE RANGE: Pinckneya is a tree of the coastal plains of Georgia, northern Florida, and extreme southern South Carolina, and is limited to sunny wetland areas. Under cultivation in protected sites it can be grown well into USDA zone 7.

CULTURE: In the wild this species grows in the light shade of scattered pine trees, in wet acid soil along the margins of sloughs, bays, swamps, and streams, where it forms thickets by sprouting from lateral roots. In the garden it responds well to rich, loose, moist, fertile soil. Like many wetland trees, it probably grows in very wet areas not so much because it requires such conditions but because wet soil minimizes competition from upland trees.

When pinckneya is under cultivation, a well-drained soil will minimize its tendency to sucker and will slow its growth rate. Without adequate irrigation, the leaves will respond to drought by bleaching or dropping. A consistently moist soil can be maintained by mulching heavily and watering every week during dry spells. Drip irrigation techniques are ideal for watering this and other wetland trees, and planting pinckneya next to a leaky rain barrel or sump pump outlet may be a good alternative. A little afternoon shade is beneficial, and winter protection is vital in areas north of pinckneya's natural range.

Propagation by seed is simple. Gather the capsules after the leaves have fallen, allow them to dry until they begin to split open, and plant the seed in rich soil in fall. Seedlings will emerge the following spring with the onset of warm weather. Softwood cuttings taken after flowering time from twigs that grow from leaf axils below the inflorescence will root easily as well. Plan to

RIGHT: A wild pinckneya (*Pinckneya bracteata*) in Georgia. Photo by Ron Lance.

propagate this tree frequently and keep a few young plants coming along. It is quick to develop into a beautiful specimen but is frequently short lived under cultivation, and once you have grown accustomed to it you will not wish to go through a single summer without its color. Alternatively it may be managed as a large shrub by cutting the largest stems occasionally to encourage resprouting, thereby keeping some of the flower display closer to eye level.

PROBLEMS: On old cotton land, pinckneya trees may succumb to root diseases. If your tree dies, plant another one in a different spot and modify heavy soil with peat moss and pulverized pine bark. Pinckneya may become stressed under drought conditions and is intolerant of both deep shade and dry, sunny exposures. This is a short-lived tree for warm climates only and is not adaptable (except as a greenhouse plant) to the majority of North America where winters are cold.

Few nurseries carry pinckneya except those specializing in southern native species, probably because this tree doesn't become showy until several years after propagation and because its color develops in early summer, which is the off-season for nursery sales in the hot climates where pinckneya grows best.

CULTIVARS: Some nurseries are selecting informally for plants with red sepals, but pink forms seem at least as

attractive and useful in the landscape. 'Larry's Party' is intriguing at least for its name, if not for its intense salmon-toned coloration. With the growing interest in pinckneya, the variable flower color, and the ease of propagation of selected forms from cuttings, more improved cultivars should appear in the future.

SIMILAR AND RELATED SPECIES: Pinckneya is the only species in its genus. Most of its woody relatives are tropical plants, with the unique exception of buttonbush (***Cephalanthus occidentalis***), which is hardy north into central Canada. This wetland species ranks among our most flood-tolerant woody plants but also thrives when planted in moist upland landscapes. It is found over a vast range from Montreal south to Cuba, west to Nebraska and Texas, down through much of Mexico, again in Arizona and California, and is even reported to occur in China. Despite its common name, buttonbush can become a multiple-stemmed tree reaching 20 feet (6 m) or more in height in the southeastern and western parts of its immense natural range.

Buttonbush blooms in summer when few other woody plants display effective color. Its intricate starburst flower clusters are all the more impressive when seen in the context of its otherwise coarse texture, with heavy, irregular branches and large, opposite or whorled leaves. 'Sputnik' is a beautiful pink-flowered cultivar found in a native stand in Oklahoma by my friend Steve Bieberich. Buttonbush seed clusters can be collected by canoeing into flooded wild stands in early fall, and the seeds will germinate promptly without pretreatment if kept sufficiently wet. They are an important source of food for migrating waterfowl. Wetland birds use the emergent stems of flooded buttonbush trees as safe nesting sites, seasonally isolated by water from many small predators.

COMMENTS: Pinckneya has also been called Georgia fever-bark for the use of its bark as a malaria treatment. In colonial times malaria affected many people in the southern coastal plain areas where pinckneya grew, particularly where rice was cultivated in impounded water and rice farmers were exposed to relentless attacks by mosquitoes. Pinckneya is a close relative of the cinchona tree (*Cinchona ledgeriana*) of South America, the original source of quinine, so many attempts were made to use it as a home remedy. Its effectiveness in this regard is uncertain.

LEFT: The beautiful flowers of pinckneya (*Pinckneya bracteata*). Photo by Ron Lance.

Pinus banksiana

JACK PINE

DESCRIPTION: Several small to medium, short-needled pine species thrive on some of the most difficult growing sites occupied by forest trees. All these species are similar, and most are very closely related. The most common one at the northernmost edge of forests across eastern North America is jack pine. This tree is in the group known collectively as the hard pines (subgenus *Pinus*, or *Diploxylon*), which includes most of our eastern pines.

Jack pine forms a ragged crown of long, uneven branches. It is a short-lived but tough little tree that colonizes dry, sandy areas after forest fires. It seeds in by the thousands on such sites and often grows in dense, pure stands. Unlike most other pines, whose branches grow in whorls at annual nodes, jack pine and some of its relatives develop internodal branches due to a phenomenon called lammas growth. In this type of growth, some of the next year's terminal growth buds open and develop during the current season, leading to multiple growth whorls from subapical buds the following year. Consequently the age of a young jack pine tree is difficult to estimate by counting whorls of limbs.

On good sites, and with protection from competition and from the frequent fires that are common in jack pine habitat, this species can grow reasonably large. The U.S. record tree, in Lake Bronson State Park, Minnesota, is 56 feet (16.8 m) tall with a trunk 3 feet (0.9 m) in diameter, but bigger specimens exist in Canada. This species is one of our fastest-growing pines when young and is one of the fastest-growing conifers wherever it has a long enough growing season to reach its potential.

LEAVES: The curled, flat, dark yellow-green needles of jack pine grow in pairs from the rough, scaly twigs. They mature at less than 2 inches (5 cm) in length and are pointed but not especially prickly. The foliage is evergreen and persists for three or four years.

CONES AND SEEDS: Staminate and pistillate strobili occur separately on the same tree. Bumping into a jack pine, or any pine, at the peak of pollen release will leave you coated with a solid dusting of pollen, with plenty left over to form a dense cloud. Pines are wind-pollinated species, so copious amounts of the stuff are needed to ensure that some of it drifts to the right place.

The crooked pine cones that follow do not have long-lasting sharp spines like those of many other hard pines. However, each scale on the cones does have a dorsal umbo, a common characteristic among all hard pines. Unlike the shingle-like overlap of scales seen on soft pines (subgenus *Strobus*, or *Haploxylon*) or spruces (*Picea*), the surfaces of unopened hard pine cones are tightly sealed with interlocking armor plates, resembling the surface of a pineapple. The cones grow to about 2 inches (5 cm) in length and persist indefinitely, sometimes becoming ingrown and enclosed by wood as the branch thickens.

This species has serotinous cones that often remain closed (but viable) for decades unless the heat of a forest fire loosens them, simultaneously releasing many years' worth of seeds to be blown throughout the ashy seedbed of a burned forest. Trees from the southern part of the natural range usually have at least some cones open each year, with or without the stimulation of fire.

BEST SEASONS: WINTER (any evergreen tree is most appreciated during bright winter days, with a little dusting of snow, and jack pine makes a great windbreak and wildlife shelter). SPRING and SUMMER (especially for its critical importance as nesting habitat for birds).

NATIVE AND ADAPTIVE RANGE: Jack pine is our northernmost pine species. It nearly reaches the Arctic Circle in northwestern Canada, extending eastward across the continent only as far south as the Gulf of St. Lawrence except for spotty distribution in New Brunswick and New England. It also follows the western Great Lakes to the southwest and occurs across the northern portions of the Lake States.

Winter hardiness is obviously not a concern for jack pine, since it grows as far north as USDA zone 1 in the wild. Surprisingly, however, it also seems to do nicely when planted as far south as USDA zone 6. This overlaps the northernmost point where the very similar Virginia pine (*Pinus virginiana*) may be used, further extending the effective range of this combination of species down into the highlands of central Alabama. From

there, other short-needled hard pines, all closely related and very similar, continue south into Florida and west to the Pacific Coast.

CULTURE: Jack pine and its relatives will grow well on many different soils and in many climate zones if planted. It must be given good drainage and absolute freedom from shade, and it prefers acid soils. It is simple to transplant with a soil ball in either spring or early fall. Ripe cones may be soaked in hot water overnight, then left on a sunny window sill to open, and the seeds can be shaken out. They require no stratification and may begin to germinate within a week of sowing.

PROBLEMS: Three physiological stresses cause more problems for cultivated jack pines than any insect or disease organism: shade, heat, and wet feet. In natural stands, fire is responsible for the death of many individ-

LEFT: Jack pine (*Pinus banksiana*) is one of our hardiest native trees in severe winter conditions. BELOW: Jack pine cones can cling for decades. TOP RIGHT: Staminate strobiles on jack pine. RIGHT: Jack pine is dense and uniform when young.

ual trees, but it also creates the conditions that ensure reproduction and survival of the species. In cultivation south of its natural range, jack pine can be killed by the same pine-wilt nematodes (*Bursaphelenchus xylophilus*) that attack European hard pine species, and insects such as the pine sawfly (*Neodiprion sertifer*) can cause substantial damage. See *Pinus echinata* for a more detailed account of insect and disease problems.

CULTIVARS: A few prostrate and weeping forms are grown in botanical gardens. 'Uncle Fogy' is probably the most interesting, and bizarre, with its random growth patterns. For gardeners in most of the eastern part of North America, trees of southern provenance (such as the Lake States) should perform best.

SIMILAR AND RELATED SPECIES: A complex of hard pines with short needles growing in pairs occurs across our continent. Virginia pine (**Pinus virginiana**) is the southeastern mountain and Piedmont look-alike of jack pine. It has spiny cones, typically grows a little larger, and has slightly longer, twisted needles. It shares the jack pine's enthusiasm for eroded, burned, inhospitable terrain and is not fussy about soil pH or texture as long as it has reasonably good drainage. Virginia pine has become a favorite species for use as a Christmas tree in the Deep South, where other suitable pine species do not grow as well.

BELOW: Virginia pine (*Pinus virginiana*) tolerates poor, rocky soils. RIGHT: Sand pine (*P. clausa*) is the southern counterpart of jack pine.

Virginia pines from the northern edge of their natural range (Pennsylvania and southern Indiana) perform equally well as jack pine when planted side by side in my arboretum in USDA zone 5. 'Wate's Golden' is an unusual selection that turns intense gold in winter. The famous Hennepin Virginia pines outline a square block of the town of Hennepin, in northern Illinois, surrounding the site of the town's first schoolhouse. These thirty-five trees were planted in 1857, and they remain in good condition despite being located far northwest of their native habitat. The largest known Virginia pine, in North Carolina, is about 90 feet (27 m) tall and well more than 3 feet (0.9 m) in diameter.

Table mountain pine (***Pinus pungens***) is a stiff cousin of Virginia pine, endemic to scattered sunny exposures in the Blue Ridge and adjacent mountains. It has sharp needles, attractive purple staminate strobiles, and large cones covered with fierce claws that compare favorably with medieval caltrops. This is a picturesque evergreen when seen along the borders of steep mountain roads in winter, and it has also grown robustly at my Illinois arboretum. The U.S. record tree, in North Carolina, stands 94 feet (28.2 m) tall with a diameter of nearly 3 feet (0.9 m).

Table mountain pine is sometimes called poverty pine for its ability to thrive on degraded soils that could not sustain most other trees. Wild stands depend on periodic disturbances such as forest fires and severe ice storms to kill their competition and facilitate seedling recruitment. Forest ecologists are studying ways to help this species maintain its position in Appalachian forest

stands because of its great values for many wildlife species and for soil protection.

In the Low Country across the Deep South, Virginia pine and table mountain pine give way to spruce pine (***Pinus glabra***). Beautiful old specimens of this short-needled pine can be seen growing at the north end of its natural range in the Francis Biedler Wildlife Sanctuary in South Carolina. It grows larger than the average Virginia pine and tolerates light shade and wet soil much better than most pines. The bark is different from that of our other native pines, looking almost like that of an oak (*Quercus*). Its shade-tolerant lower limbs tend to remain alive like those of its namesake, spruce (*Picea*), and do not shed as quickly as those of other pines, making it a very useful tree for screening or windbreaks. The biggest spruce pine known, in Louisiana, is 112 feet (33.6 m) tall with a straight trunk more than 4 feet (1.2 m) thick. Further south is sand pine (***Pinus clausa***), the equivalent of jack pine in the sandy barrens of Florida. Sand pine is usually smaller than jack pine, but the record tree is 91 feet (27.3 m) tall and more than 2 feet (60 cm) in diameter.

Westward, jack pine yields to lodgepole pine (***Pinus contorta***), which itself is divided into several varieties or subspecies. Lodgepole pine has prickly cones like Virginia pine, but otherwise is barely distinguishable from jack pine until it grows large. The Rocky Mountain type found in our region, *P. contorta* var. *latifolia*, is a tall, slender tree that follows fire and frequently falls victim to it, as with jack pine. It was used by western Native Americans for poles to support their dwellings, and it is the arboreal emblem of Alberta. It can be grown in the East, but I have found that it grows more slowly for me in Illinois than jack pine, table mountain pine, or Virginia pine. In its prime habitat in Idaho, the record lodgepole pine is 155 feet (46.5 m) high with a long trunk more than 3 feet (0.9 m) thick.

COMMENTS: Jack pine and some of its closest relatives are viewed with disdain by many self-proclaimed tree lovers, who consider them scrubby runts that occupy space more rightfully devoted to more stately species. Over much of its territory, however, the lowly jack pine exists simply because other trees cannot survive the winter cold, sterile sand, and relentless wind that seek to convert the forest, such as it is, to boreal desert. This value is so appreciated in such areas that jack pine has been designated the official Territorial Tree of the Northwest Territories of Canada. I'd bet my lunch that if the inhabitants of Nunavut ever vote for a provincial tree, jack pine will be on their short list as well—after all, what else could survive so far north?

A well-grown and thoughtfully tended jack pine, planted in a friendlier environment, can rise to an aesthetic standard that might surprise some folks who have seen it only as a weather-beaten survivor of some of the most inhospitable conditions in North America. It is also an important nesting site for many birds. In the Pine Barrens of Michigan it accommodates the globally endangered ground-nesting Kirtland's warbler.

LEFT: Spruce pine (*Pinus glabra*) can become large and tolerates wet soils. RIGHT: Table mountain pine (*P. pungens*) is a tough tree for sunny, dry, sterile sites.

Pinus echinata

SHORTLEAF PINE

DESCRIPTION: The large, valuable, coniferous timber trees of the southeastern United States are known collectively to many people as the southern pines. These trees are the ubiquitous symbols of the South, perhaps more so than any other trees, and pollen research indicates that they have been a dominant forest type in the region for at least five thousand years. One of the hardiest and most adaptable species of this group is shortleaf pine, the most widespread pine of the eastern United States. Shortleaf pine is the state tree of both North Carolina and Arkansas, although some in Arkansas claim the related loblolly pine (*Pinus taeda*).

Though typically an upland tree, this pine grows just as well in sandy, well-drained stream valleys. It does well on farmed-out old fields and acidic, infertile ridgetops, where competition from faster-growing pines and from hardwood trees is minimal. While sometimes not as large as other southern pines growing on more productive sites, it is definitely a forest-canopy species. The largest shortleaf pine is located in Putnam County, Georgia. It is 112 feet (33.6 m) tall and has a stout trunk nearly 5 feet (1.5 m) thick. Even larger specimens grew in the Ozarks until about a century ago, when the virgin pines there were eliminated in less than three decades by voracious logging. A beautiful remnant stand can still be seen in the Pioneer Forest of southern Missouri.

LEAVES: The common name of this tree is misleading, for the leaves are short only in comparison with other southern pines. The evergreen needles are borne in fascicles of either two or three on the same tree. They are dark yellow-green, flexible, reach 5 inches (12.5 cm) in length, and persist for several years in mild-winter areas.

CONES AND SEEDS: The southern pines, like other pines, have wind-pollinated strobili, with male and female structures in separate clusters on the same tree. Shortleaf pine cones are smaller than those of other

RIGHT: Shortleaf pine (*Pinus echinata*) thrives on sunny exposures.

southern pines, less than 3 inches (7.5 cm) long, and are armed with small umbo spines. Southern pines are hard pines (subgenus *Pinus*, or *Diploxylon*), so their cone scales each have a dorsal umbo, like those of jack pine (*P. banksiana*), rather than the shingle-like scales of soft pines (subgenus *Strobus*, or *Haploxylon*), such as white pine (*P. strobus*).

BEST SEASONS: FALL (in mixture with xeric hardwoods on rocky hillsides and bluffs, this tree provides green accents for the fall colors of other species). WINTER (this tree has all the value of other evergreens, and because it is the hardiest southern pine it can be planted in the Midsouth and more northern areas where the others cannot be grown; it occasionally suffers foliage discoloration in severe winters but survives nonetheless).

NATIVE AND ADAPTIVE RANGE: Shortleaf pine grows in dry soils from the Gulf Coastal Plain northwest

LEFT: Shortleaf pine (*Pinus echinata*) grows with hardwoods in the Ozark forest. BELOW: Staminate strobiles on shortleaf pine. BELOW RIGHT: A shortleaf pine cone.

through the Ozark Plateau into southern Illinois, northeast along the Cumberland Plateau to southern Ohio, and east to the Pine Barrens of New Jersey and coastal areas of Rhode Island Sound. While it is generally not as prevalent or vigorous as other southern pines in mild-climate areas of the Southeast, it is the predominant pine of the Ozark Plateau and Ouachita Highlands west of the Mississippi River, where it grows best. If occasional winter burn of the needles can be tolerated, it does well under cultivation north into USDA zone 5.

CULTURE: This tree grows in sandy or rocky soils or on well-drained silty clays. Like most southern pines, it must have full sun. Along with pitch pine (*Pinus rigida*), shortleaf pine has adapted to its fire-prone natural habitat by developing the ability to sprout from dormant buds on old wood if the top is damaged. This ability is commonly seen among hardwood trees from fire-prone habitats but is almost unknown in the pine genus.

Shortleaf pine is hard to transplant unless its taproot has been severed in the nursery at an early age, but it grows easily from seed. It has a reputation as a slow grow-

er, due mostly to the marginal sites where it is found in the wild. A specimen growing in the irrigated herb fields at Jim Wilson's Savory Farm developed quickly into a dense, picturesque, spreading tree, demonstrating the capability of this species to respond to favorable conditions. The Missouri Department of Conservation recognizes this potential and is promoting the restoration of shortleaf pine to its former habitat in the state.

PROBLEMS: All southern pines are attacked by outbreaks of boring beetles, especially the southern pine beetle (*Dendroctonus frontalis*) and engraver beetles (*Ips avulsus, I. grandicollis,* and *I. calligraphus*). They are also very vulnerable to damage from ice storms due to their tendency to collect large amounts of freezing rain on their long needles. The needles are eaten by the redheaded pine sawfly (*Neodiprion lecontei*). Shortleaf pine is resistant to the *Sphaeropsis sapinea* leaf blight that attacks some of the others, but is subject to damage from the twig-boring Nantucket pine tip moth (*Rhyacionia frustrana*). It is also susceptible to various root-rot organisms, especially following construction disturbance.

Native pines grown under stressful conditions might be susceptible to the pinewood nematode (*Bursaphelenchus xylophilus*), which is deadly to exotic hard pine species. All pines and pine products are subject to regional quarantine in the United States because of the European pine shoot beetle (*Tomicus piniperda*). This pest was recently brought from Europe, where it is the most serious beetle pest of pines.

CULTIVARS: No horticultural cultivars have been selected for shortleaf pine. All the southern pines, however, have been examined for genetic variation that might affect their performance as timber trees, and trees of selected provenance are recommended for timber plantations in various areas.

SIMILAR AND RELATED SPECIES: Pitch pine (***Pinus rigida***) is the only other pine in most of our area with the ability to sprout from old wood, and it is the hardiest southern pine. A small, irregular, picturesque species, it grows on barren highlands and sands in the Appalachian Mountains and New England. The record-sized tree is an exceptional specimen found at the northern edge of the range, in New Hampshire. It is nearly 100 feet (30 m) tall with a heavy trunk well more than 4 feet (1.2 m) thick. Pitch pine is also one of the few hard pines reported to be resistant to the pinewood nematode.

This pine has been used in plant breeding programs as one parent of *Pinus* ×*rigitaeda*, the other parent being the closely related loblolly pine (***P. taeda***). The intent was to combine the hardiness and site adaptability of pitch pine with the larger size, superior straightness, and fast growth rate of loblolly pine. Both pitch pine and the hybrid are hardy and fast-growing in my test plantings in central Illinois, but neither has a tall straight trunk.

Loblolly pine is popular throughout the Deep South but cannot survive the occasional severe winters of central Illinois, USDA zone 5. It is very susceptible to fusiform rust disease (*Cronartium quercuum*). Nonetheless, this is without doubt the most commonly seen plantation pine tree in southern forest plantations and in wet areas where most other southern pines cannot live. It is one of our largest and most productive pines. The U.S. national champion, in King William County, Virginia, is 135 feet (40.5 m) tall with a trunk nearly 7 feet (2.1 m) thick. At the other end of the spectrum is the ornamental 'Nana', propagated for its compact growth.

Another southern pine, the longleaf pine (***Pinus palustris***), grows for me in USDA zone 5 but only as a struggling botanical curiosity. In the sandy pine savannas of the South, this species becomes a magnificent and very ornamental tree. Its needles, the longest of any native North American pine, grow in bundles of three, each up to 18 inches (45 cm) in length, and droop gracefully from the coarse, stubby branches. It also has the most valuable wood and the largest pine nuts (seeds) of any southern pine. New seedlings don't put forth much stem growth for several years and tend to resemble clumps of ornamental grass. Even the older sapling trees are sparsely branched, often looking like giant chimney brushes. The cones are decorative as well, growing up to 10 inches (25 cm) long. This beautiful pine is the state tree of Alabama and is thought to have dominated 60 million acres (24 million ha) of the South before it was logged nearly to oblivion. The largest specimen left standing is in Georgia. It is 120 feet (36 m) tall and has a long, clear trunk more than 3 feet (0.9 m) thick.

Slash pine (***Pinus elliottii***) has needles nearly as long as those of longleaf pine. It is a fast-growing timber tree but is not at all hardy north and shares loblolly pine's susceptibility to fusiform rust. The U.S. national champion, in Florida, is 129 feet (38.7 m) tall with a trunk almost 4 feet (1.2 m) in diameter. Slash pine will tolerate flooding, but it thrives on sandy ridges where it has moved in to replace longleaf pines that have been logged.

Pond pine (***Pinus serotina***) resembles a slender loblolly

RIGHT: Loblolly pine (*Pinus taeda*) is the most common tree species of the southern pine forest.

pine and can grow on even wetter sites. It shares the ability of shortleaf and pitch pines to sprout from dormant buds on small trees and is found mostly in swamps and pocosins on the coastal plains. The record tree, in Georgia, is 132 feet (39.6 m) tall and just under 3 feet (0.9 m) in diameter.

In the Southwest, another three-needled hard pine can be seen in a few areas at the fringe of our region. Chihuahua pine (**Pinus chihuahuana,** syn. *P. leiophylla* var. *chihuahuana*) is an attractive small tree with waxy needles adapted to a hard life under desert conditions. It serves as the northern scout of a large cadre of magnificent Mexican pine species.

COMMENTS: The southern pines are so ubiquitous in

those areas where they do well that many people fail to appreciate the wonderful evergreen resource with which they have been blessed. Piney woods have probably been invaded more by new home construction recently than any other forest type in the southeastern United States. Many fashionable new subdivisions emerging around major population centers like Atlanta are being carved from these forests. For the most part the trees seem to cope surprisingly well, sharing their landscape with the new human tenants in quiet dignity. However, they occasionally take revenge for the root damage inflicted during careless construction by dropping huge dying limbs onto cars or toppling onto the roofs of encroaching houses.

BELOW: The classic beauty of a young longleaf pine (*Pinus palustris*). RIGHT: Chihuahua pine (*P. chihuahuana*) in the Coronado National Forest.

Pinus resinosa

RED PINE

DESCRIPTION: Red pine is the northern counterpart of the southern timber pines. It is a hard pine (subgenus *Pinus*, or *Diploxylon*) and shares many characteristics with other members of this group. The coarse twigs and flaky bark have a reddish cast, unlike those of other native pines of the North. This is a tree of sandy soil. It prefers more moisture and organic matter than required by the scrubby little jack pine (*Pinus banksiana*) with which it often grows, but it thrives on poorer sites than those usually dominated by white pine (*Pinus strobus*), with which it also often grows. Where the three species are seen together, they are among the easiest pines to tell apart.

Red pine becomes a large tree. The U.S. national champion, in Watersmeet, Michigan, is 124 feet (37.2 m) tall and has a ship mast of a trunk more than 3 feet (0.9 m) in diameter. It is the state tree of Minnesota, and I have seen some of the best-looking specimens growing along the shorelines of lakes there and in northern Wisconsin and Ontario, in situations where they have sandy soil with good drainage but access to a shallow water table.

LEAVES: Red pine's slender yellow-green needles are bundled in pairs within each fascicle and generally last for two full years before falling. They are long for a northern pine, up to 6 inches (15 cm), and very flexible, but will snap cleanly went bent too far. The needles usually don't persist as long as those of other hard pines, and the branching pattern is very coarse on young trees (due to limited early formation of lateral buds), so unsheared saplings have a very open, fluffy look reminiscent of slash pine (*Pinus elliottii*). Of course, these two species could never be confused because they are allopatric and never come close to meeting in the wild.

CONES AND SEEDS: The staminate strobili of red pine are a striking violet color and develop conspicuously at the ends of the branches. The cones that grow from pistillate strobili, usually high in the tree, are not as large as those of most southern pines, barely reaching 2 inches (5 cm) in length. The unopened cones are smooth and without prickles, like those of jack pine, and each cone scale has a dorsal umbo, giving the surface of a tightly closed cone the look of a ceramic-tiled floor.

BEST SEASONS: WINTER (the fluffy foliage looks so appealing when coated with hoarfrost that red pine Christmas trees are frequently flocked with artificial snow to duplicate the effect). ALL YEAR (the evergreen needles and reddish bark make a striking combination in any season).

NATIVE AND ADAPTIVE RANGE: Red pine is a prominent forest tree in the Lake States and eastern Canada. It extends northwest to Lake Winnipeg in Manitoba and eastward to Lake St. John and the Gaspe Peninsula of Quebec, with disjunct populations as far as the island of Newfoundland. To the south it can be found through northern New England and the northern portions of the Lake States, with outlying natural groves as far away as Illinois and West Virginia. The cold tolerance of this tree is not a question, since it grows without cultivation in its natural habitat north into USDA zone 2. Summer heat might be more of a problem, but healthy specimens can be found as far south as USDA zone 6.

CULTURE: Red pine must have full sun and very good drainage, although it does well for me in tight soils on slopes where water cannot puddle. It is the most difficult northern pine to transplant, due to its long-ranging, coarse root system. Small trees can be dug by hand with a deep soil ball; mechanical tree movers, with deep, conical configurations, work well for larger sizes. The seed has no dormancy requirement and will germinate within a week or two of planting.

PROBLEMS: Red pine is a favorite target of the European pine sawfly (*Neodiprion sertifer*). It is tolerant of ozone pollution but ranks among the most sensitive pines to the allelopathic effects of walnut (*Juglans*) roots, so it should not be planted in the same backyard as walnut trees. *Sphaeropsis sapinea* needle blight, *Sirococcus conigenus* shoot blight, and *Dothistroma pini* needlecast disease affect this tree, but not as badly as they do some of the European pine species seen more often in cultivation. See *Pinus echinata* for more information on problems associated with hard pines.

In areas south of its natural range, where snow blizzards often turn into ice storms, red pine can sustain

major damage as the ice builds up on its long needles. This might be more limiting to its use in the Midsouth than summer heat. The primary limitations that affect it, though, are poor drainage and shade.

Double leaders sometimes result from the lack of a symmetrical ring of subapical buds on young saplings; red pine seedlings develop only one to three buds each year until they are five or more years old. This problem is easy to notice and simple to correct with a pruner while the tree is still small. Christmas tree growers shear the new candles on young red pines to induce more bud development and to limit the lengths of internodes, thus producing denser trees.

CULTIVARS: Red pine is notably devoid of genetic variation, and the only cultivars likely to become available will probably develop from witches'-brooms or mutations. While the unusual genetic uniformity of this tree might be cause for some concern regarding the species' resistance to any potential future disease epidemic, it also means that provenance is of little importance when planting this species. Therefore, any red pine should grow equally well in any area where any other red pine can grow.

SIMILAR AND RELATED SPECIES: Along with the southern pines and the short-needled hard pines, red pine is allied with the hard pines of western North America, Europe, and Asia. Notable among these are the three-needled ponderosa pine (***Pinus ponderosa***) and its varieties, some of which grow well when planted in the eastern part of the continent north into USDA zone 3. Rocky Mountain ponderosa pine (*P. ponderosa* var. *scopulorum*) is the state tree of Montana and does much better throughout much of our region than does the larger Pacific Coast form. The largest known Rocky Mountain ponderosa pine grows in the Lolo National Forest in Montana. It is an ancient tree with beautiful patchy

LEFT: A young red pine (*Pinus resinosa*) at Starhill Forest. BELOW: The irregular limb structure of an old-growth red pine in Canada.

orange bark, standing nearly 200 feet (60 m) tall with a diameter of more than 6 feet (1.8 m).

Arizona pine (**Pinus arizonica**), with its needles sometimes in clusters of five, and Apache pine (**P. engelmannii**) are slightly smaller southwestern allies of ponderosa pine and are sometimes lumped in with it as varieties. Apache pine has very long needles and is reminiscent of the longleaf pine (*P. palustris*) of the Southeast.

Several exotic hard pines are commonly seen in cultivation in our area, including Scots, or Scotch, pine (**Pinus sylvestris**), Austrian pine (**P. nigra**), and the shrubby mugo pine (**P. mugo**). All three are quite variable, with numerous ecotypes, varieties, and subspecies.

COMMENTS: There is a red pine fireplace mantle in our home, wrought from the beams of a barn built generations ago by family ancestors in Iowa. The barn had been a massive five-level affair, held together with hand-mortised joints and oak pegs. The combination of strength, lightness, and workability made red pine the logical species of choice for a barn-raising in the days before cranes, gasoline engines, and stamped-steel gusset plates made easy work of lifting and connecting the bones of such a structure on the open prairie.

We used to grow red pine for Christmas trees on our Illinois tree farm, too. It taught me much about the willful nature of some trees to resist the attempts of humans to mold a loose, airy species into a tight cone of artificially colored foliage. It also taught me about red pine's many guests, the various nesting songbirds who resent being disturbed during the extremely narrow window of opportunity when this tree responds favorably to shearing. Since 1988, I have left the pine plantation for their undisturbed use.

Although it served well as barn beams, and grudgingly as Christmas trees, I have come to appreciate red pine most as a majestic large conifer with beautiful fluffy needles. It should be left alone, free to improve steadily with age. I am reminded of this whenever I look at our old mantle and at the healthy, maturing remnant trees in our abandoned Christmas tree plantation.

BELOW LEFT: Staminate strobiles of red pine (*Pinus resinosa*). BELOW: The characteristic bark pattern of old-growth ponderosa pine (*P. ponderosa*). RIGHT: Old ponderosa pines become rough but stately.

Pinus strobus
WHITE PINE

DESCRIPTION: White pine is the tallest tree native to eastern North America. It is the state tree of Maine and Michigan, and the arboreal emblem of Ontario. The long, straight, strong stems of this tree were coveted for masts during the days of sailing ships. None of its associates can match its mature stature, although its wood has been so valuable that virtually all the giant old pines of the primeval forest were harvested long ago.

Massive white pine logs were cut during the nineteenth century—one tree logged in 1899 was 12 feet (3.6 m) thick—but isolated stands such as the one at Hearts Content in the Allegheny National Forest remain to offer a hint of this tree's former greatness. The largest known white pine today is 150 feet (45 m) tall and more than 5 feet (1.5 m) in diameter. It grows in Porcupine Mountain State Park, Michigan.

LEAVES: White pine is the only soft pine (subgenus *Strobus*, or *Haploxylon*) in eastern North America, and it bears its aromatic blue-green needles in fascicles of five. The evergreen needles are flexible and friendly to the touch, unlike the prickly needles of many other conifers, and have white stomatal (pore) lines along the lower surface. They reach about 5 inches (12.5 cm) long and droop from the twigs, giving the tree a graceful weeping look and an unmistakable sound in the wind. This is the tree that accompanies the loon in providing haunting nightly music for those of us who have visited areas such as the Quetico wilderness of Ontario.

White pine needles develop only toward the ends of the twigs, rather than along their full length, and fall after their second year. This gives vigorous young specimens a see-through structure. The see-through stage is eliminated by increasing age and branching (or, on Christmas trees, by shearing), until trees reach what production foresters call overmaturity, when they lose enough limbs to become as gappy as the smile of an "overmature" human. I find white pines (and people, for that matter) to be most interesting and venerable at this stage.

CONES AND SEEDS: The staminate and pistillate strobili of white pine are borne in separate clusters. The mature cones are longer and proportionately more slender than those of most of our other pines, reaching up to 8 inches (20 cm) long and maturing in two years. Each scale has a terminal umbo, rather than the dorsal umbo of the hard pines (subgenus *Pinus*, or *Diploxylon*), which makes them overlap loosely like shingles. They are smooth but gummy to touch. Unripe cones look like green hotdogs hanging from the upper limbs of mature trees.

BEST SEASONS: WINTER (this is one of our most massive evergreen trees and one that holds its color well throughout winter; its picturesque silhouette is visible for miles when adjacent deciduous trees shed their foliage). ALL YEAR (especially for the fragrance and for the haunting sound of the wind in its crown).

NATIVE AND ADAPTIVE RANGE: This is one of our most adaptable pines, thriving from southeastern Manitoba across the Lake Country of western Ontario to the southern shore of Lake Nipigon, and from the northeastern shore of Lake Superior across to the Gulf of St. Lawrence and the island of Newfoundland; then south throughout the Lake States and New England, and in the Appalachians to northern Georgia. During earlier postglacial times it existed further southwest, and isolated relic populations remain in pockets of Indiana, western Kentucky, and, as *Pinus strobus* var. *chiapensis*, even as far as southern Mexico.

Due to its timber value, many provenance studies have been conducted for this tree. It has been shown to have clinal (genetic) variation in response to climate extremes, so locally adapted stock performs best. In general, white pine from appropriate sources will grow as far north as USDA zone 2, and as far south as USDA zone 8 on cool north slopes with adequate soil moisture.

CULTURE: As pines go, white pine is a mesic tree. It grows in many soil types, from fairly moist to quite dry soil and from silty clay to dune sand, but it does best on good soil. It loves full sun but can tolerate a little more shade than most hard pines. It is very easy to transplant

RIGHT: A mature white pine (*Pinus strobus*) planted 150 years ago.

with a soil ball, either in fall or spring. Seed should be sown outside in fall for best results, and several years are required for the tiny seedlings to reach the point where they begin rapid growth. Once they take off, they outgrow most other pines on good sites, sometimes adding annual "candles" of growth 4 feet (1.2 m) long.

PROBLEMS: White pine is extremely sensitive to salt and air pollution, so it should not be planted close to highways. The smooth, thin bark of young trees is damaged easily by fire or careless use of string trimmers. Twig-boring white pine weevils (*Pissodes strobi*) and the exotic white pine blister rust (*Cronartium ribicola*) can be problems in portions of the tree's natural habitat. Other insects such as pales weevil (*Hylobius pales*), pine bark

aphid (*Pineus strobi*), and white pine aphid (*Cinara strobi*) also cause problems locally. Mound-building ants (*Formica integra*) inexplicably kill sapling white pines within about 20 feet (6 m) of their nests at my tree farm in Illinois.

Among our native pines, white pine is one of the most resistant to the deadly pinewood nematode (*Bursaphelenchus xylophilus*), and it is less prone to attack by the defoliating European pine sawfly (*Diprion similis*) than are the hard pines. Leaf diseases such as tip blight (*Sphaeropsis sapinea*) only very occasionally spread from the more susceptible hard pines to the more resistant white pine. Even though white pine is subject to a greater variety of minor diseases than any other North American pine species, it is still among the most trouble-free trees in terms of serious problems.

CULTIVARS: Many dwarf selections have been propagated from the frequently seen witches'-brooms of white pine. Of the selections that become real trees I particularly like 'Fastigiata', because its broadly ascending form is more believable and elegant than the orthotropic, exclamation-point branching habit of most fastigiate trees, and because its branching angle makes it much

LEFT: The typical fluffy branching pattern of white pine (*Pinus strobus*). BELOW: The soft, touchable needles of white pine. RIGHT: Limber pine (*P. flexilis*) displays its typical blue color at Starhill Forest. FAR RIGHT: Southwestern white pine (*P. strobiformis*), like this specimen at Starhill Forest, is a splendid, adaptable tree.

less subject to collapse under the weight of ice or snow. 'Pendula' and 'Inversa' are weeping forms, and 'Contorta' has twisted needles. Several selections have been propagated for their leaf color, including 'Alba', 'Gracilis Viridis', 'Variegata', 'Winter Gold', and the impressive blue form 'Glauca'.

SIMILAR AND RELATED SPECIES: Western white pine (***Pinus monticola***) is a closely related species found high in the northern Rocky Mountains and to the west beyond our region. It is the state tree of Idaho and becomes a very large tree in its native habitat, but it will also grow (albeit more slowly) further east and at lower elevations under cultivation. It is hardy at Starhill Forest, in USDA zone 5. This is the species most troubled by white pine blister rust and by the white-spotted pine sawyer (*Monochamnus scutellatus*).

Limber pine (***Pinus flexilis***) has a more extensive range from the Canadian Rockies in the North to central New Mexico, at very high elevations. Its close relative southwestern white pine (***P. strobiformis***) is confined to the southern end of the Rocky Mountains but does better than limber pine under cultivation in the humidity of the East at lower elevations. Both are hardy in USDA zone 5, and limber pine from northern seed zones will grow north through USDA zone 4. They typically develop a candelabra habit of upward-curving, ascending limbs that give them striking character as they mature, and they are more tolerant of alkaline soil than white pine and some of their other close relatives. The *P. flexilis* cultivars 'Glauca' and 'Cesarini Blue' have spectacular blue-green needle color, and 'Vanderwolf's Pyramid' makes a striking, upright pyramid of steely blue foliage.

Another western relative, bristlecone pine (***Pinus aristata***), whose westernmost form is considered by some authorities to be **P. longaeva,** is the longest-lived tree species in the world. It tolerates high pH and short growing seasons, and can be planted in the East but should not be expected to live for five thousand years there like it does in the West. The similar whitebark pine (**P. albicaulis**) is a rare timberline tree of the northern Rockies, with strong populations in the Yellowstone region of Wyoming. The seeds of this pine are of critical importance to bears and other wildlife. Each of these trees is hardy at least to USDA zone 4, but none enjoys being planted in low-elevation sites.

The group of little trees known as pinyons comprises several southwestern species with large, edible seeds. ***Pinus edulis,*** the principle pinyon species and the state tree of New Mexico, is found throughout the southern Rockies in the states bordering the Four Corners area. It and Utah juniper (*Juniperus osteosperma*) are the primary species that make up the pinyon-juniper vegetation type there. Under cultivation in a suitably dry soil, *P. edulis* will survive in USDA zone 5. This pinyon can be separated from its close relatives by its needles, borne in fascicles of two.

The similar Mexican pinyon (***Pinus cembroides***) has three needles per fascicle and a more southerly range confined to southern New Mexico and adjacent areas of Texas, Arizona, and Mexico. A very similar species, the papershell pinyon (**P. remota**), is the western Texas counterpart of Mexican pinyon. The border pinyon (**P. discolor**), another three-needle pinyon, is encountered occasionally in the boot heel of New Mexico.

Singleleaf pinyon (***Pinus monophylla***) is similar, but unusual for a pine in having only one needle per fascicle. It is a more westerly species, confined mostly to the Great Basin area west of our region. Still another western species, **P. quadrifolia,** has four needles per cluster and is found only to the west in southern California and south into Baja California. Additional pinyon species, and many other soft pines, are found in Mexico.

The Pacific Coast mountain ranges also have several fine pine species that do not extend east to our region, and there are many soft pines in Asia, several of which are found in cultivation in parts of our area. Himalayan pine (***Pinus walichiana***), Chinese white pine (**P. armandii**), and Korean pine (**P. koreana**) are the main species hardy enough to be seen occasionally in cultivation east of the Rockies.

COMMENTS: The crown of white pine is made up of long, fluffy limbs that give mature trees a layered appearance when viewed from a distance. These same plumelike limbs, when seen from above, make this species one of the easiest conifers to identify from an airplane. An illustrated training manual for aerial timber survey work, published by the Canada Department of Forestry (Sayn-Wittgenstein 1960), shows the characteristic star-shaped crowns of white pines emerging above the surrounding forest canopy like starfish on an ocean floor.

A tradition among early American settlers moving west was to plant "coffin pines" at their new homes. The native forests of the frontier were composed of hardwoods that could not be worked quickly into coffins in the event of the settlers' untimely deaths, so white pine was brought from the East for this purpose. Typically a matched pair of pine trees was planted for husband and wife. Sawmills soon sprang up near settlements and began manufacturing commercial lumber from local native timber, and some settlers relocated after planting their coffin pines. As a result, many of these trees still survive.

Although conifers and broadleaved trees are not closely related, members of each group have evolved in a parallel fashion to fill analogous positions in natural communities. In many ways the various pines (*Pinus*), our largest and most important conifer genus, parallel the oaks (*Quercus*), our largest and most important genus of broadleaved trees. Pines and oaks both invade habitats that have been opened, or kept open, by diverse forces such as fire, logging, or poor soil. Both are drought resistant but low to intermediate in shade tolerance, so without periodic disturbance or dry, sterile soil to keep other species under control, they can be replaced in succession by more shade-tolerant species. Many individual oak and pine trees survive to become huge, dominating their corners of the woods, and some live to be very old; thus, the disturbances that set the stage for their reproduction need occur only once every few centuries to keep the species in place.

RIGHT: White pine (*Pinus strobus*) is one of our hardiest pines for cold climates.

Platanus occidentalis
SYCAMORE

DESCRIPTION: The word "sycamore" means different things to different people. In Europe it is the name for a common maple species, *Acer pseudoplatanus*, and in the Middle East, where it is spelled "sycomore," it refers to fig trees (*Ficus sycomorus*). But in North America it is the great white tree of the winter valley. For the four to six months of our winter dormancy period each year, the huge, white-speckled boles and limbs of this tree make it the most conspicuous living organism along every river within its range. It commonly grows with eastern cottonwoods (*Populus deltoides*), walnuts (*Juglans nigra*), bottomland oaks (*Quercus*), and other trees with rough, dark bark and is visible among them like a white fire in the night.

Sycamores never seem to slow down in growth, and those that manage to outgrow storm damage, stream undercutting, and heart rot can become the most massive trees in eastern North America. I have seen some exceeding 150 feet (45 m) in height and 6 feet (1.8 m) in trunk thickness. The largest one currently known is only 95 feet (28.5 m) tall but nearly 9 feet (2.7 m) in diameter. This patriarch may be seen growing in Bath, Virginia.

This species follows soil disturbances normally associated with floods and channel braiding along rivers, as well as those caused by human activity on some upland sites. It bears great quantities of windblown seeds, which find every available nook and cranny of open land, and with sufficient sunlight and moisture it can outgrow most potential competitors.

LEAVES: Sycamore leaves are variable in size on the same branch. Those that develop in midseason on vigorous stems can reach more than 10 inches (25 cm) in width and nearly as much in length. They have three or five very shallow lobes and a hollow petiole that encloses the bud. The creamy early spring color of woolly new sycamore leaves adds to the spectacle of the white bark, but fall color is usually only a dull tan.

FLOWERS AND FRUIT: Spherical reddish flower clusters emerge with the leaves in spring. The pistillate flower clusters develop into seed heads about 1 inch (2.5 cm) in diameter, and many hang from the tree on long flexible stalks through most of the winter. They gradually break apart in spring storms, just in time to cast seed across the sandbars and mudflats exposed by receding floods.

BEST SEASONS: WINTER (sycamore has no peer among its associates for winter brilliance in a large tree). SPRING (the colorful young foliage and flowers are noteworthy when unmarred by disease).

NATIVE AND ADAPTIVE RANGE: Sycamore, in its varieties and forms, grows from Iowa south into Mexico, east across Ontario (south of Georgian Bay) to southern Maine, and southeast throughout most of the eastern United States except for the Gulf Coast and peninsular Florida. It does best in the central part of this broad range but can be cultivated north into USDA zone 4. This is one of the few trees that does better when planted one zone north of its source provenance. Planting in such areas results in more vigorous, disease-resistant trees.

CULTURE: Among our native trees, sycamore is one of the simplest to grow. It transplants so easily that I once moved a 27-foot (8.1-m) tree successfully with a 3.5-foot (1-m) transplanting machine. This cannot be done with many other trees. Sycamores may be grown from cuttings or from seed, or wild seedlings can be transplanted from appropriate disturbed areas that they overpopulate. Trees grown from cuttings might be used to select for the whitest bark, a trait that is variable from tree to tree. The cuttings should be taken in early summer after the new growth becomes firm but is not yet woody. They will root in sterile, moist sand or perlite under partial shade, preferably with bottom heat but without hormone applications. If grown from seed, the seeds should be fresh and sown thickly on the surface of a wet seedbed. They require only sunlight and ample moisture for optimum growth. My seedlings have grown up to 4 feet (1.2 m) tall the first year.

Rapid growth can be expected to continue almost indefinitely under ideal conditions. Undamaged seedlings

RIGHT: Sycamore (*Platanus occidentalis*) is one of our most ornamental large trees in winter.

usually develop a strong central leader and require no corrective pruning, but double leaders emerge occasionally. Trees that develop wide multiple forks become very picturesque as they age, but those with narrow forks should be pruned to a single leader while small in order to preserve structural soundness.

PROBLEMS: The most important, and least recognized, problem with this tree is that the fuzz on its leaves, fruits, and young twigs can cause allergic reactions, including temporary blindness, if the branches are handled roughly during pruning. This hazard is magnified greatly if a brush chipper is used to dispose of the trimmings. When in doubt, wear protective goggles and a dust mask when working with a sycamore, especially in late spring or summer.

A less serious but more widely known problem is the spring anthracnose disease (*Apiognomonia veneta* or *Gnomonia platani*), which annually kills young leaves and sometimes even twigs on susceptible individuals, in association with sycamore twig blight (*Diaporthe arctii*). The symptoms of anthracnose look like the results of a late frost, browning the first new leaves. As secondary shoots develop, the weather generally warms and dries to the point where the fungus disease shuts down for the year, and little harm is done. In very wet years, though, and on especially susceptible trees, this anthracnose disease leads to significant twig blight and noticeable delays in leaf development, which alarm many people with sycamores in their yards.

I have observed native sycamores growing wild along Rock Creek in central Illinois for many years and found that they consistently show much less damage from anthracnose and twig blight than dozens of trees of unknown provenance planted a few miles away in Springfield. I have also noticed that a few of the Springfield trees are consistent from year to year in being more severely affected than others, showing the knobby growth that results from repeated twig dieback. It would be interesting to learn how much of this apparently variable disease resistance is genetic and how much is environmental. Some people have noted the pleasant (or unpleasant, depending upon the person) balsamlike aroma of sycamores after a rain, while others cannot detect the scent. We still have a lot to learn about this great tree.

Sycamore hosts a variety of canker diseases and wood-rotting organisms. Most of them gain entry through

pruning wounds or other damage, so proper tree care will generally prevent them. Prune them in the dormant season, and sterilize tools before moving from infected limbs to healthy ones. Many old streamside sycamores are hollow due to the decay that gains entry through wounds from winter ice flows or gets into stump sprouts via the old stump. Some of these hollow trees live on for centuries, serving as bear dens and children's playhouses, but their structural integrity is always in doubt and they shouldn't be trusted too close to a house. Members of the genus also host many insects, though few are serious. The shedding bark, large leaves, and blight-killed twigs cause significant littering throughout the year. The fallen leaves are allelopathic and can be toxic to turf, and the roots can be invasive, so there are additional reasons to keep this tree at a comfortable distance in the landscape, where it can be underlain by mulch or native forest understory.

CULTIVARS: Available cultivars seem to be selections of a hybrid with the Asian species *Platanus orientalis*. *Platanus* ×*acerifolia* is known as London plane because it has been grown for centuries in England. It is more resistant to pollution, drought, and anthracnose than the native species, but it usually has duller bark and is plagued by serious canker problems and frost cracks. Many of the London planes grown in North America seem to be backcrossed to our native species, but there are some that have retained their intermediate appearance.

Selections certainly should be made from native sycamores for bark color and anthracnose resistance, since these traits show great variability and account for the best and worst aesthetic qualities of this species. Sycamores from the southwestern part of the natural range, especially Texas and Mexico, have smaller, fuzzier, tougher leaves and might be useful for cultivar selection on that basis if they were more winter hardy. Several are classified as separate species.

SIMILAR AND RELATED SPECIES: Arizona sycamore (**Platanus wrightii**), a beautiful tree with more deeply lobed leaves and pythonlike limbs, grows along streams in the canyons of the Southwest. Wonderful specimens of this tree, including the U.S. national champion, may be seen at Sycamore Ranch in the Animas Valley of New

Mexico. They remain there only because the landowners and other friends of the trees successfully fought against an ill-advised initiative to dam the valley in the 1990s. The greatest tree is 114 feet (34.2 m) tall with a trunk more than 7 feet (2.1 m) thick below its fork. Arizona sycamore is not commonly seen in cultivation outside its natural range, but it will grow at least as far north as USDA zone 7 and perhaps zone 6.

A similar but less hardy species, **Platanus racemosa,** is found in California. It is not adapted to cultivation east of the Rockies. Several additional species are recognized in Mexico, Europe, and Asia. The buttery-barked **P. ori-**

FAR LEFT: Fall color on a sycamore (*Platanus occidentalis*). TOP LEFT: Sycamore flowers as the leaves begin to expand. LEFT: The fruit balls of sycamores release their seeds gradually in late winter. RIGHT: This large sycamore in Illinois is several centuries old.

entalis is widely planted in Europe, along with the hybrid London plane.

COMMENTS: In terms of evolution, our eastern sycamore species is considered the most advanced of the genus and is certainly first in at least one respect: a sycamore now growing across from Independence Hall in Philadelphia was germinated from seed carried to the moon and back in 1971 by Apollo Astronaut Stuart Roosa, a former U.S. Forest Service firefighter. Several of its sister seedlings, all germinated by the Forest Service upon Roosa's return to Earth, can be found in other locations. The sycamore genus is the only member of its plant family and has survived for one hundred million years since the late Cretaceous Period, making it one of the true elders of the tree tribe.

Across the United States, big old sycamores are the stuff of legend. One famous tree, the Worthington sycamore growing on the Dixon Farm in Greene County, Indiana, was 150 feet (45 m) tall and more than 14 feet (4.2 m) in diameter when it was measured in 1915. It fell in 1924, but a cross section of one of its two main limbs, taken above a fork, was preserved and can still be seen in a shelter building in the Worthington town park.

In 1889 noted ornithologist Robert Ridgeway wrote that the cerulean warbler was "the most abundant of the summer-resident members of the family in Illinois" (Vanderah 1993). Today this migratory bird has become a threatened species because of habitat destruction. Cerulean warblers seem to set up their mating territories around venerable old sycamores, which they prefer above all other trees for singing perches.

A good friend once gave me a photograph of Ridgeway, taken in 1882 at the Wabash River in southern Indiana. In it he and his brother Charles pose beside a sycamore with two trunks. The larger half measured 15.5 feet (4.6 m) in diameter and was 168 feet (50.4 m) tall. It was the largest tree of any species ever measured in North America east of California. It might still be there for us to admire, but its short-sighted owner reportedly cut it down shortly after the photo was taken, to prevent being inconvenienced by more spectators.

Stewardship connotes responsibility to the future. I often ponder the wisdom of giving individual humans rights of ownership over such wonders of nature.

LEFT: Arizona sycamore (*Platanus wrightii*) is adapted to grow along desert streams in the Southwest.

Populus deltoides

EASTERN COTTONWOOD

DESCRIPTION: "Cottonwood" is a name applied to different trees in different regions, but they are all closely related. Cottonwoods of various species and varieties are found almost throughout North America, all looking and behaving very much alike. They are rugged, water-seeking trees that grow more quickly and attain greater size than nearly all of their associates in any region of the continent. But they are also weak and very prone to damage and decay, and female trees release the summer snow of cottony seeds that become entangled in window screens from the Atlantic to the Pacific.

Cottonwoods are most appreciated in the Great Plains and the Southwest, where other large shade trees are not so readily available and easily grown. Here they make vast riparian gallery forests that cool the rivers, and they furnish the structural bones upon which wildlife habitat is built. Kansas, Wyoming, and Nebraska have each designated a cottonwood as their state tree, but there is some confusion whether the tree of choice is the eastern cottonwood or the closely allied plains cottonwood (*Populus sargentii*), considered by some authorities to be a variety of the eastern species. Their ranges merge in Kansas and Nebraska.

Old hollow cottonwoods can become roomy enough inside for a poker game. The current U.S. national cochampion, in a pasture near Minadoka Dam, Idaho, far west of the accepted natural range of the eastern species, has the spreading form characteristic of plains cottonwood. It is only 85 feet (25.5 m) tall but has a trunk 11.5 feet (3.5 m) thick. A comparable specimen, also 85 feet tall and with a trunk nearly 12 feet (3.6 m) in diameter, has a slightly smaller wingspan and grows in Nebraska. In contrast, the specimen recognized as the U.S. national champion for the taxon we recognize as plains cottonwood is in northern Colorado at the western edge of the range for that taxon, measuring 105 feet (31.5 m) tall with a sprawling forked trunk 11.5 feet (3.5 m) thick.

For many years the recognized U.S. national champion eastern cottonwood grew along the Illinois and Michigan Canal in Illinois. Before it fell in 1991, entire grade school classes could convene within its hollow base (although the entrance opening was too small to admit most teachers). This tree was much taller, as is more typical of eastern cottonwoods.

LEAVES: Toothed and triangular, the leaf blades average about 4 inches (10 cm) long and wide, on petioles about the same length. Those on vigorous shoots grow much larger, while those on the western species and varieties are generally smaller and more leathery. I have found that trees from different regions planted together at Starhill Forest retain the foliage characteristics of their home habitat.

The leaves hang from flattened, flexible petioles and clack against one another even during breezes too subtle to be felt on the ground. The motion makes a sound like rain on cardboard and is especially noticeable and pleasant in late summer when the leaves begin to dry and their sounding boards resonate in the wind. If an insect-free summer and a gradual transition into early fall allow their autumn color to develop, cottonwoods offer a good yellow, made more dramatic by the typical early abscission of the oldest leaves, thus highlighting the structural form of the branching.

FLOWERS AND FRUIT: All cottonwoods are dioecious, so only female trees bear the cottony seeds for which they are notorious. The fruit capsules begin as strings of green pearls in early spring, and the ripe capsules split open synchronously to fill the late spring air with a beautiful but messy shower of cottony snow. In areas where litter is not a concern, a cottonwood blizzard is a beautiful experience.

BEST SEASONS: FALL (there is something unforgettable about a grizzly old cottonwood with a smattering of golden leaves, rattling in a breezy sunbeam against a lowering autumn sky). LATE SPRING (the cotton is truly the best and worst of this tree, but it is festive in wild areas where it may be experienced without inconvenience).

NATIVE AND ADAPTIVE RANGE: A combination of eastern cottonwood and plains cottonwood blankets low ground and riparian habitats across the East and Mid-

west. Plains cottonwood, the midwestern representative, extends into Alberta and Saskatchewan, north at least to Saskatoon. Other species, analogous and similar in most details, range north throughout much of Canada, west to the Pacific Ocean, and southwest into Mexico, where the cottonwoods are known as *los alamos*. Eastern cottonwood is adapted from the Gulf Coast north into USDA zone 3, but local races exist, so trees of selected provenance should be sought if this tree is planted.

CULTURE: Cottonwood is probably our fastest-growing large tree. It is fairly easy to transplant in small sizes, but it grows so readily and quickly from unrooted cuttings that transplanting an established tree seems pointless. Seed is perishable and difficult to handle. Tiny seedlings volunteer everywhere, though, and may be moved about with abandon as they germinate, if the need is there and the trowel is at hand.

The trick with propagating cottonwood is to start in late winter with a hardwood cutting (of known gender, if desired). Plant it in open soil free of all competition from weeds, give it excessive amounts of water, and get out of its way or it will knock you down as it grows. I have seen groves of cottonwood that were more than 100 feet (30 m) tall but less than twenty years old. Soil type is not critical, but the trees must have ample water, full sun, and complete control of weed competition to do their best.

PROBLEMS: Whole books have been written about the insects and diseases of cottonwood. While the cottonwood leaf beetle (*Chrysomela scripta*) is among the most voracious defoliators in the bug business, of more immediate concern is the recently introduced Asian longhorned borer beetle (*Anoplophora glabripennis*), which considers cottonwood a favorite treat. Two cankers, *Cytospora chrysosperma* and *Dothichiza populea*, are especially troublesome on trees damaged by pruning or extreme weather. Cottonwoods are notorious for the damage they sustain from lightning, beavers, ice, wind, insects, decay, and nearly every other force known to nature. Yet they are so resilient that some live to take their place among our largest deciduous trees.

If cottonwoods grow with enough vigor, they can outgrow most of these maladies for a long time. And while they don't live for millennia, there are some venerable old cottonwoods along the Missouri River that were already large enough to shade Lewis and Clark on their Voyage of Discovery from 1804 to 1806. One group of trees even found a place in Lewis's journal.

The worst problems with cottonwoods are amplified by the tremendous sizes of mature trees. This translates into massive, brittle, falling limbs and extensive systems of invasive roots. And there is the cotton, of course, if the trees are female: some communities have passed ordinances prohibiting the planting of female cottonwoods. The cottonwood is a picturesque, fast-growing giant best relegated to locations where these negative traits are of no consequence.

CULTIVARS: Because cottonwood has commercial value for paper pulp, many superior production clones with elaborate pedigrees exist in forestry plantations.

LEFT: A cottonwood (*Populus deltoides*) shows its fall color. RIGHT: Cottonwoods can become great, impressive trees with lots of character.

Likewise, cottonwood has been used as a primary parent species in a vast forestry hybridization program with European, Asian, and western North American poplar species. Several nurseries offer "cottonless" ornamental cultivars, which are nothing more than staminate trees grown from cuttings. Anyone interested in growing one need only look among trees of local provenance during the blooming period for a male tree, and return in late winter to harvest a dormant cutting.

SIMILAR AND RELATED SPECIES: Eastern cottonwood and plains cottonwood are the primary species in the East and Great Plains respectively. People in the northern part of our area will find balsam poplar (***Populus balsamifera***), an aromatic species that ranges north as far as the Arctic Circle. It has narrower leaves and a narrower form than cottonwood, and it seldom grows as large, although the record tree in Michigan is 128 feet (38.4 m) tall and more than 4 feet (1.2 m) thick. Walking through

LEFT: The typical upright form of young cottonwoods (*Populus deltoides*). BELOW: A vigorous young cottonwood can grow as tall as a person in one year.

a forest of balsam poplar in spring, when the fragrant buds are bursting and releasing their aroma, will convince you to plant one.

Swampy areas in the eastern United States sometimes support swamp cottonwood (***Populus heterophylla***). It has beautiful emerging foliage in early spring and becomes large and tall like eastern cottonwood. The Little Big Tree by the Black River in Spencer, Ohio, was 140 feet (42 m) tall with a straight trunk nearly 9 feet (2.7 m) thick. The current U.S. national champion, in Mississippi, stands 93 feet (27.9 m) tall with a trunk 4 feet (1.2 m) in diameter. Swamp cottonwood is hardy in USDA zone 5.

Other cottonwood-like poplars grow in portions of western North America. They include black cottonwood (***Populus trichocarpa***), a giant tree of the Northwest; narrowleaf cottonwood (***P. angustifolia***) of the Rocky Mountains; and several varieties of Fremont cottonwood (***P. fremontii***) of the Southwest, mostly represented in our area by what is usually accepted as a distinct species, Rio Grande cottonwood (***P. wislizeni***).

Of these, narrowleaf cottonwood is a tree of mountain stream valleys, where it is more slender than the others but occasionally nearly as tall. Hardy to USDA zone 3, it has leaves that resemble those of willows (*Salix*), giving it a finer texture than other cottonwoods. The record tree is not particularly tall but has a short, forked trunk more than 8 feet (2.4 m) across.

Black cottonwood is a tall and massive tree, occurring mostly west of our area but found overlapping with its very close relative, balsam poplar, in the northern Rockies. The largest black cottonwoods are found in the Pacific Northwest, where they become the largest of all poplars. Rio Grande cottonwood always becomes a stout tree with smaller, waxy leaves, providing welcome shade in its desert habitat. The largest currently known specimen is 92 feet (27.6 m) tall with a much larger branch spread, and a trunk nearly 10 feet (3 m) in diameter. It is probably hardy north into USDA zone 6.

The aspens are poplars too, although they share much more in common with European and Asian species than they do with other North American poplars. See *Populus tremuloides*.

COMMENTS: When you enter a cottonwood grove on a hot summer day, the trees offer a standing ovation with their clapping leaves and comfort you with dappled shade. In the nearly treeless landscape of the Great Plains this can be a very memorable and appreciable experience. If modern human enterprise were not so dependent

upon window screens, air conditioners, swimming pool filters, and other things that are easily clogged, we also might appreciate the aesthetic summer snow of cottonwood seeds, just as they must have been admired by the early Native Americans who revered this great tree.

The Arapaho believed the stars were cast into the sky

LEFT: Cottonwood (*Populus deltoides*) is winter hardy throughout the Northeast. BELOW: A mature Rio Grande cottonwood (*P. wislizeni*) provides welcome shade in the Chihuahuan Desert.

by great cottonwoods shedding their cotton, and many Native American tribes found myriad uses for every part of the tree. The famous photographic portfolios of Edward Sheriff Curtis, compiled at the beginning of the twentieth century as the sun was setting on the ancient ways of Native American life, help to document the importance of cottonwoods to his photographic subjects. Two of his more dramatic images depict a Navaho weaver's loom set beneath the exposed root of a huge cottonwood and a ceremonial hat made from cottonwood leaves for the Sun Dance of the Cheyenne.

Populus tremuloides

QUAKING ASPEN

DESCRIPTION: Aspen is a tree born of fire, landslide, and disaster. It colonizes disturbed areas, massing at the sunny edges of forests and meadows, where its white bark and gentle grace make it one of our most highly sought trees for nature photography. It is a montane species in the West, a tree of moist sandy soils in the East, and the arboreal emblem in the boreal province of the Yukon. Aspens grow as clones, comprising colonies of stems with a common root system. Every periodic recurrence of fire or other natural disturbance clears away the older stems and the competition, allowing ever more vigorous new sprouts room to grow.

Most individual aspens are tall, slender, graceful trees, not known for their massive proportions. Their bark color and delicate branching pattern contribute to the illusion of small size, but aspens can become large on favorable terrain. The largest known quaking aspen is in Ontonagon County at the western end of upper Michigan. It is 109 feet (32.7 m) tall and more than 3 feet (0.9 m) in diameter. In areas where white-barked birches (*Betula*) are plagued by borers, the equally white-barked aspens might become popular as replacement trees.

LEAVES: Quaking aspen derives its common and scientific names from its foliage. The round leaves hang from flexible, flattened petioles and quake in the lightest of breezes. *Tremuloides* actually means "like *tremula*," a reference to the nearly identical European aspen (*Populus tremula*), known for its similar shivering movement. The leaves are very finely toothed along their margins.

I have an experimental provenance plot of aspen at Starhill Forest, propagated vegetatively from more than thirty locations across nearly the entire natural range. The leaves vary in size, shape, fall color, and phenology depending upon the source location. Most turn bright gold in fall, but some clones from the Rocky Mountains include a little orange. Those from the East generally have the largest leaves, with blades up to 3 inches (7.5 cm) in diameter, and those from central Alaska and the southern Rocky Mountains seem to have the smallest. These test plants vary in many other characteristics as well.

FLOWERS AND FRUIT: Aspens, like other poplars, are dioecious. In high mountain locations staminate clones seem to survive better than pistillate ones, but the genders are evenly mixed in most areas. The flowers are small catkins similar to those of willows (*Salix*) and are not particularly conspicuous.

Female trees release great quantities of seed in early summer every few years, but the tiny seeds are so perishable that few remain viable long enough to establish new trees. This is not a problem for the aspen, since the few seeds that do make it have the potential to develop into clones that can survive for millennia.

BEST SEASONS: FALL (the golden foliage, backlit and held shivering on white stems among clumps of associated dark evergreens, is perhaps the most popular of all nature subjects for calendar photographs). WINTER (for the bark). EARLY SPRING (as the misty, lime-green new leaves expand) and SUMMER (when the foliage does its dance).

NATIVE AND ADAPTIVE RANGE: If you live anywhere in the cooler portions of North America, you probably live near quaking aspen. It ranges from northern Alaska to the mountains of central Mexico, eastward across every portion of Canada that has a growing season long enough to support tree growth, south in the moist, cool highlands to Virginia and Missouri, and throughout the mountains of the West. Plantings near the limits of quaking aspen's natural range should use material of local origin if possible. Trees of locally adapted provenance are hardy north into USDA zone 1.

CULTURE: Aspen seed is difficult to deal with because of its small size and perishable nature. Any damage incurred by established trees during transplanting will doom the trees to cankers, insect attack, bark blemishes, and premature death, so aspens are best established from root cuttings set directly into the permanent planting location. Small sprouts may be lifted in the dormant season from disturbed areas at the edge of a clone, the

RIGHT: Young quaking aspens (*Populus tremuloides*) in fall color.

tops pruned back to soil level, and the roots set at the same depth they originally grew. I have seen attempts to transplant larger specimens, and they seldom thrive unless they are cut back and allowed to resprout.

Aspen tolerates many soil extremes, from sandy fields to cinder ballasts to rocky talus to peaty bogs. It does best in full sun on moist, well-drained soils of limestone origin and responds well to control of competing weeds and protection from the devastation of marauding deer and elk.

Aspen will not sucker very much if the original tree is protected from damage and stress (thus maintaining high levels of the auxin production needed to suppress sprouts) and if the soil is kept shaded and cool with mulch. Soil conditions warmer than room temperature, as in those natural settings where ground fires have opened the forest floor to sunlight, stimulate the most suckering. If you grow aspen as a clone and periodically remove older stems as they become damaged to allow new sprouts to fill in, you will have an attractive landscape plant. Better still, preserve the area around a natural aspen copse and allow it to develop on its own, interfering only to cut damaged stems and surplus shade-tolerant tree species that try to invade and overtop the clone.

PROBLEMS: Aspens as a group are very sensitive to environmental degradation and are host to more than five hundred species of parasites, herbivores, diseases, and other dependent organisms. They share most of the same diseases and pests of other poplar species. While these trees thus contribute much to the health of the ecological communities in which they live, this does not bode well for the long-term outlook of individual aspen stems in the home landscape.

Bark injuries, even superficial scratches from climbing squirrels, become permanent scars. The aboveground parts of these trees are also extremely susceptible to fire and other forms of mechanical damage—some people claim you could say "Boo" and scare them to death. New stems always emerge to replace old damaged ones unless drainage impairment or herbicides have killed the roots. This sprouting ability is great for the survival of the clone but frustrates attempts to grow aspen as a single-stem shade tree. Many of the aspens dug in the wild in the Rockies and sold to unsuspecting homeowners become disappointments, something that

LEFT: A mixed planting of aspen species at Starhill Forest. RIGHT: The striking bark of quaking aspen.

may sour the public on what could be a spectacular landscape plant under more suitable circumstances.

CULTIVARS: Quaking aspen will hybridize with our other native aspen species, bigtooth aspen (*Populus grandidentata*), and can be crossed with European aspen and perhaps with some Asian species. There are many such hybrids, developed mostly for pulpwood production, but ornamental cultivars of either of our native species are not commonly seen. Variations in bark color, branching structure, foliage characteristics, growth rate, and regional adaptability would lead to many beautiful cultivars of both species if they were better adapted to cultivation as lawn trees and easier to propagate from cuttings. I have found that quaking aspens of eastern provenance seem much better adapted to my test location in Illinois than most of the western ones I have tried, and the reverse would probably be equally true for a western test site.

SIMILAR AND RELATED SPECIES: Bigtooth aspen (***Populus grandidentata***) is much better adapted to dry sites than quaking aspen and can handle hotter, more humid

conditions. It can be a tenacious tree. A bushy specimen has been growing on the tile roof of the Decatur County Courthouse in Greensburg, Indiana, since 1870, with its roots sustained only by the windblown dust that accumulates in the cracks between the tiles. Although normally smaller than quaking aspen, bigtooth aspen can potentially grow large. One specimen in Marquette, Michigan, is 132 feet (39.6 m) tall, and a venerable old tree in Kentucky has a trunk nearly 4 feet (1.2 m) thick.

Bigtooth aspen shares much of the same range in the East as quaking aspen, but it does not extend west very far beyond the Mississippi River valley and is absent from Newfoundland. It can be grown a little further south, in the hot, humid Southeast, and north through USDA zone 3. The foliage is similar but has coarse, irregular teeth along the margins. A nursery in Manitoba has introduced 'Sabretooth', a cultivar with exceptional fall color.

The two species are easy to tell apart in early spring because bigtooth aspen is later to leaf out and because its new foliage is covered with a white wool that gives the appearance of cotton balls throughout the crown of the tree. This difference is so pronounced in early spring that mixed forests of both aspens can be separated easily into the component species even when viewed from airplanes. The flowers of bigtooth aspen also seem to open later than those of quaking aspen, which helps to prevent excessive natural introgression. The two species are more difficult to distinguish from a distance during other seasons. Both species have amazing fall color, but quaking aspen typically has brighter bark, and bigtooth aspen is more impressive in spring with its woolly new foliage.

Our native aspens are closely allied to the European *Populus tremula* and *P. alba,* and to the Asian *P. tomentosa* and *P. sieboldii.* Some taxonomists have advanced a case for making quaking aspen a variety of *P. tremula,* but most don't buy it. Of all the aspens I have seen in their respective native lands, I think our two American species are the most spectacular in bark and fall color.

This entire group of poplars is more distantly related to other native poplars, such as cottonwood (*Populus deltoides*). The genus is in the same family as the willows (*Salix*), with which it shares many horticultural characteristics including preferred habitat, rapid growth rate, and susceptibility to disease.

COMMENTS: Known to loggers across the North as popple, aspen is a premier pulp tree for paper. It also hosts an amazing array of birds, mammals, and butterflies, and if the damage these animals cause can be tolerated, aspen will serve as a premier wildlife tree in your landscape. It is a pleasure to work old damaged stems into some of the best and most beautiful fireplace kindling available, knowing that replacement stems are waiting to spring up.

Quaking aspen is a tree for the record books. It occupies a larger range than any other North American tree, spreading more than 110 degrees longitude (nine time zones), 47 degrees latitude (northern Canada to central Mexico), and from sea level up to timberline. Some individual aspen clones are among the largest living organisms known anywhere. A single clone in Utah has 47,000 stems and is estimated to have a total mass at least three times greater than the world's largest individual tree of any other species. And while this is one of the few trees with individual stems that have an average life span no longer than that of humans, trunks have been found as old as 275 years. A clone in Minnesota that has been "born again" many times from the same root system has been estimated to be 8000 years old, which would rank it very high on the antiquity scale as well.

LEFT: Quaking aspen (*Populus tremuloides*) leaves in fall color.

Prosopis glandulosa

HONEY MESQUITE

DESCRIPTION: Traveling the nooks and crannies of southwestern North America, we sometimes encounter fanciful native woody legumes that leave us with vivid images of how they might have attained their natural fit into their regional landscape situations. These plants might be limited in their general usefulness as landscape trees for any of several reasons. For example, many are winter hardy only in the southernmost portions of our area. Others typically grow as shrubs and can reach tree stature only under the right growing conditions or with advanced age. Some have troublesome thorns or poisonous seeds that restrict their potential usefulness. However, they often have gorgeous, fragrant flowers and can be the closest thing to a shade tree that can survive under harsh desert climate conditions. I have decided to present them here as a group, using honey mesquite (*Prosopis glandulosa*, syn. *P. juliflora*) as their flagship species.

Mesquite (*Prosopis*) is viewed with disdain by those who manage their ranches for livestock, because its competition reduces pasture forage under excessive grazing pressure, and because the thorns of vigorous sprouts can cripple livestock and destroy tires. Along with other desert trees and shrubs (and some of the wildlife that depend upon them), mesquite is destroyed by people dragging large anchor chains, root plows, or heavy chopping rollers across the range with bulldozers. It is often thought of as nothing more than fine firewood (the best of which is said to come from the large roots exposed by chaining or root-plowing), but in the native landscape, rather than the agricultural one, this tree and its kin are major players in the web of life.

Mesquites can also adapt well to the cultivated landscape and be tamed into amenable little trees. Several trees planted in 1974 on the campus of New Mexico State University have already lost their thorny juvenile habit under cultivation on that irrigated site. The U.S. national champion, growing along a rural road near Leaky, Texas, is 55 feet (16.5 m) tall, much broader than that, and 3 feet (0.9 m) in diameter.

LEAVES: The rachis of the deciduous, bipinnately compound, feathery leaves of mesquite is forked, with each of the two halves bearing seven to eighteen pairs of narrow leaflets about 1 inch (2.5 cm) long. On older branches they arise in clusters from knobby spur branches.

FLOWERS AND FRUIT: Mesquite flowers are light yellow and borne in 3-inch (7.5-cm) spikes in late spring. They can bloom periodically again all summer after heavy rains. My tree-loving friend Art Plotnik noted in *The Urban Tree Book* (2000) that the flowers are "more allergenic than ornamental, but they excite the bees that manufacture gourmet mesquite honey." They definitely are quite fragrant, and mature into attractive, dark red, lumpy pods that eventually ripen to tan, with each bean, or seed, showing as a swelled segment. The pods are high in carbohydrates and very nutritious for both wildlife and livestock, which gladly consume them and spread the seeds.

BEST SEASONS: SPRING (for the fragrant flowers). SUMMER (for the decorative ripening pods, the fine texture of the leaves, and the light, welcome shade; during summer this is the greenest tree in the desert). WINTER (for the persistent pods and picturesque silhouette).

NATIVE AND ADAPTIVE RANGE: Honey mesquite is the most widespread member of the genus in our region. It is native on hillsides, along arroyos, and increasingly in old pastures that have been overgrazed in the past, throughout most of Texas and southwestern Oklahoma, west into Arizona and beyond, and south throughout Mexico. Mesquite is spread by livestock that eat the pods. It can be found naturalizing in isolated pockets of rangeland much further north, probably due to overgrazing and the resultant reduction in grass cover, which lowers the intensity of range fires below the threshold necessary to control it. Honey mesquite has naturalized at elevations from 6000 feet (1829 m) down to 3000 feet (914 m) north all the way to the Colorado border and even into Kansas. The path of naturalization is obvious when seen from the air along the Kings Highway (El Camino Real) in New Mexico and the major north-south

highways. It is reliably hardy on well-drained, high pH soils in USDA zone 7 and may be tried in zone 6.

CULTURE: Mesquite loves heat. Like many other legumes, it adapts to poor soil by fixing atmospheric nitrogen via *Rhizobia* symbiosis through its roots, and enriches soil with its leaf litter. It prefers well-drained limestone soils but grows best in riparian situations where its roots can find a permanent water table.

The seeds can remain dormant for years if left to dry out, and then require scarification to germinate well. Fresh seeds, sown immediately, usually germinate more quickly. The most effective, albeit not most pleasant, way to obtain properly scarified seeds is to walk behind cattle and pick the seeds from their excrement. Young trees develop very deep roots in a hurry, as they must do to survive in their chosen habitat, so they should be grown in containers or with root-control measures until they are planted in their permanent locations. The seedlings must have full sunlight, but older trees can tolerate light shade.

These trees usually have very deep taproots and require little supplemental irrigation. Once established, they should be soaked infrequently for strong, vigorous growth, but not necessarily subjected to the same daily watering regime necessary to keep many exotic plants alive in the desert. With no irrigation following establishment, they will survive as shrubs; occasional deep irrigation will release their full potential as trees.

Existing old trees are much like Osage-orange (*Maclura pomifera*) in that they can be diamonds in the rough. With careful, sculptural pruning and removal of thorny juvenile sprouts, many can be transformed from brushy weeds into attractive small trees loaded with twist and character. Try to prune live wood only in fall or early winter to minimize excessive bleeding of sap.

PROBLEMS: Insects are not a big problem with this genus, but many seeds are destroyed by the tiny bruchid beetles (*Algarobius prosopis* and *Neltumius arizonensis*) that bore into the pods. The paired thorns (single thorns in one variety) may be clipped if they occur within reach and pose a hazard, but not all trees are very thorny and older ones are even less so.

CULTIVARS: 'Maverick' is a thornless selection of honey mesquite that is hardy to USDA zone 7. There are other thornless cultivars that may be hybrids with South American species.

LEFT: A mature honey mesquite (*Prosopis glandulosa*) in the Chihuahuan Desert.

SIMILAR AND RELATED SPECIES: The U.S. national champion velvet mesquite (***Prosopis velutina***), at the west edge of our region in Arizona, is a grizzly old tree 46 feet (13.8 m) tall with a short trunk more than 5 feet (1.5 m) thick. It has shreddy bark and ferny foliage very much like honey mesquite but with smaller, tomentose leaflets and a more westerly range. It follows desert streams and can be grown in cultivation north at least into USDA zone 7. One provenance selection from the Gila River valley is being grown successfully in USDA zone 6 by my friend Mike Melendrez in New Mexico. This species and honey mesquite were formerly given variety status under the old species name *P. juliflora*.

Screwbean mesquite (***Prosopis pubescens***) is also similar to honey mesquite but with fascinating decorative seedpods wound as tightly as watch springs. It does not get as large—the biggest known is 27 feet (8.1 m) tall and about 1 foot (30 cm) in diameter—and it is primarily a tree of the upper Rio Grande Valley in New Mexico and westward into Arizona and California. The northern end of the natural range, north of Albuquerque along the Rio Grande, is in USDA zone 6. Screwbean is riparian and needs a perched water table or regular irrigation under desert conditions. Other mesquite species seen frequently in cultivation originate from Central and South America.

Palo verde (***Parkinsonia aculeata***), also called retama, is the only tree-sized member of its genus. It is a fast-growing small tree with green twigs, very tiny leaflets, and beautiful yellow flowers. Unlike most other desert trees, it likes poorly drained soils. During severe droughts it sheds its leaves and relies upon the green bark of its branches to carry out photosynthesis. It is hardy in cultivation in USDA zone 8 and makes a fine-textured, ornamental small tree. Another yellow-flowering, green-barked tree, ***Cercidium texanum,*** is also known as palo verde and is the only representative of this attractive Mexican genus that grows naturally in our region. It is confined to southern Texas and is not known to be hardy north of USDA zone 8.

Mescal bean (***Sophora secundiflora***) is a tough, glossy little evergreen tree with bubble-gum-scented, wisteria-blue flowers that appear in late winter to early spring. Its

TOP LEFT: Honey mesquite (*Prosopis glandulosa*) foliage and thorns. LEFT: Seedpods on honey mesquite. RIGHT: The decorative seedpods of screwbean mesquite (*P. pubescens*). FAR RIGHT: A large velvet mesquite (*P. velutina*) growing along a desert stream.

bright red-orange seeds, as large as marbles and borne in silver fuzzy pods, are poisonous. This tree's natural range enters our area from Mexico only in southern and western Texas, where it is hardy at least to USDA zone 7, and in isolated populations in New Mexico. This species has been known to survive with minimal damage at 7000 feet (2100 m) in the Guadalupe Mountains along the Texas–New Mexico border. It is one of the few trees that thrives in caliche soils, with impermeable, leached calcareous horizons. Mescal bean has been found in the Organ Mountains and the Franklin Mountains of New Mexico at elevations that would be USDA zone 6, but these areas are protected by snow cover in winter and are subjected to a winter monsoon season that the Texas populations do not have.

The related necklace tree (**Sophora affinis**) is deciduous and has pink flowers and a more northeasterly range, in the calcareous blackland prairies of central Texas, north into Oklahoma, and east into Louisiana. It makes a small tree in sunny exposures and becomes more of a vine in the shady understory. Coralbean (**Erythrina herbacea**), another legume with poisonous seeds, can be found from the Gulf Coastal Plain of the Deep South west through eastern Texas and south into Mexico. It dies back in cold winters, becoming shrubby, but forms a small tree in warmer parts of its range. The flowers and seeds are bright scarlet, making it popular as a landscape plant.

Acacias are spiny, feathery shrubs and trees with worldwide distribution in warm climates. The native species that can become small trees in our region include huisache (**Acacia farnesiana**), catclaw (**A. greggii**), Roemer's acacia (**A. roemeriana**), Wright acacia (**A. wrightii**), and whitethorn (**A. constricta**). The acacias are great

honey plants and valuable for wildlife food and cover. Huisache is probably the species most widely cultivated beyond its natural range, throughout the South and in Europe. It develops a graceful spreading form with attractive yellow or orange flowers and purplish pods and can tolerate a wide range of soil and watering conditions. The largest known Roemer's acacia is located at the Alamo in San Antonio, Texas, where it goes largely unnoticed among crowds too busy imagining the ghosts of Davy Crockett and Jim Bowie. None of these acacias is likely to be hardy north of USDA zone 7.

Texas ebony (**_Pithecellobium flexicaule_**) is similar to honey mesquite and can grow larger, but it is evergreen and not as cold hardy. It is prized in cultivation in warm-climate areas worldwide for its fragrant white flowers and valuable hard wood but is confined to southern Texas in the wild. The Texas lead trees, goldenball (**_Leucaena retusa_**) and white lead tree (**_L. pulverulenta_**), round out this sampler of southwestern legumes. Both are popular landscape trees, but only goldenball is hardy north of USDA zone 9. It can be planted safely at least in USDA zone 8 and is native to New Mexico's southwestern and southeastern corners in mountain foothill areas in USDA zone 7. Under cultivation by Mike Melendrez in central New Mexico it is hardy to a microclimate in USDA zone 6 with some minor tip damage, but during extremely cold winters it dies to the ground in the Guadalupe Mountains and surrounding desert.

COMMENTS: Honey mesquites are usually seen as small trees or scrub on the open range, but the old ones on lands that have not been chained, roller-chopped, or sprayed with herbicides can become decent-sized trees, especially in riparian habitats. Some old specimens have been uprooted and found to have taproots penetrating more than 160 feet (48 m) to a permanent water table, and large specimens can be more than two hundred years old. In some photographs taken in the Old West in the 1800s, the only things recognizable today are the distant mountains and some old mesquite trees that still grow where they were seen by the photographers.

You might find mesquite or some of these other interesting native legume species growing wild on your property, or you might have a particular need in your landscape and the urge to try something different. Each of these plants merits consideration for its ornamental, conservation, or wildlife values. The mesquite genus (_Prosopis_) probably comprises the most valuable group of wildlife trees in the Southwest. Planting or preserving the unusual within the matrix of your landscape will contribute on a local scale to that critical ecological concept known as biodiversity. As the old saying goes, "A good tinker will save all the parts!"

LEFT: Whitethorn (_Acacia constricta_) in the Organ Mountains.

Prunus americana

WILD PLUM

DESCRIPTION: The genus *Prunus* includes two of our most ornamental groups of native trees: cherries and plums. Most plums are quite similar, and none is more spectacular in bloom nor more widespread in the landscape than the common wild plum, also known as the American plum. A thicket-forming small tree in the wild, similar to the wild crabapples (*Malus*), wild plum can be domesticated into a splendid flowering specimen for the ornamental garden.

When the competition of its own suckers is eliminated, wild plum develops into a fruit tree of substantial proportions. The U.S. national champion in Gadsden County, Florida, is 48 feet (14.4 m) tall with a trunk 1 foot (30 cm) thick. Several closely related species become at least as large, although most prefer to exist as dense thickets of small stems unless they are trained into tree form.

LEAVES: Wild plum leaves closely resemble those of their domesticated cousins. They are usually recurved and keeled down the midrib, reaching up to 5 inches (12.5 cm) long. They have toothed margins and rough, rugose surfaces with deeply set veins. Leaves of this species emerge after the flowers, while those of most other plum species develop concurrently with the flowers. If the leaves survive early defoliation or disfigurement by fungus diseases, they can exhibit a nice yellow-orange fall color, with colored leaves and green leaves often mixing on the same tree like a Monet painting.

FLOWERS AND FRUIT: Plum flowers, especially those of wild plum, rival those of any popular exotic flowering trees. Wild plum flowers are pure white, emerging from a showy red calyx that sets them off sharply. They bloom early, at the same time as the exotic ornamental pears (*Pyrus calleryana*), and are every bit their equal.

The plum flowers appear in clusters and reach their peak as redbud (*Cercis canadensis*) begins to bloom, making a rich color sequence along roadsides and fence rows. Many people remark on the beautiful combination of redbud flowers with dogwood (*Cornus florida*) flowers,

which appear later, but the earlier combination of plum and redbud is just as spectacular. Plum bark is curly and dark, often nearly black on some species, and the contrast of the snowy flower clusters against such bark makes them seem to glow.

The tangy fruits that develop later in summer are a colorful plum-red with yellow flesh and grow to about 1 inch (2.5 cm) in diameter. You would expect plum fruits to be a valuable source of food for birds, but their usefulness is limited mostly to foxes and other mammals, including humans. Woodpeckers, jays, and robins will take some of the plums, and quail feed on them after they fall.

BEST SEASONS: SPRING (wild plum is one of our finest flowering trees). FALL (for those trees that develop good fall color) and LATE SUMMER (for the fruit harvest).

NATIVE AND ADAPTIVE RANGE: This is one of our most adaptable plums. It grows naturally from southeastern Saskatchewan east to New England and south to northern Florida. This species and several of its close relatives can be grown north through most of USDA zone 3.

CULTURE: Plums like sunny sites and good soil drainage. They benefit from the same spray program that can be used for the home orchard, especially if insect- and disease-free fruits and attractive foliage are desired, but they don't require such attention to survive. They are easy to raise from seed, picked and cleaned as soon as the fruits are completely ripe and planted in early fall. Be sure to protect the seedbed from mice. Plums are shallow rooted and easy to transplant in early spring, and suckering clumps may be divided and relocated.

PROBLEMS: Wild plum and its relatives are subject to many leaf spot fungi, black knot disease (*Dibotryon morbosum*) of the stem, and the common brown rot fungi (*Monilinia*) that destroy many stone fruits in the home orchard. They can be attacked by the same clearwing borers (*Sanninoidea exitiosa*) and other insects that bother stone fruits in the orchard, including ubiquitous pests like yellownecks (*Datana ministra*), Japanese beetles (*Popillia japonica*), tent caterpillars (*Malacosoma americanum*), and fall webworms (*Hyphantria cunea*). Plums are also susceptible to a newly discovered virus disease called plum pox potyvirus.

The sharp spur branches of plums can be hazardous if trees are planted too close to activity areas, and the falling fruits are messy if they land on a patio or driveway. Vigilance is important when monitoring for the appearance of unwanted suckers, which should be mowed, or preferably pulled, as soon as they are noticed, unless a plum thicket is desired.

CULTIVARS: Many selections of wild plum are available for fruit production and wildlife habitat use in local areas. The species is also useful in hybridization pro-grams and as a rootstock for grafting domestic plums. I have not found any cultivars selected for ornamental use.

SIMILAR AND RELATED SPECIES: The similar Chicka-saw plum (***Prunus angustifolia***) is more of a southern species, hardy to USDA zone 6. It has narrow leaves and thus makes a more finely textured tree, almost like an olive (*Olea europaea*). This is our largest plum species. The record reportedly belongs to a specimen planted very far from its natural range, in Oregon, that stands 86 feet (25.8 m) tall and is more than 3 feet (0.9 m) in diameter. Since I have not seen it, however, I cannot vouch for its identification or the accuracy of its unusually large measurements.

LEFT: Wild plum (*Prunus americana*) in bloom at Starhill Forest. BELOW: Wild plums blooming along a field border.

Canada plum (**Prunus nigra**) is very hardy, to USDA zone 3, and is limited to the states and provinces bordering the United States–Canada international boundary from Manitoba eastward. It can become a fairly large tree and, like wild plum, blooms before the leaves emerge. This species is used widely as a food source, and several ethnobotanists have noted that it is found at many locations known to have been aboriginal village sites of Native Americans. Whether they cultivated it or merely left the seeds behind to grow is open to debate. One cultivar, 'Princess Kay', is listed.

Mexican plum (**Prunus mexicana**) also becomes a nice tree more often than it does a thicket, and with USDA zone 5 hardiness it is at home as much in the United States as in Mexico. It has a broad natural range covering much of the central United States from Nebraska and Ohio south into Mexico. Its tart reddish purple fruits ripen later than those of most other plums and are used mostly for preserves. Sloe plum (**P. umbellata**) is similar but smaller and is found more in low, sandy areas across the Deep South.

The wildgoose plums, **Prunus hortulana** and **P. munsoniana,** are smaller species restricted to the lower Midwest, and they bloom later, when the leaves are beginning to expand. Their small yellow fruits are edible but used primarily by small mammals. *Prunus munsoniana,* known as Munson's wildgoose plum, is more valuable for its fruit than for its flowers and has furnished several pomological selections. I discovered the largest *P. munsoniana* ever found, at New Salem, the Illinois village

where Abraham Lincoln lived in the early 1800s. It was nearly 18 inches (45 cm) in diameter, growing east of the first store Lincoln operated as a young businessman in the 1830s. A tornado later damaged the old plum, but I am working with the manager of the historic site to protect and restore it. Despite the loss of much of its crown, its large diameter is sufficient to allow it to remain the U.S. national champion. Hog plum (***P. rivularis***) is nearly identical to Munson's wildgoose plum and ranges further southwest into Texas. Its fruits are not as large or sweet as those of the wildgoose plums, and it tends to form shrubby thickets more than the others.

Other native plum species exist only as low shrubs or, like ***Prunus murrayana*** of Trans-Pecos Texas, as rare, indistinct taxa unlikely to be encountered. Plums belong to the same genus as the stone-fruited trees of orchards, a genus that includes more than two hundred species worldwide.

COMMENTS: Archaeologists have documented the value of wild plums to Native Americans and found evidence of their prehistoric use of these trees. They were first mentioned in historical literature in connection with the 1524 expedition of Giovanni di Verrazano, who was probably describing the beach plum (*Prunus maritima*), a shrubby species popular in cultivation today. Wild plums were recorded as a food source as early as May 30, 1539, in a journal entry of the Hernando de Soto expedition, and they remain high on the list of wild edible plants today.

Plums are not as valuable for wildlife food as it would seem they should be, but they join hawthorns (*Crataegus*) as some of the most valuable nesting cover available throughout their extensive range. They are also useful for erosion control due to their tolerance of poor, dry soil and because of the thicket-forming nature of most species. They host many butterflies, including several colorful hairstreaks and the giant cecropia moth, with its 6-inch (15-cm) wingspan.

FAR LEFT: Wild plum (*Prunus americana*) in natural habitat at the edge of a midwestern prairie. TOP LEFT: The flowers of wild plum are short-lived but spectacular. CENTER LEFT: Fall color on wild plum. LEFT: Ripening fruits of wild plum.

Prunus serotina

WILD CHERRY

DESCRIPTION: This species is far and away the preeminent forest tree of all the world's cherries and plums. It is a classic dominant species of the Allegheny Mountains, where it becomes a tall, straight canopy tree and a superior source of fine hardwood lumber for furniture. Cherry can also be a more modest, sprawling inhabitant of almost every farm fence row from the Atlantic Seaboard to the prairies of the Midwest. The largest wild cherry on record grows in Great Smoky Mountains National Park, measuring 134 feet (40.2 m) in height and nearly 6 feet (1.8 m) in diameter.

Wild cherry is a tree that follows disturbances, seeding in as birds, who eat the fruits whole and pass or regurgitate the pits, visit forest openings torn apart by tornadoes, fire, logging, or other calamities. Seedlings also attempt to establish under the forest canopy but fail or stagnate unless a subsequent windfall opens the area to sunlight within a few years. Those that survive form tall, slender trees when challenged by their neighbors, but they become spreading, heavy-limbed trees with arching branches and slightly weeping twigs when allowed to grow free from competition.

LEAVES: Wild cherry leaves resemble those of cultivated cherries but are acuminate and have smooth, glossy upper surfaces and finely toothed margins. Cherry leaves are very uniform in size and shape, growing to about 5 inches (12.5 cm) long. They are often pocked with harmless, acnelike pouch galls caused by *Eriophyes padi* mites. They turn a deep yellow or orange in autumn but are not always as impressive as their forest neighbors.

FLOWERS AND FRUIT: The flowers are white and hang in racemes 5 inches (12.5 cm) long in early summer after the leaves have developed. Trees sometimes seem covered by these flower clusters, but the foliage detracts somewhat from their beauty. The clusters of tiny pungent cherries that follow the flowers are at first green, then red, and finally a dark purplish black. The fruits of some trees are tolerably edible but only when totally black and absolutely ripe. They ripen sequentially within each cluster, so it is not possible to strip entire clusters at once. Generally they become suitable to the human palette about a day after the birds have already taken them.

BEST SEASONS: LATE SPRING (for the flowers). SUMMER (for the colorful fruit clusters, where they are not a messy problem, and for the shiny foliage).

NATIVE AND ADAPTIVE RANGE: There are several geographic races of wild cherry, and they combine to cover a lot of ground. The species in its various forms grows from Nova Scotia west to central Minnesota, south to central Florida and the Edwards Plateau of Texas, then southwest through Mexico to Guatemala. Locally adapted selections are hardy into USDA zone 3.

CULTURE: Wild cherry prefers mostly full sun and moderate soil conditions. Good drainage is probably the factor most critical to its success, as is true with many plants of this genus. Seeds germinate readily under a variety of conditions. I have seen wild cherry seedlings emerge from beneath deep layers of mulch, from the middle of a gravel driveway, and from piles of old leaves, as well as the thousands that volunteer into cultivated perennial beds. Growing them intentionally, however, requires stratification or fall planting, with foolproof protection from mice. Entire seedbeds can be cleaned out by a relatively minor mouse population, to be cached in their nests for winter food.

This tree does not appreciate being transplanted and should be taken in early spring with a good-sized soil ball. Be sure not to plant it too deep or it will wither almost as soon as it tries to leaf out. If your cherry seedling struggles into a nondescript leaning form for a year or two after transplanting, cut it to the ground in the dormant season and it will respond with a vigorous, straight shoot.

PROBLEMS: Wild cherry belongs to one of our most disease- and insect-prone tree families, but this species is more trouble-free than most. Many of the problems that frustrate orchardists also take their toll on wild cherry (see *Prunus americana*). The most conspicuous scourge is surely the eastern tent caterpillar (*Malacosoma americanum*), which totally defoliates entire fence rows of cherry and leaves them covered with its webs. Trees weak-

RIGHT: A young wild cherry (*Prunus serotina*) in bloom.

ened by these insects, or by any of several other defoliators or fungus diseases, can be attacked by several species of borers, some of which cause gummy sap globules to form on the trunk and limbs. This light, clear yellow, sticky gum is the stuff of Jurassic Park—the type of resin that trapped and preserved so many insects millions of years ago, to be converted slowly into amber with their DNA (and that of the dinosaurs they fed upon?) supposedly intact.

Wild cherry bark is the original source of cherry cough medicine, and its chemical combination of sugar and cyanide reportedly acts as a sedative. The leaves and seeds contain sufficient hydrocyanic acid to be toxic to browsing animals, especially if the acid is concentrated by wilting on broken or pruned branches. The acid content is diluted as the leaves mature and becomes less of a problem later in the season.

Wild cherries in forest settings frequently fall victim to fires, deer, porcupines, and other natural hazards of the woods. Those in exposed settings in the South are often stunted and disfigured by burls, which are coveted

by woodworkers. In cultivation these trees can be allelopathic to some other garden plants. They are sensitive to soil disturbance, bark injury, and the chainsaws of impatient homeowners who tire of the messy fruits and ceaseless twig litter.

CULTIVARS: Geographic races are known to exist over the broad natural range of this tree, but horticultural selections are virtually unknown. Upright, weeping, and cutleaf forms are mentioned in the literature but are not commercially available. 'Spring Sparkle' is the one most commonly listed.

SIMILAR AND RELATED SPECIES: Pin cherry (**Prunus pensylvanica**) is a slender look-alike that becomes a vigorous early pioneer on disturbed sites. It is more colorful and faster growing than wild cherry but not very long lived. A cold-climate species hardy in USDA zone 3, it ranges across most of Canada and southward into the Lake States, New England, and the Appalachians. 'Jumping Pond' and 'Stockton' are listed as cultivars. I've not seen them, but I have seen brilliant fiery orange fall color on specimens along the north shore of Lake Superior and in the Adirondacks. Old specimens that survive long enough can reach 80 feet (24 m) in height, with thin, straight trunks. A similar species, bitter cherry (**P. emarginata**), grows in the western mountains of North America. It is generally smaller with more bitter fruits and is often shrubby on poor sites.

Chokecherry (**Prunus virginiana**) is a shrubby, suckering tree that, in its several varieties, covers an immense natural range that includes forty states and almost every Canadian province. It is an understory species with remarkable shade tolerance for a cherry, and it tends to form clumps of upright stems. Chokecherry has impressive resilience under variable growing conditions and can be grown north into USDA zone 2, but it is not as happy in the South as many other species.

Unfortunately, the only well-known cultivar of chokecherry commonly available for purchase is a selection variously called 'Canada Red' or 'Shubert', a purple-leaved form totally incongruous with the natural settings that suit this species best. Luckily, wild plants can be propagated easily from seed or by dividing the clumping stems. The Canadian Ornamental Plant Foundation has released 'Halward's Choice', a weeping form selected by an Ontario nursery. The Canadian Prairie Farm Rehabilitation Administration's Shelterbelt Centre in

LEFT: Flower detail on wild cherry (*Prunus serotina*).
RIGHT: Wild cherry in fall color.

Saskatchewan is testing selections of chokecherry for use on the northern Great Plains, so selected releases for conservation planting may become more available in the future.

Laurel cherry (**Prunus caroliniana**) is an erect, evergreen, southeastern species with inedible shiny black fruits, popular in residential landscapes across the Deep South. Identical U.S. national champion specimens found at opposite ends of the natural range, in Florida and Texas, are 47 feet (14.1 m) tall and just over 3 feet (0.9 m) in diameter. This tree is useful in cultivation north to USDA zone 6 in protected sites.

Wild cherry and its native kin are also closely related to the cultivated cherries that originated in Europe and Asia, and less closely related to cultivated plums, apricots, peaches, and almonds, all in the genus *Prunus*.

COMMENTS: Approximately thirty species of *Prunus* are native to North America, and together they constitute some of our most valuable wildlife plants. The half of this group that includes the native cherries is especially important; despite the cyanide content of the foliage, cherries provide a major proportion of the food supply for more than one hundred species of wildlife, and wild cherry is a primary host plant for over two hundred species of butterflies and moths.

Wild cherries in midwestern fence rows are often among the first, and easiest, trees climbed by farm children. The limb structures of a few trees (right foot here, left foot there, handhold above left) remain sharply engraved in my own memory, as do the spacious rural panoramas that became visible from high in those trees, and the feelings of freedom and exhilaration that increased with each step upward. Though my climbing days are behind me, some of my favorite old climbing trees remain, ready to thrill new generations of children awakening to the miracles of their natural environment.

LEFT: A wild cherry (*Prunus serotina*) loaded with fruit.

Quercus alba
WHITE OAK

DESCRIPTION: Oaks suffer from a short-sighted demand for instant gratification in the landscape that often results in a misguided preference for trendy but short-lived exotics. As we tree planters gain the wisdom and patience of experience and begin to focus more on the potential immortality of our work, native oaks are the trees we turn to throughout most of North America.

Oaks occur naturally in vast numbers in each of the forty-eight contiguous states but Idaho, though cultivated oaks grow there. More than sixty oak species are native to the United States and Canada, and many more can be found in Mexico. Much of what I cover for white oak applies as much to the rest.

Just as maple is the official tree of Canada, oak has been selected as the national tree of the United States. And the tree that might claim to be the flagship species of the genus is white oak, the state tree of Connecticut, Maryland, Iowa, and Illinois. White oak is a dominant tree of many landscapes. It lives for several centuries under favorable conditions, becoming more massive and picturesque with every passing human generation. Like most oaks, it establishes from acorns sown by wildlife into openings caused by windthrow, fire, logging, or other disturbance, and grows slowly but relentlessly to become, after the first century or two, the lord of its locality.

The U.S. national champion white oak was the famous old Wye Oak, which grew in its own park, Wye Mills State Park, Maryland, until a storm brought it down in June of 2002. Nothing else ever quite matched it, even though every portion of its natural range boasts notable and noble white oaks. It was 80 feet (24 m) tall with a canopy that spread more than 100 feet (30 m), and its huge limbs were supported by a hollow trunk 10 feet (3 m) in diameter. Its enormous spreading crown was braced and cabled for many years to postpone its inevitable death from windstorms or lightning. Consequently it lived as it had since before the birth of the na-

tion, well exceeding what otherwise would have been its natural life span, to awe every visitor who knew enough about trees to comprehend its antiquity.

LEAVES: White oak leaves show the classic rounded outline used by graphic artists everywhere to symbolize the genus. The logo of the Nature Conservancy, one of our finest natural heritage preservation organizations, consists simply of the silhouette of a white oak leaf. The leaves emerge white or pink in spring, turning medium green as they expand to about 7 inches (17.5 cm) long. In fall they are among the most colorful of all oak leaves, turning various shades of crimson.

FLOWERS AND FRUIT: Oak flowers develop as the leaves expand in spring. The axillary pistillate flowers are minute and not easily noticed, but staminate catkins, seen en masse from a distance, give the entire tree a veil of pastel green smoke. Oaks are wind-pollinated, so tremendous numbers of these catkins are produced to ensure that some of the pollen fulfills its destiny. Individual trees exhibit protandry and thus encourage cross-pollination of early-blooming trees by later-blooming ones.

The fruits are acorns, familiar to anyone who ever walked an oak woods in early fall. White oak is in the taxonomic subdivision of oaks known collectively as the white oaks (section *Quercus*, formerly subgenus *Lepidobalanus* or *Leucobalanus*; see the taxonomic discussion under *Quercus shumardii*). Acorns of oaks in this group ripen in one year. The acorns will sprout without a dormancy period and begin to germinate as soon as they fall from the tree. They are among the very best sources of food for wildlife and are gathered and hoarded by birds and rodents.

BEST SEASONS: FALL (for the rich fall color and the acorn crop, which draws a fascinating array of wildlife like a magnet). SPRING (when the tiny new leaves and staminate catkins combine to lay a pastel tint on the artistic superstructure of limbs). WINTER (for the character of the tree's architecture and bark) and SUMMER (as a superior shade tree).

NATIVE AND ADAPTIVE RANGE: The natural range of this species is a nearly perfect square, the points of the square being Minneapolis, Minnesota; Augusta, Maine; Brunswick, Georgia; and Houston, Texas. This range

extends across southern Ontario and the edge of Quebec, and trees from northern sources can be planted safely in USDA zone 3.

CULTURE: Give white oak a neutral to acidic soil. Water and fertilize young trees to promote double-flushing (acceleration of growth by developing two years' worth of shoots in one year). Control competition from weeds and turf. Then wait. Planting a white oak is symbolic of faith in the future and should not be undertaken by anyone with plans only for the present human generation. As people grow older and become more conscious of their legacy for humanity, they tend to plant white oaks.

Kids plant them sometimes too, because propagation is so simple and fun. Healthy acorns (those not infested with insect larvae) should be planted on their sides in fall, as soon as they mature, and protected from squirrels and mice for the entire first growing season. If the young seedlings are being grown for eventual transplanting, place the acorns in a sealed bag in the refrigerator until the hypocotyls (primary roots) emerge, and lightly pinch back the tips of those roots before planting. This will encourage a branched root system, without which oaks can be difficult to transplant.

Unclipped acorns grown in pots tend to develop long,

LEFT: A white oak (*Quercus alba*) grove in early spring.
BELOW: The colorful acorns of white oak.

circling roots, which become girdling roots years later in the landscape. Some container nurseries fight this problem by using deep, ribbed pots. I prefer root-control pots coated inside with copper, or bottomless pots (on raised benches or pallets), which cause air-pruning of the taproots. The best solution, if possible, is always to plant the acorn directly where you want the tree to be growing for the next five hundred years.

PROBLEMS: Many of the common problems discussed here apply to other oaks and for the sake of brevity will not be fully repeated elsewhere. White oaks will not survive long in shade and are intolerant of poor drainage and alkaline soil, which cause chlorosis. Old trees are extremely sensitive to construction disturbance within their root zones and do not appreciate the conversion of a forest duff groundcover to competitive turf. The acorns can be a litter problem, but birds and squirrels usually clean them up before winter. Anthracnose (*Gnomonia quercina*) disfigures many oaks during wet years and can be particularly severe on white oak, but it generally does not cause permanent damage. New foliage that develops in summer as a second growth flush can be particularly susceptible to mildew from *Microsphaera* species and related fungi. Oak tatters, a physiological foliage problem, is speculated to be caused by herbicide damage or cold temperatures during budbreak.

As the preeminent genus of hardwood trees in North America—that is, the genus with the most species, the most individual trees, and the widest distribution—oaks in general are subject to many other nuisance diseases and insects that are generally not serious. They are famous for the beauty and variety of the galls they support, most of which are harmless.

The crown of an oak sometimes has forks or whorls of limbs that can affect the structural strength of the tree. These are formed from development of clustered subapical buds, which tend to be dominant over the median lateral buds scattered along the twig. Whorls may be thinned and narrow forks trimmed to a single leader when the tree is still small to encourage development of a strong crown.

A benign bark fungus, *Corticium* patch, causes interesting smooth patchy patterns on the bark of this and some other white oak species. Damaged and overwatered

TOP LEFT: The rugged limbs of an old white oak (*Quercus alba*). LEFT: Staminate catkins and new leaves of white oak. TOP RIGHT: White oak leaves display the classic "oakleaf" shape. RIGHT: Fall color of white oak.

roots are subject to decay by the fungi *Armillaria tabescens*, *A. gallica*, and *A. mellea*. Some trees die quickly from *Armillaria*, while others persist in a seemingly healthy condition until their root systems are nearly gone and they fall onto the nearest house. The most well known oak disease, oak wilt (*Ceratocystis fagacearum*), is not as virulent on white oak as it is on some other species.

Young oaks of all species can be defoliated by yellow-necks (*Datana ministra*) and other gregarious caterpillars. If they are newly transplanted or otherwise stressed, they will be prone to attack by chestnut borers (*Agrilus bilineatus*). Sucking insects like lace bugs (*Corythucha arcuata*), mites (*Oligonychus bicolor*), and various scales can weaken trees. And unless you have big dogs or tall fences, deer are bound to take their toll on young trees. Livestock, chiefly horses and goats, can girdle centuries-old trees in barnyards, unwittingly destroying the shade needed so badly in the heat of summer.

All oaks are cake and ice cream to the notorious Gypsy moth (*Lymantria dispar*), introduced from Europe in the 1860s. This insect defoliates more than 6000 square miles (15,540 sq. km) of forest each year, killing some trees and stressing others. Oaks are our most important hardwood timber genus, so many forestry scientists are working furiously to bring this epidemic under control. Specimen trees may be sprayed by an arborist, if necessary, to minimize Gypsy moth damage.

A better long-term solution will be to enlist the aid of biological controls such as the fungus *Entomophaga maimaiga*, which is showing great success in controlling this pest in experimental evaluations. Other promising tools for control include the braconid endoparasite *Rogas lymantriae*, an ichneumon fly; *Cotesia melanoscela*, a small parasitic wasp; a nucleopolyhedrosis virus marketed under the name Gypchek; and several parasitic *Microsporidia* organisms.

Oaks hold great promise for landscaping but have been held back due to several other perceived problems. Until recently they were difficult to propagate from cuttings or even by grafting, so that exceptional selections could not be replicated easily. Many oak species are difficult to transplant as well, but root-training techniques used in modern nurseries have solved this. Old oaks growing on upland sites also often experience problems related to the sudden increases in competition and irrigation in newly established lawns. All of these challenges can, and should, be overcome.

CULTIVARS: A few variant forms of white oak are described in the literature. 'Jasper' is a compact selection

from Indiana with dependable fall color. I selected a deeply lobed form a few years ago from a tree near the tomb of Abraham Lincoln and gave scionwood as a gift to Dick van Hoey Smith, director of the Trompenburg Arboretum in Holland; he was very pleased with it and named it 'Lincoln'. It is being distributed mostly in Europe. 'Elongata' is a form with long narrow leaves, again seen mostly in the arboreta of Europe. I have several other trees under evaluation.

White oak can be hybridized with other oaks in its subgenus, and some of the hybrids are magnificent. 'Crimson Spire' is a fastigiate selection of *Quercus* ×*bimundorum*, the hybrid of white oak with the upright European oak (*Q. robur* 'Fastigiata'). I have studied hybrid oaks for three decades and have selected several white oak hybrids for potential release to the nursery trade. The first of these to be released, 'Atlas', is a superior cultivar of *Q.* ×*saulii*, the hybrid of white oak with chestnut oak (*Q. montana*).

SIMILAR AND RELATED SPECIES: Several other white oak species are common on the West Coast. Garry oak (***Quercus garryana***) is the white oak of the Pacific North-

west, ranging from northern California north into western Canada. It grows for me in Illinois, though very slowly. Valley oak (***Q. lobata***) and blue oak (***Q. douglasii***) are common in California. All these species can be grown under cultivation in the East, north at least into USDA zone 6, but they much prefer the climate of their native region.

A few European oaks are common in cultivation. These include sessile oak (***Quercus petraea***), Hungarian oak (***Q. frainetto***), and especially the common European, or English, oak (***Q. robur***) and its many cultivars. Many other members of the white oak group (section *Quercus*) grow in North and Central America, Europe, Asia, and northernmost Africa, and many additional oaks grow in the Western Hemisphere, including red oaks (section *Lobatae*, formerly subgenus *Erythrobalanus*) and intermediate, or golden, oaks (section or subgenus *Protobalanus*). Worldwide there are several hundred species and countless hybrids within the genus, including the additional Asian section or subgenus *Cyclobalanopsis*, and many more among the closely allied tanoaks (*Lithocarpus*). Oaks are in the same family as chestnuts (*Castanea*) and beeches (*Fagus*).

COMMENTS: Ancient white oaks probably appear on more inventories of historic trees, over a broader area, than any other tree species. Due to their predominance in the landscape within their broad range, many historic events have taken place near them. And due to their longevity, many have survived as living witnesses to those events.

The Brompton Oak shaded a Union field hospital during the Civil War battle of Fredericksburg and still stands today. The Lincoln Vault Oak shaded the choir that sung at Lincoln's funeral but was destroyed in 1992 by a misguided public agency charged with managing the historic site in which it stood. Subsequent dissection confirmed that it was solid, vigorous, and could probably have borne witness to that sad funeral for another few centuries if its human stewards had not removed it.

The Pemberton Oak in Bristol, Tennessee, saw Revolutionary War action. Fortunately, the generations of humans that lived around it after that time were appreciative of its history; it survived in silent testimony until it was taken by a storm in 2002. Among the most impressive white oaks is the Richards Oak in Cecil County,

LEFT: The patchy bark type commonly seen on white oak (*Quercus alba*). RIGHT: Old white oaks develop impressive character.

Maryland, which was depicted as a landmark on a map made for William Penn in 1681. It subsequently served as a camp shelter for General Lafayette in 1781 and for a cavalry unit during the Civil War. By 1965 it shaded an area 115 feet (34.5 m) across.

I once stumbled upon an impressive white oak in an old rural cemetery in southern Illinois. Subsequent research revealed the origins of the cemetery, named Hopewell Cemetery after the church that was built beside it in 1831. During the time of the Lewis and Clark expedition, a westward-bound pioneer family was camped at a nearby spring. Their young child died and was buried under what even then was a landmark tree, so that the family could find the grave if they ever returned from wherever they finally settled. I don't know if they ever did return, but other pioneers, taking the same wagon trail and seeing the grave, followed suit with their own dearly departed, and the cemetery came into existence. The Hopewell Oak is there today, off a country road a few miles west of Pinckneyville. Thousands of such stories abound in written and oral history.

Think of a century-old white oak as being at the same life stage as a twenty-five-year-old human, and a two-hundred-year-old white oak as a fifty-year-old human. Then think of us at seventy-five, and at one hundred, and use the same equation to view the life stages of your oldest trees. A white oak grows for about a hundred years, lives for another hundred years, and mellows and declines for another hundred to two hundred years or more. But it can do so only if each human generation that comes and goes during its life span respects, protects, and honors it. We all inherit such responsibilities.

Quercus bicolor

SWAMP WHITE OAK

DESCRIPTION: Swamp white oak is another member of the white oak group (section *Quercus*, formerly subgenus *Lepidobalanus* or *Leucobalanus*) and a close mimic of bur oak (*Q. macrocarpa*), which shares much of its adaptability to various site conditions. As its name implies, swamp white oak is extremely tolerant of poor drainage, but it does equally well when planted on upland sites and is very tolerant of compacted soils. In nature it is found on upland flatwoods sites with hardpan soils, along the borders of swamps, and in river floodplains, where it is a common associate of pin oak (*Quercus palustris*).

This is a striking tree with peeling bark on its young limbs, almost like that of sycamore (*Platanus*) or river birch (*Betula nigra*). As the tree gets older the lower bark becomes furrowed, much like that of bur oak. After two or three centuries trees become very stout. The record tree in Washington County, Ohio, is only 75 feet (22.5 m) tall but spreads half again that wide, and another record holder in Virginia has a trunk just under 8 feet (2.4 m) through. A previous record tree in Maryland is 120 feet (36 m) tall but has a more slender trunk, measuring in at a mere 6 feet (1.8 m) in cross section.

LEAVES: The crenate leaves earn the specific epithet *bicolor* for their two-toned appearance, being dark green above with a tomentose, whitened abaxial surface that flashes in the wind. They reach 3 to 7 inches (7.5 to 17.5 cm) in length by about half as wide and often have a middle tooth on each side that is conspicuously longer than the others, giving them a diamond-shaped outline. Fall color is a gold or orange hue, fading to a pleasant warm brown that holds on marcescent young trees well into early winter.

FLOWERS AND FRUIT: The flowers are similar to those of white oak (*Quercus alba*). The acorns are among the sweetest of all, and those from some trees can be eaten fresh without leaching or roasting. The large acorns mature in one season and have some of the longest peduncles in the genus, which helps to identify the species.

BEST SEASONS: FALL (for fall color and acorn crop). SUMMER (a beautiful shade tree, especially with its leaves blowing in a breeze). WINTER (for the appealing bark on young trees and the rugged silhouette of old trees).

NATIVE AND ADAPTIVE RANGE: This is a northeastern species, growing from the Great Lakes region and southern Ontario south to the Ohio River valley and eastward to the Atlantic. It reaches its western limit in the Missouri River valley of eastern Nebraska and Kansas, probably due to its need for acid soil. Under cultivation it is hardy north to USDA zone 4.

CULTURE: Because this particular white oak is among the easiest to transplant, it has become popular with nurseries. Avoid high pH soils but don't worry about poor drainage or compaction. It may be propagated by sowing seed in fall, as with other oaks. This species has a stronger seed dormancy than many other white oaks and usually does not germinate as quickly during stratification. See *Quercus alba* for more information about oak culture.

PROBLEMS: Swamp white oak shares most of the same suite of pests as white oak (*Quercus alba*) but is much easier to transplant and much more tolerant of compacted or poorly drained soil. It is also so adaptable to the stresses of city life that it was selected by the Society of Municipal Arborists in 1998 as their Urban Tree of the Year.

CULTIVARS: I have seen no selections from this species, but it is a progenitor of some great hybrid cultivars. Crosses with the fastigiate form of European oak (*Quercus robur*) have yielded 'Regal Prince', a broadly fastigiate tree with superior foliage and enhanced mildew resistance, and my own new selection, 'Windcandle', with the added features of strong branching angles and a more graceful form, like a candle flame.

SIMILAR AND RELATED SPECIES: Further south, below USDA zone 5, swamp white oak is gradually replaced by its southern counterpart, overcup oak (**Quercus lyrata**). Overcup oak is the most flood tolerant oak of all, thriving in swamps that sometimes remain under water for the entire growing season. The overcup oak acorn is al-

RIGHT: A grove of swamp white oak (*Quercus bicolor*) on poorly drained soil.

most fully enclosed by the involucre, or cup, and falls from the tree with cup intact. The cups provide flotation, helping to disperse the seeds under flood conditions. The foliage on many specimens displays beautiful shades of crimson in both early spring and fall, while others turn dull gold before dropping their leaves. The largest overcup oak is 156 feet (46.8 m) tall and nearly 7 feet (2.1 m) in diameter.

Oglethorpe oak (**Quercus oglethorpensis**) becomes a medium-sized tree with unlobed leaves and, like live oak (*Q. virginiana*), can become infected with chestnut blight (*Cryphonectria parasitica*). Although it is a very rare species known only from a few isolated populations in South Carolina and Georgia, it is surprisingly hardy when planted further north. Vigorous specimens can be seen at the Morton Arboretum near Chicago in USDA zone 5, where they display nice fall color.

The leaves of bluff oak (**Quercus austrina**) and the similar Durand oak (**Q. sinuata**, syn. *Q. durandii*) are shallow-lobed—very shallow-lobed on the Durand oak, more deeply lobed on the bluff oak. Bluff oak is a relatively obscure southeastern species that grows on low, sandy bluffs overlooking wet ground. Its leaves look like underdeveloped white oak (*Q. alba*) leaves that are glabrous and green on both surfaces. Durand oak occupies a spotty but comparable range on low ridges and poorly drained soils much like those favored by swamp white oak further north, though Durand oak has a greater tolerance of high pH. Bigelow oak (**Q. sinuata var. breviloba**, syn. *Q. breviloba*) is a western tree, distinct from Durand oak and occupying very different habitat, yet most authorities classify the two as varieties of the same species. It has shaggy gray bark, is generally more shrubby, and loves alkaline soils. Like Oglethorpe oak, these trees all seem more hardy than would be expected from their lim-

ited natural distribution, north at least into protected locations in USDA zone 6.

COMMENTS: Though one of our hardiest native oaks, swamp white oak nonetheless has problems when planted abroad in the benign climate of Britain and parts of western Europe. Because it has evolved in our continental climate of hot, sunny summers and cold winters, it becomes confused by the mild, cloudy summers and comparatively gentle winters across the pond. Thus it lowers its guard and begins to break dormancy before the last frost in early spring. Regardless of cold hardiness during dormancy, once any tree begins to grow it becomes more sensitive to freeze damage. Many American oaks of this and related species experience almost annual dieback of their new twigs, giving them a ratty, unkempt appearance nothing like the dignified bearing they have in their native land. This is yet another example of the benefits of planting species and ecotypes that are native to the local area, whether that area is Manitoba, Alabama, or Great Britain.

TOP FAR LEFT: Fall color on swamp white oak (*Quercus bicolor*). BOTTOM FAR LEFT: An ancient swamp white oak. LEFT: The fall color of swamp white oak fades to a warm tan in winter. BELOW: The unique acorns of overcup oak (*Q. lyrata*). RIGHT: A mature Durand oak (*Q. sinuata*).

Though I have seen many splendid swamp white oaks, my favorite is a tree in Starhill Forest Arboretum. It has no special ornamental qualities, but I grew it from an acorn I picked up decades ago at the Mohawks Club along the Kankakee River in northern Indiana, where I was out fishing with my grandfather. He died in the 1970s, but I can still see his face and hear his infectious laughter whenever I walk under that tree. I'm glad it's such a long-lived, hardy species, and doubly glad I came home with that acorn instead of just a fish.

Quercus gambelii

GAMBEL OAK

DESCRIPTION: Gambel oak (*Quercus gambelii*, syn. *Q. utahensis*), also known as Rocky Mountain oak, is the white oak of the southern Rocky Mountains. It is variable enough that if you saw just a few selected specimens you'd bet your lunch they were different species. But there is no sharp line of distinction from one form to the next, and seeing enough of them should convince any taxonomical splitter to give up trying to compartmentalize them.

Traditionally known as a sprawling, suckering species, Gambel oak can form straight, single-stemmed trees up to 75 feet (22.5 m) tall. The current record tree in New Mexico is much shorter at 47 feet (14.1 m), but its wingspan is twice that large and its trunk is nearly 6 feet (1.8 m) across. Most specimens develop massive underground woody structures called lignotubers, which produce clonal regrowth after fires or other damage to the original stem. I have chosen this species to carry the banner for the many other white oaks in the Southwest.

LEAVES: Anyone who has seen the classic lobed leaves of white oak (*Quercus alba*) will have no problem recognizing Gambel oak as a close relative. The leaves are a little thicker than those of white oak, a concession to the dry climate of the West, and on average they are a little smaller. Sometimes they turn a nice russet in fall, but often not.

FLOWERS AND FRUIT: Gambel oak flowers mimic those of white oak. The acorns are also similar but only about half the size, seldom reaching 1 inch (2.5 cm) long.

BEST SEASONS: SUMMER (for the shade, particularly at hotter, lower elevations). FALL (for the acorn crop that is so valuable to wildlife, and for fall color on some trees). WINTER (for the picturesque form of large, old trees).

NATIVE AND ADAPTIVE RANGE: This is the classic montane oak of the Four Corners states. Outlier populations can be found in western Texas and southern Wyoming, but the main range is continuous at elevations from the lower foothills up to almost 10,000 feet (3000 m) throughout Colorado, Utah, New Mexico, and most of Arizona. It is the hardiest of the Southwest oaks, succeeding under cultivation throughout USDA zone 5.

CULTURE: Seedlings are tough to transplant, and many small plants are not even seedlings but originate from root sprouts, so this tree is best grown from seed. Fortunately, as with most other oaks, this is easily done, following the procedures suggested for white oak (see *Quercus alba*).

Gambel oak tolerates many soil types, including high pH soils, as long as it has good drainage and full sun. It is very drought resistant once established. Unlike some western oaks, it is not fond of excessive heat and usually does much better at high elevations than it does in the low foothills.

PROBLEMS: See *Quercus alba* for a general review of pests and problems. Suckering, clonal individuals are difficult to grow in tree form. This seems to be a genetic trait rather than a response to local environmental conditions, so seed source is very important in predicting growth habit.

CULTIVARS: Cultivar selections should be made for growth habit and fall color. Unfortunately, no one has as yet accepted this challenge.

SIMILAR AND RELATED SPECIES: Scrub live oak (**Quercus turbinella**) grows with Gambel oak at middle elevations over much of its range and is the hardiest of our evergreen oaks (borderline in USDA zone 5). A small species with prickly little leaves and intricate branching, it is extremely tolerant of drought and heat. This and several other related species often cross with Gambel oak to create the nothospecies grex known as wavyleaf oak (**Q. ×undulata**). The obscure Toumey oak (**Q. toumeyi**) of the Diablo Mountains in the Gila River valley is similar, even more shrubby, and has smoother leaves.

Arizona white oak (**Quercus arizonica**) and gray oak (**Q. grisea**) are nearly identical to each other, separated mostly by the average shape of their variable leaves and by the lengths of their peduncles. They are desert trees with what I like to call Civil War foliage (blue-gray) that is mostly subevergreen in gray oak and more deciduous in Arizona white oak. They grow in most average soils

RIGHT: Gambel oak (*Quercus gambelii*) often forms clonal groups.

found in their region and are hardy up to USDA zone 6 or 7. I recently nominated the U.S. national champion gray oak in a remote part of southern New Mexico, a grizzly old veteran 55 feet (16.5 m) tall with a rugged trunk more than 6 feet (1.8 m) in diameter. Mohr oak (*Q. mohriana*) is a smaller but similar species found on

caprock limestone in Texas and New Mexico. Two friends and I nominated the U.S. national champion Mohr oak in Guadalupe Mountains National Park, Texas. It stands 18 feet (5.4 m) tall with a trunk 1 foot (30 cm) thick, quite substantial for this normally shrubby species.

Mexican blue oak (***Quercus oblongifolia***) is similar to gray oak and occupies some of the same habitats. Its rich, glaucous, blue evergreen foliage is distinctive. It is more southerly in distribution, but some outlier populations near Roswell, New Mexico, north of the main range, could hold the largest specimens ever found. It is possible these trees have reached such size due to infusion of a few stray genes from gray oak, so further study is needed. Lacey oak (***Q. laceyi***) is a small, semideciduous tree from central Texas. Its leaves are very similar but are lightly lobed, whereas those of Mexican blue oak are oblong, as the scientific name implies. This tree becomes more deciduous the further north it is planted, which helps it avoid snow damage while also giving it a nice gold to red fall color. Many books refer to Lacey oak as *Q. glaucoides*, a name more correctly applied to a Mexican species and sometimes misapplied to an Asian one. Lacey oak is rated hardy to USDA zone 6, and Mexican blue oak is probably hardy only to USDA zone 7, but both are tolerant of heat and alkaline soil.

Monterrey oak (***Quercus polymorpha***) is a Mexican evergreen species recently discovered growing in a remote area of southern Texas. It has potential for use in USDA zone 8. This species may be the true long-lost ancestor of another putative nothospecies, the endangered Organ Mountain oak (***Q. ×organensis***) of the Organ Mountains in southern New Mexico. Long thought to have arisen from a cross of Arizona white oak and gray oak, the only other tree-size white oaks in the area, Organ Mountain oak looks more like Monterrey oak than either of those suggested parent species.

Another primarily Mexican evergreen species, the netleaf oak (***Quercus rugosa***), has beautiful foliage and is found in the wild in a few isolated spots in southern New Mexico. It makes an attractive landscape tree and is doing well in cultivation at least as far north as Albuquerque, USDA zone 7. It is a very precocious species, flowering in my conservatory collection in Illinois at only three to four years of age. Several other Mexican

TOP LEFT: Gambel oak (*Quercus gambelii*) acorns ripen in late summer. LEFT: The rough bark of a large Gambel oak. RIGHT: Scrub live oaks (*Q. turbinella*) at high elevation in San Augustine Pass, Organ Mountains.

oaks not found in the wild in the United States are sometimes planted in Texas.

Two closely allied shrubby species, the evergreen sandpaper oak (***Quercus pungens***) and the slightly larger, semievergreen Vasey oak (***Q. vaseyana***), can be seen in canyons in western Texas and southern New Mexico. Older texts often lump them together as varieties of the same species. Both are hardy in USDA zone 7. Three rare oak shrubs, ***Q. intricata, Q. depressipes,*** and ***Q. hinckleyi,*** are found in remote places in Texas and are among our rarest, and smallest, oak species. Fortunately they all grow on protected land: the first one under federal ownership, the second under Nature Conservancy ownership, and the third under diligent, watchful private ownership.

COMMENTS: It should be noted that winter cold is not the only climate difference to be overcome when planting oaks from the West and Southwest further east. They are, in effect, exotic species that evolved in very different climate cycles. Most western oaks are damaged by artificial irrigation, since they are accustomed to dry summer conditions similar to those in the Mediterranean areas of southern Europe. In fact several exotic oak species from Asia are better adapted to eastern North America than are any of those from the western part of the continent, having evolved in analogous climates.

Conversely, though many eastern oaks can stand much more brutal winters than their western counterparts, they shrivel under the dry western climate and gag and pale on alkaline western soil. While those of us who study trees for a living or as a hobby will not be dissuaded from moving them around and watching them fight for survival, saner people should be content to plant the beautiful oaks that are native to their local habitats. There are great local species to choose from in any state or province within our region.

Quercus macrocarpa
BUR OAK

DESCRIPTION: Anyone who grew up on the prairies of the Midwest knows the classic North American savanna tree species, bur oak. It belongs to the white oak group (section *Quercus*, formerly subgenus *Lepidobalanus* or *Leucobalanus*), the most widespread subdivision of oaks. Although bur oak as a species is widespread as well, it is surely most appreciated on the Great Plains, where it stands resolute for centuries against the elements that devour all lesser trees.

Bur oak is the preeminent tree of midwestern savannas just as white oak (*Quercus alba*) is the lord of the eastern deciduous forest, although each extends considerably into the habitat of the other. It is a majestic, rugged tree, extremely variable even for an oak, and tolerates a very wide range of habitats. In the extreme northwest part of its range, it toughs it out as a shrub; yet under more favorable conditions, it ranks among the most impressive of all trees. The U.S. national champion bur oak, protected by a rail fence on a horse farm in Paris, Kentucky, is 95 feet (28.5 m) tall and more than 8 feet (2.4 m) thick. Luckily its owners, taking great pride in the tree, protect it and have propagated its acorns for planting around the farm.

LEAVES: If bur oak had better fall color, instead of its dull tan, it might be rated the king of oaks. Its summer foliage is beautiful nonetheless, with dark adaxial surfaces accented in the wind by shimmering pale undersides. The mature leaves reach about 7 inches (17.5 cm) long, although the size varies much from region to region. The leaf blades have a pair of deep indentations, or sinuses, which separate the tip of the leaf from the basipetal end.

FLOWERS AND FRUIT: Bur oak flowers are similar to those of other white oaks (see *Quercus alba*). The fruits can be among the largest of all acorns, sometimes exceeding 2 inches (5 cm) in diameter, but they vary from

RIGHT: The tough bur oak (*Quercus macrocarpa*) makes a majestic, long-lived shade tree.

tree to tree, and in the northwestern part of their range they are quite small. The nuts come equipped with a cap fringe that makes them appear even larger than life. They mature in one season and are an extremely valuable food source for wildlife, especially on the prairies where other mast is scarce.

BEST SEASONS: WINTER (perhaps no other tree can match the rugged venerability of an old bur oak in winter, with frost or snow accenting its rough bark and corky twigs). SUMMER (a most appreciated shade tree on the hot prairie).

NATIVE AND ADAPTIVE RANGE: Bur oak, among the hardiest of all oaks, grows from well north of Winnipeg, Manitoba, down to the Gulf Coast of Texas, and northeast across southern Ontario to isolated populations in New Brunswick. It will grow under cultivation from USDA zone 2 south.

CULTURE: Young bur oaks can be babied into faster growth than white oaks but should still be considered a slowly developing, permanent investment. I have studied cross sections and cores of many old bur oaks. While some very large specimens were two hundred years old or less, others were more than four hundred years old. This oak, like white oak, prefers mesic conditions, and the two species often grow together. Bur oak, however, will tolerate environmental extremes better. Floods, droughts, limey soils, and even prairie fires can be considered nothing more than a good day's work for this species. Like white oak, it is easy to propagate and difficult to transplant.

PROBLEMS: Bur oak was named Urban Tree of the Year in 2001 by the Society of Municipal Arborists. It is a tough tree, yet it remains subject to most of the same insect and disease problems that affect other white oaks (see *Quercus alba*). It is more resistant to oak wilt (*Ceratocystis fagacearum*) than most members of the genus. In addition to common problems such as Gypsy moth (*Lymantria dispar*), deer, and galls, old bur oaks are subject to a unique stress factor: frequently constituting the only substantial sources of shade on the open prairie, they are crowded by root-trampling livestock and brutalized by home builders trying to cozy up to them. Even the mighty bur oak has its limits, and the ravages of con-

TOP LEFT: The staminate catkins of bur oak (*Quercus macrocarpa*). CENTER LEFT: Leaves of bur oak vary considerably from tree to tree. LEFT: The typical muted fall color of bur oak. RIGHT: Two midwestern bur oak savannas.

struction often bring it to an untimely end, centuries before its natural life span would expire from other causes.

CULTIVARS: The USDA has released two vigorous seed germplasm selections of bur oak from Oklahoma, called 'Boomer' (from Boomer Creek) and 'Lippert' (from Payne County), for windbreak use on the Great Plains. Other bur oaks collected from the entire western range of the species in the United States and Canada are being tested by the USDA Laboratory in Mandan, North Dakota. I have some of these same selections under concurrent evaluation at Starhill Forest, together with specimens from further east. The Prairie Farm Rehabilitation Administration of Canada is conducting similar provenance tests in Saskatchewan.

Another seedling strain called 'Sweet Idaho' was selected for its palatable acorns. The parent is of unknown provenance; it grows in northern Idaho, where no oaks are native. Some seedlings exhibit red fall color, so I suspect it to be of hybrid origin. 'Kreider' is a cultivar chosen by nut grower Ralph Kreider from a tree he found in eastern Illinois, selected for nut production. Some nurseries offer seedlings of 'Ashworth', a precocious, hardy northern selection, and several bur oak hybrids.

SIMILAR AND RELATED SPECIES: Bur oaks found on the Northern Plains are very much different from those found further south or east. They have very small acorns with comparatively little fringe, and they are stunted and picturesque. I have found in our test plantings in Illinois that they also mature much earlier, beginning to bear acorns in as few as five years, while other bur oaks may take up to thirty years to start flowering. Some botanists believe the northwestern types should be segregated as **Quercus mandanensis,** and others prefer *Q. macrocarpa* var. *olivaeformis* or *Q. macrocarpa* var. *depressa*. Most, however, throw up their hands at the thought of trying to define the exact point at which one type grades into another, and lump them all together as a classic ochlospecies.

COMMENTS: Bur oak is among our most variable oak species and is very prone to hybridize with other white oaks. Many intermediate forms show genetic influences from white oak, swamp white oak, and other neighboring species. Natural hybrid populations of bur oak and Gambel oak (*Quercus gambelii*) can be found in southeastern Colorado and the Bear Lodge Mountains of Wyoming, as relics from a time millennia ago when the two species grew together there. Bur oak is also one of the oaks most commonly used in hybrid cultivar development programs and has been successfully crossed with other North American, European, and Asian oak species.

Wayne Lovelace showed me a superior acorn-producing tree he is naming *Quercus* 'Kimberley', found by Judy Lovelace in a woods on the family farm in Lincoln County, Missouri. It appears to be a bur oak with some swamp white oak (*Q. bicolor*) blood, and it is self-pollinating and annual-bearing with consistently heavy seed crops. This is unusual, since most oaks are substantially protandrous and have variable seed crops from year to year. I have additional bur oak hybrids under study in Illinois for possible introduction as landscape cultivars.

Due to its preferred open-country habitat, bur oak often develops into a picturesque, spreading shade tree, which is the form most familiar to its admirers. Many historic old pioneer cemeteries on the Great Plains were located, and remain, in the shade of spreading bur oaks. I know of old monarch bur oaks growing in the deep woods of northern Indiana, the Bootheel of Missouri, and the terrace forests of the Wabash River valley in southeastern Illinois, with tall, straight trunks reaching up a distance nearly half the length of a football field, and bare of side limbs for half that height.

Bur oak is among the toughest and hardiest species of the genus *Quercus*, which is saying a lot. The noted horticulturist John Evelyn remarked, during a presentation before one of the first meetings of the respected British Royal Society, that "oaks prosper exceedingly even in gravel and moist clays, which most other trees abhor; yea, even the coldest clay-grounds that will hardly graze . . . there grow oaks . . . out of the very walls of Silcester in Hantshire, which seem to strike root in the very stones."

Evelyn made these observations on October 15, 1662. The evidence of ensuing centuries confirms them, and some of the oaks that were growing back then are still around today.

Quercus marilandica

BLACKJACK OAK

DESCRIPTION: There are a few small to medium trees among the red oaks (section *Lobatae*, formerly subgenus *Erythrobalanus*; see the taxonomic discussion under *Quercus shumardii*), found mostly on xeric soils or in other rugged habitats. One of the most widespread and well known is blackjack oak. In the most inhospitable locations, it is seen as a ratty little fiddle-leaved shrub; but when cultivated in good soil and given room to develop, it can grow into a pleasant surprise with a perfect, symmetrical crown. The U.S. national champion tree in Peach County, Georgia, reaches 94 feet (28.2 m) tall atop a trunk almost 4 feet (1.2 m) thick.

Blackjack oak grows very, very slowly and is nearly impossible to transplant unless the roots were trained or pruned during early growth in the nursery. It develops a dense, twiggy crown and makes a good screen or windbreak species where existing mature specimens can be retained in the landscape. Nurseries would do a great service if they would start producing this tree using root-control techniques.

LEAVES: The pear-shaped, leathery leaves of blackjack oak superficially resemble those of the post oaks (*Quercus stellata*), with which this species frequently associates. Some on vigorous sprouts become huge, reaching 1 foot (30 cm) in length, but most are 3 to 6 inches (7.5 to 15 cm) long. They turn great shades of crimson or orange in fall and are often marcescent through most of the winter.

FLOWERS AND FRUIT: Blackjack oak flowers develop as prominent staminate catkins and tiny pistillate axillary flowers, resembling those of *Quercus alba* and other oaks. However, this tree belongs to the red oak group, and its acorns take two years to mature. First-year acorns, called acornetts by those of us who like to assign silly names to things, are not much larger than the flowers. During their second season they expand to full size, generally a little more than half an inch (1.25 cm).

BEST SEASONS: FALL (for the great fall color on nearly every tree). WINTER (for the picturesque silhouette and the often marcescent foliage that provides screening and shelter for birds). SPRING (for the colorful staminate catkins and expanding foliage).

NATIVE AND ADAPTIVE RANGE: This tree occurs from New Jersey and southern Iowa south to the Gulf Coast and westward into Oklahoma and Texas. It is restricted by competition to sandy soils, hardpans, bluff ledges, and similarly rigorous habitats. It is hardy in USDA zone 5.

CULTURE: Do not try to transplant this tree, and do not plant an acorn expecting to see any shade on your roof during your lifetime. But plant it or preserve it on any well-drained, acid soil for a trouble-free, long-lived, colorful landscape tree, loaded with character, that will take both heat and drought in stride.

PROBLEMS: The main problems specific to blackjack oak center around its slow growth—which can be a plus if you have an existing tree that you don't want to get larger too quickly—and the difficulty encountered in transplanting it. It retains many old, dead lower branches, so if wild trees on your site are to become nice specimens they will probably need some grooming. It is completely intolerant of shade and dislikes having wet feet or alkaline soil conditions. Beyond that, it shares the same general range of pests that affect white oak (see *Quercus alba*).

The red oaks as a group are not susceptible to exactly the same leaf diseases as those affecting white oaks, such as anthracnose, but they host others, such as leaf blister (*Taphrina caerulescens*). They generally host a different gang of gall insects as well, though the overall picture is about the same. They are more threatened by oak wilt (*Ceratocystis fagacearum*) and bacterial leaf scorch (*Xylella fastidiosa*), but blackjack oak may be less so than some other red oaks. The red oaks are the oaks most likely to be susceptible to the California sudden oak death disease (*Phytophthora ramorum*) if that epidemic spreads eastward into our region.

CULTIVARS: No cultivars of blackjack oak have been selected. The western form, *Quercus marilandica* var. *ashei*, has much smaller leaves and is even more drought tolerant, and the species in general has enough variability that it could benefit from selection if it were not so difficult to transplant, graft, defoliate for cold storage in the nursery, and induce into more rapid growth. Some

European nurseries are fascinated by *Q.* ×*bushii*, a commonly encountered hybrid of blackjack oak and black oak (*Q. velutina*).

SIMILAR AND RELATED SPECIES: Arkansas oak (***Quercus arkansana***) resembles a slender blackjack oak with smaller leaves. It inhabits sandy or rocky sites, and its distribution is very localized in southwestern Arkansas and scattered areas of Alabama, Georgia, and the Florida Panhandle. It can become a relatively tall tree but usually does not. The largest known specimen is in Mississippi and stands 95 feet (28.5 m) tall with a trunk nearly 4 feet (1.2 m) thick. I have found it to be surprisingly hardy in cultivation, surviving in USDA zone 5 in Illinois.

Turkey oak (***Quercus laevis***), not to be confused with Turkish oak (***Q. cerris***), is a common shrub or small tree of sandy scrub woodlands of the Low Country of the

LEFT: An old blackjack oak (*Quercus marilandica*) in late summer. BELOW: Most blackjack oaks are beautifully symmetrical and marcescent. RIGHT: The leathery, pear-shaped leaves of blackjack oak.

Southeast. Isolated trees on fertile sites can become as large as blackjack oaks, but the species usually grows in dwarf thickets. Turkey oak leaves are deeply and narrowly lobed, resembling turkey footprints, and provide brilliant red fall color. Curiously enough, the leaves of young seedlings orient north and south like a compass. This is strictly a Coastal Plain tree, barely hardy in USDA zone 7.

Bear oak (*Quercus ilicifolia*) is a hardy and colorful scrub species, becoming a small tree only after much coaxing. It grows north along the Atlantic Coast from Virginia all the way to Maine, and survives well for me in USDA zone 5 in the Midwest. A clone in France originated from a single seedling planted over two hundred years ago and now covers several acres of land. Clones don't count in the record books, however: the largest single known specimen is a tree in Romney, West Virginia, that is 41 feet (12.3 m) tall and just shy of 1 foot (30 cm) in diameter.

Myrtle oak (*Quercus myrtifolia*) is a semievergreen shrub or small tree confined to warmer parts of the Coastal Plain. The largest I have seen was at Fort Clinch in northeastern Florida, growing amidst such a substantial thicket of its peers as to make measurement nearly impossible. It was about 35 feet (10.5 m) tall. *Quercus inopina* is very similar but has convex leaves and is not found north of central Florida.

COMMENTS: Survivability in the wild does not always give a tree the tools to adapt to our typical landscape scenario. For those who live in blackjack oak country, this tough little tree abounds to such an extent that the appropriate tactic is to protect the most choice specimens from construction damage and thereby inherit an instant landscape on soils that would preclude successful establishment of lesser trees.

The alternative, to allow the contractor to clumsily scrape the site clean and replant from scratch, fails to recognize the time factor. I recall one picturesque little blackjack oak I found on a sandstone outcrop in Georgia. It had three stems, and one had been cut off. I counted more than two hundred annual growth rings in the cut stub, using a hand lens to see them. The stub was no bigger than a baseball bat, and the entire tree was no taller than I was, but it had been there since the American Revolution.

TOP LEFT: The rich fall color of blackjack oak (*Quercus marilandica*). LEFT: An old turkey oak (*Q. laevis*) preserved for shade along a city street.

Quercus muhlenbergii

CHINKAPIN OAK

DESCRIPTION: Several species within the white oak group (section *Quercus*, formerly subgenus *Lepidobalanus* or *Leucobalanus*) have handsome leaves with serrate margins like those of chestnuts (*Castanea*). They are called chestnut oaks, and I separate them from the other white oaks merely on the basis of their foliage; all white oak types are closely related.

The most adaptable and widespread chestnut oak is chinkapin oak, also called chinquapin oak or yellow chestnut oak. It is unusual among our eastern native oaks in that it is very well adapted to alkaline soil. I have found this species growing on xeric limestone bluffs, in floodplains, and in mesic forests and savannas, without apparent preference. It seldom dominates any ecological community, but it plays a minor part in many different settings over a broad range.

Chinkapin oak is at its best in the Midwest, where many outstanding specimens can be seen. The current U.S. national champion chinkapin oak grows on a farm near Lexington, Kentucky. It is 110 feet (33 m) tall with a nearly equal spread and a trunk almost 7 feet (2.1 m) in diameter. Forester Pete Kovalic, a neighbor of the owner, has done much to preserve this incredible tree, and has shown it proudly to me and to other tree enthusiasts from around the world.

LEAVES: The leaves of this species are unlobed but consistently serrate along the margins with acute, incurved teeth. They grow up to 8 inches (20 cm) long on vigorous young trees, usually stopping at about 6 inches (15 cm) on mature specimens. They can be more than half as wide as they are long but are often very narrow on mature trees and quite attractive, with light-colored undersides that contrast with the lustrous yellow-green upper surfaces. Chinkapin oak usually develops a pleasant yellow or light orange fall color, standing out among associated oaks that turn red or tan. Fall color is accented by the bright gray bark and by the convoluted branch structure on picturesque old specimens.

FLOWERS AND FRUIT: The chestnut oaks as a group have flowering characteristics like those of white oak (see *Quercus alba*). Chinkapin oak has the smallest acorns of any chestnut oak, and some of the most precocious. They begin to form on trees that are only a few years old, mature in one year, and in humid climates can begin to germinate even before falling from the tree.

BEST SEASONS: SUMMER (the attractive foliage of this species makes it one of our most beautiful shade trees). SPRING (for the pastel smoke of the catkins). FALL (not the best oak for fall color, but not bad) and WINTER (for the bright bark and picturesque branching).

NATIVE AND ADAPTIVE RANGE: Chinkapin oak grows in a diagonal band from scattered areas in New England and southern Ontario southwest through the central states to isolated populations in Mexico and New Mexico. It is hardy north into USDA zone 4, with attention to provenance.

CULTURE: Chinkapin oak is not particularly easy to transplant. Oaks in general respond very well to the deep, cone-shaped soil balls excavated by mechanical transplanting machines and are best moved in early spring. This species is very easy, though, to start from seed. The acorns should be sown in fall as soon as they can be picked easily from the cups without tearing at the hilum. They absolutely must be protected from rodents for the entire first growing season. I have lost seedlings in late summer due to chipmunks digging them up to eat the remaining food in the cotyledons of the attached acorns.

Unlike other chestnut oaks, and unlike oaks in general, chinkapin oak loves alkaline soil. It will grow very rapidly, for an oak, under attentive cultivation, given water, fertilizer, and mulch as needed.

PROBLEMS: The chestnut oaks are susceptible in varying degrees to the same problems that affect other white oaks, with the notable exception that chinkapin oak will not suffer chlorosis on alkaline sites. See *Quercus alba* for additional information.

CULTIVARS: Chinkapin oak is a variable tree and deserves some attention in this regard. My friend Mike Melendrez already has one western cultivar, *Quercus muhlenbergii* 'El Capitan', on the market in New Mexico. I am working with several superior hybrids involving chinkapin oak and others with rock chestnut oak (*Q.*

montana, syn. *Q. prinus*), some of which may become available in the future.

SIMILAR AND RELATED SPECIES: The other chestnut oaks are not as widespread as chinkapin oak but are often more common where they do occur. Rock chestnut oak (***Quercus montana***) is a mountain tree of the ranges that comprise the Appalachians and their foothills and extensions. Swamp chestnut oak (***Q. michauxii**,* syn. *Q. prinus*) grows in well-drained bottomlands of the Southeast. Both are large, magnificent trees. Dwarf chinkapin oak (***Q. prinoides***) is a shrubby species that forms thickets in dry, rocky or sandy areas in the Midwest, Southeast, and southern Canada. All three are hardy north in USDA zone 5, and I have seen wild populations of dwarf chinkapin oak on the shore of Lake Huron near zone 4.

Rock chestnut oak is among the few white oaks available from many nurseries. It is a handsome and durable tree with rich fall color that varies from old gold to deep maroon, and its large acorns are nearly as quick to sprout as those of chinkapin oak. Like chinkapin oak, it is very resistant to drought once established, but it prefers neutral or acid soil. Its bark is dark and deeply furrowed, an unusual trait for a native white oak and something more commonly seen among Asian species. It was a prime source of tannic acid for the leather industry in our early history, as was American chestnut (*Castanea dentata*). The two species also shared the same habitats, so where one was seen, the other would not be far away. This, rather than the superficial similarity of their leaves, might be the true origin of the name "chestnut oak." This was also the primary species that expanded its role to fill the niche left by American chestnut as the chestnut blight took its toll throughout their common range. The biggest rock chestnut oak of all is found at the heart of this natural range, in Great Smoky Mountains National Park, with a height of 144 feet (43.2 m) and a trunk almost 6 feet (1.8 m) in diameter.

Swamp chestnut oak may have the most brilliant combination of scarlet fall foliage and striking whitened bark of any oak. It is not truly a swamp tree but prefers deep, rich soils that are subject to seasonal flooding. In such conditions it grows straight and tall to immense size. The largest one known stands in a forest opening in Fayette County, Alabama. It is the tallest of all U.S. national champion oaks, rising 156 feet (46.8 m) on a clear trunk more than 5 feet (1.5 m) thick. Rock chestnut oak

LEFT: This fine chinkapin oak (*Quercus muhlenbergii*) is several centuries old.

and swamp chestnut oak both have large, sweet acorns that are relished by wildlife and livestock, which is why swamp chestnut oak is known in the South as cow oak.

Dwarf chinkapin oak is a shrubby species, otherwise very similar to chinkapin oak. Since it was described first it takes priority taxonomically, for those who argue that one is a variety of the other. Some authorities therefore list chinkapin oak as *Quercus prinoides* var. *acuminata* (busy, busy, those taxonomists!). Assisted by two friends from the Nebraska Statewide Arboretum, I nominated the U.S. national champion for this species, found in a rural area near Salem. It has become a source of pride for its owner and for tree lovers throughout the state. It stands 25 feet (7.5 m) tall and has a short, single trunk 1

foot (30 cm) in diameter, which is enormous for this species.

Like other oaks, chestnut oaks commonly hybridize with other species in their taxonomic section. Rock chestnut oak is one of the parent species of my oak cultivar *Quercus ×saulii* 'Atlas'. I also nominated the U.S. national champion Deam oak (*Q. ×deamii*), a cross between *Q. macrocarpa* and *Q. muhlenbergii*, which I found in Sangamon County, Illinois. It is a stately specimen 77 feet (23.1 m) tall with a branch spread of more than 100 feet (30 m) and a trunk nearly 5 feet (1.5 m) in diameter. Rules were later enacted to discontinue such records for nothospecies, so this is one record that should never be broken. It is also a seedless, sterile tree, as are some other hybrids, and I am considering introducing it into the trade as a cultivar for those who like magnificent oak trees but dislike acorn litter. Dwarf chinkapin oak and swamp chestnut oak are also known to cross with other white oaks, particularly *Q. alba*, yielding some very ornamental hybrids. See *Q. alba* for additional information on related species.

COMMENTS: During a trip into the isolated cloud forests of Mexico, I encountered strange oaks of every shape and size. Many were evergreen and tropical in appearance. Some were dwarf and reminiscent of the chaparral oak species of the western United States. Among more than two hundred of these unfamiliar species I found one old friend: the chinkapin oak. It is the only oak from the eastern United States and Canada that is adaptable enough to grow side by side with the unusual oaks of the Mexican mountains. It can also be found at Frijole Ranch and in canyons of Guadalupe Mountains National Park in Texas, and in the Capitan Mountains of New Mexico. Seeing these eastern trees thriving in that western habitat feels about like seeing a banana grove in Saskatchewan.

In eastern North America, chinkapin oak can be a huge, dominant tree or a sprawling midstory species. Its form varies from a deliquescent limb structure to an excurrent one, and its leaves can be narrow and finely textured or wide and obtuse. Its bark is normally thin and scaly, but some populations, like the one at Frijole Ranch, have very thick, shaggy bark. It is one of our most

fascinating species to tinker with in common-garden testing, where specimens originating in different areas from Mexico to Canada are planted together under identical conditions of climate and soil, so that genetic variations will be directly comparable without environmental influence.

This species also has great potential for hybridization experiments. Traits such as its alkaline soil tolerance, narrow serrate foliage, rapid early growth, and picturesque growth habit might be combined with the red fall color, large leaves, or persistent foliage of some other white oaks to derive unique offspring with exceptional ornamental value and adaptability. Due to hybrid vigor, some of these crosses will also be faster growing than either parent species, a trait that is very valuable when working with the oaks. Stay tuned!

TOP LEFT: The colorful ripening acorns of chinkapin oak (*Quercus muhlenbergii*). LEFT: The picturesque form of a mature chinkapin oak. TOP RIGHT: Fall color of chinkapin oak. RIGHT: The brilliant fall color of swamp chestnut oak (*Q. michauxii*).

Quercus nigra
WATER OAK

DESCRIPTION: Water oak is a southern wetland species that does nicely, despite its name, even on high, dry sites. It has striking, smooth bark, often painted with lichens, and smooth, variable, spatula-shaped leaves. This adaptable oak is also brittle. If a specimen can be kept intact, it can grow large in a very short time. The U.S. national champion, in Mississippi, is 118 feet (35.4 m) tall and more than 7 feet (2.1 m) thick. A nearly identical tree has been found at Roseland Plantation in Louisiana, and the Vagabond Oak in Montz, Louisiana, is gorgeous.

LEAVES: Extremely variable, the leaves of old trees are usually small and spatulate while those on young trees and vigorous sprouts can be long and narrow like those of willow oak (*Quercus phellos*), with or without a lobe or two. They range in length up to about 5 inches (12.5 cm) but average half that size. Many trees are semievergreen or tardily deciduous, and some leaves turn a nice red while others on the same twig remain green, providing a Christmas-like display during Thanksgiving (just like shopping malls). Many oaks labeled as hybrids in European botanical gardens seem to be nothing other than juvenile water oaks.

FLOWERS AND FRUIT: The separate staminate and pistillate flowers are similar to those of other oaks (see *Quercus alba*). The acorns ripen the second year, like those of most red oaks (see *Q. marilandica*), and are very small, about the size of a garden pea.

BEST SEASONS: FALL (for the late green leaves, in the North turning red at the end of the normal color season for most other trees). WINTER (for the nice bark) and SUMMER (for the welcome shade this tree provides in less time than most other oaks).

NATIVE AND ADAPTIVE RANGE: Water oak is found on many habitats throughout the Southeast, from Delaware Bay south to central Florida, and west to the Bootheel of Missouri and eastern Texas. It can be grown north through USDA zone 6 and guardedly into zone 5. Some planted trees occasionally suffer a little winter damage in my zone 5 central Illinois arboretum, but the trees I have from northernmost provenance sources, including seedlings from the Kentucky State champion, near Kentucky Dam, have not done so.

CULTURE: Careful attention to early pruning is needed to keep this species from developing a weak limb structure and breaking apart in ice storms. It is easy to transplant, for an oak, and easy to grow from seed. See *Quercus alba* for more information on oak culture.

PROBLEMS: Freeze-damaged young trees near the northern limit of their adaptive range, or those browsed by deer, recover quickly but may develop multiple leaders. This problem requires quick attention to prevent formation of a weak crown. Some specimens seem particularly prone to mistletoe (*Phoradendron*) infestation. Water oak shares many of the same problems experienced by oaks in general and red oaks in particular. See *Quercus alba* and *Q. marilandica* for additional information.

CULTIVARS: I have seen no cultivars of this species, but there must be a few good local selections somewhere. Evaluations should be made for hardiness and adaptability to the northern edge of the range and beyond, as well as for strong crown habit.

SIMILAR AND RELATED SPECIES: Two other large oaks resemble water oak, and both are called laurel oak. Swamp laurel oak (***Quercus laurifolia***) is a bottomland species with leaves intermediate between those of willow oak (*Q. phellos*) and water oak. This is one of our most flood-tolerant and shade-tolerant oaks. A taxon formerly recognized as diamondleaf oak (*Q. obtusa*) has been combined with swamp laurel oak. Identical U.S. national champion swamp laurel oaks are located in Chesapeake, Virginia, and in Florida, standing 80 feet (24 m) tall and almost 7 feet (2.1 m) in diameter.

The similar Darlington oak (***Quercus hemisphaerica***), also called upland laurel oak, has thicker, narrower, leathery leaves with sharper points and is more evergreen. Some authorities still don't distinguish between this and swamp laurel oak, but most agree it is very distinct. Typically this is a large tree of upland, sandy soils in the Southeast. It grades gradually into a small tree or

RIGHT: Late fall color on a mature water oak (*Quercus nigra*).

clumping shrub by the time it reaches its western limit in eastern Texas. The U.S. national champion Darlington oak is found in Florida. It stands 80 feet (24 m) tall with a trunk about 7 feet (2.1 m) thick. Both laurel oak species are considered hardy north in USDA zone 6 but might require some protection there.

COMMENTS: This is one of the most ubiquitous street trees of the South. It does not rank in most peoples' minds with "quality" oak species; rather, it is planted because it adapts to almost any site and can grow very rapidly. Its reputation is tarnished because most people have seen it as a beaten-up junk tree with its roots con-fined by pavement, its limbs carelessly hacked back from the road or sidewalk, its top cut back to accommodate overhead utility lines, and its trunk scarred by car bumpers and thoughtless vandals.

I believe we all should rethink our approach to trees like this. Consider its strengths and weaknesses up front, then plant it where it has an opportunity to perform well, and give it the early training it needs to form a strong crown architecture. I have seen a few water oak trees grown under such circumstances, and they were exceptionally beautiful.

LEFT: The smooth bark of water oak (*Quercus nigra*) brightens the winter landscape. TOP LEFT: The mature foliage form of water oak. ABOVE: Water oak bark is a favorable substrate for many decorative lichens. TOP RIGHT: Swamp laurel oak (*Q. laurifolia*) in a floodplain along the Apalachicola River. RIGHT: The leaves of Darlington oak (*Q. hemisphaerica*).

Quercus palustris
PIN OAK

DESCRIPTION: Pin oak needs no introduction. It is probably the most familiar American oak in cultivation across all of North America, for better or for worse, depending upon how well it likes its planting site. It has an excurrent, pyramidal juvenile habit recognizable from a block away. This tree is a favorite of nursery professionals because it is easy to transplant, grows rapidly, and develops an attractive, uniform branching structure when very young.

The U.S. national champion pin oak is a beautiful, tall tree growing in Bell County, Kentucky. It is 134 feet (40.2 m) high and more than 6 feet (1.8 m) in diameter. Many other large specimens exist but are often mistaken for other species because as they age they lose their classic shape and are not as easily recognized from a distance.

LEAVES: Pin oak leaves are smaller than those of most similar species, with the blades ranging up to about 4 inches (10 cm) long and wide. They are deeply divided, usually with five primary lobes. Most pin oaks display a beautiful crimson fall color, and many are marcescent through most of the winter, providing shelter for roosting birds.

FLOWERS AND FRUIT: These characteristics are similar to those of other red oaks. Pin oak acorns are small, averaging about half an inch (1.25 cm) long and wide, and have a very shallow cap. They are a favorite food of waterfowl when they fall into shallow impounds or flooded riparian areas.

BEST SEASONS: FALL (this oak is among our most dependable trees for autumn color). WINTER (for the symmetrical form of young trees).

NATIVE AND ADAPTIVE RANGE: Pin oak is found on poorly drained, acidic soils from southern Michigan and Massachusetts south into Tennessee and west to Kansas and Oklahoma. In cultivation it can be grown north into parts of USDA zone 4 if soil conditions are suitable.

CULTURE: I expect to see the sales of pin oak decline as more adaptable oak species and hybrids become more widely known and grown, but it is a beautiful tree if planted in the right place. Pin oak grows vigorously and tolerates considerable flooding. Like all oaks, it sprouts readily from seed sown in fall, and it transplants more easily than almost any other oak. It maintains its excurrent form for its first century or two before broadening into a more typical oaklike silhouette. See *Quercus alba* for more general information on the genus.

PROBLEMS: Pin oak is the classic example every botany or horticulture student learns about when studying plants intolerant of alkaline soils. Many people might believe the natural color of pin oak is yellow because every tree they see is chlorotic. This species must have acid soil, and preferably wet feet, to perform at its peak potential.

Several galls also take a heavy toll on this species, especially where the trees are predisposed to such problems due to stress. The woody galls caused by some related wasp species (variously listed as *Plagiotrochus punctatus*, *P. cornigerus*, and *Callirhytis cornigera*) are particularly harmful to pin oak and shingle oak (*Quercus imbricaria*). They are among the few oak galls that can affect the health of the host tree. Most other oak galls, especially those that do not infect woody tissue, are benign and often quite beautiful.

The lower limbs of pin oaks habitually descend in a graceful cascade effect like those of many conifers. This is beautiful from a distance but problematic where trees are planted along streets or sidewalks. Pin oak is also subject to most problems affecting red oaks in general.

CULTIVARS: Two selections, 'Sovereign' and 'Crownright', were once popular due to their more upright branching habits. They are seldom found in the nursery trade anymore, due to a peroxidase enzyme incompatibility problem that causes frequent graft union failures on all oaks in this taxonomic section, thus complicating the asexual propagation that is necessary for cultivar propagation. 'Green Pillar' was selected for its upright form, and one or two dwarf selections, such as 'Forest Pygmy', can be found in some botanical collections. These will all probably become much more commonly

RIGHT: This large, fast-growing pin oak (*Quercus palustris*) is only forty years old.

available as soon as more nurseries start propagating them by cuttings.

SIMILAR AND RELATED SPECIES: Nuttall's oak (***Quercus nuttallii***) is a very close relative of pin oak. The reason Texas Shumard oak (*Q. buckleyi*) is no longer called *Q. texana* is that this name was once reassigned to Nuttall's oak. This was not done out of any sense of logic but merely because a botanist had mixed up his specimens decades before and the error was finally noticed (see *Q. shumardii* for more details). The unfortunate nomenclatural nit-picking with this species has caused many problems for nontaxonomists, because the name *Q. texana* is used by many foresters, nurseries, and ecological researchers without author attribution, so no one really knows which species is being discussed. Enlightened taxonomists will hopefully follow provisions in the *International Code of Botanical Nomenclature* for conservation of names, declaring *Quercus texana* to be *nomen ambiguum* and conserving *Q. nuttallii* as the *nomen conservandum* for Nuttall's oak. Until then most of us should probably ignore *Q. texana* as a valid name for any species. Thus I will stick with *Q. nuttallii*, which is discrete and can refer to only this one species.

Nuttall's oak, by whatever name, is a southern look-alike of pin oak and was not classified as a separate species until 1927. In the wild it is confined to wet ground in the lower Mississippi River valley and adjacent lowlands, but it grows very well when planted on higher ground. Its leaves are usually longer than those of pin oak and carry an extra pair of lobes, and its acorns are twice the size with much deeper caps. The red fall color is at least equal to that of pin oak but is displayed much later in fall and sometimes does not develop before a hard freeze toasts the leaves. Many fine specimens can be seen in New Orleans City Park, more famous for its live oaks (*Quercus virginiana*).

I discovered the former U.S. national champion Nuttall's oak at the other end of its range, on an island in Horseshoe Lake, southern Illinois, in 1972. It was 85 feet (25.5 m) tall and almost 7 feet (2.1 m) in diameter. At that time Nuttall's oak was not known to occur as far north as Illinois, and it is still listed as an endangered species there, perhaps owing its hardiness to some pin

TOP LEFT: Pin oak (*Quercus palustris*) leaves. LEFT: The excurrent branching pattern of pin oak. RIGHT: A spring and autumn view of a Nuttall's oak (*Q. nuttallii*) at Starhill Forest.

oak blood in its ancestry. The giant old tree at Horseshoe Lake is now broken and declining and is no longer the largest one known (the current record is held by a tree in Louisiana). A few other Illinois Nuttall's oaks have been found on a nature preserve near the old tree, and some are rumored to occur even further north along the Mississippi River valley in eastern Missouri.

The potentially unique genetic qualities of the Illinois ecotype, and other northern examples of Nuttall's oak that together constitute the northernmost natural populations of this tree in the world, can be useful to extend the adaptive horticultural range of the species. As is the case with many trees propagated from wild populations growing in climatic extremes at the edges of their natural ranges, offspring from the Illinois Nuttall's oaks are proving to be winter hardy through USDA zone 5, well north of the natural range of the species. The Illinois trees are being preserved through propagation by seeds and, using an emerging technology, by cuttings.

COMMENTS: I have found old references to "pine oak" in the literature, probably due to the excurrent, conifer-shaped juvenile form. This might have been shortened to the present name, but the tree also has numerous small twigs that make it look like a loaded pin cushion. In addition, the lumber is too knotty to have much value for making boards, but it was a favorite for making the pins, or pegs, that held old barn beams together before the days of bolts, nails, and perforated steel gusset plates. Then again, my old mentor Floyd Swink at the Morton Arboretum wryly claimed that wood from this tree was probably used to make the wooden puppet Pinocchio (pin-oak-io)!

Quercus phellos

WILLOW OAK

DESCRIPTION: A surprising number of oaks have narrow leaves that look anything but oaklike. My friend Art Plotnik calls them the no-lobers, and the name is simple and exact. Most of our native no-lobers belong to the red oak group (section *Lobatae*, formerly subgenus *Erythrobalanus*), endemic to the Western Hemisphere, and many more can be found in Asia in the section or subgenus *Cyclobalanopsis*, which is endemic there. The narrow-leaved species in our group are mostly southern in distribution, and the most widely known example is probably the willow oak.

Willow oak is an upright, fast-growing red oak species native to alluvial soils in warm, humid areas. It is frequently planted in southeastern landscapes due to its fine-textured foliage, rapid growth, and easy transplantation. It is not always one of the largest oak species, but huge specimens can be found on moist, well-drained sites. The record tree is located in Virginia. It is 121 feet (36.3 m) in height with a nearly equal spread, and more than 7 feet (2.1 m) in diameter.

LEAVES: Willow oak leaves are among the narrowest leaves of any oak, reaching about 4 inches (10 cm) long and less than 1 inch (2.5 cm) wide. They are without lobes or teeth on the margins. Like those of all our narrow-leaved oaks, the leaves stay green late into fall, sometimes persisting into winter in mild climate areas. Some willow oaks develop a rich yellow fall color in November.

FLOWERS AND FRUIT: The flowering characteristics of willow oak and the other oaks in this section are identical to those for white oak (*Quercus alba*), with one major exception: this and nearly all our other native oaks in section *Lobatae* require two years to mature their acorns. Pistillate flowers are located along the current year's twigs, but by the time the acorns ripen they are found on two-year-old wood. The acorns of most of our narrow-leaved oaks, particularly those of willow oak, are

RIGHT: A monarch specimen of willow oak (*Quercus phellos*).

very small and do not cause a significant litter problem in turf. They are valuable to many species of wildlife that cannot handle the large acorns of other oaks.

BEST SEASONS: FALL (for those trees with the best gold fall color). SUMMER (the fine texture of the foliage is the primary aesthetic attribute). SPRING (during the blooming period).

NATIVE AND ADAPTIVE RANGE: Willow oak is native on moist sites throughout the Southeast, north to southern Illinois and New Jersey. It is among the hardiest narrow-leaved oaks, and trees of northern origin can be planted north into USDA zone 5.

CULTURE: Willow oak is a popular street tree in the South and seems capable of adapting to a variety of growing conditions. It likes moisture and full sun and does best in acid soil. With care, fairly large trees can be transplanted successfully. Seeds may be sown (and protected from rodents) in fall as soon as they are ripe, or stratified until early spring, since they have a dormancy period during which they do not germinate. Most no-lober oaks tend to develop weak crotches, so saplings should be trained and pruned to a strong form.

PROBLEMS: The open-porous wood structure of red oak types, like willow oak, makes them much more susceptible to oak wilt (*Ceratocystis fagacearum*) than most white oaks (section *Quercus*). Oak wilt is a fatal vascular disease that moves through the pores of a tree's conductive system. It should be avoided by promptly removing dead trees, cutting root grafts to adjacent oak trees, and avoiding summer pruning in areas where it is known to occur.

The red oaks in general are subject to severe damage from Gypsy moth (*Lymantria dispar*) and suffer most other problems of the white oaks (see *Quercus alba*). The primary foliage problems in this group are pine-oak rusts (*Cronartium*) and leaf blister (*Taphrina caerulescens*), rather than anthracnose, which affects the white oaks. Some red oaks are very susceptible to bacterial leaf scorch (*Xylella fastidiosa*), a slowly fatal disease with symptoms that resemble oak wilt.

CULTIVARS: Due to difficulties with vegetative propagation of red oak species, few if any cultivars of willow oak and its relatives have entered the nursery trade. Researchers are finding ways to graft them and to propagate them from cuttings and tissue culture, so we should expect to see a surge in cultivars in the future.

SIMILAR AND RELATED SPECIES: Shingle oak (**Quercus imbricaria**) is the closest mimic of willow oak in the Midwest and certainly the hardiest of this group. Its leaves are about twice as large as those of willow oak, and it is not restricted to bottomland sites but occurs in disturbed areas across a variety of habitats. Shingle oak leaves sometimes turn dark red or yellowish in fall but may remain green until browned by a hard freeze, clinging until spring. Unfortunately shingle oak is proving to be one of the oak species most susceptible to bacterial leaf scorch. Several fine specimens ranging from twenty-five to about seventy-five years of age have died from this disease at Starhill Forest.

Shingle oak is primarily a riparian and upland species that grows naturally as far north as the southern edge of the Great Lakes and can be planted into USDA zone 4. The largest known shingle oak is located in Cincinnati, Ohio, and is 105 feet (31.5 m) tall with a trunk more than 5 feet (1.5 m) thick.

Bluejack oak (**Quercus incana,** syn. *Q. cinerea*) is a small understory tree of sandy pine forests. It has attractive

LEFT: Willow oak (*Quercus phellos*) has slender twigs and narrow leaves that give the tree a fine texture.
RIGHT: The bright fall color of willow oak.

blue-green foliage that is nearly as narrow as that of willow oak and becomes wine-colored in fall in northern climates. This species has been surprisingly root hardy in USDA zone 5 in Illinois under my limited testing. Bluejack often forms thickets in the wild, but individual trees can reach into the forest canopy. The record-sized tree, in Florida, is 56 feet (16.8 m) in height with a broader spread. Its trunk is well more than 2 feet (60 cm) thick.

The related, thicket-forming runner oak (**Quercus pumila**) is another narrow-leaved dwarf tree of sandy soils in the Coastal Plain. It lives as an understory shrub in piney woods, where it forms waist-high clonal colo-

nies by sprouting from the roots after every ground fire. It is nearly unique among red oaks in having acorns that ripen in one season, like those of white oak (*Q. alba*). I suspect this might be an adaptation to the frequent fires of its natural habitat; the acorns minimize their risk of exposure to fire by falling to the ground the first year. See *Q. alba* and other oak profiles for more information on related species.

COMMENTS: In 1908, Fort Massac State Park was dedicated as the first state park in Illinois, and for good reason. The site has a commanding, strategic view of the lower Ohio River and has been occupied for military purposes in turn by Hernando de Soto (1540), an early French trading post (1702), the French Fort de L'Ascension (1757), the French Fort Massiac (1759–1760), the British Fort Massac (1763–1770s), the American Fort Massac (1794–1814), and a Civil War training camp (1861–1862). It was the actual setting for Edward Hale's famous historical novel, *The Man Without a Country*, a true story about Aaron Burr's plot to conquer Mexico.

Three willow oaks grow at Fort Massac, within throwing distance of the restored American fort. A few historians had suggested that all the scenic old trees in the area be removed to create the freshly cleared landscape that would have existed around a fort to deprive enemies of cover. Luckily they did not prevail, and much care was taken during the initial reconstruction to protect significant trees in the project area, including the willow oak trees, two of which are very large. As the state's landscape architect involved with the project, I was proud to be responsible for the actions taken to preserve the trees.

These efforts proved worthwhile. The willow oaks and surrounding trees now offer a picturesque backdrop for views and photographs of the fort, helping to screen the visual intrusion of the new Interstate Route 24 bridge across the Ohio River. Since the Endangered Species Act was created, willow oak has been recognized as a protected, state-threatened species in Illinois, where it reaches the extreme northwestern limit of its natural range. Willow oak seedlings from the hardy provenance at Fort Massac can be planted far north of the natural range of the species with great success, providing northerners with willow oaks they might not otherwise be able to enjoy.

TOP LEFT: Bluejack oak (*Quercus incana*) leaves in early winter. LEFT: Young leaves of shingle oak (*Q. imbricaria*) emerge rolled inward. RIGHT: The uniform crown characteristic of shingle oak (*Q. imbricaria*).

Quercus rubra

RED OAK

DESCRIPTION: Red oak (*Quercus rubra*, syn. *Q. borealis*)—or, more precisely, northern red oak—is the king of the northern oak species in eastern North America and belongs to the group known collectively as the red oaks (section *Lobatae*, formerly subgenus *Erythrobalanus*). It is the state tree of New Jersey and the arboreal emblem of Canada's Prince Edward Island. This familiar oak can be seen in nearly every mesic deciduous forest area of the East, its huge columnar trunk rising half its height to the first massive limb, and its dark bark striped with long smooth plates separated by deep furrows. The smooth, striped bark is a nice ornamental feature, but many beautiful red oaks planted in gentler climates in Europe, where the tree is quite popular, and in the Pacific Northwest have not yet begun to develop furrows in their bark, even though they exceed 2 feet (60 cm) in diameter. Called slick-bark oaks, they are equally attractive, almost beechlike.

Red oak is a tree of coves, northern exposures, and moist but well-drained soils. It grows rapidly and becomes one of the largest trees in the deciduous forests of eastern North America. Many red oaks reach more than 120 feet (36 m) tall with massive boles. The sprawling U.S. national champion in New York is shorter, at 80 feet (24 m) tall, but its forked trunk is more than 10 feet (3 m) in diameter.

LEAVES: Red oak leaves are smooth and lustrous but thin compared with those of similar species. They have pointed, shallow lobes, each ending in several small, flexible bristles, called aristae. They grow up to 9 inches (22.5 cm) long by half as wide and are broadest at the middle. Most species in section *Lobatae* have nice fall color, and red oak can turn crimson, golden orange, or russet.

FLOWERS AND FRUIT: The flowers are like those of willow oak (*Quercus phellos*) and develop into mature acorns after two years. The acorns are some of the largest of any species in the red oak group, often exceeding 1 inch (2.5 cm) in length and width, with a shallow, plate-like cup that covers only the end of the nut. Both of our northernmost oaks, red oak and bur oak (*Quercus macrocarpa*), develop giant acorns in the South, but neither does so in the northern parts of its range. It seems that big acorns either confer no competitive advantage up north, or perhaps they just take a longer time to mature and the northern trees have learned to make small acorns in order to reproduce successfully, as is the case with pecans (*Carya illinoinensis*).

BEST SEASONS: FALL (many red oaks develop nice fall color). WINTER (the clean, open branching pattern and smooth, striped bark are attractive and best seen in the dormant season). SPRING (during the blooming period) and SUMMER (a clean, attractive shade tree).

NATIVE AND ADAPTIVE RANGE: Together with bur oak, red oak is our hardiest species for northern climates, and the most widely distributed oak in Canada. Although its stature is reduced in the far northern end of its range, it can be found from northern Minnesota around the northwest shore of Lake Superior and eastward north of Lake Huron and Lake St. John to Chaleur Bay in Quebec. From there it is distributed south throughout the eastern United States to the Coastal Plain, and southwest to eastern Oklahoma. Red oak can be grown north through USDA zone 3.

CULTURE: Red oak prefers everything in moderation: moist but well-drained, neutral or acidic soil and lots of light but not necessarily full sun. This is one of our more shade-tolerant large oaks and can develop well under a broken canopy of older trees. For an oak it is relatively easy to transplant and should be moved with a deep soil ball in early spring.

Acorns may be sown in fall or stratified for spring sowing. Either way, protect them from rodents during the first growing season. See *Quercus alba* for more details on seed propagation. Ohio State University conducted experiments with cultural techniques for growing red oak and has perfected the Ohio Production System for producing 7-foot (2.1-m) seedlings in containers, from acorns, in six months.

PROBLEMS: All species in section *Lobatae* are very sus-

RIGHT: Red oak (*Quercus rubra*) is a popular landscape tree.

ceptible to oak wilt (*Ceratocystis fagacearum*), which is becoming epidemic in the northwestern part of the range of red oak. Infected trees should be removed immediately, and root grafts with adjacent susceptible trees should be cut to prevent vascular infection. The primary beetle vectors are attracted to pruning wounds, so avoid pruning any red oak species growing in wilt-infested areas during the growing season, when these insects are active. Injection systems using fungicides are available from professional arborists to protect high-value specimens that are at risk.

Red oak can be infected by bacterial leaf scorch (*Xylella fastidiosa*), which also kills many shingle oaks (*Quer-*

cus imbricaria), and is very prone to *Armillaria* root rot. Many red oaks planted in France have been subject to ink disease (*Phytophthora cinnamomi*). This may be aggravated by the different growing environment, or perhaps resistance is low because of a narrower genetic pool in foreign plantations. See *Q. alba* and *Q. phellos* for more information on oak problems.

Some of the most fascinating insects that prefer red oaks for food plants are the common walkingstick (*Diapheromera femorata*) and the giant walkingstick (*Megaphasma dentricus*), neither of which normally require control. *Quercus rubra* is less subject to weather damage than most other red oaks.

CULTIVARS: This tree is so predictably variable from region to region that natural geographic varieties have been separated on the basis of acorn size, but taxonomists now seem reluctant to maintain such distinct classifications. Foresters have invested much research into the effects of provenance and of genetically induced improvements in form and growth rate, so many superior strains and geographically adapted types have been identified and propagated for timber management purposes.

Such variability should result in discovery of cultivars with exceptional horticultural or ornamental merit as well, but little of this has happened yet. As is the case with many American oaks, Europe has taken the lead with developing cultivars, including 'Magic Fire' and spectacular variegated forms like 'Regent'. I have one called 'Yates' under study. With very attractive, deep lobing and great fall color that continues to show up in the second generation, it might become a useful seed germplasm selection. Now that old problems with vegetative propagation are being solved, I expect to see more red oak cultivars in the nursery trade in the future.

SIMILAR AND RELATED SPECIES: The Southwest has a couple of very nice red oaks that are becoming more available in the nursery trade in that part of North America.

Emory oak (**Quercus emoryi**) is a semievergreen tree that has a pleasing form, attains great age, and tolerates the hottest and driest climates, with USDA zone 6 hardiness. It is one of the few southwestern oak species that prefers acid soil. Two friends and I nominated the cur-

rent U.S. national champion Emory oak tree, found at Los Olmos in Glenwood, New Mexico. It grows on private land but is easily visible from the highway. Only a shell of its former self (two of its three primary ascending limbs have fallen), it is still larger than any other Emory oak ever measured. The broken crown has been reduced to less than half its former width and is 81 feet (24.3 m) tall by 72 feet (21.6 m) across, but its massive trunk is nearly 6 feet (1.8 m) in diameter.

Emory oak, like runner oak (*Quercus pumila*), is one of the few red oaks that matures its acorns in a single season. Another one is the striking silverleaf oak (**Q. hypoleucoides**). This is primarily a high-elevation red oak species of the Southwest and Mexico with brilliant white pubescence coating the abaxial surfaces of its narrow leaves, like those found on the European *Populus alba*. Its acorns may be either annual or biennial, and it is rated hardy through USDA zone 8 and perhaps 7. Usually fairly small but very erect, it can grow into a canopy tree in southern Arizona and New Mexico. On windy mountainsides, its two-toned leaves give an extraordinary color display.

The lateleaf oak (**Quercus tardifolia**) is probably the rarest oak in North America. It was described decades ago from a few specimens found in Big Bend National Park, then lost for decades. As it turned out, everyone had been looking in the wrong place because the original description included a trail that was later relocated. Texas biologist Jackie Poole followed the original trail route and showed me the only known surviving tree, right where it had been all along. This tree does not bear fruit, either because it is sterile or because it has no pollinator. It could be of hybrid origin, and its taxonomic status is uncertain. But it is thrilling for any tree nut to

TOP LEFT: The colorful red petioles of red oak (*Quercus rubra*). CENTER LEFT: Red oak leaves in fall. BOTTOM LEFT: Red oak acorns. LEFT: The smooth, striped bark of red oak. RIGHT: The attractive foliage of silverleaf oak (*Q. hypoleucoides*).

hike up steep desert mountain trails for half a day and finally arrive at the only known tree of its kind in the world.

See *Quercus velutina* and *Q. shumardii* for discussion of similar species.

COMMENTS: Many old red oaks are associated with historical events. The Salt Fork Oak growing in Champaign County, Illinois, was Abraham Lincoln's landmark for finding the ford he used to cross the Salt Fork of the Vermilion River on his trips as an attorney to the circuit court in Danville. Another historic Illinois specimen growing near Sheffield was the surveyor's witness point as the Rock Island Railroad was built in 1851.

Red oak is becoming steadily more popular in the nursery trade and might soon take the number one position ahead of pin oak (*Q. palustris*). It is also the most intensively managed native oak species for timber production, due to the combination of its growth rate, good form, site adaptability, and wood quality. Red oak is the most popular of our native oaks for planting as an exotic species in Europe, and it grows there with great vigor. Worldwide conferences are held periodically just to review the state of knowledge on genetic improvement and physiology of red oak.

LEFT: A large silverleaf oak (*Quercus hypoleucoides*) in a canyon in the Southwest. BELOW: Emory oak (*Q. emoryi*) is a common dryland oak species of the Southwest.

Quercus shumardii

SHUMARD OAK

DESCRIPTION: Shumard oak is a giant bottomland tree in the East and a smaller upland tree in the West. Its columnar trunk, striped smooth bark, branching pattern, lobed leaves, big acorns, and great proportions all remind one of red oak (*Quercus rubra*). It is the flagship species of a host of closely related oaks. For many years I admired the U.S. national champion Shumard oak, one of a grove of comparable trees at Beall Woods in southern Illinois, until it died in 1982. An even larger tree has been found since then in Overton Park Forest, Tennessee. This record holder is 147 feet (44.1 m) tall with a trunk nearly 6 feet (1.8 m) thick.

LEAVES: Every botany or horticulture student knows the Shumard oak leaf from the cover of *Gray's Manual of Botany* or the spine of *Manual of Cultivated Broad-Leaved Trees and Shrubs*. The leaves are the size of red oak leaves but are proportionately wider and more deeply and intricately lobed. Most Shumard oaks develop beautiful red color in fall, and they are among the first native oaks to change color each year.

FLOWERS AND FRUIT: Characteristics of both flowers and fruit are similar to those of red oak (*Quercus rubra*).

BEST SEASONS: FALL (this oak and its close relatives are among our most spectacular trees for autumn color). SUMMER (an excellent shade tree with glossy, deeply lobed leaves). SPRING (during the blooming period, when the colorful staminate catkins sway in the wind).

NATIVE AND ADAPTIVE RANGE: This is a dominant tree of the lower Mississippi River valley, but it can be found over a considerable natural range from Pennsylvania, Indiana, and Missouri southward. It even grows in southern Ontario, where it is rare enough to be listed as a vulnerable species, and on upland habitats in western Oklahoma. The range is not precisely defined because this species grades into other, similar species on upland habitats and toward its western limit. Shumard oak is a popular tree in cultivation and has performed well north at least through USDA zone 5, depending upon provenance.

CULTURE: Certain geographic races of this species, particularly the Oklahoma trees, have proven to be quite tolerant of alkaline soil, an unusual quality in eastern oaks. Shumard oak also tolerates short-term flooding, but not shade. It grows very rapidly for an oak and becomes very large. It is relatively easy to transplant and to grow from seed. See *Quercus alba* and other oak profiles for more general information.

PROBLEMS: Shumard oak is subject to the same problems that affect red oaks in general.

CULTIVARS: *Quercus shumardii* is becoming popular as a landscape tree, but few cultivars have become available. Trees with deeper acorn caps were once segregated as variety *schneckii*, but this subtle distinction is not followed by most modern taxonomists. A Texas selection with vigorous growth has been named 'Andersons'. As far as I know, nobody else is even studying the species in an attempt to identify superior ornamental selections. This may be due in part to a peroxidase enzyme incompatibility problem that frequently causes graft union failures on oaks in section *Lobatae*, thus complicating the asexual propagation necessary for cultivar development. Alternatively, perhaps no one has found any reason to improve upon this outstanding ornamental species.

SIMILAR AND RELATED SPECIES: Oak nomenclature has been confused for many years, partly because these variable and cross-fertile trees refuse to fit precisely into the categories, or species, humans have used to classify living organisms, and partly because our taxonomist friends relentlessly continue trying to do so, constantly changing the names in the process. There is a smaller, upland tree that was considered a variety or form of Shumard oak until 1993. At that time my old buddy Bill Hess, the herbarium curator for the Morton Arboretum, who studied this tree in great detail, affirmed that this tree is sufficiently and consistently distinct enough to be classified as a separate species. This species, **Quercus acerifolia,** is found growing wild only on Magazine Mountain, the highest point in Arkansas, and in a few mountainous localities nearby, but it does fine in cultivation north through USDA zone 5 and makes a beautiful medium-sized tree.

RIGHT: Shumard oak (*Quercus shumardii*) becomes a large shade tree similar to red oak (*Q. rubra*).

The Stone Mountain oak (***Quercus georgiana***) is a very interesting little Shumard-like oak found in the wild only on a few granitic balds in Georgia, South Carolina, and Alabama. It is a beautiful species with small leaves shaped more like those of bear oak (*Q. ilicifolia*), and it resembles that species in size. When rescued from the stark environs of its natural habitat and placed in a more hospitable setting, Stone Mountain oak makes a nice small tree with brilliant red fall color and fine texture. The best part is that it grows just fine north at least through USDA zone 5.

The southwestern upland version of Shumard oak has been separated into a distinct species as well. Texas Shumard oak, until recently called *Quercus texana* or *Q. shumardii* var. *texana*, has been renamed **Q. buckleyi.** This oak, like *Q. acerifolia*, does not get so large nor grow so quickly as the eastern lowland Shumard oak, but it is tolerant of drought and very alkaline soils. Texas Shumard oak is not reliably hardy much north of USDA zone 6, but I have a promising selection of *Q. buckleyi* × *Q. shumardii* propagated from a fine-textured tree found near Dallas, Texas. The second-generation seedlings are showing dependable winter hardiness in USDA zone 5, fine diminutive foliage, and brilliant fall color. I am honored to report that Professor Reinhold Luebbert of the Langeneicker Eichen Archiv project in Germany has named this attractive nothospecies *Q.* ×*sternbergii*.

The reason Texas Shumard oak can no longer be called *Quercus texana* is that this name was reassigned to another oak, *Q. nuttallii*, due to a nomenclatural technicality (a mislabeled specimen). The name has also been applied in the past to the Chisos red oak (**Q. gravesii**), a species from the Chisos Mountains. This tree, "the other *Q. texana*," has leaves much like those of Stone Mountain oak but is otherwise very similar to Texas Shumard oak. It is the main oak species seen painting the mountains of Big Bend National Park red in fall. Populations can be seen also in the Glass Mountains, Davis Mountains, and surrounding areas of western Texas. It has reliable hardiness in USDA zone 7 and might be recommended for one or even two zones further north following more testing in areas with dry heat and alkaline soils. A rare evergreen relative, **Q. graciliformis,** is found at higher elevations in Blue Creek Canyon, a remote area of Big Bend, but is not seen elsewhere and is unlikely to be hardy very far north of its restricted range, USDA zone 8.

Shumard oak and its kin are very closely related to scarlet oak (**Quercus coccinea**), the official tree of the District of Columbia. A beautiful specimen planted by President Benjamin Harrison grows next to Pennsylvania Avenue at the White House. Scarlet oak is more easily distinguished from Shumard oak where their ranges overlap by its habitat (dry uplands with sandy or rocky soils) than by any conspicuous differences in general appearance. The best way to identify all Shumard-like

TOP LEFT: The deeply lobed leaves of Shumard oak (*Quercus shumardii*). LEFT: Shumard oak has dependable, brilliant fall color. RIGHT: Shumard oak in winter.

species is to look at the acorns and buds, with an identification key and magnifying lens in hand, and to examine the leaves for abaxial tufts of hairs.

Like Shumard oak, scarlet oak is popular in the nursery trade. Its common name hints at its breathtaking fall color. This tree has the reputation of being difficult to transplant unless it has been grown in the nursery using root-training techniques, but Paul Cappiello at Bernheim Arboretum has told me that he moves them easily and that he believes the problem is overstated. The U.S. national champion scarlet oak is part of a rural fence row in Powell County, Kentucky. It reaches 120 feet (36 m) tall and has a trunk more than 6 feet (1.8 m) in di-

ameter. This is a very common species of sandy upland sites in the South, but it also grows naturally in scattered locations as far north as southern Michigan and coastal Maine. Some botanists believe the northern stands of scarlet oak are actually northern pin oak (**Q. ellipsoidalis**).

Northern pin oak is hardy in USDA zone 3 and shares much of the northwestern range of red oak (*Quercus rubra*). It is similar to black oak (*Q. velutina*) in general appearance, with comparable susceptibility to damage and decay, but it has scarlet oak leaves, and in youth it maintains a classic pyramidal form. Its red fall color is outstanding. Northern pin oak is usually a smaller species on the poor soils where it grows, but the largest specimen is 128 feet (38.4 m) tall and almost 5 feet (1.5 m) thick. My urban forester friend Dave Shepard has studied this tree intensely and believes it is simply a northern expression of scarlet oak. Others suggest it might be a stabilized hybrid of some combination of scarlet oak, red oak, black oak, and possibly pin oak (*Q. palustris*).

COMMENTS: There might be no better route to humility for an amateur botanist than to dive headlong into the oaks. The genus *Quercus* consists of hundreds of species throughout the Northern Hemisphere, some in areas so remote that their acorns or other diagnostic characteristics have yet to be observed.

There are the red oaks (section *Lobatae*, formerly subgenus *Erythrobalanus*), with acorns that mature in two years, barring a few exceptions; the white oaks (section *Quercus*, formerly subgenus *Lepidobalanus* or *Leucobalanus*), with fruits that are annual, also barring exceptions; and some intermediate, or golden, oaks (section or subgenus *Protobalanus*), with certain characteristics borrowed from red oaks and others from white oaks. In Asia there are oaks classified in a completely different section or subgenus, *Cyclobalanopsis*, with ringed acorn cups and leaves that resemble anything but those of a traditional American oak. There are also several subsets of section *Quercus* in Europe and Asia that should probably be segregated, such as the Turkish oak group and the Holm oak group.

Many oaks are either nothospecies or ochlospecies and may be lumped or split defensibly almost at whim. There are tanoaks (*Lithocarpus*), which are not true oaks but do bear acorns. They are separated mostly on the basis of having erect staminate catkins like those of chestnuts (*Castanea*). Some references divide tanoaks into two genera as well, adding *Pasania*. These are all part of the family Fagaceae, which also includes several other genera.

Parallel centers of speciation and diversity for the oak genus exist in North America and Asia. There are evergreen oaks and deciduous oaks (and many in between), giant tree oaks and sprawling scrub oaks, desert oaks and swamp oaks, tropical oaks and boreal oaks. This surely must be our most fascinating family of trees, as well as one of the most useful.

It is never quite clear where to draw the imaginary lines of compartmentalization for many oaks. While some oak species are distinct and consistent, many resemble one another and seem to melt imperceptibly into each other where their ranges overlap. Sometimes this is caused by introgressive hybridization among species, which in itself is something that no self-respecting species is supposed to do very often. Much of their variation can be attributed to heterozygosity, a natural genetic variation and drift within species, and from natural selection for specific genetic traits within particular habitat types in response to environmental pressures. Soon after a habitat changes, so do its oak inhabitants. As new ecological niches become available (due to climate change, and even to the more local and rapid impacts of human activity) oaks seem to diversify even further in a race to occupy them.

The oaks are evolving—perhaps exploding—as a genus, right before our eyes. It is exciting and inspiring for students of trees to be able to watch some of the action. And one of the best places to begin looking is among the confusing, interrelated group of magnificent trees that comprise the Shumard oak group.

FAR LEFT: Scarlet oak (*Quercus coccinea*) is a spectacular tree in fall. TOP LEFT: Staminate catkins of Stone Mountain oak (*Q. georgiana*). CENTER LEFT: Stone Mountain oak leaves in fall color. LEFT: Marcescent leaves of Stone Mountain oak coated with frost.

Quercus stellata
POST OAK

DESCRIPTION: Post oak is an even slower-growing version of white oak (*Quercus alba*). It is the ultimate drought-resistant tree; I have found stunted four-hundred-year-old post oaks growing on xeric south-facing rock ledges with their roots in hot, thin, sterile soils. It also tolerates flatwoods soils that are soggy in spring and brick-hard in summer.

Post oak makes a fine, firm tree on a good site but normally does not attain the size of some other white oaks. Nonetheless, the record tree in Surry County, Virginia, is 85 feet (25.5 m) tall and more than 6 feet (1.8 m) in diameter, and a nearly identical specimen was recently measured in Jackson County, Georgia. Old trees appear to have more limbs than twigs, and the twigs they do have can wander in the type of plagiotropic confusion that might remind you of the random pattern of cracks in the mud of a dry puddle. Post oak really excels aesthetically as an ancient, weather-beaten, gnarly "hangman's tree" in a xeric setting too severe for any lesser tree to survive, and such specimens should be preserved wherever they occur.

LEAVES: Having two large, spatulate lobes directed outward near the tip of the blade like the arms of an iron cross, post oak leaves are stiff, lustrous, and substantial. They reach 3 to 8 inches (7.5 to 20 cm) in length. Fall color is subdued and often late but can be a rich russet or burnt orange. Many leaves cling into early winter.

FLOWERS AND FRUIT: These characteristics are similar to white oak (see *Quercus alba*). The acorns of post oak are smaller, reaching less than 1 inch (2.5 cm) in length.

BEST SEASONS: WINTER (for the marcescent foliage on young trees and the remarkable architecture of monumental old trees). FALL (for those trees with nice fall color). SUMMER (for the welcome shade on a strong, durable tree).

RIGHT: The typical, irregular form of post oak (*Quercus stellata*).

NATIVE AND ADAPTIVE RANGE: Post oak is common on poor or dry soils throughout the Southeast, south of a line from Cape Cod west through central Ohio and southern Iowa to the Texas Panhandle. In cultivation it does fine throughout USDA zone 5, with attention to provenance.

CULTURE: Post oak, like its common associate black-jack oak (*Quercus marilandica*), should not be transplanted and should not be expected to grow quickly regardless of the quality of soil or care it is given. On the plus side, count on it still being around four hundred years from the day you plant an acorn. For best growth, give it acid soil, full sun, and freedom from competition from other trees or turf.

TOP LEFT: Leaf and acorn of post oak (*Quercus stellata*). LEFT: The craggy limbs of an old post oak. BELOW: The marcescent leaves of post oak catch winter frost. RIGHT: A giant post oak in the Ozarks of Arkansas, several centuries old.

Seeds germinate readily, following the same procedure for white oak (see *Quercus alba*), and almost any soil texture will do. Protection of existing trees during construction, especially old scenic ones, is paramount. Most post oaks found in residential landscapes were planted there by nature's critters long before the homeowners (or the homeowners' grandparents) were born.

PROBLEMS: Post oak is subject to the same problems that affect white oak (see *Quercus alba*). Its extensive root system is especially sensitive to construction disturbance and excessive artificial irrigation, so be extra careful around this tree.

CULTIVARS: I am unaware of any attempts to develop cultivars of this species.

SIMILAR AND RELATED SPECIES: Sand post oak (***Quercus margaretta***) is a smaller variant that often suckers to form mottes (dense clonal groves) on dry, sandy soils from the southeast coast west through southern Oklahoma. Benny Simpson of Texas A&M University once told me he thought it would be hardy in USDA zone 5,

and my one trial plant in that zone in Illinois has done well its first three winters. Its leaves are not as strongly lobed nor as large as those of post oak, and its twigs are glabrous instead of tomentose. Exceptional trees will grow fairly large, and one in Augusta, Florida, is 87 feet (26.1 m) high, broader than tall, and 4 feet (1.2 m) in diameter. Sand post oak is thought by some to be a stabilized natural hybrid of post oak with Gambel oak (*Q. gambelii*). If this is true, the establishment of such a hybrid swarm would have to date back to a prehistoric time when the two parent species had overlapping ranges.

Drummond post oak (**Quercus ×drummondii**) is a Texas tree midway between post oak and sand post oak. It is presumed to have originated as a hybrid between the two and is found on intermediate habitats. It does well north to USDA zone 5. Boynton's post oak (**Q. boyntonii**) is similar but shrubby, rhizomatous, and extremely rare, occurring in a few isolated locations in Alabama and Texas. Delta post oak (**Q. similis**) is a little more common and grows very large. It favors wet soils, and its leaves are more shallow-lobed than those of post oak. It could be the result of genetic introgression between post oak and overcup oak (*Q. lyrata*), based upon its appearance and ecology. Post oak also crosses with swamp white oak (*Q. bicolor*), bur oak (*Q. macrocarpa*), and just about any other white oak type within reach of its pollen, leading to many confusing hybrid forms.

Shin oak (**Quercus havardii**) occurs in sandy soils in the southwestern part of our region but is always shrubby and clonal. Hybrids between shin oak and post oak or sand post oak are commonly seen within the range of shin oak, standing as taller clumps within the groundcover mattes of pure shin oak. Chapmann oak (**Q. chapmannii**) is a similar southeastern species, suited to dry, sandy soils in full sun. It grows naturally on sand hills and dunes of coastal Georgia and south into Florida. Usually shrubby, it can grow to 45 feet (13.5 m) tall in the southern part of its range, beyond the limits of our area of coverage.

COMMENTS: For nearly a century the students of Texas A&M University maintained a tradition of building an annual bonfire the night before the big football game with rival Texas University. The woodpile was stacked nearly six stories high and took weeks to assemble. Born of a less environmentally conscious era, the bonfire was not composed of logging slash or dead wood from urban tree removals but of five thousand solid post oak logs, each of which probably took more than one hundred years to grow. This wasteful tradition finally ended in tragedy when the pile collapsed in 1999, killing several students.

Among my family's collection of tree memorabilia is a much smaller piece of post oak wood, from the ruins of the frontier fort of Jacob Zumwalt built in the 1790s northwest of St. Louis, Missouri. This structure hosted Daniel Boone and Chief Blackhawk, was passed by the Lewis and Clark expedition on May 22, 1804, and was the site of the first Missouri battle of the War of 1812. From 1817 to 1853 it was occupied by Nathan Heald, who had been the commander during the August 16, 1812, massacre of Fort Dearborn, the outpost settlement that would rise again to become Chicago.

Zumwalt's Fort sheltered its builder and his successors for about a century, then was abandoned to the elements for another century; yet our scrap of wood remains solid and rock-hard. The fort's logs were described as "white oak" in early literature, but post oak is seldom segregated from white oak (*Q. alba*) in forestry parlance. Post oaks can still be seen in the area, perhaps having descended from the trees used more than two centuries ago to build the old fort.

Our piece of wood holds a special meaning for my wife, Edie, who is Jacob Zumwalt's great-great-great-great-great-granddaughter.

Quercus velutina
BLACK OAK

DESCRIPTION: Black oak is another member of the red oak group (section *Lobatae*, formerly subgenus *Erythrobalanus*). Among the most massive eastern oaks, black oak is also one of the most drought resistant, ranking close to its frequent associates blackjack oak (*Quercus marilandica*) and post oak (*Q. stellata*). It is also common on much better sites, growing in association with red oak (*Q. rubra*) and white oak (*Q. alba*). This is truly an adaptable tree.

Black oak accepts almost any soil type, from sand dunes to tight clay. It is very intolerant of shade and more prone to structural damage and decay than red oak, but some trees escape such injury to reach massive proportions on better soils. The largest known black oak, in Virginia, is a full-crowned specimen 108 feet (32.4 m) high, broader than it is tall, and nearly 9 feet (2.7 m) in diameter.

LEAVES: Black oak leaves are thick, glossy, and stiff, and they often turn deep orange or dark red in fall. Their early spring color, a bright, velvety red, is just as attractive. They vary in size, averaging 4 to 8 inches (10 to 20 cm) in length but occasionally reaching nearly twice that size.

FLOWERS AND FRUIT: The yellow staminate catkins of black oak are among the longest and most colorful and showy of the genus. Flowering and fruiting tendencies are similar to those of blackjack oak, with which it frequently crosses in the wild. The scales on the margins of its acorn cups are slightly loose or raised at their tips, like shingles being blown up in a strong wind.

BEST SEASONS: SPRING (for the red, velvety new leaves and the yellow catkins). FALL (for those trees with the best fall color). SUMMER (for the attractive, glossy foliage).

NATIVE AND ADAPTIVE RANGE: Black oak is a very common tree over a broad area from the Lake States and southern Ontario south to the Gulf Coast and west to eastern Kansas, Oklahoma, and Texas. It covers much the same southern and central range as red oak but stops near Kingston, Ontario, in the North. Trees from northern provenance can be grown in USDA zone 4.

CULTURE: This oak is extremely difficult to transplant and is best grown from seed or preserved in place. It is also very sensitive to soil disturbance and grade changes, so give it a wide berth during construction. Seeds germinate in spring following fall planting. They usually devote more of their initial energy to root growth than top growth, so root control techniques are useful when growing seedlings for transplanting. Young trees may develop forked leaders, which should be thinned as soon as possible to leave only the straightest or strongest one.

PROBLEMS: Most of the problems that affect blackjack oak (*Quercus marilandica*) and red oak (*Q. rubra*) apply to this species. Black oak and most related oaks are very susceptible to oak wilt (*Ceratocystis fagacearum*) and other problems specific to the red oak group.

CULTIVARS: Black oak cultivars are mostly of European cultivated origin and largely reflect subtle differences in leaf shape or size. Named selections include 'Albertsii', 'Angustifolia', 'Macrophylla', and 'Magnifica'. The genetic base of this species is narrow in Europe, so it seems that anything found there that looks a little different is given a name. If European horticulturists were able to spend a few weeks touring black oak habitats throughout eastern North America, they would likely come away with a better appreciation of the diversity of this species. To expand the scope of cultivar selection for black oak in Europe, I am cooperating with Professor Eike Jablonski of Luxembourg to propagate a new cutleaf form I found in Illinois, tentatively named 'Oakridge Walker'.

SIMILAR AND RELATED SPECIES: Another North American tree called black oak, **Quercus kelloggii**, is a California species not found in our region. Southern red oak (**Q. falcata**) is a southern associate of black oak and can subsist on some of the most abused, degraded red soils found anywhere in the South. Old southern red oaks frequently appear weather-beaten and unkempt due to the hard life they have lived, but southern red oak can make a remarkable tree when grown in a favorable location, and it can grow rapidly in good soil. The enormous U.S. national champion southern red oak grows in Upson County, Georgia. It is 150 feet (45 m) tall with an equal branch spread and a trunk more than 8 feet (2.4 m) in diameter.

Southern red oak has such variable foliage that botanists have argued for years about the existence, or number, of taxonomic varieties and forms that should be recognized. I have observed that seedlings propagated from trees with different leaf forms are not readily matched to their parents by leaf shape. Some have three lobes, some more. Some have long, tail-like central lobes, while others are barely lobed at all or have stubby leaves shaped more like those of blackjack oak. Some have rich crimson fall color, and others are drab. I have seen some southern red oaks with spring, summer, and fall foliage that ranked among the most beautiful of any tree. I grow some of these trees in Illinois and have found that trees of northern origin can be grown in at least the warmer parts of USDA zone 5.

A closely allied species, often listed as a variety of southern red oak, is cherrybark oak (**Quercus pagoda,** syns. *Q. pagodaefolia* and *Q. falcata* var. *pagodaefolia*). This tall, massive tree is a fast-growing canopy species of rich, fertile bottomlands. It may be the most valuable oak for timber production in the South, and it makes an attractive landscape tree as well, north at least to central Illinois, USDA zone 5. The straight, columnar trunks of forest-grown cherrybark oaks really do resemble those of wild cherry (*Prunus serotina*) with their dark, curly, cherrylike bark. Like black oak and southern red oak, this is one of our largest and most vigorous oaks. The biggest of all grows in Sussex County, Virginia, standing 124 feet (37.2 m) tall with an even bigger wingspan, supported on a trunk almost 9 feet (2.7 m) thick.

COMMENTS: Black oak is a tree for all seasons. In spring its emerging leaves and staminate catkins are among the most colorful of the oaks. Its dark, glossy foliage remains attractive all summer and often turns a nice crimson in fall. The heavy twigs, with their large, fuzzy buds that look almost like brown pussy willow (*Salix discolor*) catkins, catch the sunlight of winter. And black oak is one parent of two of the most frequently seen oak hybrids in eastern North America. Wherever it grows on clay or loam soil near shingle oak (*Quercus imbricaria*), the nothospecies *Q.* ×*leana* is likely to be found; and where it shares a drier habitat with blackjack oak,

LEFT: The staminate catkins of black oak (*Quercus velutina*) are among the showiest of all oak flowers. TOP RIGHT: The red, velvety emerging spring foliage of black oak. CENTER RIGHT: Young leaves and staminate catkins of black oak. RIGHT: Mature foliage and acorns of black oak.

watch for the nothospecies *Q. ×bushii*. Both taxa can be found in cultivation as well.

For early Americans the inner bark of this tree was a primary source of quercitron, a yellow dye material, which they harvested for export. The straight logs of moderate-sized trees were favored for rail splitting and

LEFT: Black oak (*Quercus velutina*) grows with post oak in dry woods. BELOW: The symmetrical form of a young southern red oak (*Q. falcata*).

log home construction. But ornamental flare and exploitation aside, consider the primeval savannas of black oak encountered in Georgia by naturalist William Bartram on his travels more than two hundred years ago, as recorded in his journal, published in 1791 (Van Doren 1928): "The most magnificent forest I have ever seen . . . I can assert that many of the black oaks measured eight, nine, ten, and eleven feet in diameter five feet above the ground . . . from thence they ascend perfectly straight with a gradual taper, forty or fifty feet to the limbs."

Quercus virginiana
LIVE OAK

DESCRIPTION: The southern live oak is the emblematic tree of landscapes throughout the Deep South. In the forest it becomes an erect tree up to 100 feet (30 m) tall, but it is best known as an awesome, spreading tree with sinuous limbs that arch over to bounce along the ground on old specimens. The squat, leaning, tapering trunks of such trees grow larger in diameter than those of any other oak.

Many trees have been described as the largest or the oldest live oak, and their irregular growth forms make it difficult to discern between specimens of roughly equal bulk. The recognized U.S. national champion is the Seven Sisters Oak located near Lewisburg, Louisiana. Although only 55 feet (16.5 m) tall, its sprawling canopy shades an area 132 feet (39.6 m) across and its short trunk, divided into seven arching sister stems, is almost 12 feet (3.6 m) thick.

The oldest and most picturesque live oak might be the famous Angel Oak on John's Island, South Carolina. Although no one really seems to have accurate data on the longevity of this species, such venerable specimens are almost certainly among the oldest oaks in North America. The most majestic specimen could be the Middleton Oak at Middleton Place, a plantation up the Ashley River from Charleston. It has perfect, symmetrical form and approaches within inches the overall size of the Seven Sisters Oak, with a much taller, single trunk. Live oak is the state tree of Georgia, which also proudly points to its own magnificent signature specimen, the Majestic Oak of Savannah.

Perhaps most inspirational, though not quite as large, are the old planted trees that make up the cathedral-like alleys lining the approaches at places such as Boone Hall in Mount Pleasant, South Carolina; Oak Alley in Vacherie, Louisiana; and Rosedown in St. Francisville, Louisiana. The most haunting specimen is surely the Windsor

RIGHT: The famous Majestic Oak, an old live oak (*Quercus virginiana*) in Savannah.

426

Oak near Port Gibson, Mississippi, unforgettable when viewed at dusk through the remaining columns of the burned antebellum plantation house.

LEAVES: Unlike the leaves of most oaks discussed up to this point, those on live oak are subevergreen, falling gradually over late winter as new leaves replace them. They reach about 3 inches (7.5 cm) long by 1 inch (2.5 cm) wide and have smooth margins or, especially on vigorous shoots and second (summer) growth flushes, scattered teeth. The leaves are waxy and resistant to salt spray, allowing this tree to grow where others can't, in coastal dune areas and on barrier islands.

FLOWERS AND FRUIT: Live oak is a member of the white oak group (section *Quercus*, formerly subgenus *Lepidobalanus* or *Leucobalanus*) and has acorns that mature in one season. The acorns are narrow and tapered, very dark when ripe, and less than 1 inch (2.5 cm) long. They are the primary food for many wildlife species in coastal habitats.

BEST SEASONS: WINTER (this is functionally an evergreen tree and shows to best advantage when its neighbors are bare). SUMMER (for the welcome shade it provides in the hot, humid climate of its home range).

NATIVE AND ADAPTIVE RANGE: Live oak grows throughout Florida and extends in narrow coastal bands north to Virginia and west into Texas. It may be hardy into the warmer parts of USDA zone 7, although many of the trees seen at the cold fringe of the range could be Texas live oak (*Quercus fusiformis*) or hybrids. Provenance is important with this species, so trees from Florida should not be propagated for planting in Virginia. Within the warm, humid environment of its natural range it is among the strongest, largest, and longest-lived trees. It does not do well very far inland of the Coastal Plain and becomes semideciduous and very slow growing when planted in the Piedmont.

CULTURE: This oak, like most others, grows readily from seed; but unlike many oaks, it can also be transplanted without difficulty. The Ol' Man Oak at Dixie Landing, Disney World, in Florida, was transported 12 miles (19 km) and replanted successfully. Its trunk is 3.5 feet (1 m) in diameter. Specimen-sized live oaks are the trees of choice for many landscaping projects because they transplant so easily and because of their value as they mature.

Live oak seeds should be planted as soon as they ri-

RIGHT: An allée of live oaks (*Quercus virginiana*) planted in 1835.

pen. See *Quercus alba* for hints on propagation. Once established, live oak is drought resistant, so it thrives on sandy soils in coastal cities. It also tolerates more shade in summer than most other oaks, since its nearly evergreen leaves can function through most of the winter, and it is very resistant to salinity. Young trees grow quickly but need to be trained to an upright form for use in parkway planting strips and similar areas where their natural, sprawling nature will be unwelcome.

PROBLEMS: Live oak is unusual among our large native oaks in its ability, and proclivity, to send up vegetative sprouts from surface roots some distance from the base of the parent tree, resulting in clonal thickets. While this is great for erosion control on coastal dunes, it can be annoying in the garden. Trees in wild habitats are damaged severely by fires, which kill the bark and leave the wood exposed to decay.

Live oak is similar to the red oaks (section *Lobatae*, formerly subgenus *Erythrobalanus*) in its susceptibility to leaf blister from *Taphrina caerulescens*, and it and its close relatives are the only white oaks seriously bothered by oak wilt (*Ceratocystis fagacearum*) and bacterial leaf scorch (*Xylella fastidiosa*). See *Quercus phellos* for more details on these problems. Oak wilt can be devastating in live oaks because many trees might originate from the same, interconnecting root system, but valuable trees in wilt-infested areas can be protected with fungicide injections applied by a certified arborist.

Live oak is also one of several oaks known to be somewhat susceptible to chestnut blight (*Cryphonectria parasitica*). This disease persists rather cryptically on "carrier" oaks, waiting to reinfect its preferred host, chestnut (*Castanea americana*), which might be planted within reach of its spores. The Spanish moss (*Tillandsia usneoides*) that drapes many live oaks is a beautiful and harmless epiphyte, valuable to many birds for nesting material. See *Quercus alba* for additional discussion of problems.

CULTIVARS: As popular and variable as this tree is, it might seem surprising that few cultivars are available. 'Highrise' is a cutting-propagated upright selection from South Carolina, and 'Southern Shade' is a Florida selection with a more traditional form. Still, almost any seedling live oak makes a great tree. Irregular, unpredictable form is considered characteristic and desirable for this species, and fall color and flowering are not issues upon which to base cultivar selection with evergreen oaks.

SIMILAR AND RELATED SPECIES: There are several other evergreen oaks in the Southeast, most of which were once (or still are) considered varieties or forms of live oak. Reference books list them in various ways. The current approach, which I follow, is to separate several of them into distinct species. All belong to the white oak group.

An inland western form called Texas live oak (**Quercus fusiformis,** syn. *Q. virginiana* var. *fusiformis*), also known as escarpment live oak, grows in interior parts of Texas. I have collected this species from the temperate mountains of eastern Mexico and from western Oklahoma. It is more tolerant of alkaline soils and much hardier than *Q. virginiana*. Planted specimens have survived to maturity through the winters of USDA zone 6 in the moun-

TOP LEFT: Leaves and staminate catkins of live oak (*Quercus virginiana*). LEFT: Leaves and acorns of Texas live oak (*Q. fusiformis*). RIGHT: An ancient sand live oak (*Q. geminata*).

tains of New Mexico and on the High Plains of Oklahoma and Kansas. The record specimen grows in a yard in Real County, Texas, standing 42 feet (12.6 m) tall, with a spread more than twice as broad, and sporting a twisted, picturesque trunk almost 8 feet (2.4 m) thick. More often, clonal groups are formed from root sprouts, and a grove of these trees might have originated from a single acorn.

I am testing plants of this species for hardiness from sources in Oklahoma. They tend to be partially deciduous in Illinois in USDA zone 5, and some seedlings even develop a bit of red fall color. They will probably not be fully hardy in our most severe winters and might survive only as shrubs, but their tolerance of winter cold has

been surprising thus far. This tree is identical to the eastern coastal species except for its larger, spindle-shaped, pointed acorns, smaller ultimate size, and greater hardiness, so it would make a good substitute for use in the Midsouth where the coastal species cannot survive.

Sand live oak (***Quercus geminata,*** syn. *Q. virginiana* var. *maritima*) was named for its Gemini-twin acorns born in pairs and for its sandy habitat. Its leaves are slightly rolled under along the edges and have deeply set veins, but there are few other differences between this tree and live oak. Young trees are more erect, and the dark leaves show nicely against the light gray branches. It cannot match the size of a mature southern live oak, but some fine specimens can be seen in Florida. The biggest, in

Gainesville, is 81 feet (24.3 m) tall with a wingspan of 106 feet (31.8 m) and a trunk 5 feet (1.5 m) in diameter. Another similar species, dwarf live oak (*Q. minima*), remains a shrub and grows as an understory plant in sandy woods under southern pines (*Pinus*).

Our eastern live oaks resemble the live oaks of California in many ways, but none of those species are classified in the same taxonomic section. The coast live oak (*Quercus agrifolia*) and the interior live oak (*Q. wislizeni*) are red oaks, while the canyon live oak (*Q. chrysolepis*) and its relatives are intermediate, or golden, oaks (section or subgenus *Protobalanus*). Engelmann oak (*Q. engelmannii*), a semideciduous species, is probably the closest counterpart of our eastern live oaks on the Pacific Coast; it even has fused cotyledons in its acorns, like southern live oak.

COMMENTS: In the South, live oak is the venerated tree of history, and every town seems to have its own famous resident tree. In fact, they are so numerous that there is a National Live Oak Society through which they are registered. To be eligible a live oak must meet strict minimum size or age requirements: full members must be at least 5 feet (1.5 m) in diameter, and junior members must be at least half that size. Seven Sisters is the current president, and Middleton is vice president. My favorite junior member is the Guy Sternberg Oak in Metairie, Louisiana, named for me by the chairman of the Live Oak Society.

One notable member is the Jim Bowie Oak located at the Bowie Museum in Opelousas, Louisiana, on land once owned by Bowie's father. The Lafitte Oaks, a pair of trees at Jefferson Island, Louisiana, supposedly conceal the lost buried treasure of Jean Lafitte, the infamous pirate. The Sunnybrook Oaks near Covington, Louisiana, sheltered Andrew Jackson on his way to the Battle of New Orleans. The Big Oak at Thomasville, Georgia, is listed in the National Register of Historic Places.

Judge Toulemin of Baldwin County, Alabama, held court among the limbs of the Blakely Jury Tree in 1820 before the courthouse was completed. The Treaty Oak in Jacksonville, Florida, with its Medusa-like silhouette, is the central focus of its own city park, created decades ago to save the old monarch from the "progress" of urban development. This tree also graces the cover of *America's Famous and Historic Trees*, written by my friend Jeff Meyer. And the list goes on, throughout the South.

These living landmarks are not immortal, and one succumbs every now and then to a hurricane or disease. Far worse, however, is the magnetic appeal such ancient and inspirational trees seem to have for the vandalous dregs of our society. The Treaty Oak in Texas, last living witness to the many peace treaties and boundary agreements negotiated under its canopy among various Native American tribes, was to have been removed in 1937 by the owner of the property upon which it grew. The town leaders intervened and made the site a city park. This worked for more than half a century, but the tree was eventually poisoned with herbicide by a vandal. Arborists from around the world flocked to the site and attempted to revive it, but none were successful.

The ancient Inspiration Oak at Magnolia Springs, Alabama, has a similar story. During a property dispute in 1990, a thoughtless nitwit spitefully girdled this giant tree with a chainsaw. After three years of bridge-grafting, watering, misting, fertilizing, pruning, and hoping, the arborists who had volunteered their efforts to try to reverse the damage finally gave up. One of them injected the tree with preservatives, so its structure will at least remain intact as a reminder of the centuries of life that can be truncated by the momentary acts of a sick individual.

Rhamnus caroliniana
NATIVE BUCKTHORN

DESCRIPTION: I call *Rhamnus caroliniana* (syn. *Frangula caroliniana*) the native buckthorn, though it is most commonly known as Carolina buckthorn or Indian cherry, to emphasize how distinct it is from several exotic buckthorn species that have become serious weeds in North America. Some botanists even favor splitting the genus, placing this species in sister genus *Frangula*. This native tree, as well as its smaller native relative *R. lanceolata,* is safe to plant without fear of it becoming another biological pest. Native buckthorn is the more colorful and treelike of the two, sometimes reaching 40 feet (12 m) tall.

Identical U.S. national champion native buckthorns can be seen in Clarksville, Tennessee, and Middleburg, Virginia. They are 25 feet (7.5 m) tall with an equal span, and their trunks are just over 1 foot (30 cm) in diameter. Most specimens are much smaller, making round-headed small trees or large shrubs.

LEAVES: Buckthorn leaves are rich and rounded, usually maintain their good condition all summer, and turn a nice yellow or occasionally dark red in fall. They average 2 to 5 inches (5 to 12.5 cm) long by less than half as wide, and they display a nice rugose texture with impressed, parallel veins and a glossy surface.

FLOWERS AND FRUIT: The flowers are small, pale green, and inconspicuous, but the tree has attractive fruits that resemble small dark cherries in late summer. They are most decorative while still red, eventually turning shiny black.

BEST SEASONS: LATE SUMMER and FALL (for the ripening fruits and fall color). SPRING and SUMMER (for the attractive foliage).

NATIVE AND ADAPTIVE RANGE: Buckthorn likes limestone soils but grows in almost anything and is found on well-drained sites from New York south to Florida in the East, and west to Nebraska, Texas, and Mexico. It is reliably hardy in USDA zone 5, and some selections could go north at least another zone.

CULTURE: This tree is not difficult to grow or transplant. Each fruit contains up to four seeds, and I have grown it from fall-planted seed with no problem. It tolerates sun or shade, becoming much more dense in full sun but thriving in the forest understory, and accepts almost any soil pH.

PROBLEMS: This is a favorite browse species for rabbits and deer, so keep the critters at bay. Old specimens can become lopsided if they have grown in the forest edge and leaned over to reach light, and their wood is very brittle, so ice storms take their toll. This is not much of a problem for symmetrical, open-grown trees or for those found in the deep woods where leaning confers no advantage.

CULTIVARS: I have found no cultivars listed for this species. In fact, I have never seen it offered at nurseries, except for those that specialize in native or unusual plants, and it is not common in cultivation. However, the future holds promise: Iowa State University and the Landscape Plant Development Center of Minnesota are studying the species, and some interesting and hardy forms are already being identified.

SIMILAR AND RELATED SPECIES: Lanceleaf buckthorn (**Rhamnus lanceolata**) is a more diminutive species with narrower leaves and a more slender aspect. Lacking the very attractive fruit display of its cousin, it is one of those invisible plants that blends in with its surroundings. I walked the same trail in our woods for several years before noticing a specimen growing right beside the path; it finally gave away its position by slapping me in the face, having grown enough to place its foliage and small black fruits at eye level directly over the trail. This species is hardy in USDA zone 5. Another small buckthorn, **R. betulifolia,** is the Rocky Mountain counterpart of the eastern species. Several more American species can be found outside our region, and perhaps another hundred worldwide.

Bluewood (**Condalia hookeri**) is a southern member of the same family. Found in south-central Texas, it can become a small tree or a thorny, clonal shrub with edible purple fruits. **Condalia globosa** is another bluewood species native further west and south, sometimes seen in cultivation. Most of the small leaves of bluewoods are crowded on short, sharp spur branches and are valuable food for wildlife because of their high protein content.

In all probability neither species can be grown north of USDA zone 8.

Woolly bumelia (***Bumelia lanuginosa***) and its southern relative, smooth bumelia (***B. lycioides***), epitomize the concept of the tough native tree. While not closely related to buckthorns or bluewoods, they offer similar performance. Woolly bumelia is the hardier of the two, growing throughout USDA zone 5. This small tree will thrive in wet soil or on barren rocky bluffs, in sun or partial shade, and will tolerate road salt, heat, and drought with impunity. Old plants growing in severe, exposed locations can be very picturesque, but those on better sites can achieve the stature of the U.S. national champion located in Robertson County, Texas, which is 80 feet (24 m) tall with a trunk almost 3 feet (0.9 m) in diameter. The olive-like fruits are edible and are used for food by wildlife. Seed should be scarified and planted in fall. Its leaves are tenacious in the North and may be subevergreen in the South. Smooth bumelia is a riparian species with narrow leaves and smooth twigs. It is also rated hardy to USDA zone 5 but is not quite as hardy as woolly bumelia.

Ironwood bumelia (***Bumelia tenax***) is a smaller tree of the southeast coast. Another small species, saffron plum (***B. celastrina***) of southern Texas and peninsular Florida, is subtropical, thorny, and has small, evergreen leaves. Some describe it as having the appearance of a small live oak (*Quercus virginiana*) with thorns. Neither ironwood bumelia nor saffron plum is reliably hardy north of USDA zone 8.

Some authors have separated these four native bumelias into a different genus, ***Sideroxylon***.

COMMENTS: Mike Dosmann of the Arnold Arboretum, a fellow Purdue graduate and one of the best young plantspeople I know, has nothing but praise for native buckthorn, especially when compared with most other species of the genus. He finds it remarkable for its ecological amplitude and ornamental quality, thriving as it does in low or high pH soils, along streams and high on rocky slopes, in full sun or heavy shade.

I had seen it growing in most of those situations in the wild, primarily in southern Illinois or further south. Then one day I visited Mike when he was still doing graduate work in Ames, Iowa, during the blizzard of the century, and we talked about this tree and the studies being done at Iowa State University. To think that this southern plant could do well in such country, and even to the north in Minnesota, told me a lot about how tough and adaptable trees can be.

LEFT: A native buckthorn (*Rhamnus caroliniana*) in the forest understory at Starhill Forest. TOP RIGHT: Foliage and fruits of native buckthorn. CENTER RIGHT: Foliage of lanceleaf buckthorn (*R. lanceolata*). RIGHT: Foliage of woolly bumelia (*Bumelia lanuginosa*).

Rhus typhina
STAGHORN SUMAC

DESCRIPTION: The sumacs are a genus of striking small trees and shrubs with some very special attributes. Their clumping habit, outstanding fall color, picturesque branching, large pinnate leaves, and persistent fruit clusters help to identify most members of the genus from a distance.

The largest and one of the hardiest native sumacs is staghorn sumac, which gets its common name from its hairy, velvet-antler twigs. Like most other sumacs, it sprouts readily from the roots to form clonal thickets. The individual stems in such thickets seldom attain the size of those that grow as individual trees, but original stems in old thickets can easily exceed 30 feet (9 m) in height. The largest known staghorn sumac tree (though not the largest clone) is 61 feet (18.3 m) tall with a trunk 15 inches (37.5 cm) thick. It was found growing in Tallapoosa County, Alabama, south of its natural range.

Staghorn sumacs were once trees of the prairie-forest interface. Now they have found homes along fence rows, rocky ballasts of railroads, roadway embankments, and in pastures and thickets—all places that make them highly visible and offer the required combination of full sun and good drainage. These trees expand into disturbed areas and have greatly benefited from the human colonization of North America.

LEAVES: The leaves of most sumac species are pinnately compound and quite large. Staghorn sumac leaves are typically composed of up to thirty-one toothed leaflets, each about 4 inches (10 cm) long, supported by a rachis almost 2 feet (60 cm) long. The fall color of this species, a glowing flame-orange, is lighter than that of most other sumacs.

FLOWERS AND FRUIT: Sumacs are dioecious, with greenish yellow flowers. Clonal thickets are uniform in being either all male or all female, and more seem to be female than male. Female staghorn sumacs produce sticky, fuzzy, dark red clusters of small berries. The dense fruit clusters are erect, often exceed 6 inches (15 cm) in height, and remain showy throughout winter until they are taken by birds or picked by nature buffs looking to make sumac lemonade.

The seeds, though rich in vitamins and fat, are not a tasty first choice for most birds, so fruit clusters remain intact in winter and are consumed when other foods are gone. Some authors have observed that female clones might live longer than males, persisting in the landscape as taller trees begin to overtop them. The tallest clones I recall seeing have all been females.

BEST SEASONS: FALL (the early fall colors of any native sumac species rank them among the elite trees of autumn). WINTER (for the branching architecture and clinging fruit clusters of females). EARLY SUMMER (for the flowers).

NATIVE AND ADAPTIVE RANGE: Staghorn sumac is found from Cape Breton Island in Nova Scotia and Lake St. John in Quebec south through the Blue Ridge and Cumberland Plateau of Tennessee, and northwest out to eastern Minnesota. It tolerates winter cold and summer heat with equal aplomb, north to USDA zone 3.

CULTURE: Most sumacs need only a sunny location and well-drained soil. Staghorn sumac will respond to good soils and adequate moisture with more vigorous growth. It should be planted or preserved where it can be allowed to form thickets, if possible. This is the natural growth habit, and the blaze of fall color at eye level from such a thicket is splendid. Individual specimens, if trained and restrained from suckering, make artistic small trees with sinuous limbs and graceful, leaning trunks. When a sumac stem is wounded it becomes prone to attack by various borers and cankers; it is often best to remove it to ground level and let a sucker take its place. Such replacement stems easily reach eye level in one season.

Sumacs are simple to transplant in the dormant season as small suckers or root cuttings from the edges of established clones of known gender, thus ensuring the desired mix of male and female plants. They frequently consist of a sprout from a ropelike, unbranched horizontal root and may be cut back and allowed to regenerate new tops in proportion to root development. They

RIGHT: A tall staghorn sumac (*Rhus typhina*) at Starhill Forest.

436

can also be grown from seed but may take two or three years to sprout without the right combination of acid scarification and stratification. Established seedlings or previously transplanted suckers that have developed branching root systems can be relocated without difficulty.

PROBLEMS: Sumacs are favorite targets of the Gypsy moth (*Lymantria dispar*) and are subject to various cankers and vascular wilt fungi. Like many other clonal trees, sumacs develop root sprouts as an adaptation to a fire-prone environment. With their sprouting capability, they have little need to invest their metabolic resources into thick, protective bark, so their thin skin

makes them sensitive to fires and to damage from lawn-mower bumps and string-trimmer abrasions. White gummy sap bleeds from such injuries, drying to a persistent black varnish that is very noticeable. Serious wounding causes sumacs to abandon the existing, damaged stems and triggers the development of sucker stems. Those who desire a thicket should cut back their sumacs every few years, and those who don't should be careful to avoid injuring the bark.

A significant problem centers around the toxicity, or perceived toxicity, of sumacs. They can be toxic to other plants, through allelopathic chemicals released by their roots, and some are toxic to humans as well. Because one native species, poison sumac (*Rhus vernix*), causes severe skin inflammations in sensitive people, some folks fear all sumacs. Conversely, because most familiar sumac species are benign, many people don't give that one toxic species the prudent respect it is due. Unless you are certain that you are, and always will be, immune to the toxic power of the poison sumac, admire its rare beauty only from a safe distance. There is no similar reason not to appreciate staghorn sumac and the other native species at close range.

CULTIVARS: Two female cultivars of staghorn sumac are popular for their deeply lobed foliage. These selections, 'Dissecta' and 'Laciniata', tend to be more spreading and suckering than the species type, and 'Laciniata' also develops fernlike bracts in its flower clusters.

Although no other cultivars have been named, I have noticed that staghorn sumac clones are variable in form, from tall and upright to low and spreading. Since sumacs can be propagated asexually from root cuttings, growth form could be a practical criterion for selection of a specimen or patio tree.

SIMILAR AND RELATED SPECIES: Smooth sumac (**Rhus glabra**) normally keeps its head down but occasionally grows as large as staghorn sumac. One measured in Dry-branch, Georgia, is 52 feet (15.6 m) tall with a trunk about 1 foot (30 cm) in diameter. This species has the most colorful fruit clusters of any of our common native sumacs and is among the hardiest, north into USDA zone 2. Smooth sumac tolerates a broader range of conditions than any other species and has the largest natural range. It grows from the southern edge of Ontario

TOP LEFT: Foliage and fruits of staghorn sumac (*Rhus typhina*). LEFT: A cutleaf selection of staghorn sumac displays the fiery fall color typical of the species. RIGHT: Winged sumac (*R. copallina*) in autumn.

and the vicinity of Lake Manitoba south throughout eastern North America to the Coastal Plain. 'Laciniata' is a terrific cultivar, and variety *cismontana* is a dwarf Rocky Mountain form that stays shrubby. Three additional selections of smooth sumac are under final evaluation for conservation use by the USDA. Botanists separate the geographic races of this small tree into distinct varieties, and the Rocky Mountain variety is becoming popular in cultivation.

Winged sumac (**Rhus copallina**), also called shining sumac, has more slender twigs, grows more slowly, and becomes less coarse than staghorn and smooth sumacs as it matures. 'Prairie Flame' is a compact cultivar found in eastern Illinois, and 'Creel's Quintet' is another listed cultivar. I recommend male winged sumac clones for landscape use; the dull, drooping fruit clusters of females are not very impressive, and the staminate flowers of the males are much more conspicuous than those of females (or those of most other sumac species). The leaves are glossy and provide a dressy background for the flowers, which bloom later than those of staghorn sumac. Although it is most at home in the South, winged sumac is hardy in USDA zone 5, and perhaps parts of zone 4.

Prairie sumac (**Rhus lanceolata**) looks like a more slender western version of winged sumac. It is found on disturbed sites in the Cross Timbers region and the Great Plains and is hardy to USDA zone 5. Fragrant sumac (**R. aromatica**) is one of several trifoliate shrub sumacs frequently seen in cultivation. It is usually more of a

groundcover than an erect plant, but some do try to become little trees. It is encountered frequently in cultivation.

Poison sumac is classified by some botanists as **Rhus vernix** and by others under the genus *Toxicodendron*, with poison ivy and poison oak. Poison sumac is unique in its preference for swampy ground, which is just as well since its ability to cause contact dermatitis would create havoc if it grew in upland areas frequented by people sensitive to its toxins. It is best admired from a distance, and the simplest barrier to use in preventing people from getting too close is to allow the wetland habitat this tree prefers to remain undisturbed. The most striking fall color of all sumacs might be the translucent ruby red of this untouchable species. When viewed in bloom or during the peak of fall color, reflected in shallow water from the safety of a shoreline or boardwalk, this swamp tree immediately becomes the aesthetic focus of the landscape. Poison sumac has a polka-dot natural range, in response to its wetland habitat requirements, throughout the eastern United States and the southern edge of Ontario.

A couple of sumacs thrive in the deserts of the Southwest. The evergreen sumac (**Rhus virens**) has gorgeous glossy foliage and bright red fruits that seem undaunted by desert winds and heat. The leaves are pubescent and friendly to the touch, making the plant useful in situations where it will be up close and personal. It seems to be a well-behaved species that typically does not form clonal mottes like other sumacs. **Rhus choriophylla** is similar except for its glabrous leaves and smaller, axillary fruit clusters, and it may be a more westerly variety of evergreen sumac. Both are southwestern species probably not hardy much north of USDA zone 8. Littleleaf sumac (**R. microphylla**) lives up to its name, with tiny leaves that give it a very fine texture quite unlike other members of the genus. It is commonly found in the Chihuahuan Desert and the dry mountain ranges of the Southwest. Like the other southwestern sumacs, it is more often a shrub than a tree in the wild, but can become a small tree under more favorable conditions under cultivation.

Other sumac species are found in Mexico and Asia. See *Cotinus obovatus*.

COMMENTS: Native Americans once valued sumacs for the variety of tonics and dyes that could be brewed from the fruits and bark. Modern woodcarvers might be tempted as well by the satiny, sulfur-green heartwood of a large sumac stem. Sumacs are as valuable for use as conservation plants, providing erosion control and wildlife habitat, as they are for ornamental planting. Once established, a sumac clone is capable of replacing cut or damaged stems with great vigor.

John Eastman, my favorite guru of tree lore, notes in *The Book of Forest and Thicket* (1992) that sumac stems have a thick, soft pith that can be poked out easily to make an effective blower for starting a campfire. But Henry David Thoreau might have been the first to document the resilience of sumac. He recorded the following in 1854 among his other notable observations regarding Walden Pond: "The sumach grew luxuriantly about the house, pushing up through the embankment which I had made, and growing five or six feet the first season." He went on at some length about the sumac's pleasant leaves, large buds, graceful form, crimson fruit, and how the young sprouts could be bent and broken under the weight of the hordes of bees that were attracted to the plant.

LEFT: The beautiful male flowers of winged sumac (*Rhus copallina*).

Robinia pseudoacacia
BLACK LOCUST

DESCRIPTION: Black locust is both admired and despised. It has been planted far beyond its limited natural range and has escaped from cultivation to invade pastures, prairies, and savannas with a tenacity equaled by no other native tree. It has caused considerable damage and expense as huge specimens deteriorate from borer damage and collapse upon roofs, fences, and automobiles. Yet it is one of the most beautiful, fast-growing, hardy, and durable trees in the landscape when healthy and is among the most effective species for erosion control and soil enrichment.

Black locust is the largest representative of a predominantly shrubby genus, and healthy trees on sunny sites become huge and singularly picturesque. The U.S. national champion grows in a front yard in Dansville, New York, well beyond its natural range, standing 96 feet (28.8 m) tall with a dark, fluted trunk 7.4 feet (2.3 m) thick. Such venerable old specimens, regardless of their physical condition, are always among the most photogenic of trees, especially when silhouetted against a colorful dawn sky. Often they are burly and contorted, assuming a character far beyond their years.

LEAVES: This tree is late to leaf out in spring, remaining bare until the sun warms the ground around its roots. When the leaves do emerge, they are pinnately compound and ferny in appearance, with smooth, oval leaflets each about 1 inch (2.5 cm) long, and cast a light, open shade. They are blue-green, contrasting beautifully with the dark, furrowed bark. On vigorous twigs they are joined at their bases by paired stipular spines. Some trees display no significant fall color, remaining green until blasted by a hard freeze, while others develop a nice yellow.

FLOWERS AND FRUIT: The legume flowers of this species are bright white, while those of several related species are pink. Locusts in general are among the most attractive and fragrant of all trees, their flowers developing in conspicuous clusters. Like many legume flowers, locust flowers are valuable as a honey source and are a favorite of hummingbirds. Black locust seeds are borne in clustered, brown legume pods about 4 inches (10 cm) long, resembling those of redbud (*Cercis canadensis*).

BEST SEASONS: LATE SPRING (during the spectacular blooming period). SUMMER (the ferny foliage is held on gracefully arching branches and is not so dense as to hide the rugged, fluted architecture of the tree). FALL (for exceptional trees with good fall color) and WINTER (for the character of the branching structure and bark on old trees).

NATIVE AND ADAPTIVE RANGE: Black locust has been cultivated intensively for so long that the exact limits of its original range are not known with much precision. In general it is a native tree of the Appalachian Mountains and the Ozark Plateau. As a naturalized species it has become thoroughly established over the majority of eastern North America and in portions of the West, and it has been planted successfully in South America, Europe, Africa, Asia, Australia, and New Zealand. It is rated hardy in cultivation north to USDA zone 3.

CULTURE: The operative instruction with black locust is "plant it and get out of the way." Given any well-drained soil, with or without nitrogen (locust fixes its own), and a sunny exposure, it will outgrow anything else in the woods. Once established, its clonal root system can dominate the surrounding area with root suckers unless the tree is maintained as a single stem by periodic sucker removal. Open-grown trees develop narrow crotches that should be pruned out, preferably in late summer or fall to avoid excessive bleeding of sap.

Black locust can be grown from root cuttings or by dividing thickets of suckers in the dormant season, and young trees either of seedling or sucker origin transplant without difficulty. Seeds germinate quickly once the hard seed coats have been cracked or scarified to allow them to soak up water.

PROBLEMS: The classic black locust pest is the locust borer (*Megacyllene robinae*), and of equal but more recent concern is the related, imported Asian longhorned borer beetle (*Anoplophora glabripennis*). Both insects can make Swiss cheese out of pole-sized trees, which commence to break in the wind wherever borer tunnels are most concentrated. Another insect, the locust twig borer (*Ecdytolopha insiticiana*), attacks seedlings and smaller twigs of old trees. Vigorous locusts growing in combination with

other trees in a forest setting are seldom damaged by borers. As is the case with many borer situations, stressed trees in monotypic stands invite attack. Some black locusts seem resistant to locust borer attack, but for most of these the cause has not been confirmed as being genetic versus environmental.

Other problems with this tree are due mostly to its untamed nature. Vigorous young twigs have sharp, strong thorns paired at each leaf axil, making leather gloves mandatory when pruning. Black locust roots are allelopathic to some other plants (but encourage turf growth), and in turn are suppressed by the allelopathy of goldenrod (*Solidago*), the food plant of the adult locust borer. As the locust tries to shade out the goldenrod, the goldenrod responds by working with the insect as an ally to attack the locust.

When the tree is comfortable on a mesic site with its roots undisturbed and growing in loamy, neutral soil, suckering is not an unmanageable problem. I have to remove no more than one or two suckers annually near my tree. Understory shade also seems to inhibit suckering. However, trees growing on strip-mine tailings, degraded pastures, or sandy prairies and savannas seem almost desperate to claim territory and soon dominate their neighborhoods with an impenetrable maze of thorny suckers.

Black locust is also notable for the problems it resists. Gypsy moth (*Lymantria dispar*), the scourge of the deciduous forest, won't touch it. Drought has no effect on established trees, nor does salt spray from road deicing. Sterile, infertile soils are perfectly satisfactory for its growth and are improved by its presence. The wood is as strong as that of any native tree, unless it has been damaged by borers, and resists damage from ice, wind, and decay.

CULTIVARS: Europeans have been fascinated with this American tree for centuries and have been responsible for developing most of its cultivars, such as the pink-flowered hybrids 'Idaho' and 'Decaisneana'. There are cultivars with no thorns ('Crispa', 'Inermis'), with unique foliage ('Aurea', 'Dissecta', 'Frisia', 'Macrophylla', 'Unifolia'), and with unusual form ('Pendula', 'Pyramidalis', 'Tortuosa', 'Twisty Baby', 'Umbraculifera'). 'Umbraculifera' is called parasol locust in the nursery trade. It is a fanciful lollipop-tree consisting of a shrubby form

LEFT: A black locust (*Robinia pseudoacacia*) blooming. TOP RIGHT: Black locust flowers. RIGHT: The typical deliquescent form of open-grown black locust .

grafted high on a standard trunk, and unfortunately it is much too common in the gardens of North America.

The Steiner Group consists of 'Appalachia', 'Allegheny', and 'Algonquin', vigorous USDA seed germplasm selections reportedly resistant to locust borer. The group originated from trees in Virginia and West Virginia and excelled in tests for growth rate and straightness. 'Appalachia' was named in 1956, while the others were added to the group in 1987 following many years of evaluation.

SIMILAR AND RELATED SPECIES: Hojalito (***Robinia neomexicana***) is a smaller but erect tree that looks identical to black locust until it blooms. Rich pink to purple flower clusters make this species a very attractive ornamental tree, prized by plant breeders as a source of pink pigment for hybridization. It is found in the mountainous "sky islands" of the Southwest and forms clonal thickets just like black locust. Some of the tallest specimens are found around Emory Pass in the Black Range of the Gila National Forest in New Mexico and up to 9500 feet (2850 m) elevation on Hillsboro Peak. The largest specimen grows in the Tonto National Forest of Arizona and is 71 feet (21.3 m) tall with a trunk diameter of more than 2 feet (60 cm).

A complex of species called bristly locust consists of ***Robinia fertilis,*** a diploid species, and **R. hispida,** a triploid. Both are low, suckering plants with prominent pink flowers. *Robinia hispida* 'Arnot' is a selection promoted by the USDA for erosion control. It tends to do its job too well, spreading and suckering with a vengeance. Clammy locust (**R. viscosa**) is a small, pink-blooming tree from the southern Appalachian Mountains.

COMMENTS: Black locust sleeps at night: the leaves fold together like the pages of a book and wait for daylight before unfolding again. This trait is shared with many tropical and herbaceous legumes but is unusual among temperate trees.

This species was among the trees cultivated by Native Americans prior to the arrival of European colonists. They planted it near their dwellings along the Atlantic Coast and used the wood for bows. Later, pioneers found the decay-resistant wood ideal for the sills of their buildings, for fence posts, and for firewood. Following the War of 1812, in which locust pegs served so well in holding together the American fleet, the British parliament was so impressed that it ordered enough American locust

wood to refit the entire English navy. (Weapons-grade locust, anyone?) Trees growing in dense groves make very tall, arrow-straight trunks, while those in open areas are arching, recurved, and quite picturesque as they mature.

Although the genus is endemic to North America, true locust lovers seem to be concentrated in Europe, where locust borer, a North American insect, is apparently not a problem. Gardener Jean Robin brought black locust seeds to Paris as early as 1601, and his son Vespasien transplanted one of those locusts in 1636. This specimen, the oldest on record, still grows in the great garden of the Paris Museum of Natural History, its old limbs propped up with bars and its trunk adorned with a crude sign that outlines its history and reveals its remarkable antiquity.

LEFT: *Robinia pseudoacacia* 'Frisia' is a gold selection of black locust. RIGHT: The pink flowers of bristly locust (*R. hispida*).

Sabal palmetto

CABBAGE PALM

DESCRIPTION: Cabbage palm, the state tree of South Carolina and Florida, is unique among the trees in this book because it is a monocot. This makes it a closer relation to grasses and cereal grains than to the conifers and broadleaved dicots commonly thought of as trees. The palms as a family are the most valuable of all trees for food, shelter, and barter material in tropical regions throughout the world, but very few can be seen in our area. Cabbage palm is the most common large palm in eastern North America, and it and some of its relatives are the hardiest of all palms.

Palms don't add growth rings to their diameter as they grow, as other trees do. A palm's thickness depends mostly upon its relative vigor at the point in its history when the terminal growth bud was located at the height where the trunk is being measured. I have never seen a cabbage palm 2 feet (60 cm) in diameter, but some come close. The U.S. national champion has a long trunk nearly 2 feet thick and 60 feet (18 m) tall. Cabbage palms grow slowly, so this specimen truly must be one of the senior citizens of central Florida.

LEAVES: Cabbage palms are evergreen, shedding older leaves, stalk and all, as new ones emerge from the growing tip, and maintaining a constant array of thirty to forty leaves at any one time. The feathery leaves are supported by hard, woody stalks that form the functional branches of the tree, in total reaching as much as 8 feet (2.4 m) out from the trunk on all sides.

FLOWERS AND FRUIT: Huge clusters of tiny flowers hang several feet from the crown of the tree, originating at the growing point among the new leaves. They are greenish white in color and develop into dark, pea-sized, spherical, edible fruits. Each fruit contains a brown pit, or seed. Ground-foraging birds like turkeys eat the fruits as they fall, and gulls and jays pick them from the trees.

BEST SEASONS: WINTER (for its evergreen foliage). ALL YEAR (a graceful accent plant in any season).

NATIVE AND ADAPTIVE RANGE: This is a tree of Florida and the Atlantic Coastal Plain, following the coastline up to Cape Fear in southern North Carolina. It can tolerate hard winter freezes and can be grown in cultivation north into the warmer parts of USDA zone 7, especially in the coastal habitats it prefers.

CULTURE: Cabbage palm is a carefree tree that likes full sun but will grow in partial shade. It inhabits sandy soils in the wild but seems willing to adjust to tighter soils in cultivation as long as it has good drainage. It seems immune to the salt spray of its coastal habitat, joining live oak (*Quercus virginiana*) on beachheads and barrier islands.

This tree grows slowly in the nursery, but large old specimens can be transplanted easily with virtually no root balls, since new adventitious roots regenerate from the base of the tree rather than from cut root ends. This combination of characteristics can lead to "palm rustling" for landscaping and to gradual localized depletion of our once-vast native palm stands.

Most landscapers now remove the leaves, or fronds, when transplanting these trees in order to reduce transpiration until the roots regenerate. The alternative, and the standard practice with most other palm species, is to remove the lower leaves and tie up the rest during reestablishment. Transplanting should be done during the active growing season, when roots regenerate most quickly. Plant all palms shallowly to place their root regeneration zone high in the soil profile, and stake as needed—without puncturing or abrading the trunk—until they reestablish.

Old leaves will turn brown and hang from the base of the crown for long periods unless they are trimmed away. They make great habitat for birds and bats but also for some of the undesirables of rodent persuasion. The decision to trim or not to trim is a matter of aesthetic preference; the palm does fine either way, as long as the trimming is done correctly. Try to leave the wishbonelike frond bases, or boots, instead of skinning the trunk (this can be an art form when done by a practiced professional), and take care to avoid damaging the trunk or bud. Tall specimens should be trimmed by a certified arborist who knows about proper palm maintenance and is trained

RIGHT: Cabbage palm (*Sabal palmetto*) grows with oaks on a coastal barrier island.

and equipped to do the job safely. You may also choose to have fruit clusters removed before they begin to shed, especially if the tree overhangs a driveway or sidewalk.

Propagation from freshly collected seed is best. Soak the cleaned seeds for a few days, then sow them in a moist, sterile peat-sand mix or commercial soil-less potting medium. The mix should be maintained at room temperature, or preferably higher, and watered as necessary. The seeds will begin to send up little spears—their first fronds—within a few weeks.

PROBLEMS: This primitive tree has one apical meristem, or growing point, which is located in the cabbage-like bud at its tip. If the bud is destroyed, the tree cannot grow new leaves and eventually dies. Because it has no cambium, it is also unable to overgrow or heal trunk wounds. These characteristics must be remembered when climbing or trimming this tree, since any such damage will not be forgiven. Never use climbing spikes or other devices that pierce the trunk, and preserve the terminal bud at all costs.

A widespread decline is affecting some cabbage palm groves in Florida. It is most noticeable in low areas and has been attributed to the intrusion of salt water into the root zone. Scientists believe this may be due to subtle rises in sea level caused by global warming. Several palms, including this one, are also susceptible to the fatal fungus *Ganoderma zonatum*, introduced from Malaysia. Cabbage palm seems to be more resistant than many other palm species to lethal yellowing (LY) phytoplasma disease.

CULTIVARS: Since cabbage palms cannot be grafted or grown from cuttings, cultivars have not been developed and propagated.

SIMILAR AND RELATED SPECIES: A smaller relative, bush palmetto (**Sabal minor**), extends further west along the Gulf Coast and grows as far north as Albemarle Sound in northern North Carolina. Besides the bush palmetto, there are a few other shrubby species of this genus and of the similar genus *Serenoa* in our area. They are known by names such as dwarf palmetto, saw palmetto, and scrub palmetto, and seldom develop erect, treelike stems of any significant size. *Sabal minor* and **Serenoa repens** form understory thickets and are among the hardiest of all palms.

LEFT: Cabbage palms (*Sabal palmetto*) can have their dead fronds removed, or they may be left for wildlife habitat. RIGHT: Bush palmetto (*Sabal minor*) is an understory palm.

Sabal mexicana is a large species from southern Texas and subtropical Mexico and is similar to cabbage palm. **Sabal louisiana** is similar to bush palmetto and occupies much the same range but more often reaches tree size. Several thousand other palm species can be found in tropical areas around the world.

COMMENTS: The hardy palmetto palms can be powerful design tools for the landscape, their presence creating the illusion of a tropical paradise in a warm-temperate climate. However, as with any tree that is unique and conspicuous among its neighbors, placement of a palm in a landscape should be tempered with a liberal dose of harmony. Strong design elements like palms call attention to themselves and look ridiculous if they don't fit the design theme. On the other hand, they always look great in their natural setting and should be preserved wherever they occur in the wild.

Cabbage palms serve a vital ecological function among trees on the seashore as the first, and most tenacious, line of defense against hurricanes and tropical storms, bending and recoiling before winds that shatter other trees. My wife and I once watched a group of cabbage palms on the seaward side of Hunting Island, South Carolina, during one of those notorious Atlantic storms. With their roots firmly anchored in the beach at the high tide mark, on the very battlefront of land and sea, they rolled with every punch of the wind like the flexible sea oat grass that fought beside them, impervious to gusts, waves, and salt spray. The next morning they stood in the warm Carolina sun with every leaf intact, as if nothing had happened, just as their species has done through countless storms in the past.

Salix lucida

SHINING WILLOW

DESCRIPTION: Willows are the ubiquitous trees and shrubs of bright light and moist soils throughout the temperate climate areas of the world. Some become huge trees, while others, like shining willow and its related species, show their stuff closer to eye level. The genus comprises countless species and hybrids and, like the oaks (*Quercus*), seems to evolve before our eyes. Many willows offer highly ornamental bark, flowers, or foliage. In the foliage category, the finest of all must be the shining willow.

This species is always admired when seen in landscapes, perhaps in part because it mimics bay willow (*Salix pentandra*), an Old World species used in European ornamental horticulture for centuries. It has a densely pyramidal growth habit when grown in the open, generally topping out as a bushy small tree in cultivation but often forming shrubby thickets in the wild. The largest recorded shining willow was measured in Traverse City, Michigan, in 1985 at 74 feet (22.2 m) tall with a trunk more than 3 feet (0.9 m) in diameter.

LEAVES: Some willows are planted for their early spring catkins, others for their colorful winter bark. If you are looking for a native willow that offers gorgeous, lustrous foliage for the entire growing season, plant shining willow. The leaves resemble those of wild cherry (*Prunus serotina*) in general outline and are similar in size, growing to about 5 inches (12.5 cm) long. Green on both sides, the glossy leaves, and the young twigs that support them, are smooth as if lacquered, shimmering in the sun. Like most willow leaves, they turn yellow in fall.

FLOWERS AND FRUIT: All willows are dioecious, and their pistillate flowers and fruits are miniature versions of those of poplars (*Populus*), with which they share a common lineage. The flowers of many staminate willows are the "pussy" catkins seen in early spring wherever these plants grow. Those of male shining willows emerge late, after the leaves, and their rich yellow anthers highlight the gloss of the leaves.

BEST SEASONS: SUMMER (the shiny foliage adds life to any landscape). ALL YEAR (the first-year twigs are attractive as well and show to advantage even after the foliage has dropped; many other willow species are at their best in winter or early spring).

NATIVE AND ADAPTIVE RANGE: Shining willow covers the Laurentian Shield of eastern Canada, dipping to encircle the Great Lakes, and extends eastward throughout New England and the Acadian provinces. Many willow species exhibit amazing cold tolerance; I have hiked on groundcovers of alpine willows in central Alaska, and a few shrubby species grow on tundra and permafrost right up to the Arctic Ocean. Shining willow can be grown from USDA zone 2 south into the cooler, moister portions of the eastern United States. Its nemesis is not cold but summer drought.

CULTURE: All willows have basic, imperative requirements: full sun; uninterrupted access to moisture during the growing season; loose, sandy or organic soil; and occasional control of the myriad organisms that attack them. Given this, they are fascinating plants to work with.

The perishable seeds of all willows are tricky to germinate unless you catch them within hours of their ripening, but most species, including shining willow, can be propagated from dormant hardwood cuttings simply by jamming a fresh stick into the ground, top end up, in late winter. The more scientific method is to clip a finger-sized section about 12 inches (30 cm) long from a vigorous stem of the desired gender in early spring, immerse its bottom half in water at room temperature for a few days, in total darkness, and pot it up as soon as root primordia (little white bumps) and adventitious roots begin to break through the bark. Willow cuttings contain salicylic acid, a rooting stimulant as well as a headache remedy, and are useful in promoting rooting of other cuttings immersed in water with them.

Willows grow very quickly—at least most tree forms do—and can be transplanted without difficulty. Seedlings sometimes spring up by the thousands in newly disturbed sites if the conditions and timing are exactly right, and may be moved with a trowel to preferred locations if desired. The ornamental values of willows (bark,

RIGHT: Shining willow (*Salix lucida*) along the pondshore at Starhill Forest.

male flowers, foliage) are enhanced by vigorous growth, which in turn is stimulated by adequate water and heavy, but judicious, pruning. Such pruning is also necessary to remove broken and diseased wood.

PROBLEMS: Willows are brittle and messy. They have aggressive roots that exploit the moisture found in drains and sewers. They are typically short lived, quick to decay, and prone to damage from nearly every insect and canker that lives. I have had willows in our study collection in Illinois disfigured by antler-rubbing deer, cut by beavers, skinned by rabbits, peeled by squirrels, mutilated by fungus diseases, and defoliated by almost every species of phytophagous insect that ever lived. They are particularly tasty to the imported Gypsy moth (*Lymantria dispar*) and Asian longhorned borer beetle (*Anoplophora glabripennis*). Some people have little good to say about willows, but others are willing to overlook their many faults and admire their seasonal beauty and optimistic vigor.

CULTIVARS: There are no cultivars of shining willow on the market. It is difficult enough to find the plant for sale as a species, and much simpler to propagate it by cuttings from a wild plant found down by an old ditch. Other willows, chiefly those that have been cultivated in

Europe for millennia, are available as selected clones. Willows also hybridize without shame, and some of the hardy weeping forms have developed from such crosses.

SIMILAR AND RELATED SPECIES: Pussy willow (**Salix discolor**) is a small native tree or shrub, famous for its satiny male catkins. Actually, staminate plants of many willows have outstanding catkin displays in late winter or early spring, including native species like Bebb willow (**S. bebbiana**) as well as some popular exotic species. Bebb willow can become a small tree but usually does so reluctantly, often crawling artistically across the ground for a bit as a decumbent shrub before finally ascending toward the sky in a sinuous fashion. It can be found from Alaska to Mexico and eastward across the entire continent via the northern Great Plains to Newfoundland and Maryland.

Sandbar willows (**Salix interior** in the East, **S. exigua** in the West) occasionally reach tree size but more often form stoloniferous thickets that serve well for soil stabilization and wildlife cover along streams and lakeshores. They are similar, sometimes even considered varieties of the same species. Both are very erect and slender in leaf and twig. *Salix interior* (syn. *S. exigua* var. *pedicellata*) has fewer teeth on the leaves and minor differences in the seed capsules. *Salix exigua*, also known as coyote willow, often has beautiful, bright bark. Both types are hardy north well into Canada. Some superior sandbar willow clones are being tested, and the winners will be released by the USDA for erosion control.

Willows are basically northern trees, but the South has the Carolina willow (**Salix caroliniana**). It grows into an upright small tree in wetlands from Pennsylvania and Kansas south to the Florida Everglades. Missouri willow (**S. eriocephala**) is very similar and is found mostly in the Missouri River valley. The Southwest also has a few willows. Yew willow (**S. taxifolia**) is found as a small tree growing along streams in western Texas. It has tiny leaves with a silvery hue and is very ornamental. Unlike most willows in our region, it is hardy north only in USDA zone 7. Arroyo willow (**S. lasiolepis**) is the common species found along washes and gullies throughout the West. Yew and arroyo willows are both small, erect trees.

In all, there may be close to one hundred willow species in North America, two hundred more worldwide, and innumerable hybrids. See *Salix nigra* for additional information.

COMMENTS: Many of our most beautiful butterflies are drawn to willows, including the distinctive mourning cloak, the red-spotted purple, the twin-spotted sphinx moth, the giant poplar sphinx moth, several underwing moths, the magnificent cecropia, and the monarchlike viceroy, with its larvae that mimic bird droppings. Each causes a little damage, but they should be encouraged in moderation for their aesthetic contributions to the landscape. If the larvae become too concentrated they may be relocated by hand to wild willows nearby or to acceptable alternate food plants.

Willows require a certain tolerance of their problems, a commitment to routine maintenance, and the realization that nothing is forever. Once these things are understood, they are simple to propagate and transplant, vigorous in growth, graceful in form, attractive to wildlife, and colorful. As they grow and decline, to be cut and grow again, willows remind us that the living garden is a dynamic entity, constantly in flux.

LEFT: An expanded staminate catkin on a male shining willow (*Salix lucida*). BELOW: Staminate catkins of Bebb willow (*S. bebbiana*). BOTTOM: Fall color on sandbar willow (*S. interior*). RIGHT: Sandbar willow can grow either as a slender tree or a shrub.

Salix nigra

BLACK WILLOW

DESCRIPTION: Various willows can be seen alongside every stream, puddle, and swamp throughout North America. Some are small but nonetheless grow into tree form. Some are large and become massive trees, but these are brittle and seldom grown in developed landscapes. The ubiquitous black willow is typical of these larger types. It is a huge species with clumping, leaning stems. This species and the similar peachleaf willow (*Salix amygdaloides*) are the most common large native willow trees of North America.

Black willow can be found wherever there is standing or flowing water and bright sun. It is a pioneer tree on floodplains, colonizing new bars and the bases of caving banks. If it grows quickly enough to stay above the shade of competing trees, and if it is able to avoid major damage from ice, wind, flood, or myriad other hazards, it can become a very large tree. One specimen in Grand Traverse County, Michigan, stands 76 feet (22.8 m) tall with a trunk that is 10 feet (3 m) thick.

LEAVES: The leaves of this species typify what we think of as willow leaves. They are 2 to 4 inches (5 to 10 cm) long and very narrow, with tiny teeth along the margins, tapering from an abrupt base to a long point. They are green on both surfaces and turn yellow in fall, color being better some years than others. Each leaf is joined at the base by a pair of stipules.

FLOWERS AND FRUIT: Staminate and pistillate flowers are found on separate trees. Black willow catkins are not particularly conspicuous compared with those of some other willows. Seeds are shed early in summer, hopefully landing on the wet exposed mud or sand of a creek bank just after the spring floods.

BEST SEASONS: SPRING (the emerging new foliage gives this tree nice texture). SUMMER (a picturesque, often artistic shade tree) and FALL (for fall color).

NATIVE AND ADAPTIVE RANGE: Black willow is found in wet areas through eastern North America from southern Maine to northern Florida and west to Minnesota, southeastern Nebraska, and central Texas, then in a more spotty distribution all the way to the Pacific. It is hardy in USDA zone 3.

CULTURE: Willows as a genus need full sun, adequate water, and freedom from weed competition. They are tricky to grow from seed but are easy to transplant and can be grown readily from cuttings, which give the added advantage of gender predetermination (see *Salix lucida* for more cultural details). Black willow grows very quickly, and well-grown specimens can make attractive, fine-textured lawn trees, casting a filtered shade that is friendly to turf and other undergrowth. It will perform much better, however, if competition is controlled. Periodic pruning is necessary to remove broken or cankered limbs and to maintain the desired structure.

PROBLEMS: All large willows are litter factories, requiring vigilant ground patrol if tidy turf is desired beneath them. See *Salix lucida* for discussion of other willow problems.

CULTIVARS: I have found no reference citing cultivars of black willow.

SIMILAR AND RELATED SPECIES: Peachleaf willow (**Salix amygdaloides**) is another large species. Its leaves are bigger and broader than those of black willow and are silvery underneath. This, coupled with its yellow twigs and slightly weeping form, make it active and colorful on windy days. Like most willows it is very hardy, at least into USDA zone 3, but it can also be found along desert streams and arroyos in the hot Southwest. While its range is generally more westerly than that of black willow, the record-size tree grows in Wisconsin and has about ten stems that combine to reach 80 feet (24 m) in height.

Scouler willow (**Salix scouleriana**) is a very hardy mountain species found above 5000 feet (1500 m) elevation and up nearly to timberline throughout the Rockies and more western ranges from Alaska south, extending east in Canada past the north shore of Lake Winnipeg and along the Nelson River valley nearly to Hudson Bay. It has colorful reddish yellow twigs and shorter, spatulate leaves that are not toothed. This is one of our best willows for conspicuous staminate catkin displays in

RIGHT: Black willows (*Salix nigra*) growing along a prairie stream.

454

early spring, and it will tolerate more shade in an open wooded setting than most other willows. It is hardy north into USDA zone 2. Scouler willow does not grow as large as black willow but still can become a good-sized tree up to 60 feet (18 m) tall. The largest known specimen, found in Washington State by my tree-hunter friends Bob Van Pelt and Ron Brightman, is a shade under 4 feet (1.2 m) in diameter.

The Gooddings willow (*Salix gooddingii*) is a broadly spreading southwestern species similar to black willow. The U.S. national champion, located in New Mexico, is only 45 feet (13.5 m) tall but has a trunk more than 9 feet (2.7 m) through. Pacific willow (*S. lasiandra*) is much like a larger version of shining willow (*S. lucida*). This is chiefly a northwestern species; its distribution is spotty in the northern Rockies, and it becomes more prevalent west of our region.

Salix is among our most complex and confusing genera, and many willows are too obscure or too shrubby to be described. The European crack willow (*S. fragilis*) and white willow (*S. alba*) are widely naturalized and grow to be very large. Several selections and hybrids of white willow are seen in cultivation, displaying the traditional weeping-willow form or the customary gold or red bark.

COMMENTS: Several black willows have grown spontaneously along Rock Creek at Starhill Forest. During the past two decades I have watched them develop from head-high seedlings into mature trees more than 60 feet (18 m) tall. Some people believe that such fast-growing but often short-lived trees are best planted by old gardeners who have no time to waste. I disagree. Old gardeners have acquired the patience and wisdom to know that a tree can become a memorial to its planter, so they plant the most permanent species available. It is the young gardener, the novice with the impatience of youth, to whom we should introduce the willow. Give a child an unrooted black willow cutting the size of a pencil, photograph that child standing next to it with each passing birthday, and watch the child's fascination grow with the tree as it reaches massive proportions by the time he or she is ready to introduce it to his or her own children.

TOP LEFT: The attractive slender leaves of black willow (*Salix nigra*). LEFT: Black willow makes an irregular, picturesque silhouette in winter. TOP RIGHT: Gooddings willow (*Salix gooddingii*) shades a wet area on the Great Plains. RIGHT: Peachleaf willow (*Salix amygdaloides*) thrives in the West from Canada to Mexico.

Sapindus drummondii
SOAPBERRY

DESCRIPTION: *Sapindus drummondii* (syn. *S. saponaria* var. *drummondii*), our native soapberry, is the hardiest member of a genus comprising perhaps forty species, mostly tropical and ranging here and there from Hawaii to Florida, Mexico, and Asia. Surprisingly, this distinctive little tree is not very well known in cultivation except within its natural range. I have admired soapberry at the Missouri Botanical Garden in St. Louis for many years, but it seems nearly impossible to find in the nursery trade.

This species is adaptable to many site conditions, including some of the most severe ones, but makes its best growth on rich limestone soils. It often forms streamside thickets of small clonal stems in the southern Great Plains, though isolated individuals can become much larger. The current U.S. national champion is located in Corpus Christi, Texas. It stands 62 feet (18.6 m) high with a trunk more than 3 feet (0.9 m) in diameter. Three trees previously shared the record, growing in Texas, Oklahoma, and Alabama. The former champions are more slender, like most large specimens I have seen, but approach the height of the current record tree.

LEAVES: Soapberry leaves are pinnately compound, leathery, and fine in texture. They reach about 12 inches (30 cm) in length and are like those of black walnut (*Juglans nigra*) in that the terminal leaflet is seldom present. They turn a rich gold in autumn.

FLOWERS AND FRUIT: Flowers are dioecious, forming showy white clusters in early summer. Pistillate trees bear grapelike clumps of yellow spherical fruits that become translucent as they ripen, each with a single black seed. They look a bit like fat golden raisins, but they are not palatable. In fact, these attractive fruits are reportedly poisonous, at least to the fish that inhabit ponds where they fall. The toxic substance they contain is called saponin. Most fruit clusters persist into or through the

RIGHT: Groves of soapberry (*Sapindus drummondii*) are common in the southern Great Plains.

following winter, giving female trees a golden sparkle when backlit on bright winter days. The hard seeds polish to a beautiful ebony color and may be drilled and strung as beads.

BEST SEASONS: FALL (for the golden foliage and lacy appearance, and for the mature fruits on female trees). SUMMER (this attractive, tough, small tree with heavy, strong wood has a deceptively delicate appearance and nice flowers that appear in early summer). WINTER (for the combination of bark, picturesque form, and clinging fruits, which bring life to the bleakest of winters).

NATIVE AND ADAPTIVE RANGE: Our primary native soapberry species is called western soapberry to distinguish it from two subtropical eastern species, and it is encountered most commonly in the southwestern United States and adjacent Mexico; but it also thrives from Texas north through Oklahoma and most of Kansas, eastward into Missouri, and southeast to portions of Louisiana. Under cultivation I have found it hardy north into the warmer parts of USDA zone 5, making it one of our hardiest Southwest desert trees.

CULTURE: Full sun is needed, but soapberry will grow well (and usually slowly) in most soils, tolerating a higher pH than most eastern forest trees. It seems to thrive on the prairie soils of the lower Midwest. Small soapberry trees are easy to transplant if grown under cultivation in decent garden soil with ample water to encourage a shallow root system. The severed roots left

TOP LEFT: Fall color of soapberry (*Sapindus drummondii*). LEFT: Bark and fruit clusters of soapberry. BELOW: The translucent ripe fruits of soapberry glisten in the winter sun. RIGHT: A large Mexican buckeye (*Ungnadia speciosa*) grows along an arroyo in the Texas desert.

behind will send up sprouts that may be dug the following year to propagate more ramets of the same gender. Once established they tolerate drought, heat, wind, poor soil, air pollution, and most other hazards of the natural or urban environment.

The seeds should be scarified to ensure uniform germination and planted outdoors in fall or early winter. Wear rubber gloves to guard against skin irritation when removing seeds from the gummy pulp of the fruits. Seedlings are easy to start and occasionally volunteer under older trees, where they can be difficult to tell from root sprouts until you try to dig them. They develop taproots, so they should be transplanted early, undercut, or grown in a moist, friable planting bed to discourage this trait until they reach their permanent home.

PROBLEMS: The fruits become leathery and dry during early winter and usually don't create the slimy litter problem you might expect from their appearance unless they are crushed underfoot and then soaked by rain. They can be hazardous, however, if small children or pets try to eat them. Soapberry might form clonal thickets if permitted to do so, which can be good or bad, depending upon the landscape objective. The worst problem is lack of commercial availability: *Sapindus* seems to be a well-kept secret. I have found no records of diseases or insects bothering this species.

CULTIVARS: No cultivars are available commercially, and one or two selections should be made, at least for gender. Individual specimens selected for form, vigor, hardiness, or gender may be grown from stem cuttings

taken in spring or from root cuttings taken during the dormant season, so I wouldn't be too surprised if someone was looking into cultivar development.

SIMILAR AND RELATED SPECIES: Other soapberries are tropical or subtropical trees or shrubs. Wingleaf soapberry (**Sapindus saponaria**), considered by some to include variety *drummondii*, is found in southern Florida. Florida soapberry (**S. marginatus**) is a coastal species found in hammocks in northern and central Florida.

Mexican buckeye (**Ungnadia speciosa**) is a relative that can become a small tree in desert canyons of Texas and New Mexico. It is used in cultivation in the Southwest for its pink flowers. Its small, poisonous fruits look very much like those of the unrelated true buckeyes (*Aesculus*). Mexican buckeye is not reliably hardy much north of USDA zone 8. Soapberry's most popular other relatives are the exotic goldenrain trees (**Koelreuteria**).

The fuzzy, evergreen wild-olive (**Cordia boissieri**) is an unrelated tree equally at home in the desert landscape. It has showy white trumpet flowers that rebloom after every summer rain, and bears small, fleshy fruits. I have found it very easy to grow from fresh seed, but it has a more difficult reputation in the literature, so perhaps I was just lucky. Wild-olive can be grown as a tree from USDA zone 8 south into Mexico, and as a shrub in USDA zone 7 where it frequently freezes back. The U.S. record specimen, in southern Texas, is 25 feet (7.5 m) tall with a broader spread and a trunk about 2 feet (60 cm) in diameter. However, I have seen bigger specimens of this hot-blooded tree in Mexico.

Anacua (**Ehretia anacua**) is related and is similar to wild-olive but has stiff, sandpapery leaves. Like wild-olive, it needs a warm climate, and most of the same cultural notes apply. Its original Native American name, anaquatal, is reflected in its vernacular name and specific epithet. A little hardier than wild-olive, it can be grown in USDA zone 7 and is less likely to be killed back by freezing. The U.S. national champion, one of many beautiful specimens planted along the streets of Victoria, Texas, is 42 feet (12.6 m) tall, even a little broader than that, and well more than 4 feet (1.2 m) in diameter.

COMMENTS: The novice tree propagator always remembers that first encounter with soapberry because of the lather its fruits make in water. Native Americans living in the southern Great Plains knew about the soap value of this tree as well, just as they seemed to be aware of the potential uses of almost every other native plant. The pulp of most tree species with fleshy fruit is normally removed from the seed to facilitate scarification or storage, and a common process for cleaning small amounts of such seed is to squeeze and rub the fruits under water. In this case, however, the cleaning becomes literal, as the pulp unexpectedly erupts into such a soapy froth that you wonder if there is something in the water besides the berries.

I had such an introduction to soapberry years ago while trying to process fruit from a nice tree growing at Fort Massac State Park in southern Illinois. The tree was a large and handsome specimen that I later nominated as champion soapberry of Illinois. The record stood until Illinois decided to limit its big-tree program to state-native species, eliminating all records for exotic trees and trees native to other parts of North America. Thus, in a bit of tree irony, it's a record that no longer stands but will never be broken. When the park's historic fort was reconstructed with a big new parking lot and visitor center in the early 1970s, I was the state's historic landscape architect. I made sure the soapberries and other significant trees on the grounds were protected during design and construction. Most of them live on today.

RIGHT: The stunning flower display of wild-olive (*Cordia boissieri*).

Sassafras albidum

SASSAFRAS

DESCRIPTION: The aromatic sassafras is among our most colorful trees. It is very fast growing in good soil and is common in many forest openings, fence rows, and old fields. Sassafras frequently forms clonal thickets by suckering, which tends to limit the ultimate size and growth rate of all the ramets, due to competition. Single-stemmed individual trees more than 60 feet (18 m) tall and 3 feet (0.9 m) in diameter are not uncommon under favorable conditions.

The largest sassafras known anywhere, in Owensboro, Kentucky, is 78 feet (23.4 m) tall and 7 feet (2.1 m) in diameter. I have seen ancient wild trees in old-growth forests in Illinois that exceeded 100 feet (30 m) in height. A grove of venerable 60-foot (18-m) trees at the Helm farm near Tuscola, Illinois, was planted during the Civil War by then-owner Oliver Hackett. It remains a traffic stopper each autumn as the trees turn a brilliant orange.

The sympodial branching structure of sassafras forms graceful horizontal layers, as happens with some dogwoods (*Cornus*). This is caused by prolepsis. Sassafras wood is light and brittle (it can be pruned by slapping twigs off), but the excellent architecture of the branching makes the tree more resistant to storm damage than might be expected.

LEAVES: The leaves are smooth, sweetly fragrant when crushed, and 3 to 7 inches (7.5 to 17.5 cm) long. They are frequently unlobed on young seedlings and on the basipetal portions of twigs, but mitten shaped with one or two lobes on the upper parts of saplings and on vigorous shoots and suckers. The color is bright yellow-green in spring, maturing to blue-green in summer, and turning brilliant shades of red, gold, orange, or purple in autumn. All stems originating from a single clone turn the same color in fall.

FLOWERS AND FRUIT: Clusters of small yellow flowers appear in early spring before the leaves, making trees look like clouds of gold dust when viewed against a dark background. Most trees are dioecious, the female individuals bearing lustrous dark blue fruits on bright scarlet pedicels in late summer. The ripe fruits are sought by squirrels and many birds, who spread the seeds along fence-row perching areas. Among the greatest fans are bluebirds, catbirds, vireos, and quail.

BEST SEASONS: FALL (for the persistent scarlet fruit pedicels on female trees and the brilliant, dependable foliage color). EARLY SPRING (for the yellow flowers and branching pattern). WINTER (for the green twigs and artistic sympodial branching) and LATE SUMMER (for the dark fruit with contrasting pedicels).

NATIVE AND ADAPTIVE RANGE: Sassafras is native and well adapted throughout most of the East, South, and Midwest, north through USDA zone 5 into southern Ontario and west to eastern Oklahoma and the Big Thicket region of Texas.

CULTURE: Sassafras requires full sun for best growth. It is difficult to transplant from the wild unless true seedlings, rather than sprouts from roots, are selected. Transplant small wild seedlings in late winter (in the South) or early spring. Current-year seedlings can often be found in mulch beds under the trees and are easy to dig and relocate. New trees may be started from seeds planted outdoors in fall. Individual trees or clonal thickets display different growth forms and fall color patterns that can be reproduced vegetatively by taking root cuttings.

Maintain the young tree as a single stem by removing the occasional suckers, or cut back the stem and encourage sprouts to form a thicket for a mass of fall color at eye level. Once established, sassafras adapts to most soils, from dune sands to silty clays with hardpans. Clumps of sassafras can even be seen spreading along the rock ballast of abandoned railroads.

PROBLEMS: This tree is not readily available from most nurseries due to its reputation as being hard to transplant. However, I have moved trees up to 5 inches (12.5 cm) in diameter with success. The key is to avoid those that have developed from root suckers, and to dig a young tree with a large root ball in late winter. Better yet, buy or grow a small container-grown seedling, which can be transplanted with proper care in any season as long as the ground is not frozen.

Sassafras is intolerant of heavy shade and road salt and can be subject to vandalism when young because of

its brittle wood. A damaged young tree may be cut back to the ground; it will sprout a straight, vigorous replacement shoot, which should be protected from further abuse. Sassafras has no serious insect or disease problems and is resistant to decay.

Root-suckering is considered a problem when it creates unwanted additional trees. This can be reduced by avoiding damage or disturbance to the roots or stem of your sassafras, and any unwanted suckers can be pulled before they become woody. Sassafras is also allelopathic and can discourage the growth of some other plants within its root zone.

CULTIVARS: No named cultivars are available at present, but the natural beauty and variability of this tree make it a good candidate for horticultural selections. Propagation and transplantation methods should be researched further, encouraging the development of cloned varieties with predictable form, fall color, and gender.

SIMILAR AND RELATED SPECIES: No other sassafras species are found in the United States or Canada, although some botanists recognize varieties based upon superficial characteristics that are inconsequential to most of us. There is a similar species in central China. Other aromatic plants from the same family can be found in our area, such as spicebush (**Lindera benzoin**).

LEFT: A male sassafras (*Sassafras albidum*) in bloom at Starhill Forest. BELOW: Sassafras flowers brighten the early spring landscape. TOP RIGHT: Each sassafras may display a different color in fall, but all are brilliant. RIGHT: The humble sassafras can become a giant forest tree, towering over its neighbors.

This dioecious plant typically grows in shrub form with multiple stems, but as it can reach more than 20 feet (6 m) tall, it can be considered a small tree. A spicebush shades the rear patio at my house, reaching high enough to provide additional shade for the deck above. This species has such appealing red fruit (on female plants), early yellow dew-drop flowers (best on male plants), and spicy-fragrant leaves with bright yellow fall color that it can't be ignored. Spicebush grows north to USDA zone 4. It requires a moist, rich site but will tolerate shade very well. Selected cultivars include 'Green Gold', 'Rubra', and 'Xanthocarpa'. Seedlings germinate easily from seed sown in fall.

Red bay (**Persea borbonia**) is another attractive small tree in the same family. The hardiest member of the avocado genus, red bay grows along the Coastal Plain north to the Delmarva Peninsula, USDA zone 7. A handsome broadleaved evergreen tree of sandy soils, usually restricted in the wild to wetlands, it does well in cultivation on a variety of soil types where it is winter hardy. It may reach 50 feet (15 m) or more in height, and it is essentially free from pests. Seeds should be extracted from the small blue drupes and planted in fall. The spicy leaves may be used as bay leaves for flavoring casseroles. This should come as no surprise, because the exotic spices bay-leaf (**Laurus nobilis**), cinnamon (**Cinnamomum zeylanicum**), and camphor (**C. camphora**) are in the same family.

COMMENTS: Sassafras is among our most striking and aromatic trees, valued in the herbal traditions of Native Americans and used by many wildlife species. The medicinal bark was among the first products exported by the American Colonies, in as early as 1603; and the roots, dug in early spring, have been used to provide the rootbeer flavor of sassafras tea. I have enjoyed chewing sassafras twigs and drinking sassafras tea from our own trees over the years, but safrole, the active ingredient, was listed in 1976 as a mild carcinogen by the U.S. government, so sassafras tea can no longer be purchased in interstate commerce. Still, the famous filé of Creole cooking is made from powdered sassafras leaves.

If it weren't so well known for its culinary values and amazing fall color, sassafras might be called the lemondrop tree for its flower display. Seen among a grove of redbuds (*Cercis*) when both are in bloom, the tasty appearance is akin to a raspberry-lemon sherbet. Sassafras also serves as a host plant for some spectacular moths and butterflies, including the colorful palamedes and spicebush swallowtails; the giant promethea, imperial, and io silkmoths; the furry little crinkled flannel moth; and the tiny sassafras leafroller.

The giant old champion sassafras tree in Owensboro would not be there today except for a bit of legendary insurgency in 1957. The highway department had planned to widen Route 431, and the tree was in the way. As the bulldozers headed for the tree they were met by the lady of the house and her shotgun, loaded with double-ought buckshot. After a long standoff that some say lasted for days, the governor of Kentucky was called to resolve the matter. The governor looked at the tree, looked at the shotgun, looked at the highway, and finally looked across the highway. "Why can't we just widen it over there?" he asked, pointing to the other side of the road. Thankfully that confrontation occurred in a simpler period in our history, before SWAT teams and suicide terrorists. Nothing bad happened, either to the tree or to its stalwart guardian.

BELOW: Bright red fruits light up a female spicebush (*Lindera benzoin*). RIGHT: Red Bay (*Persea borbonia*) can become a fairly large tree with age. Photo by Ron Lance.

Sorbus americana

MOUNTAIN-ASH

DESCRIPTION: This decorative small tree is one of the most colorful inhabitants of boreal and montane forests. Its European and Asian cousins are more well known in cultivation, but our native species is every bit their equal within its natural range. It loves granitic rock outcrops, stream banks, and acidic soils and mixes with scattered conifers, bog plants, and birches (*Betula*), all of which combine in the natural landscape to create spring and fall scenes of postcard beauty.

Partly by nature and partly due to environmental circumstance, mountain-ash usually remains a small tree or large shrub. The largest specimen in the United States, in West Virginia, is 62 feet (18.6 m) tall and 2 feet (60 cm) in diameter. Other specimens at least as large can surely be found within the vast Canadian range of the species. Bigger is not always better, however. I have admired many mountain-ash shrubs on mountain balds where their colors are displayed at eye level, and many others clinging to rocky crags in Canada where their fall colors are backlit against the dark rock; and aesthetically, they would be tough to beat. Mountain-ash trees are equally impressive when viewed from an escarpment rim looking down, with their bright red fruits and orange fall foliage held high and showing nicely against the smooth, dark bark and the shaded valley floor. And they always look great in the garden if they are healthy and well maintained.

LEAVES: Mountain-ash leaves are pinnately compound, the eleven to seventeen leaflets sharply toothed and pointed, with each leaflet up to about 3 inches (7.5 cm) in length. The leaflets turn gold-orange in fall, each clinging to its bright red rachis and combining with the ripe fruit to create one of the most colorful displays of a very colorful season.

FLOWERS AND FRUIT: The fragrant flowers develop on new growth in late spring, after the foliage, but are positioned conspicuously at the ends of twigs rather than hidden among the leaves. They consist of broad white corymbs, about 4 inches (10 cm) across, and are very showy. The fruit clusters that follow are even showier, with their flame-red color and extended season. They ripen to full color in late summer and may cling all winter unless harvested by birds. Each fruit is a small pome, containing several small seeds.

BEST SEASONS: FALL (the color combination of leaflet, rachis, and fruit ranks this tree with the finest of all autumn standouts). LATE SPRING (during the blooming period).

NATIVE AND ADAPTIVE RANGE: Most members of this genus do best at high latitudes or high altitudes, and ours is no exception. Mountain-ash flourishes in eastern Canada north to Hudson Bay, penetrating southward into the United States mostly around cool bogs and in mountainous areas down through the Appalachians. It prospers in USDA zones 2 and 3, and declines gradually southward, becoming very unhappy from USDA zone 6 on down.

CULTURE: Mountain-ash is related to the cultivated fruit trees and was at one time classified in the same genus with the pome fruits. It benefits from the same insect- and disease-management programs used in the home orchard, since virtually every borer and foliage disease that plagues fruit orchards also attacks mountain-ash.

Young trees can be transplanted easily, and seed can be germinated successfully if stratified over winter or sown early in fall. The fruits may be crushed or fermented to remove the seeds, but I have grown seedlings by squeezing the fruits to break the skin and sowing them without further cleaning. Mountain-ash is sought by rabbits, deer, moose, and other browsing mammals for winter forage, so protection of the young stems and thin bark may be needed. This tree requires a cool, mulched root zone and acidic soil. It is unusual within its family for its tolerance of wet soil, but it does best with good drainage. It will grow in full sun or, especially near its southern limit, in light shade.

PROBLEMS: Mountain-ash is vulnerable to the same insects and diseases that affect downy serviceberry (see *Amelanchier arborea*) and also experiences problems with

RIGHT: A mountain-ash (*Sorbus americana*) shows its fall color in Ontario.

sunscald, anthracnose (*Glomerella cingulata*), and the introduced European mountain-ash sawfly (*Pristiphora geniculata*). In warm climates the round-headed apple borer (*Saperda candida*), a striped beetle with larvae that tunnel into the base of the tree, can be devastating. The thin bark is sensitive to sapsucker pecks and to mechanical damage and must be protected from misguided mowers and string-trimmers. This tree is weak wooded and develops multiple leaders, making it prone to ice breakage in portions of the Midwest and upper South where freezing rain often replaces snow.

Although many people in the Midwest and South try to grow mountain-ash, it is almost always a struggle that leads to an undignified specimen meeting an untimely end. Like paper birch (*Betula papyrifera*), this tree should be conceded to the gardeners of the North and the coolest mountain areas.

CULTIVARS: 'Tangerine Treasure', from Alberta, is a compact form. Most other cultivars of mountain-ash are derived from exotic species and hybrids. 'Belmonte' was selected from our native tree, but the selection was made from plantations in an arboretum in Holland. Given the propensity of this genus toward rampant hybridization, there might be reasonable doubt that such a selection is not a cross.

SIMILAR AND RELATED SPECIES: Showy mountain-ash (*Sorbus decora*) differs only in subtle ways: its leaflets are a little wider and toothed only about halfway to the base, its fruits shade toward vermilion, and its individual florets are a little larger. It is also hardy in USDA zone 2 and has similar problems in the hot summers of the South. Greene mountain-ash (*S. scopulina*) is our Rocky Mountain species, found at very high elevations in the southern Rockies and northward in progressively lower habitats nearly to the Arctic Circle. Sitka mountain-ash (*S. sitchensis*) is more westerly, entering our region only in the northern Rockies. Both western species are usually shrubby.

Perhaps seventy more mountain-ashes can be found in Europe and Asia. Several of these are popular landscape trees, and at least one, the European mountain-ash (*Sorbus aucuparia*), is widely naturalized across the boreal forests of North America. Whitebeam (*S. aria*), Korean mountain-ash (*S. alnifolia*), and several hybrids

TOP LEFT: Leaves of mountain-ash (*Sorbus americana*) in fall color. LEFT: Striking red fruits cling to a mountain-ash in late fall high in the Appalachians. RIGHT: Mountain-mahogany (*Cercocarpus montanus*).

are seen in cultivation in cool-climate areas. The true ashes (*Fraxinus*) are not related to mountain-ash.

Mountain-mahogany (**Cercocarpus montanus**) is a related western species that tolerates excessive heat, although it does imitate mountain-ash in preferring a high-elevation site. It will grow in either acidic or alkaline soils and is impervious to drought. The fruits resemble a needle and fuzzy thread. When they land on suitable soil, the feathery, threadlike awn acts as a parachute to ensure that the needlelike seed lands end-first and knifes into the ground. There are several forms or varieties of this species, which are sometimes separated into distinct species. The various taxa range from the United States–Mexico border north into Montana and east into Kansas. Where marauding deer can be kept away long enough, mountain-mahogany becomes a nice small tree with heavy, extremely hard wood.

The related curlleaf mountain-mahogany (**Cercocarpus ledifolius**) can become larger than mountain-mahogany and has narrower, smooth leaves. This is the biggest species, and the U.S. national champion is 21 feet (6.3 m) tall and 2 feet (60 cm) in diameter. Another relative,

the Chisos rosewood (**Vauquelinia angustifolia**), is our only native rosewood tree. This is a small evergreen tree with striking narrow leaves like those of desert-willow (*Chilopsis linearis*) and white flowers. It barely enters our area, in Big Bend National Park, but is seen occasionally in landscape plantings in southern Texas.

COMMENTS: The mountain-ash genus is a prime example of what botanists grudgingly call a plastic taxon. It refuses to stay between taxonomic lines, its many species interbreeding not only with one another but even with *Aronia*, *Amelanchier*, and other members of the great rose family. Mountain-ash species that overlap in range with each other blend through introgression to the extent that the individual species cannot be distinguished.

Tidy botanists in ivory towers don't like this, since they consider their precise concept of species to be inviolate. A species by definition is a taxonomic unit that does not interbreed readily with other species, and a genus is a higher class still, a collection of related species. Natural intergeneric crossing, therefore, should be utterly impossible. But mountain-ash is a taxonomic rebel of the first order.

Taxodium distichum

BALDCYPRESS

DESCRIPTION: Baldcypress, the state tree of Louisiana, is the universal symbol of the southern swamp. It sometimes grows slowly in its watery habitat, but it can do so for a thousand years or more. Old-growth baldcypress strands from southern Florida to southern Indiana and Illinois contain the oldest trees of any species in eastern North America.

Although they grow in excess of 100 feet (30 m) during their first century or two, older trees often become stag-headed due to drainage changes in their habitat or as a result of the cumulative effects of fire, wind, and lightning. The misshapen U.S. national champion on Cat Island, Louisiana, is therefore only 83 feet (24.9 m) tall. Its forked, buttressed trunk, however, is 17 feet (5.1 m) thick, making it one of the most impressive tree bases in North America or anywhere else. Another contender, the Senator Tree in Florida, is much more massive overall but has a more typical shape without the exaggerated base. I have measured other baldcypress trees, some entering their second millennium, with tall boles and diameters at least half as large. Most were damaged or hollow and thus useless for timber; many more would be here today if their durable wood had not been so valuable to loggers.

LEAVES: Baldcypress is one of our few deciduous conifers, losing its foliage each fall after turning a coppery-bronze tone. The unique feathery foliage is composed of small individual leaves arranged alternately in tight, flat sprays along small twiglets, which themselves are deciduous, falling with the needles in the unusual process of cladoptosis.

CONES AND SEEDS: The conspicuous staminate strobili of this tree are the first signs of swamp life in the new year, expanding in winter when the deciduous forest is bare of foliage. The small, round pistillate cones develop into spherical structures about 1 inch (2.5 cm) through, patterned like miniature brown soccer balls and composed of oddly shaped seeds. Reassembling a shattered cypress cone would make a great three-dimensional jigsaw puzzle.

BEST SEASONS: FALL (seeing this conifer turn a glowing copper in a good fall-color year is reason enough for a canoe trip in the swamp). WINTER (the strobiles are a hint of life outdoors in this dormant season and combine nicely with the reddish bark and artistic form of the tree). SPRING (for the pale green color of new growth) and SUMMER (for the airy shade in a sweltering climate and the fine, graceful texture).

NATIVE AND ADAPTIVE RANGE: This low-elevation tree grows wild in the Coastal Plain and in the broad, flat valleys of the lower Mississippi River and its tributaries and bayous. It ranges north to southern Illinois and Indiana in the interior, and up to Delaware Bay along the Atlantic Coast, but probably nowhere exceeds 500 feet (150 m) in elevation above sea level.

The northern limitations are not due to lack of cold tolerance but to specific reproductive requirements. Seed must have constant moisture to germinate, young seedlings must have constant access to surface water until they sink their roots below the water table, and saplings must have seasonal flooding to kill the hardwood competitors that would otherwise outgrow them. Such flooded areas are subject to freezing in the North, and the annual formation of heavy ice would kill the seedlings before they could grow large enough to withstand it. When saplings are planted and tended, making such flooding unnecessary, baldcypress can be grown on upland sites north into USDA zone 4 in Minnesota and Ontario.

CULTURE: Baldcypress prefers a heavy soil, or one rich in organic matter. Seed will germinate in spring following a winter of wet stratification and should be sown on sphagnum moss or some similar substrate that can be kept constantly moist. Small trees can be transplanted but become very deep rooted on upland sites and can be a job to move as larger specimens. Baldcypress trees in swamps are more shallow rooted. I have read about mature wild trees that survived being plucked from swamps

RIGHT: The fall color display of baldcypress (*Taxodium distichum*), a deciduous conifer.

(with a great sucking sound, I imagine) by giant helicopters and replanted with whatever muck clung to their roots.

New trees should be watered regularly until their roots are able to penetrate lower soil horizons to reach constant moisture. Once well established, they tolerate any amount of flooding. Specimens around Reelfoot Lake in Tennessee have survived continuous inundation since being dropped into very deep water by the New Madrid Earthquake in the early nineteenth century. Baldcypress can also grow fairly quickly in cultivation. Specimens planted around 1850 at Spring Grove Cemetery in Cincinnati, Ohio, look like forest giants, and many young trees less than twenty years old in other cities are 30 feet (9 m) tall or more. Forestry research has found that baldcypress will tolerate a wide hydrological range

LEFT: A baldcypress (*Taxodium distichum*) swamp in late fall. BELOW: A large baldcypress approximately one thousand years old.

but is most vigorous in shallowly but almost permanently flooded sites.

If they are planted in well-drained locations, baldcypress trees will not develop many of the stalagmite-like root growths called pneumatophores, or knees, for which cypress swamps are famous. In those that do, the knees may be pruned off at ground level in areas where they constitute a hazard. In a mulched planting bed, out of the way of mowers and foot traffic, these knees become living sculptural pieces. I have seen magnificent knees in virgin baldcypress swamps that were taller than I am. And to put this in perspective I should note that I am 6 feet 6 inches (2 m) and the knees on our cultivated pondside specimens in Illinois grow about 1 inch (2.5 cm) every four years.

PROBLEMS: Once this tree is established it is extremely carefree. As a deciduous conifer, it resists damage from the ice storms that can tear apart evergreen trees whose needles collect freezing rain. Its light, strong wood is not very vulnerable to insects, cankers, or wind and is very

resistant to decay once it ages for a century or two, though it can fall victim to the host-specific pecky rot fungus (*Stereum taxodii*). A biochemical called cypressene is believed to act as a natural preservative in the heartwood, but it takes many decades to build up in the tree, making lumber cut from old-growth trees much more resistant to decay than lumber from younger trees. The cypress bark beetle (*Phloeosinus taxodii*) can weaken trees by tunneling under the bark, and deer love to polish their antlers at the expense of young baldcypress. The tiny leaves do not cause a significant litter problem, and the airy canopy allows other plants to be grown below. Alkaline soil can result in chlorosis, and some trees are susceptible to superficial damage from gall-forming mites and midges such as *Taxodiomyia cupressiananassa*, the cypress twig gall midge.

CULTIVARS: A nice weeping form, 'Cascade Falls', originated from a cultivated specimen found in New Zealand. Another weeping selection, 'Pendens', has been around for over a century. It has a conical form with slightly pendulous twigs. My old friend Earl Cully of Jacksonville, Illinois, has made several selections, including 'Monarch of Illinois', a broadly pyramidal tree, and 'Nelson', which is similar but with much better limb structure. 'Shawnee Brave', another Cully tree, has a narrowly upright form, at least while young, and is commonly planted. 'Autumn Gold' was chosen for its overall appearance and good fall color. Unless grafted trees are used, some plantings (like the old one at Spring Grove) are so variable that no two trees look alike.

SIMILAR AND RELATED SPECIES: Montezuma cypress (***Taxodium mucronatum***) grows along rivers in southern Texas, Mexico, and Guatemala. This species is more weeping in habit and looks much like *T. distichum* 'Pendens' in this regard. Some taxonomists classify it as *T. distichum* var. *mexicanum*. I once saw a beautiful Montezuma cypress grove along the Rio Purificación in Mexico, and a giant two-hundred-year-old planted tree at an old hacienda nearby in Tamaulipas. This species becomes a great, spreading, weeping tree, nearly evergreen, in its native habitat. The giant Tule Cypress, a Montezuma cypress in southern Mexico, has the thickest trunk of any tree on Earth, approximately 190 feet (58 m) in girth.

TOP LEFT: Knees of baldcypress (*Taxodium distichum*) emerge among Atamasco lilies and azaleas in a wetland garden. LEFT: The pendulous twigs of Montezuma cypress (*T. mucronatum*). RIGHT: Montezuma cypress is closely related to baldcypress and occupies similar habitats in the Southwest.

The related pondcypress (**Taxodium ascendens**) is smaller than baldcypress, more restricted in natural distribution, and not quite as hardy, to USDA zone 6 or maybe 5. Many authorities argue that it is merely a smaller, southern variety of baldcypress (*T. distichum* var. *imbricarium* or, incorrectly, *T. distichum* var. *nutans*), but I'm not buying the argument. It has thicker, ridged bark and linear foliage sprays that look like thick strands of green

yarn. It resembles a young and very small version of Sierra redwood (*Sequoiadendron giganteum*) and would be discernable to the most uninitiated observer if seen side by side with baldcypress. 'Prairie Sentinel' was selected from a cultivated pondcypress tree found in southern Illinois. Several arboretums and nurseries are testing other selections for hardiness, looking for marketable cultivars with superior cold tolerance.

The closest living relative and mimic of the baldcypress and its clan is dawn redwood (**Metasequoia glyptostroboides**), the "fossil tree" that was thought to be extinct until it was discovered alive in China in 1945. The oldest specimens in North America, including the beautiful grove at Missouri Botanic Garden in St. Louis, date back only to 1947. Many other members of this family really do exist now only as fossils, while two are the largest trees of the Pacific Coast.

COMMENTS: Wherever it has been preserved in old swamp forests of the South, baldcypress is invariably the largest and oldest tree. In such settings it attracts everything that likes high places over water, including eagles, ospreys, anhingas, cormorants, herons, and lightning.

A friend and I once took a canoe trip from the Suwannee Canal west into the heart of Okefenokee National Wildlife Refuge in Georgia, and the birds, alligators, and carnivorous plants were sensational. My most lasting impression, however, was of a black night spent camping among islands of beautiful baldcypress trees draped with ghostlike moss and alive with tree frogs. The roots of some trees were anchored in nothing more than drifting batteries of peat that had floated up from the bottom of the swamp.

There are more convenient places to admire ancient baldcypress trees, of course—beautiful places like Corkscrew Swamp in Florida, Heron Pond in Illinois, Reelfoot Lake in Tennessee, and Francis Beidler Refuge in South Carolina, where boardwalks serve as dry sidewalks elevated above the real world of water and snakes. But a solitary wilderness trip across Okefenokee Swamp is truly unique.

LEFT: Bark of Montezuma cypress (*Taxodium mucronatum*).

Thuja occidentalis
ARBORVITAE

DESCRIPTION: Often known as northern whitecedar, a name that can lead to confusion with other trees also called cedars, the arborvitae is a fragrant evergreen of the boreal forest. It grows slowly and lives to a venerable age on cliff faces and in swamp forests of the North.

Arborvitae seedlings germinate on rotting logs, organic peats, and moist, calcareous mineral soils laid bare by fire. They can persist under the shade of taller trees for decades until they slowly claim their place in the sun. Those that grow on rocky upland sites assume bonsai forms with twisted, forked, and gnarly crowns, looking totally unlike the slender, erect trees found in dense stands in swamps. This is solely a function of environmental influence and not due to genetic variation between the two types.

Arborvitae is a compact tree that seldom attains the stature of its neighboring conifers, but very old individuals on productive upland sites can surprise gardeners who buy arborvitae as foundation shrubs. The U.S. national champion in Leelanau County, Michigan, is 113 feet (33.9 m) tall and 5.7 feet (1.7 m) in diameter. Since arborvitae is primarily a Canadian tree, expect to find comparable specimens to the north.

LEAVES: The foliage of arborvitae is soft and pleasant to the touch, and very fragrant. The flat, filigree sprays of tiny, scaly leaves are popular as background foliage for cut-flower arrangements and wonderful to scratch and sniff on walks through the woods. Some trees remain bright green all winter, while others turn a bronze tone, greening up again in spring. Some leaves remain attached to the primary twigs even after they have turned brown and been replaced by younger ones, eventually popping off as the twig expands in girth. The secondary twigs are shed with them through the natural thinning process of cladoptosis.

CONES AND SEEDS: Tiny male and female strobili are borne on separate twigs of the same tree. The female strobili grow into oval, pea-sized seed cones with a few overlapping scales, ripening to a warm brown in late summer.

BEST SEASONS: WINTER (evergreens become dominant in any landscape during the dormant season). ALL YEAR (a pleasant, fragrant, fresh-green foliage plant in youth and a picturesque tree as it matures).

NATIVE AND ADAPTIVE RANGE: This hardy tree grows from the north end of Lake Winnipeg in Manitoba across eastern Canada to the Gulf of St. Lawrence, around the Great Lakes, and in isolated areas of suitable habitat south into Illinois, Ohio, and the Appalachians. It can be grown in cultivation north into USDA zone 2 but becomes stressed by heat and drought south of USDA zone 6 unless carefully sited and tended.

CULTURE: Arborvitae thrives in moist soil, loves limestone areas, and can take full sun or light shade. It grows slowly but is easy to transplant. Seeds should be sown in fall and should not be allowed to dry out. Wild plants often propagate by layering, their lower branches sweeping the ground and becoming covered with a litter mulch. Favorite selections are easy to propagate by cuttings taken in winter.

PROBLEMS: Many small arborvitae are destroyed each winter by rabbits, deer, moose, and other browsing mammals, and by snowmobiles. They must be given protection from such abuse, as well as from foliage browning caused by male dogs and cats marking their territory. Scale insects (*Carulaspis carueli* and *Lecanium fletcheri*), leaf miners (*Argyresthis thuiella*), and spider mites (*Oligonychus ununguis*) take their toll on this tree. Bagworms (*Thyridopteryx ephemeraeformis*) seem to prefer arborvitae above all others but cannot survive in the cold climate that prevails over much of the tree's natural range. Bags should be picked over winter to reduce the number of eggs hatching next spring, and heavy infestations can be controlled with timely application of *Bacillus thuringienus* (Bt), a biological control spray.

Summer drought is a serious problem in hot-climate areas, and low humidity desiccates trees planted in the Southwest. Within its natural habitat, arborvitae is affected most by animal damage and fire. It will tolerate urban air pollution and heat as long as it has its roots in cool, moist soil. It is tough, flexible, and more resistant to damage from ice and snow than many other conifers, but some ornamental cultivars with multiple leaders will split under heavy snow loads.

CULTIVARS: This plant has attracted many horticulturists, who have found and propagated more than two hundred selections for foliage color, growth form, and dwarfism. There is a plant of 'Hetz Midget' at Starhill Forest that I propagated from a cutting in 1967. It is robust and healthy but has yet to reach waist height, and probably never will. Some of the best tree-sized cultivars, including 'Nigra' and 'Techny Mission', have been grown for their green winter color. 'Pyramidalis', 'DeGroot's Spire', 'Smaragd' (syn. 'Emerald'), the corkscrewlike 'Spiralis', and 'Hetz Wintergreen' are narrowly upright types;

LEFT: Arborvitae (*Thuja occidentalis*) trees can be seen planted in many old cemeteries. BELOW: Pyramidal arborvitae cultivars are popular landscape trees. RIGHT: Foliage and young cones of arborvitae.

'Sunkist' and 'Yellow Ribbon' have gold-tipped branches; and 'Wandsdyke Silver' has white-tipped branches. 'Brandon' is a vigorous, narrow type tailored specifically for the harsh climate of the Canadian Great Plains. 'Affinity', a seed germplasm strain, is a tall, pyramidal type released in 1993 by the USDA. It was propagated by seed from a vigorous cultivated specimen in Indiana for conservation use in the Midwest.

SIMILAR AND RELATED SPECIES: Western redcedar (***Thuja plicata***) is a giant conifer of the Pacific Northwest that shows surprising adaptability under cultivation in the eastern United States. It is found in our region only in moist areas of the northern Rocky Mountains, growing from there westward, where it becomes a giant conifer. It is the arboreal emblem of British Columbia. A plant in my Illinois collection that was propagated from Idaho, the interior part of its range, seems denser and perhaps hardier than other specimens propagated from populations near the Pacific Coast. Western redcedar has yielded some cultivars, including the densely pyramidal 'Elegantissima' and 'Virescens', the more open 'Excelsa', the golden 'Sunshine', and the popular 'Green Giant', which is thought to be a hybrid with a Japanese species. Four additional species are found in Asia, some of which are frequently used in landscaping. Some Asian species are separated into their own genus, *Platycladus*.

The Atlantic whitecedar (***Chamaecyparis thyoides***) is our only eastern North American native representative of a similar genus. It is a lowland tree of the Coastal Plain, from Maine to the Mississippi River, and is slow growing and long lived. One ancient tree in Alabama is 88 feet (26.4 m) tall and 5 feet (1.5 m) in diameter. In the wild this species is found in scattered freshwater wetlands, usually growing in peat deposits. Unlike arborvitae, it prefers acidic soils. 'Red Star' is a cultivar that turns a nice russet in fall. Two related species grow on the Pacific Coast, and numerous cultivars have been derived from them and from several Asian species.

Cypress (*Cupressus*) are closely related as well, and one species, Arizona cypress (***C. arizonica***), is found near the southwestern limits of our region in western Texas, southern New Mexico, and Arizona. The record-sized tree in Arizona is 93 feet (27.9 m) tall and more than 6 feet (1.8 m) in diameter. Its hardiest form, variety *glabra*

(sometimes considered a separate species), is widely cultivated in the Southwest for ornamental use and for Christmas trees and is hardy in USDA zone 7. See *Juniperus virginiana* for information on other related trees.

COMMENTS: *Arborvitae* means "tree of life," and this species is among the most commonly seen trees in old cemeteries, planted ceremoniously to commemorate the afterlife of the deceased. It has been used for this and other horticultural purposes since the 1530s, when the French voyageur Jacques Cartier learned from Native Americans to drink cedar tea to treat scurvy (apparently with at least some success, prompting the king of France to confer the vernacular name). Arborvitae then became the first of our native conifers to be introduced into cultivation in Europe.

Even before that time, Native Americans left offerings at a natural shrine known as the Witch Tree, which grew on the exposed rocks of Hat Point along the northwest shore of Lake Superior, across from Isle Royale. This crooked old arborvitae served as a landmark for voyageurs on their way to Grand Portage and was noted as a very old tree by explorer Sieur de la Verendrye as he passed by it in 1731. The Witch Tree lives on, and when I inspected it a few years ago I noticed several offerings left by modern Native Americans. I touched the tree, imagining the stories it could tell, and left in silence.

LEFT: Western redcedar (*Thuja plicata*) is a large and adaptable relative of arborvitae (*T. occidentalis*).
RIGHT: 'Zebrina' is a popular gold-variegated cultivar of western redcedar.

Tilia americana

BASSWOOD

DESCRIPTION: Basswood, also called linden (or bastwood, the original name derived from the bast), is a tenacious tree that can survive under remarkably adverse growing conditions. That said, it becomes a stately shade tree or timber tree only in locations where its roots have access to deep, moist, silt-loam soils. It is a climax species of sheltered valleys, lower portions of north-facing slopes, and the cool forests of the Great Lakes region.

This tree is frequently found growing in clumps or as a single tree with several basal sprouts. It excels in its ability to regenerate by sprouting vigorously from the root collar following fire or other damage, and the sprouts often seem too impatient to wait for the main stem to be killed before racing to take its place. This sprouting ability has enabled basswood, which is generally a slow-growing species from seed, to dominate many forest areas subjected to disturbances that have killed competing species. It also results in some very artistic clumps.

Given enough time, basswood can become extremely large. The U.S. national champion growing in Montgomery County, Pennsylvania, is a typical clump-forming tree that stands 94 feet (28.2 m) tall with a main trunk that is nearly 8 feet (2.4 m) in diameter at its base. Such giants don't develop overnight, however. During a historical reconstruction project at the Lincoln Home National Historic Site in 1993, it was discovered that several average-looking basswoods on the site that appeared to be about fifty years old actually dated back to before the Civil War.

LEAVES: Heart-shaped, lop-sided, sharply toothed leaves emerge from red buds and grow to nearly 8 inches (20 cm) long. They closely resemble the unlobed leaves of red mulberry (*Morus rubra*). The foliage is arranged on the tree in an efficient pattern that captures every vestige of sunlight that falls within the spread of the tree's canopy, leaving the ground below in darkness. Basswoods often don't color well in fall, although some turn a very nice yellow.

FLOWERS AND FRUIT: Basswood blooms in early summer after the leaves are grown. Fragrant yellowish flowers hang in cymes from the bottoms of unique, narrow, leaflike bracts called cladodes. Basswood is among our most important trees as a source of nectar for honey. Bees quickly find the flowers as they open and can drop by in such numbers that the whole tree buzzes like a power line in a storm. Clusters of dry, crusty, pea-sized round fruits follow the flowers and fall in early winter while still attached to the cladodes.

BEST SEASONS: SUMMER (for the cool, dense shade and the flowers) and FALL (for those trees that color nicely). WINTER (for the arching form and red buds).

NATIVE AND ADAPTIVE RANGE: This tree can be found in mesic forests from Winnipeg, Manitoba, south to northeastern Oklahoma, east across southern Ontario and Quebec to the St. John River valley in New Brunswick, and southeast to the mountain coves of North Carolina. Under cultivation it rates hardy from USDA zone 2 southward.

CULTURE: Although basswood is very easy to transplant and can survive on a variety of sites, it will not perform well as a landscape tree unless given deep, moist soil. It grows in sun or shade and is indifferent to soil pH but very sensitive to salt. In native stands, this tree is among the best soil builders, bringing nutrients up from the subsoil and depositing them on the soil surface in its leaf litter, where they become available to understory plants. Because it likes to grow in clumps, pruning is mandatory in order to develop and maintain the desired growth form, either a single stem or uniform clump. Caution is needed when removing surplus basal sprouts to avoid damaging the smooth, thin bark of the main stems. If your tree is a persistent clumper, consider allowing it to do its thing. Such specimens can be very graceful.

Growing these trees from seed can be frustrating. The seed remains dormant for up to four years until its re-

RIGHT: A mature basswood (*Tilia americana*) casts a dense shade.

quirements have been met, and on top of that, much of it is not filled and is therefore not viable. The best advice I can offer is to obtain much more seed than you think you will need and then divide it into several batches, treating each batch differently. Stratify some, remove the seed coat from some, soak some in warm water, scarify some with acid or a file, and pick some before it's fully ripe in late summer and plant it immediately. Then be prepared to wait. If you have a foolproof protocol for this, please pass it along, because I do not.

PROBLEMS: Basswoods can be defoliated by larvae of the linden leafroller moth (*Pantographa limata*) and by yellowneck caterpillars (*Datana ministra*) and Gypsy moths (*Lymantria dispar*). They are sometimes blasted by late spring frosts, for which they seem to have little tolerance, and their soft wood and narrow crotches result in some storm damage. The foliage is subject to scorch from drought and to blotching from anthracnose (*Gnomonia tiliae*), but neither problem is serious. Canker diseases and heartrot fungi affect many wild trees, and vascular wilt from *Verticillium albo-atrum* is found on some landscape trees.

Basswoods of all species seem prone to stunting due to development of girdling roots. This is usually caused when a container-grown tree is planted without cutting or spreading the roots that have circled inside the container, but it sometimes results from regenerating roots on field-dug trees that grow out at right angles to the "wheel spokes" of severed lateral roots. Young basswoods in the landscape should be inspected for a couple of years after they are established. To do this, wash or gently brush soil away from their bases to make sure everything is okay, cutting any circling roots that may have developed.

Browsing animals love basswood and cause significant damage to young seedlings and sprouts. Deer also seem to prefer the smooth bark and soft wood of this tree for shadowboxing in fall, and they clean and test their new antlers by scraping the bark away. Basswood can be difficult to place in the landscape because of its dense shade, which restricts the options available for groundcover planting beneath its canopy.

CULTIVARS: 'Boulevard' and 'Front Yard' are forms selected for their strong central leaders. This characteristic

TOP LEFT: Basswood (*Tilia americana*) flowers hang from cladodes. LEFT: Basswood often grows naturally as a clump with several stems. RIGHT: This basswood has exceptional fall color.

develops naturally on forest-grown trees, but open-grown basswoods often form multiple leaders, which weakens their structure. 'Pyramidal' and 'Fastigiata' were selected for their narrow crowns, while 'Douglas' and 'Legend' have broad crowns and strong central leaders. 'Dakota' is a hardy round-headed selection from a nice cultivated tree found in South Dakota, and 'Rosehill' is a rounded pyramidal form. 'Lincoln', from northern Illinois, is more compact than most. A few selections with variant foliage characteristics can be seen in botanical gardens.

'Redmond' may be the most popular *Tilia* cultivar on the market. It is often listed as a selection of our native basswood, but it seems to have developed from a hybrid (and possibly a backcross) involving basswood and some European linden species. Other cultivars have been derived from European and Asian lindens, which are also known as limes, though they are not related to the edible limes of the genus *Citrus*.

SIMILAR AND RELATED SPECIES: Taxonomy in this genus is hopelessly confused by variability and hybridization, some authorities recognizing five times as many species as others. Most agree that the distinctive white basswood (***Tilia heterophylla***) of the Southeast is our only other native species of consequence, although some believe that it too is just a tomentose variant of American basswood. It is very ornamental, particularly when the woolly white undersides of its leaves are flashing in a breeze. The record tree, located in the Pisgah National Forest in North Carolina, is 116 feet (34.8 m) tall with a trunk 6 feet (1.8 m) in diameter.

Some botanists also recognize the smaller Carolina basswood (***Tilia caroliniana***) and Florida basswood (***T. floridana***) as distinct species. Both are bottomland trees of the Coastal Plain. Several more southeastern species are segregated in older literature. Other varieties or species occur in Mexico, and numerous species and hybrids are found in Europe and Asia. Many street trees planted in North America are selections from exotic varieties, particularly the littleleaf linden (***T. cordata***).

COMMENTS: Basswood was among the first trees cultivated in North America, grown as a honey plant and for its light, carvable wood and fibrous bast. Most authorities cite a confirmed introduction date of 1752, as given by English horticultural author John Loudon; but at least one record indicates that trees were grown in London in 1730 from seed collected by Mark Catesby in Carolina in 1726. (I suspect it may have taken the four intervening years just to germinate the seed.) Going even further back in time, basswood bark has been identified in the cords of ceremonial jewelry found in Native American graves in Canada that date back to more than two thousand years ago. Basswood bast was used by aboriginal people to make ropes and twine for lashing everything from lodge poles to utensils. And the drawing boards used by generations of architects to plan the development of the New World were made of basswood.

Knowing that basswood is a tree of the mesic forest, I was startled to see one years ago, while visiting the Indiana Dunes of Lake Michigan, emerging from the lakeward (retreating) side of an active sand dune. Closer inspection revealed that this scraggly little tree had developed adventitious roots as the dune advanced upon it, nearly to its top; the dune then moved past and began to fall, and some of those roots now reached more than 20 feet (6 m) down to the receding sand surface below, making the tree look like a tropical fig or banyan with stilt roots. This specimen would not have made an acceptable lawn tree or sawlog, but its tenacity was stunning.

LEFT: Bark of basswood (*Tilia americana*).

Tsuga canadensis
CANADA HEMLOCK

DESCRIPTION: Landscape professionals often speak of "quality plants" that are long lived, refined in character, and have no off-season. Hardwood trees such as sugar maple (*Acer saccharum*), beech (*Fagus grandifolia*), and white oak (*Quercus alba*) come to mind, along with conifers like white pine (*Pinus strobus*). Hemlocks (*Tsuga*) share the spotlight with these elite trees, also sharing many of the habitats where they grow best. Canada hemlock (*Tsuga canadensis*), the state tree of Pennsylvania, is a member of the quality-tree fraternity throughout its range.

Hemlocks can be recognized from a distance by their nodding leaders, which are similar to those of some exotic cedars (*Cedrus*). No other native conifer genus in eastern North America typically has this growth form. Large hemlocks are found only in old-growth forest areas or in the oldest cultivated landscapes, and they are impressive. The U.S. national champion in Great Smoky Mountains National Park is 165 feet (49.5 m) tall with a rugged trunk almost 6 feet (1.8 m) in diameter. Many magnificent hemlocks, several centuries old, can be seen in the Joyce Kilmer Memorial Forest in North Carolina and in the Tionesta Scenic Area of the Allegheny National Forest in Pennsylvania. The Tionesta Grove offers an interesting contrast between virgin forest and a swath cleared by a tornado, allowing early-successional species to reestablish among the hemlocks.

LEAVES: The evergreen needles of Canada hemlock are dark green with whitened bands of stomates underneath and reach about half an inch (1.25 cm) in length. They are borne in flattened, two-ranked horizontal sprays on slender twigs. Canada hemlocks are willowy and flexible, lacking any vestige of the stiffness and sharpness that characterize most conifers, and the foliage moves gracefully with the slightest breeze.

CONES AND SEEDS: The brown staminate strobili are tiny and inconspicuous. Pistillate strobili mature in a single season into seed cones at the ends of lateral twigs, less than 1 inch (2.5 cm) long but slightly larger than those of tamarack (*Larix laricina*). Many cones open to release their seeds early in fall and then drop before the next spring, crunching like popcorn underfoot.

BEST SEASONS: SPRING (for the two-toned pattern of fresh new foliage seen against the dark older growth). WINTER (the dark evergreen needles also contrast sharply with snow, and the lacy form of the tree is best viewed during the dormant season when neighboring deciduous trees no longer hide it). ALL YEAR (Canada hemlock casts a deep, cool shade in summer and looks dark and regal among the bright colors of other trees in autumn).

NATIVE AND ADAPTIVE RANGE: This is a tree of mesic sites and stream corridors in the Lake States, the Appalachians south to Alabama, and New England. It extends north into Nova Scotia, New Brunswick, southern Quebec, and the vicinity of Algonquin Provincial Park in Ontario. Isolated relict populations, left behind following the last glacial period, can be seen in cool canyons such as those in and around Turkey Run State Park in Indiana. These trees modify their microclimate to their own advantage by retarding soil heating and reducing evaporation. Canada hemlocks can be grown in cultivation from USDA zone 3 southward but will fail south of the cooler parts of USDA zone 7 unless precautions are taken to keep the roots cool and moist.

CULTURE: Like many of our other most prestigious landscape trees, Canada hemlock needs moderate conditions. Cool-climate areas with moist, acidic soil and good drainage are best. This tree survives well in the shade, and prefers it in the South, but becomes more dense in full sun. Locations that are windy in summer or winter should be avoided. Canada hemlock responds to pruning and shearing by becoming more dense and is more forgiving in this regard than most conifers. Still, its character and the graceful movement of its foliage are most evident when it is left unsheared.

Transplanting should be done with a soil ball in either spring or early fall. Take care not to set the new tree deeper than it originally grew. Mulch a wide area around its base, and water it regularly but not excessively during its first year. Incorporate acidic organic matter into a slightly mounded planting bed rather than just in the planting hole. Canada hemlock is sensitive to provenance, so native local sources should be used if possible.

Seedlings may be grown from seed sown in fall or stratified until spring. The cones should be picked just as they begin to open and then left in paper sacks for a few days until the seed can be shaken free. The warm, dry air rising from behind a refrigerator is great for drying and opening cones. New seedlings are tiny and fragile and must be given protection from wind and strong sunlight. Spreading a layer of compost on bare soil beneath a mature Canada hemlock and allowing nature to produce a few volunteer seedlings (to be transplanted about two years later), might be the easiest method to obtain a few starts of this beautiful tree.

PROBLEMS: Canada hemlock is sensitive to environmental extremes. Heat, drought, wind, salt spray, air pollution, soil compaction, and poor drainage must be avoided. It tolerates winter cold but can be damaged by unseasonable frosts. It will bend and recover under the weight of ice and snow but may uproot in wind due to its shallow roots. It can live for nearly a thousand years but grows slowly. During Canada hemlock's long life, it does not adapt well to changes in its local habitat. It is one of the indicator species that environmental scientists will watch closely in the future, as it will probably be among the first of our native trees to decline from the effects of global warming.

Our native hemlock is not related to the herbaceous poison hemlock (*Conium maculatum*) that killed Socrates. In fact, it is all too palatable to deer and porcupines. Rabbits can damage small specimens, and black vine weevils (*Otiorhynchus sulcatus*) feed on the roots. The most serious pest problem, however, is the hemlock woolly adelgid (*Adelges tsugae*), accidentally introduced from Asia. It can be fatal in the forest, but local infestations can be controlled easily with horticultural oil sprays or with certain systemic pesticides. The insects are white, making heavy infestations easy to spot among the dark needles. Since they spread mostly by sticking to birds' feet, avoid placing bird feeders too close to hemlocks. The Japanese lady beetle (*Pseudoscymnus tsugae*), a natural predator, has been released in some heavily infested areas. The parasitic mite *Diapterobates humeralis* comes from the adelgid's home range in Japan. It works by eating the anchor threads that hold the eggs on the tree, dislodging them and causing them to fall harmlessly to the ground. Three other predatory beetles currently under study may be used in the future as additional biological controls.

Canada hemlock needles are arranged in flat, overlapping sprays that intercept virtually all sunlight falling on the tree's crown. Unlike the translucent foliage of neighboring broadleaved trees, Canada hemlock needles are opaque. The shallow roots of hemlock are very efficient at absorbing moisture from upper soil layers, and this tree grows well in very acidic soils. All this does not bode well for the successful establishment of turf under a hemlock canopy; but a single specimen tree, limbed up to allow entry of morning and evening light, can be maintained successfully in a lawn with some extra care given to the grass. Better still, permit your Canada hemlock to remain branched to the ground, and let its needles and cones form a maintenance-free mulch under the canopy. Call the result a miniature wildlife refuge, because that's what it will be, even if the only wildlife around is the family dog.

CULTIVARS: This species has produced more than fifty prominent horticultural selections. Most are procumbent or dwarf and would not fall within our concept of a tree as such, but they are among the most prized plants for rock gardens and dwarf conifer collections. A few selections have been made for specimens with variegated or unique foliage, or compact, dense growth. 'Albo-Spica' has white-tipped branches, and 'Golden Splendor' and 'New Gold' are yellow forms.

LEFT: A Canada hemlock (*Tsuga canadensis*) planted in a cemetery during the Civil War. RIGHT: A Canada hemlock branch with old cones begins new growth in spring.

SIMILAR AND RELATED SPECIES: Carolina hemlock (*Tsuga caroliniana*) can be found only in the southern Appalachians. It is a more compact tree and is perhaps not quite as graceful as its larger cousin, but it is reportedly a little more tolerant of heat in urban plantings if there is some shade present. It can be distinguished from Canada hemlock by its foliage, which wraps around the twigs rather than arranging itself in flat sprays. The largest known specimen is in North Carolina and stands 99 feet (29.7 m) tall with a trunk more than 4 feet (1.2 m) thick.

Two other hemlocks, *Tsuga heterophylla* and *T. mertensiana,* are giant timber trees of the far West. They are strikingly beautiful when seen in their natural habitat but have not proven to be very adaptable to cultivation in our area. Several more hemlock species are found in Asia, and some are seen occasionally in North American gardens.

LEFT: Ancient Canada hemlocks (*Tsuga canadensis*) in the Allegheny National Forest. BELOW: One of the many dwarf, weeping cultivars of Canada hemlock .

COMMENTS: Canada hemlock is a patient tree. Although it grows at a moderate rate under ideal conditions, suppressed specimens no taller than a person but more than one hundred years old have been found in the wild. George Washington planted a Canada hemlock at Mount Vernon in 1785, and it has not yet reached 30 inches (75 cm) in diameter. This species can afford to grow so slowly because it is extremely shade tolerant; it can succeed, over time, even where faster-growing neighbors initially overtop it. After two or three centuries, the persistent Canada hemlock usually wins out, rising through the crowns of other trees to claim preeminence in the climax forest.

A climax forest is defined as such because once it has become dominated by mature hemlocks no further natural succession takes place under their dark shade. A fire or storm, like the tornado at the Tionesta Grove, must open the dense hemlock canopy enough to allow fast-growing, sun-loving, early-successional species to regain a temporary foothold. Without droughts, natural disasters, and human impacts, climax forests would eventually cover much of the natural world, and hemlocks would rule many forests in the North.

Ulmus americana
AMERICAN ELM

DESCRIPTION: The American elm once reigned supreme as the most favored of all shade trees. It is massive, long lived, tough, easy to grow, adaptable, and blessed with an arching, wine-glass-like silhouette, making it the perfect street tree. It is also valuable as a builder and stabilizer of forest soils and for the nutrient-rich leaves it sheds each fall that feed beneficial soil organisms. It was selected as the state tree of Massachusetts, then of North Dakota, and was a favorite of many areas in between. Then, beginning in the 1930s, a disease epidemic turned our urban monocultures of elm into firewood.

This malady, commonly known as Dutch elm disease (DED) because it was first described in the Netherlands (where it had invaded from Asia), has killed millions of elms of several species across North America and in Europe. Many elms live on, though, to remind us of the great potential of this tree. Some survivors have merely escaped the infection temporarily, and a few of them succumb each year. Others are resistant to the disease and give us hope for the future. In fact, research has given us not only hope but confidence that the stately elm will be back.

American elm is notable as an exception to the rule that narrow crotches make weak limbs. The wood of our native elms is so tough and cross grained that the trees can develop, with impunity, massive crowns full of weak-looking but resilient forks. If you doubt this, try splitting elm firewood by hand. There are two U.S. national champion American elms. One, in Michigan, has a crown spread of 115 feet (34.5 m) and is 112 feet (33.6 m) tall. The other, in Tennessee, spreads only 84 feet (25.2 m) but is 122 feet (36.6 m) tall. Both are more than 7 feet (2.1 m) in diameter.

The Louis Vieux Elm was the former record holder, standing even larger at 100 feet (30 m) tall with a girth of

RIGHT: Yellow leaves rain down from an American elm (*Ulmus americana*) in autumn.

494

26 feet (7.8 m). A huge, leaning, historic specimen, it grew along the Oregon Trail near Louisville, in northeastern Kansas, where it was isolated from other elms and had not yet become infected by DED. It was the centerpiece of the only state forest in Kansas, a piece of rural land the size of a city lot, set aside specifically for the tree. Unfortunately, vandals started a fire in its hollow trunk and the living landmark of the Oregon Trail is no more.

LEAVES: Elliptical and pointed, with prominent veins and asymmetrical bases, the leaves of all our native elms look substantially alike. Those of American elm are large but variable in size, up to 6 inches (15 cm) long but usually half that size, doubly serrate along the margin, and relatively smooth on the upper surface compared with those of other elms. They often turn a rich gold in fall, as do those of most other native elm species.

FLOWERS AND FRUIT: Drooping clusters of small flowers appear early, before the leaves, on American elm and most other native elms. Because of their flowers, native elms are among the earliest trees to show signs of life in spring, adding a soft pastel red tint to the crowns of blooming trees. The flowers expand into small, circular-winged seeds, which scatter by the thousands, riding on the late spring winds.

BEST SEASONS: FALL (on trees that exhibit the best fall color). SPRING (the early flowers and young leaves accentuate the characteristic arching limb structure). SUMMER (this is an ideal shade tree when healthy) and WINTER (for the silhouettes of picturesque old specimens).

NATIVE AND ADAPTIVE RANGE: American elm is among our most resilient and tractable trees. It grows in habitats ranging from rocky bluffs to floodplains and from mesic forests to prairie valleys. It is ubiquitous, growing wild in almost every county in North America

east of Wyoming and south of a line from Prince Albert in central Saskatchewan to the Gaspe Peninsula of Quebec, skipping southern Florida. Under cultivation it is hardy anywhere south of USDA zone 2.

CULTURE: Elms are adaptable to almost any climate and soil, wet or dry, in sun or partial shade, and are very easy to transplant at virtually any size. Seeds of most species sprout immediately upon ripening, with no dormancy. Once established in the right setting, our several native elm species have only one significant cultural requirement, and that is management for control of Dutch elm disease and a few other problems.

PROBLEMS: Elm roots are invasive and shallow, with flaring buttresses. They may lift adjacent sidewalks unless root barriers are installed. Small seedlings sprout in every flowerbed and sidewalk crack within reach of the windblown seeds, so periodic weeding is necessary where they are unwanted. Elms are susceptible to several vascular diseases caused by various fungi and viruses. Rabbits girdle many small elms in winter, so young trees should be protected. The exotic Asian longhorned borer beetle (*Anoplophora glabripennis*) includes elms on its menu. Spiny elm caterpillar (*Nymphalis antiopa*) and yellowneck caterpillar (*Datana ministra*) are among the many defoliators that like these trees. Elm leaf beetles (*Pyrrhalta luteola*) also feed on native elms but cause more serious damage on exotic elm species.

A disease called elm yellows (*Phytoplasma ulmi*, complex 16SrV) causes serious problems in outbreak areas. Formerly known as phloem necrosis, it is spread chiefly by leafhopper insects (*Scaphoideus luteolus*). Leafhoppers are not hardy north of USDA zone 5, so the disease is not a problem further north. It looks much like Dutch elm disease, for which it is often mistaken, but can be identified in the field by the faint wintergreen odor it imparts to infected inner bark, or phloem. There are reports that an injection of the antibiotic oxytetracycline may be effective in curing elm yellows.

The European elm bark beetle (*Scolytus multistriatus*) and a native bark beetle (*Hylurgopinus rufipes*) are the major problems for American elm and its kin, partly because of the direct damage they inflict by burrowing under the bark as larvae, but mostly because they spread Dutch elm disease when feeding on the twigs as adults. Dutch elm disease (*Ophiostoma ulmi*, formerly *Ceratocystis*

LEFT: The doubly serrate leaves of American elm (*Ulmus americana*). RIGHT: A single mature American elm can shade an entire home.

ulmi) originated in Asia and was introduced into North America via Europe. An especially aggressive strain, now predominant in North America, has been given separate taxonomic status as *O. novo-ulmi* by some pathologists. Since Dutch elm disease is such an overwhelming concern with elms, it merits some discussion here.

Asian elms are resistant to this disease, but most European and North American elms are not. Because elms are so valuable for landscape use, a horticultural war is being waged on several fronts against the disease and its vectors. One successful technique has been to use Asian elms, either directly or in hybridization programs with native elms to breed disease-resistant trees. My friend George Ware, a dendrologist at the Morton Arboretum

in Illinois, has led this effort since 1972. He furnished the resistant *Ulmus davidiana* planted at the Lincoln Home National Historic Site, and I am testing a few of his most promising selections in my own arboretum.

Other research efforts are focused on management of existing, potentially susceptible specimen trees. One approach is to control the bark beetles that spread the disease. Since they are attracted to stressed elms, maintaining tree vigor will help minimize exposure. Insecticides can be used to protect historic or valuable trees from beetles, but they should be narrow-spectrum types that limit damage to nontarget organisms. Fungicide injections that kill or block the fungus can be applied every three years by qualified professional arborists, and these

provide nearly failsafe results at a modest cost per tree, especially when compared with the cost of removal.

Some researchers in the Netherlands are experimenting with low-level inoculation of elms with the fungus *Verticillium dahliae* and reporting some success from the antibody responses of the trees. Scientists in Ontario are vaccinating elms with proteins extracted from weak cultures of the Dutch elm disease fungus, causing the injected trees to manufacture substances called mansonones, which attack the fungus. By inspecting my elms regularly during the growing season, I have successfully cured the disease on two of my trees simply by pruning out the "flags" of dying foliage that start at the points of disease infection in small twigs, where the beetles feed. Such pruning must be done immediately, with tools sterilized after every cut, several feet basipetal to the lowest detectable sapwood stain caused by the fungus. The disease can also spread to adjacent elms

through natural root grafts, so dying elms should be removed and have their root systems isolated from healthy ones by cutting with a trencher.

Callus-culture laboratory techniques can be used to expedite screening for natural resistance in native elms, and such resistance is being found. Susceptibility may vary with the size of vascular openings in the wood: an elm will be more resistant if it is managed to encourage strong but moderate growth as a sapling, minimizing the open pores that occur in rampant growth, since the disease must move through the xylem against the sap flow to become systemic. Such resistance in individual trees increases with age, and seasonally after the initial spring growth flush. Hot summer temperatures also control spread of the fungus, so it is not as serious a problem in the Deep South as it is in the North. However, natural selection by Dutch elm disease has removed many of the most susceptible trees in the North, so the remaining elm population there has a higher proportion of resistant trees than in the South and is a better source of native breeding stock for research.

Professor Ray Guries and his predecessors and associates at the University of Wisconsin have tested thousands of American elms since 1957 and found varying degrees of disease resistance. Several of their first selections have been propagated by the Elm Research Institute in New Hampshire and are available commercially as the 'American Liberty' multiclone. The university began work on an improved "second generation" of resistant elms in 1986, incorporating the best genes of the original trees with some new ones. I look forward to seeing the results of this work planted across the continent.

CULTIVARS: Most older cultivars, selected for growth form and other ornamental characteristics, are susceptible to Dutch elm disease. 'Princeton' from New Jersey and 'Delaware 2' from Delaware, Ohio, are reportedly disease resistant. 'Moline', an upright selection from Illinois, is susceptible but has some latent resistance and has been one of the more useful parent clones in the Wisconsin breeding programs for disease resistance. 'American Liberty' consists of a mixture of six different selections bred from 'Moline' and other partially resistant trees chosen from across northern North America. Most are known only by experimental numbers, but one has been named 'Independence'.

TOP LEFT: *Ulmus americana* 'Independence' is one of the new disease-resistant cultivars of American elm. LEFT: Red elm (*U. rubra*) flowers in very early spring.

'New Harmony' from Ohio and 'Valley Forge' from Pennsylvania are disease-tolerant American elm selections introduced by the USDA. Most studies report that these two, along with 'Princeton', are the most promising.

SIMILAR AND RELATED SPECIES: Red elm (***Ulmus rubra,*** syn. *U. fulva*), also called slippery elm, is a forest tree of the eastern United States and southern Canada, west to the Great Plains. It is more stiffly erect than American elm and has larger, rougher leaves and more conspicuous flowers. Its bark is soft and corky, helping to distinguish it from American elm in the forest where no leaves are within reach for examination. This species is as susceptible to Dutch elm disease as American elm, but 'Lincoln' is a disease-resistant hybrid. The two largest slippery elms grow in Ohio. Each are 100 feet (30 m) tall with at least that much wing span and trunks more than 6 feet (1.8 m) in diameter.

Rock elm (***Ulmus thomasii,*** syn. *U. racemosa*) grows primarily in the Lake States and southern Ontario. It is an upright tree with decorative corky twigs and beautiful gold fall color. Although usually seen as a smaller tree, this species can grow as large as red elm. The current record holder, growing beside a country road near Cassopolis, Michigan, is 117 feet (35.1 m) tall, at least as broad, and more than 5 feet (1.5 m) in diameter.

Several smaller elms grow in the southern United States. Winged elm (***Ulmus alata***) is a tough, drought-resistant tree of old fields and rocky bluffs. It develops very broad wings on its most vigorous twigs, and some specimens I have seen in western Kentucky are spectacular in this regard. On productive sites this tree can grow fairly large, but it is more often seen as a subdued inhabitant of poor, dry soil. 'Lace Parasol' is a weeping selection. Cedar elm (***U. crassifolia***) is similar, with smaller leaves and less pronounced wings. It prefers moister sites but takes severe drought in stride, and blooms in late summer. It has wonderful, fine texture, tiny leaves, artistic form, and great fall color that peaks very late, after most other trees are bare.

All these species are susceptible to Dutch elm disease to some extent, but none so readily as American elm or slippery elm, and individual trees can be quite resistant. I grow them all at Starhill Forest in USDA zone 5. September elm (***Ulmus serotina***) is another small southern species. It blooms early in fall. I have not tested its hardiness and have seen no ratings for it, but I would expect it to be hardy to about USDA zone 6.

Several other elms from Europe, and many from Asia, will grow in cultivation in North America. Water-elm (***Planera aquatica***) is a small member of the elm family that grows in southern swamps. Hackberries (*Celtis*) are also related to elms.

COMMENTS: Some elms will survive on their own, but remember that it will cost much less to have an arborist inject protective fungicide into a healthy or recently infected elm this year than it will to have it removed next year. If you need further reason to take proper care of your elm, you might find inspiration from one of the majestic two-hundred-year-old bicentennial elms that can still be found in some places, or from the six hundred historic American elms that form colonnades along the Capitol Mall in Washington, D.C.

Many people decide to cut down the healthy elms on their properties, reasoning that the trees are likely to die anyway. But any mature native elm that has survived this long in disease-infested localities might have some degree of natural resistance and should be preserved at least until its response to the disease can be tested and its potential use for breeding evaluated. Fossil pollen research in England reveals that something nearly exterminated elms in that region five thousand years ago. Maybe it was something like Dutch elm disease, or maybe it was something else; but the English elms came storming back, without our help, and flourished there until Dutch elm disease laid them low again, several decades before it crossed the pond to invade North America. The elms probably relied upon the genetic resistance of a few survivors to repopulate. And if they did it before, they can do it again, in England as well as in North America.

Viburnum prunifolium

BLACKHAW

DESCRIPTION: Viburnums, both native and exotic, are familiar to most of us as choice landscape shrubs for the discriminating gardener. Left to their own devices, though, several of these fine species will grow into small ornamental trees. One of the largest, toughest, and most widely adapted of these is the blackhaw viburnum, known simply as blackhaw.

Blackhaw is most likely to form an erect tree when pressed by the competition of other understory species growing in a forest opening. As its crown emerges above the foliage mass of its shorter neighbors, it spreads into an arching form with pendent outer branches. A rough, alligator-hide bark forms on old individuals, adding much to the personality of the tree. Where time and conditions permit, these old plants attain considerable size. The U.S. national champion blackhaw, a cultivated specimen at George Washington's birthplace in Wakefield, Virginia, is 24 feet (7.2 m) tall and broader than high, with a trunk 20 inches (50 cm) thick.

LEAVES: The oppositely arranged oval leaves of blackhaw are smooth, glossy, bluntly pointed, and finely toothed along the margin. They reach about 3 inches (7.5 cm) in length and turn from a rich dark green in summer to an even richer crimson in fall.

FLOWERS AND FRUIT: The flowers are borne in fragrant white clusters in late spring, which show to advantage above the lustrous foliage. Blackhaw begins to bloom around Victoria Day (late May) in southern Ontario, blooming progressively earlier as it moves southward. This tree-type viburnum takes much longer to reach blooming age than most smaller viburnum species, sometimes requiring ten years or more from seed, but blooming plants can be propagated from layers to speed the process along.

The clustered, raisinlike fruits are small drupes that darken from pink-purple to nearly black as they ripen. They are often sweet enough to the human palate to be eaten fresh. Wildlife find them too, of course; they are enjoyed by many songbirds and by most of our frugivorous mammals, all of whom help distribute the seeds.

BEST SEASONS: FALL (when the combination of ripe fruits and shiny red foliage can be seen together). SPRING (a very close second, for the flowers). SUMMER (for the clean, lustrous foliage and unripe fruit) and WINTER (for mature specimens with dark, checkered bark and picturesque form).

NATIVE AND ADAPTIVE RANGE: Blackhaw occupies a band of territory roughly equivalent to USDA zones 5 and 6, from the entire western boundary of Missouri eastward, then extends down the Appalachian Mountains and Piedmont into the higher parts of South Carolina. Scattered populations can be found on the Cumberland Plateau and south along the Appalachians into Georgia and Alabama. It can be grown north through USDA zone 4.

CULTURE: All viburnums tolerate shade much better than drought, but blackhaw is much less picky than most shrubby viburnums. It is very easy to transplant and not fussy regarding soil as long as it has good drainage. Old wild specimens found on wooded building sites retain copious amounts of dead twigs and suckers and, like some long-abandoned orchard tree, will benefit aesthetically from a careful cleaning and thinning to remove this unwanted material.

Propagation is easy from layers or suckers, which are frequently available around old plants. Larger quantities may be obtained by rooting softwood cuttings. Seeds will germinate well but often not until a full two years after planting. They have an involved dormancy that requires scarification and alternating periods of warm and cold stratification, so it might be easier to look for surplus volunteer seedlings under the fences used as perches by the many birds that eat the fruit.

PROBLEMS: These small trees have no major native insect enemies or disease problems. Their lush foliage usually remains in top condition throughout the growing season, although trees under drought stress are sometimes affected by mildews. One imported pest, the viburnum leaf beetle (*Pyrrhalta viburni*), is spreading in eastern Canada and the Atlantic States, where it attacks some other viburnums but has yet to display undue affection for blackhaw. Viburnum species in general are sensitive to salt spray along highways or coastlines, and they don't do well in extreme soil conditions.

CULTIVARS: Most viburnum cultivars come from other species and hybrids. 'Mrs. George Large' is a compact selection, and Mike Dirr refers to a selection called 'Early Red'. I have seen no cultivars available in the nursery trade; they seem to be limited to arboreta and the gardens of viburnum collectors.

SIMILAR AND RELATED SPECIES: Rusty blackhaw (***Viburnum rufidulum***), with its red-bearded buds, is the southern counterpart to *V. prunifolium*, growing from the Ozark Plateau of Missouri and the Ohio River valley in southern Indiana south to the Florida Panhandle and central Texas. The leaves of rusty blackhaw, also known as southern blackhaw, are particularly shiny and may have either rounded or bluntly pointed tips. The young leaves and twigs are coated with feltlike hairs that give them an auburn halo in the sun. One tree in Knox County, Tennessee, is 30 feet (9 m) tall with a trunk that is 20 inches (50 cm) in diameter. This species will grow in cultivation north through most of USDA zone 5.

Nannyberry (***Viburnum lentago***), with its tadpole-shaped buds, can grow even taller but is more slender. It is inclined to sucker more than the blackhaws and will form a clonal thicket if given the opportunity. One nannyberry in Oakland County, Michigan, has a crown 50 feet (15 m) tall with a main stem 11 inches (27.5 cm) thick. The leaves are wider than those of the two blackhaw species, sometimes nearly round, but are otherwise similar and turn reddish purple in fall. In my collection in Illinois, nannyberry is the latest of the three species to bloom, finishing just before the onset of really hot weather. 'Pink Beauty' is a selection with fruits that don't darken as they ripen, and 'Deep Green' reportedly has extra nice foliage.

Nannyberry is found to the north of blackhaw and rusty blackhaw, from central Illinois northwest to southern Saskatchewan and from West Virginia northeast to Georgian Bay in Ontario, the southern margin of Quebec, and the southern tip of New Brunswick. It is hardy in cultivation north into USDA zone 2. While the ranges of these three species overlap, and each is adaptable in the South considerably beyond its home ground, species

TOP RIGHT: Tiny white flowers appear in large clusters on blackhaw (*Viburnum prunifolium*). RIGHT: Fall color and fruits of blackhaw.

selection in the North is best guided by the microclimate of the planting area.

Also classified in this group of viburnums is possumhaw (***Viburnum nudum***), a related species confined in the wild mostly to wet areas in the Coastal Plain and Piedmont. Its leaves have smooth margins, but it otherwise looks like a small version of rusty blackhaw. The largest of three U.S. national champion possumhaw trees is located in the Chattahoochee National Forest in Georgia and is 23 feet (6.9 m) tall with a main stem 3 inches (7.5 cm) thick. Like the others, this is a very ornamental species, and it is widely planted as far north as

USDA zone 6, often in the form of 'Count Pulaski', 'Pink Beauty', or 'Winterthur'. A shrubbier version of possumhaw, **V. cassinoides,** grows in the Great Lakes area and the Appalachians.

Cranberry viburnum (***Viburnum trilobum***) is normally a large shrub with lobed leaves and bright red, persistent fruit. It can grow up to 30 feet (9 m) tall, but any claim to tree status must be made on the basis of height rather than form. Named cultivars have been introduced for fruiting qualities and compact growth. Most other native viburnums are strictly shrubs. Many exotic viburnum species and hybrids are popular in cultivation, and some have naturalized locally.

Elders (*Sambucus*) are closely related to viburnums. Most are shrubs, but two species can become small trees in the western part of our region. Blue elder (**S. caerulea**) makes a rugged specimen that often looks much older than it is. Ranging throughout the western mountains, it can grow up to 40 feet (12 m) tall with an equal spread, supported by a clump of stocky, craggy trunks. It has pinnate, compound, opposite leaves with five to nine leaflets and creamy white flowers in saucer-sized corymbs, followed by steely blue, edible fruits. It is adaptable north into USDA zone 5.

Mexican elder (***Sambucus mexicana***) is similar but more southerly in distribution. It grows nearly as large and has nicely textured bark on rough, irregular stems. Its leaves have smaller and fewer leaflets, and it is drought resistant but probably not quite as cold hardy.

Both species are used commonly in cultivation in the Southwest.

COMMENTS: For years I have admired blackhaws in cultivation, generally maintained as large shrubs by pruning. So in 1976 when my wife and I established Starhill Forest Arboretum, we were pleased to find some blackhaws there among the forest understory. As we surveyed and mapped our land, we encountered a few old blackhaws growing in one valley that were as large as fully grown hawthorns (*Crataegus*). This is their natural mature growth form, seldom seen in cultivation except in old landscapes that have not been "maintained" by removing the primary stems of every small tree to keep it growing as a shrub.

Such pruning is neither right nor wrong but a matter of choice; blackhaws are amenable plants and will perform with color and character either way. They make such fine flowering trees, however, that more of them should be planted or preserved as such and encouraged to develop to their full potential. Certainly any old, wild blackhaw found growing on a wooded building site—a specimen with all the character that many decades of wildness can bestow—should be preserved if possible, as a valuable amenity in the future home landscape.

BELOW LEFT: The rusty-velvet new growth of rusty blackhaw (*Viburnum rufidulum*). BELOW: Late fall color on rusty blackhaw. RIGHT: A blooming nannyberry (*V. lentago*) at Starhill Forest.

Tree Selection Guide

The following guide divides native trees into groups with particular design or horticultural characteristics. Categories include trees tolerant of seasonally wet or dry soils, hot or cold climates, or shady sites; trees with evergreen or subevergreen foliage, good autumn color, notable flowers, or notable fruit; and large or small trees. Some trees appear in several categories.

Trees tolerant of seasonally wet soils or flooding

Abies balsamea
Acer ×freemanii
Acer negundo
Acer rubrum
Acer saccharinum
Aesculus discolor
Aesculus pavia
Aesculus splendens
Aesculus sylvatica
Alnus maritima
Alnus oblongifolia
Alnus rugosa
Alnus serrulata
Alnus tenuifolia
Amelanchier alnifolia
Amorpha fruticosa
Aralia spinosa
Asimina parviflora
Betula fontinalis
Betula nigra
Betula papyrifera
Betula uber
Carpinus caroliniana
Carya aquatica
Carya illinoinensis
Carya laciniosa
Catalpa bignonioides

Catalpa speciosa
Celtis laevigata
Celtis occidentalis
Cephalanthus occidentalis
Cercis canadensis
Chamaecyparis thyoides
Chilopsis linearis
Chionanthus pygmaeus
Chionanthus virginicus
Cliftonia monophylla
Cornus amomum
Cornus foemina
Cornus obliqua
Cornus sericea
Crataegus aestivalis
Crataegus erythropoda
Crataegus mollis
Crataegus opaca
Crataegus rivularis
Crataegus viridis
Cyrilla racemiflora
Diospyros virginiana
Forestiera acuminata
Forestiera segregata
Fraxinus caroliniana
Fraxinus nigra
Fraxinus pennsylvanica

Fraxinus tomentosa
Gleditsia aquatica
Gleditsia triacanthos
Gordonia lasianthus
Gymnocladus dioicus
Ilex cassine
Ilex coriacea
Ilex decidua
Ilex glabra
Ilex montana
Ilex verticillata
Ilex vomitoria
Illicium floridanum
Illicium parviflorum
Juglans nigra
Juniperus silicicola
Larix laricina
Leitneria floridana
Liquidambar styraciflua
Maclura pomifera
Magnolia grandiflora
Magnolia virginiana
Myrica pensylvanica
Nemopanthus mucronatus
Nyssa aquatica
Nyssa biflora
Nyssa ogeche

Nyssa sylvatica
Osmanthus americanus
Parkinsonia aculeata
Persea borbonia
Picea mariana
Pinus elliottii
Pinus glabra
Pinus serotina
Pinus taeda
Planera aquatica
Platanus occidentalis
Platanus racemosa
Platanus wrightii
Populus angustifolia
Populus balsamifera
Populus deltoides
Populus fremontii
Populus heterophylla
Populus sargentii
Populus tremuloides
Populus trichocarpa
Populus wislizeni
Prosopis glandulosa
Prosopis pubescens
Prosopis velutina
Prunus maritima
Prunus umbellata

LEFT: White ash (*Fraxinus americana*).

505

Ptelea trifoliata
Quercus arizonica
Quercus arkansana
Quercus austrina
Quercus bicolor
Quercus imbricaria
Quercus laurifolia
Quercus lyrata
Quercus macrocarpa
Quercus michauxii
Quercus muhlenbergii
Quercus nigra
Quercus nuttallii
Quercus oglethorpensis
Quercus pagoda
Quercus palustris
Quercus phellos
Quercus shumardii
Quercus similis
Quercus sinuata
Quercus virginiana
Rhus vernix
Sabal louisiana
Sabal mexicana
Sabal minor
Sabal palmetto
Salix amygdaloides
Salix bebbiana
Salix caroliniana
Salix discolor
Salix eriocephala
Salix exigua
Salix gooddingii
Salix interior
Salix lasiandra
Salix lasiolepis
Salix lucida
Salix nigra
Salix scouleriana
Salix taxifolia
Sambucus caerulea
Sambucus mexicana
Sapindus marginatus
Serenoa repens
Staphylea trifolia
Styrax americanus
Styrax grandifolius
Symplocos tinctoria
Taxodium ascendens
Taxodium distichum
Taxodium mucronatum
Thuja occidentalis
Thuja plicata
Tilia americana
Tilia caroliniana
Tilia floridana
Ulmus americana
Ulmus crassifolia

Ulmus racemosa
Ulmus rubra
Ulmus serotina
Viburnum cassinoides
Viburnum lentago
Viburnum nudum
Viburnum prunifolium
Viburnum rufidulum
Viburnum trilobum
Zanthoxylum americanum
Zanthoxylum clava-herculis

Trees tolerant of dry soils
Abies concolor
Acacia constricta
Acacia farnesiana
Acacia greggii
Acacia roemeriana
Acacia wrightii
Acer grandidentatum
Acer negundo
Aralia spinosa
Arbutus texana
Arbutus xalapensis
Artemisia tridentata
Betula populifolia
Bumelia celastrina
Bumelia lanuginosa
Bumelia lycioides
Bumelia tenax
Carya floridana
Carya glabra
Carya laciniosa
Carya myristicaeformis
Carya ovalis
Carya ovata
Carya pallida
Carya texana
Carya tomentosa
Castanea alnifolia
Castanea dentata
Castanea ozarkensis
Castanea pumila
Catalpa bignonioides
Catalpa speciosa
Celtis lindheimeri
Celtis occidentalis
Celtis pallida
Celtis reticulata
Celtis spinosa
Celtis tenuifolia
Cercidium texanum
Cercocarpus ledifolius
Cercocarpus montanus
Chilopsis linearis
Condalia globosa
Condalia hookeri
Cordia boissiera

Cornus asperifolia
Cornus drummondii
Cornus racemosa
Cotinus obovatus
Crataegus arnoldiana
Crataegus crusgalli
Crataegus douglasii
Crataegus marshallii
Crataegus mollis
Cupressus arizonica
Diospyros texana
Diospyros virginiana
Ehretia anacua
Erythrina herbacea
Forestiera angustifolia
Forestiera ligustrina
Forestiera neomexicana
Forestiera phillyreoides
Forestiera pubescens
Forestiera reticulta
Fraxinus anomala
Fraxinus berlandieriana
Fraxinus cuspidata
Fraxinus greggii
Fraxinus lowellii
Fraxinus quadrangulata
Fraxinus texensis
Fraxinus velutina
Garrya wrightii
Gleditsia triacanthos
Gymnocladus dioicus
Juglans major
Juglans microcarpa
Juglans nigra
Juniperus ashei
Juniperus coahuilensis
Juniperus communis
Juniperus deppeana
Juniperus erythrocarpa
Juniperus flacida
Juniperus horizontalis
Juniperus monosperma
Juniperus osteosperma
Juniperus pinchottii
Juniperus scopulorum
Juniperus silicicola
Juniperus virginiana
Leucaena pulverulenta
Leucaena retusa
Maclura pomifera
Magnolia grandiflora
Malus angustifolia
Malus coronaria
Malus diversifolia
Malus ioensis
Morus microphylla
Myrica cerifera
Myrica pensylvanica

Nyssa sylvatica
Ostrya chisosensis
Ostrya knowltonii
Ostrya virginiana
Parkinsonia aculeata
Picea pungens
Pinus albicaulis
Pinus aristata
Pinus arizonica
Pinus banksiana
Pinus cembroides
Pinus chihuahuana
Pinus clausa
Pinus contorta
Pinus discolor
Pinus echinata
Pinus edulis
Pinus elliottii
Pinus engelmannii
Pinus flexilis
Pinus leiophylla
Pinus longaeva
Pinus monophylla
Pinus monticola
Pinus palustris
Pinus ponderosa
Pinus pungens
Pinus quadrifolia
Pinus remota
Pinus resinosa
Pinus rigida
Pinus strobiformis
Pinus strobus
Pinus taeda
Pinus virginiana
Pistacia texana
Pithecellobium flexicaule
Platanus occidentalis
Platanus racemosa
Platanus wrightii
Populus deltoides
Populus fremontii
Populus grandidentata
Populus sargentii
Populus wislizeni
Prosopis glandulosa
Prosopis pubescens
Prosopis velutina
Prunus americana
Prunus angustifolia
Prunus emarginata
Prunus hortulana
Prunus maritima
Prunus mexicana
Prunus munsoniana
Prunus murrayana
Prunus nigra
Prunus pensylvanica

Prunus serotina
Prunus virginiana
Pseudotsuga menziesii
Ptelea trifoliata
Quercus acerifolia
Quercus alba
Quercus arizonica
Quercus arkansana
Quercus austrina
Quercus boyntonii
Quercus breviloba
Quercus buckleyi
Quercus chapmannii
Quercus coccinea
Quercus depressipes
Quercus ellipsoidalis
Quercus emoryi
Quercus engelmannii
Quercus falcata
Quercus fusiformis
Quercus gambelii
Quercus garryana
Quercus geminata
Quercus georgiana
Quercus graciliformis
Quercus gravesii
Quercus grisea
Quercus havardii
Quercus hemisphaerica
Quercus hinckleyi
Quercus hypoleucoides
Quercus ilicifolia
Quercus imbricaria
Quercus incana
Quercus inopina
Quercus intricata
Quercus laceyi
Quercus laevis
Quercus macrocarpa
Quercus margaretta
Quercus marilandica
Quercus minima
Quercus mohriana
Quercus montana
Quercus muhlenbergii
Quercus myrtifolia
Quercus nigra
Quercus oblongifolia
Quercus polymorpha
Quercus prinoides
Quercus pumila
Quercus pungens
Quercus rugosa
Quercus shumardii
Quercus similis
Quercus sinuata
Quercus stellata
Quercus tardifolia

Quercus toumeyi
Quercus turbinella
Quercus vaseyana
Quercus velutina
Quercus virginiana
Rhamnus betulifolia
Rhamnus caroliniana
Rhamnus lanceolata
Rhus aromatica
Rhus choriophylla
Rhus copallina
Rhus glabra
Rhus lanceolata
Rhus microphylla
Rhus typhina
Rhus virens
Robinia fertilis
Robinia hispida
Robinia neomexicana
Robinia pseudoacacia
Robinia viscosa
Sabal louisiana
Sabal mexicana
Sabal minor
Sabal palmetto
Sambucus caerulea
Sambucus mexicana
Sapindus drummondii
Sassafras albidum
Serenoa repens
Shepherdia argentea
Sophora affinis
Sophora secundiflora
Staphylea trifolia
Tecoma stans
Tilia americana
Ulmus alata
Ulmus americana
Ulmus crassifolia
Ulmus racemosa
Ulmus rubra
Ungnadia speciosa
Vaccinium arboreum
Vauquelinia angustifolia
Viburnum prunifolium
Viburnum rufidulum
Zanthoxylum americanum
Zanthoxylum clava-herculis

Trees tolerant of hot climates
(USDA zone 7 and south—
some may also be hardy
further north)
Acacia constricta
Acacia farnesiana
Acacia greggii
Acacia roemeriana
Acacia wrightii

Acer grandidentatum
Acer leucoderme
Acer negundo
Acer rubrum
Acer saccharinum
Aesculus arguta
Aesculus discolor
Aesculus flava
Aesculus parviflora
Aesculus pavia
Aesculus splendens
Aesculus sylvatica
Alnus maritima
Alnus oblongifolia
Alnus rugosa
Alnus serrulata
Alnus tenuifolia
Amelanchier alnifolia
Amelanchier utahensis
Amorpha fruticosa
Aralia spinosa
Arbutus texana
Arbutus xalapensis
Artemisia tridentata
Asimina parviflora
Asimina triloba
Betula nigra
Betula uber
Bumelia celastrina
Bumelia lanuginosa
Bumelia lycioides
Bumelia tenax
Carpinus caroliniana
Carya aquatica
Carya floridana
Carya glabra
Carya illinoinensis
Carya laciniosa
Carya myristicaeformis
Carya ovalis
Carya ovata
Carya pallida
Carya texana
Carya tomentosa
Castanea alnifolia
Castanea dentata
Castanea ozarkensis
Castanea pumila
Catalpa bignonioides
Catalpa speciosa
Celtis laevigata
Celtis lindheimeri
Celtis occidentalis
Celtis pallida
Celtis reticulata
Celtis spinosa
Celtis tenuifolia
Cephalanthus occidentalis

Cercidium texanum
Cercis canadensis
Cercis mexicana
Cercis occidentalis
Cercis reniformis
Cercis texensis
Cercocarpus ledifolius
Cercocarpus montanus
Chamaecyparis thyoides
Chilopsis linearis
Chionanthus pygmaeus
Chionanthus virginicus
Cladrastis kentuckea
Cliftonia monophylla
Condalia globosa
Condalia hookeri
Cordia boissiera
Cornus amomum
Cornus asperifolia
Cornus drummondii
Cornus foemina
Cornus obliqua
Cornus racemosa
Cornus sericea
Cotinus obovatus
Crataegus aestivalis
Crataegus crusgalli
Crataegus douglasii
Crataegus erythropoda
Crataegus marshallii
Crataegus mollis
Crataegus opaca
Crataegus phaenopyrum
Crataegus pruinosa
Crataegus punctata
Crataegus rivularis
Crataegus succulenta
Crataegus viridis
Cupressus arizonica
Cyrilla racemiflora
Diospyros texana
Diospyros virginiana
Dirca palustris
Ehretia anacua
Elliotia racemosa
Erythrina herbacea
Euonymus americanus
Euonymus atropurpureus
Fagus grandifolia
Forestiera acuminata
Forestiera angustifolia
Forestiera ligustrina
Forestiera neomexicana
Forestiera phillyreoides
Forestiera pubescens
Forestiera reticulta
Forestiera segregata
Franklinia alatamaha

Fraxinus americana
Fraxinus anomala
Fraxinus berlandieriana
Fraxinus biltmoreana
Fraxinus caroliniana
Fraxinus cuspidata
Fraxinus greggii
Fraxinus lowellii
Fraxinus pennsylvanica
Fraxinus quadrangulata
Fraxinus texensis
Fraxinus tomentosa
Fraxinus velutina
Garrya wrightii
Gleditsia aquatica
Gleditsia triacanthos
Gordonia lasianthus
Gymnocladus dioicus
Halesia diptera
Halesia monticola
Halesia parviflora
Halesia tetraptera
Hamamelis macrophylla
Hamamelis vernalis
Hamamelis virginiana
Ilex cassine
Ilex coriacea
Ilex decidua
Ilex glabra
Ilex montana
Ilex opaca
Ilex verticillata
Ilex vomitoria
Illicium floridanum
Illicium parviflorum
Juglans major
Juglans microcarpa
Juglans nigra
Juniperus ashei
Juniperus coahuilensis
Juniperus communis
Juniperus deppeana
Juniperus erythrocarpa
Juniperus flacida
Juniperus horizontalis
Juniperus monosperma
Juniperus osteosperma
Juniperus pinchottii
Juniperus scopulorum
Juniperus silicicola
Juniperus virginiana
Kalmia latifolia
Leitneria floridana
Leucaena pulverulenta
Leucaena retusa
Lindera benzoin
Liquidambar styraciflua
Liriodendron tulipifera

Maclura pomifera
Magnolia acuminata
Magnolia ashei
Magnolia cordata
Magnolia fraseri
Magnolia grandiflora
Magnolia macrophylla
Magnolia pyramidata
Magnolia tripetala
Magnolia virginiana
Malus angustifolia
Malus coronaria
Malus diversifolia
Malus ioensis
Morus microphylla
Morus rubra
Myrica cerifera
Myrica pensylvanica
Nemopanthus mucronatus
Nyssa aquatica
Nyssa biflora
Nyssa ogeche
Nyssa sylvatica
Osmanthus americanus
Ostrya chisosensis
Ostrya knowltonii
Ostrya virginiana
Oxydendrum arboreum
Parkinsonia aculeata
Persea borbonia
Picea glauca
Picea pungens
Pinckneya bracteata
Pinus arizonica
Pinus cembroides
Pinus chihuahuana
Pinus clausa
Pinus contorta
Pinus discolor
Pinus echinata
Pinus edulis
Pinus elliottii
Pinus engelmannii
Pinus flexilis
Pinus glabra
Pinus leiophylla
Pinus monophylla
Pinus palustris
Pinus ponderosa
Pinus pungens
Pinus quadrifolia
Pinus remota
Pinus rigida
Pinus serotina
Pinus strobiformis
Pinus taeda
Pinus virginiana
Pistacia texana

Pithecellobium flexicaule
Planera aquatica
Platanus occidentalis
Platanus racemosa
Platanus wrightii
Populus angustifolia
Populus deltoides
Populus fremontii
Populus grandidentata
Populus heterophylla
Populus sargentii
Populus wislizeni
Prosopis glandulosa
Prosopis pubescens
Prosopis velutina
Prunus americana
Prunus angustifolia
Prunus caroliniana
Prunus hortulana
Prunus maritima
Prunus mexicana
Prunus munsoniana
Prunus murrayana
Prunus rivularis
Prunus serotina
Prunus umbellata
Prunus virginiana
Pseudotsuga menziesii
Ptelea trifoliata
Quercus acerifolia
Quercus alba
Quercus arizonica
Quercus arkansana
Quercus austrina
Quercus bicolor
Quercus boyntonii
Quercus breviloba
Quercus buckleyi
Quercus chapmannii
Quercus coccinea
Quercus depressipes
Quercus emoryi
Quercus engelmannii
Quercus falcata
Quercus fusiformis
Quercus gambelii
Quercus geminata
Quercus georgiana
Quercus graciliformis
Quercus gravesii
Quercus grisea
Quercus havardii
Quercus hemisphaerica
Quercus hinckleyi
Quercus hypoleucoides
Quercus ilicifolia
Quercus imbricaria
Quercus incana

Quercus inopina
Quercus intricata
Quercus laceyi
Quercus laevis
Quercus laurifolia
Quercus lyrata
Quercus macrocarpa
Quercus margaretta
Quercus marilandica
Quercus michauxii
Quercus minima
Quercus mohriana
Quercus montana
Quercus muhlenbergii
Quercus myrtifolia
Quercus nigra
Quercus nuttallii
Quercus oblongifolia
Quercus oglethorpensis
Quercus pagoda
Quercus palustris
Quercus phellos
Quercus polymorpha
Quercus prinoides
Quercus pumila
Quercus pungens
Quercus rubra
Quercus rugosa
Quercus shumardii
Quercus similis
Quercus sinuata
Quercus stellata
Quercus tardifolia
Quercus toumeyi
Quercus turbinella
Quercus vaseyana
Quercus velutina
Quercus virginiana
Rhamnus betulifolia
Rhamnus caroliniana
Rhamnus lanceolata
Rhododendron catawbiense
Rhododendron maximum
Rhus aromatica
Rhus choriophylla
Rhus copallina
Rhus glabra
Rhus lanceolata
Rhus microphylla
Rhus typhina
Rhus vernix
Rhus virens
Robinia fertilis
Robinia hispida
Robinia neomexicana
Robinia pseudoacacia
Robinia viscosa
Sabal louisiana

Sabal mexicana
Sabal minor
Sabal palmetto
Salix amygdaloides
Salix caroliniana
Salix discolor
Salix eriocephala
Salix exigua
Salix gooddingii
Salix interior
Salix lasiolepis
Salix taxifolia
Sambucus caerulea
Sambucus mexicana
Sapindus drummondii
Sapindus marginatus
Sassafras albidum
Serenoa repens
Shepherdia argentea
Sophora affinis
Sophora secundiflora
Staphylea trifolia
Stewartia malacodendron
Stewartia ovata
Styrax americanus
Styrax grandifolius
Symplocos tinctoria
Taxodium ascendens
Taxodium distichum
Taxodium mucronatum
Tecoma stans
Tilia americana
Tilia caroliniana
Tilia floridana
Tilia heterophylla
Ulmus alata
Ulmus americana
Ulmus crassifolia
Ulmus rubra
Ulmus serotina
Ungnadia speciosa
Vaccinium arboreum
Vauquelinia angustifolia
Viburnum nudum
Viburnum prunifolium
Viburnum rufidulum
Viburnum trilobum
Zanthoxylum americanum
Zanthoxylum clava-herculis

Trees tolerant of cold climates (USDA zone 5 and north—some may also grow further south)
Abies balsamea
Abies lasiocarpa
Acer ×freemanii
Acer glabrum

Acer leucoderme
Acer negundo
Acer nigrum
Acer pensylvanicum
Acer rubrum
Acer saccharinum
Acer saccharum
Acer spicatum
Alnus rugosa
Alnus tenuifolia
Amelanchier arborea
Amelanchier canadensis
Amelanchier ×grandiflora
Amelanchier interior
Amelanchier laevis
Amelanchier neglecta
Amelanchier sanguinea
Amelanchier spicata
Amelanchier stolonifera
Amelanchier utahensis
Amorpha fruticosa
Artemisia tridentata
Betula alleghaniensis
Betula fontinalis
Betula lenta
Betula nigra
Betula papyrifera
Betula populifolia
Betula uber
Carpinus caroliniana
Carya cordiformis
Carya glabra
Carya laciniosa
Carya myristicaeformis
Carya ovalis
Carya ovata
Carya texana
Carya tomentosa
Castanea dentata
Catalpa speciosa
Celtis laevigata
Celtis occidentalis
Celtis reticulata
Celtis tenuifolia
Cephalanthus occidentalis
Chionanthus virginicus
Cladrastis kentuckea
Cornus alternifolia
Cornus amomum
Cornus asperifolia
Cornus drummondii
Cornus obliqua
Cornus racemosa
Cornus sericea
Cotinus obovatus
Crataegus arnoldiana
Crataegus crusgalli
Crataegus erythropoda

Crataegus mollis
Crataegus phaenopyrum
Crataegus pruinosa
Crataegus punctata
Crataegus rivularis
Crataegus succulenta
Crataegus viridis
Diospyros virginiana
Dirca palustris
Euonymus americanus
Euonymus atropurpureus
Fagus grandifolia
Forestiera acuminata
Fraxinus americana
Fraxinus biltmoreana
Fraxinus nigra
Fraxinus pennsylvanica
Fraxinus quadrangulata
Gleditsia triacanthos
Gymnocladus dioicus
Halesia monticola
Halesia tetraptera
Hamamelis vernalis
Hamamelis virginiana
Ilex decidua
Ilex glabra
Ilex montana
Ilex verticillata
Juglans cinerea
Juglans nigra
Juniperus communis
Juniperus horizontalis
Juniperus scopulorum
Juniperus virginiana
Larix laricina
Larix lyallii
Larix occidentalis
Leitneria floridana
Lindera benzoin
Liquidambar styraciflua
Liriodendron tulipifera
Maclura pomifera
Magnolia acuminata
Magnolia ashei
Magnolia cordata
Magnolia fraseri
Magnolia macrophylla
Magnolia pyramidata
Magnolia tripetala
Magnolia virginiana
Malus angustifolia
Malus coronaria
Malus diversifolia
Malus ioensis
Morus rubra
Myrica pensylvanica
Nemopanthus mucronatus
Nyssa sylvatica

Ostrya virginiana
Picea engelmannii
Picea glauca
Picea mariana
Picea pungens
Picea rubens
Pinus albicaulis
Pinus aristata
Pinus banksiana
Pinus contorta
Pinus echinata
Pinus flexilis
Pinus longaeva
Pinus monticola
Pinus palustris
Pinus ponderosa
Pinus pungens
Pinus resinosa
Pinus rigida
Pinus strobiformis
Pinus strobus
Pinus virginiana
Platanus occidentalis
Populus angustifolia
Populus balsamifera
Populus deltoides
Populus grandidentata
Populus heterophylla
Populus sargentii
Populus tremuloides
Prunus americana
Prunus angustifolia
Prunus hortulana
Prunus maritima
Prunus munsoniana
Prunus nigra
Prunus pensylvanica
Prunus rivularis
Prunus serotina
Prunus virginiana
Pseudotsuga menziesii
Ptelea trifoliata
Quercus acerifolia
Quercus alba
Quercus bicolor
Quercus coccinea
Quercus ellipsoidalis
Quercus falcata
Quercus gambelii
Quercus georgiana
Quercus ilicifolia
Quercus imbricaria
Quercus lyrata
Quercus macrocarpa
Quercus marilandica
Quercus michauxii
Quercus montana
Quercus muhlenbergii

Quercus nigra
Quercus oglethorpensis
Quercus pagoda
Quercus palustris
Quercus phellos
Quercus prinoides
Quercus rubra
Quercus shumardii
Quercus stellata
Quercus turbinella
Quercus velutina
Rhamnus betulifolia
Rhamnus caroliniana
Rhamnus lanceolata
Rhododendron catawbiense
Rhododendron maximum
Rhus aromatica
Rhus copallina
Rhus glabra
Rhus lanceolata
Rhus typhina
Rhus vernix
Robinia fertilis
Robinia hispida
Robinia pseudoacacia
Robinia viscosa
Salix amygdaloides
Salix bebbiana
Salix discolor
Salix eriocephala
Salix exigua
Salix interior
Salix lasiandra
Salix lucida
Salix nigra
Salix scouleriana
Sapindus drummondii
Sassafras albidum
Shepherdia argentea
Sorbus americana
Sorbus decora
Sorbus scopulina
Sorbus sitchensis
Staphylea trifolia
Styrax americanus
Taxodium ascendens
Taxodium distichum
Thuja occidentalis
Thuja plicata
Tilia americana
Tilia heterophylla
Tsuga canadensis
Tsuga caroliniana
Ulmus alata
Ulmus americana
Ulmus crassifolia
Ulmus racemosa
Ulmus rubra

Viburnum cassinoides
Viburnum lentago
Viburnum prunifolium
Viburnum rufidulum
Viburnum trilobum
Zanthoxylum americanum

Trees tolerant of shady sites or forest understory

Abies balsamea
Acer barbatum
Acer ×freemanii
Acer glabrum
Acer grandidentatum
Acer leucoderme
Acer nigrum
Acer pensylvanicum
Acer rubrum
Acer saccharum
Acer spicatum
Aesculus arguta
Aesculus discolor
Aesculus flava
Aesculus glabra
Aesculus parviflora
Aesculus pavia
Aesculus splendens
Aesculus sylvatica
Amelanchier alnifolia
Amelanchier arborea
Amelanchier bartramaniana
Amelanchier canadensis
Amelanchier ×grandiflora
Amelanchier interior
Amelanchier laevis
Amelanchier neglecta
Amelanchier sanguinea
Amelanchier spicata
Amelanchier stolonifera
Amelanchier utahensis
Aralia spinosa
Asimina parviflora
Asimina triloba
Betula alleghaniensis
Carpinus caroliniana
Catalpa bignonioides
Catalpa speciosa
Cercis canadensis
Cercis mexicana
Cercis occidentalis
Cercis reniformis
Cercis texensis
Chionanthus pygmaeus
Chionanthus virginicus
Cladrastis kentuckea
Cliftonia monophylla
Cornus amomum
Cornus asperifolia

Cornus drummondii
Cornus florida
Cornus foemina
Cornus obliqua
Cornus racemosa
Cornus sericea
Dirca palustris
Elliotia racemosa
Euonymus americanus
Euonymus atropurpureus
Fagus grandifolia
Forestiera acuminata
Franklinia alatamaha
Halesia diptera
Halesia monticola
Halesia parviflora
Halesia tetraptera
Hamamelis macrophylla
Hamamelis vernalis
Hamamelis virginiana
Ilex cassine
Ilex coriacea
Ilex decidua
Ilex glabra
Ilex montana
Ilex opaca
Ilex verticillata
Ilex vomitoria
Illicium floridanum
Illicium parviflorum
Kalmia latifolia
Lindera benzoin
Magnolia acuminata
Magnolia ashei
Magnolia cordata
Magnolia fraseri
Magnolia grandiflora
Magnolia macrophylla
Magnolia pyramidata
Magnolia tripetala
Magnolia virginiana
Morus rubra
Nyssa aquatica
Nyssa biflora
Nyssa ogeche
Osmanthus americanus
Oxydendrum arboreum
Picea engelmannii
Picea glauca
Picea rubens
Pinus glabra
Planera aquatica
Prunus virginiana
Ptelea trifoliata
Quercus incana
Quercus minima
Quercus pumila
Quercus rubra

Quercus virginiana
Rhamnus betulifolia
Rhamnus caroliniana
Rhamnus lanceolata
Rhododendron catawbiense
Rhododendron maximum
Rhus aromatica
Robinia pseudoacacia
Sabal louisiana
Sabal mexicana
Sabal minor
Sabal palmetto
Serenoa repens
Staphylea trifolia
Stewartia malacodendron
Stewartia ovata
Styrax americanus
Styrax grandifolius
Symplocos tinctoria
Thuja occidentalis
Thuja plicata
Tilia americana
Tilia caroliniana
Tilia floridana
Tilia heterophylla
Tsuga canadensis
Tsuga caroliniana
Ulmus americana
Ulmus rubra
Ulmus serotina
Vaccinium arboreum
Viburnum cassinoides
Viburnum lentago
Viburnum nudum
Viburnum prunifolium
Viburnum rufidulum
Viburnum trilobum
Zanthoxylum americanum
Zanthoxylum clava-herculis

Trees with evergreen or subevergreen foliage

Abies balsamea
Abies concolor
Abies fraseri
Abies lasiocarpa
Arbutus texana
Arbutus xalapensis
Artemisia tridentata
Bumelia celastrina
Celtis pallida
Celtis spinosa
Cercidium texanum
Chamaecyparis thyoides
Cliftonia monophylla
Cupressus arizonica
Cyrilla racemiflora
Gordonia lasianthus

Ilex cassine
Ilex coriacea
Ilex glabra
Ilex opaca
Ilex vomitoria
Illicium floridanum
Illicium parviflorum
Juniperus ashei
Juniperus coahuilensis
Juniperus communis
Juniperus deppeana
Juniperus erythrocarpa
Juniperus flacida
Juniperus horizontalis
Juniperus monosperma
Juniperus osteosperma
Juniperus pinchottii
Juniperus scopulorum
Juniperus silicicola
Juniperus virginiana
Kalmia latifolia
Magnolia grandiflora
Magnolia virginiana
Myrica cerifera
Osmanthus americanus
Persea borbonia
Picea engelmannii
Picea glauca
Picea mariana
Picea pungens
Picea rubens
Pinus albicaulis
Pinus aristata
Pinus arizonica
Pinus banksiana
Pinus cembroides
Pinus chihuahuana
Pinus clausa
Pinus contorta
Pinus discolor
Pinus echinata
Pinus edulis
Pinus elliottii
Pinus engelmannii
Pinus flexilis
Pinus glabra
Pinus leiophylla
Pinus longaeva
Pinus monophylla
Pinus monticola
Pinus palustris
Pinus ponderosa
Pinus pungens
Pinus quadrifolia
Pinus remota
Pinus resinosa
Pinus rigida
Pinus serotina

Pinus strobiformis
Pinus strobus
Pinus taeda
Pinus virginiana
Pithecellobium flexicaule
Prunus caroliniana
Pseudotsuga menziesii
Quercus depressipes
Quercus emoryi
Quercus fusiformis
Quercus geminata
Quercus grisea
Quercus hemisphaerica
Quercus hinckleyi
Quercus hypoleucoides
Quercus inopina
Quercus intricata
Quercus minima
Quercus mohriana
Quercus myrtifolia
Quercus polymorpha
Quercus pumila
Quercus pungens
Quercus rugosa
Quercus toumeyi
Quercus turbinella
Quercus vaseyana
Quercus virginiana
Rhododendron catawbiense
Rhododendron maximum
Rhus choriophylla
Rhus virens
Sabal louisiana
Sabal mexicana
Sabal minor
Sabal palmetto
Serenoa repens
Sophora secundiflora
Symplocos tinctoria
Thuja occidentalis
Thuja plicata
Tsuga canadensis
Tsuga caroliniana
Vauquelinia angustifolia

Trees with good autumn color
Acer barbatum
Acer ×freemanii
Acer glabrum
Acer grandidentatum
Acer nigrum
Acer pensylvanicum
Acer rubrum
Acer saccharum
Acer spicatum
Aesculus parviflora
Amelanchier alnifolia

Amelanchier arborea
Amelanchier bartramaniana
Amelanchier canadensis
Amelanchier ×grandiflora
Amelanchier interior
Amelanchier laevis
Amelanchier neglecta
Amelanchier sanguinea
Amelanchier spicata
Amelanchier stolonifera
Amelanchier utahensis
Asimina triloba
Betula alleghaniensis
Betula lenta
Betula papyrifera
Betula populifolia
Betula uber
Carpinus caroliniana
Carya cordiformis
Carya floridana
Carya glabra
Carya laciniosa
Carya myristicaeformis
Carya ovalis
Carya ovata
Carya pallida
Carya texana
Carya tomentosa
Castanea dentata
Castanea ozarkensis
Castanea pumila
Celtis laevigata
Celtis tenuifolia
Cercis canadensis
Chionanthus pygmaeus
Chionanthus virginicus
Cladrastis kentuckea
Cornus drummondii
Cornus florida
Cornus racemosa
Cotinus obovatus
Crataegus aestivalis
Crataegus arnoldiana
Crataegus crusgalli
Crataegus phaenopyrum
Crataegus pruinosa
Crataegus punctata
Cyrilla racemiflora
Diospyros virginiana
Elliotia racemosa
Euonymus atropurpureus
Fagus grandifolia
Fraxinus americana
Fraxinus nigra
Fraxinus pennsylvanica
Fraxinus quadrangulata
Gleditsia triacanthos
Gordonia lasianthus

Gymnocladus dioicus
Hamamelis macrophylla
Hamamelis vernalis
Hamamelis virginiana
Juglans nigra
Larix laricina
Larix lyallii
Larix occidentalis
Leitneria floridana
Lindera benzoin
Liquidambar styraciflua
Liriodendron tulipifera
Maclura pomifera
Morus rubra
Nyssa sylvatica
Ostrya chisosensis
Ostrya knowltonii
Ostrya virginiana
Oxydendrum arboreum
Pistacia texana
Platanus occidentalis
Platanus racemosa
Platanus wrightii
Populus angustifolia
Populus balsamifera
Populus deltoides
Populus fremontii
Populus grandidentata
Populus sargentii
Populus tremuloides
Populus trichocarpa
Populus wislizeni
Prunus emarginata
Prunus pensylvanica
Prunus serotina
Quercus acerifolia
Quercus alba
Quercus bicolor
Quercus buckleyi
Quercus coccinea
Quercus ellipsoidalis
Quercus falcata
Quercus gambelii
Quercus georgiana
Quercus gravesii
Quercus ilicifolia
Quercus incana
Quercus laceyi
Quercus laevis
Quercus lyrata
Quercus margaretta
Quercus marilandica
Quercus michauxii
Quercus montana
Quercus muhlenbergii
Quercus nigra
Quercus nuttallii
Quercus oglethorpensis

Quercus pagoda
Quercus palustris
Quercus phellos
Quercus prinoides
Quercus rubra
Quercus shumardii
Quercus sinuata
Quercus stellata
Quercus velutina
Rhamnus betulifolia
Rhamnus caroliniana
Rhus aromatica
Rhus copallina
Rhus glabra
Rhus lanceolata
Rhus typhina
Rhus vernix
Salix bebbiana
Salix exigua
Salix gooddingii
Salix interior
Salix lasiandra
Salix lasiolepis
Salix scouleriana
Sassafras albidum
Sorbus americana
Sorbus decora
Sorbus scopulina
Sorbus sitchensis
Stewartia malacodendron
Stewartia ovata
Taxodium ascendens
Taxodium distichum
Tilia americana
Ulmus alata
Ulmus americana
Ulmus crassifolia
Ulmus racemosa
Ulmus serotina
Vaccinium arboreum
Viburnum lentago
Viburnum prunifolium
Viburnum rufidulum
Viburnum trilobum

Trees notable for blooming

Acacia constricta
Acacia farnesiana
Acacia greggii
Acacia roemeriana
Acacia wrightii
Acer rubrum
Acer spicatum
Aesculus arguta
Aesculus discolor
Aesculus flava
Aesculus glabra
Aesculus parviflora

Aesculus pavia
Aesculus splendens
Aesculus sylvatica
Amelanchier alnifolia
Amelanchier arborea
Amelanchier bartramaniana
Amelanchier canadensis
Amelanchier ×grandiflora
Amelanchier interior
Amelanchier laevis
Amelanchier neglecta
Amelanchier sanguinea
Amelanchier spicata
Amelanchier stolonifera
Amelanchier utahensis
Amorpha fruticosa
Aralia spinosa
Arbutus texana
Arbutus xalapensis
Carya cordiformis
Castanea alnifolia
Castanea dentata
Castanea ozarkensis
Castanea pumila
Catalpa bignonioides
Catalpa speciosa
Cephalanthus occidentalis
Cercidium texanum
Cercis canadensis
Cercis mexicana
Cercis occidentalis
Cercis reniformis
Cercis texensis
Cercocarpus ledifolius
Cercocarpus montanus
Chilopsis linearis
Chionanthus pygmaeus
Chionanthus virginicus
Cladrastis kentuckea
Cliftonia monophylla
Cordia boissiera
Cornus alternifolia
Cornus amomum
Cornus drummondii
Cornus florida
Cornus foemina
Cornus obliqua
Cornus racemosa
Cornus sericea
Cotinus obovatus
Crataegus aestivalis
Crataegus arnoldiana
Crataegus crusgalli
Crataegus douglasii
Crataegus erythropoda
Crataegus marshallii
Crataegus mollis
Crataegus opaca

Crataegus phaenopyrum
Crataegus pruinosa
Crataegus punctata
Crataegus rivularis
Crataegus succulenta
Crataegus viridis
Cyrilla racemiflora
Ehretia anacua
Elliotia racemosa
Erythrina herbacea
Forestiera acuminata
Franklinia alatamaha
Fraxinus cuspidata
Garrya wrightii
Gordonia lasianthus
Halesia diptera
Halesia monticola
Halesia parviflora
Halesia tetraptera
Hamamelis macrophylla
Hamamelis vernalis
Hamamelis virginiana
Illicium floridanum
Illicium parviflorum
Kalmia latifolia
Leucaena pulverulenta
Leucaena retusa
Lindera benzoin
Liriodendron tulipifera
Magnolia acuminata
Magnolia ashei
Magnolia cordata
Magnolia fraseri
Magnolia grandiflora
Magnolia macrophylla
Magnolia pyramidata
Magnolia tripetala
Magnolia virginiana
Malus angustifolia
Malus coronaria
Malus diversifolia
Malus ioensis
Osmanthus americanus
Oxydendrum arboreum
Parkinsonia aculeata
Persea borbonia
Pinckneya bracteata
Pithecellobium flexicaule
Prosopis glandulosa
Prosopis pubescens
Prosopis velutina
Prunus americana
Prunus angustifolia
Prunus caroliniana
Prunus emarginata
Prunus hortulana
Prunus maritima
Prunus mexicana

Prunus munsoniana
Prunus murrayana
Prunus nigra
Prunus pensylvanica
Prunus rivularis
Prunus serotina
Prunus umbellata
Prunus virginiana
Quercus marilandica
Quercus velutina
Rhododendron catawbiense
Rhododendron maximum
Rhus aromatica
Rhus choriophylla
Rhus copallina
Rhus glabra
Rhus lanceolata
Rhus typhina
Rhus vernix
Rhus virens
Robinia fertilis
Robinia hispida
Robinia neomexicana
Robinia pseudoacacia
Robinia viscosa
Sabal mexicana
Sabal palmetto
Salix bebbiana
Salix discolor
Sambucus caerulea
Sambucus mexicana
Sassafras albidum
Sophora affinis
Sophora secundiflora
Sorbus americana
Sorbus decora
Sorbus scopulina
Sorbus sitchensis
Stewartia malacodendron
Stewartia ovata
Styrax americanus
Styrax grandifolius
Symplocos tinctoria
Tecoma stans
Ungnadia speciosa
Vaccinium arboreum
Vauquelinia angustifolia
Viburnum cassinoides
Viburnum lentago
Viburnum nudum
Viburnum prunifolium
Viburnum rufidulum
Viburnum trilobum

Trees notable for conspicuous or edible fruits

Acer rubrum
Aesculus arguta

Aesculus discolor
Aesculus flava
Aesculus glabra
Aesculus parviflora
Aesculus pavia
Aesculus splendens
Aesculus sylvatica
Amelanchier alnifolia
Amelanchier arborea
Amelanchier bartramaniana
Amelanchier canadensis
Amelanchier ×grandiflora
Amelanchier interior
Amelanchier laevis
Amelanchier neglecta
Amelanchier sanguinea
Amelanchier spicata
Amelanchier stolonifera
Amelanchier utahensis
Aralia spinosa
Arbutus texana
Arbutus xalapensis
Asimina parviflora
Asimina triloba
Carya floridana
Carya glabra
Carya illinoinensis
Carya laciniosa
Carya myristicaeformis
Carya ovalis
Carya ovata
Carya pallida
Carya texana
Carya tomentosa
Castanea alnifolia
Castanea dentata
Castanea ozarkensis
Castanea pumila
Catalpa bignonioides
Catalpa speciosa
Celtis tenuifolia
Cephalanthus occidentalis
Cercocarpus ledifolius
Cercocarpus montanus
Chionanthus pygmaeus
Chionanthus virginicus
Condalia globosa
Condalia hookeri
Cornus alternifolia
Cornus amomum
Cornus drummondii
Cornus florida
Cornus foemina
Cornus obliqua
Cornus racemosa
Cornus sericea
Cotinus obovatus
Crataegus aestivalis

Crataegus arnoldiana
Crataegus crusgalli
Crataegus douglasii
Crataegus erythropoda
Crataegus marshallii
Crataegus mollis
Crataegus opaca
Crataegus phaenopyrum
Crataegus pruinosa
Crataegus punctata
Crataegus rivularis
Crataegus succulenta
Crataegus viridis
Diospyros texana
Diospyros virginiana
Erythrina herbacea
Euonymus americanus
Euonymus atropurpureus
Forestiera acuminata
Fraxinus americana f. iodocarpa
Gleditsia triacanthos
Gymnocladus dioicus
Ilex cassine
Ilex coriacea
Ilex decidua
Ilex montana
Ilex opaca
Ilex verticillata
Ilex vomitoria
Juglans cinerea
Juglans major
Juglans microcarpa
Juglans nigra
Leucaena pulverulenta
Leucaena retusa
Lindera benzoin
Liquidambar styraciflua
Maclura pomifera
Magnolia acuminata
Magnolia ashei
Magnolia cordata
Magnolia fraseri
Magnolia grandiflora
Magnolia macrophylla
Magnolia pyramidata
Magnolia tripetala
Magnolia virginiana
Malus angustifolia
Malus coronaria
Malus diversifolia
Malus ioensis
Morus microphylla
Morus rubra
Nemopanthus mucronatus
Nyssa aquatica
Nyssa biflora
Nyssa ogeche
Nyssa sylvatica

Oxydendrum arboreum
Pinus arizonica
Pinus cembroides
Pinus discolor
Pinus edulis
Pinus elliottii
Pinus engelmannii
Pinus monophylla
Pinus monticola
Pinus palustris
Pinus ponderosa
Pinus pungens
Pinus quadrifolia
Pinus remota
Pinus strobiformis
Pinus strobus
Pinus taeda
Pistacia texana
Platanus occidentalis
Platanus racemosa
Platanus wrightii
Prosopis glandulosa
Prosopis pubescens
Prosopis velutina
Prunus americana
Prunus angustifolia
Prunus caroliniana
Prunus emarginata
Prunus hortulana
Prunus maritima
Prunus mexicana
Prunus munsoniana
Prunus murrayana
Prunus nigra
Prunus pensylvanica
Prunus rivularis
Prunus serotina
Prunus umbellata
Prunus virginiana
Ptelea trifoliata
Quercus acerifolia
Quercus alba
Quercus arizonica
Quercus arkansana
Quercus austrina
Quercus bicolor
Quercus boyntonii
Quercus breviloba
Quercus buckleyi
Quercus chapmannii
Quercus coccinea
Quercus depressipes
Quercus ellipsoidalis
Quercus emoryi
Quercus engelmannii
Quercus falcata
Quercus fusiformis
Quercus gambelii

Quercus garryana
Quercus geminata
Quercus georgiana
Quercus graciliformis
Quercus gravesii
Quercus grisea
Quercus havardii
Quercus hemisphaerica
Quercus hinckleyi
Quercus hypoleucoides
Quercus ilicifolia
Quercus imbricaria
Quercus incana
Quercus inopina
Quercus intricata
Quercus laceyi
Quercus laevis
Quercus laurifolia
Quercus lyrata
Quercus macrocarpa
Quercus margaretta
Quercus marilandica
Quercus michauxii
Quercus minima
Quercus mohriana
Quercus montana
Quercus muhlenbergii
Quercus myrtifolia
Quercus nigra
Quercus nuttallii
Quercus oblongifolia
Quercus oglethorpensis
Quercus pagoda
Quercus palustris
Quercus phellos
Quercus polymorpha
Quercus prinoides
Quercus pumila
Quercus pungens
Quercus rubra
Quercus rugosa
Quercus shumardii
Quercus similis
Quercus sinuata
Quercus stellata
Quercus toumeyi
Quercus turbinella
Quercus vaseyana
Quercus velutina
Quercus virginiana
Rhamnus betulifolia
Rhamnus caroliniana
Rhus aromatica
Rhus choriophylla
Rhus glabra
Rhus lanceolata
Rhus typhina
Rhus virens

Sabal louisiana
Sabal minor
Sabal palmetto
Sambucus caerulea
Sambucus mexicana
Sapindus drummondii
Sapindus marginatus
Sassafras albidum
Sophora affinis
Sophora secundiflora
Sorbus americana
Sorbus decora
Sorbus scopulina
Sorbus sitchensis
Staphylea trifolia
Symplocos tinctoria
Tecoma stans
Ungnadia speciosa
Vaccinium arboreum
Viburnum cassinoides
Viburnum lentago
Viburnum nudum
Viburnum prunifolium
Viburnum rufidulum
Viburnum trilobum
Zanthoxylum americanum
Zanthoxylum clava-herculis

Tall or large trees
Abies balsamea
Abies concolor
Abies fraseri
Abies lasiocarpa
Acer barbatum
Acer ×freemanii
Acer grandidentatum
Acer negundo
Acer nigrum
Acer rubrum
Acer saccharinum
Acer saccharum
Aesculus flava
Aesculus glabra
Alnus maritima
Alnus oblongifolia
Amelanchier arborea
Amelanchier interior
Amelanchier laevis
Betula alleghaniensis
Betula lenta
Betula nigra
Betula papyrifera
Betula populifolia
Betula uber
Carya aquatica
Carya cordiformis
Carya floridana
Carya glabra

Carya illinoinensis
Carya laciniosa
Carya myristicaeformis
Carya ovalis
Carya ovata
Carya pallida
Carya texana
Carya tomentosa
Castanea dentata
Catalpa bignonioides
Catalpa speciosa
Celtis laevigata
Celtis occidentalis
Chamaecyparis thyoides
Cladrastis kentuckea
Cupressus arizonica
Diospyros virginiana
Fagus grandifolia
Fraxinus americana
Fraxinus biltmoreana
Fraxinus caroliniana
Fraxinus nigra
Fraxinus pennsylvanica
Fraxinus quadrangulata
Fraxinus texensis
Fraxinus tomentosa
Fraxinus velutina
Gleditsia aquatica
Gleditsia triacanthos
Gordonia lasianthus
Gymnocladus dioicus
Halesia diptera
Halesia monticola
Halesia tetraptera
Ilex opaca
Juglans cinerea
Juglans major
Juglans nigra
Juniperus deppeana
Juniperus scopulorum
Juniperus silicicola
Juniperus virginiana
Larix laricina
Larix lyallii
Larix occidentalis
Liquidambar styraciflua
Liriodendron tulipifera
Maclura pomifera
Magnolia acuminata
Magnolia cordata
Magnolia fraseri
Magnolia grandiflora
Magnolia macrophylla
Magnolia pyramidata
Magnolia tripetala
Morus rubra
Nyssa aquatica
Nyssa biflora

Nyssa ogeche
Nyssa sylvatica
Oxydendrum arboreum
Persea borbonia
Picea engelmannii
Picea glauca
Picea mariana
Picea pungens
Picea rubens
Pinus arizonica
Pinus banksiana
Pinus chihuahuana
Pinus contorta
Pinus echinata
Pinus elliottii
Pinus engelmannii
Pinus flexilis
Pinus glabra
Pinus monticola
Pinus palustris
Pinus ponderosa
Pinus resinosa
Pinus rigida
Pinus serotina
Pinus strobiformis
Pinus strobus
Pinus taeda
Pinus virginiana
Platanus occidentalis
Platanus racemosa
Platanus wrightii
Populus angustifolia
Populus balsamifera
Populus deltoides
Populus fremontii
Populus grandidentata
Populus heterophylla
Populus sargentii
Populus tremuloides
Populus trichocarpa
Populus wislizeni
Prunus emarginata
Prunus pensylvanica
Prunus serotina
Pseudotsuga menziesii
Quercus alba
Quercus arizonica
Quercus arkansana
Quercus austrina
Quercus bicolor
Quercus coccinea
Quercus ellipsoidalis
Quercus emoryi
Quercus engelmannii
Quercus falcata
Quercus fusiformis
Quercus gambelii
Quercus garryana

Quercus geminata
Quercus graciliformis
Quercus gravesii
Quercus grisea
Quercus hemisphaerica
Quercus hypoleucoides
Quercus imbricaria
Quercus laceyi
Quercus laurifolia
Quercus lyrata
Quercus macrocarpa
Quercus margaretta
Quercus marilandica
Quercus michauxii
Quercus montana
Quercus muhlenbergii
Quercus nigra
Quercus nuttallii
Quercus oblongifolia
Quercus oglethorpensis
Quercus pagoda
Quercus palustris
Quercus phellos
Quercus polymorpha
Quercus rubra
Quercus rugosa
Quercus shumardii
Quercus similis
Quercus sinuata
Quercus stellata
Quercus tardifolia
Quercus velutina
Quercus virginiana
Robinia neomexicana
Robinia pseudoacacia
Sabal palmetto
Salix amygdaloides
Salix caroliniana
Salix gooddingii
Salix lasiandra
Salix nigra
Sapindus drummondii
Sassafras albidum
Taxodium ascendens
Taxodium distichum
Taxodium mucronatum
Thuja occidentalis
Thuja plicata
Tilia americana
Tilia caroliniana
Tilia floridana
Tilia heterophylla
Tsuga canadensis
Tsuga caroliniana
Ulmus alata
Ulmus americana
Ulmus crassifolia
Ulmus racemosa

Ulmus rubra
Ulmus serotina

Short or shrubby trees

(some may be larger in
certain habitats)
Acacia constricta
Acacia farnesiana
Acacia greggii
Acacia roemeriana
Acacia wrightii
Acer glabrum
Acer grandidentatum
Acer leucoderme
Acer pensylvanicum
Acer spicatum
Aesculus arguta
Aesculus discolor
Aesculus parviflora
Aesculus pavia
Aesculus splendens
Aesculus sylvatica
Alnus rugosa
Alnus serrulata
Alnus tenuifolia
Amelanchier alnifolia
Amelanchier arborea
Amelanchier bartramaniana
Amelanchier canadensis
Amelanchier ×grandiflora
Amelanchier interior
Amelanchier laevis
Amelanchier neglecta
Amelanchier sanguinea
Amelanchier spicata
Amelanchier stolonifera
Amelanchier utahensis
Amorpha fruticosa
Aralia spinosa
Arbutus texana
Arbutus xalapensis
Artemisia tridentata
Asimina parviflora
Asimina triloba
Betula fontinalis
Betula populifolia
Bumelia celastrina
Bumelia lanuginosa
Bumelia lycioides
Bumelia tenax
Carpinus caroliniana
Castanea alnifolia
Castanea ozarkensis
Castanea pumila
Celtis lindheimeri
Celtis pallida
Celtis reticulata
Celtis spinosa

Celtis tenuifolia
Cephalanthus occidentalis
Cercidium texanum
Cercis canadensis
Cercis mexicana
Cercis occidentalis
Cercis reniformis
Cercis texensis
Cercocarpus ledifolius
Cercocarpus montanus
Chilopsis linearis
Chionanthus pygmaeus
Chionanthus virginicus
Cliftonia monophylla
Condalia globosa
Condalia hookeri
Cordia boissiera
Cornus alternifolia
Cornus amomum
Cornus asperifolia
Cornus drummondii
Cornus florida
Cornus foemina
Cornus obliqua
Cornus racemosa
Cornus sericea
Cotinus obovatus
Crataegus aestivalis
Crataegus arnoldiana
Crataegus crusgalli
Crataegus douglasii
Crataegus erythropoda
Crataegus marshallii
Crataegus mollis
Crataegus opaca
Crataegus phaenopyrum
Crataegus pruinosa
Crataegus punctata
Crataegus rivularis
Crataegus succulenta
Crataegus viridis
Cyrilla racemiflora
Diospyros texana
Dirca palustris
Ehretia anacua
Elliotia racemosa
Erythrina herbacea
Euonymus americanus
Euonymus atropurpureus
Forestiera acuminata
Forestiera angustifolia
Forestiera ligustrina
Forestiera neomexicana
Forestiera phillyreoides
Forestiera pubescens
Forestiera reticulta
Forestiera segregata
Franklinia alatamaha

Fraxinus anomala
Fraxinus berlandieriana
Fraxinus cuspidata
Fraxinus greggii
Fraxinus lowellii
Fraxinus texensis
Garrya wrightii
Gordonia lasianthus
Halesia diptera
Halesia parviflora
Halesia tetraptera
Hamamelis macrophylla
Hamamelis vernalis
Hamamelis virginiana
Ilex cassine
Ilex coriacea
Ilex decidua
Ilex glabra
Ilex montana
Ilex verticillata
Ilex vomitoria
Illicium floridanum
Illicium parviflorum
Juglans microcarpa
Juniperus ashei
Juniperus coahuilensis
Juniperus communis
Juniperus erythrocarpa
Juniperus flacida
Juniperus horizontalis
Juniperus monosperma
Juniperus osteosperma
Juniperus pinchottii
Kalmia latifolia
Larix lyallii
Leitneria floridana
Leucaena pulverulenta
Leucaena retusa
Lindera benzoin
Magnolia ashei
Magnolia fraseri
Magnolia macrophylla
Magnolia pyramidata
Magnolia tripetala
Magnolia virginiana
Malus angustifolia
Malus coronaria
Malus diversifolia
Malus ioensis
Morus microphylla
Myrica cerifera
Myrica pensylvanica
Nemopanthus mucronatus
Nyssa ogeche
Osmanthus americanus
Ostrya chisosensis
Ostrya knowltonii
Ostrya virginiana

Oxydendrum arboreum
Parkinsonia aculeata
Persea borbonia
Pinckneya bracteata
Pinus albicaulis
Pinus aristata
Pinus banksiana
Pinus cembroides
Pinus chihuahuana
Pinus clausa
Pinus discolor
Pinus edulis
Pinus leiophylla
Pinus longaeva
Pinus monophylla
Pinus pungens
Pinus quadrifolia
Pinus remota
Pinus rigida
Pinus virginiana
Pistacia texana
Pithecellobium flexicaule
Planera aquatica
Prosopis glandulosa
Prosopis pubescens
Prosopis velutina
Prunus americana
Prunus angustifolia
Prunus caroliniana
Prunus emarginata
Prunus hortulana
Prunus maritima
Prunus mexicana
Prunus munsoniana
Prunus murrayana
Prunus nigra
Prunus pensylvanica
Prunus rivularis
Prunus umbellata
Prunus virginiana
Ptelea trifoliata
Quercus acerifolia
Quercus arkansana
Quercus austrina
Quercus boyntonii
Quercus breviloba
Quercus buckleyi
Quercus chapmannii
Quercus depressipes
Quercus fusiformis
Quercus gambelii
Quercus geminata
Quercus georgiana
Quercus graciliformis
Quercus gravesii
Quercus grisea
Quercus havardii
Quercus hinckleyi

Quercus hypoleucoides
Quercus ilicifolia
Quercus incana
Quercus inopina
Quercus intricata
Quercus laceyi
Quercus laevis
Quercus margaretta
Quercus marilandica
Quercus minima
Quercus mohriana
Quercus myrtifolia
Quercus prinoides
Quercus pumila
Quercus pungens
Quercus rugosa
Quercus toumeyi
Quercus turbinella
Quercus vaseyana
Rhamnus betulifolia
Rhamnus caroliniana
Rhamnus lanceolata

Rhododendron catawbiense
Rhododendron maximum
Rhus aromatica
Rhus choriophylla
Rhus copallina
Rhus glabra
Rhus lanceolata
Rhus microphylla
Rhus typhina
Rhus vernix
Rhus virens
Robinia fertilis
Robinia hispida
Robinia neomexicana
Robinia viscosa
Sabal louisiana
Sabal minor
Salix bebbiana
Salix caroliniana
Salix discolor
Salix eriocephala
Salix exigua

Salix interior
Salix lasiolepis
Salix lucida
Salix scouleriana
Salix taxifolia
Sambucus caerulea
Sambucus mexicana
Sapindus drummondii
Sapindus marginatus
Sassafras albidum
Serenoa repens
Shepherdia argentea
Sophora affinis
Sophora secundiflora
Sorbus americana
Sorbus decora
Sorbus scopulina
Sorbus sitchensis
Staphylea trifolia
Stewartia malacodendron
Stewartia ovata

Styrax americanus
Styrax grandifolius
Symplocos tinctoria
Tecoma stans
Thuja occidentalis
Tilia caroliniana
Tilia floridana
Ulmus alata
Ulmus crassifolia
Ulmus serotina
Ungnadia speciosa
Vaccinium arboreum
Vauquelinia angustifolia
Viburnum cassinoides
Viburnum lentago
Viburnum nudum
Viburnum prunifolium
Viburnum rufidulum
Viburnum trilobum
Zanthoxylum americanum
Zanthoxylum clava-herculis

U.S. Department of Agriculture
Plant Hardiness Zone Map

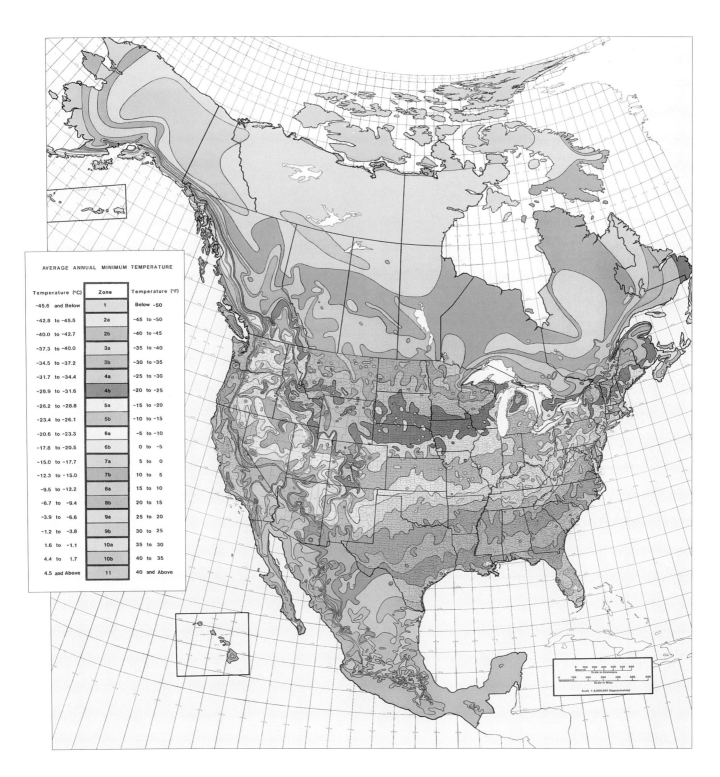

AVERAGE ANNUAL MINIMUM TEMPERATURE		
Temperature (°C)	Zone	Temperature (°F)
−45.6 and Below	1	Below −50
−42.8 to −45.5	2a	−45 to −50
−40.0 to −42.7	2b	−40 to −45
−37.3 to −40.0	3a	−35 to −40
−34.5 to −37.2	3b	−30 to −35
−31.7 to −34.4	4a	−25 to −30
−28.9 to −31.6	4b	−20 to −25
−26.2 to −28.8	5a	−15 to −20
−23.4 to −26.1	5b	−10 to −15
−20.6 to −23.3	6a	−5 to −10
−17.8 to −20.5	6b	0 to −5
−15.0 to −17.7	7a	5 to 0
−12.3 to −15.0	7b	10 to 5
−9.5 to −12.2	8a	15 to 10
−6.7 to −9.4	8b	20 to 15
−3.9 to −6.6	9a	25 to 20
−1.2 to −3.8	9b	30 to 25
1.6 to −1.1	10a	35 to 30
4.4 to 1.7	10b	40 to 35
4.5 and Above	11	40 and Above

Natural Heritage Directory

These groups can help you learn about the trees in your area and locate nursery sources for native trees. Unfortunately, some of the best native-plant nurseries are ephemeral because they are operated by plantspeople rather than business-people; so it is difficult to publish a listing that will be comprehensive or remain current. Experts working for local government agencies and nongovernment organizations such as plant societies are the best resources for current, accurate information.

FEDERAL AGENCIES

Agriculture Canada
Plant Research Center, Building 99
Ottawa, Ontario K1A 0C6
phone: (613) 996-1665

Bureau of Land Management
U.S. Department of the Interior
1849 C Street, NW, Suite 5600
Washington, D.C. 20240
phone: (202) 208-5717

Canadian Council on Ecological Areas
Environment Canada
Ottawa, Ontario K1A 0H3
phone: (819) 953-1444

Environment Canada
International Trade in Endangered
   Species
Ottawa, Ontario K1A 0H3

Forestry Canada
351 St. Joseph Boulevard
Place Vincent Massey
Hull, Quebec K1A 1G5
phone: (819) 997-1107

National Invasive Species Council
U.S. Department of the Interior
South 1951 Constitution Avenue, NW,
   Suite 320
Washington, D.C. 20240
phone: (202) 208-6336

National Park Service
U.S. Department of the Interior
1849 C Street, NW
Washington, D.C. 20240
phone: (202) 208-7351

National Weather Service
General Information
phone: (301) 713-0622

U.S. Environmental Protection Agency
401 M Street, SW, Suite 1200W
Washington, D.C. 20460
phone: (202) 382-2090

U.S. Fish and Wildlife Service
U.S. Department of the Interior
1849 C Street, NW
Washington, D.C. 20240

U.S. Forest Service
Urban and Community Forestry
210 14th Street, SW
Washington, D.C. 20250
phone: (202) 205-9694

U.S. Geological Survey
National Center
Reston, Virginia 22092
phone: (703) 648-4000

STATE & PROVINCIAL AGENCIES & ORGANIZATIONS

ALABAMA
Alabama Wildflower Society
11120 Ben Clements Road
Northport, Alabama 35475

Department of Conservation and
   Natural Resources
State Lands Division
Folsom Administration Building
64 North Union Street, Room 752
Montgomery, Alabama 36130
phone: (205) 242-3007

ARKANSAS
Arkansas Native Plant Society
P.O. Box 250250
Little Rock, Arkansas 72225

Arkansas Natural Heritage
  Commission
225 East Markham, Suite 200
Little Rock, Arkansas 72201
phone: (501) 324-9332

COLORADO
American Wildlands
6551 South Revere Parkway, Suite 160
Englewood, Colorado 80111
phone: (303) 649-9020

Colorado Native Plant Society
P.O. Box 200
Fort Collins, Colorado 80522

CONNECTICUT
Connecticut Botanical Society
P.O. Box 9004
New Haven, Connecticut 06532

Connecticut Natural Diversity
  Database
Natural Resources Center
Department of Environmental
  Protection
State Office Building, Room 553
165 Capital Avenue
Hartford, Connecticut 06106

DELAWARE
Delaware Natural Heritage Inventory
Division of Parks and Recreation
89 Kings Highway
Dover, Delaware 19903
phone: (302) 739-5285

Mount Cuba Center for the Study of
  Native Piedmont Flora
P.O. Box 3570
Greenville, Delaware 19807

Northern Nut Growers
P.O. Box 550
Townsend, Delaware 19734

DISTRICT OF COLUMBIA
American Association of Nurserymen
1250 I Street, NW, Suite 500
Washington, D.C. 20005
phone: (202) 789-2900

American Forests
1515 P Street, NW
Washington, D.C. 20005
phone: (202) 667-3300

American Society of Landscape
  Architects
4401 Connecticut Avenue NW
Washington, D.C. 20008
phone: (202) 686-2752

Botanical Society of Washington
Department of Botany, NHB
166 Smithsonian Institution
Washington, D.C. 20560

Defenders
1244 19th Street, NW
Washington, D.C. 20036
phone: (202) 659-9510

Ecological Society of America
2010 Massachusetts Avenue, NW, Suite
  420
Washington, D.C. 20036
phone: (202) 833-8773

National Tree Trust
1455 Pennsylvania Avenue, Suite 250
Washington, D.C. 20004
phone: (202) 628-8733

Save America's Forests
4 Library Court, SE
Washington, D.C. 20003
phone: (202) 544-9219

Wilderness Society
900 17th Street, NW
Washington, D.C. 20006
phone: (202) 833-2300

FLORIDA
Famous and Historic Trees
8701 Old Kings Road
Jacksonville, Florida 32219
phone: (800) 320-8733

Florida Natural Areas Inventory
1018 Thomasville Road, Suite 200C
Tallahassee, Florida 32303
phone: (904) 224-8207

Tall Timbers Research
Route 1, Box 678
Tallahassee, Florida 32312
phone: (904) 893-4153

GEORGIA
Georgia Botanical Society
2 Idlewood Court NW
Rome, Georgia 30165

Georgia Native Plant Society
2 Idlewood Court, NW
Rome, Georgia 30165

Georgia Natural Heritage Program
Department of Natural Resources
2117 U.S. Highway 278, SE
Social Circle, Georgia 30279
phone: (404) 918-6411

IDAHO
Idaho Native Plant Society
P.O. Box 9451
Boise, Idaho 83707

ILLINOIS
Division of Natural Heritage
Illinois Department of Natural
  Resources
One Natural Resource Way
Springfield, Illinois 62702
phone: (217) 785-8774

Illinois Native Plant Society
Forest Glen Preserve
20301 East 900 North Road
Westville, Illinois 61883

International Society of Arboriculture
P.O. Box 3129
Champaign, Illinois 61826
phone: (217) 355-9411

Natural Areas Association
320 South Third Street
Rockford, Illinois 61104

North American Fruit Explorers
Route 1, Box 94
Chapin, Illinois 62628
phone: (217) 245-7589

TreeKeepers
Chicago Openlands Project
25 East Washington Street
Chicago, Illinois 60602
phone: (312) 427-4256 ext. 232

INDIANA
Indiana Division of Nature Preserves
402 West Washington, Room W267
Indianapolis, Indiana 46204
phone: (317) 232-4052

Indiana Native Plant and Wildflower
  Society
2606 South 600 West
Morgantown, Indiana 46106

International Oak Society
Department of Biology, Saint Mary's
    College
Notre Dame, Indiana 46556

IOWA
Bureau of Preserves and Ecological
    Services
Iowa Department of Natural Resources
Wallace State Office Building
900 East Grand Avenue
Des Moines, Iowa 50319
phone: (515) 281-8967

Soil and Water Conservation Society
7515 NE Ankeny Road
Ankeny, Iowa 50021
phone: (515) 289-1227

Trees Forever
770 7th Avenue
Marion, Iowa 52302
phone: (319) 373-0650

KANSAS
Holly Society of America
11118 West Murdock
Wichita, Kansas 67212

Kansas Natural Heritage Inventory
Kansas Biological Survey
2041 Constant Avenue
Lawrence, Kansas 66047
phone: (913) 864-3453

Kansas Wildflower Society
R. L. McGregor Herbarium
University of Kansas
2045 Constant Avenue
Lawrence, Kansas 66047

KENTUCKY
Kentucky Native Plant Society
Department of Biological Science
Eastern Kentucky University
Richmond, Kentucky 40475

Kentucky State Nature Preserves
    Commission
407 Broadway
Frankfort, Kentucky 40601
phone: (502) 564-2886

Pawpaw Foundation
147 Atwood Research Facility
Kentucky State University
Frankfort, Kentucky 40601

LOUISIANA
Louisiana Native Plant Society
216 Caroline Dormon Road
Saline, Louisiana 71070

Louisiana Natural Heritage Program
Louisiana Department of Wildlife and
    Fisheries
P.O. Box 98000
Baton Rouge, Louisiana 70898
phone: (504) 765-2821

MAINE
Josselyn Botanical Society
566 North Auburn Road
Auburn, Maine 04210

Maine Natural Areas Program
Office of Community Development
State House Station 130
Augusta, Maine 04333
phone: (207) 624-6800

MANITOBA
Manitoba Naturalists Society
302-128 James Avenue
Winnipeg, Manitoba R3B 0N8
phone: (204) 943-9029

Manitoba Natural Resources
314 Legislative Building
Winnipeg, Manitoba R3C 0V8
phone: (204) 945-3730

MARYLAND
American Association of Amateur
    Arborists
5455 Wingborne Court
Columbia, Maryland 21045

American Conifer Society
P.O. Box 3422
Crofton, Maryland 21114
phone: (410) 721-6611

Association of Consulting Foresters
    of America
5410 Grosvenor Avenue, Suite 205
Bethesda, Maryland 20814
phone: (301) 530-6795

Audubon Naturalist Society of the
    Central Atlantic States
8940 Jones Mill Road
Chevy Chase, Maryland 20815
phone: (301) 652-9188

Magnolia Society
6616 81st Street
Cabin John, Maryland 20818
phone: (301) 320-4296

Maryland Native Plant Society
P.O. Box 4877
Silver Spring, Maryland 20914

Maryland Natural Heritage Program
Department of Natural Resources
E-1 Tawes Building
Annapolis, Maryland 21401

Society of American Foresters
5400 Grosvenor Lane
Bethesda, Maryland 20814
phone: (301) 897-8720

Wildlife Habitat Enhancement Council
1010 Wayne Avenue, Suite 1240
Silver Spring, Maryland 20190
phone: (301) 588-8994

MASSACHUSETTS
Massachusetts Natural Heritage and
    Endangered Species Program
Division of Fisheries and Wildlife
100 Cambridge Street
Boston, Massachusetts 02202
phone: (617) 727-9194

New England Wild Flower Society
180 Hemenway Road
Framingham, Massachusetts 01701

MICHIGAN
Michigan Botanical Club
7951 Walnut Avenue
Newaygo, Michigan 49337

Natural Heritage Program
Michigan Department of Natural
    Resources
Box 30028
Lansing, Michigan 48909
phone: (517) 373-1263

MINNESOTA
Minnesota Native Plant Society
220 Biological Science Center
University of Minnesota
1445 Gortner Avenue
St. Paul, Minnesota 55108

Scientific and Natural Areas Program
Minnesota Department of Natural
    Resources
Box 7, 500 Lafayette Road
St. Paul, Minnesota 55155
phone: (612) 297-2357

MISSISSIPPI
Mississippi Native Plant Society
Mississippi Museum of Natural Science
111 North Jefferson Street
Jackson, Mississippi 39202

Mississippi Natural Heritage Program
State Museum of Natural Science
Department of Wildlife, Fisheries and
    Parks
111 North Jefferson Street
Jackson, Mississippi 39201
phone: (601) 354-7303

MISSOURI
Center for Plant Conservation
P.O. Box 299
St. Louis, Missouri 63166
phone: (314) 577-9450

Missouri Native Plant Society
P.O. Box 20073
St. Louis, Missouri 63144

Natural History Division
Missouri Department of Conservation
2901 West Truman Boulevard
Jefferson City, Missouri 65109
phone: (314) 751-4115

MONTANA
Craighead Wildlife-Wildlands Institute
5200 Upper Miller Creek Road
Missoula, Montana 59803
phone: (406) 251-3867

Montana Native Plant Society
P.O. Box 8783
Missoula, Montana 59807

NEBRASKA
National Arbor Day Foundation
211 North 12th Street
Lincoln, Nebraska 69508
phone: (402) 474-5655

Nebraska Natural Heritage Database
Nebraska Game and Parks Commission
2200 North 33rd Street
Lincoln, Nebraska 68503
phone: (402) 471-5469

NEW BRUNSWICK
Department of Natural Resources
Box 6000
Fredericton, New Brunswick E3B 5H1
phone: (506) 453-2510

NEW HAMPSHIRE
National Arborist Association
P.O. Box 1094
Amherst, New Hampshire 03031
phone: (603) 673-3311

New Hampshire Natural Heritage
    Inventory
Department of Resources and
    Economic Development
P.O. Box 856
Concord, New Hampshire 03302
phone: (603) 271-3623

NEW JERSEY
Native Plant Society of New Jersey
P.O. Box 231, Cook College
New Brunswick, New Jersey 08903

New Jersey Natural Heritage Program
Office of Natural Lands Management
22 South Clinton Avenue, CN 404
Trenton, New Jersey 08625
phone: (609) 984-1339

NEW MEXICO
Native Plant Society of New Mexico
734 North Reymont Street
Las Cruces, New Mexico 88002

NEW YORK
American Nature Study Society
5881 Cold Brook Road
Homer, New York 13077
phone: (607) 749-3655

Champion Tree Project
44 Gilligan Road
East Greenbush, New York 12061
phone: (518) 477-6100

Finger Lakes Native Plant Society of
    Ithaca
532 Cayuga Heights Road
Ithaca, New York 14850

National Audubon Society
700 Broadway
New York, New York 10003
phone: (212) 797-3000

New York Flora Association
New York State Museum 3132 CEC
Albany, New York 12230

New York Old Growth Forest Associa-
    tion
Landis Arboretum
P.O. Box 186
Esperance, New York 12066
phone: (518) 875-6935

New York State Department of
    Environmental Conservation
Natural Heritage Program
700 Troy-Schenectady Road
Latham, New York 12110
phone: (518) 783-3932

Niagara Frontier Botanical Society
Buffalo Museum of Science
1020 Humboldt Parkway
Buffalo, New York 14211

NEWFOUNDLAND
Department of Environment and Lands
Parks Division
Box 4750
St. John's, Newfoundland A1C 5T7

Department of Tourism and Culture
P.O. Box 8700
St. John's, Newfoundland A1B 4J6
phone: (709) 729-0659

Wildflower Society of Newfoundland
    and Labrador
c/o MUN Botanical Garden
Memorial University of Newfoundland
St. John's, Newfoundland A1C 5S7

NORTH CAROLINA
North Carolina Natural Heritage
    Program
P.O. Box 27687
Raleigh, North Carolina 27611
phone: (919) 733-7701

North Carolina Wildflower
    Preservation Society
North Carolina Botanical Garden
Totten Garden Center 3375
University of North Carolina
Chapel Hill, North Carolina 27599

Yellow Creek Botanical Institute
P.O. Box 1757
Robbinsville, North Carolina 28771

NORTH DAKOTA

North Dakota Natural Heritage
 Inventory
604 East Boulevard, Liberty Memorial
 Building
Bismarck, North Dakota 58505
phone: (701) 224-4892

NOVA SCOTIA

Department of Natural Resources
P.O. Box 698
Halifax, Nova Scotia B3J 2T9
phone: (902) 424-5935

Nova Scotia Forestry Association
P.O. Box 1113
Truro, Nova Scotia B2N 5G9
phone: (902) 893-4653

Nova Scotia Museum
1747 Summer Street
Halifax, Nova Scotia B3H 3A6
phone: (902) 424-6478

Nova Scotia Wild Flora Society
Nova Scotia Museum
1747 Summer Street
Halifax, Nova Scotia B3H 3A6

OHIO

Cincinnati Wild Flower Preservation
 Society
9005 Decima Street
Cincinnati, Ohio 45242

Native Plant Society of Northeastern
 Ohio
2651 Kerwick Road
University Heights, Ohio 44118

Ohio Department of Natural Resources
Division of Natural Areas and Preserves
1889 Fountain Square Court, F-1
Columbus, Ohio 43224
phone: (614) 265-6453

Ohio Native Plant Society
6 Louise Drive
Chagrin Falls, Ohio 44022

OKLAHOMA

Oklahoma Native Plant Society
Tulsa Garden Center
2435 South Peoria
Tulsa, Oklahoma 74114

Oklahoma Natural Heritage Inventory
Oklahoma Biological Survey
2001 Priestly Avenue, Building 605
Norman, Oklahoma 73019
phone: (405) 325-1985

ONTARIO

Algonquin Wildlands League
160 Bloor Street East, Suite 1335
Toronto, Ontario M4W 1B9
phone: (416) 324-9760

Canadian Chestnut Council
Department of Biology
University of Guelph
Guelph, Ontario N1G 2W1

Canadian Forestry Association
185 Somerset Street West, Suite 203
Ottawa, Ontario K2P 0J2
phone: (613) 232-1815

Canadian Institute of Forestry
151 Slater Street, Suite 1005
Ottawa, Ontario K1P 5H3
phone: (613) 234-2242

Canadian Nature Federation
453 Sussex Drive
Ottawa, Ontario K1N 6Z4
phone: (613) 238-6154

Canadian Ornamental Plant
 Association
652 Aberdeen Avenue
North Bay, Ontario P1B 7H9
phone: (705) 495-2563

Canadian Parks and Wilderness Society
160 Bloor Street East, Suite 1335
Toronto, Ontario M4W 1B9
phone: (416) 972-0868

Conservation Council of Ontario
489 College Street, Suite 506
Toronto, Ontario M6G 1A5
phone: (416) 969-9637

Federation of Ontario Naturalists
355 Leamill Road
Don Mills, Ontario M3B 2W8
phone: (416) 444-8419

Field Botanists of Ontario
RR 1
Acton, Ontario L7J 2L7

Nature Conservancy of Canada
794A Broadview Avenue
Toronto, Ontario M4K 2P7
phone: (416) 469-1701

North American Native Plant Society
P.O. Box 84, Postal Station D
Etobicoke, Ontario M9A 4X1
phone: (416) 680-6280

Ontario Forestry Association
150 Consumers Road, Suite 509
Willowdale, Ontario M2J 1P9
phone: (416) 493-4565

Ontario Shade Tree Council
5 Shoreham Drive
North York, Ontario M3N 1S4
phone: (416) 661-6600

Parks and Policy, Heritage Branch
Ministry of Natural Resources
90 Sheppard Avenue East
North York, Ontario M3N 3A1
phone: (819) 953-1444

Thames Valley Wildflower Society
1 Windsor Crescent
London, Ontario N6C 1V6

Toronto Wildflower Society
43 Anaconda Avenue
Scarborough, Ontario M1L 4M1

Waterloo-Wellington Wildflower
 Society
Botany Department
University of Guelph
Guelph, Ontario N1G 2W1

Wildlife Habitat Canada
1704 Carling Avenue, Suite 301
Ottawa, Ontario K2A 1C7
phone: (613) 722-2090

PENNSYLVANIA

American Association of Botanical
 Gardens and Arboreta
351 Longwood Road
Kennett Square, Pennsylvania 19348
phone: (610) 925-2500

Botanical Society of Western
 Pennsylvania
5837 Nicholson Street
Pittsburgh, Pennsylvania 15217

Delaware Valley Fern and Wildflower
    Society
263 Hillcrest Road
Wayne, Pennsylvania 19087

Pennsylvania Native Plant Society
1001 East College Avenue
State College, Pennsylvania 16801

Pennsylvania Natural Diversity
    Inventory
Pennsylvania Department of Natural
    Resources
Bureau of Forestry
P.O. Box 1467
Harrisburg, Pennsylvania 17105
phone: (717) 783-0388

PRINCE EDWARD ISLAND
Department of the Environment
P.O. Box 2000
Charlottetown, Prince Edward Island
    C1A 7N8
phone: (902) 368-5340

Island Nature Trust
Box 265
Charlottetown, Prince Edward Island
    C1A 7K4
phone: (902) 892-7513

QUEBEC
Department of Recreation, Fish, and
    Game
Place de la Capital 150 East
St. Cyrille Boulevard
Quebec City, Quebec G1R 4Y1
phone: (418) 643-6527

Direction des Reserves Ecologique et
    Sites Naturels
Environment-Quebec
3900, Rue Marly
Ste-Foy, Quebec G1X 4E4

Flora Quebeca
83 rue Chenier Saint-Eustache
Quebec City, Quebec J7R 1W9

Quebec Forestry Association
(Association Forestiere Quebecoise)
175 rue Saint-Jean, 4e etage
Quebec City, Quebec G1R 1N4
phone: (418) 529-2991

RHODE ISLAND
Rhode Island Natural Heritage
    Program
Department of Environmental
    Management
83 Park Street
Providence, Rhode Island 02903
phone: (401) 277-2776

Rhode Island Wild Plant Society
P.O. Box 114
Peace Dale, Rhode Island 02883

SASKATCHEWAN
Saskatchewan Environment
3085 Albert Street
Regina, Saskatchewan S4S 0B1
phone: (306) 787-6133

Saskatchewan Natural History Society
Box 4348
Regina, Saskatchewan S4P 3W6
phone: (306) 780-9273

Saskatchewan Natural Resources
5211 Albert Street
Regina, Saskatchewan S4S 5W6
phone: (306) 587-2930

SOUTH CAROLINA
South Carolina Department of Natural
    Resources
Non-Game and Heritage Trust Section
P.O. Box 167
Columbia, South Carolina 29202
phone: (803) 734-3893

South Carolina Native Plant Society
P.O. Box 759
Pickens, South Carolina 29671

Southern Appalachian Botanical
    Society
Newbury College
2100 College Street
Newberry, South Carolina 29108

SOUTH DAKOTA
Great Plains Native Plant Society
P.O. Box 461
Hot Springs, South Dakota 57747

South Dakota Natural Heritage
    Program
South Dakota Department of Game,
    Fish, and Parks
523 East Capitol Avenue
Pierre, South Dakota 57501
phone: (605) 773-4345

TENNESSEE
American Association of Field Botanists
P.O. Box 23542
Chattanooga, Tennessee 37422

Ecological Conservation Division
Tennessee Department of Environment
    and Conservation
401 Church Street, 8th Floor Tower
Nashville, Tennessee 37243
phone: (615) 532-0431

Tennessee Native Plant Society
Department of Botany
University of Tennessee
Knoxville, Tennessee 37996

Wildflower Society
Goldsmith Civic Garden Center
750 Cherry Road
Memphis, Tennessee 38119

TEXAS
National Wildflower Research Center
2600 FM 973 North
Austin, Texas 78725
phone: (512) 929-3600

Native Plant Society of Texas
P.O. Box 891
Georgetown, Texas 78627

Texas Endangered Resources Branch
Texas Parks and Wildlife Department
3000 South IH 35, Suite 1000
Austin, Texas 78704
phone: (512) 448-4311

UTAH
Utah Native Plant Society
P.O. Box 520041
Salt Lake City, Utah 84152

VERMONT
American Chestnut Foundation
P.O. Box 4044
Bennington, Vermont 05201

Vermont Non-Game and Natural
  Heritage Program
Center Building
103 South Main Street
Waterbury, Vermont 05671
phone: (802) 244-7340

VIRGINIA
American Chestnut Cooperators'
  Foundation
2667 Forest Service Road 708
Newport, Virginia 24128

National Woodland Owners Association
374 Maple Avenue East, Suite 210
Vienna, Virginia 22180

Nature Conservancy
1815 North Lynn Street
Arlington, Virginia 22209
phone: (703) 841-5300

Virginia Department of Conservation
  and Recreation
Division of Natural Heritage
Main Street Station
1500 East Main Street, Suite 312
Richmond, Virginia 23219
phone: (804) 786-7951

WEST VIRGINIA
North American Plant Preservation
  Council
HC 67, Box 539B
Renick, West Virginia 24966
phone: (304) 497-2208

West Virginia Native Plant Society
P.O. Box 75403
Charleston, West Virginia 25375

West Virginia Natural Heritage
  Program
P.O. Box 67
Elkins, West Virginia 26241
phone: (304) 637-0245

WISCONSIN
Botanical Club of Wisconsin
Wisconsin Academy of Arts, Sciences,
  and Letters
1922 University Avenue
Madison, Wisconsin 53705

Society for Ecological Restoration
University of Wisconsin Arboretum
1207 Seminole Highway
Madison, Wisconsin 53711

Wilderness Watch
P.O. Box 782
Sturgeon Bay, Wisconsin 54235
phone: (414) 743-1238

Wild Ones Natural Landscapers
P.O. Box 1274
Appleton, Wisconsin 54912
phone: (877) 394-9453

Wisconsin Department of Natural
  Resources
Bureau of Endangered Resources
Box 7921
Madison, Wisconsin 53707
phone: (608) 267-7479

WYOMING
Wyoming Native Plant Society
1604 Grand Avenue, Suite 2
Laramie, Wyoming 82070

Web Directory

I have spent many hundreds of midnight hours surfing for information related to native trees. Why not share the best sites I have found and give you a head start? These are not commercial sites. Most are agencies or nongovernment organizations, each one a valuable resource in itself as well as a source of links to additional sites.

Sites are listed in informal categories, including plant databases, government agencies, universities and museums, nongovernment organizations, directories and links, forums and listserves, ranges and geographic information, big- and historic-tree sites, glossaries and nomenclature, and miscellaneous reference sites. Please keep in mind that information on the Web is constantly changing. If you have trouble locating any of these sites using the address I've provided, try using a search engine.

Enjoy—but don't stay up too late!

PLANT DATABASES

Atlas of Florida Vascular Plants.
   http://www.plantatlas.usf.edu/default.asp
Authority Files and Checklists.
   http://www.nearctica.com/syst/author/pcheck.htm
Common Trees of Pennsylvania.
   http://www.dcnr.state.pa.us/forestry/commontr/
   common.htm
Flowering Threatened and Endangered Plants.
   http://ecos.fws.gov/webpage/
   webpage_vip_listed.html?&code=F&listings=0#Q
Garden Watchdog.
   http://gardenwatchdog.com/
Global Plant Checklist.
   http://www.bgbm.fu-berlin.de/IOPI/GPC/default.htm
Gymnosperm Database.
   http://www.conifers.org/
HortiPlex Database.
   http://plants.gardenweb.com/plants/

Identification of Common Trees of Iowa.
   http://www.extension.iastate.edu/pages/tree/
Identifying Trees of Michigan.
   http://www.msue.msu.edu/msue/imp/modft/
   23320001.html
Illinois Plant Information Network.
   http://www.fs.fed.us/ne/delaware/ilpin/ilpin.html
Index Herbariorum.
   http://www.nybg.org/bsci/ih/ih.html
Invasive Species.
   http://tncweeds.ucdavis.edu/
List of Native Trees for Use Along Roadsides in Illinois.
   http://www.inhs.uiuc.edu/~kenr/treetable.html
Missouri Trees.
   http://www.conservation.state.mo.us/nathis/plantpage/
   flora/motrees/index.htm
National Germplasm System.
   http://www.ars-grin.gov/npgs/searchgrin.html
Native Plants Database.
   http://www.epa.gov/grtlakes/greenacres/
Noxious Weeds and Invasive Non-Native Plants Lists.
   http://www.fs.fed.us/r9/weed/index.htm
Phytochemical and Ethnobotanical Databases.
   http://www.ars-grin.gov/duke/ethnobot.html
Plant Answers.
   http://aggie-horticulture.tamu.edu/plantanswers/
   web.html
Plant Database.
   http://www.hort.uconn.edu/plants/
Plant Database.
   http://www.neoflora.com/
Plants Database.
   http://plants.usda.gov/
Right Tree Handbook.
   http://www.mpelectric.com/treebook/

Silvics Manual.
  http://www.na.fs.fed.us/spfo/pubs/silvics_manual/
  volume_2/vol2_Table_of_contents.htm
Threatened Species.
  http://www.redlist.org/
Tree Guide.
  http://www.treeguide.com/
Trees of Alabama and the Southeast.
  http://www.forestry.auburn.edu/samuelson/dendrology/
  index.html
Trees of Florida.
  http://www.floridaplants.com/trees_fl.htm
Trees, Shrubs, and Groundcovers.
  http://ohioline.ag.ohio-state.edu/lines/trees.html
Trees and Shrubs of Ontario.
  http://gaia.flemingc.on.ca/~dhendry/
Tropicos Database.
  http://mobot.mobot.org/W3T/Search/vast.html
Web Garden.
  http://webgarden.osu.edu/
What Tree Is It?
  http://www.oplin.lib.oh.us/products/tree/
Woody Plants Database.
  http://www.hort.net/woodyplants/
World Dictionary of Trees.
  http://www.wdt.qc.ca/
World Species List.
  http://envirolink.org/species/
Worldwide Flowering Plant Family Identification.
  http://www.colby.edu/info.tech/bi211/plantfamilyid.html

GOVERNMENT AGENCIES

Canadian Forest Service.
  http://www.pfc.cfs.nrcan.gc.ca/
Environment Canada.
  http://www.ec.gc.ca/
U.S. Agricultural Research Service.
  http://www.ars.usda.gov/
U.S. Forest Service.
  http://www.fs.fed.us/
U.S. National Agricultural Library.
  http://www.nal.usda.gov/
U.S. National Arboretum.
  http://www.ars-grin.gov/ars/Beltsville/na/
U.S. National Invasive Species Council.
  http://www.invasivespecies.gov/council/main.shtml
U.S. National Museum of Forest Service History.
  http://www.nfs-museum.org/
U.S. Plant Conservation Alliance.
  http://www.nps.gov/plants/

UNIVERSITIES & MUSEUMS

Arkansas Plant Evaluation Program, University of Arkansas.
  http://www.uark.edu/campus-resources/cotinus/
  arboretum_html/planteval.html
Biological Information Browsing Environment (BIBE),
  University of Illinois.
  http://www.biobrowser.org/

Entomology Index of Internet Resources, Iowa State
  University.
  http://www.ipm.iastate.edu/list/
Home, Yard, and Garden Pest Newsletter, University of
  Illinois.
  http://www.ag.uiuc.edu/cespubs/hyg/
Museum Link, Illinois State Museum.
  http://www.museum.state.il.us/muslink/
Pawpaw Information Web Site, Kentucky State University.
  http://www.pawpaw.kysu.edu/
Purdue Landscape and Nursery Thesaurus, Purdue University.
  http://bluestem.hort.purdue.edu/plant/
Questions on University Extension Regional Resource Information (QUERRI), Midwest University Extension Publica-
  tions.
  http://ncremp.ag.iastate.edu/idea/querri/index.asp
Virtual Library of Botany, University of Oklahoma.
  http://www.ou.edu/cas/botany-micro/www-vl/

NONGOVERNMENT ORGANIZATIONS

American Association of Amateur Arborists.
  http://dir.gardenweb.com/directory/aaaa/
American Association of Botanical Gardens and Arboreta.
  http://www.aabga.org/
American Chestnut Cooperators' Foundation.
  http://www.accf-online.org/
American Chestnut Foundation.
  http://chestnut.acf.org/
American Conifer Society.
  http://www.conifersociety.org/
American Forests.
  http://www.americanforests.org/
American Horticultural Society.
  http://www.ahs.org/
American Nursery and Landscape Association.
  http://www.anla.org/
American Phytopathological Society.
  http://www.apsnet.org/
American Society for Horticultural Science.
  http://www.ashs.org/
Biota of North America Program.
  http://www.bonap.org/
Botanical Society of America.
  http://www.botany.org/
Botanique: Portal to Gardens, Arboreta, and Nature Sites.
  http://www.botanique.com/
Canadian Chestnut Council.
  http://www.uoguelph.ca/~chestnut/
Center for Plant Conservation.
  http://www.mobot.org/CPC/welcome.html
Earth Day Network.
  http://www.earthday.net/
Elm Research Institute.
  http://www.libertyelm.com/
Flora of North America.
  http://hua.huh.harvard.edu/fna/

Friends of the Trees Society.
   http://www.geocities.com/RainForest/4663/index2.html
Future Forests.
   http://www.futureforests.com/
Garden Writers' Speakers Bureau.
   http://www.gwaa.org/bureau/index.html
Global Tree Campaign.
   http://www.wcmc.org.uk/trees/Background/ack.htm
International Oak Society.
   http://www.saintmarys.edu/~rjensen/ios.html
International Society of Arboriculture.
   http://www.isa-arbor.com/
International Society for Horticultural Science.
   http://www.actahort.org
International Union of Forest Research Organizations.
   http://iufro.boku.ac.at/
Metria: The Metropolitan Tree Improvement Alliance.
   http://fletcher.ces.state.nc.us/programs/nursery/metria/
National Arbor Day Foundation.
   http://arborday.org/
National Gardening Association.
   http://www2.garden.org/nga/
National Tree Trust.
   http://www.nationaltreetrust.org/
Native America.
   http://www.nativeamerica.org/
Nature Conservancy.
   http://nature.org/
Nature Serve.
   http://www.natureserve.org/
North American Fruit Explorers.
   http://www.nafex.org/
Northern Nut Growers Association.
   http://www.icserv.com/nnga/
Ontario Nut Growers.
   http://www.songonline.ca/
Plants for a Future.
   http://www.comp.leeds.ac.uk/pfaf/
Society for Ecological Restoration.
   http://www.ser.org/
Travels of William Bartram.
   http://www.bartramtrail.org/
Tree Folks.
   http://www.treefolks.org/
Trees Forever.
   http://www.treesforever.org/
Vermont Tree Society.
   http://www.vermonttreesociety.org/
Wildflower.
   http://www.wildflowermag.com/
Wildlands Project.
   http://www.twp.org/
Wild Ones Natural Landscapers.
   http://www.for-wild.org/

DIRECTORIES & LINKS

Best Environmental Directories.
   http://www.ulb.ac.be/ceese/meta/cds.html
Botany Links.
   http://www.pocketflora.com/PocketFlora_Guides/
   botany_links.htm
Botany Resources.
   http://biodiversity.uno.edu/cgi-bin/hl?botany
Browsing 4 Gardens.
   http://www.browsing4gardens.com/
Forestry Index.
   http://www.forestryindex.net/
Forestry Sites.
   http://dnr.state.il.us/conservation/forestry/
   internetsite.htm
Garden Gate.
   http://www.prairienet.org/ag/garden/homepage.htm
Gardening Resources.
   http://www.digital-librarian.com/gardening.html
Garden Web.
   http://www.gardenweb.com/
Henri D. Grissino-Mayer's Science of Dendrochronology.
   http://www.valdosta.edu/~grissino/
I Love Plants.
   http://www.iloveplants.com/
Index to American Botanical Literature.
   http://www.nybg.org/bsci/iabl.html
Internet Directory for Botany.
   http://www.botany.net/IDB/
Landscape On Line.
   http://www.landscapeonline.com/
Midwest Plants.
   http://midwestplants.com/
Nearctica: The Natural World of North America.
   http://www.nearctica.com/
Our Backyard Forest.
   http://w3.one.net/~markws/links.html
Plant Search.
   http://www.natureserve.org/servlet/natureserve
Scott's Botanical Links.
   http://www.ou.edu/cas/botany-micro/bot-linx/
Southeastern Rare Plant Information Network.
   http://serpin.org/
SoVerNet: Vermont's Sovereign Connection.
   http://www.sover.net/%7esubzero/links.html
Virtual Library of Forestry.
   http://www.metla.fi/info/vlib/forestry/
Yu-Fai Leung's Natural Resources Research Information.
   http://www4.ncsu.edu/~leung/nrrips.html

FORUMS & LISTSERVES

Champion Tree Listserve.
   http://www.championtrees.org/listserv.htm
Conifers Forum.
   http://forums.gardenweb.com/forums/conif/
Native Plants Forum.
   http://forums.gardenweb.com/forums/natives/

Plant Society.
  http://plantsociety.com/
Trees Forum.
  http://forums.gardenweb.com/forums/trees/
Trees Listserve.
  http://trees@treelink.org/docs/trees.phtml

RANGES & GEOGRAPHIC INFORMATION
Broadleaf Tree Range Maps.
  http://greenwood.cr.usgs.gov/pub/ppapers/p1650-a/
  pages/hardwoods.html
Conifer Range Maps.
  http://geology.cr.usgs.gov/pub/ppapers/p1650-a/pages/
  conifers.html
Geography Division Map Gallery.
  http://www.census.gov/geo/www/mapGallery/index.html

BIG- & HISTORIC-TREE SITES
Champion Trees and Ancient Forests.
  http://www.championtrees.org/
Historic Trees Project.
  http://home.earthlink.net/~jeffkrueger/index.html
Laboratory of Tree-Ring Research.
  http://tree.ltrr.arizona.edu/
Laboratory of Tree-Ring Science.
  http://web.utk.edu/~grissino/ltrs/
National Register of Big Trees.
  http://www.americanforests.org/resources/bigtrees/
  register.php
World Community of Old Trees.
  http://www.nyu.edu/projects/julian/

GLOSSARIES & NOMENCLATURE
Dictionary of Botanical Epithets.
  http://www.winternet.com/~chuckg/dictionary.html
Glossary of Botanical Terms.
  http://glossary.gardenweb.com/glossary/
Glossary of Roots of Botanical Names.
  http://garden-gate.prairienet.org/botrts.htm

Integrated Taxonomic Information System.
  http://www.itis.usda.gov/
International Code of Botanical Nomenclature.
  http://www.bgbm.fu-berlin.de/iapt/nomenclature/
  code/SaintLouis/0000St.Luistitle.htm
International Code of Nomenclature for Cultivated Plants.
  http://www.ishs.org/sci/icracpco.htm
International Plant Names Index.
  http://www.ipni.org/

MISCELLANEOUS REFERENCE SITES
Colors of Fall.
  http://muextension.missouri.edu/xplor/agguides/
  forestry/g05010.htm
Community and Urban Forestry.
  http://forestry.tqn.com/science/forestry/msub11.htm
Forestry Images.
  http://www.forestryimages.org/
Genetically Engineered Trees.
  http://www.americanlands.org/forestweb/getrees.htm
Genetically Modified Technology in the Forest Sector.
  http://www.panda.org/resources/publications/forest/gm/
Illinois Flowering Trees.
  http://dnr.state.il.us/lands/education/kids/KIDSCONS/
  Spring2001/ILfloweringTrees.htm
Leopold Dippel's Handbuch der Laubholzkunde.
  http://www.mpiz-koeln.mpg.de/~stueber/dippel/
  index.html
Plant World.
  http://www.plantworld.com/
Propagating Shrubs from Cuttings.
  http://www.ces.uga.edu/pubcd/b641-w.html
U.S. Drought Monitor.
  http://www.drought.unl.edu/dm/index.html
Woody Plant Seed Manual.
  http://wpsm.net/

Glossary

Abaxial. Outer or lower; said of the surface of a leaf or other plant part. Compare with *adaxial*.

Abscission. The natural process by which trees wall off and shed unneeded parts such as ripe fruit, old leaves, and dead branches.

Acuminate. Long-pointed, as in a leaf blade.

Adaxial. Inner or upper; said of the surface of a leaf or other plant part. Compare with *abaxial*.

Adventitious. Developing in abnormal positions from cambial meristem. Adventitious roots or buds often develop in response to the loss or damage of normal buds or root growth.

Allelopathy. A biochemical process wherein one plant suppresses the growth or health of another.

Allopatric. Having completely separate ranges of natural distribution. Compare with *sympatric*.

Apical dominance. The release of growth hormones by the tip of a stem or branch, resulting in suppressed growth of lateral buds.

Apomixis. Reproduction without pollination from a male element.

Arboriculture. The professional care of trees.

Auriculate. Having earlike lobes, pertaining to the base of a leaf blade.

Autochthonous. Aboriginal; said of an organism with a distribution remaining in the area where it evolved.

Axillary. In the axil; said of a lateral bud or flower that develops at a node, or leaf axil.

Backcross. To cross a first-generation hybrid back to one of the parent species or varieties; also, a plant resulting from such a cross.

Bast. The fibrous inner bark of some trees, used by aboriginal people to make twine or paper.

Bipinnate. A doubly compound leaf with a branched rachis.

Bog. A wetland area formed by the gradual filling of a marsh, lake, or pond with organic material. Compare with *marsh* and *swamp*.

Bole. The main stem or clear trunk of a tree.

Bottomland. Floodplain; a flat, low area subject to occasional flooding by a nearby stream.

Broadleaved evergreen. An angiosperm (not a conifer) with leaves that remain green throughout the dormant season.

Canopy. In a forest area, the general level of the tops of the average tree crowns; on an individual tree, the branch spread.

Catkin. A spike- or tassel-like flower structure with scaly bracts; may be either staminate or pistillate.

Chlorosis. The abnormal loss of chlorophyll, or green pigment, in a leaf, sometimes caused by a chemical imbalance such as a deficiency of iron or magnesium.

Cladoptosis. The annual shedding of twigs, either as a natural crown-thinning process or in response to stress.

Climax forest. The ultimate population of plant and animal species that will come to dominate a site in the absence of disturbance.

Climax species. The tree species that typically achieve dominance in a climax forest.

Cline. A gradual shift in morphology across a range of distribution. Compare with *ochlospecies*.

Clone. A ramet or a sum of ramets, frequently seen as a thicket of coppicing trees. A clone may be propagated, named, and registered as a cultivar.

Codominance. A structural defect in the branching pattern of a tree formed when two or more competing growing tips, or leaders, develop. Codominant leaders form included bark and weak crotches that can be split easily by ice or wind.

Compound. Said of a leaf having a multiparted blade composed of leaflets, which in our native trees may be palmate, pinnate, or bipinnate.

Conifer. A cone-bearing tree that is often, though not always, evergreen. Conifers are the most familiar tree-sized order of gymnosperms native to North America.

Copse. A small grove or thicket; also, a sprout cluster or coppice.

Cotyledon. The primary leaf of a seedling, formed as the seed matures. Trees such as palms, Joshua trees, and bamboos are monocots, with single cotyledons, while most other temperate trees are dicots, with paired cotyledons.

Cove. A protected lower mountain slope, concave in profile, that accumulates moisture and nutrient runoff from surrounding areas and provides an ideal site for mesic tree growth; also, a protected coastal bay or inlet.

Cultivar. A plant variety known only in cultivation (*culti*vated *vari*ety) and, in the strictest sense, not reproducible except by asexual processes; often a named clone. A cultivar name is capitalized, enclosed in single quotes, and usually written in English. Like a variety name, a cultivar name follows the specific epithet. Most authorities also accept the concept of using cultivar names for closely related, seed germplasm groups, hybrid series, and so forth, and many incorrectly equate them with trade names.

Deciduous. Remaining leafless during the dormant season, which, for the purposes of this book, is winter.

Deliquescent. Spreading or arching; said of a branching habit that results from the development of lateral buds into ascending limbs. Compare with *excurrent*.

Dentate. Having teeth that do not point forward like saw teeth; said of the margin of a leaf. Compare with *serrate*.

Dichogamy. A combination of protandry and protogyny, in which the male and female flowers of a given tree mature at different times.

Dioecious. Having functionally staminate and functionally pistillate flowers on separate individuals. Only pistillate dioecious trees bear fruit. Some species are predominantly or functionally, but not absolutely, dioecious. Compare with *monoecious*.

Diploid. Having a double set of chromosomes, the typical genetic form of an organism.

Dripline. The edge of the shadow of a tree at noon; literally, the circle beneath a tree where rain drips from the outer edge of the canopy and where much of the absorptive root system is concentrated.

Drupe. A type of fleshy fruit with a hard seed, or stone, such as a cherry or plum.

Ecotypes. Individual organisms within a species that share similar characteristics such as size, growth form, or hardiness due to their common evolution within a particular habitat or provenance.

Endangered species. The most critical rank in legal classification systems in the United States and Canada for organisms at risk either of extirpation from portions of their range or of complete extinction. Lesser degrees of risk are also recognized under some laws enacted to protect endangered species, such as *threatened* (at risk of becoming endangered), *vulnerable* (at risk of becoming threatened), *candidate* (nominated for listing), and *watch-list*. Any tree or other living organism protected under state endangered species laws in the United States is automatically protected by federal law.

Endemic. Restricted to a specific region or habitat. Compare with *exotic* and *pandemic*.

Entire. Smooth, toothless; said of the margin of a leaf.

Epigeal. A seed that raises its cotyledons above the soil as it germinates, as with a beech or pawpaw. Compare with *hypogeal*.

Ex situ. Off site; said of a plant cultivated outside its natural habitat. Compare with *in situ*.

Excurrent. Having a single central stem extending up through the crown of the tree to its tip, as is prevalent in many conifers and some juvenile hardwoods; also said of an element projecting beyond the surface or tip, such as a leaf bristle. Compare with *deliquescent*.

Exotic. Not native to the area under consideration; cultivated or naturalized due to human activity. Compare with *endemic* and *pandemic*.

Fascicle. A bundle or cluster, as of pine needles arising from a common point on the twig.

Fastigiate. Narrowly upright in form due to the orthotropic growth of lateral branches.

Fertile soil. Literally, soil with ample amounts of mineral nutrients; in practice, soil capable of sustaining vigorous plant growth due to additional factors such as pH, aeration, moisture-holding capacity, structure, depth, organic matter, and microbial activity.

Follicle. A fruit capsule that splits open on one side at maturity.

Friable. Crumbly and easily penetrated by root growth; said of soil.

Fruit. A fertilized ovary containing one or more seeds; may or may not be edible or fleshy.

Genus (pl. **genera**). A group of closely related species. Some major genera, like the oaks (*Quercus*), maples (*Acer*), and pines (*Pinus*), are divided into distinct groups called subgenera, sections, series, and so on. Genus names are written in Latin and are italicized and capitalized.

Glabrous. Without hairs or tomentum.

Glaucous. Waxy; covered with a frostlike coating.

Grex. A group of closely related hybrids or very similar species that are not always mutually distinct; a hybrid swarm.

Habit. The natural shape of a tree: spreading, excurrent, fastigiate, columnar, pyramidal, weeping, and so forth.

Habitat. The specific natural environmental conditions within which a tree grows. Compare with *range*.

Hardiness zone. See USDA zone.

Hypogeal. A seed that germinates with its cotyledons remaining below the surface of the soil, as with an oak or hickory. Compare with *epigeal*.

In situ. On site; said of a plant managed within its natural habitat. Compare with *ex situ*.

Included bark. The bark sometimes trapped in a narrow fork between two adjacent limbs as they each grow and expand in girth; a structural weakness in trees.

Indumentum. A hairy or fuzzy covering on the surface of a leaf or other plant part.

Introgression. A merging of species via progressive hybridization.

Lammas growth. Precocious growth of the apical bud during the same year it is formed. This results in formation of multiple whorls of subapical buds and facilitates what appears to be internodal lateral growth the following year on certain pines and other trees. Compare with *prolepsis* and *syllepsis*.

Layering. The development of roots on a lateral branch by covering with soil; used to propagate some trees, and occasionally occurs under natural conditions in the wild.

Leaflet. One element of a compound leaf, consisting of a blade and its petiolule.

Marcescent. Persistent but not evergreen; said of leaves or other plant parts. Marcescent oaks, for example, hold some of their dead foliage through most of the dormant season, providing wildlife cover and windbreak value.

Marsh. A type of wetland with slowly flowing or fluctuating water, supporting mostly herbaceous plant growth. Compare with *bog* and *swamp*.

Mesic. Said of a moist, median type of habitat condition; neither wet nor dry.

Microclimate. A localized climate condition, showing the effects of factors such as wind protection, shade, heat reflection from a building, or temperature moderation by a nearby body of water. Microclimate conditions should be considered when selecting planting locations for sensitive species or those of marginal hardiness.

Micropropagation. Tissue culture; the laboratory culture of tissue cells to replicate a plant; a high-tech form of asexual propagation.

Monoecious. Having staminate and pistillate flowers or flower parts on the same individual. Compare with *dioecious*.

Mulch. The natural or artificial accumulation of a layer of loose material such as bark pieces or leaf and twig litter beneath a tree. Mulch conserves soil moisture, moderates temperature extremes, inhibits weed growth, and promotes mycorrhizal development, thus contributing to better tree growth.

Mycoplasma. An infectious organism without cell walls, similar to a virus and appearing intermediate between fungi and bacteria; it lives outside the cells of its host organism and causes diseases such as yellows. Compare with *phytoplasma*.

Mycorrhiza (pl. mycorrhizae). A beneficial fungus that grows symbiotically with the roots of a tree; more correctly used to describe the combination of the fungus and tree.

Nothospecies. A named interspecific hybrid, occasionally found in nature at the boundary of two different habitat types that support different but cross-compatible species. Oaks are notorious for forming groves of nothospecies under such circumstances.

Ochlospecies. A species comprising many forms that grade gradually and continuously into one another from one part of the range to another. Such trees from opposite ends of the species' range might be classified as distinct species except for the clinal merging of their characteristics, thus providing no clear distinction from one form to another. Compare with *cline*.

Old growth. A forest condition approaching or synonymous with virgin forest; characterized by a predominance of ancient trees, the remains of even older trees, and the complex, dependent web of life associated with them.

Organic matter. High-carbon soil components such as litter, duff, leaf mold, humus, and peat; the portion of soil comprising the remains of living organisms.

Ortet. The original ancestral organism from which a clone of ramets develops.

Orthotropism. The vertical growth habit found in the leader and trunk of young trees and the limbs of many fastigiate tree cultivars. Compare with *plagiotropism*.

Palmate. Having lobes or veins radiating from a central point; said of leaves.

Pandemic. Present nearly everywhere. Compare with *endemic* and *exotic*.

Panicle. A compound-branched tuft of flowers or fruits, composed of several combined racemes.

Pedicel. The stalk of an individual flower or fruit in a cluster, or of a solitary flower or fruit. Compare with *peduncle*.

Peduncle. The basal stalk that supports a flower or fruit cluster, or a solitary inflorescence. Compare with *pedicel*.

Persistent. Continuing to adhere even when not necessarily living or functional; said of leaves and fruits that cling to the twig through the dormant season, or of structures such as bristles or tomentum that do not shed.

Petiole. The stalk of a leaf, connected to the twig.

Petiolule. The stalk of a leaflet of a compound leaf. Compare with *rachis*.

Phenology. The timing and sequence of biological phenomena such as flowering, leaf development, and fruit ripening.

Phyllotaxy. The arrangement of leaves on a twig, an important characteristic for identification. Opposite leaves occur in pairs, whorled leaves develop in groups of three or more, and alternate leaves are borne singly in a zigzag or spiral pattern along the twig.

Phytophagous. Feeding on plants; usually said of insects and other invertebrates. Phytophagous vertebrate animals are more commonly referred to as herbivorous.

Phytoplasma. A pathological cluster of organelles that behaves like a bacterium, causing systemic yellowing and wilting diseases in some trees; formerly known as a mycoplasma-like organism, or MLO. Compare with *mycoplasma*.

Pinnate. Featherlike; said of the arrangement of leaflets of a compound leaf along a rachis.

Pistillate. Having a pistil; describes a female flower or a functionally female dioecious plant. Compare with *staminate*.

Plagiotropism. The branching pattern seen on mature trees when the branches begin to spread at apparent random angles instead of continuing to extend vertically; caused by loss of apical dominance as the tree matures. Compare with *orthotropism*.

Plumule. The initial bud or shoot that arises from the epicotyl of a seed, from which the trunk develops.

Pocosin. A shallow, upland bog that supports woody plant species.

Pod. A dehiscent fruit, usually dry, woody, or leathery.

Pome. A fleshy fruit with seeds in a multicelled core, such as an apple or pear.

Prairie. A natural community dominated by grassy herbaceous plants.

Prolepsis. A growth process involving lateral (especially sub-apical) buds that break dormancy during the same season they are formed, creating sympodial branching. Compare with *lammas growth* and *syllepsis*.

Propagation. Generating additional organisms by seeds, cuttings, layers, or other means.

Protandry. A phenological condition involving maturation of staminate flowers prior to pistillate flowers on the same individual; encourages outcrossing among neighboring trees, with the earlier blooming one being primarily a seed bearer and the later one being a pollen donor. Protandry is predominant in some tree genera, like oaks. Compare with *protogyny*.

Protogyny. A phenological condition involving maturation of pistillate flowers prior to staminate flowers on the same individual; encourages outcrossing among neighboring trees, with the earlier blooming one being primarily a pollen donor and the later one being a seed bearer. Compare with *protandry*.

Provenance. A specific combination of soil and climate factors that may lead to the evolution of a particular ecotype; also, the ecotype itself. Provenance considerations are very important with some species in selecting individual trees or cultivars for planting in particular areas, especially in marginal or stressful habitat locations.

Raceme. A branched tuft of flowers or fruits.

Rachis. The stalk of a pinnate compound leaf. Compare with *petiolule*.

Radicle. The embryonic root that first emerges from a seed during germination.

Ramet. An asexually propagated individual, genetically identical to the ortet from which it originated; one member of a clone.

Range. The geographic area within which a tree grows. Compare with *habitat*.

Rhizome. An underground stem.

Riparian. Occurring along a stream bank.

Rugose. Wrinkled; having indented veins.

Samara. A winged, papery, wind-dispersed seed.

Semievergreen. Intermediate between fully evergreen and deciduous.

Serotinous. Blooming or opening late; blooming in fall. Serotinous seedpods or cones do not open immediately when ripe unless triggered by a stimulus, such as fire.

Serrate. Sharply saw-toothed, with the teeth pointing forward; said of the margin of a leaf. Compare with *dentate*.

Simple. Unbranched, not compound; said of a leaf or solitary flower structure.

Speciation. The development or evolution of new species.

Species. A group of similar, freely interbreeding individual organisms that consistently produce similar offspring; the taxonomic level below genus (or subgenus, if there is one). Species names, or specific epithets, are written in italic, lowercase Latin and always follow the genus name.

Stag-headed. Coarse and antlered in appearance. A severely stressed tree may become stag-headed due to branch die-back in the upper canopy.

Staminate. Bearing stamens; describes a male flower or a functionally male dioecious plant. Compare with *pistillate*.

Stratification. In plant propagation, the treatment of seed in layers of cold, moist medium for several weeks or months to simulate wintering and break dormancy.

Strobile. A conelike flower structure with tough, persistent bracts.

Swamp. A low, wooded wetland without surface drainage. Compare with *bog* and *marsh*.

Syllepsis. The precocious growth of lateral buds during the year they are formed, resulting in a branched one-year-old twig on some trees, such as alders. This is common on stump sprouts and in tropical trees but rare in temperate ones. Compare with *lammas growth* and *prolepsis*.

Sympatric. Sharing a common distribution range. Compare with *allopatric*.

Sympodial. Candelabra-like; describes branching caused by prolepsis. Sympodial branching contributes to the attractive architecture of trees such as sassafras.

Taxon (pl. **taxa**). Any unit in the scientific classification of organisms, such as genus, species, or variety. The study of such classification of taxa is called taxonomy, and those who do so are taxonomists.

Terminal. Occurring at the tip or distal end, as of a twig, leaf, or fruit.

Tetraploid. Having four sets of chromosomes. Tetraploid plants often display hybrid vigor and may be more robust than their diploid relatives.

Tomentum. A woolly coating on a leaf or twig.

Twig. The end of a branch, representing the growth increment of the most recent or current growing season.

Umbo. The point of a cone scale.

USDA zone. A widely accepted plant hardiness zone based on average minimum winter temperature as depicted on the Plant Hardiness Zone Map published by the U.S. Department of Agriculture.

Variety. A taxonomic subdivision of a species, with minor but consistent differences from other such varieties and with the general capacity to transmit those differences to offspring by normal (sexual) reproduction. If sexual reproduction produces inconsistent offspring with random variation in the diagnostic characteristics under consideration, the classification is reduced in status from variety to form. Most cultivars do not breed true and are actually cultivated forms. Variety names are written in lowercase Latin.

Vegetative propagation. Nonsexual reproduction of plants using cuttings, layers, grafting, or any method other than seeds.

Volunteer. A tree that becomes established in a location spontaneously, as by seed, suckering, or layering.

Xeric. Dry or excessively well drained, or preferring such conditions.

Xeriscaping. The development of landscaping for dry habitats or drought-prone areas, using low-maintenance techniques with little or no long-term supplemental irrigation.

Bibliography and Recommended Reading

American Association of Nurserymen. 1993. *State Association Listing*. Washington, D.C.

American Forests. 2002. *National Register of Big Trees*. Washington, D.C.

Bacon, Francis. 1627. *Sylva Sylvarum: A Naturall Historie in Ten Centuries*. London: William Lee.

Bailey, Liberty Hyde. 1917. *The Standard Cyclopedia of Horticulture*. 2d ed. New York: Macmillan.

Bailey, Liberty Hyde, and Ethel Zoe Bailey. 1976. *Hortus Third: A Concise Dictionary of Plants Cultivated in the United States and Canada*. Revised and expanded by the staff of the Liberty Hyde Bailey Hortorium. New York: Macmillan.

Baron, Robert C., ed. 1987. *The Garden and Farm Books of Thomas Jefferson*. Golden, Colorado: Fulcrum.

Barton, Barbara J. 1993. *Taylor's Guide to Specialty Nurseries*. Boston: Houghton Mifflin.

Benvie, Sam. 2000. *The Encyclopedia of North American Trees*. Buffalo, New York: Firefly.

Bir, Richard E. 1992. *Growing and Propagating Showy Native Woody Plants*. Chapel Hill: University of North Carolina Press.

Boutcher, William. 1775. *A Treatise on Forest-Trees*. Edinburgh: R. Fleming.

Boyce, John Shaw. 1948. *Forest Pathology*. New York: McGraw-Hill.

Bowers, Janice Emily. 1993. *Shrubs and Trees of the Southwest Deserts*. Tucson, Arizona: Southwest Parks and Monuments Association.

Braun, E. Lucy. 1961. *The Woody Plants of Ohio*. Facsimile. New York: Hafner Press, 1969.

Britton, Nathaniel Lord. 1907. *Manual of the Flora of the Northern States and Canada*. New York: Henry Holt.

Britton, Nathaniel Lord, and Addison Brown. 1913. *An Illustrated Flora of the Northern United States, Canada and the British Possessions*. 2d ed. New York: Charles Scribner's Sons.

Brooks, A. B. 1920. *West Virginia Trees*. Parsons, West Virginia: McClain. Reprint. West Virginia University Agricultural Experiment Station Bulletin 175, 1976.

Brown, Clair A. 1945. *Louisiana Trees and Shrubs*. Baton Rouge: Louisiana Forestry Commission.

Brown, Claud L., and L. Katherine Kirkman. 1990. *Trees of Georgia and Adjacent States*. Portland, Oregon: Timber Press.

Brown, David E., ed. 1982. Biotic communities of the American Southwest: United States and Mexico. *Desert Plants* 4 (1–4).

Brown, H. P. 1921. *Trees of New York State: Native and Naturalized*. Technical Publication 15. Syracuse: New York State College of Forestry.

Brown, Russell G., and Melvin L. Brown. 1972. *Woody Plants of Maryland*. Baltimore, Maryland: Port City Press.

Brown, Wilson. 1969. *Reading the Woods: Seeing More in Nature's Familiar Faces*. Harrisburg, Pennsylvania: Stackpole Books.

Browne, Daniel Jay. 1846. *The Trees of America*. New York: Harper.

Brzuszek, Robert F. 1993. *Native Trees for Urban Landscapes in the Gulf South*. Picayune, Mississippi: Crosby Arboretum.

Bryant, Arthur, Sr. 1871. *Forest Trees for Shelter, Ornament, and Profit*. New York: Henry T. Williams.

Burns, G. P., and C. H. Otis. 1979. *The Handbook of Vermont Trees*. Rutland, Vermont: Charles E. Tuttle.

Canada Department of Northern Affairs and National Resources, Forestry Branch. 1956. *Native Trees of Canada*. 5th ed. Bulletin 61. Ottawa, Ontario: Edmond Cloutier.

Carter, J. Cedric. 1964. *Illinois Trees: Their Diseases*. Circular 46. Urbana: Illinois Natural History Survey.

Carter, Jack L. 1997. *Trees and Shrubs of New Mexico*. Boulder, Colorado: Johnson Books.

Clarke, John. 1839. *A Treatise on the Mulberry Tree and Silkworm*. Philadelphia: Thomas, Cowperthwait.

Clemson Agricultural College. 1944. *Common Trees of South Carolina*. Columbia: South Carolina State Commission of Forestry.

Coker, William Chambers, and Henry Roland Totten. 1937. *Trees of the Southeastern States*. Chapel Hill: University of North Carolina Press.

Cole, Rex Vicat. 1915. *The Artistic Anatomy of Trees*. London: Seeley, Service.

Cole, Trevor. 1996. *Gardening with Trees and Shrubs in Ontario, Quebec, and the Northeastern United States*. Toronto: Whitecap Books.

Craighead, F. C. 1950. *Insect Enemies of Eastern Forests*. Miscellaneous Publication 657. Washington, D.C.: U.S. Department of Agriculture.

Dame, Lorin L., and Henry Brooks. 1901. *Handbook of the Trees of New England*. Reprint. New York: Dover, 1972.

Daubenmire, R. F. 1959. *Plants and Environment: A Textbook of Plant Autecology*. New York: John Wilet and Sons.

Davis, Richard C., ed. 1983. *Encyclopedia of American Forest and Conservation History*. New York: Macmillan.

Davison, Verne E. 1967. *Attracting Birds: From the Prairies to the Atlantic*. New York: Thomas Y. Crowell.

Deam, Charles C. 1931. *Trees of Indiana*. 2d ed. Fort Wayne, Indiana: Fort Wayne Printing.

Dean, Blanche Evans. 1988. *Trees and Shrubs of the Southeast*. Birmingham, Alabama: Birmingham Audubon Society Press.

de Forest, Elizabeth Kellam. 1982. *The Gardens and Grounds at Mount Vernon: How Washington Planned and Planted Them*. Mount Vernon, Virginia: Mount Vernon Ladies' Association of the Union.

de Klemm, Cyrille. 1990. *Wild Plant Conservation and the Law*. Environmental Policy and Law Paper 24. Cambridge, United Kingdom: International Union for Conservation of Nature and Natural Resources.

Dirr, Michael A. 1998. *Manual of Woody Landscape Plants: Their Identification, Ornamental Characteristics, Culture, Propagation, and Uses*. 5th ed. Champaign, Illinois: Stipes.

Dix, Mary Ellen, Judith Pasek, Mark Harrell, and Frederick P. Baxendale, eds. 1986. *Common Insect Pests of Trees in the Great Plains*. Great Plains Agricultural Council Publication 119. Lincoln: Nebraska Cooperative Extension Service.

Downing, A. J. 1849. *A Treatise on the Theory and Practice of Landscape Gardening*. New York: George P. Putnam.

Duncan, Wilbur H. 1988. *Trees of the Southeastern United States*. Athens: University of Georgia Press.

Dwelley, Marilyn. 1980. *Trees and Shrubs of New England*. Camden, Maine: Down East Books.

Eastman, John. 1992. *The Book of Forest and Thicket*. Harrisburg, Pennsylvania: Stackpole Books.

Elias, Thomas S. 1987. *The Complete Trees of North America*. New York: Gramercy.

Elliott, Simon B. 1912. *The Important Timber Trees of the United States*. Boston: Houghton Mifflin.

Elmore, Francis H. 1976. *Shrubs and Trees of the Southwest Uplands*. Tucson, Arizona: Southwest Parks and Monuments Association.

Elton, Charles S. 1958. *The Ecology of Invasions by Animals and Plants*. London: Methuen.

English, L. L. 1968. *Illinois Trees and Shrubs: Their Insect Enemies*. Circular 47. Urbana: Illinois Natural History Survey.

Evelyn, John. 1729. *Silva: or, a Discourse of Forest Trees and the Propagation of Timber in His Majesty's Dominions*. London: Royal Society.

Everitt, James H., and D. Lynn Drawe. 1993. *Trees, Shrubs and Cacti of South Texas*. Lubbock: Texas Tech University Press.

Fernald, Merritt Lyndon. 1970. *Gray's Manual of Botany*. 8th ed. New York: Van Nostrand Reinhold.

Flagg, Wilson. 1890. *A Year Among the Trees: or, The Woods and By-Ways of New England*. Boston: Educational.

Flint, Harrison L. 1997. *Landscape Plants for Eastern North America Exclusive of Florida and the Immediate Gulf Coast*. 2d ed. New York: John Wiley and Sons.

Foster, John H. 1951. *Trees and Shrubs of New Hampshire*. Concord, New Hampshire: Society for the Protection of New Hampshire Forests.

Fowells, H. A. 1965. *Silvics of Forest Trees of the United States*. Agriculture Handbook 271. Washington, D.C.: U.S. Forest Service.

Gallagher, Arlene. 1993. *Directory of Natural Area Programs*. Mukwonago, Wisconsin: Natural Areas Association.

Gerhold, Henry D., Willet Wandel, and Norman Lacasse, eds. 1993. *Street Tree Factsheets*. University Park: Pennsylvania State College of Agricultural Sciences.

Gibson, Henry H. 1913. *American Forest Trees*. Chicago: Hardwood Record, Regan Printing House.

Gleason, Henry Allen, and Arthur Cronquist. 1963. *Manual of Vascular Plants of Northeastern United States and Adjacent Canada*. Princeton, New Jersey: D. Van Nostrand.

Godfrey, Robert K. 1988. *Trees, Shrubs, and Woody Vines of Northern Florida and Adjacent Georgia and Alabama*. Athens: University of Georgia Press.

Gordon, Rue E., ed. 1993. *Conservation Directory*. Washington, D.C.: National Wildlife Federation.

Green, Charlotte Hilton. 1939. *Trees of the South*. Chapel Hill: University of North Carolina Press.

Gupton, Oscar W., and Fred C. Swope. 1981. *Trees and Shrubs of Virginia*. Charlottesville: University Press of Virginia.

Harlow, William M. 1942. *Trees of the Eastern United States and Canada*. New York: McGraw-Hill.

Harlow, William M., and Ellwood S. Harrar. 1941. *Textbook of Dendrology Covering the Important Forest Trees of the United States and Canada*. New York: McGraw-Hill.

Harper-Lore, Bonnie, and Maggie Wilson. 2000. *Roadside Use of Native Plants*. Washington, D.C.: Island Press.

Harrar, Ellwood S., and J. George Harrar. 1946. *Guide to Southern Trees*. Reprint. New York: Dover, 1962.

Haworth, Paul Leland. 1915. *George Washington: Farmer*. Indianapolis, Indiana: Bobbs-Merrill.

Hepting, George H. 1971. *Diseases of Forest and Shade Trees of the United States*. Agriculture Handbook 386. U.S. Forest Service.

Hightshoe, Gary L. 1988. *Native Trees, Shrubs, and Vines for Urban and Rural America*. New York: Van Nostrand Reinhold.

Holmes, J. S. 1922. *Common Forest Trees of North Carolina*. Chapel Hill: North Carolina Geological and Economic Survey.

Horn, Henry S. 1971. *The Adaptive Geometry of Trees*. Princeton, New Jersey: Princeton University Press.

Hosie, R. C. 1979. *Native Trees of Canada*. Don Mills, Ontario: Fitzhenry and Whiteside.

Hough, Romeyn Beck. 1947. *Handbook of the Trees of the Northern States and Canada East of the Rocky Mountains.* New York: Macmillan.

Hunter, Carl G. 1989. *Trees, Shrubs, and Vines of Arkansas.* Little Rock: Ozark Society Foundation.

Hyland, Fay, and Ferdinand H. Steinmetz. 1944. *The Woody Plants of Maine.* Orono, Maine: University Press.

Illick, Joseph S. 1928. *Pennsylvania Trees.* Pennsylvania Department of Forests and Waters Bulletin 11.

Iverson, L. R., A. M. Prasad, B. J. Hale, and E. K. Sutherland. 1999. *An Atlas of Current and Potential Future Distributions of Common Trees of the Eastern United States.* General Technical Report NE-265. Northeastern Research Station, U.S. Forest Service.

Jaynes, Richard A., ed. 1969. *Handbook of North American Nut Trees.* Knoxville, Tennessee: Northern Nut Growers Association.

Johnson, Warren T., and Howard H. Lyon. 1976. *Insects that Feed on Trees and Shrubs.* Ithaca, New York: Cornell University Press.

Jones, Warren, and Charles Sacamano. 2000. *Landscape Plants for Dry Regions.* Tucson, Arizona: Fisher Books.

Krüssmann, Gerd. 1985. *Manual of Cultivated Conifers.* Portland, Oregon: Timber Press.

Krüssmann, Gerd. 1986. *Manual of Cultivated Broad-Leaved Trees and Shrubs.* Portland, Oregon: Timber Press.

Kurz, Herman, and Robert K. Godfrey. 1962. *Trees of Northern Florida.* Gainesville: University of Florida Press.

Leake, Dorothy VanDyke, John Benjamin Leake, and Marcelotte Leake Roeder. 1993. *Desert and Mountain Plants of the Southwest.* Norman: University of Oklahoma Press.

Leighton, Ann. 1986. *American Gardens in the Eighteenth Century, "For Use or for Delight."* Amherst: University of Massachusetts Press.

Leopold, Donald L., William C. McComb, and Robert N. Muller. 1998. *Trees of the Central Hardwood Forests of North America: An Identification and Cultivation Guide.* Portland, Oregon: Timber Press.

Li, Hui-Lin. 1963. *The Origin and Cultivation of Shade and Ornamental Trees.* Philadelphia: University of Pennsylvania Press.

Li, Hui-Lin. 1972. *Trees of Pennsylvania, the Atlantic States, and the Lake States.* Philadelphia: University of Pennsylvania Press.

Little, Elbert L., Jr. 1953. *Check List of Native and Naturalized Trees of the United States (Including Alaska).* Agriculture Handbook 41. Washington, D.C.: U.S. Forest Service.

Little, Elbert L., Jr. 1971. *Atlas of United States Trees.* Vol. 1, Conifers and Important Hardwoods. Miscellaneous Publication 1146. Washington, D.C.: U.S. Forest Service.

Little, Elbert L., Jr. 1976. *Atlas of United States Trees.* Vol. 3, Minor Western Hardwoods. Miscellaneous Publication 1314. Washington, D.C.: U.S. Forest Service.

Little, Elbert L., Jr. 1977. *Atlas of United States Trees.* Vol. 4, Minor Eastern Hardwoods. Miscellaneous Publication 1342. Washington, D.C.: U.S. Forest Service.

Martin, Alexander C., Herbert S. Zim, and Arnold L. Nelson. 1951. *American Wildlife and Plants: A Guide to Wildlife Food Habits.* Reprint. New York: Dover, 1961.

Mattoon, W. R., and J. M. Beal. 1936. *Forest Trees of Mississippi.* State College: Mississippi State College.

McCoy, Doyle. 1981. *Roadside Trees and Shrubs of Oklahoma.* Norman: University of Oklahoma Press.

Meehan, Thomas. 1853. *The American Handbook of Ornamental Trees.* Philadelphia: Lippincott, Grambo.

Meier, Lauren, and Betsy Chittenden, compilers. 1990. *Preserving Historic Landscapes: An Annotated Bibliography.* Washington, D.C.: National Park Service.

Michaux, F. André. 1819. *A Treatise on the Resinous Trees of North America.* Paris: D'Hautel.

Mielke, Judy. 1993. *Native Plants for Southwestern Landscapes.* Austin: University of Texas Press.

Ministere de l'Energie et des Ressources. 1982. *Les Principaux Arbres du Quebec.* Gouvernement du Quebec.

Ministere des Terres et Forets. 1974. *Quebec Forests.* Quebec: Service de l'Information.

Moll, Gary, and Stanley Young. 1992. *Growing Greener Cities: A Tree-Planting Handbook.* Los Angeles: Living Planet Press.

Morin, Nancy R., ed. 1993. *Flora of North America: North of Mexico.* Vol. 2, Pteridophytes and Gymnosperms. New York: Oxford University Press.

Morin, Nancy R., ed. 1997. *Flora of North America: North of Mexico.* Vol. 3, Magnoliophyta: Magnoliidae and Hamamelidae. New York: Oxford University Press.

Nelson, Gil. 1994. *The Trees of Florida.* Sarasota, Florida: Pineapple Press.

Nokes, Jill. 2001. *How to Grow Native Plants of Texas and the Southwest.* Austin: University of Texas Press.

Nowak, David J., and T. Davis Sydnor. 1992. *Popularity of Tree Species and Cultivars in the United States.* General Technical Report NE-166. Radnor, Pennsylvania: U.S. Forest Service.

Oosting, Henry J. 1956. *The Study of Plant Communities.* San Francisco: W. H. Freeman.

Otis, Charles Herbert. 1931. *Michigan Trees.* Ann Arbor: University of Michigan.

Otteson, Carole. 1995. *The Native Plant Primer.* New York: Harmony Books.

Peattie, Donald Culross. 1950. *A Natural History of Trees of Eastern and Central North America.* Boston: Houghton Mifflin.

Peattie, Donald Culross. 1953. *A Natural History of Western Trees.* Boston: Houghton Mifflin.

Petrides, George A. 1988. *A Field Guide to Eastern Trees.* Boston: Houghton Mifflin.

Petrides, George A. 1992. *A Field Guide to Western Trees.* Boston: Houghton Mifflin.

Pinchot, Gifford. 1898. *The Adirondack Spruce.* New York: Critic.

Plotnik, Arthur. 2000. *The Urban Tree Book.* New York: Three Rivers Press.

Pool, Raymond J. 1951. *Handbook of Nebraska Trees.* 3rd ed. Nebraska Conservation Bulletin 32. Lincoln: University of Nebraska.

Powell, A. Michael. 1998. *Trees and Shrubs of the Trans-Pecos and Adjacent Areas.* Austin: University of Texas.

Pyle, Robert Michael. 1981. *The Audubon Society Field Guide to North American Butterflies.* New York: Alfred A. Knopf.

Radford, Albert E., Harry E. Ahles, and C. Ritchie Bell. 1981. *Manual of the Vascular Flora of the Carolinas*. Chapel Hill: University of North Carolina Press.

Randall, Charles Edgar, and Henry Clepper. 1977. *Famous and Historic Trees*. Washington, D.C.: American Forestry Association.

Rehder, Alfred. 1940. *Manual of Cultivated Trees and Shrubs Hardy in North America*. 2d ed. New York: Macmillan.

Richard, J., and Joan E. Heitzman. 1987. *Butterflies and Moths of Missouri*. Jefferson City: Missouri Department of Conservation.

Riffle, Jerry W., and Glenn W. Peterson, technical coordinators. 1986. *Diseases of Trees in the Great Plains*. General Technical Report RM-129. Fort Collins, Colorado: U.S. Forest Service.

Rosendahl, Carl Otto. 1955. *Trees and Shrubs of the Upper Midwest*. Minneapolis: University of Minnesota Press.

Rowe, J. S. 1972. *Forest Regions of Canada*. Canadian Forestry Service Publication 1300. Ottawa, Ontario: Department of the Environment.

Rupp, Rebecca. 1990. *Red Oaks and Black Birches*. Pownal, Vermont: Storey Communications.

Sargent, Charles Sprague. 1905. *Manual of the Trees of North America (Exclusive of Mexico)*. Boston: Houghton Mifflin.

Sayn-Wittgenstein, L. 1960. *Recognition of Tree Species on Air Photographs by Crown Characteristics*. Technical Note 95. Ottawa, Ontario: Canada Department of Forestry.

Schopmeyer, C. S., technical coordinator. 1974. *Seeds of Woody Plants in the United States*. Agriculture Handbook 450. U.S. Forest Service.

Schwarz, G. Frederick. 1902. *Forest Trees and Forest Scenery*. New York: Grafton Press.

Settergren, Carl, and R. E. McDermott. 1974. *Trees of Missouri*. Columbia: University of Missouri Press.

Simmons, James Raymond. 1919. *The Historic Trees of Massachusetts*. Boston: Marshall Jones.

Simpson, Benny J. 1988. *A Field Guide to Texas Trees*. Austin: Texas Monthly Press.

Spurr, Stephen H. 1964. *Forest Ecology*. New York: Ronald Press.

Snyder, Leon C. 1980. *Trees and Shrubs for Northern Gardens*. Minneapolis: University of Minnesota Press.

Stephens, H. A. 1969. *Trees, Shrubs, and Woody Vines in Kansas*. Lawrence: University Press of Kansas.

Stephens, H. A. 1973. *Woody Plants of the North Central Plains*. Lawrence: University Press of Kansas.

Sternberg, Guy, and Jim Wilson. 1995. *Landscaping with Native Trees: The Northeast, Midwest, Midsouth, and Southeast Edition*. Shelburne, Vermont: Chapters.

Taber, William S. 1937. *Delaware Trees*. Publication 6. Dover: Delaware State Forestry Department.

Taylor, Norman. 1991. *Taylor's Guide to Gardening Techniques*. New York: Houghton Mifflin.

Taylor, Richard B., Jimmy Rutledge, and Joe Herrera. 1999. *A Field Guide to Common South Texas Shrubs*. Austin: Texas Parks and Wildlife Press.

Thoreau, Henry David. 1854. *Walden*. Apollo Edition. New York: Thomas Y. Crowell, 1966.

Thwaites, Reuben Gold, ed. 1904. *Original Journals of the Lewis and Clark Expedition*. New York: Dodd, Mead.

Trehane, P., C. D. Brickell, B. R. Baum, W. L. A. Hetterscheid, A. C. Leslie, J. McNeill, S. A. Spongberg, and F. Vrugtman, eds. 1995. *The International Code of Nomenclature for Cultivated Plants (ICNCP or Cultivated Plant Code): Adopted by the International Commission for the Nomenclature of Cultivated Plants. Regnum vegetabile* 133. Wimborne, United Kingdom: Quarterjack Publishing.

Tripp, Kim E., and J. C. Raulston. 1995. *The Year in Trees*. Portland, Oregon: Timber Press.

Turnbull, Cass. 1991. *The Complete Guide to Landscape Design, Renovation, and Maintenance*. White Hall, Virginia: Betterway.

Tyrrell, Lucy E. 1991. *Old-Growth Forests on National Park Service Lands: NPS Views and Information*. Great Lakes Cooperative Park Studies Unit. Madison: University of Wisconsin.

U.S. Department of Agriculture. 1949. *Trees: The Yearbook of Agriculture*. 81st Congress, House Document 29.

U.S. Department of Agriculture. 1961. *Seeds: The Yearbook of Agriculture*. 87th Congress, House Document 29.

U.S. Forest Service. 1979. *A Guide to Common Insects and Diseases of Forest Trees in the Northeastern United States*. Broomall, Pennsylvania.

van der Linden, Peter, and Donald R. Farrar. 1984. *Forest and Shade Trees of Iowa*. Ames: Iowa State University.

Van Dersal, William R. 1938. *Native Woody Plants of the United States: Their Erosion-Control and Wildlife Values*. Miscellaneous Publication 303, Soil Conservation Service. Washington, D.C.: U.S. Department of Agriculture.

Van Doren, Mark, ed. 1928. *Travels of William Bartram*. New York: Macy-Masius. Reprint. New York: Dover, 1955.

Vanderah, Glendy C. 1993. *Cerulean Warbler Habitat*. Report 320. Urbana: Center for Biogeographic Information, Illinois Natural History Survey.

Vines, Robert A. 1960. *Trees, Shrubs, and Woody Vines of the Southwest*. Austin: University of Texas Press.

Walker, Laurence C. 1990. *Forests: A Naturalist's Guide to Trees and Forest Ecology*. New York: John Wiley and Sons.

Wandell, Willet N., project leader. 1989. *Handbook of Landscape Tree Cultivars*. Gladstone, Illinois: East Prairie.

Wandell, Willet N. 1993. *Hardiness of Landscape Tree Cultivars*. Gladstone, Illinois: East Prairie.

Westcott, Cynthia. 1971. *Plant Disease Handbook*. 3rd ed. New York: Van Nostrand Reinhold.

Wharton, Mary E., and Roger W. Barbour. 1973. *Trees and Shrubs of Kentucky*. Lexington: University Press of Kentucky.

Wilson, Brayton F. 1984. *The Growing Tree*. Amherst: University of Massachusetts Press.

Wooton, E. O., and Paul C. Standley. 1915. *Flora of New Mexico*. Contributions from the United States National Herbarium 19. Washington, D.C.: Smithsonian Institution.

Young, James A., and Cheryl G. Young. 1992. *Seeds of Woody Plants in North America*. Portland, Oregon: Dioscorides Press.

Index